Windows NT
& UNIX

Windows NT & UNIX
Administration, Coexistence, Integration, & Migration

G. Robert Williams

Ellen Beck Gardner

Addison-Wesley

An imprint of Addison Wesley Longman, Inc.

READING, MASSACHUSETTS   HARLOW, ENGLAND   MENLO PARK, CALIFORNIA
BERKELEY, CALIFORNIA   DON MILLS, ONTARIO   SYDNEY
BONN   AMSTERDAM   TOKYO   MEXICO CITY

Many of the designations used by manufacturers and sellers to distinguish their products are claimed as trademarks. Where those designations appear in this book and Addison-Wesley was aware of a trademark claim, the designations have been printed in initial caps or all caps.

The authors and publisher have taken care in the preparation of this book, but make no expressed or implied warranty of any kind and assume no responsibility for errors or omissions. No liability is assumed for incidental or consequential damages in connection with or arising out of the use of the information or programs contained herein.

The publisher offers discounts on this book when ordered in quantity for special sales. For more information, please contact:

Corporate, Government, and Special Sales Group
Addison Wesley Longman, Inc.
One Jacob Way
Reading, Massachusetts 01867

Library of Congress Cataloging-in-Publication Data

Williams, G. Robert, 1948–
      Windows NT & UNIX : administration, coexistence, integration, &
   migration / G. Robert Williams, Ellen Beck Gardner.
            p.   cm.
      ISBN 0-201-18536-9 (alk. paper)
      1. Microsoft Windows NT.   2. UNIX (Computer file)   3. Operating
   systems (Computers)   I. Gardner, Ellen Beck.   II. Title.
   QA76.76.063W5547   1998
   005.4′476--dc21   97-48514
                                                                          CIP

ISBN 0-201-18536-9
Text printed on recycled and acid-free paper.

1 2 3 4 5 6 7 8 9 10 -CRS- 02 01 00 99 98
First printing, March 1998.

Brief Contents

Contents

PART II **System Administration Primer for UNIX
and Windows NT**   **31**

CHAPTER 3   UNIX Structure, Processes, and Users   **33**

PART III Coexistence and Migration with UNIX and Windows NT   267

CHAPTER 9   Planning and Implementation Issues   269

PART IV Windows NT and UNIX Integration   329

CHAPTER 12   UNIX and Windows NT Network Overview   331

Michael Borowski

CHAPTER 13   UNIX and Windows NT Network Integration   349

Michael Borowski

CHAPTER 14   Electronic Mail Integration   387

Mark E. Walla

CHAPTER 15   Windows NT and UNIX as Web Servers   420
Barrie Sosinsky

PART V   Epilogue and Quick Reference Guides   445

CHAPTER 16   A Look at the Future   447

APPENDIX A   Windows NT Commands and Utilities   453

Preface

The continued growth of UNIX coupled with the overwhelming market acceptance of Windows NT Server has created a window of opportunity. Professionals with skills appropriate to manage both of these operating systems are rare. This book is written for information managers and system administrators who are seeking combined operating system skills or who require quick reference guides.

We utilized three primary sources of information to prepare this book. First, we relied heavily on our combined decades of experience in application development and system administration for UNIX and Microsoft operating systems. Our recommendations have not emerged from a vacuum, but are based on hard-fought reality. We have experienced both successes and blunders in managing UNIX and Windows NT systems. It is our hope that the experience we bring to this book assists fellow system administrators to better manage an enterprise.

Secondly, observations and interviews with system administrators in the field were also utilized to provide "reality checks" for our conclusions. Theoretic understanding of UNIX and Windows NT is a nice beginning, but it is no substitute for actual experience.

Thirdly, we utilized the operating systems and associated documentation. Microsoft Windows NT references are based primarily on Version 4.0. Occasionally we refer to the early Windows NT Version 3.51 and associated products like Windows 3.1, Windows 95, and Windows for Workgroups. The server and client versions of Windows NT are largely the same, with the exception of a few administrative tools. Therefore, much of the discussion assumes both the client and server versions of the Windows NT operating system.

The task of analyzing UNIX is not as straightforward because of the existence of so many variant UNIX versions. Although they have underlying similarities of form and function, the actual implementation can vary significantly. Therefore, we elected to utilize generic UNIX System V, Release 4, as our baseline operating system. References to special adaptations made for other versions of UNIX are noted whenever appropriate. The following commercial versions of UNIX were utilized to prepare this book:

- AT&T UNIX V4.2
- AIX 3.x and 4.x
- Digital UNIX 4.0
- HP-UX 9.x and 10.x
- SCO UNIX 3.x and Open Desktop
- Sun OS 4.x
- Sun Solaris 2.x
- UnixWare 2.1

We also occasionally refer to LINUX. Although LINUX is not technically a UNIX variant because it was not derived from the original AT&T source code, this "freeware" UNIX-like operating system is gaining acceptance in some sectors. It is anticipated that it will play a part in many mixed UNIX and Windows NT enterprises.

AUDIENCE FOR THE BOOK

This book is written for a very special breed of system administrators—those who are involved in managing both UNIX and Windows NT environments. Specifically, we envision three primary audiences who should find this book useful:

1. UNIX system administrators who must now also manage Windows NT
2. Windows NT system administrators who must learn basic UNIX management
3. Individuals new to both UNIX and Windows NT system administration

We acknowledge the fact that some system administrators have extensive formal training, whereas others inherit responsibility through organizational default. Therefore, the level of direct UNIX and Windows NT knowledge varies widely. Any individual who even occasionally struggles with system management issues can use this book as a reference document.

HOW TO USE THIS BOOK

Windows NT and UNIX: Administration, Coexistence, Integration, and Migration adheres to the following style conventions to facilitate reading clarity and to underscore emphasis:

- **Bold** is used for specific Windows NT fields, tabs, or buttons that the user should access to accomplish the task being discussed. Otherwise, bold is used to bring attention to a specific term or concept.
- **Semibold** is used to depict a series of Windows NT options for a specific action.
- *Italic* is used to highlight terms and commands.
- `Monospace` is used to denote sample code and specific strings of code or keystrokes to be entered by the user.

 This symbol is used to note information of special interest or shortcuts associated with the UNIX operating system.

 This symbol is used to note information of special interest or shortcuts associated with the Windows NT operating system.

ORGANIZATION OF THE BOOK

This book is divided into five parts:

- *Part I: Introduction* – This part outlines both real and perceived strengths and weaknesses of the two operating systems.
- *Part II: System Administration Primer for UNIX and Windows NT* – This part is a primer and quick reference guide for the administration of UNIX and Windows NT. Each operating system is reviewed from the following three perspectives:

  1. Operating system structure, processes, and user intervention
  2. Common tasks encountered by system administrators
  3. Advanced operating system topics

- *Part III: Coexistence and Migration with UNIX and Windows NT* – This part defines the key issues and considerations concerning coexistence and migration between the operating systems. Part III begins with Chapter 9 about planning and implementation issues. Chapter 10 describes key technologies that augment operating system coexistence. The final chapter in this part, Chapter 11, reviews issues related to migrating UNIX applications to Windows NT.

- *Part IV: Windows NT and UNIX Integration* – The cornerstone of the integration of these premier network operating systems rests on common utilization of the Transmission Control Protocol/Internet Protocol (TCP/IP) and related services. We begin Part IV with a review of networking operations and a specific analysis of TCP/IP in Chapter 12. Chapter 13 describes methods for networking integration. Chapter 14 focuses on e-mail interoperability. We conclude Part IV with Chapter 15, a view of the roles played by Windows NT and UNIX with the Internet and the specific management of Web servers.

- *Part V: Epilogue and Quick Reference Guides* – In Chapter 16 we provide a glimpse into our crystal ball to see the probable future of Windows NT 5.0 and UNIX. Appendices A and B detail the use of common Windows NT and UNIX commands and utilities, respectively. We cross-reference the commands and utilities that are similar in function in both operating systems.

WHERE TO GET RECENT INFORMATION

An Internet Web site has been established to provide you with additional information and files to download. We also hope that you will share your experiences and post them on our Web site. If you want to obtain updated information or share your experiences, surf the net and land at `http://www.unint.com/book.html`.

Throughout this book we provide the relevant addresses, e-mail addresses, and Web site locations of software and hardware vendors, educational and governmental institutions, trade associations, and other groups.

Acknowledgments

When any book is written there is a number of people, both in the foreground and in the background, who help the authors make their publication deadlines. This book is no exception. We would like to pay tribute to those individuals who helped us succeed.

First, we would like to thank the staff at Addison Wesley Longman for having the vision to understand the need for this book and the professionalism to follow through and make it happen. In particular we would like to recognize Mary Treseler O'Brien, Carter Shanklin, Rachel Beavers, and Elizabeth Spainhour. Additionally, we want to acknowledge our copy editor, Catherine Ohala; the Addison-Wesley production coordinator, Marilyn Rash; and Judy Strakalaitis of Bookworks. We also want to thank our marketing manager, Tracy Russ.

The book would have taken much longer to complete without the assistance of our contributors: Mark Walla, Barrie Sosinsky, and Michael Borowski. Mark Walla also provided technical reviews.

We also would like to acknowledge the work and effort of our technical reviewers. These are the people who kept us on the straight and narrow: Brooks Cutter of Microsoft; Les G. Farkas, John Hart, Brian Helvey, and Jeff Gitlin of Lucent Technologies; Bill Mansfield of CIBER; Brad TerEick; Stephen Walli of Softway Systems; and Fred Zlotnick.

Microsoft Corporation has been very cooperative in the development of this book. Gary Schare, Windows NT Server Product Manager, was instrumental in providing technical information and other vital resources that proved extremely valuable. Ed Muth and Chris Preston also provided support. Insight into Microsoft marketing and strategic relationships was garnered from the dynamic support of John Ford. Technical and professional training support was also provided by Barbara Staub and Liz Brackett. The authors send a very special thanks to Gary, Ed, Chris, John, Barbara, Liz, and many other Microsoft personnel.

In addition to new friends in the Windows NT community, we must also thank many individuals involved in UNIX. First and foremost, thank you to the many people of the old Decathlon Data Systems, including Edward Nichols, Martha McGavin, Larry Bridges, Mark Chance, Paul Bailey, Kayla Hulse, Ken Gamauf, Katherine Griffin, Eric Taylor, and the late Kenneyth Griffin. And we cannot forget UNIX friends Nicky Hull-Itkin, Rich Itkin, Cliff Mangum, Manuel Diaz, Frank Mancusco, and many others.

Coauthor Robert Williams was privileged to be a featured speaker on UNIX and Windows NT interoperability in the international road show Integration97. Much additional insight was garnered from the exceptional team in this traveling circus. In addition to the previously acknowledged Microsoft personnel, we want to thank Hewlett-Packard's remarkable Lee Rodberg, Scott Cicora, and Frank Sancho. We also want to acknowledge the exceptional team from Tech Data, including Raymond Doucette (fellow dancing bear), John Mayeux, Steve Brunk, Scott Maentez, Jack Shortway, and so many others.

A very special thank-you needs to go to coauthor Ellen Beck Gardner's husband, Kevin, whose patience and understanding was remarkable and cannot be understated. Thanks, Kev! Their daughter, Emily, who is also Bob's goddaughter, was the light that kept all of the craziness in perspective. To both Kevin and Emily, your love, understanding, and support never went unnoticed, although it may not have been frequently acknowledged. Personal thanks is also given by Ellen to Bob and Arleen Beck for years of support and love. Ellen also gives a special thanks to Bob for his vision, his sense of humor, and his determination that helped to keep this book on track.

Bob Williams gives special acknowledgment to the people of Productive Data Systems, including Joe Martinez, Sally Tulk, and Dave Perry for providing new opportunities. Jeff Howell and Bruce Batkey of Batkey-Howell Education Training Centers also deserve a special note. A special thank you also goes to Doug Miller of Software Systems and to the folks at DataFocus. Bob extends personal thanks to Ellen, Flora Williams, Sue and Mike Montgomery, and supportive friends Ivory Curtis, Scott Woodland, Mark Sehnert, Jim Fry, and Karen Bircher.

Finally, we thank the many professional associates we have been honored to meet over the years. This book belongs to them.

About the Authors and Contributors

THE AUTHORS

G. Robert Williams, PhD, is currently president of PDS Advanced Technologies, Inc., a national system integration firm involved in designing, planning, and deploying Windows NT and UNIX enterprises. Previously he was president and founder of Decathlon Data Systems, Inc., the leading publisher of the GOLDMEDAL office automation suite and the industry's first groupware suite, TEAMWARE. He has been a senior executive at other computer companies, such as UNISYS and System Development Corporation. He was a dean of research at the University of California, Los Angeles, and California State Polytechnic University. An author or contributor to a number of other books and articles, Dr. Williams is also a lecturer at many industry trade shows. Recently he was the keynote speaker at the Windows NT and UNIX Summit with Microsoft's Bill Gates. He also was the featured speaker for Integration '97 and '98—the international road show on UNIX and Windows NT interoperability sponsored by Microsoft, Hewlett-Packard, and Tech Data.

Ellen Beck Gardner, MBA, is an authority on the UNIX operating system who was faced with the challenge of learning Windows NT to incorporate it into a UNIX environment. Her UNIX experience began at NCR Corporation, where she was responsible for managing technical support services for their field locations throughout the United States. Ms. Gardner further refined her UNIX expertise as a senior vice president at Decathlon Data Systems, Inc., a pioneer in UNIX office automation and groupware applications. Currently, she is an independent consultant who specializes in training and support of both UNIX and Windows NT operating systems. She contributed to the *Microsoft Back-Office Bible* published by IDG Books in 1997. She is also Emily's mom.

THE CONTRIBUTORS

Mark Walla is a director of PDS Advanced Technologies. He is a technical leader with extensive UNIX, Windows NT, and networking experience. He has most recently consulted for Microsoft Corporation and Hewlett-Packard, where he helped develop the companies' integration strategy and presentation materials for their current national tour, Integration '98. While consulting for US West, Mr. Walla evaluated network management tools. At Bay Networks he was the technical lead for sustaining released software and customer hot site issues. Before that, he was a software engineer at Motorola, with software design and testing responsibilities, and an embedded software engineer at Storage Technology .

Barrie Sosinsky is the author or coauthor of more than forty-five computer books on a variety of subjects relating to desktop computing. Among the 1996–1997 titles he has been principle author of are *The Windows NT Answer Book* from McGraw Hill, *How to Use Microsoft Access 97* from ZD Press, *Managing Microsoft Remote Access Server* from New Riders Press, *The BackOffice Bible* and *Building Visual FoxPro Applications* from IDG Press, and the *Web Recipe Book* from PTR. Mr. Sosinsky is also the author of eighty articles in a variety of trade journals. His company, Killer Apps (Medfield, Massachusetts), specializes in custom software (database and Web-related), training, and technical documentation. Currently, Mr. Sosinsky is the editor and laboratory manager at *BackOffice Magazine*.

Michael Borowski is a senior consultant and IS manager in computer networking and integration. He has provided services to many national and international firms, including US West, QualComm, IBM, CIBER, Puerto Rico Telephone Company, and R&D Systems.

Part
I

Introduction to Windows NT and UNIX

Windows NT and UNIX are collectively emerging as the predominant server operating systems. The existence of these two operating systems in a mixed enterprise will become the norm rather than the exception. Part I of this book provides introductory thoughts on Windows NT and UNIX interoperability.

- Chapter 1, Introduction
- Chapter 2, A View of UNIX and Windows NT from 30,000 Feet

Chapter 1

Introduction

The kaleidoscope of today's technological options can easily blind even the most sophisticated information management professional. Nowhere is this fact more evident than in the deployment of UNIX and Windows NT. As we enter the next century, these two operating systems should dominate the server landscape. This book shines a light on those aspects of UNIX and Windows NT that support their use and management.

UNIX AND WINDOWS NT INTEGRATION

When UNIX first emerged more than twenty-five years ago, the newly initiated advocates treated the operating system with almost religious vigor. UNIX professionals believed that they could change the face of modern computing. In many ways, they achieved their goal. Today another type of religious war is taking place. However the nature of this war is much different than the early UNIX skirmishes against mainframe titans. As Windows NT rapidly enters the marketplace, an *evolution* rather than a revolution is emerging. We consider this event an evolution because many of the underlying paradigms that made UNIX world class have been fully embraced by Windows NT. Individuals with extensive UNIX experience will feel an immediate level of familiarity with many aspects of Windows NT. However, as with any evolution, Windows NT must be considered an entirely new species that bears its own unique power and characteristics. Microsoft has done an admirable job of incorporating the foundations of UNIX while expanding many other elements. By the same token, UNIX itself continues to grow in both form, features, and market acceptance. In most large enterprises the issue is not Windows NT *versus* UNIX, but rather Windows NT *and* UNIX.

In preparing this book, we began the project with a decidedly pro-UNIX bias. After all, we had invested decades in the development of applications for many UNIX variants. It might even be said that initially we did not even want to like Windows NT. We were extremely skeptical about Microsoft's ability to offer an operating system with the breadth and depth of power inherent in UNIX. We believe it is important for us to confess to these early prejudices in the opening paragraphs of this book because many others in the UNIX community undoubtedly share these same biases. Having now completed the book, after exhaustive use of Windows NT, our opinions have changed radically. In fact, although we both regularly utilize UNIX, Windows NT has been our primary operating system in work and play. In making this confession, it is important to underscore our belief that UNIX is not going away. The task facing both UNIX and Windows NT administrators is to rise above initial biases and to understand how to manage appropriately the interoperability of these operating systems.

UNIX has enjoyed the role as a preeminent server operating system for nearly two decades. Further, it maintains a sizable share of the workstation market. By contrast, Windows NT has risen from relative obscurity to a position of leadership in the market. Some industry analysts call Windows NT 4.0 the "UNIX killer." The death of UNIX has been predicted often; obviously, this is nonsense. To paraphrase, we believe the rumors of the death of UNIX are greatly exaggerated. The reality for the foreseeable future is that the server world will contain a mix of Windows NT and UNIX systems where each operating system will dominate in niches that best suit their respective strengths. Both UNIX and Windows NT are individually robust, and a total displacement of one over the other is highly unlikely. As a result of a strong UNIX and Windows NT installation base, system administrators are increasingly called on to become proficient with both operating systems.

The demand for professionals with high-level skills in both the UNIX and Windows NT operating systems is growing rapidly and the people with both skill sets are still rare. Scanning the want ads of any major metropolitan newspaper verifies this contention. Demand for UNIX and Windows NT system administrators, programmers, network engineers, customer service representatives, trainers, and similar professionals is readily evident. We believe those persons with existing UNIX skills possess a learning curve advantage over those with strictly Windows NT experience. The simple fact is that Windows NT is easier to learn than UNIX. For those users and administrators who have relied on Wizards and graphical interfaces, movement into a command line-oriented operating system involves a very different world. However, it should not be assumed that because an operating system is easier to learn that it is somehow less robust. Both UNIX and Windows NT are complex operating systems that require training and significant maintenance.

TRENDS AND RESULTING OPPORTUNITY

The convergence of Windows NT and UNIX is currently like a class five tornado. In most organizations of any size, Windows NT boxes are being introduced next to existing UNIX systems. The current trend appears to be that Windows NT is not replacing UNIX in any wholesale fashion, except perhaps on the desktop. It is still common to see a UNIX workstation and Windows NT-based personal computer (PC) in the same office or cubicle. Supporting two boxes is rapidly becoming unnecessary because of the ready availability of X-Servers, telnet clients/servers, and other technologies discussed in this book. As to UNIX and Windows NT server operations, many organizations still utilize these systems as islands of computing. While base-level network communication between UNIX and Windows NT servers is common, levels of true interoperability have not been widely achieved. Here again, technologies exist today that facilitate rapid and well-tested integration.

Technical evolutions do not take place in a vacuum. They are often spawned by a number of external forces. The underlying trend that is controlling the entire market movement revolves around communication. Four primary conditions can be sited.

1. *Continued demand for information* – The information age is far from over. Despite the availability of information from numerous sources, the demand continues to spiral upward. The requirement for systems to support this demand is significant accordingly.

2. *Unprecedented growth of the Internet* – The Internet explosion is something that could have not been anticipated. However, as more people come on line with enhanced functions and services, a fundamental shift in the way we communicate and conduct business is evolving. Both UNIX and Windows NT play a major role today in the expansion of the Internet, intranet, and extranet.

3. *Expanded complexity* – The days of the isolated PC and small local area network (LAN) may be limited. Complex networks based on multitiered topologies are becoming very commonplace. Although the tools needed to support this complexity have greatly improved, the fact remains that complicated solutions require sophisticated administration and management.

4. *Impact of the PC business model* – Perhaps the single driving force that has propelled Windows NT into the limelight is the impact of the PC on today's business model. A decision was made by the overwhelming majority of the marketplace that desktop business applications would reside on the Microsoft Windows environment. Had a market shift not occurred in such an overwhelming fashion, then the trend to consolidate business application work on a single

Windows-based terminal probably would be much slower. However, the days of a PC running Microsoft Windows and green dumb terminals working side by side may be numbered. The PC business model is driving much of Windows NT's acceptance.

Market share shifts are also occurring. The losers appear to be NetWare and proprietary operating systems. UNIX is projected to maintain credible market growth during the next five years. By contrast, Windows NT Server will surpass the shipment of UNIX this calendar year. Microsoft Corporation's Bill Gates has publicly stated that the future of his company may hinge on the success of next year's release of Windows NT 5.0. Many market analysts believe that by the year 2001, more than 80% of the entire server market will be nearly equally divided between UNIX and Windows NT.

IMPACT OF TRENDS AND THIS BOOK

As UNIX and Windows NT expand their stronghold on the enterprise, the types of opportunities afforded information management professionals with mixed operating system expertise dramatically increase. Customers and end users are demanding solutions that integrate the environments by asking questions such as

- How can I provide seamless access to resources?
- How can I control access with limited burden on users?
- How can I support messaging successfully?
- How can I manage the environment without duplicating resources?
- How can I develop an application just once?
- How can I leverage Web technologies to provide greater access?

This book addresses these types of specific issues inherent in UNIX and Windows NT coexistence, integration, and migration. Although these three terms may appear similar, we view them differently in the context of operating system management.

- *Coexistence* – UNIX and Windows NT coexistence refers to areas of *cooperation* and common methods of maintenance.
- *Integration* – Windows NT and UNIX integration suggests technologies that support true operating system *interoperability*.
- *Migration* – The term *migration,* as we use it in this book, refers to the *movement from* UNIX to Windows NT.

This is a resource document and is not designed to replace your system manuals. A single volume cannot address adequately all the issues inherent with either UNIX or Windows NT. These operating systems are very robust and require extensive document sets. By the same token, we seek to provide concise information organized to facilitate the administration of mixed UNIX and Windows NT environments. When greater detail is required, we provide sufficient guideposts for the user to pursue necessary assistance. To illustrate this point, new system administrators may find themselves overwhelmed by the terminology. We dissect the jargon into understandable information bits. Some of the terms utilized are obvious and logical. Unfortunately, this is not always the case, and many terms are simply silly or whimsical. For example, UNIX enlists *daemons* to manage processes such as printing and mail delivery. By the same token, Windows NT provides its *services* to perform roughly the same task as daemons. Another example is the word *domain,* which has radically different implications in UNIX and Windows NT, as described later. This book attempts to demystify the jargon and procedural mumbo jumbo.

THE GOOD, THE BAD, AND THE UGLY

When writing this book, the theme music from the 1960s western movie classic *The Good, the Bad and the Ugly* kept running through our minds. If you are managing a UNIX and Windows NT environment, the analogy is all too obvious. Both operating systems truly provide good, bad, and very ugly elements. Although we could not bundle a forty-five-rpm single record of the theme music (Remember, those seven-inch vinyl disks with grooves we utilized to reproduce sound in the good old days?), we can still offer a mental picture of Clint Eastwood shooting down oblique operating system commands. If only a symbolic bullet into the computer screen would help clarify the administration of UNIX and Windows NT! As to the good, both UNIX and Windows NT offer significant computer power to overcome the bad and the ugly.

The term *UNIX* is used in this book to describe scores of variant operating systems. Known by trade names such as AIX, HP-UX, and Solaris, they share common functionality and networking interoperability. UNIX is an eloquent, multipurpose, and multiuser computing environment. The modern-day explosion of the Internet rests on the backbone of UNIX technology. With major developmental breakthroughs including support for a 64-bit architecture, UNIX should maintain a solid place in future computing.

The relatively new Windows NT is capturing an astonishingly large market share in many market sectors. The extension *NT* stands for *new technology,* yet it owes much to UNIX as well as to the much older Digital Equipment Corporation (DEC) proprietary standby, VMS, and Microsoft's own OS/2, DOS, and Windows incarnations. Despite its many influences, Windows NT does transform the best elements of other operating systems into something truly unique.

Windows NT in its own right brings a new life and dimension to the client/server paradigm. Its familiar user interface and fresh approach to enterprise computing help to account for Windows NT's new-found acceptance.

Much of the debate between UNIX and Windows NT boils down to driving a proven utility vehicle or a hybrid new model with fancy bumpers and leather seats. They both get you to your computing destination and both require extensive maintenance. Use this book to lift the hood and kick the tires. Be aware that the lemon laws that apply to automobiles do not apply to operating systems. As you begin your test drive, we hope this book provides a map to avoid those all too common bumpy roads.

# Chapter 2

A View of UNIX and Windows NT from 30,000 Feet

Capturing the essence of Windows NT and UNIX is a daunting task that we admit cannot be achieved in a few introductory pages. This chapter is really a view from 30,000 feet so you can survey the terrain. The remainder of the book brings the issues down to earth. This chapter summarizes both the perceived and real strengths and weaknesses of two very popular operating systems. We use the word *perceived* very purposefully, because one user can view a given function as an advantage whereas another user may see it as a defect. In addition, popular perception does not always equal reality.

Describing the relative merits of UNIX and Windows NT is sometimes like arguing philosophy. Zealots on either side of the discussion will find fault in whatever is presented as a weakness or strength of the respective operating system. Therefore, we apologize in advance for any failure to present every possible argument for and against either UNIX or Windows NT. Our intent is merely to provide a broad-brush view of these operating systems as a means of establishing a foundation for the in-depth technical discussions in the following chapters. We begin our discussion with UNIX for no other reason than it is the older of the two operating systems.

UNIX: AN UNUSUAL SUCCESS STORY

UNIX is well over 25 years old. Despite its longevity, it has a widely held reputation as a technical operating system that simply overwhelms the uninitiated. This image is truly unfortunate, because behind its terse command set resides a formidable computing powerhouse.

UNIX is a general-purpose, multiuser operating system capable of support-ing a wide range of applications. Whether employed by one or one thousand users, it is designed to handle individual and group computing activities elo-quently. As a multitasking operating system, UNIX permits many processes to run in the foreground and in the background at the same time. This means that larger jobs can be activated while a user engages in one or more other com-puting processes. UNIX can be scaled to any size environment—from a single laptop to the largest computer enterprise. It is also very portable across most major computer processors. New systems can be brought on line with relative ease. UNIX also provides exceptional networking.

At first glance, UNIX appears to be a collection of snap-on tools. This view is at least partially correct. UNIX includes scores of utilities that can be used individually or as a collection of programmed events through the use of inter-connecting "pipes." These utilities and commands function within the user space. The second portion of the operating system is the kernel mode, which supervises the protected system semantics and manages hardware devices. Interestingly, this is the same basic conceptual structure employed by Windows NT. One of the first concepts UNIX users learn is that everything within the operating system is treated as a file. The characteristics of different types of files vary in terms of permission and ownership. These files can hold data or may be designed to execute programs. They take several forms, including flat (ASCII) files, binary executable code, and directories.

In saying *UNIX*, we are using a generic term that best describes dozens of commercial and research variants. Throughout this book, references are made periodically to these versions. The diversity of UNIX variants stems from the nature of its developmental history. The history of UNIX development is one of both unbridled creativity and organized chaos. This operating system was cre-ated and supplemented by dozens of creative and talented technical minds that worked both together and separately. From its humble beginnings at AT&T's Bell Laboratories, several branches of UNIX eventually evolved. During the dawning of UNIX development, AT&T was restricted by a federal court restrain-ing order from entering the commercial computer market; therefore, the re-search conducted at Bell Labs was widely shared. The academic community in particular took a real interest in the new operating system. Arguably the two most influential versions of UNIX were AT&T's own System V and the contri-bution from the University of California, Berkeley (otherwise known as the Berkeley Software Distribution or BSD). A third influential variant, XENIX, was used on Intel-class machines. This version was developed and supported by SCO and, oddly enough, Microsoft Corporation. In 1989, under the auspices of AT&T's UNIX System Labs (USL), the major features of System V, XENIX, and BSD were merged into System V, release 4 (or SVR4). Despite this effort, many vendors continued to support their own version of UNIX, such as IBM's AIX, Sun's Solaris, Hewlett-Packard's HP-UX, and Digital's Ultrix.

AT&T sold USL to Novell Corporation in 1993. Novell released its own micro-computer version of System V4.2 called *UnixWare*. Novell attempted to market UnixWare as a multiuser challenger to the Microsoft Windows environment. When Novell originally purchased USL, critics in the industry and media cried foul about the ability of this leading local area networking company to control the future of UNIX. Novell also faced a potential court battle with the University of California over certain technical and trade name rights. In a concession to critics, Novell granted the UNIX trademark to the independent X/Open industry consortium. In turn, X/Open (now merged with the Open Software Foundation and called the *Open Group*) established a set of policies and procedures known as Spec 1170 that must be met in order for a product to be branded UNIX. The Open Group has most recently published the single UNIX specification, which is required for future branding of UNIX '98 variants. As of the writing of this book, the promise of a common UNIX is merely conceptual. Major manufacturers of UNIX systems still add their own extensions to provide competitive marketplace advantage.

As with other operating systems of its day, early UNIX was originally de-signed on character-based terminals. When multiline displays became available, UNIX adjusted to this innovation. For example, the earlier *ex* or *edit* (extended line-oriented text editor) program was updated to *vi* (visual editor). In today's world of graphical user interfaces (GUIs), the thought of a "visual editor" sup-porting only character-based input is almost humorous. However, at the time, this was a major breakthrough. Even to this day the character-based command line remains a common (and for many, the preferred) way to interact with UNIX. Today UNIX also has an excellent graphical front end. Running in parallel with the development efforts at the University of California at Berkeley campus, stu-dents and faculty of the Massachusetts Institute of Technology began develop-ment of a graphical front end know today as X-Windows version X11 (or simply X11). The networking and client/server primitives provided by X-Windows has been extended with developmental tool kits (like the standard Xt tool kit) and window managers (such as Motif, TWM, OpenLook, and Common Desktop Envi-ronment [CDE]). One of the primary modern characteristics of UNIX is that users can function exceptionally well in either a character-based or GUI environment.

UNIX BENEFITS: REAL AND PERCEIVED

UNIX offers a number of strengths and benefits to its users and administrators. These benefits range from being a mature, proven operating system to recent developments such as 64-bit architecture support. A discussion of each of the benefits follows.

Command Line Orientation: Power and Intelligence

UNIX is replete with a straightforward command set. Interestingly, detractors will point to the very power of UNIX's command line structure as also a weakness. They point to it as cryptic and difficult to use. We believe the brevity of the command structure is elegant and very easy to use for those with training. Complex events can be invoked with few keystrokes. However, we do acknowledge that the learning curve can be steep for those without technical training and/or aptitude.

To illustrate the potential strength of the command structure, let us consider how a one-line command can be used to perform many tasks, as shown in the following example.

Five O'clock Crisis Averted by UNIX User

Consider the following scenario: It is Friday at 4:45 P.M. when the department manager calls an emergency meeting. It seems that the database server has crashed without completing a report that must be distributed by 8:00 A.M. on Monday. The message is clear—no completed report, don't show up for work on Monday.

Before crashing, the database server produced a flat file containing 1.5 million records with eighteen columns of data per record, all delimited by commas. Your assignment is to create a new report omitting the first 263,000 records; include only data columns one, two, nine, and fourteen; separate the data by tabs rather than commas; sort in reverse order by data item two; and print ten copies on a remote printer across the country. The only software available is the UNIX operating system.

As your coworkers panic searching for tape and scissors, you calmly go to your terminal without a word. You know that with UNIX the user can read the contents of a file with the *cat* command, change the delimiter with the translate (*tr*) command, extract the proper data items with *cut,* eliminate the first 263,000 records with the *tail* command, place the data in reverse order with *sort,* and output the data to a remote printer on the network with the *lp* command. You also know that by using a pipe (|) all of these commands can be strung together. So you calmly type

```
cat <file> | tr "," "<TAB>"|cut -f1,2,9,14|tail
+263001|sort +1 -r> lp -d <printer> -n10
```

You press <Enter> and the work is done. You also know that you could save this command as a shell script—a UNIX program that can be implemented anytime in the future.

After users become familiar with UNIX commands, the fear and loathing of the operating system usually translates to an appreciation for its power. Until that time, UNIX is formidable. The biggest challenge facing any UNIX system administrator is new user training.

Equated with Open Systems Standards

The concept of computer industry standards owes much to UNIX. In fact, the term *open systems* is often equated with UNIX, a reputation that is only partially deserved. User groups and industry consortiums have made lasting influences on UNIX. Perhaps the most important of these influences came in the form of the ISO/IEC 9945-1 specification, otherwise known as IEEE Std 1003.1–1990–Portable Operating System Interface (POSIX)–Part 1: System Application Programming Interface (API for the C language). This specification is referred to throughout this book as POSIX.1. This specification was later augmented to describe commands, and these additional specifications are commonly known as POSIX.2. Although UNIX and POSIX are mistakenly used interchangeably, POSIX is a specification and not an operating system. Therefore, other operating systems can also embrace the POSIX standard, as we later discuss regarding the degree to which the Windows NT POSIX subsystem embraces POSIX.1.

Despite the perception that UNIX is the bastion for open systems, it is also important to note that every major manufacturer of UNIX variants adds their own extensions. These additions, by their very existence, limit the openness of the UNIX operating system. In some ways, variants such as AIX or HP-UX are very proprietary.

Scalable, Portable, and Flexible

A major advantage UNIX has demonstrated since its earliest days is the ability to run on machines from the largest mainframe to modern laptops. Networks that connect these divergent machine types can be configured in peer-to-peer or hierarchical relationships. A UNIX enterprise may consist of several or hundreds of thousands of nodes. UNIX also supports multiple processor configurations. Therefore UNIX can be viewed as scalable both internally and across multiple host systems.

Built-in Programming Environment

UNIX supports both compiler-based and scripting languages. For example, the development of UNIX ran parallel to the evolution of the higher level C programming language. The C language produces software programs that require a compiler to create an executable. UNIX also supports scripting languages that do not require a compiler. A script-based program differs from a compiled executable in several important ways. The primary difference resides in the fact that a script is an easily edited, flat ASCII file. The UNIX shell (a layer of code that interprets commands) is used to create executable shell scripts.

Until very recently most commercial distributions of UNIX included bundled copies of the C language compiler. Then companies like Sun Microsystems discovered they could make more money by selling the software development kits separately, so they unbundled the C compiler. Fortunately the Free Software Foundation provides excellent C compilers that can be downloaded over the Internet without cost. The GNU C Compiler is available at `http://www.gnu.ai.mit.edu` and several other mirror sites. For C language developers, the availability of the GNU compiler across so many UNIX variants makes multiplatform application support generally as simple as a new compile. The actions of UNIX vendors ironically serve to make application support much easier through the use of single source code as well as freeware compilers. Other languages and scripting utilities such as AWK and Perl are also available from GNU.

Equal Functionality across Platforms

It is odd to think of an operating system as a vehicle for democratic standards. However, for computer hardware, UNIX is the great equalizer. When running UNIX, the computing functionality is the same for a mainframe as it is for a lowly laptop. Yes, there are differences in memory as well as disk and performance capacity; however, the functions these machines can perform with UNIX are identical.

Wide Range of User Interfaces

The availability of a wide range of user interfaces is another one of the double-edged swords wielded by UNIX. In general, three types of UNIX interfaces are most commonly used today (Figure 2.1). The first is the traditional character-based environment on workhorse standard ASCII terminals such as the Digital VT100 and VT220, the IBM 3151, and the Wyse 50/60 family. These devices are primarily used for data entry, retail businesses, and environments in which cost is a major factor. The character-based terminal remains substantially less expensive than the personal computer (PC), workstation, or X-Windows terminal. Despite the cost differential, there is a noticeable decline in the use of character-based terminals. However, it is unlikely we will see their demise as long as the price difference with other displays exists.

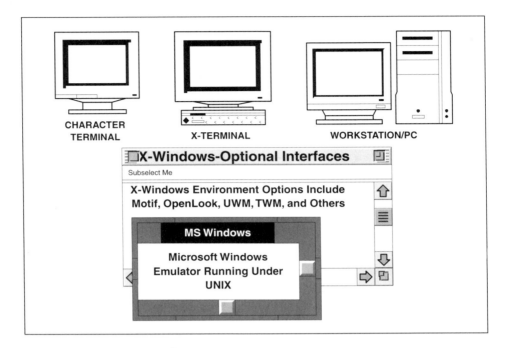

FIGURE 2.1.   User Interfaces

The second major interface is based on X-Windows on which users can run graphically based applications. In this environment a window manager creates a friendly face overlaying X-Windows. The most popular by far is the Open Software Foundation's Motif window manager. Recently, the CDE is becoming widely employed. The CDE is clearly designed to rival the ease of use available with Microsoft Windows and the Apple Macintosh. (Although this topic is discussed in later chapters, it is important to note that X-Windows is operating system independent and can therefore also reside on other systems like Windows NT.)

The final interface involves the use of yet another layer of code that either emulates the Microsoft Windows environment or provides a means of reverse displaying Windows applications from a Windows NT host onto a UNIX X11-based display. Several commercial Microsoft Windows emulators are available, including Sun's Windows Application Binary Interface (WABI), which provides limited support for Windows applications executing on UNIX systems. Another approach involves the use of the Citrix WinFrame technology that turns Windows NT into a traditional multiuser operating system and thereby permits the local execution of applications that are then displayed remotely. Tektronic's Windows Distributed Desktop (WinDD) is an example of such a commercial product.

Networking Integration

If UNIX offered nothing else, its integration with the TCP/IP suite justifies its use. While developed independently, most professionals equate the TCP/IP suite as the heart of UNIX networking. The way TCP/IP seamlessly integrates with the multitasking functions of UNIX makes the technologies a natural complement. Part IV of this book describes this important networking relationship for both UNIX and Windows NT integration.

64-bit Architecture

While Microsoft is still limited to a 32-bit architecture, a small segment of the UNIX community is ahead with commercially available 64-bit systems. The increase in flat virtual memory addressability of 64-bit architecture from 4 GB to 16,000,000 GB clearly demonstrates the value of UNIX for power system users. Digital was the first to offer 64-bit UNIX implementations commercially.

The question must still be asked: What real-world benefit does a 64-bit architecture represent? There are several obvious responses.

- The flat address space of more than 4 GB dramatically impacts the potential performance of programs with very large file structures and, in particular, massive databases.

- Native arithmetic support for very large integer sets greatly enhances scientific and engineering applications, and commercial financial software that require rapid and complex number manipulation.

- Software developers are provided greater freedom in designing software that does not have to conform to strict, flat address space parameters.

- Overall machine performance improves with the expansion of large virtual memory addresses.

Mature, Robust, and Proven

Anyone who has dealt with computer hardware and software is familiar with viewing new computer releases with some skepticism. When new software is released, people often sing the same tune: I'll wait until the bugs are worked out before I install it. The beauty of UNIX is that it has been around long enough that most of the bugs have been fixed. Even though UNIX as an operating system is continuing to grow and improve, it is solid and reliable. When choosing a UNIX operating system, system administrators are utilizing a full functioning system that has proved itself over time.

Vendor Independent

As discussed earlier in this chapter, a great number of organizations and individuals contributed to creating the UNIX operating system that we use today. This diversified approach to development created an operating system that is powerful and that can run over a wide range of hardware. It is truly a vendor-independent system. Users can choose which hardware configuration best fits their computing needs and then choose the variant of UNIX that reflects these requirements. While most of the major hardware manufacturers have their own variant of UNIX (e.g., Hewlett-Packard has HP-UX, IBM has AIX, Sun has Solaris), these versions only serve to increase the functionality of UNIX. When (and if) a unified UNIX materializes, the input and expertise of a variety of vendors can only serve to increase the strength of an already powerful operating system.

Multiuser, Distributed Applications

UNIX supports both traditional multiuser and distributed applications. In a multiuser environment the application resides on the server and is accessed through a serial terminal. All information resides on the server. Through the use of the X-Windows client/server architecture, UNIX supports the distribution of graphical applications, which means that GUI-based software and the files they generate can be shared from UNIX X-terminals or workstations. Contrast this with how Windows NT addresses applications like Microsoft Word. In the latter case, a copy of the application must reside on the workstation, with only individual files capable of being shared across the network.

UNIX WEAKNESSES: REAL AND PERCEIVED

The UNIX operating system has both real and perceived weaknesses. In this section we briefly visit its shortcomings.

Perceived by New Users as Difficult to Use

If there is a single criticism directed at UNIX, it is the difficulty novices' experience using it. Even among the strongest UNIX proponents, this argument is widely acknowledged as valid. Many powerful options can be executed from the basic UNIX prompt, but few that can be considered intuitive. New users often look at their screen and say: What do I do next?

The basis for most criticism of UNIX's unfriendliness is rooted on the command line. For the novice, UNIX command line instructions appear cryptic, and the ability to string commands together through the use of pipes can be confusing initially. By contrast, experienced users affirm appreciation for these very same attributes. As another example, the concept of a shell interpreting UNIX commands is difficult to grasp initially. Individual users (and for that matter many administrators) get confused as to which commands are Korn shell built-ins versus operating system utilities. Novices generally ask: Why is the origin of the command important? The answer must be coupled with a reminder about the diverse development of UNIX variants. Different teams developed several shells. Each shell can interpret commands and built-ins differently. The Bourne shell (sh) and its successor the Korn shell (ksh) behave similarly, whereas the C shell (csh) will interact with many commands differently. (It should be noted that the Korn and C shells are syntactically different but similar in functionality.) Therefore, the user must be aware of the shell type invoked when login occurs.

UNIX Requires Skillful Administration

As with any operating system, the need for attention to the operating system is never ending. For example, although very rare, a single misbehaved application can create runaway processes that result in system overload. Even in very small UNIX shops, a fairly high level of system administrative technical skill is required. It is not reasonable to assume that a UNIX installation will function over time without system administrative intervention. By the same token, Windows NT Server also requires system administrative support. Both operating systems require professionally trained management.

Application Binary Incompatibility across UNIX Variants

While UNIX proponents point to its portability, this does not translate to compatibility of applications across platforms. Different binaries must be maintained for each variant of UNIX and chip set. Even different versions of the same UNIX variant often must be recompiled. This means that both software vendors and end users must maintain multiple versions of the same application sets in heterogeneous environments. This is a management challenge.

As an example, one UNIX software developer has to maintain several dozen different versions of its office automation and groupware suite. To support customers with different computer systems and operating system releases, the company must support four versions of IBM AIX, three for SCO, two for Hewlett-Packard, six for Sun, three for Digital, and so forth. To make this even more complex, versions for both character-based and Motif environments are required. In the character-based arena, support for scores of terminals is maintained for each of the UNIX variants. Obviously this is a daunting task and is a real headache for system administrators supporting multivariant UNIX. If a popular application is purchased across a multiplatform enterprise, then version management is critical.

The Open Group (formerly X/Open and the Open Software Foundation) branding of UNIX may reduce these problems. Through enforcement of Spec 1170 for UNIX 95 branding, the long-term objective is to provide application binary compatibility. Frankly, this is a promise made before and broken. . . . This jury is still out.

Perception of Higher Hardware Costs

There is a perception that UNIX systems require greater system overhead, resulting in much costlier hardware solutions. Although this is a largely debatable perception, we have listed it as a negative because certain computer manufacturers have greatly inflated the cost of components on the higher end where Intel-based systems cannot play. For example, one major UNIX manufacturer is currently charging $50 per megabyte of memory for its RISC-based box while comparable memory for an Intel system is selling for one tenth of that price. Other devices from that manufacturer, such as hard disks, are similarly priced.

Another reason for the perception of higher UNIX system prices is that this operating system supports high-end machines outside the realm of Windows NT. Unlike Intel boxes that can be commodity priced, proprietary chip sets and architectures do not enjoy the quantity manufacturing runs that permit lower costs. In addition, these systems by definition are designed for larger and higher performance work tasks. Therefore, a $50,000 or much higher price tag is not out of line if performance needs are met.

When loading UNIX and Windows NT on an Intel-based machine, the overhead requirements are roughly the same. However, for some unexplained reason at least two major manufacturers charge more for a system to support UNIX than they do for a Windows NT Server system. The hardware components are identical and the operating systems bear comparable prices. Yet despite these facts, companies have elected to sell UNIX solutions at a premium. There is no logic behind this pricing differential. Therefore, the perception of UNIX being higher priced is at least partially based on artificial market practices.

WINDOWS NT: A CALCULATED SUCCESS STORY

We refer to UNIX as an unusual success story because of its emergence as the leading server operating system despite its disjointed origins. The success of Windows NT is very different. The minions at Microsoft have carefully crafted an operating system that borrows heavily from competitors while adding a familiar and friendly front end. Who would not love an operating system that incorporates some of the best of UNIX, NetWare, VMS, DOS, and OS/2, and adds a Windows 95 look and feel? To a very large extent, Microsoft has succeeded in producing a robust environment that captures the best of the old while leveraging the future.

On a superficial level, UNIX and Windows NT are very similar. They are both multipurpose, multitasking networking powerhouses. They also are considered excellent environments for application development. Windows NT also freely embraces guidelines written by industry groups long associated with UNIX, like a subset of the POSIX.1 standard. De facto standards such as native TCP/IP are also bundled within both operating system environments. However, despite these and other similarities, Windows NT is also a very different operating system in structure and execution.

The history of Windows NT is relatively short, but its parentage is nearly two decades old. Windows NT combines a number of technologies and integrates them uniquely into a power package (Figure 2.2). The formal history of Windows NT began in 1993. At that time Microsoft had recently split ways with IBM on OS/2. Windows NT was widely viewed as a curious little network operating system (NOS) designed as a challenger to IBM's OS/2 LAN Manager. Obviously, Microsoft had bigger plans than what was perceived by industry naysayers. The first upgrade came a year later as version 3.5. This offered many significant improvements in performance and scope of functionality. Unfortunately the industry was transfixed on the forthcoming release of Windows 95 (then still called *Chicago*), thus leaving Windows NT 3.5 as a back-page story. The 1995 release of Windows NT 3.51 added to the networking functionality and offered a greatly enhanced suite of server products known as BackOffice. With Windows NT 3.51, Microsoft was viewed as real threat to NOS vendors such as Novell. Since its release in late 1996, Windows NT 4.0 has experienced unprecedented market acceptance. It has eclipsed Novell's NetWare product family and taken a bite out of UNIX enterprise sales.

The single most important advancement made with the release of Windows NT 4.0 is the incorporation of the Windows 95 user interface. In fact, Microsoft internally refers to Windows NT 4.0 as the Shell Update Release, referring to the Windows 95 front end. Windows 4.0 has added the Distributed Common Object Model (DCOM) and enhanced Domain Name Server (DNS) support for its TCP/IP transport. A few enhancements to the BackOffice suite have also been added, in particular the Exchange mail server. This version also includes additional, certified security functionality for E3, C2, and F-C2 compliance.

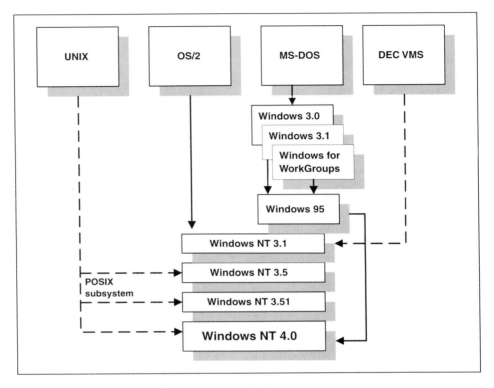

FIGURE 2.2.   Windows NT History and Influences

WINDOWS NT BENEFITS: REAL AND PERCEIVED

Windows NT provides a number of strengths and benefits to its users. These range from a friendly user interface to strong system administration support. The following is a detailed discussion of the benefits of Windows NT.

Familiar and Proven User Interface

Millions of users instantly feel comfortable with the new Windows 95 user interface shell available with the Windows NT 4.0 server and workstation. Although arguments abound regarding whether this interface is the ultimate in ease of use, there is no question that it is familiar (Figure 2.3) and in active use world wide. From the vantage of a system administrator, this becomes an important training and usability consideration. Windows NT 4.0 is being embraced in a large part because of the perception of reduced training costs.

FIGURE 2.3.   Windows NT Screen

Adherence to De Facto and Certain Industry Standards

Windows NT, at least in part, embraces two types of standards—those supported by industry groups and those that emerge naturally from market utilization as de facto. Windows NT embraces a subset of the IEEE POSIX.1.

Nowhere is Microsoft's adherence to de facto standards more evident than in terms of network technology. An example is the use of a portion of the TCP/IP network protocol suite. The marketplace, primarily through the explosion of the Internet, has dictated that TCP/IP is the enterprise network transport facility of choice. Another widely used networking standard is Novell's IPX/SPX. Microsoft bundles with Windows NT NWLink, an IPX/SPX-compatible clone. The final transport protocol shipped with Windows NT is Microsoft's own NetBEUI, an older standard for simple local area network (LAN) PC-based networks. On the UNIX side, a freeware product called SAMBA provides support of NetBEUI connectivity. Part IV of this book explores these related network issues.

Support for Commodity-based Hardware

The prevailing use of Windows NT 4.0 is on Intel-compatible PCs. With reasonably powerful Windows NT workstations coming to market at less cost than a compatible, diskless X-terminal, many corporate buyers are looking favorably at the implicit cost advantage. While UNIX-supported dumb terminals are clearly a lot less expensive, the differential is rapidly shrinking. Souped-up Intel boxes can be easily configured to accommodate the demands of the Windows NT server. One recent cost model we prepared showed a clear cost efficiency in purchasing an Intel-compatible server and workstations as opposed to a RISC-based UNIX server with dumb terminals. However, in defense of UNIX, the hardware cost of supporting that operating system in an Intel-compatible environment is the same. This might lead to the conclusion that cost factors may be merely perceptual. Despite the widely held belief that PC ownership is inexpensive, the real costs are more than the $2,000 initial purchase price denotes. Each system must support individual copies of software. Training, maintenance, and support also play into this equation. The key is that so many existing desktop computers have Windows 3.1 or Windows 95 installed; therefore, these systems are natural clients to the Windows NT server.

Cross-Platform Support (Although Limited)

Windows NT supports both 32-bit x86 Intel class CISC microprocessors and currently only one RISC-based CPU. The early industry buzz was that Windows NT platform support would sweep across all major architectures. For a while, this prophecy was being fulfilled. Digital's Alpha AXP systems have been the most successful non-Intel implementation of Windows NT to date. Although originally supported, the MIPS R4000-class processors and IBM PowerPC architecture are no longer part of the Windows NT hardware family.

Software Portability

Microsoft claims that porting applications from one platform to another requires no code changes. Because only two hardware architectures are now supported, this is somewhat a nonissue (although it could become important in the future.) As software developers for many UNIX variants, we can attest to the fact that porting applications is a costly and time-consuming nightmare. If Microsoft's claims for Windows NT prove correct, then this might be one of the single most compelling reasons to migrate to Windows NT. To a system administrator, having to maintain fewer binaries and an application set that uses the same set of device drivers equates to a potential headache removed.

Digital has an add-on product for its Alpha-based CPUs that permits applications compiled for Intel boxes to run. FX!32 provides an emulation layer that permits shrink-wrapped Windows NT applications to operate on Alpha even though they were compiled for Intel.

Interestingly, the UNIX community is taking special note of Microsoft's Hardware Abstraction Layer (HAL). SCO and Hewlett-Packard have announced an initiative to develop its own layer of code to buffer the hardware from the operating system. Theoretically, the 3DA (three-dimensional architecture) could serve the same type of function as HAL for software portability.

Easy to Install and to Configure

If you believe Microsoft's literature, the Windows NT workstation and server installation process requires minimal system administration intervention. If you are armed with basic information about your Internet Protocol (IP) address, domain name, host name, and related standard data, then the installation process is indeed effortless. Configuration is just as simple. The individual user and system administrator are walked through a menu- and dialog-based process. On the negative side, the users' ability to reconfigure their own workstations can lead to a certain level of system administrative headache, particularly if you imagine a user altering the IP addresses.

Excellent Device Support

Installation and configuration of devices is very straightforward when utilizing the Windows NT Wizard-based assistance scheme (Figure 2.4). The system automatically detects installed devices and helps the user make appropriate decisions. For the system administrator, network device support is also provided.

Contrast this support to what a system administrator faces installing devices on most UNIX systems. When performing this task from the command line, you need to be armed with extensive technical information about the device and with knowledge of how to make a device file and how to configure the operating system kernel properly. Even with modern UNIX system administrative tools, the ability to autodetect and analyze devices is still lacking.

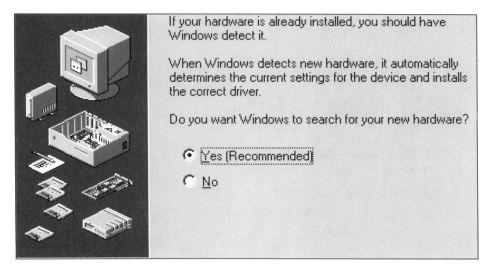

FIGURE 2.4.   Device Installation Wizard

Widely Used Application Development API

The Windows NT operating system offers support for familiar APIs that aid countless Windows programmers in developing compatible applications. Among the standards that are supported for Win32 applications are Dynamic Data Exchange, Object Linking and Embedding (OLE 2.0), and Windows socket technology. Updates to support ActiveX controls are anticipated.

Peer-to-Peer and Client/Server Support

The hallmark of Windows for Workgroups was its support for small LANs with peer-to-peer topology (Figure 2.5). Windows NT incorporates this technology and adds the hierarchical client/server architecture for enterprise-size organizations. In terms of integrating Windows NT and UNIX systems, the ability of both operating systems to support client/server and peer-to-peer relationships opens many options to a TCP/IP-based mixed operating system environment.

Security Features

One of the strengths of UNIX is its security paradigm. As we discuss in Chapters 6 through 8, Windows NT takes the concept of user and system security

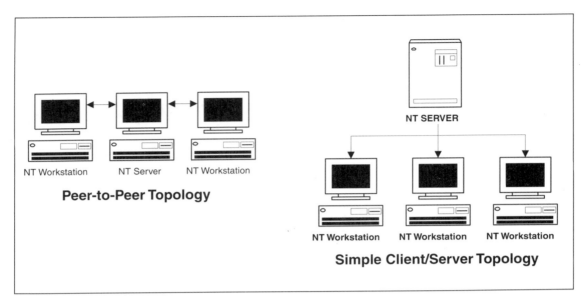

FIGURE 2.5.   Simple Network Topology

several steps beyond. Microsoft's model is both robust and easy to administer. The ability to authenticate user account logon centrally is a feature that should make the life of any system administrator much easier.

Integrated Management Tools and Applications

Microsoft put a lot of forethought into providing a suite of integrated management tools and services. For example, system performance monitoring is supported by both graphical- and character-based applications. This stands in stark contrast to many variants of UNIX in which such tools are expensive add-on products.

Built-in Fault Tolerance for System Availability

The concept of system clustering is one of the industry's hottest topics. One of the bases for clustering is system availability and fault-tolerant fail-over. Windows NT provides built-in fault tolerance technology. In addition, it supports redundant array of inexpensive disks (RAID) disk management.

WINDOWS NT WEAKNESSES: REAL AND PERCEIVED

As with any application or operating system, there is room for improvement within Windows NT. Microsoft appears to be aggressively addressing both the real and perceived "weaknesses" with software patches, documentation updates, and further development.

Limited Support for Traditional Multiuser System

As mentioned previously, Windows NT is not a true multiuser system in the tradition of UNIX. This means that access to centralized or distributed applications is not natively supported in the manner customary to UNIX. Windows NT workstations are generally loaded with their own copies of common applications. However, as discussed in Chapter 10, the Microsoft-supported WinFrame from Citrix provides an additional layer of code that converts Windows NT into a traditional multiuser system. Shared network applications are supported in the same way as older LAN-based applications.

Scalability: More Perceived Limitation than Reality

Critics of Windows NT hammer at the concept that the operating system has limited scalability. As we discuss in later chapters, Microsoft has yet to achieve its own stated goals on this front, but has achieved a level of scalability that still places Windows NT Server 4.0 in a first-class position. UNIX remains a bit more scalable, but this picture could shift rapidly. One of the major promotional themes in Microsoft literature is the fact that Windows NT now breaks new ground in its support of multiple processors. This is a significant advancement for Microsoft-based operating systems. Windows NT does provide for symmetric multiprocessors. This support is limited in both type and number of processors. Out of the box, Windows NT supports four processors. Some hardware vendors ship systems supporting up to thirty-two processors. (It should be noted that products such as Sun Solaris currently scale to sixty-four processors.)

Blue Screen of Death: System Failure

With any new operating system, one has to expect a certain number of bugs. Microsoft Windows NT 4.0 is no exception. A number of service patches have been released to overcome problems. When failure occurs, the system will display what has been dubbed by media critics as the Blue Screen of Death. Fortunately, this is now a very rare occurrence.

Limited to 32-bit Architecture

Windows is limited to a strictly 32-bit architecture. This restricts virtual memory access to 4 GB. Considering the previous generation of Microsoft operating systems had a 16-MB limit, an increase to 4 GB would seem impressive. However, Windows NT divides memory access into two 2-GB address sets—one for the system and one for applications. Contrast this to the fact that 32-bit UNIX systems permit access to the full 4 GB of virtual memory. Further, 64-bit versions of UNIX are slowly emerging. This provides 16 exabytes (18,446,744,073,709,551,616 bytes) of data access compared to merely 4 GB.

Proprietary Yet Open Interface

Windows NT is largely a closed and proprietary operating system controlled by a single vendor. This is one of those issues that can be viewed as both a weakness and strength. Yes, Microsoft does embrace third-party standards such as TCP/IP, but how the code is managed is strictly their decision. Computer hackers would prefer a world where all source code was freely available. However, in the real world, many advances are not spawned by a free exchange of information, but from the profit motive. Therefore, we must all be happy for Microsoft's good financial fortunes because it has allowed the company to invest in products like Windows NT. By the same token, detractors claim that the overwhelming market advantage of Microsoft only stifles innovation. This issue is clearly a double-edged sword when contrasting it to UNIX. When Microsoft delivers a version of Windows NT, we can generally feel assured that a unified set of binaries will be delivered. Historically, when a new version of UNIX has been released, we still count on dozens of variants.

System Administrative Attention Required

One of Microsoft's stated goals was to produce a zero-management operating system. Unfortunately, there is no operating system today that can manage itself. Windows NT is no exception. Managing a Windows NT enterprise can be as taxing as administrating UNIX for many of the same reasons. First, there is the ever-present user. Although the argument is made that the time required for managing users is reduced because of the familiar Windows 95 user interface, our interviews with system administrators suggest that this is not always the case. Users that refuse to learn or follow basic rules are just as likely to create headaches for a UNIX or Windows NT system administrator. Secondly, managing a Windows NT enterprise is still very complex. Although the consistent administrative tools available with Windows NT are generally superior to their UNIX counterparts, extensive resources are still required.

FINAL THOUGHTS

We were biased in favor of the UNIX operating system when we began this book project. After all, we have been UNIX software publishers for more years than we want to admit. However, this bias has evaporated. After close examination of Windows NT, we must conclude that Microsoft has developed a formidable competitor that can easily hold its own. Both UNIX and Windows NT have major operating system strengths. It is to these strengths and how they interrelate that we direct most of our attention in this book.

System Administration Primer for UNIX and Windows NT

A need exists for cross-operating system administrative skills. The first three chapters of Part II provide an overview of the UNIX operating system and highlight tasks and issues common to its administration. These chapters were written for Windows NT system administrators who need to acquire UNIX skills. The last three chapters take the reverse approach; they provide an overview of Windows NT and common administrative tasks and issues. These chapters are designed for UNIX system administrators who need to develop an understanding of Windows NT. When appropriate, the two operating systems are cross-referenced.

- Chapter 3, UNIX Structure, Processes, and Users
- Chapter 4, Tasks Common to UNIX System Administration
- Chapter 5, UNIX Topics
- Chapter 6, Windows NT Structure, Processes, and Users
- Chapter 7, Tasks Common to Windows NT System Administration
- Chapter 8, Other Advanced and Miscellaneous Windows NT Topics

UNIX Structure, Processes, and Users

In many ways UNIX must be regarded as the ultimate "feel good" operating system. Every user has a home. The home is protected by passwords and permissions that can be changed by the user. You are automatically granted individual privileges and retain ownership to the contents of your home environment. All users also belong to one or more groups. The community of users is monitored by a good system administrator whose primary responsibilities focus on user needs and system health. Helpers known as *daemons* scamper about to make sure that user and operating system tasks are completed. Daemons should not be confused with mystical evil demons; UNIX daemons are good things. Even when the user does not have an active login session, these daemons are hard at work delivering mail and performing maintenance jobs. Every file and process within UNIX has a parent. The parent watches over the activities of their children. In this "perfect world" no children exist without a parent. Occasionally a child will run away, but it is promptly adopted by the root operating system. On rare instances, a process goes wild and becomes a zombie. The system administrator must be ever aware of zombies taxing the system and must take action to kill the cyber living dead on behalf of the overall health of the user, file, and process communities. Home, life, death, family, and community are all part of the wonderful world of UNIX. Center stage in this drama is the UNIX system administrator. Welcome to the wonderful world of UNIX.

THE UNIX TRIANGLE: STRUCTURE, PROCESSES, AND USER INTERVENTION

UNIX must be viewed from the perspective of structure, processes, and user intervention. These three elements form a triangular relationship (Figure 3.1).

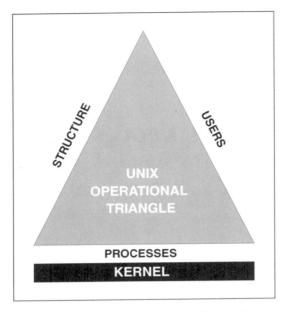

FIGURE 3.1.   UNIX Operational Triangle

As a system administrator, an understanding of the co-dependence of each side of the UNIX triangle is fundamental. In discussing structure, we refer to the role of the file as the basis of all operating system organization. UNIX processes transform files into specific actions and data storage. Finally, user intervention is the great variable that converts the predictable UNIX operating system into a dynamic, almost living, environment.

UNIX TRIANGLE SIDE 1: STRUCTURE

The structure of the UNIX operating system (Figure 3.2) is based on the concept that all elements are files. Some of the files contain data, whereas others launch processes and control devices. The UNIX kernel is the single most important file in the operating system. It regulates virtual memory, the file system, network connectivity, signals, semaphores, processes, application pipes, and hardware devices through compiled drivers. The kernel is usually called *vmunix* or just *unix*, although some vendors will use product-specific names such as *hp-ux*. If the kernel file is accidentally removed or damaged, the UNIX operating system is disabled. Kernels are dynamic files that are rebuilt periodi-

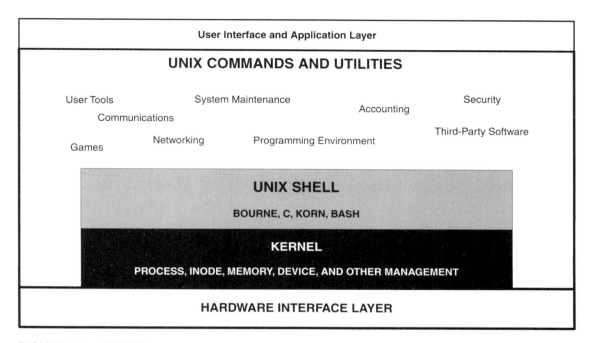

FIGURE 3.2.   UNIX Structure

cally by the system administrator to update a variety of parameters ranging from adding devices to changing inode allocations. Residing above the kernel is a command interpreter called a *shell*. It translates kernel parameters and applications into human interface terms. The Bourne shell (sh) was the first UNIX command interpreter. While still widely used, the C shell, Korn shell, and Born Again Shell (BASH) have greater functionality and are more commonly employed. The final set of components are utilities, commands, and third-party applications that are employed by the user. Each of these programs is a file that launches UNIX processes either independently or with the assistance of daemons.

UNIX Structure: Files and the File System

The basic structure of UNIX revolves around a simple and eloquently designed file system. It manages the storage of files and provides a referencing system for file utilization. It is hierarchical, with all structures centered around the root file system (noted by a forward slash). From root (/), a number of other file systems, individual files, and directories emanate. Every element within the operating system is a file.

The file system appears to the user as a neatly organized hierarchy in the form of an inverted tree. In fact, the tree structure is an illusion created for the convenience of the human mind. In reality, it contains flat file structures of numbers and pointers that track files. All file systems have three components in common:

1. *Superblock* – Information on the physical data and the file system structure itself, including the file system size, and the number, list, and index of free blocks plus the number and index of free inodes

2. *Inode list or table* – An index of information about the location and characteristics of files

3. *Data blocks* – Storage of actual data

All files systems are mounted under the root file system. A file system resides on a single slice. Before reviewing the file system structure in further detail, it is appropriate first to examine the key component—the UNIX file.

What Is a UNIX File?

The concept of a file within UNIX is very important to understand. Just as we humans are carbon based, UNIX is file based. All data and system instructions are stored in files. Every process including memory allocations filter through files. Even how hardware devices perform functions are automated through UNIX files. A file can be of different types and maintain varied characteristics. This section summarizes file types, characteristics, and relationships.

There are several types of files (Table 3.1). By far the most common are regular files that do not have a specifically imposed structure. They are either ASCII character streams or compiled executable programs. Other files within the UNIX operating system have more specific functions and/or limitations. To determine the file type rapidly, the UNIX command *file* can be utilized against the filename. For example

```
$ file  filename
filename            ascii text
```

How Files Are Tracked and Stored

Files have both a name and a system identification number (*inode*). Files also occupy physical space on a hard drive. When the user performs a long list (*ls -l*) command, it appears that the files within the working directory are neatly organized in consecutive order. This impression is very misleading. In fact, files are

TABLE 3.1.   UNIX File Types

Types	Description
Standard/regular files	This is a collection of characters that can take the form of ASCII data streams and compiled binaries (also called *executables*). Files can have multiple names by the use of hard links. The operating system imposes no structure on a regular file.
Directories	A UNIX directory is a structured file containing a paired list of inodes and filenames. While a user may get the impression that files under the directory are actually contained within, the directory is an artificial construct that points to the files. Directories can have child subdirectories and may be nested to any depth.
Linked	Files can be symbolic or hard linked. In the first case, a filename points to another file. The symbolic link is often used to execute a command outside of the normal user path in another file system. Directories can also be linked symbolically. The hard link provides a dynamic relationship of a file with two different names or a file with the same filename but often residing in different directories. A hard link must be performed within the same file system, and directories cannot be hard linked. The *ln* command creates hard-linked files. When the *-s* option is invoked with *ln,* it then becomes symbolic.
Block devices	This is a special file generally located in the */dev* directory to control the behavior of devices that use fixed memory or data blocks.
Character devices	This is a special file generally located in the */dev* directory to control the behavior of devices that do their own buffering a character at a time.
Named pipes and sockets	Named pipes (derived from AT&T UNIX) permit interaction between two unrelated processes. Sockets (BSD based) files invoke points of contact for asynchronous communication and execute noninvolved processes.

typically stored in data blocks, often on a noncontiguous basis. A block is 512 bytes (or 1,024 bytes for long blocks). If a file is only 1 byte in size, it will still occupy an entire data block. By the same token, a file with 513 bytes takes two blocks. Most UNIX systems maintain "logical" blocks of one, two, four, eight, and sixteen blocks so that some level of contiguous storage is possible. However, in large multiple-block files, the information may be scattered anywhere on the physical storage device. The operating system tracks files through the maintenance of an inode table (Figure 3.3). Think of the inode table as a giant index that points to the physical location of file blocks and stores other data. The following information is retained in the inode table:

- The owner's user and group identification number (UID and GID)
- The type of file (designated by two digits [01, named pipes; 02, character devices; 04, directory; 06, block device; 10, ordinary or regular files; 12, symbolic link; and 14, sockets])
- Date of last modification for both the content of the file and any inode data

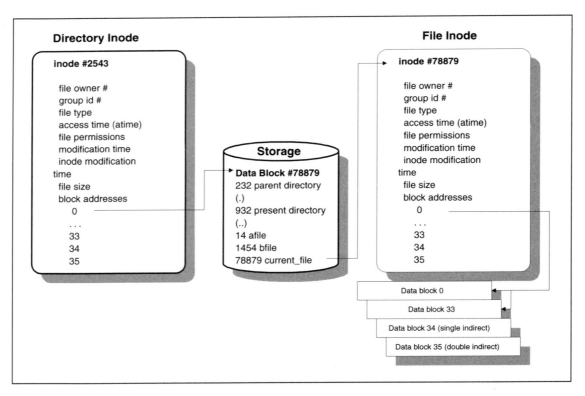

FIGURE 3.3.   Inode Relationships

- Number of bytes of data or physical size
- Number of links to the file
- Data block addresses on the disk where the file is stored

Hard links use the same inode number and therefore must exist in the same file system. This is because hard-linked files are the same file but are listed with different names for the convenience of users. Symbolic links, on the other hand, use different inode numbers. Symbolic links are pointers to a file on the same or a different file system.

File Characteristics: Permissions and Ownership

All UNIX files embody two important security-based characteristics: permissions and ownership. The concept of permissions involves how a file may be used. Ownership involves who can access the file based on established permissions. There are three levels of file ownership: user/owner, group, and all others. Eight levels of permission (also called *modes*) can be set for each file. When coupled with the three levels of ownership, a large number of possible combinations exist. At one extreme, a file cannot be viewed, modified, or executed by anyone; at the other end, all of these possibilities exist. For each ownership level, the levels of permissions or modes are

- *None* – No activity permitted including viewing the file
- *Read only* – The file can be opened for the purpose of examining its contents
- *Write only* – Seldom used; the file can be modified without being read
- *Execute only* – Seldom used; this permits execution of the file contents only
- *Read and write* – A file can be opened and modified
- *Read and execute* – A file can be examined and its contents executed
- *Write and execute* – Seldom used; the file can be modified (without opening) and executed
- *Read, write, execute* – The file has read, write, and execute permission

In addition to file permissions, a file also is characterized by three levels of ownership:

- *File owner* – The user that controls the permissions and ownership of the file
- *Group owners* – Any user belonging to the designated group (such as the engineering or marketing departments) can perform tasks as designated by the permissions
- *Other users* – Any other user with a system login can act on the file at the level set by the permissions

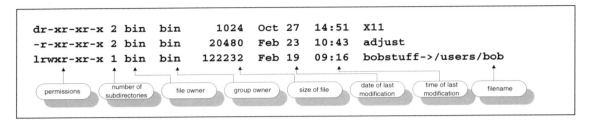

FIGURE 3.4.   Dissection of Long File Listing

When performing a long list (*ls -l*) command, information about the file type, permissions, ownership, and other data is provided. The first column identifies the type of file and its associated permissions. The second column indicates the number of links existing for a file or a directory. All files except directories register a 1, unless they are linked to another filename. The third column lists the owner of the file. It should be noted, as shown in Figure 3.4, that ownership can extend to nonhuman users such as root, bin, sys, and so forth. The next column identifies group ownership, followed by the file size. The last date and time of file modification are found in columns 6 and 7, respectively. Finally, the file name is shown. If the file is linked symbolically, a pointer is provided to the parent file.

A closer look at the first column is warranted. Note the first character in the permissions column. In most cases it is proceeded by a dash (-) to signify a normal file. A directory is designated by the letter *d*. Block and character devices begin with the letters *b* or *c,* respectively. The letter *s* is used for a sticky bit, a special type of executable file, or a socket file. A linked file is designated by the letter *l.* Finally, a named pipe is proceeded by the letter *p.*

The file type designator is followed by three sets of three permission mode characters (Figure 3.5). The first three letters define the permissions held by the file owner. A designation of *rwx* means that the owner has read, write, and execute permission on the file. The second collection of three characters are reserved for a user group. If the group permissions are *rw-*, this means that any-

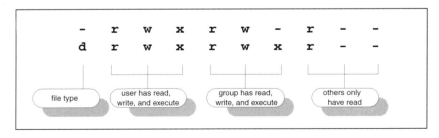

FIGURE 3.5.   Dissection of the Permissions Column

one within the designated group membership can read and modify (write) to the file, but cannot execute it. In this particular example, lacking execute permission is not too surprising since most UNIX files contain data streams and are not meant to be an executable script or UNIX program. However, it is more common for a user to provide members of the group read permission only (*r--*). The third series of letters provides permission for all others with a system login. In this case, it is very common to only provide read (*r--*) or no access (*---*). Some files have default settings. For example, symbolically linked files have read, write, and execute permissions set for all user levels (*lrwxrwxrwx*). Device files have read, write, and execute permissions set for only its owner (*brwx------*), the system itself.

Directories have a different relationship to permissions. How the directory is set will impact all those files under its structure. The read permission permits the review of files within the directory. With write permission, files can be added, deleted, moved, and renamed. Subdirectories can also be made with the write bit. Execute sanction is treated as a search bit. If the execute bit is turned off, then search programs like *find* cannot view inside the directory. This also restricts the ability to execute files within the directory.

FILE PERMISSION AND OWNERSHIP AS A SECURITY FEATURE

File permission and group ownership are the second line of defense in the UNIX security schema (the first line being the logon process with passwords). For the user inclined to change or delete a file accidentally, the ability to turn off the write bit can save problems later. In a work group environment, providing read or write permission to close associates streamlines productivity. On the other end of the spectrum, restricting group and other permissions can safeguard the user from unauthorized file intrusion. Users must be cautious when changing modes or ownership.

NOTE   A Word of Caution to System Administrators

The system administrator has a special responsibility with regard to file permissions and ownership. First, a user with root authority can override the permissions and ownership of any user. Therefore, this "power" must be treated with extreme discretion. Second, changing permissions for system-critical files or directories can seriously undermine their integrity. Third, the system administrator may establish default user file permissions with the *umask* function. Fourth, through the effective use of group creation and maintenance, department work on shared files can be greatly improved.

CHANGING PERMISSIONS AND OWNERSHIP

File permissions and ownership can be changed easily by the superuser or the file's owner. The three commands used to accomplish these actions are explained in greater detail later:

- *chmod* – change the mode or permissions of a file or directory
- *chown* – change the ownership of a file or directory
- *chgrp* – change the group ownership of a file or directory

Changing the mode with *chmod* is often used. There are several ways to change the permissions of a file. One method is to use references that involve binary or octal referencing as shown in Table 3.2. To change a file to read, write, and execute permissions for the owner, group, and other category, the *chmod* syntax in binary is as follows, although this is an old method and is not always supported.

```
chmod 111 111 111 filename
```

The *chmod* syntax in octal is

```
chmod 777 filename
```

To change a file for the owner to read, write, and execute; for the group to read only; and for others to have no access, the *chmod* syntax in binary is as follows, although this is an old method and is not always supported.

```
chmod 111 110 000 filename
```

The *chmod* syntax in octal for this example is

```
chmod 760 filename
```

TABLE 3.2.   File Permission Levels

Permission level	Permissions	Octal setting	Binary setting
None	---	0	000
Execute only	--*x*	1	001
Write only	-*w*-	2	010
Write and execute	-*wx*	3	011
Read only	*r*--	4	100
Read and execute	*r*-*x*	5	101
Read and write	*rw*-	6	110
Read, write, and execute	*rwx*	7	111

Another method in setting permissions is to use a symbolic approach. In this case, letters are used to reference the equivalent binary or octal approach symbolically (Table 3.3).

The syntax used to change a mode with the symbolic method is probably easier for new users to grasp. For example, to *chmod* all users with read and write permission, the command line string is

```
chmod a=rw filename
```

A permission can be added or removed by the use of the plus (+) or minus (–) sign. To *chmod* a file adding the write bit to the group, the command is

```
chmod g+w filename
```

Changing ownership of a file is also easily accomplished using the *chown* command. However, caution must be exercised. For example, if a user changes the ownership of a file to a coworker, the file then becomes the property of the other user—the original owner loses all ownership control. To regain control, you have two options: (1) have the other user return ownership or (2) make a copy of the file (providing you still have sufficient permissions as part of a user group). The syntax for changing ownership is

```
chown new_owner_name filename
```

The string `new_owner_name` is actually the login name of the new owner.

Changing group ownership is similar to user ownership. The syntax for changing group ownership is

```
chgrp new_group_name filename
```

The string `new_group_name` is the name of the group as identified in the */etc/group* file.

TABLE 3.3.　Symbolic Ownership and Mode References

Letter	Description
u	Owner or user ownership
g	Group ownership
o	All others with a system login
a	All of the above user levels (user, group, and other)
r	Read permission
w	Write mode
x	Execute permission

TABLE 3.4.   Summary of *umask* Settings

Permission level	Permissions	Octal setting	Binary setting
None	---	7	111
Execute only	--*x*	6	110
Write only	-*w*-	5	101
Write and execute	-*wx*	4	100
Read only	*r*--	3	011
Read and execute	*r*-*x*	2	010
Read and write	*rw*-	1	001
Read, write, and execute	*rwx*	0	000

CHANGING DEFAULT FILE PERMISSIONS

Default file permissions can be changed with the *umask* command (Table 3.4). It is usually designated in the user's *.profile, .login,* or shell resource file. The *umask* command is counterintuitive to many because it is calculated by deducting permissions from the maximum allowable 777 level. For example, to set the default permission levels to read and write for the owner, and read only for the group and all other users, the *umask* setting would be calculated by subtracting the normal permissions numbers (in the case of octal) from 777. Therefore the *umask* command is represented as

```
umask 133
```

which sets the permissions for all new files to 644 or *rw-r--r--*.

Hierarchical File System

The UNIX file system is hierarchical in structure. From the perspective of a user, a file system looks just like a directory. In fact, moving or executing data on different file systems is done in the same way as directory manipulation. However, there are also differences depending on the file system type. First let's look at the sample file system structure (Figure 3.6 and Table 3.5). (The actual structure differs between UNIX variants.)

As presented in Figure 3.7, only / (root) is a file system and the rest are directories under the / (root) file system. To determine the mounted file systems, use the *df* (or *bdf* on some systems) command. This provides a listing of recognized files plus information pertaining to utilization levels. Another alter-

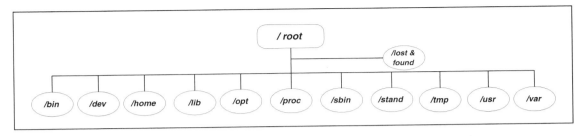

FIGURE 3.6.   First-level File System

native is to use the */etc/mount* command to view all of the currently mounted file systems.

There are several types of files systems (Table 3.6), some harkening back to early UNIX development.

Windows NT also offers optional file systems. They each provide unique capabilities and limitations. The native Windows NT file system NTFS provides the greatest security. The file allocation table (FAT) file system provides compatibility with existing DOS-based environments and is used primarily in installations where dual booting of the operating systems is desired. Finally, the high-performance file system (HPFS) provides compatibility with OS/2 (although this file system is no longer supported in Windows NT 4.0). The implications for using these file systems are discussed in Chapter 6.

File systems must be mounted to be accessible. When the system is first booted, file systems identified in the *filesystem* script are automatically checked using the *fsck* command and then mounted. Local file systems are mounted first, followed by defined network file systems. In addition to automatic action, a file system can be added by the system administrator anytime during run time. This activity is commonly done when mounting a device like CD-ROM, when adding a new disk, or when connecting network file systems (NFS). NFS are discussed in greater detail later. Before attempting to tackle this task, we recommend that you review the *man* pages for *mkfs, mount, umount, nfs, checklist,* and *exports.* The following examples illustrate how to add CD-ROM as a temporary file system, syntax for adding a new file system on a hard drive, and how to unmount both. To mount a file system or device, you must determine the device or file system name and establish a mount point. A mount is really nothing more than an existing directory (created by the *mkdir* command) that

TABLE 3.5.   UNIX File System Structure

Directory	Contents	Sample of contents
/	Root file system from which all structure is derived	Mounted file systems and standard system or user directories and files
/bin	Binary files; primarily UNIX commands that are linked symbolically to /usr/bin	*alias, batch, cal, cat, cd, chgrp, compress, cpio, date, diff, du, find, grep, ftp*
/dev	Input/output files (device files)	*dsk, mt, rdsk, mdsk, pttyX, ttyX*
/etc	Administrative files and system programs	*backup, config, cron, dump, fsck, fstab, getty, hosts, inetd, lp, mkfs, passwd*
/home	Directory where end user "home" directories are created	Some UNIX variants also store user home directories on /u, /usr, /users, and so on
/lib	Libraries used by the operating system or software applications; usually linked symbolically to other directories such as /usr/lib	Many libraries ending with .a are treated as static libraries and those ending with .sX are shared libraries that are linked symbolically to applications
/opt	Used in SVR4 systems for third-party application software	Varies among UNIX variants; examples are DCE
/proc	Process-oriented files	Not used on all UNIX systems, such as HP-UX
/sbin	System binary (executable) files	*cat, chmod, chown, date, fsck, init, ln, ls, mount, mv, rc, rm, shutdown, tar, who*
/stand	Standard configuration files are found optionally here, including the UNIX kernel	Varies depending on the operating system (sometimes these files are found in /root)
/tmp	Temporary files	Varies per boot session
/usr	Files that are invoked by the user directly or indirectly through user applications; may also contain the user's home directories	Subdirectories like /adm, /bin, /conf, /etc, /included, /lbin, /lib, /mail, /man, /spool, /include/bin
/usr/bin	More utilities	Generally the same as /bin
/usr/adm	System administration files and programs	*scct, crash, cron, lp, rc.log, streams, sulog*
/usr/include	Files used by the C compiler	Header files ending in .h that are referenced by applications at compile time
/usr/lib	More libraries (less critical than /lib)	Subclass of libraries used for specific applications needs, such as X11 support
/usr/mail	Mail	Varies depending on user activity
/usr/spool	Communication files and utilities including printer control; mail files may also be found here	*cron, locks, lp, mqueue, pcnsf, rwho, sockets, uucp*

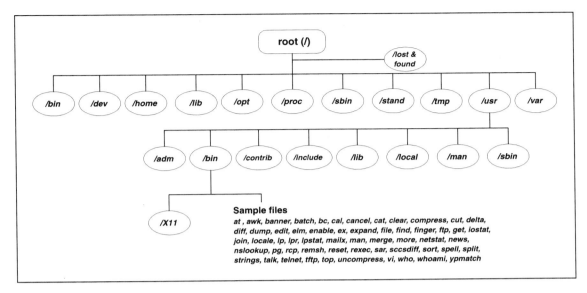

FIGURE 3.7.   File System Hierarchy

TABLE 3.6.   File System Types

Type	Characteristics
bfs	The boot file system is used particularly for system booting.
nfs	The network file system involves mounting file systems residing on a foreign host to a point on the local system using network protocols. From the vantage of the user, the network file system looks and acts like a local file system. It requires that the server share (export) its file system and the client must mount the "shared" file system.
s5	The System V file system enforces a number of specific limitations, including logical block sizes (512, 1,024, or 2,048 bytes), maximal inodes of 65,500 per file system, and fourteen-character filenames.
ufs	The universal file system is Berkeley based but is more expansive in many ways than the System V file system (s5). It supports symbolic links, maintains no inode limits, and permits filenames of 255 characters in length.
vxfs	This default file system for UNIX System V version 4.2 supports many performance and journal improvements, including expanded block allocation. Emergency "hard" shutdowns can be done without damaging the file system.

is used as a path to the mounted information. To mount a CD-ROM device (*/dev/cdrom*) at the mount point (*/cdrom*), the syntax of the command is

```
# mount -option /dev/cdrom /cdrom
```

where -option can be an option to make the device read only.

To create a file system and subsequently mount it for use, two commands must be entered. The syntax for these commands are

```
#mkfs -F filesystem_type -options device_name
#mount -option device_name mount_point
```

To unmount a file system, the syntax of the command is

```
# umount device_name
```

Directories and Paths

Files are grouped into directories (Table 3.7). A directory is really a mechanism for associating the filenames understood by humans with operating system-recognized inode data. The structure imposed by UNIX on the directory file is to pair the filename with the inode number. Directories also pair their own inode number and that of their parent. This is why a directory always appears to have a link associated with it when an *ls -l* command is executed. With the exception of / (root), all directories have a parent; they, in turn, can also support children or subdirectories. When the all long list (*ls -la*) command is invoked, the first thing a user notes is a single dot (.) followed by a double dot (..), signifying its own inode description and that of its parent, respectively. Directories help enforce relationships of one file to the other.

TABLE 3.7.   File Relationships

Type	Description
Subdirectory	Child to parent directory
Ordinary	Resides independently within a directory
Device files	Ordinary or regular files until compiled into the kernel, which controls the interaction of devices
Link file	Same file with different filename or different filename location (similar to creating a shortcut file in the Windows 95 or NT environment)
Symbolically linked	Pointer to another file

Directories form a hierarchical relationship with each other. Having sub-directories buried many levels is not uncommon. However, this also creates the problem of retrieving information from a file located in another directory. Moving between directories involves following a cyber road map known as a *path*. Three types of accesses through paths are commonly used:

1. *Export path* – Usually defined in the user's *.profile* or *.login* file using the *path* command; defines those directories that are automatically accessed when the system is searching for a file to execute

2. *Absolute path* – A method for moving between directories using the full description of the path (always starting from the / directory)

3. *Relative path* – A shortcut method of moving between directories relative to the current directory location that permits cryptic notations

The exported path can be set at login time (through *.profile*) or it can be expanded by the user at any time. For the exported path resolution to work, however, the user must have the proper execute permissions for the targeted directories. Because we discuss exporting or setting parameters in Chapter 5, it is sufficient to mention here that this is a task that instructs the operating system to assume a specific characteristic for the user's login environment. In this case, setting a path instructs the operating system to locate files within the designated directory. For example, if a user wanted to execute *calendar,* typing the command will display the function, providing the path has been set to include */usr/bin.* If the path was not set, the user would have to type /usr/bin/calendar <Enter> to execute the command. When changing the path, it is best first to see the current setting by typing

```
echo $PATH
```

This command will output results similar to the following:

```
/bin:/usr/bin:/usr/contrib/bin:/usr/local/bin:/usr/bin/X11:.
```

In this example, the user can execute commands from a number of directories containing common *bin*(ary) files. Therefore, utilities like *calendar, date,* and *sort* can be executed by typing them on the command line without having to input the full path */usr/bin/*(command). Note that each directory is separated by a colon. The string ends with a period to signify the user's own home directory.

Obviously it is not necessary to have the path set to move between directories. The absolute pathing method is the most cumbersome but the easiest for the new user. It involves simply typing the entire directory to change directory locations or to read, write, or execute a file within a specified directory (providing you have permission). The following examples show how to change a directory, and execute and open (*cat*) a file within a directory using an absolute path.

To change to a new directory, type

```
$ cd /usr/bob/special
```

To execute a program, type

```
$ /usr/bob/special/program
```

To open a file to view its contents, type

```
$ cat /usr/bob/special/program
```

The relative method is a type of shorthand that requires you first to understand in which directory the user is currently working. The *pwd* command prints the working directory to the screen. The term *relative* is used because you construct the path "relative" to your current position (Figure 3.8). Let's work through two examples of changing directories from */home/bob*—one that moves the user to a subdirectory and another that takes the user to another user's directory. The current directory is designated by a period. First, to confirm the current directory, enter the *pwd* command and observe the output.

```
$ pwd
/home/bob
```

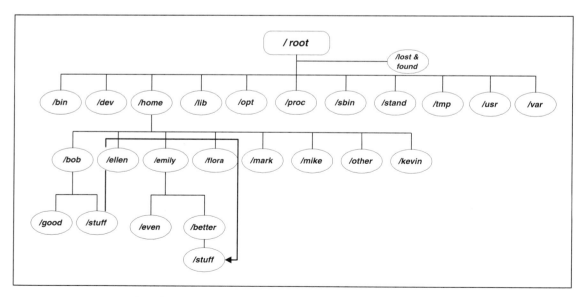

FIGURE 3.8.   Example of Relative Pathing

To change to the subdirectory */home/bob/stuff* from */home/bob,* all you must type is

```
cd ./stuff
```

If you want to move from */home/bob/special/stuff* to */home/emily/better/stuff* you move up the directory tree using the double dots (..) to define parent directories. Therefore, you type

```
cd ../../emily/better/stuff
```

NOTE   Common Directory Manipulation Actions

The following lists the most common actions (described in Appendix B) that can be taken with directories:

- *Make a directory* – Use the *mkdir* command
- *Delete a directory* – Use *rmdir* (empty directory) or *rm -r directory name*
- *Discover present directory* – Use the *pwd* command
- *Move to another directory* – Use the *cd* command

UNIX TRIANGLE SIDE 2: UNIX PROCESSES

Although the file system provides structure to UNIX, a file is nothing more than bits and bytes until an action "processes" the information. UNIX is very comparable to an organic being—from the moment of boot initialization (birth) until system shutdown (death), activities known as *processes* pulse through the operating system. Processes occur based on the kernel's defined parameters for system health and as a result of stimulation from external forces such as users, the network, or device interventions. The organism analogy doesn't stop here. All processes have parents and many can spawn children. However, unlike in nature, child processes cannot live without a parent. Occasionally, a child process does not die without its parent. When this happens, it is quickly adopted by the kindly old superuser root. Processes also have owners who keep them running or terminate them. The system administrator is responsible for ensuring that key system processes are running and unnecessary or runaway processes are destroyed.

UNIX is a true multitasking operating system. This means that many UNIX "processes" function simultaneously. This section explores the concept of UNIX processes from several perspectives.

- What are processes and how are they identified by UNIX?
- How are initialization and run-level states defined and configured?

- How are processes scheduled?
- What does the concept of processes mean to a UNIX user?

Understanding UNIX Processes

Multitasking is the operative word when discussing UNIX. Many processes function at the same time, both in the background and in the foreground. The system call that regulates the processes is *exec*. The UNIX kernel loads into memory the process through the *exec* system. Every process has a beginning and continues to run until the task is done, or killed or terminated.

Often a process will spawn one or more children. The system call that creates child processes is known as a *fork* (Figure 3.9). A new process can be created only by an already active process. In biological terms, the fork process is really more like the splitting of a single-cell organism.

As a new process is forked, the parent process first clones itself and copies its original process identification number (PID) to that of a parent process identification number (PPID). The new child is then provided its own unique PID. The new process causes the operating system to reset the virtual memory data stack and obtains a special memory address. A hierarchy of processes is thereby created.

In addition to the familiar hierarchy, the UNIX operating system tracks processes similar to how it tracks files (Figure 3.10). Like the inode table used for files, the kernel also maintains a process table. Each process has an identification number (PID) that is sequentially issued by the operating system. Once the system's maximum ID is reached, unused PIDs are then reclaimed and recycled. No process can exist without a parent. Like files, a process also retains the user ID and group ID of the individual executing the process. For persons developing UNIX applications, the programming structure for processes can be reviewed in the */usr/include/sys/proc.h* file.

FIGURE 3.9.   Process Forking

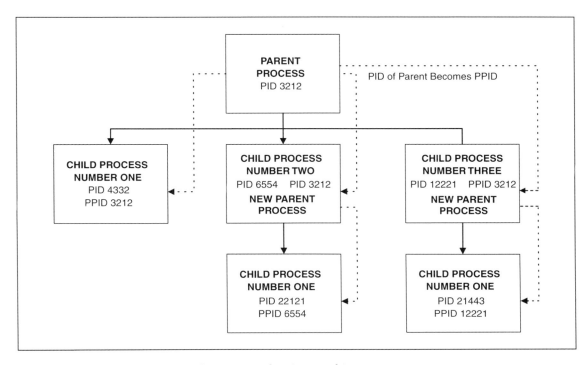

FIGURE 3.10.   Process Hierarchy Parent Identity Tracking

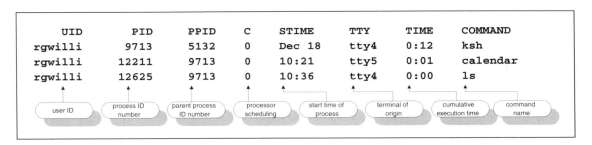

FIGURE 3.11.   Dissection of a Full Process Listing

PROCESS IDENTIFICATION

The *ps* command lists active user and system processes. When executed without options, *ps* registers the processes of the invoking user. To see every (*-e*) active process in full (*-f*) format, the *ps -ef* command provides extensive information about all running processes (Figure 3.11).

FOREGROUND AND BACKGROUND PROCESSING

Launching a process is as easy as typing a command. For example, the *ps -ef* command launches a process that was forked from the user's shell process. When UNIX first came on the market, and before X-Windows, a single line character terminal (tty) was used to invoke processes through the command line. This means that once a command was executed, the terminal could not be used until the process was completed. The developers of UNIX soon overcame this shortcoming by utilizing the operating system's multitasking functionality. Because many system processes run without the knowledge of the user, it became a logical extension to permit users to place a process in the background, thereby freeing the terminal's resources. When executing a process, the user can elect to run it in the foreground or background, depending on the amount of interaction desired by the user. The system default is to run the application in the foreground. To run a file in the background, the command string should end with an ampersand. To run *ps -ef* in the background, the user would type `ps -ef &` (although this is not a logical way to run this command because the user is running the command to observe the results that are displayed).

KILLING PROCESSES

All processes have a finite life. Some continue to run for the duration of a boot cycle, but most have a shorter life cycle. Terminating a process can be graceful or brutally hard. Most processes die of natural causes after they have completed their appointed task. Others die when the user specifically requests to end it by sending a kill signal (as embedded in well-behaved applications with a *quit* or *exit* option) or by using `<Ctrl-D>` or `<Ctrl-C>` key combinations. Still other processes are more stubborn and require the more aggressive *kill* command. Only the owner can kill the processes he owns. (Obviously the superuser has authority to kill any processes, including those owned by an individual user.) The key to successful process termination is to have the signals properly "trapped." *Trapping* means that the target process captures its signals and executes an orderly shutdown. Unfortunately, this is not always possible. There are several levels of process killing and the user should understand the implications of the most commonly employed *kill* command options (Table 3.8).

Process Use of Virtual Memory and Disk Swapping

All UNIX processes are executed in virtual memory except the kernel. The importance of the 64-bit architecture recently embraced by the newest generation of UNIX systems is obvious when considering the use of virtual memory. With 32-bit systems like older UNIX and the latest version of Windows NT, only

TABLE 3.8.   Kill Options

Kill command level	Description
kill	Regular process killing; generally forces a graceful exit; activities can be trapped; the same as executing a *kill -15*
kill -3	Terminates the process and forces the creation of a core file; activities can be trapped
kill -9	Kills with extreme prejudice; kills stubborn processes, but can result in damage to the interacting files such as databases; use with caution, activities *cannot* be trapped
kill -15	Forces a less graceful end of a process and is the default kill level; activities trapped

4 GB of virtual memory can be addressed, compared with 16,000,000 GB with a 64-bit system. Translated very simply, 64-bit UNIX is able to execute far many more processes (Figure 3.12).

When the UNIX operating system senses that it is near to full real memory utilization, it will attempt to free physical memory from the hard drive. UNIX utilizes two algorithms to perform this task. The first is known as *paging,* which allocates measured blocks of data per a free-space list maintained by the operating system. "Pages" of data are moved to the hard drive. The other method is known as *swapping,* and it transfers nonactive processes (defined in fractions of a second) in larger blocks to physical memory. When active processes are "swapped" to physical memory, a system crisis is at hand. A condition known as *thrashing* occurs in which constant disk accessing can overwhelm the system. When this occurs, the system administrator should immediately kill unnecessary processes. If the event transpires again, there are actions that system administrators can institute. For example, they can take measures to alter the real memory allocation, review the type of processes being executed, place system restrictions on the heaviest memory user, and/or increase swap space.

UNIX SYSTEM RUN LEVELS

In the most basic sense UNIX has three primary states—not running (halted), single user, and multiuser. Technically there are other gradations of run levels (Table 3.9) that can be invoked by the system administrator. Understanding the differences and uses of these run levels is fundamental to UNIX management. When a system is booted, a run level defined in the start-up scripts */etc/inittab* and */etc/rc2.d* are rendered. The run level can be increased or decreased as needed. A system administrator, before altering the system's default run level,

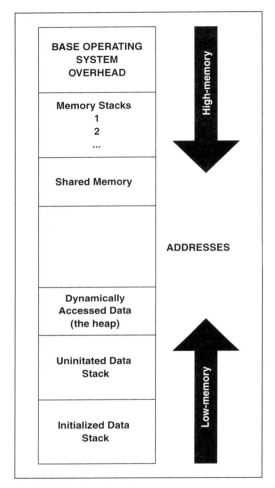

FIGURE 3.12.   Process Memory Stacks

must know the implications of changes to the system and active users. To find the run level of the system, execute the command *who -r.*

```
    run-level 3    Dec 12    14:22    3    0    S
```

EXAMINATION OF SINGLE-USER STATUS

The single-user run level, also known as the *maintenance mode,* is important for the system administrator. All unnecessary processes are terminated. Networking, mail, job scheduling, and user login functions are concluded. File systems are unmounted in some UNIX variants. This is used as a precaution so that files located elsewhere are not damaged. It also prevents other processes from

TABLE 3.9.   Run Level States

Level	Init level	Description
Level 0	*init 0*	Shut down the system
Level 1	*init 1*	Single-user mode: unmounts nonroot file systems; kills auxiliary processes; also known as *maintenance mode* and is sometimes referred to as run level *s* or *S*
Level 2	*init 2*	Multiuser mode
Level 3	*init 3*	Multiuser mode with network file-sharing level
Level 4	*init 4*	Mode defined by the user and user applications
Level 5	*init 5*	Firmware mode: used primarily for hardware upgrades
Level 6	*init 6*	Shut down and reboot the system
Level S	*init s or S*	Same as level 1, single-user mode
Level Q	*init q or Q*	Read the */etc/inittab* and verify the correct run state
Level a, b, c	*init a, b, c*	Don't change the run level but execute */etc/inittab* to update it

being written to disk. In single-user mode, the user is typically relegated to a character-based environment on the system console only. By definition, you are the superuser in this mode; therefore, the # root prompt appears on the console. The system administrator should revert to maintenance mode when severe system problems arise. The system automatically reverts to the single-user mode if the kernel, */etc/inittab,* or the / (root) file system is corrupted at login.

EXPLANATION OF SHUTDOWN INIT LEVELS

Two init levels cause a system shutdown. By executing *init 0,* the system is immediately brought down. This is generally employed in emergency situations or when no other user is logged onto the system. On some UNIX systems the *halt* command performs the same tasks as *init 0.* The *init 6* command also performs an immediate shutdown, but then reboots the system. This procedure is used to reset the system to the initial boot state. System administrators typically schedule a periodic shutdown and reboot. In some cases, executing *init 6* may be the only way to cure an unexpected problem. For example, a zombie process may be created that may begin eating extraordinary system resources. In most cases these processes can be terminated with a *kill -9,* but occasionally even this extreme kill signal will fail. The only option is to shut down and reboot the system to terminate the zombie and force a reset.

When multiple users are logged onto the system, it is recommended that the extended script, known as *shutdown,* be used. While it forces an *init 0, shutdown* provides the system administrator with control to support a more graceful system termination. For example, the time of the shutdown can be scheduled so that logged-in users may be properly notified to cease activity. The *-g(time in seconds)* option is used on most UNIX variants to define a delayed shutdown. The *-i* option permits the user to set the initialization level (e.g., *-i0* for a complete termination and *-i6* for a reboot). Shutdown also forks a *wall* command to let login users know the time at which the system will be brought down. Shutdown then sequentially reduces the run levels until all processes are successfully and gracefully terminated. Consult the *man* pages on your system to determine the supported options for *shutdown.*

DEFINING INITIATION SEQUENCES

Several UNIX files are utilized at boot time to set up the system's run level and to launch processes through the *init.d* initialization daemon. On booting, the kernel is loaded from the disk and spawns the *init* process. The *init* process is the parent of all processes and is given process number 1. Obviously, if this process somehow dies, all of its children (everything in the system) are killed. The */etc/inittab* regulates how file system processes are handled (Figure 3.13). The *inittab* fields define the kernel ID (a two- or four-character label), run level (*rstate*), action to be taken, and the command to be executed.

The following are terms common to UNIX operating systems when discussing the UNIX initialization process:

- *boot* – Executes the designated process only at boot time without waiting for completion
- *bootwait* – Same as boot, but sequences events until the identified process is completed
- *initdefault* – The run level to which the system defaults at boot time
- *off* – Temporarily disables commands or processes such as mail or printer daemons

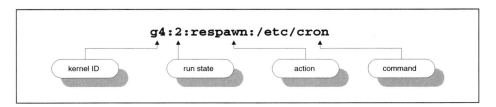

FIGURE 3.13.   Dissection of *etc/inittab*

- *respawn* – If the process has terminated, reexecutes the process
- *sysinit* – Identifies processes that are launched at the time of boot

The *inittab* first scans for all *sysinit* entries and executes them sequentially in the order listed. The *initdefault* entry is then found and that level of run time is established. System states are then reviewed and executed. System states for run level 2 are defined in the *rc2* file. The *rc2* script mounts the defined file system, starts the *cron* daemon, outputs the system hardware configuration, and starts services such as *mail, lp,* and *uucp.* Port, tty, and logging services are also initiated to complete the multiuser facility management. Other *rc* files can also be defined and executed sequentially to provide other services (Figure 3.14).

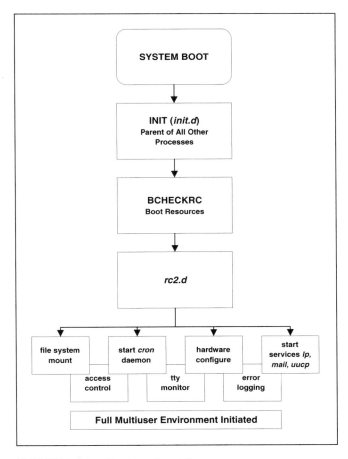

FIGURE 3.14.   System Boot Sequence

How to Schedule Processes

In addition to the processes launched at boot time through the */etc/inittab,* the system administrator and individual authorized users can schedule regular and one-time events. UNIX has a *cron* daemon that checks the system for scheduled events once a minute. The *cron* daemon "memorizes" scheduled jobs and maintains logs describing scheduled work. Three methods for scheduling jobs are supported by UNIX. The *cron* command is also known as the *clock* daemon in that it executes processes during defined time and date parameters. The *at* command only executes once, unlike *cron,* which performs regularly scheduled events. The final method, *batch,* also only executes once, but it completes a series of events sequentially.

The *cron* method maintains instructions in *crontab* files (chronological tables) that include entries regarding execution, including

- *Minute* – Defined by the number sequence 0–59 (with 0 being the first minute)
- *Hour* – Defined by the numbers 0–23 (with 0 being midnight)
- *Day of the month* – Sequences from 1–31
- *Month* – Month designations of 1–12
- *Day of the week* – Defined by the number sequence 0–6 (with 0 being Sunday)
- *Command* – The name of the executable binary or script to be executed

When defining *crontab* entries, ranges of time and wildcard regular expressions can be used. For example, if 10–18 is placed in the second field, it means the commands should be executed from 10:00 A.M. through 6:00 P.M. (1800 hours). An asterisk in the third field means the command is to be completed every day of the month (Figure 3.15).

The superuser controls who can create cron and at files. A set of files is written and modified by the root to determine who can execute scheduled jobs. Generally a normal user does not have the ability to schedule jobs. The obvious

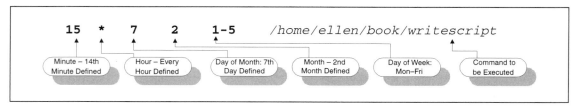

FIGURE 3.15.   Dissection of Sample *crontab* Entry

reason for this default is to provide the system administrator the greatest control in determining when and how system resources are to be used. However, the root user can precisely add or restrict a specific user's ability to schedule jobs. This is done through listing users in the following files (Table 3.10), which are typically found in the */usr/lib/cron* directory.

When a user submits a *cron* job, a file under that user's login name is created in the */var/spool/cron/crontabs* directory. The previous *crontab* for that user is destroyed. The superuser can use the *crontab -r* command to remove entries and the *crontab -l* command to list jobs. By running *crontab -e,* a privileged user can edit a *crontab* entry using the *vi* editor. To submit a *cron* job, use the following command:

```
crontab filename
```

It is important to understand that there are both system and user *cron* files. The system *cron* file can be modified only by a superuser and it is named */var/spool/cron/crontabs/root.* The user's *cron* file is created as we described earlier. When */etc/cron* is initialized at system start-up, all *cron* files that exist in */var/spool/cron/crontabs* are initialized so that they will execute when necessary.

Scheduling an event with the *at* command is a little more straightforward. The command line syntax has three parts: the *at* command with the time designation, the command to be executed, and the <Ctrl-D> key sequence. The *at* function understands time in the format of HH:MM; day and date such as

TABLE 3.10.   Process Scheduling Permissions Files

Command	Description of permission level
cron.allow	Allows only those users listed to submit *crontab* entries; if no *cron.allow* file exists, then all users except those in the *cron.deny* file can submit *cron* jobs; if no *allow* or *deny* files exist, then only the system administrator can submit jobs
cron.deny	Used to define those users restricted from submitted *cron* jobs; if no *cron.allow* file exists and the *cron.deny* file is empty, then all users can submit *cron* jobs
at.allow	Allows only those users listed to submit *at* entries; if no *at.allow* file exists, then all users except those in the *at.deny* file can submit *at* jobs; if no *allow* or *deny* files exist, then only the system administrator can submit *at* jobs
at.deny	Used to define those users restricted from submitted *at* jobs; if no *at.allow* file exists and the *at.deny* file is empty, then all users can submit *at* jobs

Monday or February 19, 1999; and words such as now, noon, next, and tomorrow. For example

```
at 13:15 next Tuesday /home/bobw/myscript <Crtl>D
```

executes *myscript* next Tuesday at 1:15 P.M.

Windows NT has provided similar scheduling functions. The UNIX *at* command is also available in Windows NT from the Virtual DOS Machine (VDM). The Command Scheduler performs like UNIX's *cron* and is available optionally through the Windows NT Resource Kit.

UNIX TRIANGLE SIDE 3: USER INTERVENTION

Understanding the structure and the processes of a UNIX system is valuable, especially when the interaction of users is added to the mix. Users create files and start processes to achieve a desired end result. Within UNIX, a user could be one created and maintained by the system or an actual human user. This section discusses the different types of UNIX users.

What Is a UNIX User?

In a UNIX environment, users are both human and system defined. The system administrator assumes control over system users. Both human and system users share several common characteristics, including ownership of certain files and processes. All UNIX variants have a number of standard users (Table 3.11).

The Superuser

The superuser or root is the most privileged user. The right to operate as the superuser must be restricted to the most trustworthy of humans to ensure system integrity. Horror stories abound involving careless, untrained, or malicious superusers. The superuser can override all system parameters, modify or delete any file (including the kernel), and kill all processes. If employed correctly, root status is employed to benefit the system and its user community. In the wrong hands, disaster occurs. Consider the impact of executing the *rm -r ** command from the root directory. That's right. *Everything* is removed—and that is not a good thing!

TABLE 3.11.   UNIX Users

Standard user	Description
adm	System accounting files and processes are owned by *adm*.
auth, auditor, audit	System auditing functions are owned by these "pseudo" users.
bin	Common UNIX commands and utilities are owned by the bin(ary) user
cron, mail, news, usenet, lp, lpd	These are special-function "pseudo" users that run selected subsystem activities.
daemon	These are really "servant" users that exist only to execute processes and manage related files.
human	These are users who have been provided accounts by the system administrator.
nobody	Another "pseudo" user that is employed by the NFS.
root	The superuser is also known as the root user, with a UID of 0.
sys	All system files are owned by the sys(tem) user.
uucp	This is the UNIX-to-UNIX copy protocol accounting ownership.

Careful control over who is granted superuser status is the first line of defense in UNIX security. Being ever mindful of unauthorized users becoming root is the second line of protection. Knowledge of who has attempted to log in as root can be very helpful. Fortunately, UNIX provides a log of all attempts to become the superuser through the file */var/adm/sulog*. As shown here, this file provides information as to the time, date, terminal of origin, and the user attempting root status. The fourth column indicates whether the attempt was a success (+) or a failure (–).

```
SU    11/15   11:47   +    tty01   root-bob
SU    11/15   12:15   –    tty10   emily
SU    11/15   01:16   +    tty03   root-ellen
```

Attempts to log in at any level by an unauthorized user should be a system administrative concern. The */var/adm/loginlog* traps events with five consecutive unsuccessful attempts to log in. Periodically running the *tail* command on */var/adm/loginlog* is recommended. This lists the last group of unsuccessful

TABLE 3.12.   Examples of Restrictions on Human User Accounts

Command string	Description
passwd -l user_name	Locks the user out of system access until changed
useradd -e mmddyy user_name	Sets up temporary accounts with expiring logins
usermod -f #n user_name	Removes inactive accounts after a specific number (#n) of days of inactivity

login attempts. While very little information is provided as to who is attempting the login, it can help flag a potential problem. Also useful is the */var/adm/wtmp* file, which accumulates all system logins. By running the *last* command against a user login name like root, a list of the most recent login information (including the terminal of origin, state, and time) is provided.

Take immediate action when unauthorized users attempt to become root. When suspected misbehavior has occurred or when additional control over a human user's account is desired, the system administrator can employ several actions. We know of some system administrators who believe in shooting first and asking questions later, so they lock out the offending user until explanations can be reviewed. Table 3.12 presents three easily employed procedures to restrict accounts.

Human User Accounts

As discussed in Chapter 4, human users are granted access through the creation of an account in the */etc/passwd* file. There is no predefined structure assigned to the user's home directory. Each account is assigned a login name or user name, a UID, and a GID. Although not required, most users have a password owned and controlled by them. A home directory is created for the user and a path is set as the standard point of entry at login.

Users are generally the master of their own home directory and files. A user may organize the home directory and create subdirectories as required. The contents of a user's home directory should be considered sacred. If the user wants to provide other users access to files, then that must be done with the knowledge of the potential drawbacks. Providing read permission to other members of the group relegates confidentiality. Granting write permission removes restrictions on modifications. Changing a file's ownership transfers all rights to a third party. For each of these conditions, valid reasons exist for altering permissions and ownership, but it is a "user beware" situation. As the system administrator, system files must not be treated so casually. Modifying ownership and permissions should be done only with a very clear understanding of the repercussions.

When a user attempts to log in, UNIX handles several key processes (Figure 3.16). First, a check is performed on the /etc/passwd and (when installed) the /etc/shadow file to authenticate the login name and password. After identifying the user's UNIX shell and determining the location of the home directory, the user's personal initialization script .profile (sh or ksh shells) or .login (csh shell) file is read and executed. Within these scripts, a number of environmental parameters are set, including the standard path and terminal or display definitions. The system administrator establishes a "standard" user environment in the /etc/login or /etc/profile file. However, users can then modify these standards by editing their own .login or .profile files.

Many of the common .login or .profile modifications made by system administrators and users relate to default terminal settings, window managers, applications to be automatically launched, paths to other directories, and e-mail

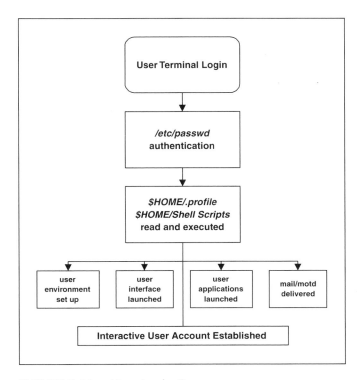

FIGURE 3.16.   User Login Processes

settings. Each of these items are discussed in detail in other sections of the book. However, the important message to remember here is that the *.login* and *.profile* files provide a flexible method to customize a user's computing session. Unlike Windows NT, which provides a graphical front end to user profiling, UNIX permits customization through its cryptic, character-based editor. When installing third-party applications, please take special note of any requirements to modify the system */etc/profile* or individual user's *.profile* (or equivalent *.login* for C shell users).

FINAL THOUGHTS

UNIX can simply be viewed as being comprised of three interrelated components. The structure of UNIX is based on the relationship of different types of files that are organized by the simple, hierarchical file system. Every file is tracked by the system by numbers known as inodes and is displayed in human terms by names. Processes convert the data bits that comprise files into actions. As a multitasking operating system, processes are conducted both in the background and as a result of user intervention in the foreground. This brings us to the third side of the UNIX triangle—the involvement of users. To the UNIX operating system, a user can be defined both in software application and human terms. These users invoke processes that in turn alter the component files of the structure.

Tasks Common to UNIX
System Administration

This chapter outlines concisely the tasks common to UNIX system administration. A broad-brush approach is taken because system administrative responsibilities are often assumed by accident rather than by design. Although many system administrators have been purposefully trained for the task at hand, a great many of the others assume responsibility to fill a void within an organization. This is particularly true for Windows NT administrators who are suddenly thrust into the UNIX world. They have to learn UNIX fundamentals while practicing management chores.

Good system administration is based on a solid UNIX knowledge foundation. This does not mean that understanding every operating system or shell command is required. In point of fact, very few system administrators have or need that depth of knowledge. An effective administrator, however, should possess core skills and the ability to seek specific information as it becomes needed.

The UNIX system administrator has two masters—the user community and the computer system itself. Both have equal weight. Many new system administrators make the initial mistake of focusing on software and hardware issues. Unless the user constituency is highly technologically oriented, demands from the user base may soon overwhelm the hapless new administrator. Therefore, striking a balance between user and system demands must be the primary objective. We profile the key tasks of the system administrator from both the user and system perspective through the following topics:

- Common user-oriented administrative tasks
  - User addition and removal
  - Group management

- User application support
- User help, education, and communication
- Basic service management such as mail and printing
- Common system-oriented administrative tasks
  - Boot-up, shutdown, and everything in between
  - Backups and restoration
  - Hardware maintenance, addition, and removal
  - System accounting and monitoring
  - System administration log management
  - System security and password aging
  - Network support
  - General troubleshooting

Using System Administrator Tools

Although UNIX system administrative functions are available from the command line, recent versions of the operating system offer interfaces to streamline management. Unfortunately, not all system administrative tools are created equal. For example, early UNIX V releases provided a program called *sysadm* or *sysadmin,* depending on vendor implementation. Despite its rather crude user interface, many functions such as adding and deleting user accounts are straightforward. Recently, some computer manufacturers have bundled exceptionally useful tools such as Hewlett-Packard's System Administration Manager (SAM), IBM's System Management Information Tool (SMIT) and Digital's SysMan Tools. Our advice is to use these tools. They are fast, fairly intuitive, and reliable. While understanding how to invoke command line administrative processes is useful, these system administrative tools have generally been designed with the particular UNIX variant in mind. We recommend that you use these tools whenever possible.

USER-ORIENTED RESPONSIBILITIES

A system administrator faces many responsibilities. Primary among them is supporting the end user. This responsibility spans the spectrum of maintaining user accounts, training, simplifying login processes, and user hand holding.

User Account Management

The first task of the system administrator is to manage user accounts. This is an obvious but deceptively important responsibility. It is really the foundation of user intervention and security. Understanding which issues are critical is of paramount importance to the system administrator. Invoking improper settings while adding a user is a sure prescription for disaster. Failure to remove a defunct user account or control a mischievous user represents a major security breach.

ADDING USERS

The system administrator must make a series of initial decisions that impact how a user interacts with the operating system and applications software. These decisions influence system security and the integrity of the workgroup. When adding a user, the system administrator must undertake a series of decisive tasks, including

- Establish the user's login name with ID number and initial password
- Assign the user to a system group (see the next section on group management)
- Assign the user to a shell environment (see Chapter 5 on shell programming)
- Create the user's home directory and set appropriate file permission levels
- Copy appropriate start-up scripts such as *.login* for the csh or *.profile* for the Bourne or Korn shell; *.mailrc, .xinitrc,* and other scripts are discussed later
- Determine and set paths to applications that will be employed by the user
- Establish password-aging rules
- Set limitations such as file size quotas for the user

Fortunately, system administration tools abound to make this job easier. Even older systems provide *adduser* scripts that automate the process. It is much safer to employ these tools than to edit vital system files like */etc/passwd* manually.

Of course it is possible to add a user by directly editing the */etc/passwd* file. First, prior to editing the file, it is important to dissect the *passwd* file itself. The *passwd* file is a flat ASCII file that allocates one line per authorized user. A sample user entry is shown in Figure 4.1.

Any user in the system can read and copy the */etc/passwd* file. However only a user with root or system administrative authority may modify */etc/passwd*. With this authority, you may add, modify, and remove users manually by using a text editor.

Another important file in most modern UNIX systems is the */etc/shadow* file. This file is only readable by the system administrator. The */etc/shadow* file

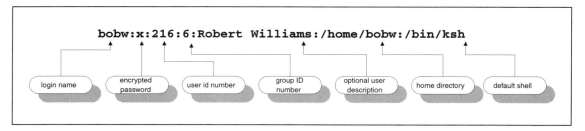

FIGURE 4.1.   Dissection of */etc/passwd*

contains the encrypted user password. It can also be used to retain information about other system privileges assigned to a user. In Figure 4.1, the "x" entry in the second field of the */etc/passwd* file signifies the existence of an encrypted password. This means that an */etc/shadow* file exists and is storing the password information. Since */etc/passwd* is available for review by any user, the use of the */etc/shadow* file enhances system security.

NOTE   **A Word of Caution**

As stated earlier we highly recommend the use of system administrative tools or common scripts available on some systems like *adduser, usermod,* and *userdel.* However, if you insist on hand coding the */etc/passwd* file, please be very careful. A common mistake is to replace the colon separator with a semicolon. This seriously impacts the entire */etc/passwd* file structure. Another common blunder is to attempt hand coding the encrypted password. We have not met the individual who can produce DES encryption on the fly. Therefore, place an asterisk in the password field and exit your text editor. Then run the *passwd* command to define a password for the new user. Again, the safest approach is to use the system administrative tools supplied with your variant of UNIX. Figure 4.2 presents a screen from one of these tools.

The modification of user accounts normally involves changing permission levels, login scripts, and/or user permission levels. In System V, release 4 versions of UNIX, this task can be streamlined by running the *usermod* command.

DELETING USERS

Expeditiously removing invalid users is equal in importance to adding users. The proper maintenance of operating system integrity is based on restricting unauthorized users or abusive behavior. In certain cases, the system adminis-

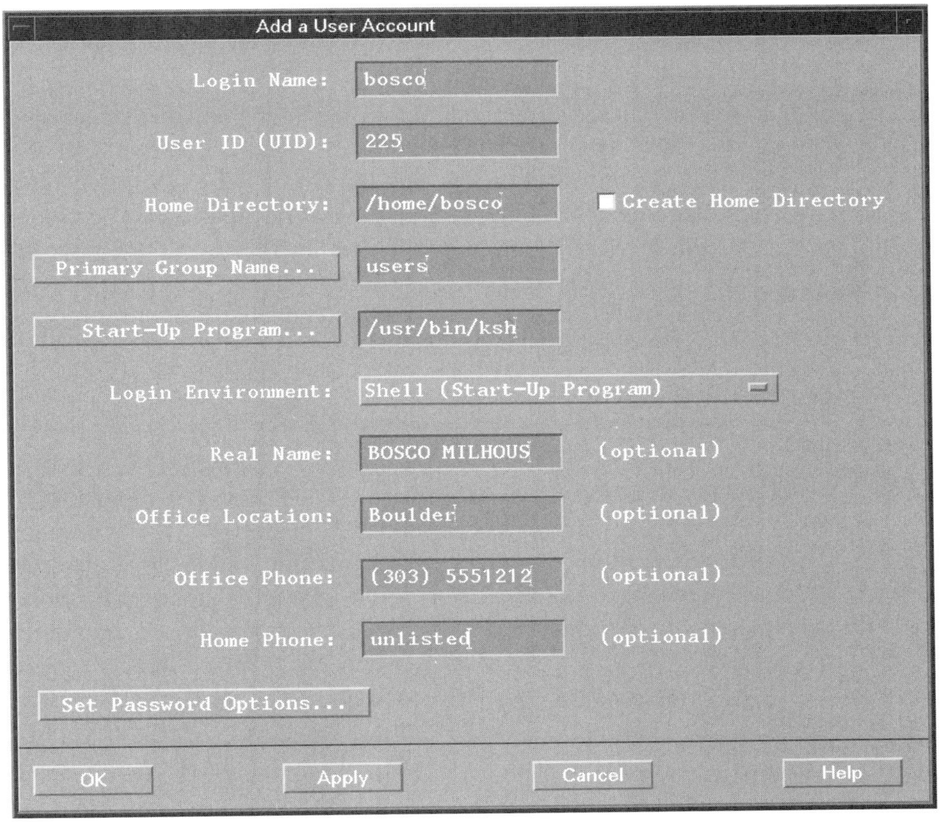

```
┌─────────────────────────────────────────────────────────────────┐
│                        Add a User Account                         │
├─────────────────────────────────────────────────────────────────┤
│                                                                   │
│           Login Name:   │ bosco            │                      │
│                                                                   │
│         User ID (UID):  │ 225              │                      │
│                                                                   │
│       Home Directory:   │ /home/bosco      │   ■ Create Home Directory │
│                                                                   │
│  │ Primary Group Name... │  │ users         │                    │
│                                                                   │
│  │ Start-Up Program...   │  │ /usr/bin/ksh  │                    │
│                                                                   │
│     Login Environment:  │ Shell (Start-Up Program)      │ ═      │
│                                                                   │
│           Real Name:    │ BOSCO MILHOUS    │   (optional)         │
│                                                                   │
│       Office Location:  │ Boulder          │   (optional)         │
│                                                                   │
│         Office Phone:   │ (303) 5551212    │   (optional)         │
│                                                                   │
│          Home Phone:    │ unlisted         │   (optional)         │
│                                                                   │
│  │ Set Password Options... │                                     │
│                                                                   │
├─────────────────────────────────────────────────────────────────┤
│  │   OK   │      │  Apply  │      │  Cancel  │      │  Help  │     │
└─────────────────────────────────────────────────────────────────┘
```

FIGURE 4.2.   Hewlett-Packard SAM Add User Interface

trator may select to restrict system access temporarily or to remove the account altogether. In the first instance, the quickest way to restrict access is to change the user's password using the *passwd* command. The user will then need to contact the system administrator to regain access. At that time, any behavioral issues can be discussed and hopefully resolved. However, we do not recommend you taking this step casually. Restricting a user's ability to complete work is a serious matter.

In many cases, initially locking the account is safer than full-fledged account deletion. In some organizations, users may return after assignments elsewhere. An easy way to accomplish this task is to "comment out" the target user by adding the pound sign as the first character on the line in the */etc/passwd* file. To restore the user, simply remove the pound sign comment. However, after an appropriate period of time, full deletion is appropriate.

For a final solution, deletion of the user's entry from the */etc/passwd* and */etc/group* files removes the account. The next step is to review the contents of the user's home directory to determine if any important information should be retained. If so, either back up the appropriate data or reassign ownership of the directory to another user using the *chown* command. If the data within the user's home directory is not important, then employ the *rm* command to delete unwanted information. Finally, purge the mail accounts and remove any *crontab* scheduled jobs established by the user. Obviously, system administrative tools and scripts such as *userdel* (or *rmuser* or *deluser,* depending on the UNIX variant) can be employed effectively to delete the user. These tools are designed for ease of use and protection.

Windows NT offers a graphical interface for adding, modifying, and deleting users that is not too dissimilar to UNIX system administrative tools. Windows NT defines three levels of user administrators: (1) the Administrator is able to perform all user management functions for the local group, (2) the Account Operators are able to perform restricted management actions, and (3) the Domain Administrator has global user and group management authority. In the latter case, the **User Management for Domain** option available from the task bar is generally used. A User Wizard is also available.

Group Management

Every user belongs to one or more groups. Group membership offers more than a sense of cyber community. Inclusion in a group provides the user certain rights and privileges shared by other members. In most cases, default group membership is assigned to the typical user. However there are times when ad hoc workgroups need to be established for which document sharing is necessary. Further, some users many be assigned certain system administrative tasks that require membership for that operating system group. Depending on the modern UNIX variant, a user may belong to as many as eight or sixteen groups. The typical user will belong to a single default group, whereas the system administrator has multiple group assignments.

Group membership is controlled by a flat file database called */etc/group*. Just like the *passwd* file, each line constitutes a complete database record, with four fields separated by colons (Figure 4.3). The first field is the name of the group, followed by an optional group password field (usually left blank), fol-

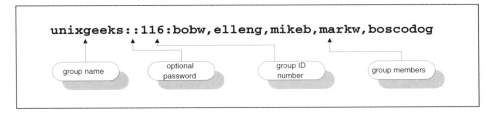

FIGURE 4.3.   Dissection of /etc/group

lowed by a group ID and finally a list of group members (user login names separated by commas). Group membership can be set through manual modification of the /etc/group file or through system administrative tools such as SAM, SMIT, or SysMan mentioned earlier.

Windows NT embraces group membership as the primary vehicle for assigning rights and privileges. If you anticipate that some users may have logins in both the UNIX and Windows NT environments, it is helpful to investigate how group membership can remain consistent across platforms. To add, modify, or delete groups, invoke the **User Manager** option or use the Administrative Wizard (**Start** ➝ **Programs** ➝ **Administrative Tools** ➝ **User Manager for Domains**).

Automating Logon Processes

At first glance, the login process seems very straightforward. In a homogeneous environment, it is very easy to establish a standard login policy. However, if you are working with different UNIX variants, it is important to understand each login process and the impact of using alternate shell environments.

As an inherently multiuser system, UNIX is constantly monitoring user execution. Several programs or daemons run to determine serial port or network access activity. When using a serial line login, UNIX invokes a process known as a *getty* (or *uugetty* on modem-connected serial lines). Each user creates a separate *getty* (get the teletype or terminal connection). On some UNIX systems the *getty* program has been renamed with a somewhat enhanced *ttymon* (tty or terminal monitor) program. These programs perform the same tasks of informing the UNIX operating system that user activity is occurring across a particular serial port interface.

In networked environments, programs like *inetd* and *xdm* take control of monitoring certain processes. The *inetd* program is a kind of superdaemon that starts other helper daemons when necessary. When a user logs in from a network interface, the *inetd* daemon manages the specified request. As discussed later, network access to UNIX may take the form of process requests such as *telnet, ftp, rlogin,* and *rcp.* Much like *inetd,* the *xdm* program regulates requests for the graphical display in X-Windows.

From the user's perspective, gaining entrance into the system involves typing the login name followed by a password. If the name and password match, the UNIX operating system updates appropriate system monitoring/accounting files and executes the login shell script. Depending on the shell environment set by the */etc/passwd* entry for that user, one or more shell programs are executed.

UNIX shells are discussed in greater depth in Chapter 5. However, as an overview, Table 4.1 outlines basic differences between shells as they relate to user logins.

The Bourne and Korn shells both support a centralized */etc/profile* script. This file impacts the actions of all users on the system. The system administrator can automate many activities by using this file properly. Environmental settings common to all users can be set in */etc/profile*. For example, if the system administrator wants to log out users who forget to terminate their own sessions, a timing parameter can be set to force a logoff after ten hours. However, invoking environmental commands for all users is also a double-edged sword. If a universal terminal type is set, for example, a user involved in a remote login session using another display type could experience very unexpected results.

The Korn and Bourne shells also utilize a local file that resides in the user's home directory called *.profile*. When a user is first added, the *.profile* that is originally created is simply a copy of the */etc/profile* file. It can then be modified to include custom items such as setting special paths, invoking the graphical

TABLE 4.1.   Shell Environment Login Scripts

Shell type	Programs/scripts executed/read at start-up
sh (Bourne shell)	*/etc/profile* – System standard profile *$HOME/.profile* – User's individual login shell
csh (C shell)	*$HOME/.login* – User's individual login script *$HOME/.cshrc* – User's C shell resource file
ksh (Korn shell)	*/etc/profile* – System standard profile *$HOME/.profile* – User's individual login shell *$HOME/.kshrc* – User's Korn shell resource file

```
# @(#) $Revision: 72.2 $

# Default user .profile file (/usr/bin/sh initialization).

# Set up the terminal:
        if [ "$TERM" = "" ]
        then
                eval ' tset -s -Q -m ':?☒' '
        else
                eval ' tset -s -Q '
        fi
        stty erase "^H" kill "^U" intr "^C" eof "^D"
        stty hupcl ixon ixoff
        tabs

# Set up the search paths:
        PATH=$PATH:.

# Set up the shell environment:
        set -u
        trap "echo 'logout'" 0

".profile.new" [Read only] 26 lines, 446 characters
```

FIGURE 4.4.   Partial Sample *.profile* Script

interface, launching UNIX commands and commercial applications, and performing other accounting tasks as directed. As a system administrator, you may want to have several alternative "canned" *.profile* scripts that can be copied into a new user's *$HOME* directory (see Figure 4.4 for a sample). By reflecting user needs in *.profile*, many hassles can be avoided later. The proper employment of the *.profile* script can ease potential user frustration and facilitate productivity.

The *csh* is most widely used on Sun Microsystems workstations. It invokes a *.login* file that operates like *.profile*. The two files perform similarly but use different syntax and structure.

During login, many other scripts can be launched. Common scripts that a system administrator may have to manage or modify periodically include those presented in Table 4.2.

Application Support

The system administrator is responsible for commercial applications employed by the user community. Beyond the obvious responsibility of providing software training, the system administrator has management duties including version and license control. On a single system this typically involves making sure that application licenses are timely. Some vendors of UNIX applications apply a

TABLE 4.2.   Other Login Scripts

Script name	Description
.dt	Is the management file for the CDE
.elm	Configures the user's *elm* mailbox (if used)
.emacs_pro	Sets defaults for the *emacs* editor
.exrc	Sets defaults for the *vi* editor
.forward	Is a user-defined file to forward mail to another mailbox
.mailrc	Configures the user's mail configuration and aliases
.mwmrc	Sets parameters for systems using the Motif window manager
.newsrc	Lists news groups of interest to the user
.openwin-init	Sets parameters for systems using the OpenLook window manager
.project	Is a crude, user-controlled project manager/calendar
.Xdefaults	Defines X-Windows setup parameters such as color, fonts, and geometry
.xinitrc	Launches X11 using *startx* or *xinit*

time stamp to their software that must be renewed periodically. Many UNIX software vendors sell their applications on an absolute user or concurrent per-user basis. In the latter case, if a ten-user license is purchased and thirteen users demand use at the same time, then an obvious conflict arises. Therefore, periodic sizing for application use is required. Log files are helpful in determining application use over time.

One of the standard administrative applications shipped with Windows NT Server 4.0 is a License Manager that automates much of the control of applications. To access this function, select **Start** → **Programs** → **Administrative Tools** → **License Manager**.

Application management across several types of UNIX systems can be very difficult. The level of complexity can be awesome. First, different sets of binary (executable) software distributions must be maintained for each UNIX variant and even for different releases of the same version of the operating system.

Second, the user environment must be considered. Most UNIX applications support only a character-based or graphical environment. For those relatively rare programs that support both, you will need to address any inherent differences in performance, look and feel, and user training. For example, the Decathlon GOLDMEDAL Office Automation Suite supports both character and graphical environments, but not for all variants of UNIX. For example, the company shipped character, OpenLook, and Motif versions for the Sun OS 4.x, but supports only character-based and Motif interfaces on Solaris 2.x.

Part of the role of the system administrator is to qualify applications for their environments. The following is a list of questions that should be addressed when purchasing and maintaining user applications.

- How is the software licensed? Once or must it be renewed periodically?
- Are user licenses based on the number of people on the system or based on concurrent utilization?
- What are the support and maintenance policies?
- What operating systems are supported by the release number?
- What level of compatibility exists with other versions and back releases?
- What GUIs are supported?
- Are character-based environments supported? If so, on what type of terminal devices?
- Is user training different for each release type or level?

User Help, Education, and Communication

An often overlooked task of the system administrator is one of communicator and educator. The system administrator could turn to some of the very excellent outside training organizations for support, but this is often expensive. However, there are times when this type of investment pays great dividends.

Another option is to perform in-house training. Large companies have entire departments to support this activity. However, in many cases, the poor system administrator must also assume responsibility as the trainer. Some system administrators also feel inadequately prepared to conduct formal classroom training. Fortunately, UNIX itself provides tools that can be utilized to train and communicate with users. The message-of-the-day (*motd*) and *news* functions can be effective training instruments. The system administrator is encouraged to use the *motd* file to educate and provide organizational news and information. Using the *vi* text editor to open the */etc/motd* file, brief sessions or pointers can be provided to users. If the */etc/motd* file is set in the */etc/profile* script, then the message of the day is displayed to the user at system login. By utilizing *motd* and *news,* users are provided information in a nonthreatening way. It is our belief that a more effective working environment evolves when the user understands the computing environment. If training can be accomplished with minimal impact on schedules and budgets, then the job of the system administrator is made easier. Using *motd* and *news* can help accomplish this goal.

The system administrator's need to communicate with users is not limited to education. UNIX mail is capable of accepting individual, group, and broadcast messages. But what about emergency situations? UNIX has a command called *wall* that permits the distribution of information to all users with a current login. For example, suppose an emergency weather warning requires immediate evacuation. The system administrator can use *wall* to broadcast evacuation orders and then invoke an immediate system shutdown, as follows:

```
# wall
The local weather bureau has identified a tornado in
our area. You should move immediately to the designated
shelter. We are shutting down the computer immediately
until the danger has passed. Please proceed to
shelter!!
Ctrl-d
# init 0
```

A *wall* message can be written to a file and broadcast at a later time. For example, before shutting down a system for routine maintenance, a *wall* message prior to shutdown is invoked by default by the system. Other messages can be stored and sent when desired. This is accomplished by simply redirecting the flat file to the *wall* command:

```
# wall < save_file
```

Basic Function Management

Most users have a single interest—getting their appointed task (such as printing or mail) accomplished. In theory, a computer system streamlines work production. However, try to make that argument when e-mail can't be sent or received, print jobs get lost, or applications stop working because of outdated licenses. The system administrator has a responsibility to be proactive in ensuring user support. This requires fundamental understanding of the primary processes commonly employed by the user community. Reference the appropriate sections of this book and other documents to perfect your knowledge base. System administrators must be as multitasking as the operating system they support.

COMMON SYSTEM SUPPORT TASKS

In addition to keeping users happy, the system administrator must also maintain the system itself. As with any computer or electronic system, periodic maintenance must be undertaken. Some of the maintenance tasks that a system administrator must provide to retain a healthy system include periodically rebooting the operating system, backing up critical files, installing additional hardware, executing system accounting, implementing security measures, and troubleshooting day-to-day problems.

Boot, Reboot, and Everything in Between

In writing this book in Colorado, we are familiar with a device called a *Denver boot*—a contraption that local police affix to the tires of a vehicle they wish to immobilize. Like the Denver boot, the process of booting UNIX also affixes certain behavior that is firm until the parameters are changed by UNIX's own law enforcer—the system administrator. You should understand what happens when UNIX is booted, who does what to whom, and how to end processes with a shutdown. This is one instance in life when responsibility and authority are equal. System behavior is your responsibility. As the system administrator, you have root authority that must be exercised efficiently and prudently.

Backups and Restoration

The responsibility for performing periodic backups should not be taken for granted. It can spell the difference between organization success and failure. Too many variables exist within modern computing that cause hardware, network, power, or software failure. A periodic backup is the primary defense against such catastrophes. Backups can be created using system administrative tools or archival tools such as *backup/restore, tar, dd, mt, volcopy, ufsdump/ufsrestore,* and *cpio.* As administrator you should execute several levels of backup, as indicated in Table 4.3.

In daily activity it is easy to overlook the importance of backing up data. However, the system administrator should not forget the reasons for backups, including

- Data restoration if lost by human error or sabotage
- Hardware failure that requires repair or replacement
- Disasters such as earthquakes or hurricanes, which don't always happen to other people
- Backups are yet another form of data security

TABLE 4.3.   Levels of Backup

Type	Description
Full system backup	Backup of the entire operating system to be used in the case of full-system failure
Full disk image	Mirror image of the disk contents (not as commonly used)
Data partition	Backup of a particular disk partition
Backup for migration	Backup of software/system files in preparation for upgrade or replacement
Incremental backup	Scheduled backup of files changed since the last full-system backup
File-specific backup	Backup of files of special importance that require special handling

Windows NT provides methods for full-system, incremental, and file-specific backups also. These are accomplished by using the NT Backup module (**Start ➤ Programs ➤ Administrative Tools ➤ Backup**).

Hardware Maintenance, Addition, and Removal

The system administrator is also responsible for maintaining devices such as terminals, printers, hard disk drives, CD ROMs, and modems. The scope of this book does not include detailing how to install or remove devices. However some basic concepts should be explored here. First, any device requires a compiled driver that is linked to the system kernel. The kernel then uses the driver information to provide instructions when executed that are understandable to the device itself. Software applications are the interface between the driver and the device.

UNIX defines two types of device drivers: character (also called *raw*) and block devices. Character devices stream data a single character unit at a time. The block device, on the other hand, moves set units of data in chunks like 512 and 1,024 bytes. When looking at the permission codes of devices, the type is normally identified by a *c* or *b* at the start of the character or block respectively. In addition, the devices are often stored in separate directories. Raw or character device directories start with *r*. For example, */dev/mt* is used for block tape devices and */dev/rmt* stores character (raw) tape devices.

Devices are found in the *dev* directory. They are organized differently on UNIX variants. In some cases the devices are all found in the *dev* directory. In other cases, the devices are nicely organized in subdirectories within *dev*. Unfortunately not all UNIX variants have identical device support. Often, guess-work is required when determining a device name. Table 4.4 lists the primary device types in subdirectory format.

When listing devices using the *ls -l* command, the operating system provides cryptic information about the nature of a device, as shown in Figure 4.5. All devices have major and minor numbers that are used by the kernel to identify it. The major number is used by the operating system to establish its behavior, whereas the minor number is vendor specific.

TABLE 4.4.   Device Directory (/*dev*) Components

Device subdirectory	Description
/dev/console	Primary-system terminal console
/dev/mem	Installed random access memory (RAM)
/dev/kmem	RAM allocated specifically for the kernel
/dev/tty(#)	Serial ports used primarily for terminals
/dev/pty(#)	Pseudo serial ports (often used in window environments)
/dev/null	Available to all users, this is really not a device; commonly described as a *bit bucket*; where standard error information is sent along with other user-directed garbage
/dev/dsk	Disk directory using block formats
/dev/rdsk	Disk directory using character or raw formats
/dev/mt	Tape devices using block formats
/dev/rmt	Tape devices using character or raw formats

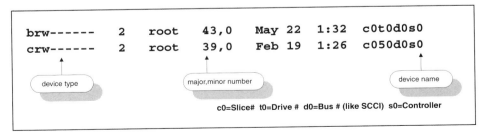

FIGURE 4.5.   Dissection of a Device File

System Accounting and Monitoring

UNIX is always a dynamic environment. Without vigilance, resource allocation becomes critical. When a UNIX file system gets too full, for example, applications may stop working or the ability to save files could cease. Fortunately, commands such as *df* (*bdf* in HP-UX) are available for some UNIX variants to support the reviewing of file system usage (or disk free space) and *du* shows disk utilization. Shareware utilities like *top* display CPU and memory utilization. Excellent and sophisticated products like Hewlett-Packard's *GlancePlus* are available for a more in-depth analysis of the system. If the operating system becomes sluggish or processes begin to fail, it is the system administrator's telephone that rings at 2:30 A.M. If you value regular sleep, then basic operating system maintenance must be a top priority. The following is a brief list of items (all discussed in detail later) that must be managed as a minimum.

- *Disk space* – Is there enough to permit the proper manipulation of files?
- *Memory* – Has a sufficient amount of memory been installed to support available applications?
- *Swap space* – Has sufficient disk space been allocated to the swap area to accommodate the periodic "swapping" of main memory during peek demand periods?
- *Network* – Are network devices such as modems, routers, and communications lines operating correctly and sufficient in size (speed, bandwidth, and so on) to handle user traffic?
- *Attached devices* – Are local and remote devices like printers and fax machines properly configured and maintained with supplies like paper and toner?
- *Runaway processes* – Have zombies been created that are unnaturally eating memory resources and can they be analyzed to prevent a reoccurrence?
- *Unusual user activity* – Is a user "abusing" the situation by utilizing too much storage or impacting the network with recreational Internet browsing?
- *Security* – Do the logs suggest that unauthorized logins have been attempted or are there indications that an authorized user has tampered with system or user files?

OTHER BASE-LEVEL TASKS

Three actions should be considered basic in operating system maintenance. First, plan to reboot the operating system periodically. This will clean up zombie processes and set daemon activity to zero. System administrators typically plan a monthly, and in noncritical environments weekly, system rebooting. Yes, some minor downtime occurs, but it is generally more than compensated by improved performance. Second, if you suspect that a file system has become corrupted, run the *fsck* command. (Special note: This may require all users to log off temporarily while some files systems are unmounted during the *fsck* process.) If users are using too much disk space, set up disk quotas with the *ulimit* command. Finally, if a process begins to run away or a user fails to log off, become a judicious user of the *kill* command.

UNDERSTANDING AND USE OF LOG FILES

The UNIX operating system records operating system and user activities with a time stamp. The *syslog* collects information from the kernel, process daemons, mail system, security command structures, *cron* jobs, network, and other sources. It not only records reports of activity but also notes errors by severity level. The *syslog* is created by the *syslogd* daemon based on entries in the *syslog.conf* file. Applications can be written to be *syslog* aware.

Other applications create *.log* and/or *.err* files to help review system and software activity. As shown later, UNIX also provides a facility to see errors automatically as they occur. Standard errors can be redirected to a file using *2> filename*. The system administrator should become familiar with log and error files.

System Security and Password Aging

The front line of maintaining system integrity is to enforce the many security features of UNIX. The file permission structure underscores both the strength and potential vulnerability of UNIX. The password is equally important in controlling unauthorized system access. The system administrator sets and enforces policies that guard file permission integrity and password aging. While no hard and firm rules exist, it is generally believed that permissions to file systems should not be changed from default settings without careful thought. Additionally, user passwords should be set to expire periodically (for example, every six months or every quarter). This restricts inactive users while providing authorized users the ability to continue with the submittal of a new password string.

General Troubleshooting

The final and perhaps most demanding role of a UNIX system administrator is troubleshooter. You are a detective on a mission that often appears impossible. Fortunately UNIX does provide clues, and reference documents abound, to decipher fingerprints on the screen. The first art learned by a system administrator is how to ask the right question. Does an occurrence appear to be due to hardware, software, or user error? Sometimes the answer is obvious; other times only reviewing log files, tracing coaxial wire connectors, or analyzing application-produced core files provides the answer. While UNIX system administration is always a challenge, it is never dull.

FINAL THOUGHTS

The job of the UNIX system administrator can never be defined as trivial. User and system demands require constant system administrative review. Various versions of UNIX provide administrative tools that range from the rather crude to the very robust. Regardless of the sophistication of these tools, we recommend that they be employed over command line intervention. If you must use the command line, refer to Appendix B for a quick reference of available options.

5 UNIX Topics

This chapter reviews topics indispensable to UNIX system administration. Each discussion in this chapter is treated as a discrete feature. The following items are covered

- Use of the UNIX *man* pages
- Operating system monitoring and performance
- Security issues
- Use of the *vi* editor
- Interfaces and user accessibility, including character-based and X-Windows environments
- Shell and UNIX programming fundamentals

USING UNIX *man* PAGES

If you follow no other recommendation in this book, at the very least take heed to become familiar with the UNIX *man*(ual) pages. A *man* page is on-line documentation for UNIX commands and certain procedures. Although the name may be politically incorrect in some circles, *man* pages are an extremely effective resource for the system administrator.

The *man* page document collection is divided into sections. They are generally stored as compressed files that uncompress with proper screen formatting when the *man* command is invoked. UNIX System V, Release 4 variants organize *man* pages as outlined in Table 5.1.

To use *man* pages (Figure 5.1), type the *man* command followed by the desired application. For example, if you want to discover how to add your own

TABLE 5.1.   UNIX *man* Page Sections*

Section	Contents
1	User-oriented commands
2	Kernel and UNIX system codes including errors
3	Calls for system and programming libraries
4	File format information and standards
5	Other documentation and files not easily categorized
6	Games and contributed code or demos
7	Drivers and device support
8	System administration commands (not available with some variants)

*BSD UNIX versions organize *man* pages with some slight differences. Devices are in Section 4, file formats are in Section 5, and other miscellaneous files are in Section 7.

man pages to a local system, you could run the *man* command on *man* itself by typing

```
man man
```

You can scroll through the *man* pages line by line. Depending on the paging utility used by your variant of UNIX, <space bar> or <Enter> moves the text by a full screen. (In most cases <space bar> scrolls to the next screen and <Enter> moves to the next line.) To find a particular word within the open *man* page, type a forward slash followed by the desired word, then press <Enter>. To terminate the review of the *man* page, type *quit* or press <Ctrl-Z>. In some cases information about a command may be located in a different section. For example, a user may want information about changing the password (using the *passwd* command) while a system administrator wants data on the structure of the */etc/passwd* file. By default, the user section is displayed first, unless a specific section identifier is provided on the command line. To provide the *man* page of interest to the user, enter

```
man passwd
```

To provide Section 4 on the file structure of the *passwd* file, enter

```
man 4 passwd
```

The *man* page facility also permits the user to search for key words. For example, if information is required on how to rename a file, the *-k* option would

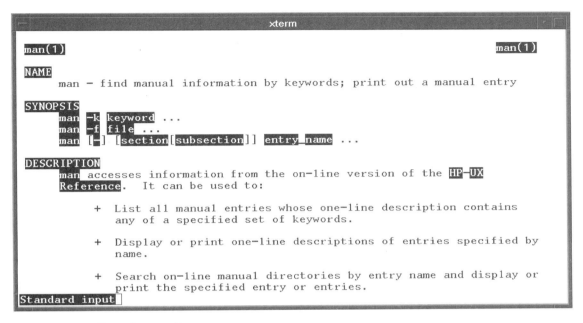

FIGURE 5.1.   Sample *man* Page

be invoked. The following command lists all the *man* pages containing the word *rename*:

```
man -k rename
```

In UNIX variants like Solaris, the *apropos* function is also available to scan the *man* pages' summary database quickly to find key words. It works very much like *grep*, but is specifically designed to search *man* pages.

Using *man* pages can save much time and effort. On many systems supporting X-Windows, a more graphical version of *man* pages is available by typing *xman* followed by the desired topic. As a system administrator, acquaint your users with *man* pages. Productivity can improve when users are provided the tools to seek their own answers.

Ironically, the process required to output *man* pages to a file or printer is not well documented by the *man* page on *man*. To output to a file or printer, it is advisable to strip the pages of the default formatting. This is done by using the *col -b* command. A *man* page can be output to a file or to a printer by the following two examples, respectively:

```
man passwd | col -b > password.file
man passwd | col -b | lp -d <printer device>
```

The Windows NT counterpart to *man* pages is a graphically oriented, hypertext-linked help system. In many ways the Windows NT implementation is considerably superior to the older UNIX *man* pages. However, if you know exactly the type of information you need, then the UNIX *man* pages are very efficient and easy to use.

MONITORING AND PERFORMANCE

UNIX system monitoring should be proactive. Unfortunately, system monitoring typically only becomes a hot issue when performance appreciably degrades. Whether proactive or reactive, the job of the system administrator is to ensure optimal system performance. Fortunately, UNIX provides a number of monitoring tools to help analyze performance by categories. In addition, a number of commercial third-party applications are available for a more comprehensive review of system parameters that may require fine-tuning. The task of determining bottlenecks in system performance is often very daunting and requires a fair amount of guesswork. Often, performance problems can stem from many sources including the following:

- *CPU* – How much of the central processor is being utilized? If the analysis indicates full processor utilization with regular wait time ratios more than 1.0, then some action is required, including limiting the applications in use or installing faster or additional CPUs.

- *Paging/swapping per second* – Does the system encounter high levels of paging or swapping memory to disk? If so, then additional virtual memory and/or swap space may be required.

- *Memory* – Is the utilization of virtual memory regularly above 75% and/or does it reach maximal levels periodically during an average workday? If so, you can limit applications or the number of user logins, or add more memory.

- *Network collisions* – Are a great number of packet collisions indicated after analysis? If so, the network setup or associated devices must be reviewed.

- *Packet errors in receiving network* – Is the number of receiving packet errors more than 5%? Although baselines vary radically, this level generally indicates a problem with the network itself or the connecting interface.

- *Input/output (I/O) load balance* – Is there a significant number of input and output requests noted in reading and writing to disk? The easiest solution is to divide commonly accessed data between multiple hard drives.

- *Zombie runaway processes* – Are there individual processes running with root as their parent ID (a PID of 1) that are taking extraordinary system resources? The system administrator should try to use the *kill* command to rid the system of the runaway processes. However, if they are truly zombies, then the processes are already dead and therefore *kill* will have no bearing. A system reboot is necessary in the most extreme case.

- *Application/process execution* – Are applications very slow or impossible to execute? Any of the previously listed items could account for this problem , but you should also look at if you are simply out of processes or out of inodes and then alter the kernel appropriately.

UNIX supports several utilities that can help the system administrator get a handle on performance issues. These utilities differ slightly between UNIX variants. It is therefore appropriate for the user to review the *man* pages of the utilities discussed next.

uptime

The *uptime* command is a very simple performance-monitoring tool. It is a rather crude utility that must be run multiple times to set a trend. Workload is measured with *uptime* and it provides a snapshot over a fifteen-minute interval. The dissection of the *uptime* output (Figure 5.2) shows current load levels as well the last five-minute and fifteen-minute period. The report can be misleading without an established baseline because loads may vary between systems. As a rule, loads larger than five should signal a mid-range load. Levels more than ten signify a heavier than healthy workload.

sar

The System Activity Reporter is more flexible than *uptime* in that it permits the collection of information over time so that it can be analyzed. The data is collected using the *sadc* utility run in conjunction with */usr/lib/sa/sa1* script. To

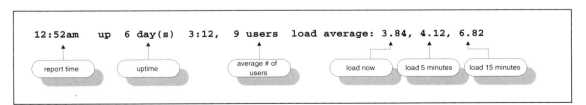

FIGURE 5.2.   Dissection of the *uptime* Output

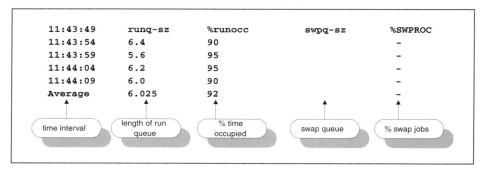

11:43:49	runq-sz	%runocc	swpq-sz	%SWPROC
11:43:54	6.4	90		-
11:43:59	5.6	95		-
11:44:04	6.2	95		-
11:44:09	6.0	90		-
Average	6.025	92		-

time interval | length of run queue | % time occupied | swap queue | % swap jobs

FIGURE 5.3.   Dissection of a *sar* Report

obtain data over time, the */usr/lib/sa/sa1* is run through *cron*. The data is added to the */usr/adm/sa/sa(date)* file. A report is generated using the following syntax:

```
sar -f <options> /usr/adm/sa/sa(date)
```

The *sar* command offers a high-level view similar to *uptime*. This is generated using the *-q* option together with settings for the queue and percentage of occupied queue time. A *sar* report using *-q* is shown in Figure 5.3.

top and Other Utilities

Depending on your variant of UNIX, other utilities can be employed to obtain information on system performance. The *top* utility is shipped with many UNIX variants and is freely available as a shareware program. When *top* is run, the system administrator can see real-time utilization of the CPU, memory, and other information in total, based on individual user processes (Figure 5.4). This is a very useful utility that we strongly urge you to employ periodically. It is most helpful when attempting to obtain system baselines or to determine the existence of runaway processes.

The Windows NT bundled Performance Monitor rivals third-party add-on applications for UNIX like Hewlett-Packard's *GlancePlus*. We examine the use of the Performance Monitor in Chapter 7. Another good resource for managing Windows NT performance is Volume 4 of the Windows NT Resource Kit.

A full file system can also create a bottleneck. The *df* command (*bfd* for HP-UX) provides a report on file system utilization. Various options can be em-

```
                                    xterm
System: grwhp                                     Tue Feb   4 08:00:37 1997
Load averages:  0.10, 0.09, 0.13
152 processes:  151 sleeping, 1 running
Cpu states:
 LOAD    USER    NICE    SYS    IDLE   BLOCK   SWAIT    INTR    SSYS
 0.10    9.9%    0.0%   6.5%   83.6%   0.0%    0.0%    0.0%    0.0%

Memory: 29152K (12276K) real, 49148K (21796K) virtual, 9864K free   Page# 1/11

 TTY    PID USERNAME  PRI NI    SIZE    RES  STATE    TIME %WCPU   %CPU COMMAND
   ?   1081 daemon    154 20   6912K  4428K sleep    44:02  4.25   4.24 X
   ?  26794 rgwilli   154 20   5352K   924K sleep     2:20  1.39   1.39 vuewm
  pc   2105 root      178 20    284K   300K run       0:00  0.94   0.68 top
   ?      3 root      128 20     0K     0K  sleep   109:30  0.26   0.26 statdaemon
   ?  29660 rgwilli   154 20    468K   572K sleep     0:02  0.16   0.16 hpterm
   ?  24169 root      154 20   1392K   532K sleep     0:35  0.12   0.12 pmd
   ?  29074 mborows   154 20    120K   232K sleep     9:59  0.12   0.12 xclock
   ?    260 root      154 20     24K    20K sleep    59:12  0.10   0.10 syncer
   ?   2068 rgwilli   154 20    472K   604K sleep     0:00  0.07   0.07 hpterm
  pb   2097 rgwilli   154 20    336K   388K sleep     0:00  0.07   0.07 xterm
   ?  26754 daemon    154 20    744K   276K sleep     0:02  0.06   0.06 pexd
   ?  24172 root      154 20   3484K   648K sleep     0:11  0.05   0.05 ovtopmd
  p8  29661 rgwilli   156 20    188K   156K sleep     0:00  0.05   0.05 ksh
   ?    411 root      127 20    108K    52K sleep    28:14  0.05   0.05 netfmt
```

FIGURE 5.4.   View of a *top* Output Report

ployed to present the data in different formats. We generally recommend maintaining file system usage at less than 80% (unless it is a particularly large file system, in which case a higher level of use is permitted). The *du* command is used to determine disk utilization. When a file system is nearing maximal usage, the system administrator can systematically employ *du* to discover where the heaviest data storage is taking place. On discovering problem areas, the larger files can be moved, and individual user storage can be restricted. A core file, a data stream collected when an application prematurely misbehaves and terminates, can occupy many megabits of storage space. It is common to have multiple core files in existence at any given time. Therefore, using the *find / -name core -print* command to locate all core files also assists the system administrator in removing these typically unneeded files.

Windows NT file management functions perform some of the same tasks as *du*. Windows NT does not support disk quotas (although third-party programs are available for this optional support).

SECURITY

UNIX provides solid security features. It also manifests areas where significant breaches can occur without the constant vigilance of the system administrator. We have discussed security preparedness with a great number of UNIX system administrators. All of them acknowledge the importance of security, but remarkably few had a comprehensive security plan, and even fewer had a real-life implementation. Security is too often treated as an afterthought. Hackers have long known this fact. Obviously, once the cows are out of barn, it is much more difficult to protect your livestock. While only the most severe security breaches ever surface in the popular press, stories abound of financial losses, theft of confidential records, system downtime, and other negative impacts. We cannot recommend more strongly that a system administrator become very proactive in matters of security.

Designing and implementing a security plan starts with understanding the type of security issues facing UNIX system administrators. A mistake often made is to assume that security measures center solely on averting attacks from unauthorized users. While guarding against malicious behavior is a very important front line, that is only one focus. Security also includes computer hardware protection, data preservation, and system accountability. A comprehensive plan includes attention to the following items at a minimum:

- *User accounts* – Monitoring authorized users and maintaining proper privileges
- *Network accessibility* – Controlling a variety of access points and protocols
- *Hardware* – Protecting the physical computer and its peripherals
- *System backups* – Managing adequate backups to support disaster recovery
- *Software and applications* – Protecting licenses and theft
- *Viruses and Trojan horses* – Preventing the flow of destructive software invaders
- *File system* – Maintaining proper permissions on system files and directories as discussed in Chapter 3 under File Permission and Ownership as a Security Feature.

User Accounts

We have previously discussed methods in which the system administrator can restrict users suspected of improper behavior. It is more likely that real security problems arise from sloppy or misinformed user activity. First among these problems is setting a user's password. It is up to the system administrator to provide guidelines on user passwords and to test for enforcement periodically.

The user should be aware of how hackers go about identifying a password. The use of proper names should be avoided. One department of a major telephone company commonly assigns the user's last name as the password. This is an obvious security time bomb. Popular words and phrases should be avoided. A good hacker will maintain a list or data dictionary of pop culture words (startrek, superman, and so forth) to break into a user account. Passwords involving hobbies or personal traits are easily cracked by invaders. Names of family pets, sports teams, locations, or special events (such as birth dates) are also fairly easily deduced passwords. One user we know used his personalized car license plate as a password until an intruder destroyed many important documents.

Password integrity can be violated in other ways. System administrators should remind users never to write their password. Also, users should be aware of who is nearby when they type their password into the system. A clever observer can effortlessly replicate keystrokes. Finally, the password should never be spoken aloud.

A good password should be easy for the user to remember and preferably easy to type. We recommend the use of a minimum of six characters with at least one nonalphabetical symbol.

Another common user-oriented security breach is making the *$HOME* directory writable to other users. Once a user permits write privileges to the *$HOME* directory for group or other system users, then personal file security has been eliminated. To share group work, a system administrator could create a special pseudo user account in which a defined group could enter and utilize the files within that *$HOME* directory. However, it is generally not a good idea to create too many special accounts. They are difficult to manage and can prove confusing to an unsophisticated user. A more secure method is to establish work groups with */etc/group* and have the users in the group set appropriate permissions on the selected files to be shared.

Another thing a system administrator should do is to set a proper *umask* level for users. The default can be set in the */etc/profile* file or individually in the user's *$HOME/.profile* file. A generally recommended level is *umask 200* (read-write for the user and no permissions for the group or all others). This is accomplished by adding a single line:

```
umask 200
```

Network Security

UNIX provides exceptional networking capabilities but also presents unique security problems. Chapters 12 and 13 discuss in greater detail the specific use of UNIX networking protocols. In this discussion, we hope merely to point to several areas in which security should be focused when implementing a networking scheme.

A common problem associated with network security is the use of what is known as equivalency files. Applicable most often when using BSD commands like *rlogin, rcp,* and *rsh,* these utilities can be configured to permit access to foreign systems without the benefit of a password. The concept of equivalency can take two forms—system and user based. In the first case, */etc/hosts.equiv* is employed. When a host name is added to this file, that system becomes "trusted." As such, all users on one system can log in (if a user account exists) on the trusted host without a password. The exception to this rule is that root is not a trusted user account. If a user's name is also added to the */etc/hosts.equiv* file, then that user can log in as any other user on the trusted system. At the user level, the file *.rhosts* in the *$HOME* directory permits users to gain access to an account on another system without the use of a password. The flow of activity when a remote login (*rlogin*) command is invoked is shown in Figure 5.5. The most obvious problem with the use of both trusted accounts and user-based *.rhosts* is password control. After a password is known for the original system, then all "trusted" accounts are in jeopardy.

Other common networking protocols connote additional security issues. The following should be noted as potential security problem areas.

- *ftp* – This File Transfer Protocol is widely used to move information from one platform to another. It generally requires a password to access a foreign directory. However, *ftp* also permits the use of an anonymous user account.

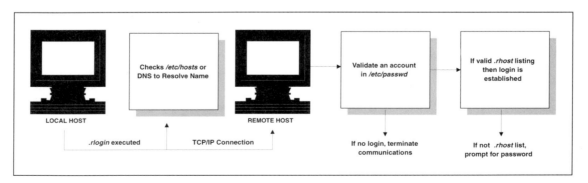

FIGURE 5.5.   Using Equivalent File *.rhosts*

This permits the free flow of information without password intervention. However, if proper permissions are not maintained in other accounts, then an anonymous user could run amok in the foreign host.

- *tftp* – The Trivial File Transport Protocol is a more relaxed version of *ftp*. Files can be transferred without a password—even system files such as */etc/passwd*. It is valuable when uploading data to a diskless device. However in other situations it could prove disastrous. Unless this facility is absolutely needed, we strong recommend that it be disabled by renaming or removing the *tftpd* file. In this case, comment out the entry from the */etc/inetd.conf* file by placing a pound sign immediately before the *tftp* line.

- *NIS* – Network Information Services is a directory services program formerly known as *yellow pages* (*yp*). It allows the system administrator to transport data effortlessly across an enterprise using defined naming conventions. The problem lies in the fact that NIS is an open environment that is not secured. Therefore, vital information pertaining to user accounts can be tapped by an intruder. Some recent versions of NIS have added some security features, although modest.

- *NFS* – The Network File System is a very convenient and widely used facility that permits file systems on foreign hosts to be shared locally. From the user's perspective, a network file system looks like a local file system. The obvious problem resides in the fact that once a network file system is mounted, it is open to any user with the proper permissions, which means that abuse is always possible. We recommend the use of NFS with all security features fully enabled and without major degradation of permissions. Export only those file systems that are required.

Windows NT also supports *ftp* directly and NFS through third-party vendors. The same problems inherent in UNIX security using these facilities apply to Windows NT. The specifications published by the National Computer Security Center offer additional guidelines on securing your network. The *Orange Book (Trusted Computer Evaluation Criteria)* is an exhaustive set of definitions established by the federal government. Many variants of UNIX provide C2-level security auditing. Implementing C2 security is certainly recommended for highly sensitive networks. However, C2 security also imposes many restrictions that could prove cumbersome in many environments. Consult the user documentation that comes with your UNIX system before implementing C2 security. We also recommend you become familiar, at the very least, with some of the baseline criteria for security outlined in the *Orange Book*.

Hardware

Consider the following scenarios: It's late at night on a weekend when an intruder pops off the top of the computer chassis and disconnects a hard drive containing massive amounts of organizational data. Or, a burst pipe floods the floor with 6 inches of water—just enough to "fry" the computer system through a series of electrical shorts. If you don't think that this could happen to you, we can attest first hand that these disasters do happen—even to nice people. These are just two examples of what can happen in the real world. A good security plan must account for protecting physical property.

Common sense dictates hardware security planning. When possible, place servers in a secure room, or otherwise lock components into place. Don't make theft easy. Also, placement of key components is critical. At the very least, secure the system console. Placing a server directly on the floor is generally begging for problems. Raise the system if possible.

Another common problem from making hardware too accessible is accidental disconnection or hitting the off switch. Whenever a UNIX system is brought down ungracefully, there is a chance that data or even an entire file system will be corrupted. Although recent versions of SVR4 have advanced journals that permit the rebuilding of the corrupted file systems, the risk of lost data is still too great to permit premature operating system termination. If it is impossible to move the hardware to a secure area, then commercial products are available that lock onto the on/off switches and that cover power cords protectively.

System Backup

The first line of defense in disaster recovery is an effective system backup plan. We have previously discussed the issues involved in creating a backup strategy. We underscore this issue again because it is so vital. There are so many things that can occur. The only remedy is to maintain backups.

It is equally important to have a backup storage strategy. Again, common sense should rule. Place backup media in a secure, dry environment. It is also recommended that periodic backups be moved away from the workplace. This does not mean, however, that backup tapes should be carried home with the system administrator. In our business we store monthly backups and copies of source code in a bank safety deposit box to insure against acts of nature.

The Windows NT backup facility has many of the same features as UNIX. The graphically based Backup Wizards walk the system administrator through the process of backing up and restoring files or an entire file system. See Chapter 7 for more detail.

Software and Application Security

Software can be one of an organization's biggest investments. Theft and piracy is a multibillion-dollar problem. A system administrator should secure copies of software to prevent unauthorized copying or outright theft. As to installed software, the system administrator is also responsible for managing licenses. Although most commercial software programs ship with built-in license authority schemes, it is important to monitor the number of authorized users and any expiration dates.

Another often overlooked issue is the installation of bootlegged copies of software. Users are sometimes known to install "cool" software that they procured from an associate. If the software is not properly licensed, the installation of such software opens your organization, and possibly you as the system administrator, to a potential legal dead zone. Federal and international copyright and patent laws are very explicit as to the use of software. Software companies, to protect their interests, are applying criminal and civil remedies.

Viruses and Trojan Horses

A Greek bearing gifts has toppled at least one fabled civilization. Seemingly harmless gifts of software can also cripple countless computer systems. Fortunately, unlike DOS or Windows environments, UNIX is less vulnerable to computer-borne viruses. A common computer virus is normally held at bay by the permissions security features inherent in UNIX.

A Trojan horse is a little more difficult to manage and detect. This is a computer program that is purported to accomplish one thing and performs something entirely different. Before installing software, make sure that you are sure of its origins. Commercial software is generally safe, as the publisher runs serious credibility and financial risks for not reviewing distributions prior to release. In the case of shareware, install it and test it as a restricted user before making it available to the general user community. Also, forbid the installation of any software by a user without the prior permission of the system administrator. If possible, obtain and compile the source code for shareware software before you test it. In this way you can review the content of the code in advance.

Viruses have regularly targeted Windows 3.1 and Windows 95. Fortunately, the Windows NT NTFS file system utilization of file permissions schema also works to enhance virus protection greatly.

TEXT EDITING WITH *vi*

A system administrator cannot survive without using a text editor periodically. Although UNIX supports a number of bundled and shareware text editors such as EMACS, we center this discussion on the *vi* editor. It is universally available on all UNIX systems and is clearly the most used text editor.

The *vi* editor is the application we love to hate. It is extremely cryptic and is counterintuitive to many users. Yet even the most sophisticated, modern word processors have difficulty matching its robustness and speed. Consider the fact that a block of text can be moved in three keystrokes with *vi* compared with Microsoft Word, which requires pulling multiple menus, and selecting the block of text and the new text location. As a friend says, "*vi* ain't pretty but it gets the job done." All system administrators should have at least basic *vi* skills.

Developed originally by a group at the University of California at Berkeley, *vi* is a full-screen version of the *ex* line editor. When single-line tty devices where replaced with the character-based CRT terminal, the ability to see a full screen of text was indeed a major "visual" improvement. In the modern context, a character-based editor is anything but visual. Yet in view of *vi*'s development, this was very visual. The *ex* and *vi* editors are essentially the same programs, with differences based on the amount of screen real estate utilized. Another variation is a utility called *view* that provides a read-only examination of a file. The *view* command is invoked using the same syntax as *vi* and *ex*.

This section assumes that you already have some level of familiarity with the *vi* editor and is a quick reference on creating, editing, and moving textual material using *vi*. The following topics are reviewed:

- Basic *vi* operational modes and commands
- Commands for moving a text file
- Techniques for editing text
- Search techniques and pattern matching
- Advanced topics such as named buffers, macros, and *.exrc*

Basic *vi* Operational Modes and Commands

The *vi* editor has two primary modes—command and input. In the command mode the user may invoke a series of instructions ranging from search to save. The input mode is employed to add text. Depending on the particular editing function being employed, the input mode can also be referred to as insert, append, and open modes. A *vi* editing session is begun by invoking the command string

```
vi (option) filename <ENTER>
```

A few notes on specifying the filename are appropriate. If a file already exists by the filename, then that is what is displayed on the screen. A directory cannot be edited with *vi*. Both flat ASCII text files and most binaries can be edited by *vi,* although we recommend never editing a binary by hand because a slipped bit can destroy an entire executable. While you are editing a preexisting file, UNIX makes a copy of the original file in memory and copies it temporarily to disk. The original is not altered at any time during the editing session. Therefore, you replace the original file only in the event that you decide to save the edited work under the same filename. Otherwise, you can elect to save the edited work under a new name, thereby retaining the original as a backup. Since a *vi* session is saved separately from the original, it can be recovered from the */lost+found* directory in the case of a premature system crash. If you invoke *vi* with the name of a file that does not exist, then you automatically create a file by the name specified. Finally, you can invoke *vi* without listing a filename. In this case you need to provide the new filename when it comes time to save the text. Several additional options exist for invoking the *vi* command, as shown in Table 5.2.

TABLE 5.2.   Options for Launching a *vi* Session

Option	Description
+	The plus sign places the cursor on the last line of the file.
+*linenum*	The plus sign with a line number (e.g., +34) places the cursor on that line.
+/*pattern*	The plus sign, slash, and a pattern places the cursor on first occurrence of the pattern.
-*r*	Using -*r* recovers the file with editing in the event of an operating system crash.
-*R*	Using -*R* enters *vi* in read-only mode—the same as invoking *view.*

TABLE 5.3. Insert Mode Commands

Key	Description
i	Standard insert mode; insert characters immediately before the current location
I	Insert characters at the beginning of the current line
a	Append mode; insert characters immediately after the current location
A	Append characters at the end of the current line
o	Open mode; insert characters on a new line immediately below the current line
O	Insert characters on a new line immediately above the current line
ESC	Terminate input mode and return to command mode

INSERT MODE

Entering the insert or input mode is accomplished by one of several methods. The only real difference between the methods involves where your cursor is initially placed. The input mode is invoked using any one of the characters listed in Table 5.3.

COMMAND MODE

Command mode is a much broader set of instructions that encompasses basic editing to robust internal programming. Basically, everything except the input mode is part of the command mode scheme. Therefore it is necessary to break this discussion into several parts for greater clarification. In this subsection we highlight the commands invoked while using the colon. While in the command mode, pressing the colon places the cursor at the bottom of the screen. The user can then invoke the appropriate command after pressing <Enter>. To terminate a colon command before it is completed, press <Esc>. Table 5.4 presents the most commonly used colon commands.

One of the often overlooked but potentially most helpful group of colon commands is the :set command structure option. There are nearly fifty :set command options. Rather than listing them all, we have selected a handful to illustrate the type of options that can be invoked (Table 5.5). To see all of the available options, invoke the following command during a *vi* editing session:

```
:set all
```

TABLE 5.4.   Colon Commands

Command	Description
:q	Quits without saving
:q!	Quits without saving after editing a file; ignores all edits
:w	Writes (saves) the document to disk
:w!	Writes the edits to disk using the existing name; overrides protections
:wq	Write and quit combination; use ! to override protection
:x	Same as :wq; to write (save) and quit
:ZZ	Same as :x and :wq; to write and quit
:b#,e#w file	Writes the lines beginning with b# and ending with e# to a new file (e.g., :5,19w test will write lines five through nineteen to the file named test)
:b#,e#w>>file	Takes lines b# through e# and adds them to the end of the specified file (e.g., :5,19w>>test2 will append lines five through nineteen to the file test2)
:set option	Invokes a number of options; they are discussed later
:e file	Opens a second file and places the current editing session in the background
:e!	Reverts back to the previous editing session
:e#	Brings the other file to the foreground
:f	Displays the file name, its size, and its current line position
:n	Brings the next file to the foreground for editing
:sh	Temporarily enters a UNIX shell to perform other tasks; <Ctrl-D> to return
:! command	Invokes a UNIX command like the date command
:r filename	Reads and inputs the specified filename's data at the current cursor location
:r! command	Inserts the results of a UNIX command, such as the date command for a time stamp

The :set command uses the same syntax to turn on an option. Add the word *no* before the option to turn it off:

```
:set ai
:set noai
```

TABLE 5.5.   Sample *:set* Command Options

Command	Abbreviation	Description
autoindent	*ai*	Inserts text using the same indent as above; default is *noai*
ignorecase	*ic*	Turns off case sensitivity in searches; default is *noic*
number	*nu*	Prints the number of the line on the left-hand side; default is *nonu*
showmode	*showmode*	Shows the current editing mode in the bottom right-hand corner; default is *off*
term	*term*	Changes the current terminal definition for the editing session
terse	*terse*	Shows shorter error messages; default is *noterse*
wrapmargin	*wm=#*	Wraps text at specified number of characters; default is *nowm* or *wm=0*

Moving about the *vi* Session

Moving the cursor in a *vi* session is one of the most difficult concepts to grasp by new users. Frankly, some of the commands are not intuitive. The original ASCII terminal had a set of keys similar to a typewriter. Familiar computer keys such as function, directional, and page up/page down keys were not available. As terminals evolved from the limited models, these keys were added. Unfortunately, each manufacturer included their own instruction set known as *termcap* or *terminfo*. Therefore, the signal sent by a Wyse50 when pressing a down arrow key is different than performing the same task on a DEC VT220 or IBM 3151 terminal. The unfortunate result for *vi* users is that using directional or other movement keys is unreliable. Occasionally, especially when using some X-terminals, *vi* will respond positively to directional keys; however in most cases very unexpected results occur. As a result, the developers devised a set of keyboard commands that permits efficient cursor movement.

The simplest and most used set of key commands are those for moving the cursor one position up, down, right, and left. By placing your little finger on the letter *l* and permitting your other fingers to straddle the next three keys, cursor movement is easily accomplished (Figure 5.6). The *h* key moves the cursor to the left, the *j* jumps the cursor down one line, the *k* key kicks the cursor up one line and the *l* moves the cursor to the right. (Yes, they did use the letter *l* to move to the right. Oh well, just think of it as your other left.)

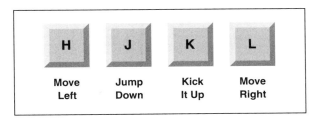

FIGURE 5.6.   Cursor Single-Key Movement Keys

When using any *vi* movement command you can combine the letter with a number to automatically move multiple positions on the page. For example, *6j* will jump the cursor down six lines. By the same token, *20h* move the cursor 20 characters to the left of the current position. The *vi* editor provides other methods for rapidly moving around the document. Tables 5.6 through 5.8 provide a common set of movement commands. As described, numbers can be combined to invoke multiple actions.

Techniques for Editing Text

Obviously anything done while in the insert mode is considered text editing. In addition, the command mode provides methods for modifying, deleting, and moving text. Some of the jargon used to accomplish these tasks may seem a bit strange at first. For example, the process of copying a block of text is called *yank* and then pasting the data is denoted as *put*. As with the movement commands, it is possible to use numbers to perform multiple actions at once. For example, *6yy* will yank (or copy) six lines of text.

It is also possible to combine numbers and movement commands with edit countermands. For example, the letter *c* indicates that you want to change an item. By typing *3cw,* the *vi* editor understands that you want to change the next

TABLE 5.6.   Movement between Lines of Text

Keystroke	Description
0	Places the cursor at the absolute first position on the line
$	Places the cursor at the absolute last position on the line
^	Places the cursor on the first character of the line
+	Moves the cursor to the next line
–	Moves the cursor to the line above the cursor

TABLE 5.7.   Movement between Words and Sentences

Keystroke	Description
w	Moves forward to the beginning of a word; *3w* moves the cursor forward three words
W	Moves forward to the beginning of a word, ignoring punctuation
b	Moves back a word; *5b* moves the cursor back five words
B	Moves back a word, ignoring punctuation
e	Moves to the end of a word, *6e* moves to the end of the sixth word
E	Moves to the end of a word, ignoring punctuation
(	Moves to the previous sentence
)	Moves to the next sentence
[	Moves to the previous paragraph (the last hard return)
]	Moves to the next paragraph (the position after the last hard return)

TABLE 5.8.   Scrolling through the File

Keystroke	Description
Ctrl-F	Scrolls forward one screen of text
Ctrl-B	Scrolls back one screen of test
Ctrl-D	Scrolls down half a screen (Caution: Pressing this twice could kill the session.)
Ctrl-U	Scrolls up half a screen
Ctrl-E	Displays an additional line at the bottom
Ctrl-Y	Moves to the top of the current window
H	Moves to the top of the screen
M	Moves to the middle of the screen
L	Moves to the bottom of screen (Caution: Do not confuse L with l [to move right])
Ctrl-G	Shows the current line number
nG	Moves to the line number specified by n
G	Moves to the end of the file
:n	Moves to the line number specified by n; same as nG

three words, or *c$* means that everything to the end of the line will be changed. The *change* command is always used in conjunction with a movement option. Tables 5.9 and 5.10 summarize the most commonly used modify commands.

TABLE 5.9.   Modify Commands

Keystroke	Description
r	Replaces the current character with the next one typed; *3r* means replace the next three characters
R	Replaces everything until <Esc> is pressed
~	Changes the case of the character
cmovement	Changes the current word by using a *movement* command such as *cw*
cc	Changes the entire current line
C	Changes to the end of the line; same as *c$*
s	Replaces the current character with a substituted text string
S	Replaces the current line with a substituted text string
xp	Reverses the next two characters

TABLE 5.10.   Text Deletion and Movement

Keystroke	Description
x	Deletes the current character; *12x* means delete twelve characters
X	Deletes the character before the cursor; *6X* means delete the six previous characters
dmovement	Deletes everything as defined by the movement command; *dw* means delete the word
dd	Deletes the current line
D	Deletes everything to the end of the line; same as *d$*
ymovement	Yanks (copies) the text defined by the *movement* command; *y$* means yank to the end of the line
yy or Y	Yanks (copies) the current line; *6yy* means yank or copy six lines to the buffer
p	Puts (pastes) saved or deleted text in the buffer on the line after the current one
P	Puts (pastes) saved or deleted text in the buffer on the line before the current one
j	Removes the hard return and joins two lines

TABLE 5.11.   Undo and Repeat Commands

Keystroke	Description
u	Undoes the last edit command
U	Undoes any changes that have been made on the current line
.	Repeats the last action

The final significant editing command is the *undo* command (Table 5.11). If your typing capabilities are as great as ours, then the *undo* command will be regularly employed. While the *undo* command is very helpful, it is not very sophisticated. Stated simply, the *undo* command is good for only one layer of command reversals. On the bright side, *vi* also provides an ability to perform the same action repetitively.

Before leaving the editing section we should acknowledge that screens particularly on character terminals occasionally become scrambled as a result of a power or communication glitch. In this case it is necessary to redraw the screen. This can be accomplished by pressing <Ctrl-L> or <Ctrl-R>.

Search Techniques and Pattern Matching

The *vi* editor provides a solid mechanism for locating words or phrases within a document. It also provides a limited capability for pattern matching and substituting. If more sophisticated pattern substitution is required, we recommend the use of *sed* (the streaming editor) or the *awk* shell command set.

Before listing the search options (Table 5.12) it is important to mention that multiple-word phrases should be enclosed with quotation marks. In addition, if you are searching for words starting with a regular expression (e.g., $, /, and so on), use a backslash to let the system know that you are seeking the literal character dollar sign or forward slash. Finally, when searching for special escape sequence characters like ⌃D (Ctrl-D), precede it with Ctrl-v followed by the ⌃D (Ctrl-D) escape sequence.

Pattern substitution combines searching with the replacement of data. The substitution command is invoked with the colon command *:s* using the following syntax:

```
:s /original_pattern/new_pattern
```

This command substitutes the first occurrence of the pattern in the current line only. To change all occurrences in the line, add the */g* command at the end to

TABLE 5.12.   Search Commands

Keystroke	Description
/*pattern*	Searches forward from the current position for a text string (*pattern*) or multiword phrase
?*pattern*	Searches backward from the current position for a text string (*pattern*) or multiword phrase
n	Searches forward for the next occurrence of *pattern*
N	Searches backward for the previous occurrence of *pattern*
/	Repeats the previous forward search
?	Repeats the previous backward search
f*character*	Finds the defined *character* in the current line; *3fc* means find the third c in the current line
F*character*	Finds the defined *character* in current line backward from the cursor position
t*character*	Finds the defined previous *character* in the current line
T*character*	Finds the defined previous *character* in the current line backward from the cursor position
;	Repeats the same search in the current line forward
,	Repeats the same search in the current line backward

designate a global replacement. The *vi* editor also permits substitutions for a defined block of text or the entire document. To define a block of text for pattern search and replacement, you need to define the specifically affected lines of text. For example, to change all occurrences of the name *bob* with *ellen* on lines 25 through 175, the syntax would be as follows:

```
:25,175s/bob/ellen/g
```

The /g command at the end is for globally replacing all defined patterns. To perform the same task globally from a particular point in the file to the end, the command syntax would be the following:

```
:25,$s/bob/mike/g
```

To make a global substitution for an entire file, two formats can be used as follows:

```
:1,$s/bob/mark/g
:%s/bob/mark/g
```

For the cautious among us, global search and replacement functions are very powerful but potentially a real problem. For example, there may be situations when the substitution of a pattern is inappropriate. Therefore, applying the conditional option may be appropriate. When used, *vi* searches for each defined pattern and asks for you to confirm the substitution. If a replacement is desired, press <y> for yes followed by <Enter>; if no substitution is desired, press <Enter>. The letter *c* added to the end of the command string invokes the conditional option. The syntax for conditional search and replace using the previous two examples is as follows:

```
:1,$s/bob/mark/gc
:%s/bob/mark/gc
```

Advanced Topics: Named Buffers, Macros, and Resources

The *vi* editor offers many advanced editing functions. Unfortunately, the scope of this book does not permit a complete exploration of all of these facets. Therefore, we confine this section to a discussion of two useful advanced topics: using named buffers and creating macros. We conclude with a discussion on the use of the *.exrc* editor resource file.

As a general rule, the *vi* editor maintains a single layer of buffered information. It is possible to add additional layers of information for later recall. This is done through a mechanism known as *named buffers*. To move a block of text from one *vi* session to another, the use of named buffers is required.

There can be up to twenty-six named buffers. A named buffer is simply a command or string that can be recalled by hitting a key sequence during the current editing session. A named buffer is created by entering the colon command mode and using the double quote mark followed by a letter (the name) and then the command. Therefore "*add* is a named buffer that is invoked with "*a* and then deletes a line of text (*dd*). The "*ap* command will put the contents of the named buffer "*a*.

There are also nine delete buffers during a particular edit session. Each time that one line is deleted, it is rolled sequentially into the delete buffer. To restore the contents of the most recently stored deleted text, use the number one before the *p* or *put* command. Therefore *1p* or *1P* pastes the last-deleted item after or before the current cursor location.

Related to macro creation is the ability to assign optional key sequences to commands to streamline the editor. This is done by assigning an escape sequence to keys in conjunction with the colon command *:map*. This information can also be stored and automatically retrieved in the editor's resource file *.exrc*. For example, if you wanted to assign the sequence Ctrl-z to insert a phrase repeatedly, type the following command:

```
Ctrl-v Ctrl-z i this is the phrase I want inserted
<Enter>
```

The `Ctrl-v` tells the editor that this is the beginning of an escape sequence, the `Ctrl-z` is the new macro key, the letter `i` invokes the insert mode, then the phrase itself is listed, followed by <Enter> to conclude the action. Each time during the editing session that Ctrl-z is pressed, the defined phrase will be inserted. If this macro key sequence is to be saved for multiple *vi* sessions, then include it in the *.exrc* file as shown here. Note that the syntax appears to be different. Do not type `^[` as this is added automatically with the Ctrl-v sequence.

Finally, the *.exrc* file is a resource flat file that is placed in the user's *$HOME* directory. When the *vi* editor is invoked, it first looks for the *.exrc* file and loads its contents. This file is particularly useful when default settings are desired. A sample *.exrc* file might include instructions on using line numbering, word wrap, and other functions available with the *:set* command. In addition, items such as optional key mapping can be included. The contents of a sample *.exrc* file is shown here:

```
$vi .exrc
set wordmargin=0
set number
set showmode
map ^[z i this is the phrase I want inserted
map ^[h  1G
```

USER INTERFACES AND ACCESSIBILITY

In this section we explore both character- and X-Windows-based interfaces. The scope of this section is restricted to a cursory look at those issues that most demand the attention of the system administrator. Unfortunately, many of the possible areas of analysis are simply too vendor dependent to address thoroughly in this book. An example is *termcap* or *terminfo,* the database definitions used by UNIX systems to control specific terminal behavior. However, we do point to common issues inherent in topics such as terminal setup and maintenance. Although we can not provide a comprehensive solution set for these topics, our hope is that you become armed with an understanding of how to tackle related problems.

Traditional UNIX Interface: Character-based Terminal

The traditional user interface known to UNIX users is the ASCII character terminal. Generally when a device is connected by a serial interface, it communicates with the host via asynchronous communications at variable baud rates. The CRT screen displays a fixed number of characters, typically eighty characters by twenty-four or twenty-five lines. It also uses additional pointing devices, like those pesky mice. Sound simple enough? Yes, if that was the entire story. Unfortunately, supporting a terminal-based environment is laden with significant system administrative headaches. So, given these problems, why are character terminals still in use? First, in shops using older legacy software systems, the character terminal many be the only reasonable option available. To run character applications on graphical devices is not very cost effective. Second, character terminals are very cost efficient, with prices well below their graphical big sibling the X-terminal or a PC. Despite the predicted demise of character-based terminals, they remain a fixture in many UNIX environs.

There is not much to the user interface on a character terminal. While some third-party software applications do provide a flat-looking version of pull-down menus, UNIX itself presents a single face to the user—the command line. (In the shell programming section we offer a sample menu system shell script that you can modify to provide your users with standard tasks.) In the strictest sense, UNIX regards the terminal as the point of standard input. Information is typed in at the keyboard and is input to the computer. This is defined as standard UNIX input. The standard UNIX outputs are characters from the computer to the terminal screen. Keystroke input is output as a character on the screen. If an error occurs that cannot be processed, it is dumped to the terminal or normally redirected by many applications to the great bit bucket called */dev/null,* which is the receptacle for UNIX's standard errors.

Issues Associated with Character Displays

Let's examine the most common issues confronted by the system administrator in working with terminals.

Hardware connectivity – Character terminals are typically connected directly to the host using an RS232 port via a modem or some form of hub routing device. The first challenge is to make sure the pin-out serial connections match the terminal manufacturer's specification. (Generally, a 25 pin-in and -out works.) The next issue is to make secure the hard connections. One of the most frequently reported problems rests simply with the fact that the terminal is disconnected. Have users check the connection first when they report a terminal problem. The screen itself has a finite life expectancy, so be prepared to replace the screen periodically. Finally, the same terminal may support several types of keyboards. Don't assume that two different keyboards for the same terminal will send the same key sequences. We have noted that some keyboards for the same terminal model have different key mapping. This may impact your software applications significantly.

Matching setup parameters – It may sound silly, but most terminal difficulties can be traced directly to the failure of matching the terminal's internal setup with the type defined on the host and within the user's environment. For example, an IBM 3151 terminal may be physically present on a user's desktop, but it could be set to emulate a Wyse 60. The unknowing user, seeing the IBM 3151 logo, assumes that an export of that type of terminal is logical, not understanding the terminal itself is really behaving like a Wyse 60. The result is garbage output. Other setup items such as baud rate and data bit and stop bit settings can impact screen output negatively. To minimize grief, the system administrator should take on the responsibility for initial terminal setup. By so doing, you can match the host system's parameters with the terminal's setup. In turn, you can modify the user's *$HOME/.profile* to export the correct terminal emulation.

Terminal definitions – UNIX systems ship with two databases of terminal definitions—*terminfo* and *termcap*. On SRV4 systems, *terminfo* is the most commonly used set of terminal definitions. When a user's environment is set to export a terminal type, these definitions are used to interpret key mapping and other behavior. Logically, a terminal definition for <F1> should always be the same, right? Unfortunately, this is not always the case. It seems that every UNIX variant maintains a slightly different set of *terminfo* and *termcap* definitions. Complicating this issue further, a different type of keyboard can completely defy logic. For example, we have a group of identical terminals from a well-known computer manufacturer—the only difference is the keyboard layout. Only one of the terminals worked properly with that manufacturer's brand of UNIX and none with other variants of UNIX. Since we commonly operate with many versions of UNIX and hardware systems, it often becomes necessary to change the *terminfo* definitions and add to the "modified" *terminfo* for each keyboard type or terminal emulation program. We do this by invoking the *infocmp* command against the terminal type to obtain a source file. Once modified, it is then recompiled with the *tic* command. Updating terminal definitions can be a constant challenge to the system administrator. Also, see your *man* pages for more information on *infocmp*(1M), *tic, terminfo*(4), and *termcap*(5) as well as for additional information on terminal definitions.

Application support – When purchasing terminals or software applications make sure that a match exists with regard to terminal support. Many software vendors support a very narrow line of terminals. In our development efforts, we supported more than fifty terminal models; yet, despite this rather extensive list of support devices, our customer service personnel regularly received calls about terminal issues like key mapping. With so many variables, there is probably no software vendor in business today that can match every possible configuration or *terminfo* definition variation. Therefore, be prepared to work with your third-party software vendor to iron out key mapping and related issues. In addition, be warned that some vendors are rapidly narrowing or abandoning entirely character-based terminal support. Your choices of software for character terminals will undoubtedly continue to decrease.

X-Windows

The X-Windows system together with a window manager like Motif or CDE provides a GUI to UNIX. From a user's perspective, a windows manager like CDE is very similar in function to the Microsoft Windows GUI family, but is very different in structure, look, and feel. The technology underlying X-Windows presents some of the pioneering developments of the client/server paradigm. Often called simply *X* or *X11,* the X-Windows system was developed originally in 1984 by individuals at the Massachusetts Institute of Technology. Conceptually, X was designed as a networking code layer to permit local computer access to applications running on another system. The idea was to use bitmap displays to open several terminal windows to different computer systems, each running different applications. This notion not only succeeded, but has also evolved into an extremely robust GUI. The current incarnation of X-Windows is very portable, with complete vendor and hardware independence. It also runs on many operating systems—from UNIX to Windows NT. In other sections of the book, we focus on how to utilize X-Windows to bridge the gap between UNIX and Windows NT.

Before discussing X-Windows specifically, a short discussion on the client/server relationship is appropriate. In the simplest terms, the server provides support to its client. In the computer world, there are countless types of clients and servers. Commonly, servers are used to handle tasks such as printing or file and mail management. In terms of X-Windows, the server provides all the information necessary to handle input (from the keyboard, mouse, or other devices) and to display this information properly in a graphical context. The individual windows that are popped up during an X session are like cyber panes of glass to the client application. When a user clicks the mouse on a client window, the X-server takes control of further input into that client and displays the output processed by the client. With the exception of input and display handling, the actual computing work is done entirely by the client. Simply remember, the job of the X server is to manage input and output.

The relationship between the X server and clients can take many forms (Figure 5.7). It is important to note that the X-server can reside within the same system as its clients or in a totally different system. In addition, users can employ an X-terminal that manages all the X-server functions locally. The X-terminal is really a diskless CPU with sufficient memory to support X-server calls. The X-server information is either generated by an on-board ROM or through a download from a target host at the time when it boots. The advantage of an X-terminal is to reduce network traffic. In addition to stand-alone X-terminals, many commercial packages exist that permit emulating the X-server on PCs. For example, in our environment we commonly run X-server applications on our Windows NT box using an X-Windows emulation program.

Three varieties of applications run in an X-Windows environment. The first utilizes specific X interface calls to permit the server to display information graphically. These applications generally employ several layers of code to achieve this end. The first layer is the X foundation, a series of networking protocols. The Xt tool kit provides library routines that permit easier programming of the user and network interface. Finally, window management tool kits including Open Software Foundation/Motif and CDE, are called for more consistent user look and feel. Applications utilizing some or all of these calls are commonly referred to as *X smart*. The second category extends the X-Windows

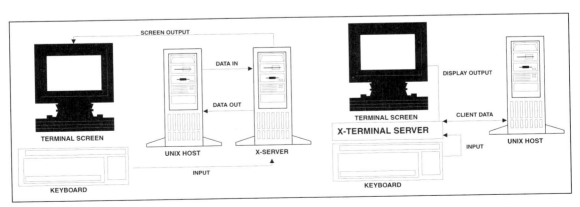

FIGURE 5.7.   X Client/Server Relationships: Two Sample, Basic X-Windows Server Topologies

environment and layers the Microsoft Windows API (or clones) to support a limited number of Microsoft Windows products. Generally, this support is restricted to 16-bit applications that support Windows 3.1. The third category of software includes those applications that were designed under the assumption that a serial interface exists between the terminal and the software. These so-called X-dumb applications run under an X client terminal emulation package known as *xterm*. They remain character based, but operate in a single non-graphical window.

The *xterm* package itself has a *terminfo* and *termcap* definition like character-based terminals. The behavior of a standard *xterm* is also command line oriented (Figure 5.8). Just like other *terminfo/termcap* definitions, *xterm* also varies between UNIX vendors. While the base *xterm* is supplied through a distribution from the X Consortium, UNIX suppliers make modifications. Therefore, compatibility issues also exist when dealing with *xterm*. Fortunately, with recent consolidations among UNIX vendors a new hybrid *xterm* (called *dtterm*) that has very similar definitions and behavior is now being shipped.

When launching *xterm* the user can freely change characteristics to reflect a desired environment. The syntax for launching *xterm* with one or more options (Table 5.13) is

```
xterm -option (option)
xterm -bg blue -fg white -geometry 80x40 -e myprogram &
```

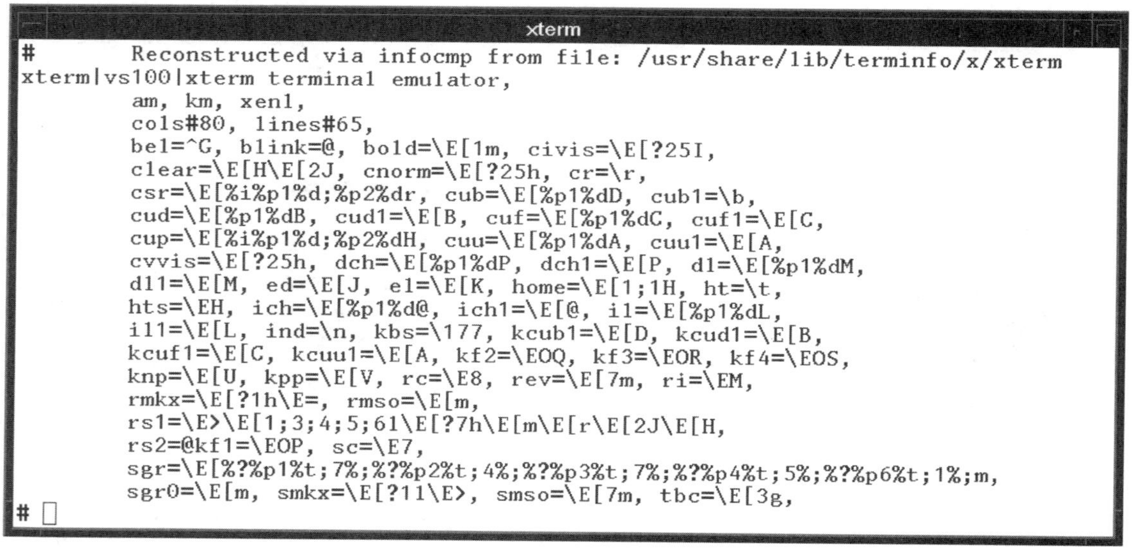

```
                              xterm
#        Reconstructed via infocmp from file: /usr/share/lib/terminfo/x/xterm
xterm|vs100|xterm terminal emulator,
        am, km, xenl,
        cols#80, lines#65,
        bel=^G, blink=@, bold=\E[1m, civis=\E[?25I,
        clear=\E[H\E[2J, cnorm=\E[?25h, cr=\r,
        csr=\E[%i%p1%d;%p2%dr, cub=\E[%p1%dD, cub1=\b,
        cud=\E[%p1%dB, cud1=\E[B, cuf=\E[%p1%dC, cuf1=\E[C,
        cup=\E[%i%p1%d;%p2%dH, cuu=\E[%p1%dA, cuu1=\E[A,
        cvvis=\E[?25h, dch=\E[%p1%dP, dch1=\E[P, dl=\E[%p1%dM,
        dl1=\E[M, ed=\E[J, el=\E[K, home=\E[1;1H, ht=\t,
        hts=\EH, ich=\E[%p1%d@, ich1=\E[@, il=\E[%p1%dL,
        il1=\E[L, ind=\n, kbs=\177, kcub1=\E[D, kcud1=\E[B,
        kcuf1=\E[C, kcuu1=\E[A, kf2=\EOQ, kf3=\EOR, kf4=\EOS,
        knp=\E[U, kpp=\E[V, rc=\E8, rev=\E[7m, ri=\EM,
        rmkx=\E[?1h\E=, rmso=\E[m,
        rs1=\E>\E[1;3;4;5;61\E[?7h\E[m\E[r\E[2J\E[H,
        rs2=@kf1=\EOP, sc=\E7,
        sgr=\E[%?%p1%t;7%;%?%p2%t;4%;%?%p3%t;7%;%?%p4%t;5%;%?%p6%t;1%;m,
        sgr0=\E[m, smkx=\E[?11\E>, smso=\E[7m, tbc=\E[3g,
#
```

FIGURE 5.8.   An *xterm terminfo* Definition Seen within a Motif Window

TABLE 5.13.   List of Common *xterm* Options

Option/command	Description
-e command	Executes the *command* or application specified with *xterm* (e.g., -e myprogram)
-bg color	Sets background color to *color* (e.g., -bg blue)
-fg color	Sets foreground color to *color* (e.g., -fg white)
-bd color	Sets border color to *color* (e.g., -bd red)
-sb	Adds scroll bars
-fn font	Sets the font to *font*
-title string	Displays the title specified by *string* at the top
-bw pixel#	Uses this number of pixels for the border
-geometry lxc	Sets the window size to the number of lines (*l*) and columns (*c*) specified (e.g., -geometry 80×40)

X-Windows, in its native form, is rather flat looking. What it does is provide a method of engaging in multiple terminal sessions on the same screen. As X evolved, additional layers of code provided a friendlier look and feel. The first major advancement was the window manager, a client program that provides a consistent operation. Early versions such as *uwm* (universal window manager) and *twm* (tom's window manager) are still commonly shipped with X-Windows distributions. The OpenLook window management system has been the default on Sun Microsystems computers for a decade. The Open Software Foundation's Motif window manager (*mwm*), however, has eclipsed this very popular window manager.

The most recent major advancement is the Common Desktop Environment (CDE). The GUI makes UNIX a real challenger to the Windows95/NT look and feel. It is friendly and robust. CDE is a polished version of the Motif tool kit combined with Hewlett-Packard's Visual User Environment (VUE). In one of the first meaningful acts of cooperation among UNIX vendors, CDE was spawned by an effort called the *Common Open Software Environment* (COSE). The UNIX community owes much to the good-faith actions of Digital, Hewlett-Packard, IBM, Novell, SCO, Sun, and other affiliated partners.

CONFIGURING X-WINDOWS STARTUP

It is not surprising to note that UNIX vendors have implemented X differently. The COSE initiative has helped to bring some commonality to X-Windows environments. However, it is impossible to detail the many variations of X that exist. In a typical SVR4 system, the user logs in to X-Windows either through a UNIX shell or via *xdm*, the X-Windows daemon. In the first case the user invokes the *startx, xstart,* or *xinit* commands to launch the X-Windows server. The clients for the session are defined globally in the *system.xinitrc* file or locally as a user in *$HOME/.xinitrc*. On the other hand, if X-Windows is already running through *xdm*, then clients are launched through the *system.xsession* or *$HOME/.xsession* files.

Most UNIX vendors include sample X applications. Usually found in the */usr/X11/bin* or */usr/contribute/bin* directories, these programs range from useless to fairly helpful utilities. Some of them, like *xclock* or *xcalc,* are commonly launched as part the user's *.profile*. As the system administrator, you may want to incorporate some of these functions into the standard user desktop.

CONFIGURING MOTIF

Motif easily supports configuration variables such as color, font, window size, location, titles, scrollbars, and many others. Motif's resource file—*/usr/lib/X11/system .mwmrc*—can be modified to change standards before launching and to modify applications to be called. For individual users the *system.mwmrc* file is generally copied to the home directory as a customized profile retained in the *$HOME/.mwmrc* file. Once the user is logged on to Motif, the configuration either uses a modified *.mwmrc* file or creates a new one.

Common X-Windows System Administrative Issues

X-Windows and its various windowing management systems provide a strong alternative to Microsoft Windows 95/NT 4.0. However, these capabilities don't come without administrative costs. In general, X11, Motif, and CDE are strong enough products that they operate without much administrative intercession. However, there remain several key potential problem areas that must be mentioned here.

Differences between X11 versions – The last distributed version of X11 is Release 6 (which is also referred to as X11-R6). The two most widely used versions are still Releases 4 and 5. There is not much operational difference between Releases 4, 5, and 6. The primary changes center on bug fixes and programming-oriented additions to the library and inclusion of *.h* file calls. It is fairly safe to have a mixed environment of hosts running X11, Releases 4 through 6. However, if you have systems with earlier versions, there are significant operational differences. Our recommendation is to upgrade systems that are running X11 versions prior to Release 4.

Use of dynamic versus static libraries, particularly with Motif – When applications are compiled, the programmer can elect to use static libraries, which bind information into the executable code, or employ dynamic library calls, which address standard link libraries on the host. Many UNIX vendors promote the use of dynamic libraries because they result in a significantly smaller block of executable code. We have noted first hand the problem with this strategy in distributing dynamically linked commercial code. A potential support nightmare emerges. As an example, during a relatively short period of time, Sun Microsystems distributed five releases of Solaris (2.1 through 2.5). Although each release was a definite improvement, backward compatibility became a problem because certain X11-based dynamic libraries were renamed. Therefore, code written for Solaris 2.1 had to be recompiled and patched for release 2.5. Our customers suddenly found that their office automation suite would not run after installing an operating system release upgrade. By recompiling our code using static libraries, this problem went away. The code was larger, but a single version supported Solaris 2.1 through 2.5. From a developer point of view, we can argue for and against the use of static and dynamic libraries. As a system administrator, you must be mindful of potential incompatibilities when installing operating system upgrades.

Network traffic – The very design of X-Windows is based on a client/server paradigm resulting in network traffic. Each keystroke and displayed character represent a network exchange of information. X traffic can become very significant. While performing system-monitoring tasks, do not overlook the potential impact of X on your enterprise.

Resource-hungry applications – X smart applications are notorious resource hogs. Many vendors of X applications suggest that the system administrator even increase swap space just to handle the potential impact of the software. Before purchasing X smart software, review the published system requirements. Note that most of these estimates are conservative. The cost of support software just begins with the purchase price; the added system resources can prove very expensive. If you already have resource-hungry applications running on your system and performance becomes an issue, consider limiting the specific users with access to the program if possible. Also, check periodically to determine whether users with open sessions of the software are actively using it. It is very common to have a user open an application and not employ it for hours at a time.

Resource-hungry users – Following our last point, some users make a habit of opening applications just for the sake of having them on screen. With

CDE's ability to support completely different workspaces, it is very simple for a user to run dozens of applications. If performance is an issue, examine user processes periodically to determine the workload being placed on the system and strongly discourage abuse.

Authority to access – Displaying applications on an X display is sometimes frustrating to new users. Two actions must always be taken. First, access must be granted. This is done by invoking the *xhost* + command. Before you telnet to the remote host, type the *xhost* + command. A message similar to the following is then displayed: "Access control disabled. Clients can connect from any host." If you want to restrict access to a single remote host, then you can type *xhost* + *hostname*. This will add that specific host to the access control list. Now you can telnet to the remote host. The next step involves setting the display variable. This is done with the Korn or Bourne shell by *DISPLAY=(ipaddress):0.0; export DISPLAY,* or in the C shell by *setenv DISPLAY (ipaddress):0.0.*

UNIX SHELLS AND FUNDAMENTALS OF UNIX PROGRAMMING

Understanding the UNIX Shell

In discussing the UNIX shell we are engaged in a discussion area that is largely alien to Windows NT. The UNIX shell is often viewed as a user front end that interprets and channels commands. Actually it is much more. The shell is not only an interpreter of commands, but it is actually a programming language that permits the customization of both system and user environments. Think of the shell as a superprocess that manages its own functions and processes called the user. UNIX can be used without the benefit of a shell. However, when employed, the shell is a giant wrapper around the user's intervention with the UNIX operating system designed to interpret commands. Typically, the first process initiated at user login is a shell; this shell, in turn, becomes the parent of subsequent processes during that session.

UNIX supports several shells. The oldest, developed by Steven Bourne, bears his name—the Bourne shell. It is by far the simplest shell and is still shipped by many UNIX vendors as the default. Users of the Bourne shell see a dollar sign ($) as the command line prompt. To enter the Bourne shell the user types /bin/sh. The next major shell was designed by Bill Joy and associates at the University of California at Berkley, and is called the C shell because its syntax structure is similar to that of the C language. Users of the C shell have a percent sign (%) command prompt. To obtain a C shell, type /bin/csh. The shell we recommend is a hybrid extension developed by David Korn, which also bears his name—the Korn shell. Since programs written for the Bourne shell run under the Korn shell, users of the Korn shell also use the dollar sign ($) as the command line prompt. To obtain a Korn shell, type /bin/ksh. Finally, BASH is distributed by the Free Software Foundation's gnu project. It is used primarily in operating system environments like freeBSD and Linux.

The UNIX shell is the system administrator's friend. With even a minimal understanding of shell programming, many routine tasks can be automated. If you are not already familiar with shell programming, it is to your benefit to learn and use shell-programming techniques.

We recommend use of the Korn shell for most computing environments because it incorporates the Bourne shell and many of benefits of the C shell. In addition it adds programming functionality. Since we are centering our attention on the Korn shell, we recommend investing in Anatole Olczak's *Korn Shell: User and Programming Manual* (Addison-Wesley, 1991). There are equally good publications for other types of shell programming.

The Korn shell has by far the richest set of built-in facilities. Among the functions supported by the Korn shell and not by the C shell are *case* statements, *export* commands (the C shell uses *set* options), *getopts, let, print,* RANDON shell, *select, until, set-uid, trap, typeset, ulimit,* coprocessing, and assorted wildcard commands. Some of these are discussed later. For additional information on these functions, see your *man* pages.

Shell Basics

Before discussing some shell programming fundamentals, it is important to understand some basic issues. The following highlights shell basics, including discussions on setting the shell environment; using metacharacters, quotes, variables, and operators; and process direction and redirection.

SETTING THE SHELL ENVIRONMENT

A user's shell environment is set in the last field of the */etc/password* file (Table 5.14). It can also be set at login time or dynamically during the session. In addition, each shell type supports its own resource file, which can be optionally created to customize environmental conditions.

TABLE 5.14.   Methods to Set Shell Environments

Method	Bourne	C Shell	Korn Shell
Setting within /etc/passwd	/bin/sh	/bin/csh	/bin/ksh
Setting within system login file	/etc/profile	/etc/login	/etc/login
Setting within user login file	.profile	.login	.profile
Exporting or setting shell environment from command line	SHELL=/bin/sh export SHELL	setenv SHELL csh —	SHELL=/bin/ksh export SHELL
Dynamic change to another shell	sh <Enter>	csh <Enter>	ksh <Enter>

To determine the current shell environment, type the following command line:

```
echo $SHELL
```

USE OF METACHARACTERS

When executing simple commands, the shell manages the process and its extension. For example, if you seek a list of files using the asterisk or splat (*), the shell executes *ls* and interprets the asterisk as a qualifier known as a metacharacter. Therefore, the command *ls b* will list all the files in the working directory starting with the letter *b*. Each shell has its own set of metacharacters (Table 5.15).

TABLE 5.15.   Common Metacharacters List

Syntax	Shell	Description
*	All	Match string, zero or more characters; *ls file**
?	All	Match single character in that position; *ls file?*
[abc12]	All	Match any character listed; *ls file[abc12]*
[a-z,1-3]	All	Match any character in the specified range; *ls file[a-z,1-3]*
[!abc1]	sh/ksh	Match all characters except those specified; *ls file[!abc1]*
?(xyz)	ksh	Pattern match, zero or once; *ls file?(xyz)*
*(xyz)	ksh	Pattern match, zero or more; *ls file*(xyz)*
+(xyz)	ksh	Pattern match, only one; *ls file +(xyz)*
!(xyz)	ksh	Pattern match, any one but the one specified; *ls file!(xyz)*

TABLE 5.16.   Syntax for Setting Command Forms

Syntax	Description
Command only	Executes the command in the foreground
&	Executes the command that ends with & in the background
;	Separates multiple commands to be executed in sequence
( )	Groups the commands together
|	Executes the first command, inputs to the second and executes, and so on
||	Executes either the first command OR the next command
&&	Executes the first command AND, if successful, executes the second command

MANAGING COMMANDS

As the shell interprets a command line string, it looks at the syntax to determine the form of the instruction set. For example, is the command to be executed in the foreground or background? Table 5.16 lists the most commonly used command forms.

EXIT STATUS: EXECUTION SUCCESS OR FAILURE

The last item in Table 5.16 underscores the ability of the shell to track the status of an executed command. When a command is given, it posts an exit status. To see the exit status of the command, simply type

```
echo $?  <ENTER>
```

The number zero will be output if the command exited successfully. If it failed, the output will be a nonzero number (Table 5.17).

If you are using the C shell, it is possible to output the exit status using a shell variable called *status*. Zero, for success, is provided for successful execution and 1 is provided for a failed job. The syntax for this command is *set status*.

TABLE 5.17.   Exit Status

Output	Description
0	Successfully executed command
Nonzero	Failed command

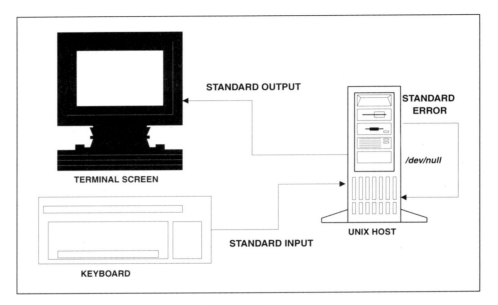

FIGURE 5.9.   Standard Input, Output, and Error

PROCESS DIRECTION AND REDIRECTION

When dealing with processes, the direction of the input and output is critical (Figure 5.9). The shell permits acceptance of both standard direction and multiple levels of redirection. There are three levels of standard direction: (1) standard input or *stdin* is any signal from the keyboard, (2) standard output or *stdout* is data displayed to the terminal, and (3) standard error or *stderr* is sent to the terminal but is often redirected to the bit bucket known as */dev/null*.

Standard input, output, and error can be redirected using several methods. The simplest form of redirection is to instruct the shell to send output from the screen to a file. The types of redirection listed in Table 5.18 are commonly utilized.

USING QUOTES

A special word is necessary regarding the use of characters that have unique meaning to shells. A shell automatically reacts and attempts to interpret events when it sees any of the following:

```
;   &   ( )   |   >   <   &   *  ?  [ ]  ~ + = @ !  "  '  \ $
```

TABLE 5.18.   Process Redirection

Syntax	Description
> *file*	Redirects the command out from the terminal to a *file*; *ls -l > filelist*
< *file*	Processes the input from the *file* using the defined command; *sort < filelist*
2> *file*	Redirects the standard error of a command to a *file*; *find / -name UNIX -print 2>/dev/null*
>> *file*	Appends the standard output to the designated *file*; *ls -l >> oldfile*
>&-	Does not use standard output
<&-	Does not use standard input
> *file* 2>&1	Redirects standard output and standard error to the *file*; *ls -l > filelist 2>&1*
(>*file1*)2>*file2*	Redirects standard output to *file1* and standard error to *file2*
>! *file*	Redirects to the *file* named only if it does not already exist (C shell only)
| tee *file*	Pipes the *tee* command so that the standard output goes to both a *file* and the terminal

There are obviously times when these characters will be used in a text string and must be treated literally and not for their special meaning by the shell. To offset this situation, the use of quote marks around the string will inform the shell to disregard the special characters and treat them as part of a literal ASCII string. In the C shell, you can set the *nonomatch* variable for the same result.

SHELL VARIABLES

The shell provides a number of options that can be executed at login or dynamically during the session. Variables for the Bourne and Korn shells are invoked using the *export* command and use the syntax *Variable=setting; export Variable.* The C shell uses a *set* command with the syntax *set Variable setting.* Tables 5.19 and 5.20 list the commonly used variables for each of the shells.

TABLE 5.19.   Sample of Korn and Bourne Shell Variables

Variable	Description
COLUMNS=*n*	Changes the number of character columns for output
ENV=*file*	Directs the reading of another file for further shell instructions
HISTFILE=*file*	Sets the input file for a list of the command history; *$HOME/.sh_history*; Korn only
HISTLIST=*n*	Sets the number of events to be remembered by HISTFILE
HOME=*directory*	Defines or redirects the user's home directory
LANG=*directory*	Some programs are language dependent; references the language directory
LINES=*n*	Sets the number of lines to be output on the display
MAILCHECK=*n*	Checks for undelivered mail every *n* number of seconds
PATH=*directories*	Lists the directory paths that a user can access by typing the absolute path; each path is separated by a colon; *PATH=$HOME:/usr/bin:/usr/bin/X11.; export PATH*
SHELL=*shell*	Sets the shell type; *SHELL=/bin/ksh; export SHELL*
TERM=*terminal*	Sets the terminal type; *TERM=xterm; export TERM*
TMOUT=*n*	Terminates the shell if no commands are executed in *n* number of seconds

OPERATORS

The Korn and C shells also utilize a number of arithmetic and logical operators that are used to string events and actions together. Table 5.21 presents the operators that are common to both the Korn and C shells.

Shell Programming Fundamentals

UNIX provides a feature-rich shell programming environment. Most system administrators take advantage of this facility to streamline work. The following highlights key shell-programming issues.

TABLE 5.20.   Sample of C Shell Variables

Variable	Description
echo	Shows the command line before it is executed
hardpaths	Forces the display of the real path of a symbolically linked file
home=*directory*	Directs or redirects the user's home directory
mail=*n*	Checks mail every *n* number of seconds (default, 300 seconds)
noclobber	Does not overwrite an existing file during a redirection of standard output
nonomatch	Ignores metacharacters and treats them as literal characters
notify	Lets the user know when the execution of a process is complete
path=*directories*	Lists the directory paths that a user can access by typing the absolute path; each path is separated by a colon; *set path=$HOME:/usr/bin:/usr/bin/X11*
savehist=*n*	Sets the number of commands that are saved in the *.history* file
term=*terminal*	Sets the terminal emulation type; *set term=xterm*

TABLE 5.21.   Common Korn and C Shell Operators

Operator	Description
+ −	Arithmetic add (+) and subtract (−)
* / %	Arithmetic multiply (*), divide (/), modulus (%)
<< >>	Shift bitwise; shift left (<<) and right (>>)
== !=	Equal (==) and not equal (!=)
< >	Less than (<) and greater than (>)
<= >=	Less than or equal to (<=) and greater than or equal to (>=)
&	and (bitwise)
|	or (bitwise)
&&	and (logical)
||	or (logical)

WHAT IS A SHELL PROGRAM?

A shell program is referred to as a *script* because the processing of the information is accomplished in the same manner as an actor might read a script of dialog. The shell examines each sequential line in a file and either executes the command or outputs an error. As opposed to a compiled binary program, the shell program is a flat ASCII file that can be viewed and modified easily by authorized users.

A SIMPLE SHELL PROGRAM

A simple program is easy to write. Remember that the shell interprets the contents of a shell in sequential order, beginning with the first line. If it encounters an item that it cannot execute, an error message is produced.

When writing a script, the first decision is to determine which shell to use. For simple and globally distributed shell scripts, writing to the Bourne shell with its lowest common denominator of functionality may be appropriate. For example, errors will occur if a script is written with C shell calls but the user's home environment is set the Bourne (*sh*) shell. By writing to the Bourne shell, you are generally guaranteed that the command will be understood in any user environment. However, in so doing, the scope and power of the script is also compromised. To overcome this shortcoming, the script itself can force the invocation of the desired shell environment during its execution. We recommend the following steps in writing a shell script:

1. Start by defining the type of shell. This *must* be on the first line. Although this is an option, it forces execution using the built-in functions of the defined shell. The syntax for the Korn shell is *!#/bin/ksh,* for the C shell is *!#/bin/csh,* and for the Bourne shell is *!#/bin/sh.*

2. Optionally include comment statements so that others looking at the shell script can understand the intent of the commands. Comments are defined by a pound sign (#) at the beginning of the statement.

3. Make sure that the commands used in the shell conform to the functions supported by the particular shell.

4. After the shell script is written, you must change the permissions by using *chmod* to add execution privileges for the user, group, and others as desired. Until the execution bit is set, the script is just another flat file.

Let's write a very simple script. Enter the *vi* editor and while in the input mode type

```
echo This is my first shell script with the time and date listed below
date
```

Save the file as *myscript* and exit the *vi* editor. Now change the permissions to permit the entire world to read, write, and execute *myscript*:

```
chmod 777 myscript
```

Now execute your script by typing `./myscript`. You should see two lines—the string of information echoed to the screen followed by today's time and date. The script performed two functions. First, it acknowledged the *echo* command and wrote the string of text to the screen as standard output. Then, it went to the second line and executed the UNIX *date* command. Writing a shell script is just that simple.

Let's try another sample script. This time assume that you want to see your current environment setting, confirmation of your present working directory, a long list of files, and this month's calendar—all displayed by typing your new shell script's name *doit*. So, open a new file called *doit* with the *vi* editor, add the lines shown in Figure 5.10, write and quit *vi*, and then execute *chmod*. Figure 5.10 dissects the script.

More Advanced Scripting Concepts

The following discussion centers primarily on the use of the Korn shell. Consult your *man* pages for information about the C and Bourne shells.

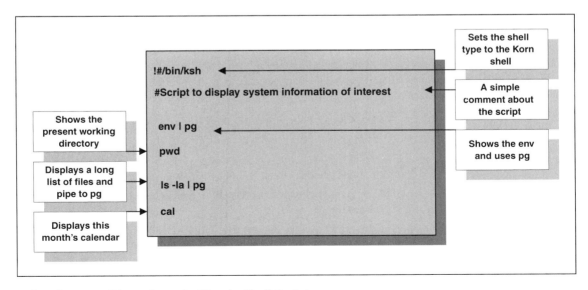

FIGURE 5.10.   Dissection of a Simple Shell Script

BUILT-IN COMMANDS

The shell is a program that includes extensions to the common UNIX command set. These extensions are called built-in commands. Most of the shell built-ins provide a series of options similar to standard UNIX commands. It is outside the scope of this book to discuss all of the built-ins and their options. However, as a matter of reference, we list some of most commonly used shell built-ins in Table 5.22.

The shell is a layer of code that includes its own "built-in" functions. Each shell type has its own unique set of built-in commands. It is sometimes difficult to determine what is a UNIX command and what is a shell command because they are executed identically. Fortunately, you can tell from where the command comes by using the *whence* utility. If you type *whence* against commands like *cd, ls,* and *mkdir,* you will notice that only *cd* was not listed with a directory listing. This means that *ls* and *mkdir* are commands that are independent binary files. On the other hand, *cd* is a shell built-in. When moving from one shell type to another, it is sometimes important to know whether a particular built-in command is available.

TABLE 5.22.   Sample of Korn Shell Built-in Commands

Built-in	Description
#	Starts a comment; the shell ignores everything after the pound sign
[ ]	Offsets a test expression
alias	Renames a command, such as changing *ls* to the DOS-like *dir* command; *ls = dir*
bg *job(s)*	Places the defined *job* using the PID in the background
case … esac	Establishes a condition with the start of *case* and ends with reverse case (*esac*)
cd	Changes the directory
do	Script language word used with *for, select, while,* and *until* statements
echo	Outputs a string of data to the standard output or redirected device
eval	Examines the expressions first and then executes commands
export	Exports *variables* such as *PATH, TERM,* and so on
for do done	A series of conditional statements *for* this occurrence, *do* something until *done*

TABLE 5.22.   *(Continued)*

Built-in	Description
if	Another conditional statement; *if* something, *then* . . . *else*; also *elif* (else if) and *fi*(nish)
jobs	Displays all running and stopped processes
kill	Using different levels, terminates processes gracefully or by a forced termination
print	An extension of the *echo* command
pwd	Displays the present working directory
r *number*	Executes the previous or designated historically numbered command
set	See the *man* pages for the long list of options that can be set
shift *number*	In positional arguments, shifts by the designated *number*
stop *PID*	Terminates the background process per the PID
test	Tests the condition of a situation; very powerful
ulimit	Displays the values of limits for items like core size, block size, stack size, CPU seconds
umask *num*	Sets the default permission levels for files
wait *PID*	Waits until all associated processes have executed in the background
while	Conditional statement; *while* this is happening *do* this until *done*

An example of a very useful Korn shell built-in is using the *set* command to keep a history of commands entered. For example, if you want to edit and execute a previously used command string easily, you should first invoke the following *set* command:

```
set -o vi
```

This sets the *vi* editor as a command line option. Now, press <Esc> and press the k to show the last command entered. Each time k is pressed, the previous command is displayed. If you passed the desired command, press j. It is just like moving between text in the *vi* editor. Use *k* to kick it up to the next command and *j* to jump down. Once you locate the desired prompt, you will find yourself in the *vi* editor's input mode. Make your changes, press <Esc> to exit the input mode and press <Enter> to execute. This can really save time and typing frustration, especially for long command lines.

TEST STATEMENTS

One of the most useful Korn shell built-in functions used in scripting is *test.* The *test* built-in examines whether the specified condition exists (Table 5.23). There are two formats used in writing a *test* condition. For example, if you wanted to test if a filename represented a directory, the two alternate formats are

```
test -d filename
[ -d filename ]
```

The brackets replace the need to use the *test* built-in name. To see if the condition was successful (e.g., that filename was a directory), you can use echo $? on the command line. Typically, *test* is used within a script to determine whether a condition has been achieved before executing the next statement.

CONDITIONAL STATEMENTS

Korn shell scripts can include specific conditional statements. These statements can be used inside one another. Think of the conditional statement as a road map for the shell to process sequentially until the conditions have been achieved. Let's briefly examine the use of conditional statements.

TABLE 5.23.   Korn Shell *test* Conditions

Condition	Description
-a *file*	Confirms the existence of *file*
-b *file*	Confirms the existence of *file* and confirms that it is a block file type
-c *file*	Confirms the existence of *file* and confirms that it is a character file type
-d *file*	Confirms the existence of *file* and confirms that it is a directory
-f *file*	Confirms the existence of *file* and confirms that it is a regular file
-g *file*	Confirms the existence of *file* and confirms that the GID bit is set
-G *file*	Confirms the existence of *file* and confirms that it is part of the current GID
-k *file*	Confirms the existence of *file* and confirms that the sticky bit is set

TABLE 5.23.   *(Continued)*

Condition	Description
-L *file*	Confirms the existence of *file* and confirms that it is a symbolic link
-n *string*	Confirms that the *string* has more than zero characters
-O *file*	Confirms the existence of *file* and confirms that the owner is the actual UID
-p *file*	Confirms the existence of *file* and confirms that it is a named pipe
-r *file*	Confirms the existence of *file* and confirms that it is set as read only
-s *file*	Confirms the existence of *file* and confirms that it is one or more bits in size
-S *file*	Confirms the existence of *file* and confirms that it is a socket
-u *file*	Confirms the existence of *file* and confirms that a set UID bit is set
-w *file*	Confirms the existence of *file* and confirms that it is set as writable
-x *file*	Confirms the existence of *file* and confirms that it is set as executable
-z *string*	Confirms that the *string* is 0 bits in length
filea -ef *fileb*	Checks to see if these two files are linked
filea -nt *fileb*	Checks to see if the first file is newer than the second file
filea -ot *fileb*	Checks to see if the first file is older than the second file
string a = *stringb*	Checks to see if the two strings are identical
stringa != *stringb*	Checks to see if the two strings are not identical
num1 -eq *num2*	Checks to see if the two numbers are equal
num1 -ge *num2*	Checks to see if the first number is greater than or equal to the second
num1 -gt *num2*	Checks to see if the first number is greater than the second number
num1 -le *num2*	Checks to see if the first number is less than the second
num1 -lt *num2*	Checks to see if the first number is less than or equal to the second
num1 -ne *num2*	Checks to see that the two numbers do not equal each other

If-Then-Else

The *if-then-else* statement follows the very simple logic: If this condition is specified, then do the specified action. If not (*else*), do the other specified things. Here is an example of an *if-then-else* script:

```
!#/bin/ksh
if  [ -f targetfile ]   #if targetfile is a regular file, then
then
      echo   "The targetfile is a regular file and it is being printed"
      lp -d laser targetfile
else
      echo   "The targetfile is not a regular file and can not be printed"
fi
```

If-Then-Else If

A variation of the *if-then-else* construct is the addition of an else if (*elif*) layer. An example of the use of *elif* is as follows:

```
!#/bin/ksh
if [ filea -nt fileb ] ; then    #if filea is new than fileb, then ..
      rm fileb      #delete fileb
elif [ filea -ot fileb ] ; then    #if filea is older than fileb, then
      rm filea      #delete filea
else
      echo  "You have successfully removed the older file"
fi
```

Loop Conditions

The loop sets a condition in which a sequence of events is run. The word *for* is special and is used to define the variable list. This is followed by the word *do,* meaning execute the following items, and *done,* when everything is completed. An example loop looks like the following:

```
#/bin/ksh
for dogs  in basset beagle collie golden husky
do
      echo "A $dogs puppy is available from the animal shelter"
      echo "Don't you want a cute little $dogs puppy"
done
```

while *and* for *Loops and* case *Statements*

More sophisticated conditions can also be set using the *for* and *while* loops. The conditions are fairly obvious: *for* these instances, do something *while* this condition is executing. The *case* statement permits the use of pseudo point-ers that support an action based on the execution of a selected case. The following sample script creates a menu system for the selection of com-mon UNIX commands as shown in Figure 5.11. It uses the *while* and *case* constructs.

```ksh
#!/bin/ksh
LINES=24
COLUMNS=80
export COLUMNS LINES
#In order to permit execution of functions in a sequential manner, a
#function called hold is first defined that sends to standard output
#(terminal) a message when selected function is completed to "Hit the
#ENTER key to continue" The function also clears the screen
hold()
{
echo
echo "Hit the ENTER key to continue"
read answer
clear
}
while :    #this loop is visible on the screen as a menu until an action
do
echo
echo
echo '                  YOUR PERSONAL COMMAND CENTER'
echo
echo '                        (1) Long List of All The File'
echo '                        (2) Confirm the Current Directory'
echo '                        (3) Display a Calendar for a Defined Year'
echo '                        (4) Telnet to the following IP Address'
echo '                        (5) FTP to the following IP Address'
echo '                        (6) View the /etc/passwd file '
echo '                        (7) Words of Wisdom'
echo '                        (8) Screen capture and print'
echo '                        (q) Quit'
echo
echo '                    Please Enter Your Choice: \c'
read answer
echo
case $answer in
```

```
1) echo ' The following is the long list of files ....'
   ls -l &
 hold
   ;;
2) pwd &
hold
;;
3) echo '       Please indicate the calendar year desired: \c'
       read answer
       cal $answer -n 5
hold
;;
4) echo '      Please Enter the IP Address: \c'
       read answer
       telnet $answer
hold
;;
5) echo '       Please Enter the IP Address: \c'
       read answer
       ftp $answer
 hold
   ;;
6) more /etc/passwd
 hold
   ;;
7) echo
   echo
   banner " life is "
   banner "   good"
   echo '                    ..... unless otherwise notified'
 hold
   ;;
8) xwd -frame -out 1.xwd
   xpr -rv -device <printer> 1.xwd | lp -option
hold
;;
q) exit
;;
*) echo 'Invalid Key'
esac
done
```

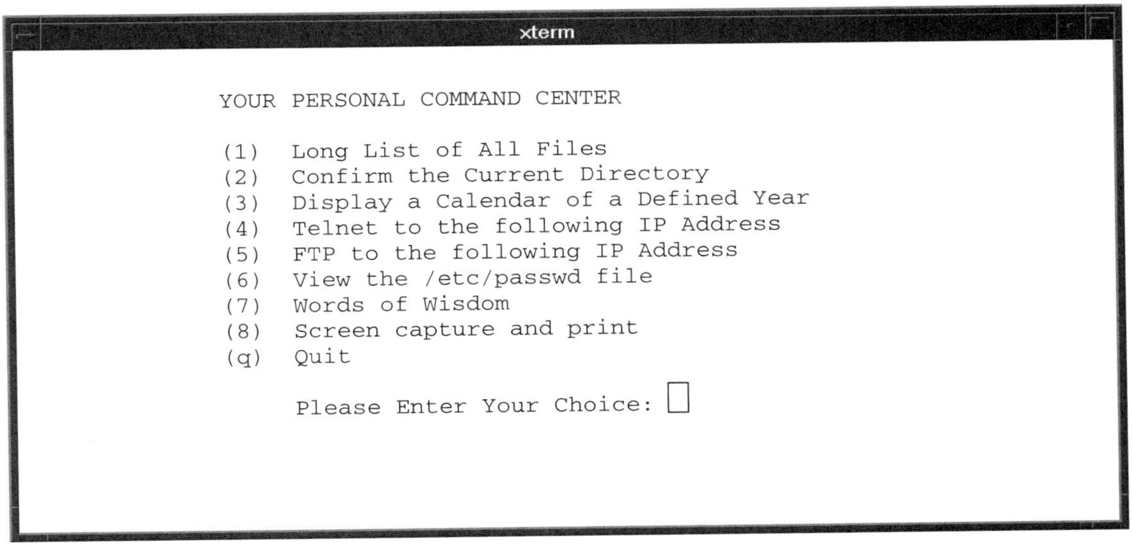

```
                                    xterm

            YOUR PERSONAL COMMAND CENTER

            (1)   Long List of All Files
            (2)   Confirm the Current Directory
            (3)   Display a Calendar of a Defined Year
            (4)   Telnet to the following IP Address
            (5)   FTP to the following IP Address
            (6)   View the /etc/passwd file
            (7)   Words of Wisdom
            (8)   Screen capture and print
            (q)   Quit

                  Please Enter Your Choice: ▯
```

FIGURE 5.11.   Output of Sample Menu Script

OTHER SCRIPTING LANGUAGES

As a system administrator becomes more proficient with basic UNIX scripting, more advanced procedures are typically sought. Fortunately, UNIX does support a number of high-grade scripting languages. While the scope of this book does not permit lengthy discussions of these languages, the following list provides a few resources.

- *sed* – The streaming editor provides many facilities not supported by *vi*. It is excellent for activities that require sophisticated pattern matching and text manipulation.
- *awk* – This is a series of scripting calls that can be easily interspersed with Korn shell scripts. One of the best references for both *sed* and *awk* is Dale Doughery's *UNIX Power Tools: sed and awk* (O'Reilly & Associates, Inc., 1992).
- *perl* – The perl language provides many of the advances of the C language with a number of script language extensions. An excellent reference for perl is Larry Wall and Randal Schwartz's *Programming perl* (O'Reilly & Associates, Inc., 1992).
- *Java* – The Java language is an excellent cross-platform development environment.

In addition to script-oriented programming, UNIX is the bastion of many compiled languages. C and C++ were developed for and on UNIX. Other mainframe-oriented languages such as Cobol, Fortran, and Ada are also UNIX supported. Other more exotic languages can also be used on UNIX. There is no lack of opportunity to develop applications of any kind on this robust operating system.

Windows NT Structure, Processes, and Users

In Chapter 3 we described UNIX as a "feel good" operating system that provides each user's files and processes a home, a parent, an identity, secured ownership, and other attributes. With the exception of the parent/child relationship, Windows NT provides an equally comfortable "feel good" environment. In some ways, Windows NT can be viewed as UNIX on steroids, with a pretty face. Users are provided a home under their login name, security, ownership, and many attributes known to UNIX users. Interestingly, these concepts are very different than the paradigms employed in Microsoft's earlier single-user MS-DOS and Windows 3.x environments. Since Windows NT utilizes the familiar Windows 95 user interface, the challenge of making the end user community comfortable with the new structure is minimized. From a user's perspective, the task is to learn where personal files are now stored and how to use best the enhanced features. For system administrators, introduction of Windows NT represents an opportunity to bring the familiar into a server environment.

Windows NT Server was designed with a number of very specific objectives. Contrary to some popular beliefs, Microsoft's corporate goal was not merely the same as exposed by the cartoon characters Pinky and the Brain of "trying to take over the world." Instead, Microsoft embarked on a mission to create a world-class client/server environment that could compete against UNIX and venerable proprietary operating systems. There is no question that Windows NT Server 4.0 has made enormous strides in this direction. Some people argue that Windows NT must now be considered the premier server operating system (at least on the low end). The following summarizes the design objectives that have been achieved in Windows NT Server 4.0:

- Preemptively multitasking
- 32-bit architecture

- Support for the new NTFS file system and the legacy FAT file system
- Subsystem support for POSIX and OS/2
- Support for 16-bit Windows and legacy MS-DOS applications
- Scalable for a symmetric multiprocessor architecture
- Portable across multiple processor types
- Security features that minimally meet C2 and eventual B1 levels
- Unified development environment with standard API calls
- Native networking support for TCP/IP, NetBEUI, and IPX/SPX

As Windows NT Server relates to UNIX, Microsoft provides technologies that support the integration of the two operating systems. By embracing a subsystem for POSIX.1, Microsoft has established a basis for third-party vendors to supply tools that permit support for all major UNIX facilities. The optional Microsoft Windows NT Resource Kit provides an assortment of utilities with functional similarity to UNIX counterparts. Native support for a subset of the TCP/IP suite ensures immediate connectivity with UNIX. Inclusion of *telnet* and *ftp* are two UNIX utilities shipped with both the Windows NT Server and Workstation. Although the TCP/IP stack is not a comprehensive port (with the most notable absence of the Simple Mail Transport Protocol [SMTP] and the NFS), Microsoft has provided a solid basis for first-level integration. Companies such as Hummingbird (www.hummingbird.com) and Softway Systems (www.softway.com) provide applications that virtually transform a Windows NT box into something that functions like UNIX with the many Windows NT enhancements. It is nice to know that a reasonably full UNIX-like implementation within Windows NT can be achieved. However, we are not suggesting that this type of extension is at all required. Windows NT Server 4.0 stands nicely as an excellent operating system on its own merits.

This chapter is a primer for system administration of Windows NT from a UNIX administrator's vantage. While not designed as the definitive study, the chapter provides a foundation in key components of the operating system. Chapter 7 centers on the major issues that affect Windows NT system administrators. Important concepts such as replication services and security are reviewed in Chapter 8. Finally, Appendix A rounds out the primer with a review of major Windows NT commands and utilities, cross-referenced where appropriate with UNIX counterparts. These chapters, coupled with Microsoft's own on-line documentation, should provide a solid basis for both operation and administration.

OPERATING SYSTEM FOUNDATION

In Chapter 3 we described UNIX as comprising three sides of an operating system triangle—structure, processes, and user intervention. Nearly everything connected with UNIX can be modified and customized. This basic view of an operating system triangle only partially fits Windows NT (Figure 6.1) in that Microsoft has added several additional dimensions. Windows NT boasts a non-configurable microkernel and the Hardware Abstraction Layer (HAL), which are significantly different than what exists in UNIX. In addition, a collection of services rests on top of the microkernel. We view the microkernel, HAL, and the operating system service components as the base on which the Windows NT operating system triangle rests. Therefore, a discussion of the microkernel, HAL, and the operating system service managers is appropriate before venturing into an analysis of structure, processes, and user intervention.

Windows NT functions in two primary modes: the privileged, processor *kernel mode* and the open, nonprivileged *user mode* (Figure 6.2). This effectively separates operating system tools from user applications. This concept of kernel and user modes is very similar to UNIX. Low-level operating system services, system data, and interfaces to hardware are controlled by the kernel mode. The kernel mode, as we discuss later, should not be confused with the

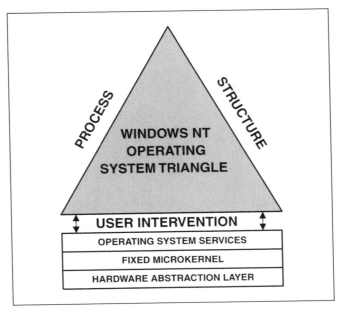

FIGURE 6.1.   Windows NT Operating System Triangle

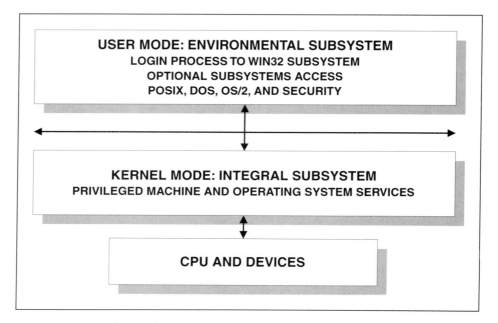

FIGURE 6.2.   Relationship of the User and Kernel Modes

Windows NT microkernel itself. The *user mode,* by contrast, handles every-thing else that is subject to user intervention, including the default Win32 sub-system, the optional subsystems, and applications. The user mode interacts with system data and hardware through a tightly integrated API.

The Windows NT Executive

The Windows NT Executive performs many of the same functions as the con-solidated UNIX kernel. In UNIX the kernel manages underlying operating sys-tem activities that are protected from direct user intervention. Windows NT breaks the Executive's operations into four segments that run within the kernel or privileged mode. These segments are the microkernel, HAL, the Executive Managers, and the Executive Services buffer.

A brief examination of the kernel, HAL, and Executive Managers is appro-priate. The kernel mode is also known as the *privileged processor mode* be-cause of the respective system responsibilities that are outside the control of a normal user. In Windows NT, the Executive controls only essential operating system functions. Other functions are pushed into the nonprivileged sector or into protected subsystems. The subsystems are configurable through APIs and built-in utilities. The objective in designing Windows NT was first to break out common functions into integrated Executive components and then to separate hardware-related issues from software applications. The elements of the Windows NT Executive are discretely independent and exchange data through defined interfaces. In concept, any component can be deleted and replaced with a technologically updated version. Assuming adherence to the interface APIs, the operating system should function without difficulty after swapping Executive components.

THE MICROKERNEL

Windows NT supports a small microkernel similar in structure to that of Carnegie-Mellon University's Mach operating system. (Ironically, the Mach kernel was being considered as the model for UNIX standardization in the early 1990s. Vendors such as Hewlett-Packard have again launched an initiative promoting a microkernel UNIX standard.) The Windows NT microkernel is designed as a nonconfigurable and nonpageable element. By *nonconfigurable* we refer to the fact that the Windows NT microkernel is never modified (Figure 6.3). Unlike UNIX, the Windows NT microkernel is never recompiled. By *nonpageable* we

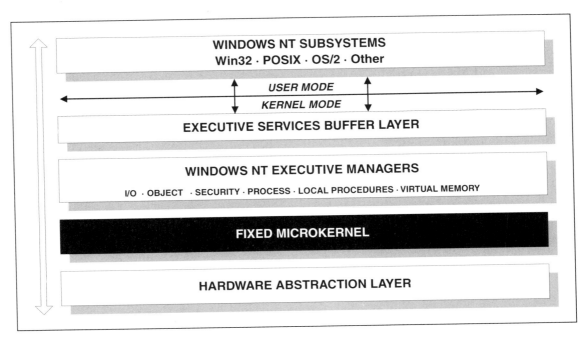

FIGURE 6.3.   Windows NT Building Blocks

refer to the fact the 4-KB memory pages associated with the microkernel are fixed and not stored in the *pagefile.sys* file where dynamic paging activities are retained. The microkernel manages the smallest unit within the operating system by *dispatching* and *controlling* threads. (When multiprocessors are involved, the kernel also synchronizes that workload.) The dispatcher objects manage the implementation and synchronization of events, semaphores, timers, threads, and mutants (mutually exclusive resource access). Control objects regulate virtual address processes, system interrupts, thread profiles, and asynchronous procedure calls.

HARDWARE ABSTRACTION LAYER

As a means of ensuring greater portability across platforms, Microsoft separated hardware-related interfaces into a separate segment of code. HAL deals with CPU- and device-dependent issues. The term *abstraction* comes from the fact that HAL hides hardware definitions from the operating system and support applications. By separating hardware drivers, a single set of instructions can be written by applications developers for a device type. Porting applications thereby becomes a matter of recompilation rather than also having to deal with process or device considerations.

In multiprocessor systems, HAL synchronizes hardware-related threads with the next-available CPU. Thread priorities ranges between real-time processes (with the highest priority) and variable or dynamic processes (lower priority).

EXECUTIVE MANAGERS

The third segment of the Windows NT operating system's kernel mode is the Executive Managers. These services allow the subsystems and user applications to access system resources. The components of the Windows NT Executive include the managers discussed in the following pages.

- *Object Manager* – In contrast to UNIX's reliance on the file as the atomic component, Windows NT uses objects. The Object Manager is responsible for the creation, deletion, and interim management of these resources. Objects specifically monitored by the Object Manager include files, directories, threads, processes, ports, semaphores, events, and shared memory segments.

- *Process Manager* – Windows NT support for program processes are controlled through a threading system. This manager specifically monitors thread and process objects. As discussed in the process section, native Windows NT does not create a parent/child relationship as with UNIX. (The POSIX subsystem together with third-party products make it possible to emulate these parent/child relationships as required by actual UNIX applications that have been ported to Windows NT).

- *Virtual Memory Manager* – The Virtual Memory Manager regulates the allocation of 32-bit linear memory. Window NT supports 4 GB of virtual, addressable memory, half of which is allocated to system tasks and the other half to application workload. As required, the Virtual Memory Manager pages information to disk or physical memory.

- *Local Process Call facility* – Operating similarly to a remote process call, the Local Process Call manages client/server relationships in the computer. As a local procedure that impacts system resources is launched from the user mode, the server elements in the kernel mode are called.

- *Security Reference Monitor* – Security is a cornerstone of Windows NT. To create or gain access to an object, the request must first flow through the Security Reference Monitor (SRM). Unlike some of the other Executive Managers, the SRM operates in both the kernel and user modes. As discussed later, each Windows NT object has a descriptor located in the Access Control List (ACL). Each item is provided an individual Access Control Entry (ACE) containing the security ID (SID) of the user and group. On logging in, users are assigned a Security Access Token (SAT) that operates as a passkey to objects that match their entry levels (Figure 6.4).

- *I/O Manager* – All input and output functions are controlled by the I/O Manager. The activities are broken into several component parts that regulate the input/output of the system cache, file system, network drivers, and specified devices (Figure 6.5).

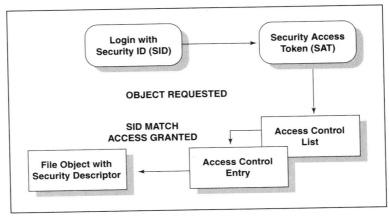

FIGURE 6.4.   Flow of Security Reference Monitoring

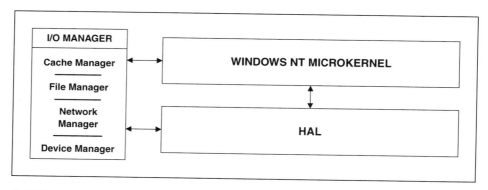

FIGURE 6.5.   I/O Manager Relationship to the Kernel and HAL

- *Windows Manager and graphics device drivers* – The Windows Manager and graphics device drivers (GDDs) were moved from the user mode, where they resided under Windows NT 3.5 and earlier versions, to the kernel mode in Windows NT Server 4.0. The reason for the move was to isolate Windows API and GDD functions in the kernel mode as equal Executive Managers. Applications could address the *win32k.sys* interface and the GDD talks directly to HAL. Microsoft believes that this transfer improved the screen and graphics handling.

EXECUTIVE SERVICES

The Executive Services buffer is a small layer of code that sits on top of the other Executive components. It is the buffer between the kernel and user modes and acts as the medium for passing API and system calls.

User Mode

The user mode is also comprised of a number of parts that act together to facilitate user and application integrity. In the most simplified terms, the user mode can be categorized in two parts.

1. *Protected subsystems* – Windows NT supports user mode subsystems that support specific requirements for native Windows (16 bit and 32 bit), POSIX, and OS/2 applications, as well as user-related system calls. An examination of protected subsystems follows.

2. *Dynamic user intervention* – The second part of the user mode is the unprotected action of individual user programs. We discuss the impact of this dynamic intervention in the processes section of this chapter.

UNDERSTANDING THE PROTECTED USER MODE SYSTEM

Windows NT uses the concept of subsystems to separate complex functions into more manageable components. The idea was to design each subsystem as a relatively discrete part of the operating system that is started when Windows NT is booted. In theory, new subsystems could be added to Windows NT without recompiling the operating system or its kernel. The subsystem structure can be viewed as a buffer mechanism between the user applications and kernel mode services structure. The term *protected* is used because the subsystems are not directly changed or modified by the administrator or the user; rather, they merely pass and manage API calls. Windows NT supports two protected subsystem types. The first is known as the *integral subsystem;* it performs underlying operating system tasks. Security management is an example of an integral or sustained subsystem. The second subsystem is called *environmental* because it establishes the grounding for applications. If a POSIX application is invoked, then the POSIX environmental subsystem is invoked for that particular process.

The use of the environmental subsystem is substantially different in form than what is present in UNIX. Therefore, an examination of the environmental subsystem is appropriate.

NOTE   As an interesting note, LINUX, the shareware upstart billed as a UNIX-like operating system, supports environmental subsystems similar to Windows NT. In fact, a freeware adaptation of NTFS is available for LINUX.

ENVIRONMENTAL SUBSYSTEM

The user mode supports three environmental subsystems or "personalities" (Figure 6.6). The intent of Windows NT was to provide an ability to run applications originally compiled for other operating systems or to make porting of applications easier to achieve. First, Microsoft needed to ensure backward compatibility with MS-DOS and Windows 3.x applications. Due to its developmental contribution to OS/2, Microsoft sought support for OS/2 version 1.x. Obviously, the new Windows NT (a 32-bit operating system) had to support new software written for its own Win32 subsystem. In all of these instances, Microsoft has succeeded. Finally, Microsoft wanted to embrace UNIX and other operating system applications through the inclusion of a POSIX subsystem. In this regard, rudimentary support has been achieved. With the inclusion of third-party applications, however, character-based UNIX applications compiled on Windows, and even X-Windows-based software, can run on top of Windows NT.

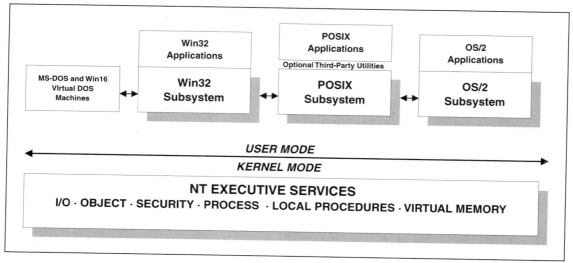

FIGURE 6.6.   Windows NT Subsystem Relationship

Microsoft has achieved the rather formidable goal of supporting multiple "personality" subsystems when running these applications. Each application runs within a single process and is managed by the Windows NT Executive. The term *protected mode* in this case means that each process is assigned its own memory register. Conflict between applications is minimized theoretically because of the discrete treatment of the individual process with its own memory allocation.

Win32 SUBSYSTEM

Win32 is the mother of all subsystems (Figure 6.7). It handles all standard Windows NT input and display output. Specifically, it controls the GUI. All Win32 applications are run directly inside this subsystem.

Win32 also takes on a sort of arm's-length relationship with the other subsystems by switching personalities when necessary. For example, when a DOS or POSIX application is invoked, Win32 does not get directly involved in the execution. Instead, Win32 detects the type of executable then invokes the appropriate subsystem.

DOS/Win16 SUBSYSTEMS

Unlike Window 3.x, which rests on top of the MS-DOS operating system, Windows NT supplies an emulator that creates a discrete virtual computing relationship. The VDM is a port of MS-DOS 5.x that makes x86-compatible calls.

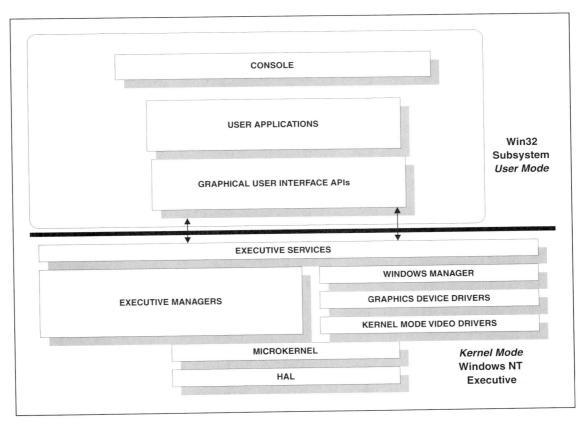

FIGURE 6.7.　Win32 Subsystem Structure

When running the VDM on an x86 box, applications can run in traditional DOS full-screen mode or within a window. Only the window mode is supported for DOS applications running on a non-x86 box like the Digital Alpha. Everything done in the VDM is emulation, including input and display output.

Windows 3.x applications utilize both the VDM and the Win32 system. The application processes technically run as a VDM process, but the display handling is off-loaded to the Win32 subsystem. Because API "stubs" are used to the old graphical drivers and dynamically linked libraries (DLLs), Win16 applications generally operate without impacting other operating system activities. It should be remembered that Windows NT is a preemptively multitasking operating system that supports numerous, single processes simultaneously. In the case of Win16 applications, Windows on Windows (WOW) is used to describe the interplay with the VDM and Win32 subsystems.

OS/2 SUBSYSTEM

The OS/2 subsystem is actually very limited in function and support. It only supports the older character-based version of OS/2 version 1.x. Users wanting to load Presentation Manager of IBM OS/2 Warp applications are out of luck. Further, the OS/2 subsystem only supports x86 computers. Although not a common requirement, RISC computer owners have to go elsewhere to run their character-based OS/2 1.x applications.

POSIX SUBSYSTEM

Given the nature of this book, the POSIX subsystem is a great point of interest. The Portable Operating System Interface Computing Environment is embraced by a number of operating systems such as VMS and CTOS. However, it is in the interface of UNIX and Windows NT that POSIX holds the greatest potential.

Only the NTFS file system supports the POSIX subsystem. By subsystem we refer solely to the implementation of a small portion of the total POSIX specification set. The IEEE 1003.1 standard for the C language API to applications and operating systems is solely supported in the standard Microsoft distribution. Fortunately, third-party vendors such as Softway Systems provide additional layers of POSIX-compatible code. With these third-party tools, it is possible to migrate existing UNIX applications to Windows NT with comparative ease. As a test we attempted to port both a character-based and an X-Windows application to Windows NT using the Softway Systems tool kit for the POSIX subsystem. The character-based application moved across with little effort. The X-Windows software took a bit more effort, but porting was also achieved. However, as expected, the performance of the X-Windows application was slower than what would be expected in a native UNIX environment.

NOTE   As of the writing of this book, a Microsoft product manager reports that OpenNT by Softway Systems, Inc., is considered the POSIX solution set for Windows NT by the Microsoft organization. Softway Systems, Inc., can be contacted through their web site at `www.softway.com`. We examine the OpenNT product suite later in the book.

WINDOWS NT TRIANGLE SIDE 1: THE STRUCTURE

Windows NT and UNIX exhibit many similarities in structure, but also deviate in several significant areas. In this discussion, we review Windows NT structural components, including the role of files, directories, and the two supported files systems. This exploration includes the issues of permissions, file tracking, and the relative merits of the NTFS and FAT file systems. We interweave UNIX compatibility items when appropriate.

Files and Objects

Windows NT 4.0 is a quasi-object-oriented operating system. (The next version, Windows NT Server 5.0 [code named *Cairo*] is billed as being a truly object-oriented operating system.) In a strictly defined object-oriented environment, client objects pass instructions to server objects. The relationship between server and client is dynamic, with the ability of the respective objects to reverse relationships. A computer object consists of attributes and the code instructions or data that controls the behavior of the object. When put in the perspective of the Windows NT operating system, everything is treated as an object. The Windows NT Object Manager regulates

- File objects
- Directory objects
- Symbolic link or alias objects
- Semaphore or event objects
- Process and thread objects
- Port objects

NOTE   Windows NT 4.0 introduced DCOM as a network-based expansion of the Common Object Model (COM) used in earlier versions. DCOM defines how reusable objects behave with one another and is related to Microsoft's OLE automation scheme. The UNIX community currently promotes a rival technology known as CORBA, the Common Object Request Broker Agent. A consortium of primarily UNIX vendors known as the Object Management Group (OMG) is attempting to build a bridge between CORBA and DCOM. As of the writing of this book, several alternate technologies are being considered by the OMG for development. Hewlett-Packard is promoting a solution that is closely aligned to Microsoft's DCOM called Distributed Environment's Remote Procedure Call. A rival group is seeking endorsement from the Internet Inter-ORB Protocol. If the UNIX community is true to form, several probably incompatible solutions will emerge. Regardless, the good news for administrators of mixed UNIX and Windows NT enterprises is that greater object interoperability is in their future. CORBA versus DCOM is explored in greater detail in Chapter 11.

For the purpose of this discussion, we center on file and directory objects within the context of the file system structure. In UNIX everything is regarded as a file. The Windows NT paradigm is very similar, except that it adds attributes, which are tracked in the kernel mode's Executive components. These attributes are actually embedded in the file. Part of the attribute information is data that identifies the file or directory as either *restricted* or *shared* to the system. In the latter case, a shared name is created to permit access to individual users or groups of users.

How File Objects Are Managed and Tracked

Windows NT Server 4.0 does not track objects in the same manner as the UNIX *inode* relationship discussed in Chapter 3. However, although the same mechanism is not used, Windows NT does track objects with equal integrity. The method by which file objects are tracked is different depending on the Windows NT file system employed. Windows NT Server 4.0 supports the native NTFS and the older FAT file systems. (The HPFS used with OS/2 and supported in previous Windows NT releases is no longer supported in version 4.0.) In a later discussion, we describe in great detail the relative strengths and weaknesses of these file systems. For this discussion, a brief description of how files are tracked in FAT and NTFS is appropriate.

FILES IN THE FAT FILE SYSTEM

The FAT file system must be regarded as a legacy file system. It was originally developed for the MS-DOS operating system and was utilized by all previous versions of Windows including Windows 95. FAT includes the following basic information about a file:

- Name of the file or directory (folder) with a structured, maximal eight-character name and three-character mandatory extension known as the *8.3 format*
- Pointer to the physical location of the first byte of data associated with the file
- Size of the file in bytes
- Designation of its attributes as hidden, read-only, archive, or system based

Within the context of how files are stored on a disk or partition, the FAT hierarchy is very simple (Figure 6.8). The first sector contains the Bios block followed by the FAT and a duplicate image. The root directory is the first set of information visible to a user. Individual files are then stored in the root directory or its subdirectories.

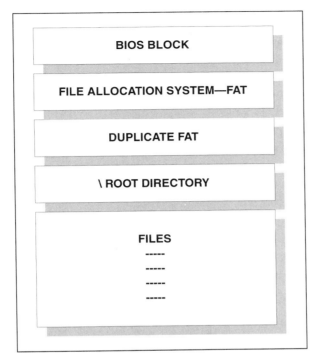

FIGURE 6.8.   Disk Structure for FAT File System

FILE OBJECTS IN THE NTFS FILE SYSTEM

NTFS boasts a relational database structure using B-tree structures to organize and streamline file object management. Microsoft publishes precious little information about the internal structure of this database, known as the *master file table* (MFT). The MFT is maintained in a mirrored format for redundancy. Pointers from the boot sector describe the location of the MFT and its mirror.

As a B-tree structure, file data is stored in what can be conceptualized as the trunk and extended branches (Figure 6.9). You can think of the MFT as the trunk of the B-tree. Small files and directory data are stored in *residence* within the MFT. Large files and directories are stored in a *nonresident* relational database (B-tree) structure in what are called *extents* (branch extensions) or *runs* (runners). Nonresident data can cross multiple extents or runs.

File and directory objects are similar in structure and utilize the same form for defining information sometimes known as *metadata,* but they differ in back end structure. NTFS treats directory objects as a special form of file objects. Both files and directories contain *standard attributes,* a *filename,* and *security*

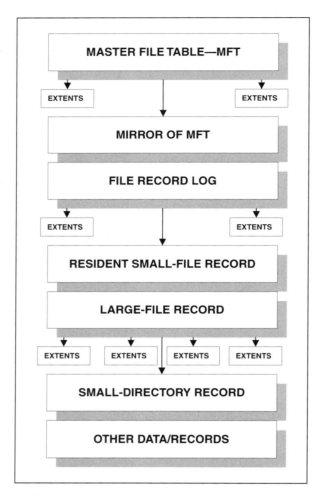

FIGURE 6.9.   Simplified View of MFT Structure

descriptors (Figure 6.10). The file also includes its raw data content, which is otherwise not managed by the operating system. The directory object also includes indexes of the relative location and size of the directory, plus a bitmap representation of the directory structure. When using the term *bitmap* we are not referring to a bitmap graphic as commonly known to any PC user. The bitmap in question is utilized by the database as a kind of road map depiction of the structure.

Filenames follow a specific convention depending on the file system utilized (FAT, with a eight-character maximum and a three-character extension [8.3] or NTFS, with a maximum of 255 characters.) Directories are separated in

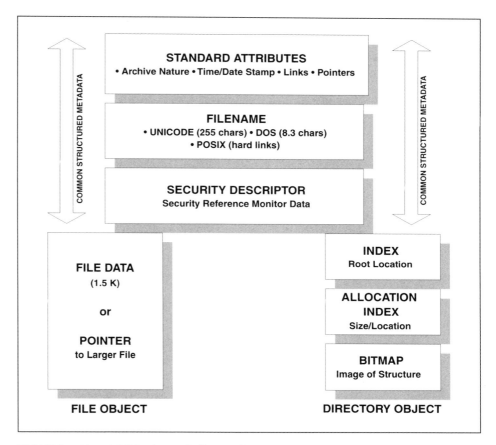

FIGURE 6.10.   NTFS View of Files and Directories

all cases with the backslash. (For the convenience of UNIX users, the familiar forward slash can be used in path definitions with the VDM.) Windows NT directories are similar to UNIX directories in that they are a special form of a file object that merely maintain information about the files they manage. When coding applications for Windows NT, current and parent directory paths are designated by either a single period (.) or double periods (..), just like UNIX.

The NTFS database structure helps to facilitate system recovery, a procedure that is not available with FAT. NTFS utilizes a transaction database methodology employing a logging process to initiate disk-writing instructions. Data enters cache memory where it is then directed to the Virtual Memory Manager (VMM) for background or lazy writing to disk. The VMM sends the data to the fault-tolerant driver (assuming the existence of a RAID structure). The disk drivers then attempt to write to the drive physically. If successful, the transaction in the database is released. If a failure occurs, the record of the logged process is retained in the transaction table until restoration. The use of small computer system interface (SCSI) controllers and RAID will impact the caching process.

HOW FILES ARE CREATED, MODIFIED, AND DELETED

Earlier we briefly discussed the role of the kernel Executive in providing services for the management of files and processes. Windows NT uses several components of the Executive to create, name, modify, and delete files. The Object Manager is the coordinating agent in this process. When a user or application issues an instruction to create or delete a file object, a sequence of events occurs within the kernel mode Executive.

1. *I/O Manager* – When a call to create a file is issued, the I/O Manager intercepts data and invokes an appropriate file system procedure (Figure 6.11). The I/O Manager utilizes a hierarchical set of drivers including caching of the data, file system instructions, and device (disk) activation to alert the Object Manager to the need to take action.

2. *Security Reference Manager* – All calls going to the Object Manager are first intercepted by the SRM. The ACL is checked based on the user's SAT. The SRM can verify the SID of the users and their associated groups, and permits the file object's requested action to occur. Authorization is then passed to the Object Manager. If permissions cannot be verified, the

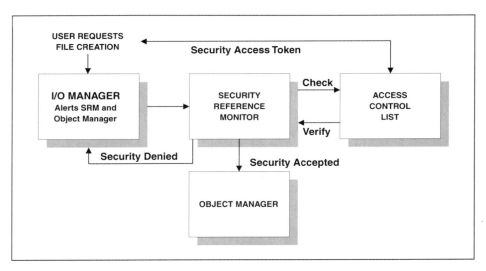

FIGURE 6.11.   Executive Manager Involvement in File Creation

Object Manager is taken out of the loop and the request is forwarded back to the I/O Manager with notification that the request was rejected.

3. *Object Manager* – After security authentication, the Object Manager then creates, names, deletes, or otherwise modifies the file object. Once this action is complete, the Object Manager forwards a success status code back to the I/O Manager.

FILE PERMISSIONS AND SECURITY

Microsoft's answer to file and directory security is well designed and flexible. Windows NT Server 4.0 utilizes a series of related ACLs to track file object permissions. User and group permissions are controlled by an ACL, with each line in the list constituting an ACE. All objects in turn have ACL. The ACL interacts with the System Access Command List and the Discretionary Access Control List. Each of the ACL's ACE has security functions that permit three types of discretionary access control, as shown in Table 6.1.

NTFS PERMISSION CATEGORIES: STANDARD VERSUS SPECIAL

When it comes to securing files, NTFS is far superior to the FAT file system. Restricting local access to files and directories cannot be established on a FAT partition. The only type of permission setting available on FAT is for shared directories with shared file names. (Shared files and directories are noted graphically by the appearance of a hand under the target icon when listed under Explorer or My Computer.) On the other hand, NTFS permits sophisticated granting of permissions on local and shared volumes (Figure 6.12).

Microsoft's NTFS significantly extends the basic read, write, and execute permission model found in UNIX. Permissions are broken into two overlapping categories—special and standard.

TABLE 6.1.   Types of Access Control Elements

Type	Description
Access allowed	Identifies users and groups that have explicit permission to utilize the object
Access denied	Identifies the permission denied expressly to a user or group based on the SID
System audit	Using the SIDs of users and groups, permits the logging of and attempted access to files, and logs audit messages

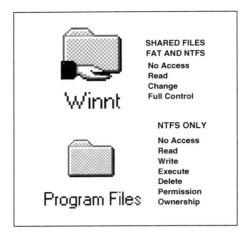

FIGURE 6.12.   File System Permission Differences

Special Permissions

There are six types of special permissions that can be combined for different results: read, write, execute, delete, permission change, and ownership change (Table 6.2).

Files and directories respond differently, depending on the special permissions that are set. Table 6.3 details the permissions that must be set for selected activities.

TABLE 6.2.   Special or Individual Permissions

Abbreviation	Type	Description
R	Read	Provides the designated user or group the ability to read the file
W	Write	Provides the designated user or group the ability to write or edit the file
X	Execute	Provides the designated user or group the ability to execute a program
D	Delete	Provides the designated user or group the ability to delete the file
P	Permission	Provides the designated user or group the ability to change permissions
O	Own	Provides the designated user or group the ability to change ownership

TABLE 6.3.   Special Permission Settings for Files and Directories

Activity permissions	File	Directory
View data	R	R
View attributes	R X	R X
Change attributes	W	W
Display permissions/filenames in directory	RWX	R
Modify data/modify directory contents	RW	W
Execute file	X	X
Change permissions	P	P
Change ownership	O	O
Delete file/directory	D	D

Standard Permissions

Standard permissions are simply operating system-defined combinations of special permissions. Windows NT Server 4.0 developers believed that a small combination of permissions cover most normal activities involving files. There are four basic types of standard permissions:

1. *No access ()* – The file is restricted from any user access. Even if the user is a member of a group with access, the "no access setting" will block access for that user to the target file object.
2. *Full control (RWXDPO)* – The opposite of no access, full control provides users full authority to fold, staple, and otherwise mutilate a file.
3. *Change or modify (RWXD)* – This permission allows users all types of access with the exception of changing permissions and ownership.
4. *Read (RX)* – This permission provides viewing of a normal file and the execution of an application.

Relationship of Directory to File Permissions

When describing the standard permissions of a file, it is important to note that it also inherits the permission of its parent directory. The first entry that is addressed is the standard permission of the directory followed by the permissions of the file itself. Standard permissions defined for directory and file relationships are

- *No access ()()* – Users cannot gain any access to the directory or it contents.
- *Full access (RWXDPO)(RWXDPO)* – The full scope of access is provided to the directory and the target file.

- *Modify or change (RWXD)(RWXD)* – A full set of permissions is granted to the directory and the target file except for changing permissions or ownership.
- *Add file (WX)()* – A new file can be added to the target directory. There are no file permissions.
- *Read (RX)(RX)* – Users can view a file or execute an application within the target directory.
- *List contents (RX)()* – A directory listing of its contents is permitted. There are no file permissions.

Managing Folder and File Permissions

As previously mentioned, there is a difference between shared permissions and those additionally permitted by NTFS. Shared permissions can be managed by either the FAT or NTFS file systems. Only NTFS has the expanded facility to micromanage local files and directories as well as those existing in other NTFS domain systems. Therefore, we briefly examine how to manage permissions in both an NTFS and shared environment, respectively. When establishing and changing permissions, you should determine the following issues.

- Which users and groups will have access?
- What level of access do you want to grant?
- Will the information be shared across the network?

The user must have an appropriate listing in the ACL for the individual user or member groups that corresponds to the privileges assigned to the file or directory (Table 6.4). When accessing a resource on a remote system over the network, the user must first have read share permission to see the folder (Figure 6.13). NTFS permissions are secondary to shared permissions when on remote systems. A user may have NTFS permission on the remote site; however, if the share permissions are not also granted, then no remote access is permitted. Shared permissions will have no effect on local disk space and only NTFS permissions will restrict local user access.

TABLE 6.4.   Shared File/Directory Object Access

Windows NT version	Number of users that can concurrently gain access
Workstation	10
Server	Unlimited

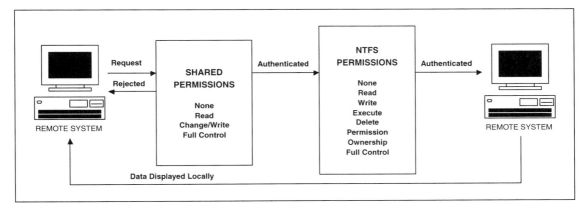

FIGURE 6.13.   Permissions Flow for Remote Access with NTFS

SETTING NTFS PERMISSIONS

From the vantage of a user or administrator, setting permissions is far less cryptic than what is experienced in the command line UNIX world. A set of graphical screens ensures an accurate and straightforward method of setting permissions. We recommend starting the process of setting permissions by first launching the Windows NT Explorer and selecting **Properties** from the **Files** menu (Figure 6.14).

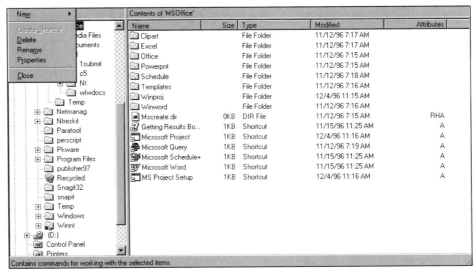

FIGURE 6.14.   Explorer Screen for Selecting File/Directory Properties

The Properties window provides three levels of information separated by tabs labeled **General, Sharing,** and **Security.** (*Remember,* if you are using the FAT file system, then you will not see the **Security** option. This is only applicable to NTFS.) Select the **Security** tab to display the **Permissions, Auditing,** and **Ownership** buttons for a file or folder (Figure 6.15).

The **Permissions** button displays a window that shows groups and users along with their respective permissions for the file or folder (Figure 6.16).

Within the **Type of Access** list, the **Special File Access** selection displays for files whereas the **Special Directory Access** selection displays for directories. Choose these options to create a special permission configuration. An example of the Special File Access window is shown in Figure 6.17, from which you select the permissions for each user or group.

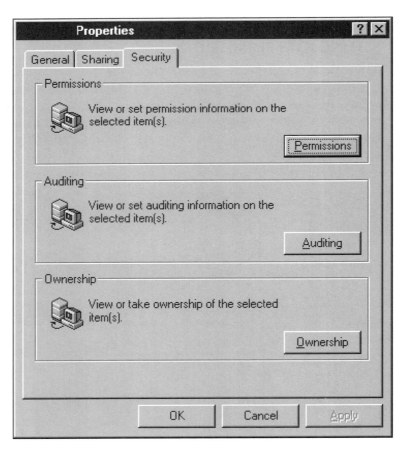

FIGURE 6.15.   NTFS File Permission Property Screen

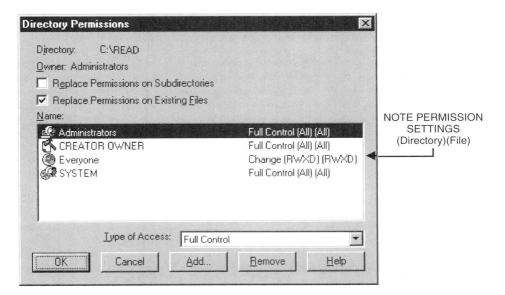

NOTE PERMISSION
SETTINGS
(Directory)(File)

FIGURE 6.16.   Users/Groups and Their Permissions

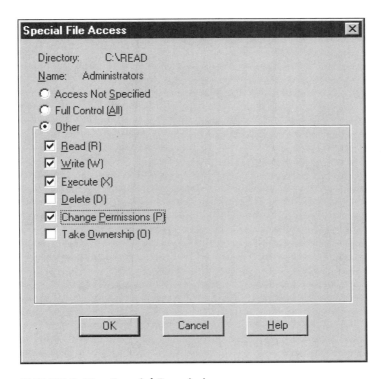

FIGURE 6.17.   Special Permissions

SHARE PERMISSIONS

Share permissions can be set with either the FAT or NTFS file system. The procedure used to set share permissions is very similar to those covered previously for local NTFS. Launch Windows NT Explorer and highlight the file or directory to be shared. Then from the menu bar select **File ➤ Properties**. As noted before, the FAT file system provides two tabs: **General** and **Sharing** (Figure 6.18). NTFS shows **General, Sharing,** and **Security** tabs. Select the **Sharing** tab.

When the **Shared As** radio button is selected, all files and folders within the selected folder will be shared. Remote users then have access to these folders using the network, providing they have an account on the system. The shared remote system must also be in a trusted domain or in the same domain as the sharing computer.

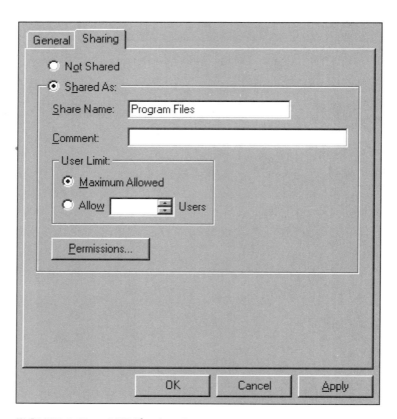

FIGURE 6.18.   FAT Sharing Property Screen

Selecting the **Permissions** button opens the share permissions (Figure 6.19). You may assign each group or user one of four permission levels.

Unlike the NTFS file/directory permission options, the shared options are only limited to the following:

- *No access* – Does not allow users access to the shared folder
- *Read* – Allows users to open files and see subfolder names
- *Change* – Allows all privileges offered by read permissions and allows users to change file contents, delete files and subfolders, and create files and subfolders
- *Full control* – Allows all privileges offered by change permissions and adds the ability to take ownership and to change NTFS permissions

The My Computer tool or Windows NT Explorer displays shared folders with a hand underneath the folder icon. It is also useful to show all folders shared out to the network regardless of their permissions. This can be accomplished by selecting **Start → Settings → Control Panel → Server** (Figure 6.20). Then select the **Shares** button to display all shared resources on the system, including shared files and directories (Figure 6.21).

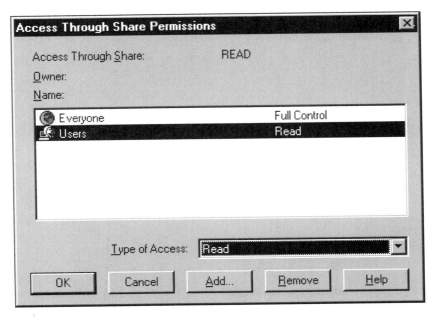

FIGURE 6.19.   Setting Share Permissions for Highlighted Group

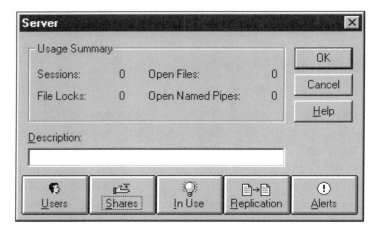

FIGURE 6.20.   Server Status Screen

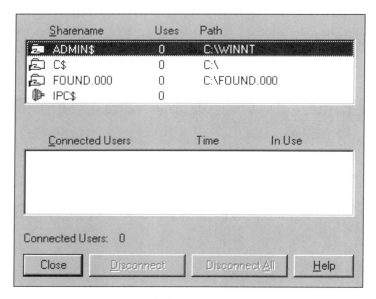

FIGURE 6.21.   Listing of Shared Resources on System

SETTING USER RIGHTS POLICY

Another action that needs to be taken when establishing network or shared access is to establish the user rights policy. User rights define those tasks that a user can perform on the network. This is accomplished by selecting **Policy** from the **User Manager for Domains** (Start ➤ Programs ➤ Administrative

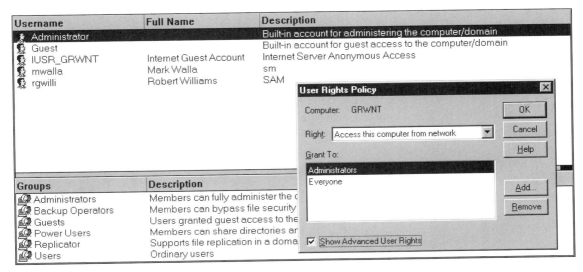

FIGURE 6.22.   User Rights Policy Screen

Tools → User Manager for Domains → Policies → User Rights). From the **Right** list box, select the **Access this computer from network** option to display groups and users that may access your system from the network (Figure 6.22). To share a folder, the user or group to which the user belongs must be included in this access list, in addition to having share rights. It makes sense that you must have access to the computer first in order to access a shared file.

File System Basics

As with UNIX, Windows NT also supports multiple files systems. Each file system has its own parentage and unique characteristics. In terms of base-level security issues, we have already established the clear advantage of utilizing the native NTFS file system. However, there are circumstances, such as a need to switch between older Windows versions and Windows NT, when retaining the FAT file system is necessary. An examination of the relative merits of each is appropriate.

FILE ALLOCATION TABLE—FAT FILE SYSTEM

FAT is a simple file system that dates back to the days in which the 5¼-inch floppy drive was the default medium and a 10-MB hard drive was an expensive luxury. In writing this section, we are using one of our test machines that is running Windows NT using the FAT file system. Due to the fact that this older computer has a number of DOS and ancient Windows applications, we decided to retain the original FAT file system and overlay Windows NT. The installation process designed by Microsoft was flawless; preserving both the old Window 3.1/MS-DOS 5.1 environment while providing Windows NT advanced functionality. When booting the system, we are provided the option of selecting among the installed operating systems (in this case, Windows 3.1, Windows 95, and Windows NT Server 4.0). One very nice feature Microsoft has included is the ability to convert the file system from FAT to NTFS (but not vice versa) when it is appropriate. This is accomplished by invoking the *convert* command from the VDM with the following syntax

```
convert [drive:] /fs:ntfs [/nametable:filename]
```

where *filename* is the name of the file created during the conversion process that contains a name translation table for unusual filenames.

The following list summarizes the major characteristics of the FAT file system:

- Support for dual booting of older Microsoft operating systems
- Filenames limited to eight characters and a three-character extension with only a single period separating the name with the extension
- Maximal length of a directory path is sixty-four characters
- Maximal file system partition size is 2^{32} bytes
- Only security permitted is restricted to remote access using the share permissions

NTFS FILE SYSTEM

NTFS was first introduced with Windows NT 3.1 and was an outgrowth of the original OS/2 HPFS. With the introduction of Windows NT Server 4.0, the NTFS file system has taken a giant leap forward to rivaling UNIX in terms of stability and flexibility. NTFS boasts of numerous advantages over the FAT file system, including

- Superior *security* that extends to files, processes, and user access protection
- *Fault tolerance* using RAID 1–5 to create duplicate copies of all files on servers (e.g., if a bad partition is detected, Windows NT can create a new sector with the stored duplicate copy of the files)
- *Unicode* support of 16-bit (64K characters) filenames for easy internationalization; FAT supports only 7- or 8-bit ASCII and ANSI

TABLE 6.5.   NTFS Files

File	Description
$	Root file name
$Bitmap	Bitmap representation used by MFT for tracking volume contents
$Boot	Boot file listing the bootable volumes
$Mft	Master File Table
$MftMirr	MFT mirror
$Volume	Volume name and version information

- *MFT redundancy* ensures recovery of system data in the case of corruption
- *32-bit virtual memory* support with 2 GB allocated to system requirements and 2 GB for applications
- *64-bit (2^{64}) volume* size for support of large, fixed disks (The 64-bit clusters for physical disks greatly enhance storage over the Windows 95 16-bit FAT system.)
- *Filename length* is 255 characters but also automatically generates the shorter DOS filenames for backward compatibility
- Unlimited maximal *path length*

The NTFS file system maintains a number of key files that should not be removed or unnecessarily modified. Table 6.5 summarizes several of the most important NTFS files.

Windows NT Tree File Structure

When looking at Windows NT from an organizational perspective, UNIX system administrators will immediately feel very comfortable. Files and directories are organized in the familiar directory tree format. The Windows NT Explorer displays this tree in a nice graphical format as shown in Figure 6.23.

When looking at the file/directory structure from a UNIX perspective, the layout looks identical (Figure 6.24). We begin at root with a series of first-layer standard directories or folders. The UNIX */home* directory is replaced by the *Profiles* folder. The */dev* directory is replaced with *Media*. The *system32* folder combines the elements of */bin, /sys, /etc,* and */usr*. With a small amount of time invested in roaming through the directory tree, an old UNIX administrator should feel comfortable with the organization of Windows NT Server 4.0.

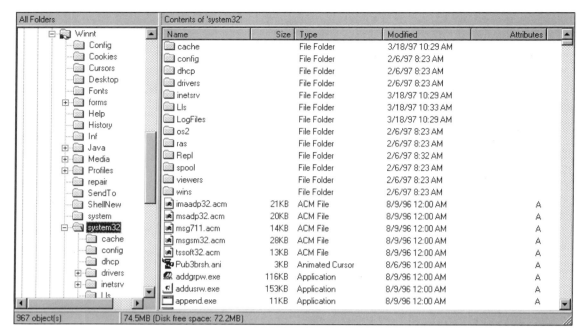

FIGURE 6.23.   Explorer View of Partial Tree Structure

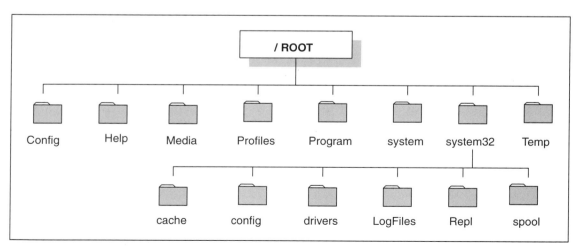

FIGURE 6.24.   Sample File Structure from a UNIX Perspective

WINDOWS NT TRIANGLE SIDE 2: PROCESSES

Windows NT Server 4.0 processes are represented by a surprisingly simple yet informative set of graphical screens. By utilizing the Task Manager (with three equally helpful screens), the Event Viewer, and the Services Manager, a system administrator can review and govern activities of the server. The Task Manager can also be effectively employed to address many performance issues rapidly.

Behind this graceful user interface resides a robust, process-oriented, multitasking operating system that differs significantly from UNIX. While both Windows NT and UNIX use many similar terms (such as interprocess communication [IPC], remote procedure calls [RPC], threads, pipes, processes, and semaphores), the actual implementation of these technologies often differs and deserves consideration. Application developers, for example, will find the porting of existing UNIX code dependent on signaling a nontrivial task. This section explores the following process-related topics:

- Fundamental understanding of Windows NT processes, threads, pipes, and handles
- Use of the Task Manager and Services Manager to identify, start, and kill processes
- Use of the Event Viewer to diagnose process success and failure
- Virtual memory model and swapping
- Boot processes, run levels, and administrators (superuser)
- How to schedule processes

Understanding Windows NT Processes, Threads, and Handles

At first glance, the concept of processes within Windows NT is very similar to that of UNIX. In both cases, processes involve the use of threads to invoke an action with a reaction, the use of pipes to connect threads, and the use of semaphores to synchronize activities. Further, Windows NT services are roughly equal to UNIX daemons. However, there are many differences, including the Windows NT concept of handles and the absence of the exec/fork replication relationship of UNIX. The fundamental UNIX concept of the parent/child process is also not universally used in Windows NT.

A Windows NT process is treated as an object. The process object has a number of characteristics, including a virtual memory address, defined resources, and a security profile. Each process has one or more thread objects associated with its execution. As an object, the thread also has its own unique memory stack and system state. The thread is an agent that does the bidding of the process. The Object Manager controls both the process and thread objects.

When a new process is created, the CreateProcess() and CreateThread() calls are made. As additional threads are required to support a given process, other CreateThread() calls are invoked. The thread should be thought of as a unit of execution. Between both ends of the thread is a pipe. Both ends of the pipe must be open; if either end is broken, then the process data is lost. Unlike UNIX, Windows NT does not permit any latency.

Threads are assigned *handles*. A handle is an index with its own table specific to a process. (Handles are also provided to events, semaphores, muxlexes, pipes, processes, and communications.) The handle is a 32-bit entity with its own characteristics, including ACLs to examine process security. Process and thread objects are tracked by their handles and a unique identification number (Figure 6.25).

Windows NT also utilizes *named pipes* to transmit information. Windows NT named pipes are viewed similarly to file objects and operate within the same security framework. The named pipe retains information in memory and dispenses the data as requested by a process. It acts like a regular data file, except

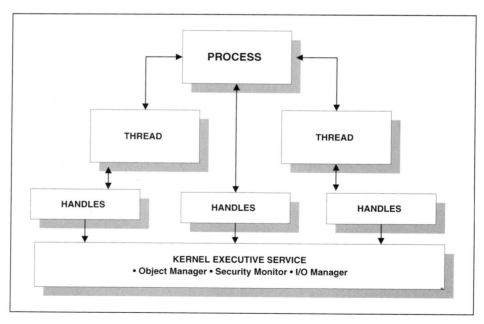

FIGURE 6.25.   Process Hierarchy

that the information is in resident memory as opposed to being physically archived on disk.

Windows NT is a multithread operating system. One of the strengths of Windows NT is its ability to manage and synchronize multiple threads. While UNIX can also be considered a multithread operating system, the implementation between variants is often different. As long-term UNIX developers, we avoided the use of threads because of the inconsistencies. The Windows NT published thread API makes the task much easier.

The concept of a handle is not used in UNIX but is critical to the Windows NT operating system. Therefore, when migrating UNIX code to Windows NT, consideration of the use of handles to create events and duplicate processes will often be required unless the application resides entirely in the POSIX subsystem. Among the calls that we found to be important to understand when porting legacy UNIX applications to the Windows NT API include OpenProcess(), WriteProcessMemory(), ExitProcess(), CreateProcess(), CreateFileMapping(), CreateThread(), CreateFile(), Create/OpenEvent(), DuplicateHandle(), WaitForObject(), ImpersonateNamedPipeClient(), and Select().

Windows NT does provide a robust process and thread priority facility. The programming API permits the setting of application process priorities or states that include idle, normal, high, and real time. Within each of these states two levels of subpriorities can also be established. However, when using this facility it is important for a programmer to consider the impact on the entire system. If a +2 high priority is set for a major task, then it can easily swamp lesser tasks.

UNIX processes assume a parent/child relationship in which the child inherits the characteristics of the parent during the initial cloning period. Windows NT processes do not go through a similar cloning process, but retain only very explicit characteristics. The UNIX fork() and exec() calls are also not emulated in Windows NT. Since Windows NT does not inherit the parent's base characteristics, the associated problems in the creation of zombie processes are eliminated. Additionally, as Windows NT was not designed as a multiuser operating system supporting dumb terminals, UNIX terminal process groups and semantics are not used.

INTERPROCESS COMMUNICATION

The concept of IPC and RPC is common to both Windows NT and UNIX. (At the risk of being overly simplistic, RPC can be regarded as the distributed network version of IPC.) Unfortunately, neither operating system conforms completely to industry-standard IPC or RPC calls. Therefore, what might be initially viewed as a major area of common ground can instead be a potential mine field for application developers and system administrators. It is important to understand where interoperability is possible and where differences exist.

RPC was originally designed by Sun Microsystems and expanded by the Open Software Foundation as a product known today as the Distributed Computing Environment or DCE (not to be confused with OSF's CDE). Microsoft claims that its implementation of RPC is compliant with DCE. The actual level of this interoperability is discussed in later networking chapters.

On the other hand, there are differences in IPC implementation. Windows NT employs a point-to-point relationship between processes and threads. At any given time there is a producer and a consumer (similar to BDS socket library calls). The objective is to achieve a very scalable operating system that permits easy load balancing of discrete, measured threads. Windows NT also employs a first-in-first-out (FIFO) message model. The unimodal approach moves messages in and out in straight, sequential order. This leaves no room for message priorities, filtering, or out-of-band messaging. UNIX uses neither FIFO nor point-to-point-based protocols for IPC and RPC calls.

WINDOWS NT SERVICES

A Windows NT service is a special class of process that is allocated fixed characteristics and must run with user credentials. The Windows NT service is the same as the UNIX daemon in that it performs tasks as defined in either the foreground or the background. Services can be managed either locally or remotely.

The Windows NT Service Manager (not to be confused with the Server Manager) provides a list of all defined services, their current status, and their status at start-up (Figure 6.26). Services can be started, stopped, paused, continued, or defined for system start-up with a simple mouse click.

The Task Manager: More Than a View from 30,000 Feet

Our first impression when looking at the Windows NT Task Manager is "Gee, this is a clever graphical view of the system." On further examination, we discovered that the Task Manager is information rich despite its straightforward interface.

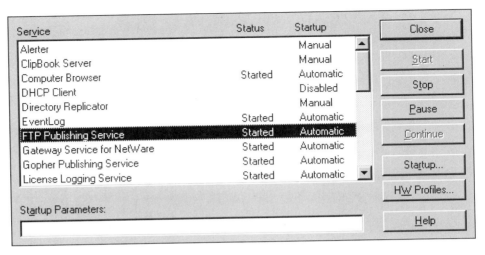

FIGURE 6.26.   Windows NT Service Manager

The Windows NT Server 4.0 Task Manager performs the equivalent UNIX functions of *ps, sar, top,* and many other utilities. Although not as robust as high-end UNIX tools such Hewlett-Packard's *GlancePlus,* the Windows NT Task Manager encompasses information that would involve the use of a number of UNIX command line procedures to achieve.

The Task Manager is readily available to an administrator at any point during a logon session. The two most common methods of executing the Task Manager are (1) click the right mouse button on the task bar and select **Task Manager,** and (2) press <Ctrl-Alt-Del> and select **Task Manager** from the Windows NT Security window.

The Task Manager provides three window tabs that provide very different views of the Windows NT process schema.

1. *Applications* – This permits the view and control of all applications that could be responsible for one or more processes.
2. *Processes* – This provides in-depth information about individual processes, including resource utilization.
3. *Performance* – This provides a graphical and numeric view of the system based on the current application and process load.

APPLICATIONS WINDOW

A simple dissection of the Applications window shows the application name in the first column followed by the current status (Figure 6.27). The bottom set of buttons permits the administrator to end the task, switch to another task, or invoke a new task. At the bottom of the screen a system summary status is presented, including the number of open processes, CPU usage, and memory utilization.

Processes are ordinarily started by invoking an application from an icon or command line instruction. Processes can also be initiated, as discussed in a later section, by using scheduling services (daemons) such as *at,* which is similar to UNIX's *at* and *cron.* The Task Manager can also be used to start a new task by selecting **New Task** at the bottom of the screen. When selected, a new dialog box appears, such as the one shown in Figure 6.28.

Ordinarily, processes are terminated by the graceful exit of the application through its own kill signals. However, from time to time more radical solutions are required. Processes can be killed easily using the Task Manager. When in the Applications window, simply highlight the offending process and select the **End Task** option on the bottom of the screen. When in the Processes window, select the **End Process** option on the bottom of the screen. In both cases, a

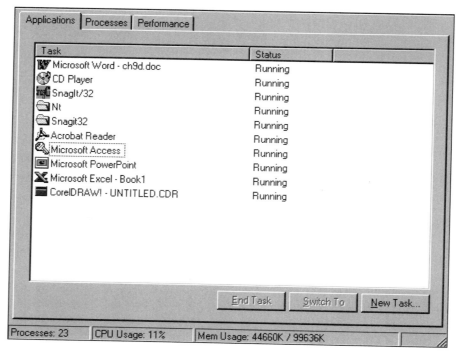

FIGURE 6.27.   Task Manager Applications List

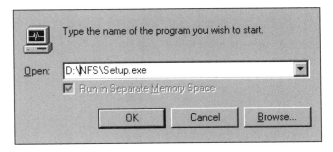

FIGURE 6.28.   New Task Dialog Box

confirming message will appear before final termination of the process occurs. At this point, all handles, threads, and pipes are destroyed. Any data being transmitted could be lost when ending a process in this manner.

PROCESSES WINDOW

The Processes window displays an array of information (Figure 6.29) that provides system administrators a very good snapshot of system activity. The default

Image Name	PID	CPU	CPU Time	Mem Usage
System Idle Process	0	98	2:18:01	16 K
System	2	01	0:00:26	120 K
smss.exe	21	00	0:00:00	120 K
csrss.exe	24	00	0:00:01	480 K
winlogon.exe	35	00	0:00:02	312 K
services.exe	41	00	0:00:04	1348 K
lsass.exe	44	00	0:00:00	928 K
Winword.exe	47	01	0:49:40	9272 K
spoolss.exe	67	00	0:00:00	120 K
ntvdm.exe	74	00	0:00:06	2836 K
wowexec.exe		00	0:00:00	
llssrv.exe	78	00	0:00:00	704 K
RpcSs.exe	83	00	0:00:01	636 K
snagit32.exe	99	00	0:00:01	344 K
nddeagnt.exe	105	00	0:00:00	88 K
inetinfo.exe	107	00	0:00:01	684 K
taskmgr.exe	149	01	0:00:00	1372 K
Explorer.exe	152	01	0:00:23	2712 K
OSA.EXE	156	00	0:00:00	116 K

Applications | Processes | Performance

End Process

Processes: 20 | CPU Usage: 3% | Mem Usage: 35032K / 99636K

FIGURE 6.29.   Task Manager Process List

screen provides five process checkpoints: image name, PID, CPU utilization, CPU time, and memory usage (Table 6.6).

A total of fourteen items may be selected for analysis by changing **Select Columns** under the **View** menu bar command. When the dialog box such as the one shown in Figure 6.30 appears, use the mouse to click on the additional reporting parameters.

TABLE 6.6.   Default Process Column Options

Attribute	Description
Image Name	Identification of processes (not an optional listing)
PID	Process identification number
CPU	CPU utilization level of each process
CPU Time	CPU time used by the process
Mem Usage	Current real or virtual memory utilization of the process

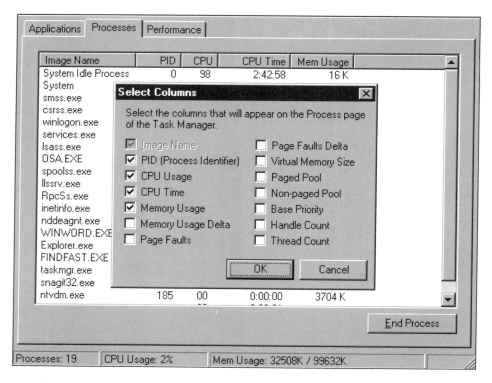

FIGURE 6.30.   Select Columns Dialog Box

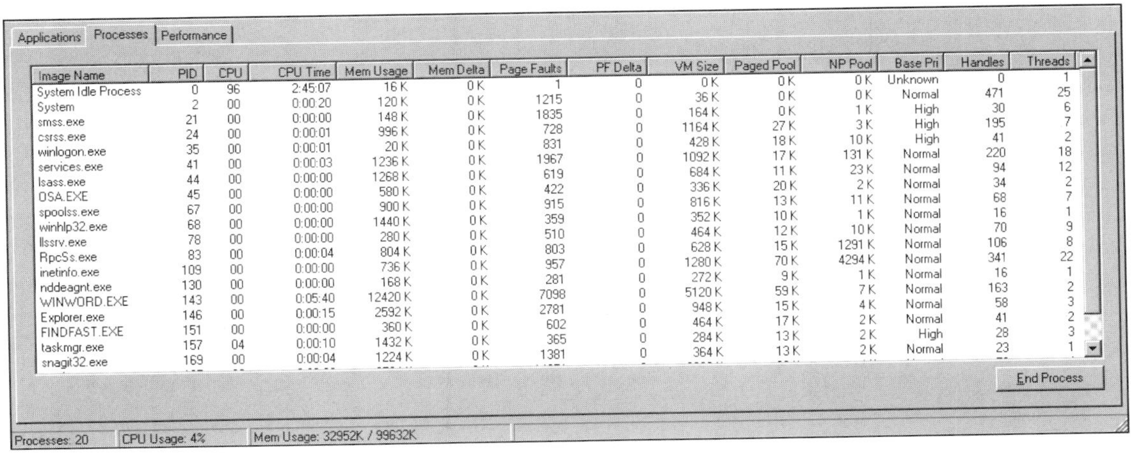

Image Name	PID	CPU	CPU Time	Mem Usage	Mem Delta	Page Faults	PF Delta	VM Size	Paged Pool	NP Pool	Base Pri	Handles	Threads
System Idle Process	0	96	2:45:07	16 K	0 K	1	0	0 K	0 K	0 K	Unknown	0	1
System	2	00	0:00:20	120 K	0 K	1215	0	36 K	0 K	0 K	Normal	471	25
smss.exe	21	00	0:00:00	148 K	0 K	1835	0	164 K	0 K	1 K	High	30	6
csrss.exe	24	00	0:00:01	996 K	0 K	728	0	1164 K	27 K	3 K	High	195	7
winlogon.exe	35	00	0:00:01	20 K	0 K	831	0	428 K	18 K	10 K	High	41	2
services.exe	41	00	0:00:03	1236 K	0 K	1967	0	1092 K	17 K	131 K	Normal	220	18
lsass.exe	44	00	0:00:00	1268 K	0 K	619	0	684 K	11 K	23 K	Normal	94	12
OSA.EXE	45	00	0:00:00	580 K	0 K	422	0	336 K	20 K	2 K	Normal	34	2
spoolss.exe	67	00	0:00:00	900 K	0 K	915	0	816 K	13 K	11 K	Normal	68	7
winhlp32.exe	68	00	0:00:00	1440 K	0 K	359	0	352 K	10 K	1 K	Normal	16	1
llssrv.exe	78	00	0:00:00	280 K	0 K	510	0	464 K	12 K	10 K	Normal	70	9
RpcSs.exe	83	00	0:00:04	804 K	0 K	803	0	628 K	15 K	1291 K	Normal	106	8
inetinfo.exe	109	00	0:00:00	736 K	0 K	957	0	1280 K	70 K	4294 K	Normal	341	22
nddeagnt.exe	130	00	0:00:00	168 K	0 K	281	0	272 K	9 K	1 K	Normal	16	1
WINWORD.EXE	143	00	0:05:40	12420 K	0 K	7098	0	5120 K	59 K	7 K	Normal	163	2
Explorer.exe	146	00	0:00:15	2592 K	0 K	2781	0	948 K	15 K	4 K	Normal	58	3
FINDFAST.EXE	151	00	0:00:00	360 K	0 K	602	0	464 K	17 K	2 K	High	28	3
taskmgr.exe	157	04	0:00:10	1432 K	0 K	365	0	284 K	13 K	2 K	Normal	23	1
snagit32.exe	169	00	0:00:00	1224 K	0 K	1381	0	364 K	13 K	2 K	Normal		

End Process

Processes: 20   CPU Usage: 4%   Mem Usage: 32952K / 99632K

FIGURE 6.31.   Expanded View of Process Activity

When all of the options are selected, the system administrator then has a reasonably comprehensive view of active processes and their impact on the overall system, as shown in Figure 6.31.

PERFORMANCE WINDOW

The Windows NT Task Manager Performance window provides four graphical representations and four numeric boxes of data for the entire system (Figure 6.32).

- **CPU Usage** – Shows current CPU utilization (in this example, the CPU has reached a critical utilization state)
- **CPU Usage History** – A longer term view generally showing CPU usage over time (Unfortunately, in this window, there is no ability to change time intervals nor is there an ability to save or print this information, although accessing **Start ➤ Programs ➤ Administrative Tools ➤ Performance Monitor** increases your options somewhat.)
- **MEM Usage** – Shows current virtual or real memory utilization
- **Memory Usage History** – Shows fluctuation of real memory over time (Unfortunately, in this window, there is no ability to change time intervals nor is there an ability to save or print this information, although accessing **Start ➤ Programs ➤ Administrative Tools ➤ Performance Monitor** increases your options somewhat.)
- **Totals** – Shows the number of currently open handles, threads, and processes
- **Physical Memory** – Summary of the system virtual memory defined as a total, currently available, and file cache available in kilobytes

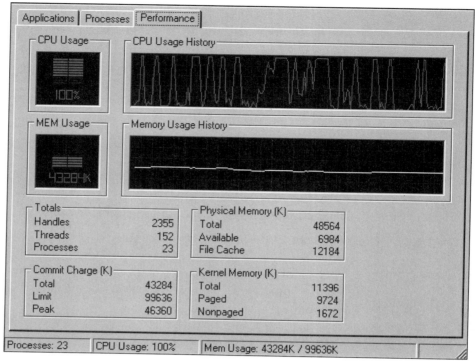

FIGURE 6.32.   Task Manager Performance Window

- **Commit Charge** – Memory allocated to programs and the system total; limit and peak memory might exceed the physical maximum, including swap memory
- **Kernel Memory** – The total memory allocated to kernel mode activities and broken down to paged and nonpaged events

Using the Event Viewer

The Event Viewer provides a nicely defined log of abnormal system events (Figure 6.33). Windows NT defines an event as any system occurrence that requires notifications. (Note that very critical events, such as application fault errors, will appear immediately on screen.) An example of the type of event that is recorded in the Event Viewer system log is a dysfunctional driver or load failure. The Source column identifies the application that initiated the message. The Category column defines the classification of the event as being related to secu-

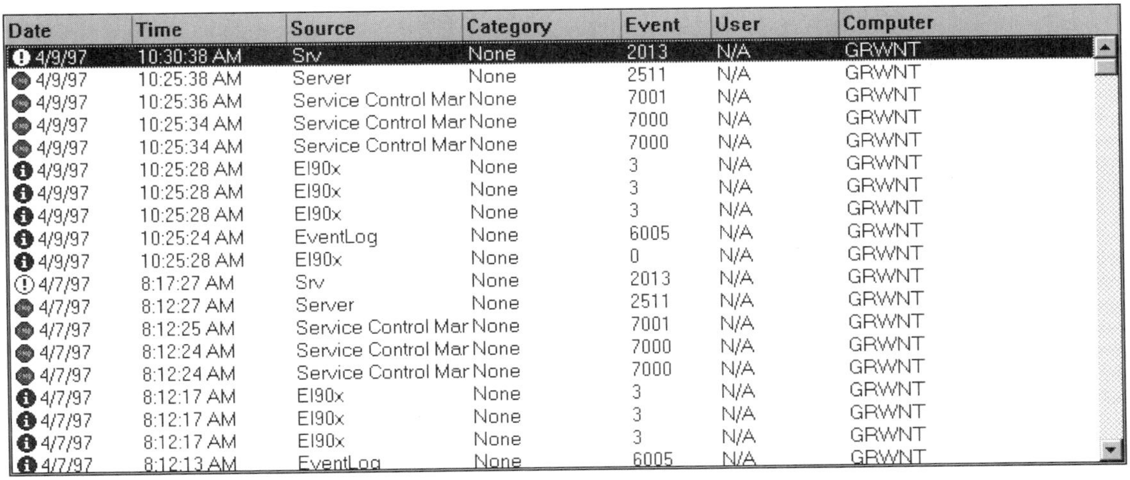

Date	Time	Source	Category	Event	User	Computer
❶ 4/9/97	10:30:38 AM	Srv	None	2013	N/A	GRWNT
● 4/9/97	10:25:38 AM	Server	None	2511	N/A	GRWNT
● 4/9/97	10:25:36 AM	Service Control Mar	None	7001	N/A	GRWNT
● 4/9/97	10:25:34 AM	Service Control Mar	None	7000	N/A	GRWNT
● 4/9/97	10:25:34 AM	Service Control Mar	None	7000	N/A	GRWNT
❶ 4/9/97	10:25:28 AM	EI90x	None	3	N/A	GRWNT
❶ 4/9/97	10:25:28 AM	EI90x	None	3	N/A	GRWNT
❶ 4/9/97	10:25:28 AM	EI90x	None	3	N/A	GRWNT
❶ 4/9/97	10:25:24 AM	EventLog	None	6005	N/A	GRWNT
❶ 4/9/97	10:25:28 AM	EI90x	None	0	N/A	GRWNT
① 4/7/97	8:17:27 AM	Srv	None	2013	N/A	GRWNT
● 4/7/97	8:12:27 AM	Server	None	2511	N/A	GRWNT
● 4/7/97	8:12:25 AM	Service Control Mar	None	7001	N/A	GRWNT
● 4/7/97	8:12:24 AM	Service Control Mar	None	7000	N/A	GRWNT
● 4/7/97	8:12:24 AM	Service Control Mar	None	7000	N/A	GRWNT
❶ 4/7/97	8:12:17 AM	EI90x	None	3	N/A	GRWNT
❶ 4/7/97	8:12:17 AM	EI90x	None	3	N/A	GRWNT
❶ 4/7/97	8:12:17 AM	EI90x	None	3	N/A	GRWNT
❶ 4/7/97	8:12:13 AM	EventLog	None	6005	N/A	GRWNT

FIGURE 6.33.   Event Viewer Screen

rity, object access, logon/logoff problems, detail tracking, system events, policy changes, account management, and miscellaneous (none) events. The level of importance of an event message is shown as an icon in the extreme left-hand column: error, informational, warning, success audit, and failure audit.

The Event Viewer has a very flexible set of options that permits long-term tracking of potential system, security, and application problems, including those listed in Table 6.7.

TABLE 6.7.   Description of Event Viewer Options

Option	Description
Logging	With a maximal log size of 512K, sets the rolling of events as needed, remove events after a defined number of days, or sets no overwriting of events (this requires manual removal of events)
Sorting	Sorts the events based on categories, sources, user, or machine
Archiving	Saves event records in native event format (*.EVT) or in a normal or comma-delimited ASCII text (*.TXT) format
Details	Provides additional information on the event (Figure 6.34)
Filtering	Filters for desired events or characteristics
Find	Locates events based on type, category, source, computer, or other criteria

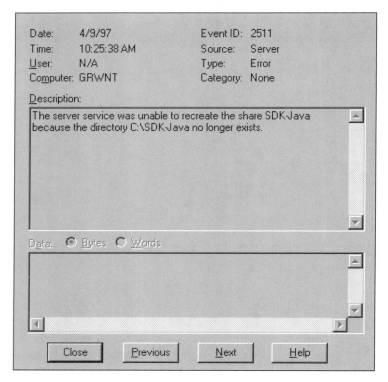

FIGURE 6.34.   Detailed Information on an Event

Virtual Memory Model and Swapping

Windows NT utilizes a flat 32-bit virtual memory scheme very similar to UNIX. However, unlike UNIX, Windows NT reserves half of the total capacity (2 GB) for system resources and the other half for applications. The VMM allocates each process to an address space. The virtual space is then mapped to physical memory in 4-KB pages. As memory is required, the system then swaps between virtual and physical memory. The concept of disk swapping is discussed in Chapter 3 and applies to both UNIX and Windows NT.

Windows NT memory management is limited to 2^{32} bytes, as are most versions of UNIX. However, some UNIX variants like Digital UNIX do support a 2^{64} architecture. Whereas 2^{32} sustains 4 GB of real memory, the 2^{64} allows 16 exabytes (or 18,446,744,073,709,551,616 bytes). In most computing environments, 4 GB is more than sufficient. However, until Windows NT ships a 64-bit version with release 5.0, the highest memory-intensive applications should continue to reside on UNIX.

The Boot Process

The Windows NT Server 4.0 booting sequence involves a series of system configuration checks, hardware activation, and application loading. The following is a brief list of the booting process:

- *Power on self-test* – This is a check of whether key hardware elements are present, such as sufficient memory, keyboard, video card, and so on

- *Start-up initialization* – The hard drive's first sector is examined for the Master Boot Record and Partition Table. If either is missing or corrupted, then the process terminates.

- *Boot loader* – When multiple operating systems are present on the system, the boot loader permits the selection of the desired environment. In x86-based systems, the system looks for NTLDR, located in the root directory (by reading *Boot.ini* and invoking *Ntdetect.com* and *Bootsect.dos*). On RISC systems, *Osload.exe* performs this function. A typical boot loader screen on an x86 system could include the following:

```
OPERATING SYSTEM Loader V4.0
Please select the operating system to start:
      Windows NT Server Version 4.0
      Windows NT Server Version 4.0 (VGA mode)
      Windows 95
Use ↑ and ↓ to move the highlight to your choice.
Press Enter to chose
Seconds until highlighted choice will be started
automatically is: 23
```

- *Hardware configuration review* – At this stage, information about the system and attached devices is gathered by *Ntdetect.com* (x86 systems) or *Osloader.exe* (RISC systems).

- *Kernel load and initialization* – As dots are drawn across the computer screen, Windows NT loads the kernel with *Ntosknrl.exe* and HAL's *Hal.dll*. The actual initialization of the kernel occurs when the blue screen appears and identifies the Windows NT version, build number, and your system configuration.

- *User logon* – The system is ready to use when the Begin Logon box appears with instructions *Press Ctrl + Alt + Delete to log on*. Windows NT does not consider the start-up procedure complete until the first user has logged on.

For x86 systems, the *Boot.ini* file includes vital information for successful execution of the operating system. The contents of this file are used during the boot load process to provide options on screen. The following is a sample *Boot.ini* file that supports both Windows NT Server 4.0 and Windows 95 options:

```
[boot loader]
timeout=30
default=multi(0)disk(0)rdisk(0)partition(1)\WINNT
[operating systems]
multi(0)disk(0)rdisk(0)partition(1)\WINNT="Windows NT
Server Version 4.00"
multi(0)disk(0)rdisk(0)partition(1)\WINNT="Windows NT
Server Version 4.00 [VGA mode]" /basevideo /sos
C:\="Microsoft Windows"
```

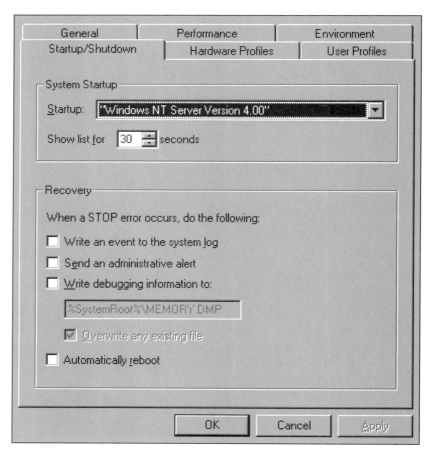

FIGURE 6.35.   System Option Screen to Change *Boot.ini*
                Timing and Default

The *Boot.ini* is divided into two sections: boot loader and operating systems. The [boot loader] defines the number of seconds before an automatic load of the default operating system (the path of which is defined in the next line). The [operating systems] lists the environments available for initiation. In this case, two modes of Windows NT (regular and vga) and Windows 95 are available.

The *Boot.ini* file is set as read only, system, and hidden to prevent unwanted editing. To change the *Boot.ini* timeout and default settings, use the **System** option available in the **Control Panel** (Figure 6.35).

How to Schedule Processes

Windows NT supports process-scheduling software that is identical in function to its counterpart in UNIX. The *at* program is invoked from the VDM command line for single-event scheduling. The Windows NT Server 4.0 Resource Kit provides what must be considered an expanded version of UNIX's *cron* called the *Command Scheduler* (Figure 6.36). This application alone justifies the purchase of the optional Resource Kit. Background on the use of *at* and *cron* is discussed in Chapter 3 and Appendix B. We recommend that you cross-reference those sections for additional conceptual information on process scheduling.

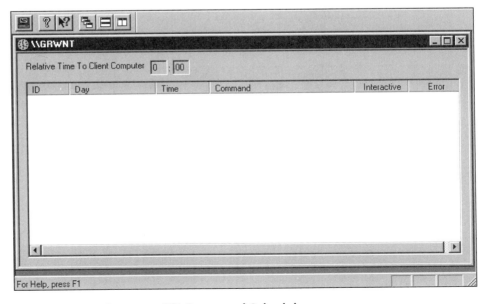

FIGURE 6.36.   Resource Kit Command Scheduler

WINDOWS NT TRIANGLE SIDE 3: USER INTERVENTION

Earlier in this chapter we discussed user and group permissions, ownership, and properties. In Chapter 7 we describe how to establish and manage user and group accounts. For the purpose of this discussion, we concentrate solely on defining standard users and groups.

What Is a Windows NT User?

Windows NT provides three basic classes of users—the *ordinary user,* the *guest* (system-specific or Internet) *user*, and the *administrative user* (with several subcategories). Each user can belong to one or more user groups. Windows NT ships with a number of predefined user groups as shown in the User Manager window in Figure 6.37. (The actual use of the User Manager is covered in Chapter 7). New user groups can be added and coupled together to form very flexible relationships.

NOTE   In describing user types, it is important to note that Windows NT classifies them as user groups. We are treating the following definitions in terms that are more akin to how users are described in UNIX.

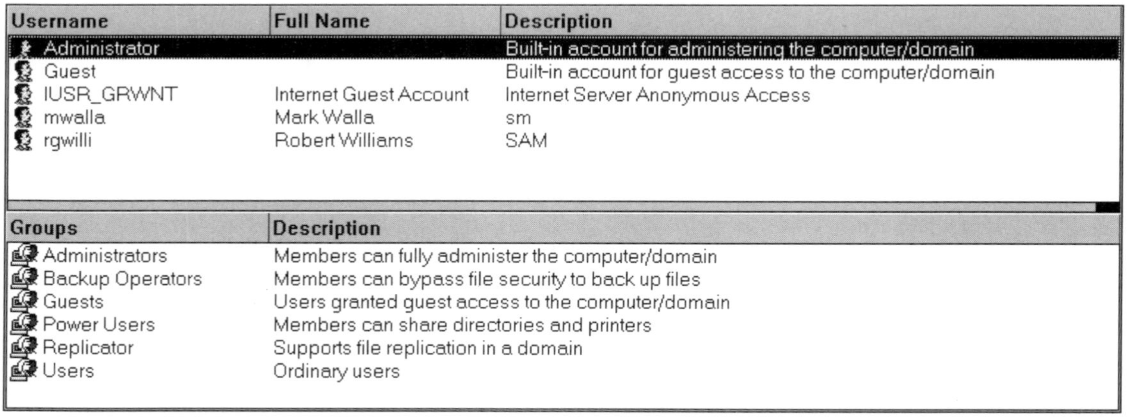

Username	Full Name	Description
Administrator		Built-in account for administering the computer/domain
Guest		Built-in account for guest access to the computer/domain
IUSR_GRWNT	Internet Guest Account	Internet Server Anonymous Access
mwalla	Mark Walla	sm
rgwilli	Robert Williams	SAM

Groups	Description
Administrators	Members can fully administer the computer/domain
Backup Operators	Members can bypass file security to back up files
Guests	Users granted guest access to the computer/domain
Power Users	Members can share directories and printers
Replicator	Supports file replication in a domain
Users	Ordinary users

FIGURE 6.37.   User Manager

ORDINARY OR POWER USERS

The ordinary user for Windows NT is very much the same as a regular UNIX user. A profile is created that defines the privileges and group memberships associated with the user. A default user folder is created for the storage of information in *\%systemroot%\Profiles\<user name>*. The folder is typically populated with subfolders that are owned by the user. An example of standard user folders is shown in Figure 6.38.

The power user is one with additional privileges associated with the ability to share folders, files, printers, and other resources. The power user was used for Windows NT 3.51 but is not a default type in Windows NT Server 4.0.

GUESTS

There are three standard types of accounts that permit limited access to specifically shared documents or folders. The ordinary Guest account is provided locally for individuals with temporary or limited need to access information. Local access is assumed. The Internet Guest is provided access to files located in the Anonymous account files. The Domain Guest is the same as the ordinary guest except that remote access is provided.

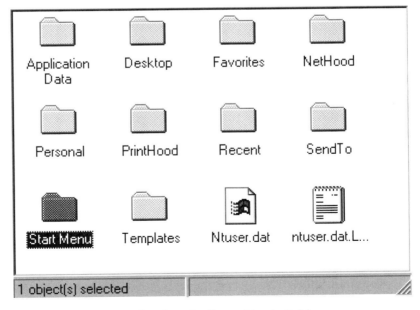

FIGURE 6.38.   Sample of an Ordinary User's Folder

TABLE 6.8.   Administrative User Types

Level	Description
Administrator	The most powerful individuals in a local domain; can control complete system configuration, user management, and so forth
Domain Administrator	Global administrative group for server domains
Account Operator	Local group that can manage user accounts and local resources
Backup Operator	Local users that can back up and restore the systems, and invoke shutdown
Printer Operator	Administers printer queues and functions
Server Operator	Local user group that controls primary and backup server controllers; cannot manage security
Replicator	Performs local folder replication

ADMINISTRATIVE USER (SUPERUSER)

Windows NT provides a number of administrative user levels. Clearly, individuals belonging to the Administrators group are equivalent to the UNIX superuser. Table 6.8 contains a list of user groups that have varying amounts of responsibility and authority.

Multiuser Versus Multiconsole Concept

Microsoft Windows NT Server can best be described as a multiconsole operating system as opposed to UNIX's multiuser status. By multiconsole, we refer to the ability of a single workstation to open application sessions from a remote server with the distinction that the actual processing and memory utilization is local. Compare that to a traditional multiuser application where the processing and resources are allocated on the remote server and displayed locally. While multiple users can obviously log on to a Windows NT system simultaneously, the operating system does not treat the actual sharing of resources and applications in the same way as UNIX.

Windows NT off-loads the work to the system and user that are requesting the applications. Rather than a user burdening a remote box with requests that sometimes have to be managed by the UNIX system administrator, the local system is used for CPU and memory crunching. This puts the burden of load balancing locally on the user. The multiconsole approach makes a lot of sense.

However, if a UNIX-style multiuser environment is still required for ported applications, then Windows NT will accept this added functionality through third-party software.

The important issue when discussing user accessibility with a multiconsole operating system is to understand where the actual processing is being completed. When sharing an application remotely, Windows NT executes the application from the disk of the remote server, but processing and memory resources are local. Process IDs, threads, and handles are local despite the fact that the application physically resides on a remote disk. By contrast, there is also an argument against this architecture. Instead of using resources in a centralized managed format, the load is duplicated over and over again across many workstations and servers. The user burden increases as do the requirements for resources on each of these systems. In Chapter 10 we explore technologies such as Citrix's WinFrame that layer Windows NT with code that transforms the operating system into a traditional (by UNIX definition) multiuser system.

Chapter 7

Tasks Common to Windows NT System Administration

Windows NT system administrators have much in common with those managing strictly UNIX enterprises. In Chapter 4, we applied a broad brush to a discussion of basic UNIX system administration responsibilities. Where administrative concerns obviously overlap, we do not repeat the issues again in this chapter. However, we do review two classes of Windows NT system administration concerns. First, there are activities that on the surface look comparable to UNIX responsibilities, but are implemented differently. Second, we address the issues that are unique to Windows NT administration.

Just like UNIX system administrators, those managing Windows NT also have two masters—the user community and computer operating system itself. Both carry equal weight. Therefore we have divided this chapter into system administrative concerns relating to both the user community and the operating system.

As a precursor to these discussions, it is important to have a fundamental understanding of how Windows NT Server 4.0 defines the concept of *workgroups* and *domains*. In working with either user or system issues, the nature of the workgroups and domains must be considered. An important duty of the system administrator is to understand workgroup and domain topology when adding and managing workstations and servers. The job of adding users is predicated on determining the intended rights of the individual within the context of the local and networked systems. The rights of users can vary radically when workgroup and various domain models are used. The chapter specifically addresses the following topics:

- Understanding the concept of workgroups and domains
  - Windows NT workgroup management
  - Windows NT domain management

- Primary and backup (secondary) domain controllers
- Domain authentication process
- Trust relationships between domains
- User-oriented system administrative concerns
  - Local versus global users
    * Adding users
    * Removing users
  - Group management
    * User rights and policies definition
    * User profiles
    * Basic services management—mail, printing, Web, and so on
- System-oriented administrative responsibilities
  - Administrative Wizard usage
  - The Registry
  - Installation issues clarification
  - Backup and restoration
  - Hardware additions and removal
  - System accounting and monitoring

UNDERSTANDING WORKGROUPS AND DOMAINS

When it comes to organizing a computer network, a system administrator should arrange systems to protect shared resources and ease the administrative burden. Classic problems with security, user convenience, and resource availability naturally evolve. To address user account setup and access, Windows NT created the concept of workgroups and domains.

NOTE   A Word about Membership Exclusivity

A Windows NT computer can belong to either a domain or a workgroup. However, this relationship is mutually exclusive. A Windows NT box cannot belong to a workgroup and domain at the same time. Switching between the membership of a workgroup and a domain is a fairly easy task. Select **Start ➤ Settings ➤ Control Panel ➤ Network ➤ Identification ➤ Change**. Caution should be taken, however, because the user may not have the expected access to shared network resources. Switching between environments is not recommended. Attempt to determine the type of membership in advance.

Managing Windows NT Workgroups

A workgroup is a logical association of systems where each host maintains its own user account and password database known as the Security Accounts Manager (SAM) (Figure 7.1). The association between workgroups is rather loose. Users can access any workstation from any other workstation as long as they have an account. This means that the user must have a predefined account on the desired system in order to log on. There are few advantages for a user to belong to a workgroup. A user is not required to stay within a workgroup. Belonging to a workgroup gives the user no special privileges.

From a system administrator's perspective, the workgroup model means extra work. In practical terms, user accounts, profiles, and group memberships must be added to individual systems. If a user is to obtain access to multiple workgroup systems, the administrator will need to repeat this procedure on each target workstation. Although Windows NT makes the addition of users straightforward, it is still time-consuming and open to possible problems relating to inconsistency and typographical errors (especially when entering logon names and password information manually and repeatedly on different machines).

Since no controlling or hierarchical relationship exists, the workgroup can include Windows NT Workstation, Windows 95, and Windows 3.x computers that operate as peers. Any computer within the workgroup can provide services

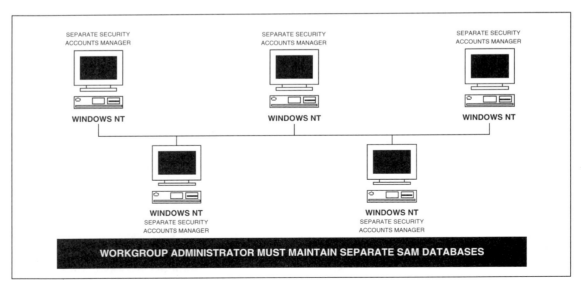

FIGURE 7.1.   Workgroup Basic Topology

like print spooling. As one system may be the focus of a particular service, it can also be a client to another workgroup computer system that is managing other services.

To view workgroup systems (Figure 7.2), run the Windows NT Explorer and select **Map Network Drive** from the **Tools** option (**Start** ➤ **Programs** ➤ **Windows NT Explorer** ➤ **Tools** ➤ **Map Network Drive**). (Note that this information is also commonly viewed using Map Network Devices.)

The workgroup model is generally employed when low cost and a minimal central function architecture are desired, such as where managing temporary machines and demo and trade show systems. However, obvious downsides exist in general administration. The workgroup model lacks the ability to manage a coordinated security policy. Since every workstation in the workgroup has its own user accounts, security policies, and SAM database, there is no ability to establish global accounts. If some level of standardization is desired, the system administrator must copy SAM databases and related files manually between workgroup systems.

Another problem is the lack of a failsafe with shared resources. If a workgroup computer performing a service goes down, then a secondary, backup system is not automatically put into service. The target service is simply termi-

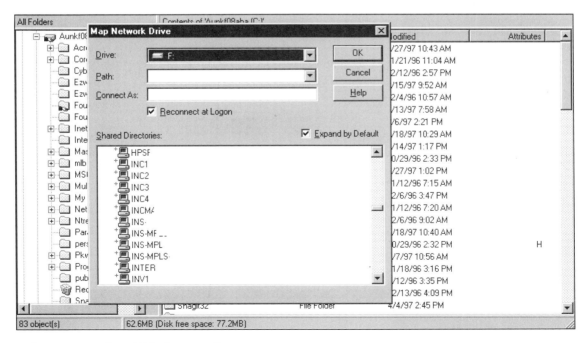

FIGURE 7.2.   List of Workgroup Computers

nated. The workgroup solution is probably not satisfactory for anything other than small networks. In large enterprises, a workgroup model cannot be managed reliably due to potential human error.

Managing Windows NT Domains

A domain model is a logical group of servers, workstations, and client computers that share a common SAM on a Windows NT server (Figure 7.3). All hosts in this domain reference this centralized SAM to verify user IDs and passwords. Users are permitted to log on to any host in the domain by using their central user account ID and password. A singular security and network policy can be constructed around the domain model.

In many ways the domain is a larger version of the workgroup model but with added, centralized login and security functionality. Workgroups remain autonomous and maintain a peer-to-peer relationship. In contrast, the domain permits the user to have roaming access to all hosts in the domain or trusted domains in hierarchical arrangements. Domains can form an assortment of peer-to-peer or hierarchical relationships. *The only prerequisite is that at least one Windows NT server must be part of the domain model.*

Domains are created only at the time that Windows NT Server is installed (or reinstalled) on a machine. Only after a domain has been created can other computers join the domain. A computer joining a domain must inform the server of its existence before a domain user can log on. This is accomplished when the Network Manager is set to join the target domain and the connection

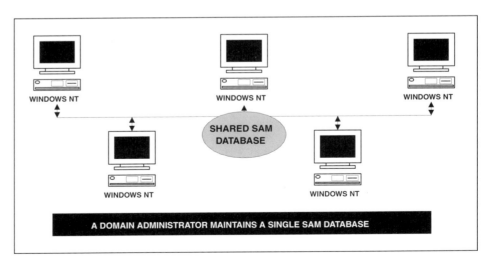

FIGURE 7.3.   Common SAM Database Used for Domains

is verified by pressing the **OK** button on the Identification window (**Start** ➤ **Settings** ➤ **Control Panel** ➤ **Network** ➤ **Identification** ➤ **Change** ➤ **Domain** ➤ **Enter the domain name** ➤ **OK**). The domain server will broadcast approval of the new relationship. This procedure assumes that the computer joining the domain already has an account in the domain's SAM. If not and you have administrative rights, select **Create a Computer Account in the Domain** from the Identification Changes window and enter a user name that belongs to either the Account Operator or Administrator groups.

NOTE   To log on to a Windows NT system within the domain, explicit approval must be granted to the user. See the discussion about user rights later in this chapter for additional information on permitting network access.

There are a number of advantages for using the domain model when constructing a Windows NT-based enterprise. First, as we shall learn, it is very flexible. The system administrator can take full advantage of the built-in functionality of a single Windows NT machine and apply it globally to a large group of systems. Shared printer and mail services are a prime example. The use of Windows NT RAID fault tolerance (NTFS configurations only) ensures greater archiving and data integrity. The graphical DNS and the Windows Internet Name Service (WINS) support dynamic address and name resolution. Folders can be shared and replicated easily to facilitate data exchange in a domain model.

The term *domain* has slightly different meanings for UNIX and Windows NT. A UNIX domain refers to a Domain Name Server (DNS) assignment or a set of Network Information Service (NIS) maps. Windows NT domains are a collection of computers with a common security and user account database. Since this is a centralized database, a Windows NT domain can be considered a single entity with multiple computers sharing a single resource.

PRIMARY AND BACKUP DOMAIN CONTROLLERS

The domain model is employed with centralized user account management and when many users require access to the same resources. At a minimum, a domain requires at least one Windows NT server that is configured as a primary domain controller (PDC). The PDC is responsible for user account authentication and maintenance of the current SAM database. Whenever users log on to the domain, they must be validated by the PDC. If for some reason the PDC is unavailable, a backup domain controller (BDC) is used (Figure 7.4). (The word *backup* is used interchangeably with secondary; therefore, a BDC is the same as a secondary domain controller.) The BDCs must be resynchronized periodically with the PDC. Approximately every five minutes, the PDC database is sent to all BDCs with an up-to-date SID and user account information. Also, any changes to each BDC are sent to the PDC. During this synchronization process only changes or differences between the SAM databases on the BDCs and PDCs are exchanged.

The synchronization process may be instigated manually from the Server Manager's **Computer** menu. You may synchronize the entire domain or just one particular BDC with the PDC. To accomplish this task, select **Start** ➤ **Programs** ➤ **Administrative Tools** ➤ **Server Manager** ➤ **View** ➤ **Servers**. After highlighting the PDC in the Server Manager window, select **Computer** ➤ **Synchronize Entire Domain**.

It may be necessary to take the PDC out of service periodically. Windows NT provides a nicely engineered solution for "promoting" a BDC to PDC status. The Server Manager is utilized to accomplish a proactive switch that explicitly instructs a BDC to assume the primary role. The previously defined PDC then relinquishes its status and may be taken out of service for needed repair, upgrade, or other purposes. Accomplish this by selecting **Start** ➤ **Programs** ➤ **Administrative Tools** ➤ **Server Manager**. Within the Server Manager window, highlight the target BDC, then select **Computer** ➤ **Promote to Primary Domain Controller**.

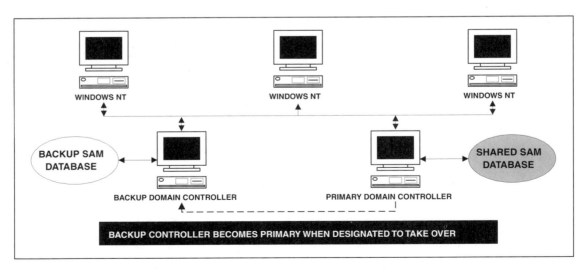

FIGURE 7.4.   Primary and Backup Domain Controllers

When a user logs on to a domain, the quickest responding BDC or PDC will authenticate the user. Remote sites should have their own local BDC to prevent authentication from occurring over a slow remote link. As a system administrator, you should consider where BDCs are physically resident in the domain to permit more rapid logon authentication.

NOTE The information that is synchronized and shared between the PDC and BDC does not include user profiles or logon scripts. To preserve this important information, the system administrator must copy the data manually between the domains. As discussed in Chapter 8, the Replicator tool can be helpful in synchronizing profiles and logon scripts.

DOMAIN AUTHENTICATION PROCESS

Some understanding of the user authentication process is useful for troubleshooting user logon problems. Windows NT employs the user name and password to verify authority to log in. Once logon is achieved, the user can invoke applications and files in which they have rights and permissions. The local security authority (LSA) verifies the user account name and password through the SAM database. An SAT, containing the user name and information, group memberships, and SID, is then granted. The SID is a numeric identifier created from information such as the user's host machine, user or group name, and computer clock time. This information is retained in a security table that remains static during the logon session. Therefore, if users are granted different group membership permissions, for example, they do not take effect until the current session is ended and the user logs on again. This unique number is changed when a user's account is deleted and then recreated.

All objects that are created with an original SID will not behave the same way toward the new SID. Every object (e.g., a process or a resource) within Windows NT carries with it an ACL. The ACL contains items called ACEs, which consist of a SID as well as the rights or actions permitted for the object. Whenever a user tries to access an object, the SRM verifies that the user's SID matches an entry in the ACL. This prevents any process from having global access to any file or resource on the Windows NT workstation. This concept is similar to the UNIX file and process permissions. However, the Windows NT security model is more advanced as it enables the administrator to allow or restrict access to an object more specifically, be it a file, a process, or a resource.

The following steps occur during a successful remote logon on a system running Windows NT workstation or server.

1. The client computer transmits the user name, password, and domain identification (which is entered manually at the Begin Logon dialog box) to the Windows NT server.

2. A comparison of the SAM database with the entered user name and password takes place.

3. If the authentication is successful, the LSA on the server creates an access token that is passed to the server to process.

4. The user ID created by the server in association with the access token is then used for all application, file, and system requests made by the user.

The following steps occur during a successful remote logon at a domain computer connecting to another system on the same domain.

1. The SAM database on the domain conducts the interactive logon for the user at the local client machine.

2. The user name, password, and client domain name are transmitted to the target remote system and in turn are sent to the domain Windows NT server.

3. The domain Windows NT server authenticates the information as matching from the central SAM database.

4. The domain Windows NT server grants permission to access the system.

This is really a classic client/server relationship. In particular, the Microsoft Client for Networks and the NETLOGON service are the programs that provide the client/server connectivity.

TRUST RELATIONSHIPS BETWEEN DOMAINS

The Windows NT trust relationship permits a user from one domain (trusted) to access the resources of another domain (trusting). The relationship is unidirectional, in which a trusting domain gives permissions to users of a trusted domain. If a bidirectional relationship is desired, then two separate unidirectional relationships must be established.

It is important to understand that trust relationships cannot be inherited or cascaded to other domains. Trust relationships are formed by invoking a very explicit action (Figure 7.5). For example, if domain #2 has a trust relationship with both domain #1 and domain #3, it does not follow that the latter two servers also are mutually trusted. To achieve a trust relationship between domain #1 and domain #3, an explicit granting of rights is required. Domains that have resources are called *resource domains*.

Five generic types of domain relationships can be implemented in a Windows NT enterprise (Figure 7.6).

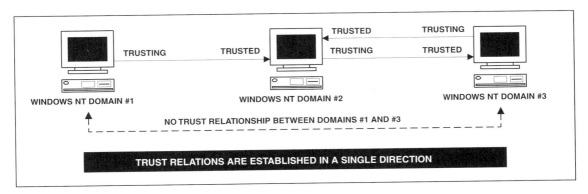

FIGURE 7.5.   Trust Relationships

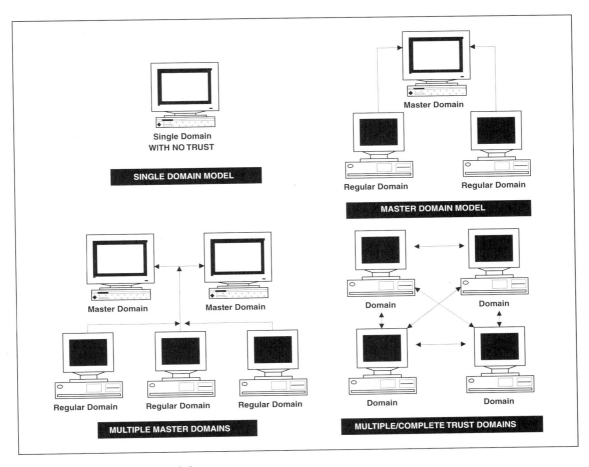

FIGURE 7.6.   Domain Models

- *Single-domain model* – In this case a single domain exists and therefore no trust relationship is required. The single domain model consists of one PDC and should have at least one BDC.

- *Master domain model* – Used for domains of forty thousand users or less, a unidirectional trust relationship is established with a master domain for the purpose of maintaining centralized user accounts and security policies for multiple trusting domains. In this model users log on to the master domain and access the other domains for resources according to the rights and permissions defined.

- *Multiple master domains model* – As the name implies, multiple master domains exist for centralized security and user account maintenance. Each of the master domains has a bidirectional trust relationship with each other, but not with the subdomains. Once again, the subdomains usually manage resources such as file sharing and printing. This model is good for organizations with more than forty thousand users.

- *Multiple trust or complete trust model* – With this model all domains maintain a complete trust relationship with each other. This permits the easy flow of information but represents an equally dicey security problem. User accounts are maintained on each of the domains. This is because they are maintained by separate administrative bodies.

- *Mixed trust model* – In larger organizations it is probable that a mixture of these models will be manifest. Organizations with different goals or requirements have varying levels of data transmission requirements. Therefore, a marketing department may adopt a complete trust domain whereas a manufacturing department could install a top-down master trust model.

The domain model provides the major advantage of being able to manage multiple domains centrally. From a user's perspective, logons are permitted anywhere across the trust (or master) domains, and resources can be accessed without the necessity of having an account on the trusting domain.

It is important to note that the establishment of trust relationships can be accomplished easily (Figure 7.7) by invoking the User Manager for Domains dialog and selecting **Trust Relationship** from the **Policies** menu (**Start** ➤ **Programs** ➤ **Administrative Tools** ➤ **User Manager for Domains** ➤ **Policies** ➤ **Trust Relationship**). Because of the sheer simplicity of the interface, it is also easy to formulate improper trusts accidentally. The potential for accidentally reducing the domain model to a complete trust relationship always exists.

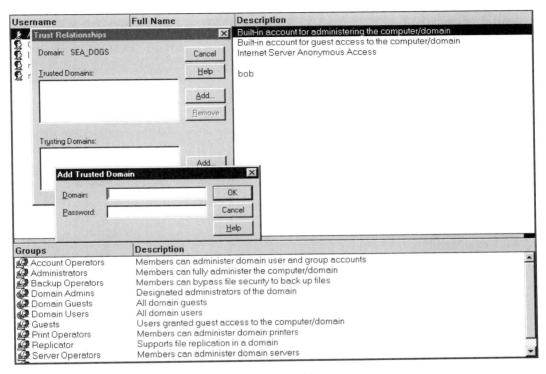

FIGURE 7.7.   Dialog for Creating Trust Relationships

USER-ORIENTED MANAGEMENT TASKS

As the system administrator for a Windows NT server or domain, you are faced with a series of standard concerns relating to the support of users. Windows NT makes several distinctions with regard to how users are managed locally and in group environments. This section discusses the nature of users and groups with specific examples on how to add and manage these accounts.

For this section we concentrate on managing users and groups from a Windows NT Server. On a server, the **User Manager for Domains** option will display on the **Administrative Tools** menu. If you upgrade from a Windows NT workstation to Windows NT Server, separate **User Manager** and **User Manager for Domains** options may display as well. (The **User Manager** option also displays on Windows NT workstations.) Choosing either of these options enables you to manage user and group accounts locally or on the domain level, respectively. In this section we refer mainly to the **User Manager for Domains** selection, but keep in mind that you may select **User Manager** to manage the users on the local system.

Understanding Users and Groups

Windows NT Server 4.0 ships with a number of built-in user and group accounts. The most important of these standard accounts is the *Administrator* user account. Among the rights and responsibilities of this user is user account management. Within the context of the domain model, the Administrator user account is equivalent in status to the UNIX superuser for management tasks. It is the only user account that cannot be removed. Given the responsibility for user management, the remainder of this section assumes that you log on as the Administrator or that you are a member of the Administrator group (thereby inheriting the full authority of the default Administrator user).

NOTE   Security

Renaming the Administrator account is usually a good policy. Since hackers are aware that every Windows NT box has an account named Administrator, the task of breaking into a domain is made easier. By changing the account name to something less obvious, the hacker's task is made more complex. When the Administrator account name is changed, none of the rights or profile information is changed.

Windows NT uses the concept of standard groups to perform the most common management tasks. These groups are built into the operating system with the idea that common tasks can be assigned to specific groups of users. Therefore, an individual can be granted just the authority to manage system backups by making the user a member of the Backup Operators group. As we shall discuss, other groups can be added to permit greater authority for particular users. The built-in groups are displayed in Figures 7.8 and 7.9.

Account Operators	Members can administer domain user and group accounts
Administrators	Members can fully administer the computer/domain
Backup Operators	Members can bypass file security to back up files
Domain Admins	Designated administrators of the domain
Domain Guests	All domain guests
Domain Users	All domain users
Guests	Users granted guest access to the computer/domain
Print Operators	Members can administer domain printers
Replicator	Supports file replication in a domain
Server Operators	Members can administer domain servers
Users	Ordinary users

FIGURE 7.8.   Standard User Groups for Domain Configuration

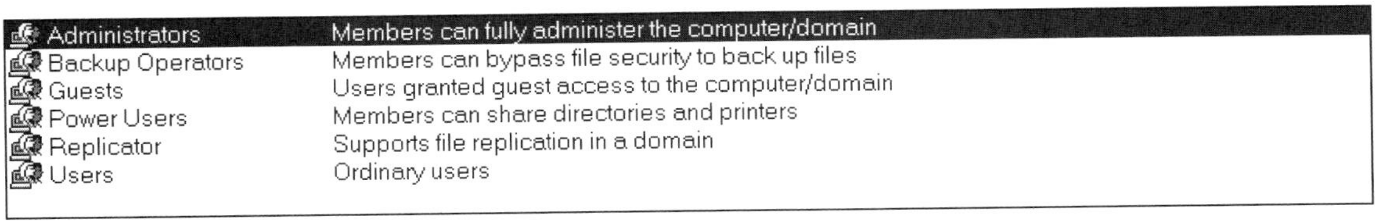

Administrators Members can fully administer the computer/domain
Backup Operators Members can bypass file security to back up files
Guests Users granted guest access to the computer/domain
Power Users Members can share directories and printers
Replicator Supports file replication in a domain
Users Ordinary users

FIGURE 7.9. **Standard User Groups for Workgroup Configuration**

Several additional groups exist with members that do not have to be assigned. The membership in these groups is generally assumed by the nature of the logon or work being performed. These groups include

- The Interactive group; usually contains only the users that are logged on to the console
- The Network group; contains those users accessing an object across the network
- The System group; doesn't contain user accounts, but is a group that allows the operating system to control access to its own resources

There is one other special group that warrants mention and that is the Everyone group. Every user belongs to the Everyone group (Figure 7.10). This

List Names From:
SEA_DOGS
Names:
Domain Admins Designated administrators of the domain
Domain Guests All domain guests
Domain Users All domain users
Everyone All Users
INTERACTIVE Users accessing this object locally
NETWORK Users accessing this object remotely
Add
Show Users
Members...
Search...
Add Names:
OK
Cancel
Help

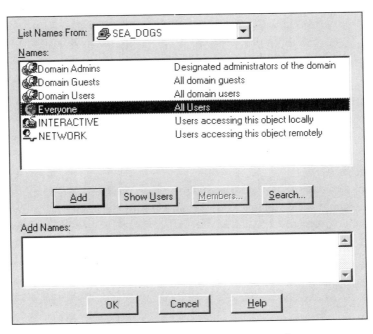

FIGURE 7.10. **Explicit Group Membership such as Everyone**

group exists primarily to simplify the task of assigning a right or permitting access to universal resources to all users in a domain. It is possible to select these groups explicitly when assigning rights by selecting the **User Rights** option from the **User Manager for Domains' Policies** menu.

ROLE OF GROUP ACCOUNTS TO INDIVIDUAL USERS

The concept of groups within Windows NT is very similar to the UNIX counterpart. The group is a mechanism for a common set of rights and attributes that are shared by a number of individual users. The difference between the two operating systems is that Windows NT permits the administrator to define more explicitly what a particular group of users may do within the enterprise.

LOCAL VERSUS GLOBAL USERS AND GROUPS

Before discussing how to add users and groups it is important to understand the differences between the available types of accounts. Actually there are four different types of accounts: local user accounts, global user accounts, local group accounts, and global group accounts.

Local Users

The purpose of the local user account is to allow a user from a workgroup or an untrusted domain to access resources in your domain. Local users cannot become members of either local or global groups. To define a new user account as local, select the **Account** button at the bottom of the New User window. (The New User window is displayed by selecting **Start ➤ Programs ➤ Administrative Tools ➤ User Manager for Domains ➤ User ➤ New User**.) Within the Account Information window, select **Local Account**. When you return to the User Manager window, you will notice that the new local user is displayed with a computer monitor behind the face icon. This computer monitor designates graphically that the user is a local user.

Global Users

A global user account is the default type of user account and it defines the user to the Windows NT server domain controller. You will also see this type of account referred to as a *domain user account* or as simply a *user account*. Global user accounts can be used to log on interactively to other systems in the domain as well as to access any shared resources. In addition, these accounts can be added to either local or global groups. Through the use of trusted domains and global user accounts, it is not necessary for a user to have an account defined in more than one domain in the network.

Global Groups

Unlike UNIX, group membership can span a number of servers. A user is not confined merely to the local server. Since each user has unique requirements, membership to multiple groups is very common. Just like there are two types of user accounts, there are two types of group accounts—local and global.

A global group account consists of a collection of user accounts that are members of its own domain. These users are usually placed in the same global group because they have similar requirements, such as similar permissions and resource access needs. A global group can be assigned privileges in its own domain as well as any trusting domain. A global group cannot contain users from another domain nor can it contain other groups. These accounts can only be created on a Windows NT server and not on a Windows NT workstation.

The User Manager window displays a list of available groups. Global groups are depicted graphically by including a world globe as part of the icon.

Local Groups

In contrast to the global group account is the local group account. A local group can only be assigned privileges in its own domain. However, the power of the local group comes from the fact that it can contain both user accounts and global groups that have been created either in its own domain or in trusted domains. Since a local group can provide privileges only for the local domain, it makes sense that it cannot contain other local groups. A local group can be created on Windows NT workstations as well as Windows NT servers. Local groups are depicted graphically in the User Manager for Domains window with a computer as the icon instead of the world globe that displays for global groups.

The local group simplifies the task of managing security on the system since it enables the administrator to assign similar permissions and rights to a large collection of users at the same time. It is recommended that rights and permissions be assigned at the local level rather than the global level to keep a tighter rein on security. Use global groups to group together domain users that need similar access to a particular local system. This way, instead of adding each individual user to a local group, you can add just the global group (Figure 7.11).

CREATING GROUPS

As discussed earlier, Windows NT provides a variety of built-in groups that pre-define the rights and permissions for commonly executed tasks. When these built-in groups are not enough to meet your needs, the creation of new local and global groups is straightforward (Figure 7.12). As the administrator, a local group account is created on a Windows NT server by selecting **Start ➜ Programs ➜**

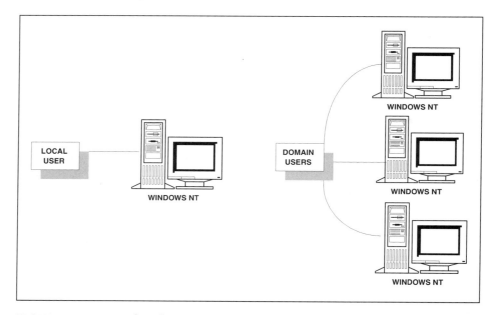

FIGURE 7.11.   Local and Domain Users

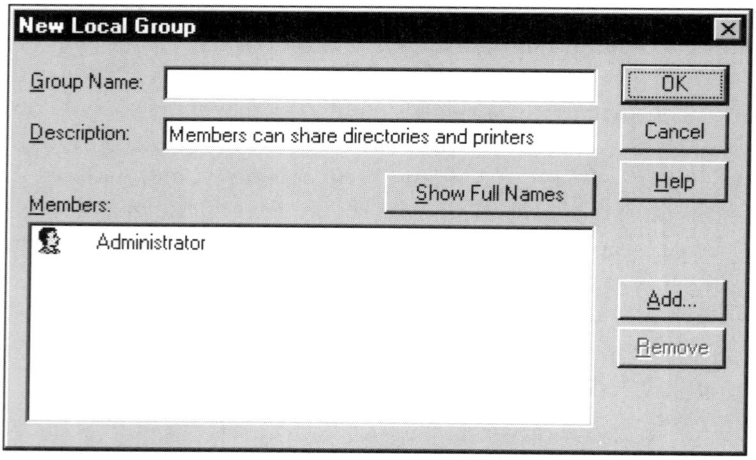

FIGURE 7.12.   New Local Group Dialog Box

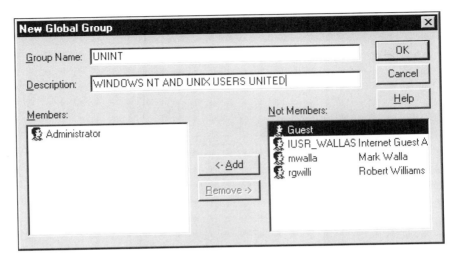

FIGURE 7.13.   New Domain or Global Group Dialog Box

Administrative Tools ➤ **User Manager for Domains** (or **User Manager**) ➤ **User** ➤ **New Local Group**.

As an administrator, a global group account is created on Windows NT servers by selecting **Start** ➤ **Programs** ➤ **Administrative Tools** ➤ **User Manager for Domains** ➤ **User** ➤ **New Global Group** (Figure 7.13).

User Maintenance

Now that you have a basic understanding of local and global users and local and global groups, it is time to understand the steps necessary to add, delete, and maintain user accounts. User maintenance is usually executed from the User Manager dialog box for Windows NT workstations and from the User Manager for Domains dialog box for Windows NT servers. For the purpose of this discussion we will concentrate on using the Windows NT server for user maintenance because the server provides more capabilities and options.

ADDING USERS

The task of adding users is supported by a fairly intuitive interface. The Windows NT Administrative Wizard steps you through each step of the process. Access the Administrative Wizard by selecting **Start** ➤ **Programs** ➤ **Administrative Tools** ➤ **Administrative Wizards** ➤ **Add User Accounts**. A more interactive approach involves the use of the User Manager for Domains dialog box. To add a user in the current domain, select **Start** ➤ **Programs** ➤ **Administrative Tools** ➤ **User Manager for Domains** ➤ **User** ➤ **New User** (Figure 7.14).

Username	Full Name	Description
Administrator		Built-in account for administering the computer/domain
Guest		Built-in account for guest access to the computer/domain
IUSR_WALLASPC	Internet Guest Account	Internet Server Anonymous Access
mwalla	Mark Walla	Network Administrator
rgwilli	Robert Williams	System Administrator

Groups	Description
Account Operators	Members can administer domain user and group accounts
Administrators	Members can fully administer the computer/domain
Backup Operators	Members can bypass file security to back up files
Domain Admins	Designated administrators of the domain

FIGURE 7.14.   User Manager

NOTE   A Word to Command Line Users

On a Windows NT workstation, the User Manager can also be started from the VDM or Run command by typing `musrmgr`. Additionally you can specify the domain (*musrmgr [domain]*) or the NetBIOS server name (*musrmgr [\\server-name]*). For Windows NT servers, the command is *usrmgr [\\servername | domainname]*.

To add a user to a domain other than the current or local domain, you must first select the domain by choosing **Select Domain** from the **User** menu on the menu bar of the User Manager for Domains window (Figure 7.15). After selecting the desired domain, you may add a new user by selecting **User ➤ New User**. This will display the New User window.

For workgroups and local servers, the form shown in Figure 7.16 is displayed. There is a difference between the local and domain new user dialog box and options. On the bottom of the dialog box are three buttons for the local new user (Figure 7.16) and six for the new domain user (Figure 7.17).

In the New User window, the only field that must be completed is the user's logon name. However, we recommend that the entire form be completed as shown here:

- **Username** – Name used for logon; a maximum of twenty characters, excluding the following reserved characters: = + [ ] / \ ; : < > ? * ,
- **Full Name** – The full name of the user; an optional field
- **Description** – The user's title, organization, or other descriptive name; an optional field
- **Password** – A unique password limited to fourteen case-sensitive characters; an optional field

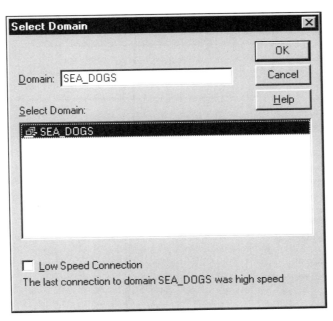

FIGURE 7.15.   Select Domain for User Members
Dialog Box

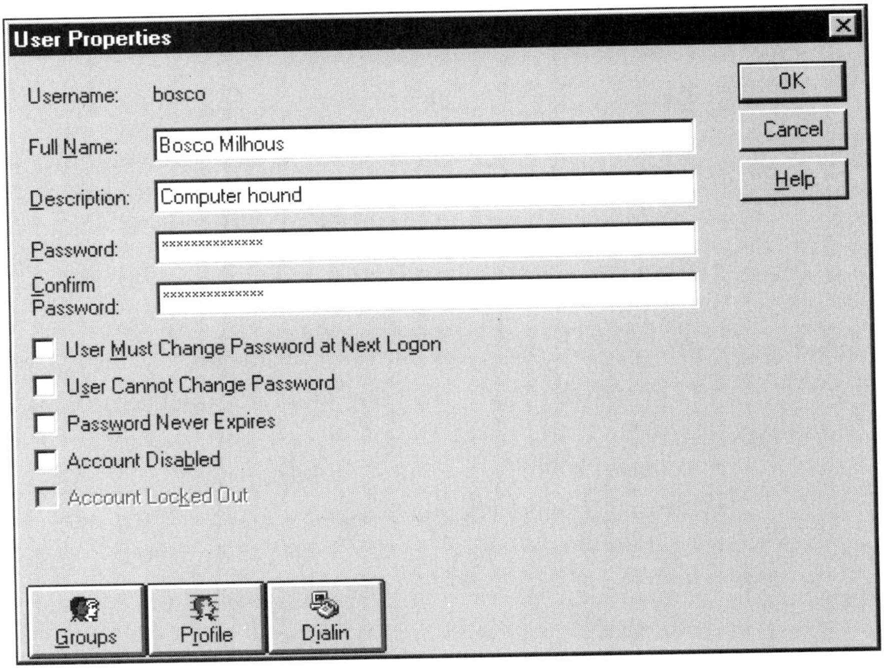

FIGURE 7.16.   New User Dialog Box—Local Administration

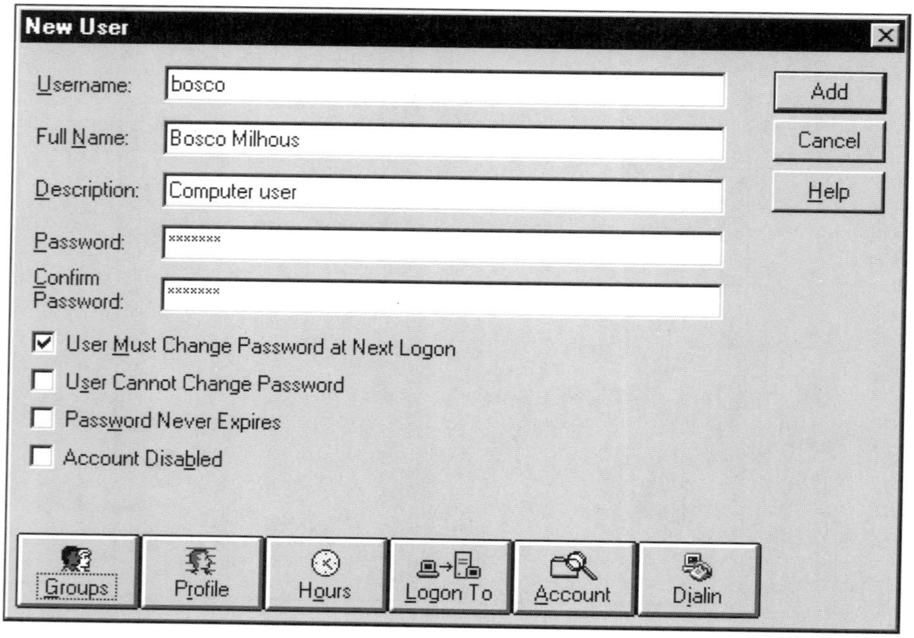

FIGURE 7.17.   New User for Domain Dialog Box with Six Bottom Options

- **Confirm Password** – Retype the previously defined password; optional only if the previous line is blank
- **Check boxes** – Check off the types of password management desired

Once the basic information has been entered you may define additional properties for the user by selecting each of the buttons displayed at the bottom of the window. These buttons enable you to define the following properties:

- **Groups** – Add the user to local and global groups
- **Profile** – Define user profile information
- **Hours** – Set the hours that the user may access the network
- **Logon To** – Identify the computers that the user may use to log on to the domain
- **Account** – Define user account information
- **Dialin** – Define whether a user can dial in to the network from a remote location

A discussion of each of these account properties follows. It is important to understand that each of these properties has default values, so it is not necessary to set or change them when you set up a new user. You can access these properties for an existing user by selecting **User ➤ Properties** from the menu bar of the User Manager window. Alternately, you can just double clicking on the user in the user portion of the User Manager window.

Adding Users to Groups (the Groups Button)

Each user belongs to the default users' group known as Everyone. It is often appropriate to add a user to other built-in or customized groups. Within the User Properties window and the New User dialog box, a button appears on the lower left-hand corner called **Groups**. To add a user to others groups, simply select the **Groups** button. Highlight the appropriate group and select the **Add** button (Figure 7.18). When group membership is added or removed, the user automatically inherits the appropriate permissions and rights associated with that group.

Setting the User's Environment (the Profile Button)

Like UNIX, Windows NT employs a profile that is called when the user logs on to the system. The User Environment Profile dialog box (accessed by selecting the **Profile** button) is used to establish a number of default settings and paths to optional scripts (Figure 7.19). The first section in the box, **User Profiles,** establishes the standard user paths to the named, optional logon scripts. If you wish to access a specific user profile that will be used when the user first logs in, enter the path for this profile in **User Profile Path**. This path can point to a shared

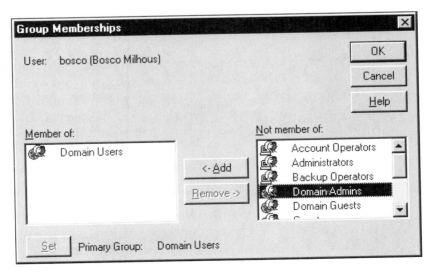

FIGURE 7.18.   Group Memberships Dialog Box

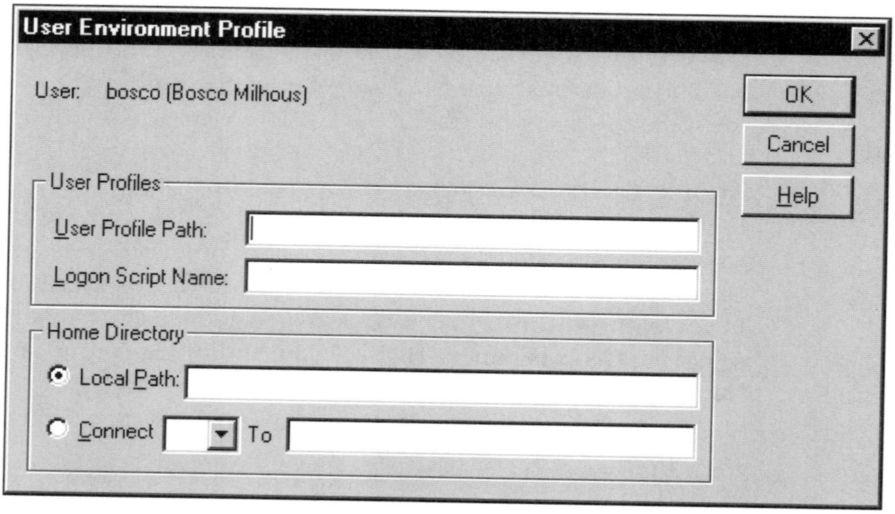

FIGURE 7.19.   User Environment Profile Dialog Box

profile directory on the network or a specially created profile on the local machine. The default directory for user profiles is *c:\winnt\profiles\username*.

If using a logon script, enter either the script name or the relative path of the script in the **Logon Script Name** field. The default path for the *.bat* logon network script is *\\SERVERNAME\winnt\system32\Repl\Import\Scripts*.

If a relative path is entered in this field, then it is appended to the default path name. Relative paths in Windows NT are very similar to those in UNIX, as described in Chapter 3.

The next section of the User Environment Profile dialog box defines the user's home directory. The home folder is the directory into which the user is put when logging on or starting a VDM window. It is normally home for personal files. This directory may be defined on the local machine by using the **Local Path** option, or it may be defined on a shared network drive using the **Connect** option.

A more in-depth discussion of profiles and logon scripts is provided later in this chapter in the More about Profiles and Scripts section.

Restricting User Hours (the Hours Button)

For reasons of security and maintenance, it may become necessary to restrict the hours that users can log on to the system. For example, if routine system backups are scheduled for several hours during the weekend, you may want to block user access during this time. The Logon Hours window displays a weekly

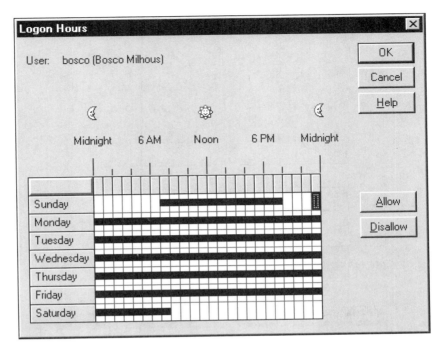

FIGURE 7.20.   Logon Hours Dialog Box

schedule (Figure 7.20). First select the hours, then select either the **Allow** or **Disallow** button to identify whether or not the user is able to access the system during that time frame.

User Logon Authority to Remote Systems (the Logon To Button)

Using the **Logon To** button, you may select to authorize user logons to all associated workstations in the domain or to those specifically listed in the dialog box (Figure 7.21).

Establishing Domain Account Information (the Account Button)

The **Account** button allows you to define the account type and the length of time that access is permitted. The default is to never have the account expire and to assign a global status to regular user logons. Through the Account Information dialog box (Figure 7.22), set a date for account expiration and restrict the user to a local access only, if so desired.

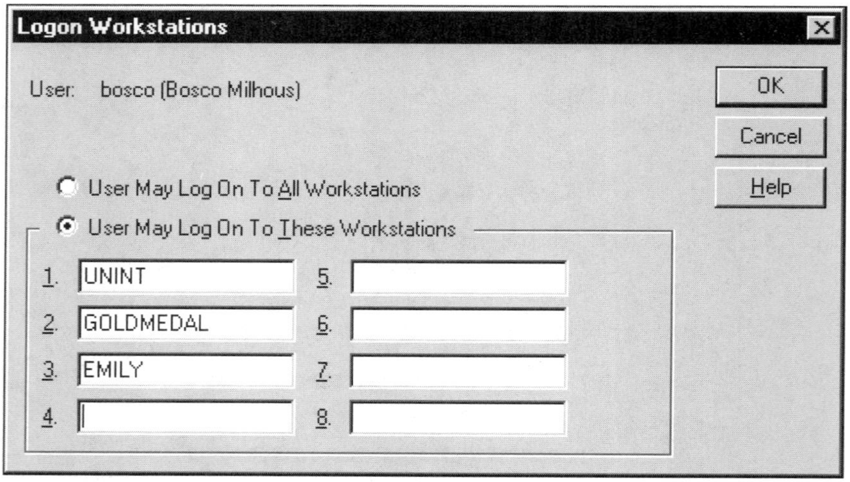

FIGURE 7.21.   Logon Workstations Dialog Box

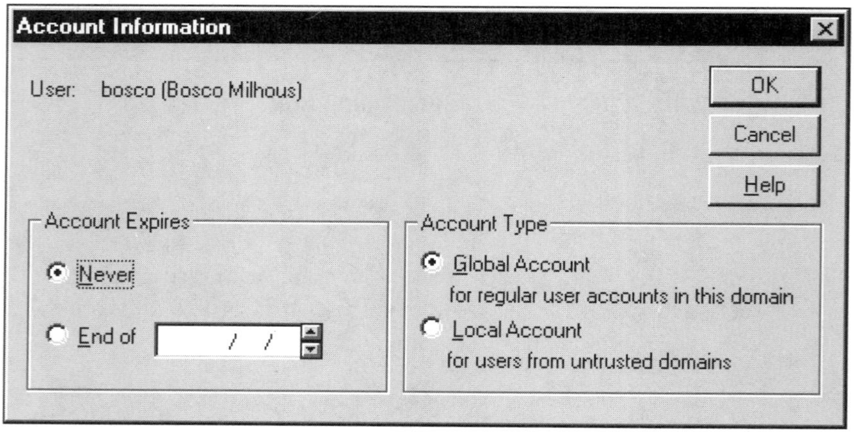

FIGURE 7.22.   Global User Accounts

Dial-in Authority (the Dialin Button)

A user can be granted access to the system through a telephone dial-in connection only if authority is given explicitly by checking **Grant dialin permission to user** in the Dialin Information window (Figure 7.23). Three options exist with regard to the treatment of dial-in authority. First, the default is to permit no callbacks. The second option permits a defined callback. This is good for

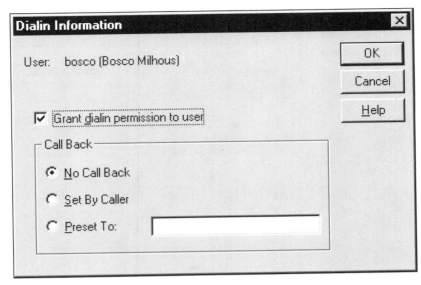

FIGURE 7.23.   Dialin Information Dialog Box

traveling folks and prevents large long-distance telephone bills at hotels. It also provides phone records of people who log in to the server. Finally, a single predefined number can be established for dial-in security purposes. Attempts made from a number other than the one listed are rejected. The ability to grant dial-in permission is new to Windows NT 4.0.

USER AND GROUP TEMPLATES

Windows NT provides a simple way of replicating the properties of one user account or group and applying them to other new accounts and groups. The trick is to select the best default source account or group to be used as the basis for other accounts.

To employ an existing user account as a template to create other user accounts, select **Start ➤ Programs ➤ Administrative Tools ➤ User Manager for Domains ➤ Highlight the source user accounts ➤ User ➤ Copy.** At this point the Copy of (user name) window displays and you may enter any additional or different information for the new user (Figure 7.24).

To employ an existing group as a template to create other groups, select **Start ➤ Programs ➤ Administrative Tools ➤ User Manager for Domains ➤ highlight the source group ➤ User ➤ Copy.** At this point enter any new or different data for the new group (Figure 7.25).

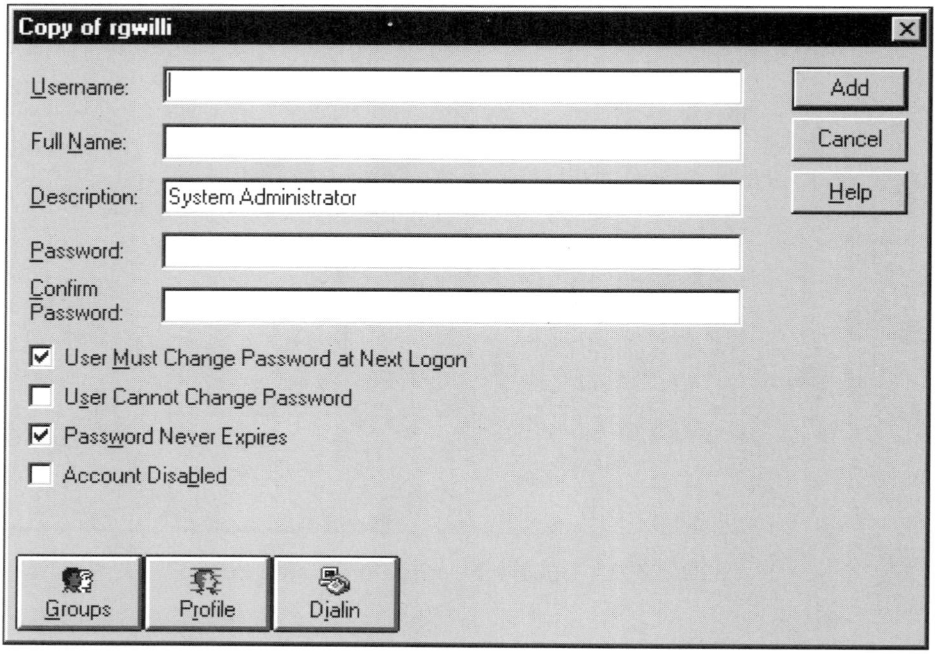

FIGURE 7.24.   Copy of User Account as a Template

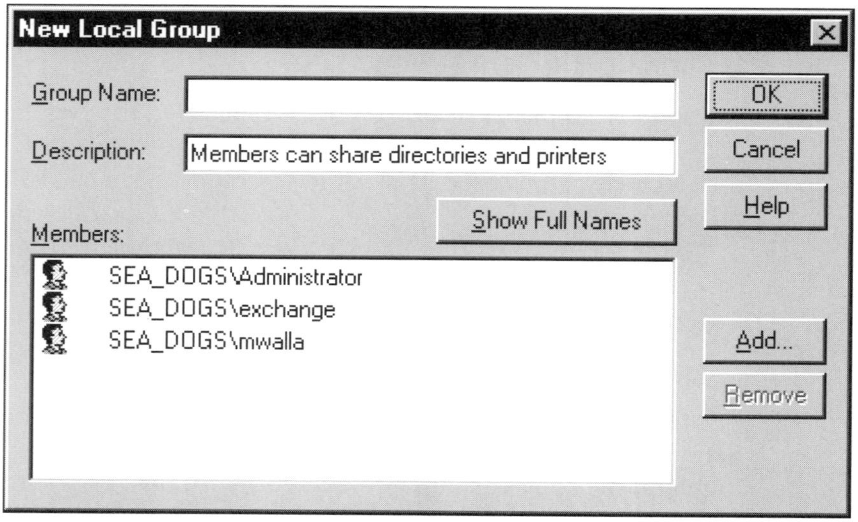

FIGURE 7.25.   Copy of Group as a Template

NOTE   Multiple-Account Generation

An interesting feature of the User Manager is the ability to select multiple users and modify their traits simultaneously. First, from the User Manager window, select multiple users by holding <Ctrl> while selecting the users with the left mouse button. After the multiple users have been selected, press <Enter> or select **User ➤ Properties** to bring up the User Properties window (Figure 7.26). Options common to all selected users are displayed. (You can also use <Shift> to select a band of users.)

DELETING USER ACCOUNTS

Deleting user accounts is very simple. This is clearly a double-edged feature. Although simplicity can streamline productivity, it can also cause major problems if users are removed without a precaution. Specifically, initially disabling a user account rather than deleting it is recommended until it has been determined whether valuable data is stored in the user's directories. After this assessment has been made, then deleting the account is appropriate.

To delete a user, simply select the user from the User Manager window and press <Delete> or select **User ➤ Delete** from the menu bar. Two warning prompts then display to make sure this action is desired (Figures 7.27 and 7.28).

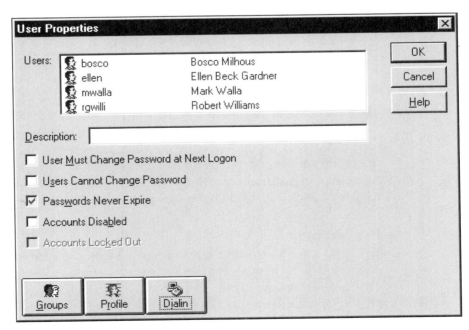

FIGURE 7.26.   List of Users with Common Accounts

FIGURE 7.27.   First User Deletion Warning

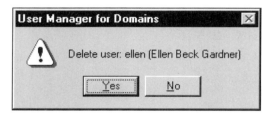

FIGURE 7.28.   Confirmation Deletion
Warning

NOTE   When a user account is removed, the folder containing the data is not auto-matically deleted. To accomplish this task, the system administrator needs to delete manually those folders and files deemed unnecessary.

POLICY MANAGEMENT

The User Manager offers three primary facilities for managing and fine-tuning user accounts. These are standard user account policies, rights, and audit para-meters for users on the server or the domain. Although these three sets fall under the same menu, it is important to note that two are global settings. The **Account** and **Audit** options apply to all users in the domain. By contrast, **User Rights** is utilized to define rights for each user and user group (Figure 7.29).

User Account Policies

The Account Policy dialog box permits a method for rapidly standardizing password and lockout security features on a server or across the domain (Fig-ure 7.30). The Account Policy dialog box is divided into two parts, which in turn provide options to set specific constraints or leave the item unrestricted. These options are listed in Table 7.1.

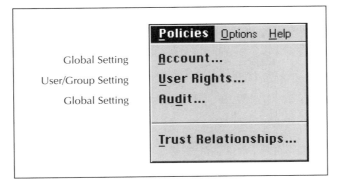

FIGURE 7.29.   Policies Menu

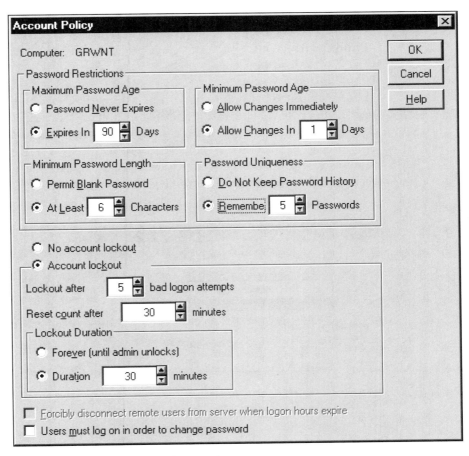

FIGURE 7.30.   Account Policy Dialog Box

TABLE 7.1.   Account Policy Options

Option	Default	Allowed value
Maximum Password Age	Never expires	1–999 days
Minimum Password Age	Allow immediate change	1–999 days
Minimum Password Length	Allow blank password	1–14 characters
Password uniqueness	Do not keep history	Remember 1–24 passwords
Account lockout	No account lockout	—
Lockout after	Five bad logon attempts	1–999 bad logon attempts
Reset logon count after	30 minutes	1–99999 minutes
Lockout duration	After 30 minutes	1–99999 minutes or forever

To access the user's Account Policy dialog box, select **Start** ➤ **Programs** ➤ **Administrative Tools** ➤ **User Manager for Domains** ➤ **Policies** ➤ **Accounts**.

User Rights

There are number of rights that can be assigned to a user group through the User Rights Policy dialog box (Figure 7.31). Table 7.2 presents a list of the standard rights granted to the default group members. A special note of the first option is appropriate as it grants the right to access a server. By default, the Administrator and Everyone are granted logon rights. If you want to restrict access, it is recommended that the Everyone group be removed and individual

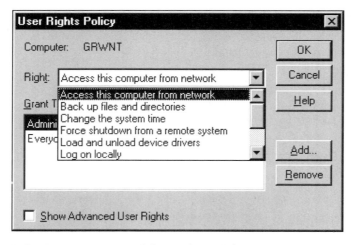

FIGURE 7.31.   User Rights Policy Dialog Box

The server-based profile is defined as either personal or mandatory. Personal and mandatory profiles are mutually exclusive. Personal profiles have a file extension of *.DAT* whereas mandatory profiles have a *.MAN* extension. The personal server-based profile for each user is maintained on the domain controller. The profile is downloaded when the user logs on to the domain. Personal profiles are utilized when user flexibility is desired. The path of this profile is identified in the User Environment Profile window. To access this window for a current user, select **Start ➤ Programs ➤ Administrative Tools ➤ User Manager for Domains ➤ select the user ➤ User ➤ Properties ➤ Profile**. When the personal profile is stored on the PDC, the profile becomes a roaming profile.

Multiple users share the mandatory server profile. Changes made during a logon session by users of the mandatory shared profile are not retained. When the user logs on again, the default shared configurations are utilized. While the personal profile provides users freedom, the mandatory profile gives the system administrator greater peace of mind. It provides a means of consistency for common connectivity, application access, and general management. Because the user cannot permanently alter the desktop, the system administrator does not have to worry about repeatedly installing applications or setting printer parameters.

NOTE   **Security**

In some environments it may be wise to consider the removal of administrative logons from the network. This approach obviously defeats some of the ease of use inherent in Windows NT because it requires physical access to the server for full access and prevents someone from making repeated remote logon attempts. However, it will also prevent global damage to the enterprise if the wrong person gains unrestricted administrative access. From the User Manager window select Policies ¤ User Rights. Make sure the Access this computer from the network selection is chosen. Select the Administrator and Everyone groups and then press the Remove button. Another possibility is to remove all groups from being able to gain access from the network and create one group called Network Users that can be accessed from the net. Members of this group would be carefully screened for administrative privileges, limiting the system's access from the network to user status.

Application Support

The system administrator is responsible for commercial applications employed by the user community. Beyond the obvious responsibility of providing software training, the system administrator has management duties, including version and license control. On a single system, this typically involves making sure that application licenses are timely. Periodic sizing for application use is also required. Log files are helpful in determining application use over time.

System administrators will find the Windows NT License Manager tool particularly helpful in tracking installed applications (Figure 7.33). It provides purchase history, product views, per-seat user allocations, and install-point information. To access the License Manager, select **Start** ➤ **Programs** ➤ **Administrative Tools** ➤ **License Manager**.

Cross-platform application management across Windows NT support systems is much more straightforward than what exists within the UNIX environment. Windows NT applications are generally shipped with code supporting both Intel- and RISC-class machines. By contrast, UNIX system administrators typically have to purchase licenses for each UNIX variant (and sometimes versions) that exist in the enterprise. The Windows NT HAL makes the task of cross-compiling code less daunting. Obviously, the argument made from the UNIX camp is that this is really an unfair comparison because Windows NT still has limited chip set support.

Part of the role of system administrators is to qualify applications for their environments. The following is a list of questions that should be addressed when purchasing and maintaining user applications:

- How is the software licensed? One time or must it be renewed periodically?
- Are user licenses based on the number of people on the system or based on concurrent utilization?
- What are the support and maintenance policies?

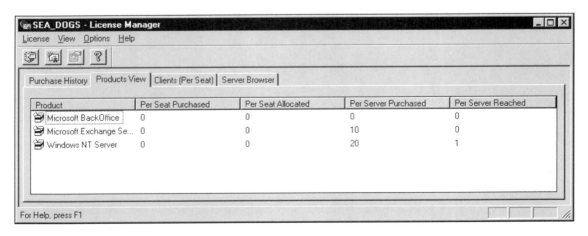

FIGURE 7.33.   License Control Tool

- Which operating systems are supported by which release number?
- What level of compatibility exists with other versions and back releases?
- Which GUIs are supported?
- Are character-based environments supported? If so, what type of terminal devices?
- Is user training different for each release type or level?

Managing Basic Functions

The Windows NT system administrator is also responsible for basic services like managing the mail and the printing networks. Issues involved in integrating Windows NT and UNIX mail services are discussed in Chapter 14.

With regard to printing, a brief explanation of how Windows NT treats local and network printer management in the context of UNIX is appropriate. As the administrator, you can regulate printer activity from any workstation and perform functions such as

- View print jobs and available printers along with their status
- Stop and pause print jobs
- Delete print jobs
- Remove print devices from service
- Determine which printer resources are to be shared

LOCAL PRINTER MANAGEMENT

The typical extent of system administrator involvement with local (directly attached) printers is minimal. Printers are defined through the **Control Panel** printer option. Most users familiar with earlier versions of Microsoft Windows operating systems are generally capable of setting default parameters for a locally connected printer (Figure 7.34). Many users are also capable of basic maintenance like toner installation. Despite these factors, you can expect to be involved in some aspect of local printer setup and maintenance. To set up a local printer, select **Start** ➤ **Settings** ➤ **Control Panel** ➤ **Printers** ➤ **Add Printer** or select **Start** ➤ **Settings** ➤ **Printers** ➤ **Add Printer**.

REMOTE PRINTER MANAGEMENT

Windows NT management of TCP/IP-based network printers bears much similarity to UNIX in the use of *lpr* and the line printer daemon (LPD). The lpr protocol takes a printer client's request and spools it to a server system. Windows NT provides both the lpr client applications and the LPD that receives job

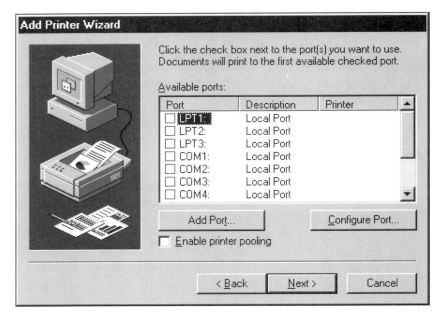

FIGURE 7.34.   Printer Manager

requests from other Windows NT boxes as well as UNIX systems. The lpr is also accessible from the VDM command line.

The lpr standard is based on early BSD UNIX design and is the basis for Request for Comment (RFC) 1179. Windows NT is modeled after RFC 1179. Therefore, it is possible to transmit print jobs between BSD UNIX and Windows NT operating systems. Interestingly, this is not as easily accomplished with variants of UNIX System V.4 that do not have a BSD subsystem.

In the next section, we discuss the use of Administrative Wizards, which is by far the easier way to install a network printer. Chapter 13 expands on the concept of setting up a network printer.

SYSTEM-LEVEL RESPONSIBILITY

In addition to keeping users content, the system administrator must also keep the system happy and running smoothly. In the UNIX world, this activity is generally defined as one box at a time. Due to the Windows NT domain model, administration takes on multiple server dimensions. One of the real strengths of Windows NT is the ability to manage systems in the domain remotely. This section explores the tools available on Windows NT to facilitate both localized and remote system management and maintenance.

Administrative Wizards

As first glance, Windows NT Server Administrative Wizards look more "cute" than substantive. However, underlying their appearance are a powerful set of graphical applications that streamline normal system administrator activities (Figures 7.35 and 7.36). The Wizards lead the user and administrator through a series of screens that largely eliminate failure due to the accidental skipping of a procedure. The Windows NT Server 4.0 Administrative Wizards provide the following eight task managers:

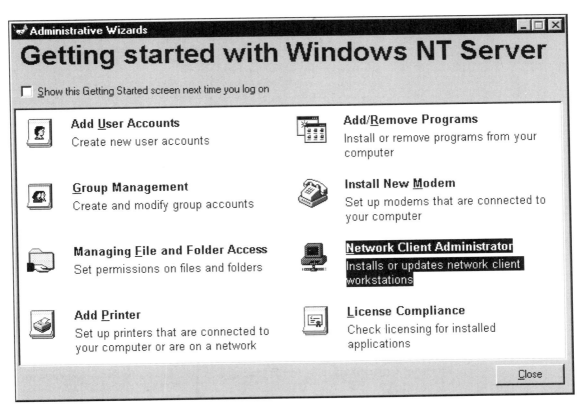

FIGURE 7.35.   Administrative Wizards Index

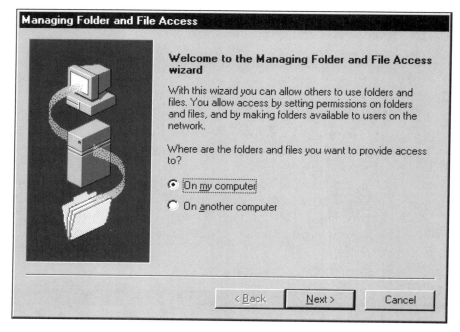

FIGURE 7.36.   Sample of Initial Wizard Prompt

1. **Add User Accounts** – The ability to create new user accounts with appropriate rights

2. **Group Management** – The ability to create and modify local and global group accounts

3. **Managing File and Folder Access** – The capacity to set permissions on NTFS and sharing for FAT-based systems

4. **Add Printer** – The capacity to set up local and remote printing devices

5. **Add/Remove Programs** – The automation of the installation and removal of applications

6. **Install New Modem** – The capacity to add a modem device with appropriate settings

7. **Network Client Administrator** – The automation of the installation of network clients and update of appropriate information

8. **License Compliance** – The licensing review of installed applications

To gain access to the Windows NT Server 4.0 Administrative Wizards, select **Start** ➤ **Programs** ➤ **Administrative Tools** ➤ **Administrative Wizards**.

The Registry

The Windows NT Registry contains operating system, hardware, folder/file, and user information. The Registry replaces the *config.sys, autoexec.bat, reg.dat,* and *.ini* files common to earlier versions of Microsoft Windows operating systems. (The exception is the *boot.ini* file, which permits the selection of which operating system to boot when the computer is first powered up and before Windows NT begins any activity.) An example of the type of information stored in the Registry is a list of all properly installed applications. Therefore, when you double-click on a file with the Windows NT Explorer, its extension is matched with a list of installed applications and launches the appropriate software. Among the other items stored in the Registry are

- Hardware configuration data
- Program group and desktop settings for each user
- User profile data
- Local language and time settings
- Network configuration data
- Security information for users and groups
- ActiveX and OLE server data

The Registry is comprised of a set of *keys* and *subkeys*. The concept of a subkey follows the same principle as subfolders within a directory tree. For each of the five primary keys, subkeys or subcategories of information are collected. The system administrator must have a basic understanding of how the Registry is organized. This is clearly different than anything connected with UNIX. The five keys are described in Table 7.6.

The keys and subkeys are stored in collections known as *hives*. This permits values to be paired to form a comprehensive profile of a user, the hardware, file components, and so forth. Hive information is coupled with associated log files in an effort to minimize corruption. When changes are made to the Registry data, they are compared with the logs before they are written. The log file is written first in a type of data-streaming mechanism. When saved to disk, changes are then updated to the hive key components. Hive files are stored in *%systemroot%\System32\Config* or for user data in *\%systemroot%\Profile\username*.

As a system administrator, you are the protector of the Registry. If the Registry is lost or damaged, Windows NT cannot function. Therefore, the care and feeding of the Registry is a critical responsibility. The first rule is to retain an emergency copy of the Registry in case of damage or loss. As stated before, the Registry information is found in *%systemroot%\System32\Config,* where *%systemroot%* is the root directory for the system, such as *\winnt*. For system

TABLE 7.6.   Registry Keys

Key	Description
HKEY_LOCAL_MACHINE	Information regarding the local system, such as hardware and operating system data
HKEY_CLASSES_ROOT	File allocation and OLE/ActiveX data; association of extensions to applications
HKEY_CURRENT_CONFIG	System startup configuration that permits changes to device settings
HKEY_CURRENT_USER	Profile for the currently active user as well as console, Control Panel, environment, printer, and software data
HKEY_USERS	Profiles for all currently active users as well as the default profile

recovery, the Windows NT Setup program also creates a *%systemroot%\Repair* folder that contains the following files:

- *Autoexec.nt* – A copy of *%systemroot%\System32\Autoexec.nt,* which is used to initialize the MS-DOS environment
- *Config.nt* – A copy of *%systemroot%\System32\Config.nt,* which is used to initialize the MS-DOS environment
- *Default.* – The Registry key HKEY_USERS\DEFAULT in compressed format
- *Ntuser.DA_* – A compressed version of *%systemroot%\Profiles\Default-User\Ntuser.dat;* the process uses *Ntuser.da_* if this area needs repair
- *Sam._* – The Registry key HKEY_LOCAL_MACHINE\SAM in compressed format
- *Security._* – The Registry key HKEY_LOCAL_MACHINE\SECURITY in compressed format
- *Setup.log* – The log of installed files with cyclic redundancy check data; this file is read only, system, and hidden by default
- *Software._* – The Registry key HKEY_LOCAL_MACHINE\SOFTWARE in compressed format
- *System._* – The Registry key HKEY_LOCAL_MACHINE\SYSTEM in compressed format

When installing Windows NT, it is recommended that you permit the system to create automatically an emergency repair disk when prompted (Figure 7.37). To update an existing emergency repair disk, invoke the VDM and type

```
rdisk /s
```

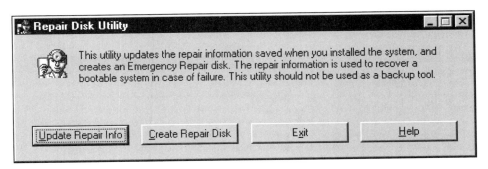

FIGURE 7.37.   Emergency Repair Disk Setup Screen

To create a new emergency repair disk, invoke the VDM and type

```
rdisk
```

The second rule is to understand how the Registry can be safely edited and managed. It is not recommended that the Registry be modified by hand or without cause. Random changes to application or device settings can render them useless. If you must change settings, utilize the handy System Policy Editor available for computer and user properties management (Figures 7.38 and 7.39). The system policies are stored in local machines at

- *%systemroot%\INF\COMMON.ADM* for user policies
- *%systemroot%\INF\WINNT.ADM* for other policies

To gain access to the System Policy Editor, select **Start** ➤ **Programs** ➤ **Administrative Tools** ➤ **System Policy Editor** ➤ **File** ➤ **Open Registry**.

NOTE   The Windows NT and Windows 95 registries are very similar in content but their structure and internal naming conventions are different. Therefore, it is not possible to exchange the binaries between the two operating systems.

Installations: Tips Not Covered or Obvious

It is our belief that Microsoft has done a very fine job in automating the installation process for both the workstation and server Windows NT versions. However, we have found several areas in which further clarification could be helpful.

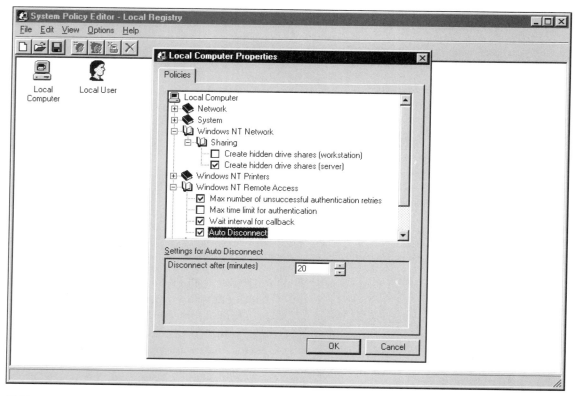

FIGURE 7.38.   System Policy Editor—Local Computer Properties

INSTALLING ON A RISC-BASED SYSTEM

The boot disks shipped with Windows NT are designed solely for Intel-class systems. To install Windows NT directly on a RISC-based system such as Digital's Alpha family, it is necessary to boot from the CD-ROM. The full device name is required. You need to invoke the system's ARC screen (which varies between systems, and you should consult the hardware documentation) and select **Run a Program**. At the prompt, type device name:\system type like ALPHA\ setupldr. For example, if the CD device is D: and the system type is ALPHA, you would enter d:\ALPHA\setupldr.

INSTALL THE PDC FIRST

If you plan to use the domain model, then it is very important that the PDC be the first system installed. During the installation process you are prompted to identify whether a system will be a PDC, BDC, or stand-alone server. The instal-

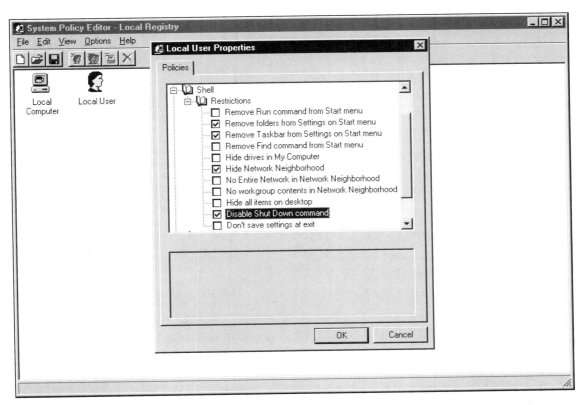

FIGURE 7.39.   System Policy Editor—Local User Properties

lation process involving domain installations requires an initial domain point or connection so that the uniqueness of the server name can be verified. Therefore, the first system should be the PDC and it should be operational before moving on to additional installations. Remember, this does not lock you into a permanent situation, as a BDC can be promoted to PDC status at a later date or you can reassign a server to a different domain.

MINIMUM SYSTEM REQUIREMENTS

Microsoft publishes recommended minimum system requirements for Windows NT of 16 MB of RAM. Although we have successfully tested the operating system with this configuration, we suggest that you at least double that level of RAM. Once you start loading applications like Office 97, the computer will begin to slow down seriously with only 16 MB of RAM. The good news is that RAM is now very cheap (at least for Intel-class machines). We recommend that the server have a minimum of 64 MB of RAM.

DOMAIN VERSUS WORKGROUP

The Installation Wizard automatically prompts you to select between joining a domain or a workgroup. The system administrator must predetermine the topological model to be used. Refer to the beginning of this chapter regarding the pros and cons of domains and workgroups. Also remember that the process of joining a domain requires that a PDC be installed first, in addition to being operational.

BE CAUTIOUS WHEN ASSIGNING DOMAIN NAMES

When assigning a domain name, make sure it is something that you can use for an extended period of time. Windows NT does not appreciate changing domain names. If the domain is changed, you will then need to reinstall new information on every server within the domain.

Backup/Restoration

The requirements for system backups and restorations are identical for both Windows NT and UNIX. The difference obviously resides with the available tools. Windows NT provides a nicely automated tool with which to perform backups and restorations (Figure 7.40). To access the Backup tool, select **Start ➤ Programs ➤ Administrative Tools ➤ Backup**.

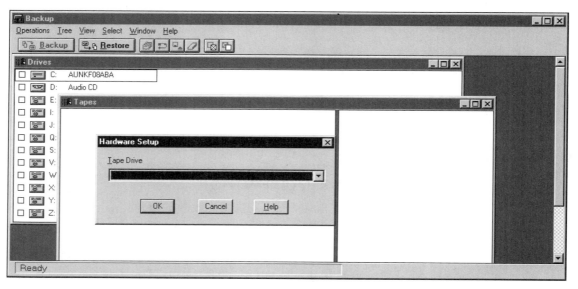

FIGURE 7.40.   Backup and Restoration Tool

TABLE 7.7.   Levels of Backup

Type	Description
Full-system backup	Backup of the entire operating system to be used in the case of full-system failure
Full disk image	Creation of a mirror image of the disk contents (not as commonly used)
Data partition	Backup of a particular disk partition
Backup for migration	Backup of software/system files in preparation for upgrade or replacement
Incremental backup	Scheduled backup of files changed since the last full-system backup
File-specific backup	Files of special importance that require special handling

The system administrator is responsible for establishing a backup scheme and should not forget the reasons for backups, including

- Data restoration, if lost by human error or sabotage
- Hardware failure that requires repair or replacement
- Disasters such earthquakes or hurricanes don't always happen to other people
- Backups are yet another form of data security

There are a number of different types of backup that must be considered as well. Table 7.7 describes these.

Hardware Addition and Removal

When contrasted with UNIX, the installation and removal of devices is child's play with Windows NT. As a system administrator you can forget about guessing which cryptic device listed in */etc/dev* is really a tape or a hard drive. You can also forget about recompiling the system kernel in order for the system to recognize a new device properly.

PLUG AND PLAY (PRAY?)

The first thing one notices with Windows NT is a feature known as Plug and Play. In theory, Windows NT searches the system and identifies all associated hardware. In our computer labs we have both brand name and off-label systems.

What we have determined is that Plug and Play works very well with brand names and more recent vintage computer systems. However, with more obscure systems, the identification process is more "plug and pray." In some cases the recognition process becomes as scary as any hardware addition under UNIX. However, this is really an exception to the rule. If you have retained the original device drivers for the hardware in question, Windows NT generally does a good job of supporting even ancient equipment.

HOW TO ADD AND REMOVE DEVICES

The Control Panel provides access to the addition, modification, and removal of most common devices (Figure 7.41). When the appropriate icon is selected, you are provided the necessary dialog boxes to accomplish the desired task. A brief examination of default Control Panel device-related objects shows the following items of interest:

- **Accessibility Options** – General, mouse, keyboard, and sound parameters
- **Devices** – Standard devices and their operational status, with the ability to enable, disable, and install other devices
- **Display** – Configuration of video adapters and display types, colors, fonts, screen saver, screen lock password, and so on
- **Keyboard** – Type and configuration of the keyboard
- **Modems** – Configuration of modem devices
- **Mouse** – Installed mouse settings
- **Multimedia** – Configuration of audio, video, MIDI, CD music, and other devices such as joysticks and mixers
- **PC Card** – Configuration of PCMIA cards
- **Ports** – Configuration of system ports
- **Printers** – Installation and setup of local and network printers including settings for device sharing
- **SCSI Adapters** – Addition and modification of SCSI adapters
- **Tape Devices** – Addition and removal of tape backup devices
- **UPS** – Setup for uninterrupted power supply

Remote Access Control

The Remote Access Service (RAS) is a facility common to UNIX systems and is fully implemented in Windows NT. It permits dial-in access that is supported over TCP/IP, IPX, or NetBEUI protocol connections. A client/server relationship

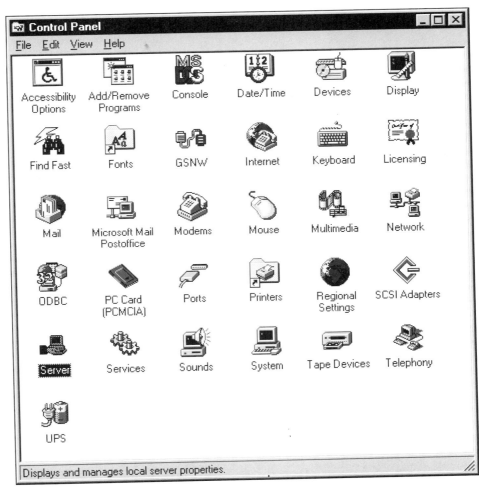

FIGURE 7.41.　Control Panel Selection of Hardware

exists between the remote client modem and the Windows NT RAS server. After a connection is made, the remote node is treated as a full client within Windows NT.

The Remote Access Administration tool supports configuration and user access. For example, if access is granted to a particular user or user group, then the system administrator can define the level of callback privileges. (See the earlier section on dial-in authority.) To gain access to the Remote Access Administration tool, select **Start ➤ Programs ➤ Administrative Tools ➤ Remote Access Admin** (Figure 7.42).

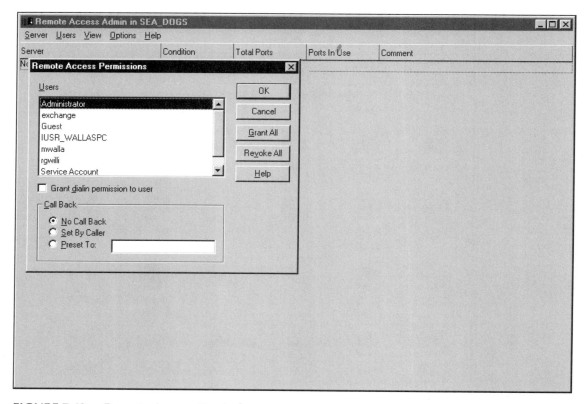

FIGURE 7.42.   Remote Access Controls

System Accounting and Monitoring

In Chapter 6, we discussed the use of the Task Manager and Event Viewer as providing additional information valuable to the administration of a Windows NT system or domain. Microsoft does not stop there in providing quality tools. The system administrator is charged with the responsibility of optimizing system performance.

Microsoft includes a performance monitoring tool that puts bundled UNIX utilities to shame and rivals third-party and expensive add-on software such as Hewlett-Packard's *GlancePlus* or Measureware. The Performance Monitor charts system activity, permits configuration of alerts, creates defined logs, and outputs appropriate reports (Figure 7.43). To gain access to the Performance Monitor, select **Start → Programs → Administrative Tools → Performance Monitor**.

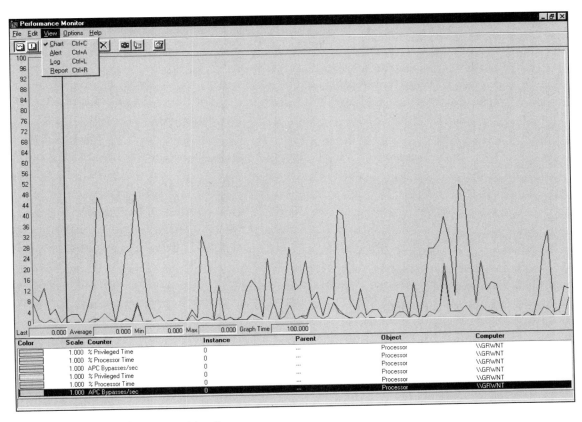

FIGURE 7.43.   Performance Monitor

The Windows NT Diagnostics tool permits the system administrator to perform more precise reviews of system activities. By selecting the appropriate tab, you can get a quick snapshot of memory, network, drive, and other activities (Figure 7.44). To access the Windows NT Diagnostics tool, select **Start ➤ Programs ➤ Administrative Tools ➤ Windows NT Diagnostics**.

There is an optional tool that is available on the Microsoft Windows NT Server 4.0 Resource Kit that provides excellent views of process activities. The Process Viewer alone justifies the price of the Resource Kit (Figure 7.45). Processor times broken down into the percent utilized by privileged processes and user processes can be helpful when memory constraints are an issue. Thread priority levels together with memory details are something that UNIX system administrators can only hope to see with some future product release.

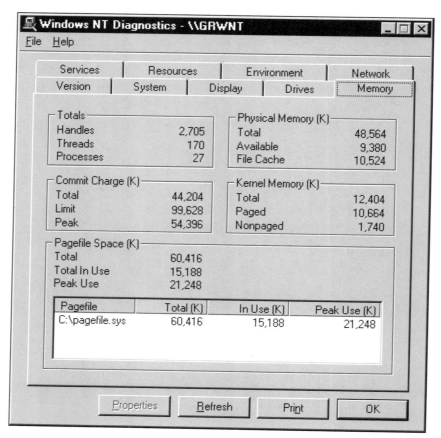

FIGURE 7.44.   System Diagnostics

Bottom Line: General Troubleshooting

The final and perhaps most demanding responsibility of any system administrator is troubleshooting. Fortunately, Windows NT provides graphically based clues in troubleshooting. In addition, good on-line reference documentation abounds to decipher fingerprints left by user or system problems. The first art a system administrator learns is how to determine the question that must be asked. Does an occurrence appear to be hardware, software, or user error? Sometimes the answer is obvious; other times only reviewing log files, tracing coaxial wire connectors, or analyzing application memory allocations will pro-

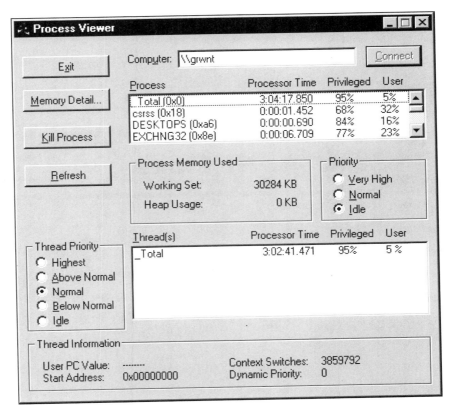

FIGURE 7.45.   Process Viewer from Resource Kit

vide the answer. As we have discussed, tools like the Task Manager, Performance Monitor, and Diagnostics applications are bundled with Windows NT and are only an expensive option with UNIX. The investigative burden with Windows NT is thereby greatly reduced. These tools notwithstanding, the job of the Windows NT system administrator is always challenging and never dull.

# Chapter 8

Advanced and Miscellaneous Windows NT Topics

Chapters 6 and 7 are billed as primers for Windows NT system administration. This chapter reviews topics not otherwise discussed in the previous chapters and items that need further elaboration. Each section in this chapter is treated as a discrete component. The following items are covered:

- Using Windows NT Help as an answer to UNIX *man* pages
- Security modeling issues
- Interfaces and user accessibility
- Replication services
- Configuring client systems
- Introduction to the BackOffice suite

Appendix A rounds out the primer with a review of common Windows NT commands, utilities, and functions.

HELP—NO *man* PAGES

Earlier we suggested that you become very familiar with the UNIX *man*(ual) pages—the on-line documentation for UNIX commands and procedures. Windows NT Server 4.0 provides an equally powerful set of on-line documentation in the form of its Help system. Windows NT Help is a well-indexed, graphic documentation set that should ease much system administrator and end user confusion. As a basic assessment, however, old UNIX hacks may find Windows NT Help to be a little too general in focus and "choppy" in presentation because large topics often span numerous screens.

The general-purpose Windows NT Help is available from the **Start** menu. Context-specific help is obtained from within utilities and applications through their respective tool bars. When invoking general Windows NT Help, a three-tab dialog box appears on screen that provides several methods of locating appropriate information.

1. **Contents** *tab* – This tab lists the primary available topics in the subject area in a format similar to a book's table of contents (Figure 8.1). By clicking on a subject, lists of subtopics are often displayed. From these lists, a selection of the desired item is made by double clicking the topic.

2. **Index** *tab* – This tab provides a comprehensive list of all related topics similar to an index in a book (Figure 8.2). By typing the first few letters of a topic on the first option line, the listings in the lower half of the dialog box will scroll to match your input.

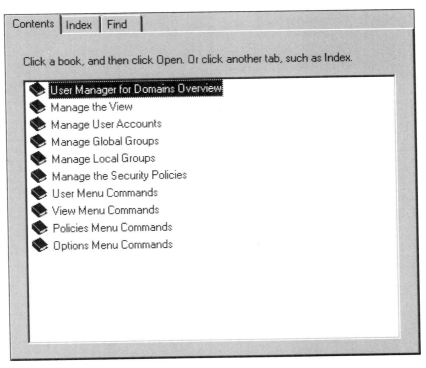

FIGURE 8.1. Windows NT Help Contents Dialog Box

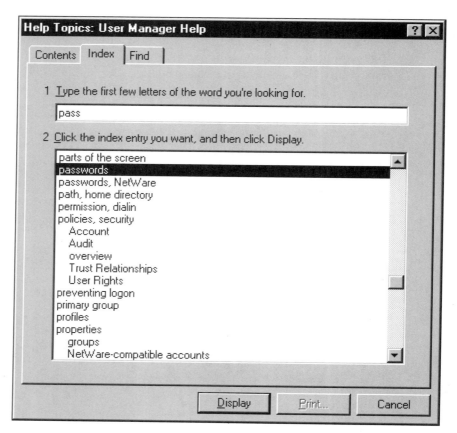

FIGURE 8.2.   Index Tab of Windows NT Help by Topic Area

3. Find tab – This tab provides a method of finding help more globally for each item entered by the user in line 1 (Figure 8.3). Alternately, you can scroll through the list and then select the desired item by double clicking the mouse or pressing the **Display** button.

The actual presentation of Help is straightforward and often contains step-by-step instructions. Hypertext links to other topics are often included, and pop-up bubble screens are used to clarify definitions as shown in Figure 8.4. Help screens can be printed, copied to other documents, or "bookmarked" for easy future reference. You can return to the previous help screen by pressing the **Back** button and return to the index listing by selecting the **Help Topics** button.

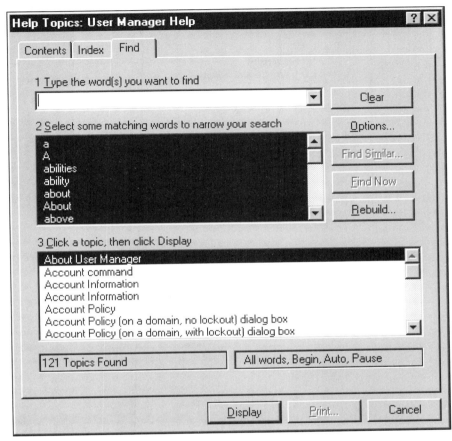

FIGURE 8.3.   Find Tab for Windows NT Help

SECURITY

Windows NT was designed with world-class security in mind. The level of security in the Windows NT operating system certainly rivals that of UNIX. The security model was designed to comply with United States and international security requirements.

Designing and implementing a security plan starts with understanding the type of security issues facing system administrators. An often-made mistake is to assume that security measures center solely on averting attacks from unauthorized users. Guarding against malicious behavior is very important, but it is not the only focus. Security also includes computer hardware protection, data preservation, and system accountability. A comprehensive plan includes attention to the following items at a minimum:

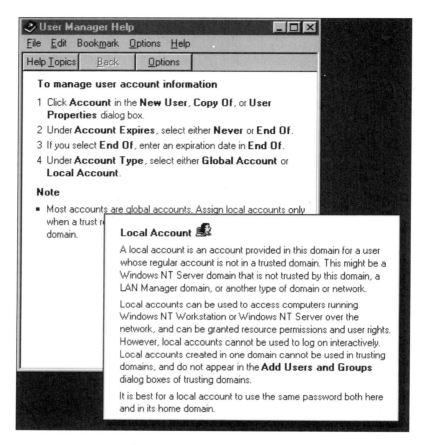

FIGURE 8.4.   Sample Help Screen with Bubble Pop-up

- *User accounts* – Monitoring authorized users and maintaining proper privileges as discussed in Chapters 6 and 7
- *Network accessibility* – Controlling a variety of access points and protocols as discussed in Chapter 12 and 13
- *Physical hardware* – Protecting the physical computer and its peripherals as discussed later in this section
- *System backups* – Managing adequate backups to support disaster recovery as discussed in Chapter 7
- *Software and applications* – Preserving software and licenses as discussed in Chapter 7
- *Viruses and Trojan horses* – Preventing the flow of destructive software invaders as discussed later in this section

- *File system* – Maintaining proper permissions on system files and directories as discussed in Chapter 6 and amplified later in this section

Security Model Components

The Windows NT security model is comprised of four primary ingredients:

1. *Logon processes* – Windows NT requires interactive logon with password dialog entry before access can be obtained.
2. *Local security authority* – This verifies that the person attempting a logon has authority by creating security access tokens in accordance with local policies. Audits and log files can be used to help detect potential abuse.
3. *Security Account Manager* – The SAM database contains information about users and group accounts, and validates appropriate rights and authorities.
4. *Security Reference Monitor* – The SRM reviews permissions when a user requests access to an object. If validated, the user can access the object to the level defined (read, write, and so forth).

Windows NT treats everything as an object with specific *security descriptors*. The object's security information is stored in the *Access Control List* (ACL), including which users and groups are allowed or denied access at various privilege levels. Each of these items is known as an *Access Control Entry* (ACE). (See Chapter 6 for additional, related information on permissions and ownership.)

On successful logon, the user is passed a Security Access Token (SAT) that contains information about the user's rights and group memberships. When a user attempts to open a file object, for example, the SRM reviews all the ACEs until access is explicitly granted or denied (Figure 8.5).

NTFS Versus FAT Security

NTFS provides clearly superior security options to the earlier FAT file system. NTFS was built from the ground up as a security-based file system. NTFS's first line of defense is access and file permissions. As discussed in Chapter 6, NTFS encompasses the levels of ownership and permissions available in UNIX and adds a number of additional features. By contrast, FAT is virtually unsecured, with the exception of logon procedures (passwords) and screen saver locks. On a network, any folder that is shared out is vulnerable to the whims of other users. FAT files cannot be protected on the basis of either permissions or ownership. The system administrator should make users of FAT-based Windows NT installations aware of these security shortcomings.

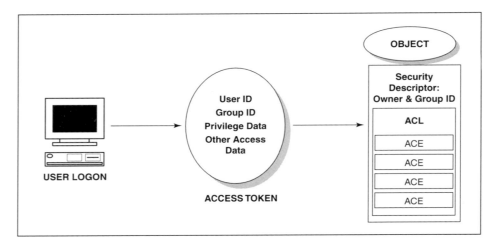

FIGURE 8.5.   Simplified View of SRM System

Physical Security

Controlling physical access to systems is one of the most overbearing issues with any operating system and especially Windows NT. Since the vast majority of Windows NT workstations and servers are run on Intel-based boxes, physical security breaches on local systems are relatively easy. With a floppy disk containing the DOS operating system, it is possible to gain access to Windows NT data using the FAT file system. By rebooting the system with the DOS diskette, the DOS system then permits access to files resident on local hard drives. The system administrator must be aware of this potential problem.

Unauthorized access can also be gained to NTFS systems if the intruder has a valid boot disk, although this takes a little more skill. Since it is not our objective to provide potential hackers a road map for destructive practices, we will not pursue the methodology involved. It is only fair to say that protecting your Windows NT Server 4.0 physically is an important consideration for any system administrator.

NOTE   In all fairness, Windows NT is not the only operating system subject to physical security breaches. Having a boot disk for UNIX systems is typically a key for intrusive security problems. Since many larger UNIX systems are big boxes with control room access, the problem may not seem as prevalent as desktop PCs that are located everywhere. However, the reality still remains that UNIX boxes are just as open to physical abuse as Windows NT if left unchecked.

C2 Security

The United States Department of Defense established the C2-level specifications under the *Trusted Computer System Evaluation Criteria* (also known as the *Orange Book*), published in 1985. The National Computer Security Center (NCSC) evaluates and certifies products for C2 compliance. Windows NT is now certified C2 compliant; this is an important designation that Microsoft needed to achieve in order to be able to play in the lucrative federal government marketplace.

C2 offers a powerful set of features. Its implementation should be considered when particularly sensitive data is involved. However, it also provides the negative impact of reduced access flexibility. It is difficult to back out C2 level functionality completely after it is installed. The scope of this book does not permit further discussion of C2 security. However, the Windows NT Server 4.0 Resource Kit does provide a tool to implement C2 security (Figure 8.6). A good resource on C2 is the Microsoft white paper entitled *Windows NT C2 Security System Administration Guide.*

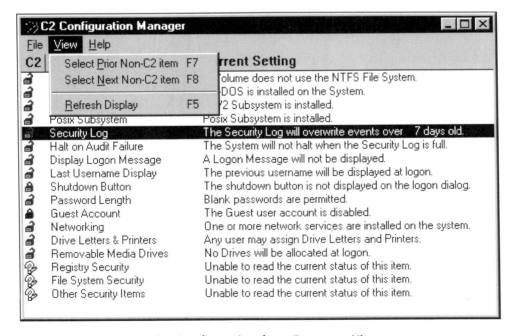

FIGURE 8.6.   C2 Security Configuration from Resource Kit

Viruses and Trojan Horses

Seemingly harmless gifts of software can cripple countless computer systems. Unlike UNIX, the older DOS and Windows environments are very vulnerable to computer-born viruses. Fortunately, most common computer viruses are normally held at bay by the permissions security features inherent in Windows NT using NTFS. However, it is still possible that an unwanted virus may attack valuable system and user files. In a trusted domain model, a wild virus can be extremely costly. The Internet is currently the single greatest vehicle for viruses. Therefore we strongly urge that antivirus software be installed on Windows NT servers and workstations together with antivirus applet plug-ins for Web browsers.

A Trojan horse is a little more difficult to manage and detect. This is a computer program that is purported to accomplish one thing but in reality executes something more sinister. Before installing software, make sure that you are sure of its origin. Commercial software is generally safe, as the publisher runs serious credibility and financial risks for not reviewing distributions prior to release. In the case of shareware, install it and test it as a restricted user before making it available to the general user community. Also, if possible forbid the installation or downloading of any software by a user without the prior permission of the system administrator. We recognize such restrictions are impossible to enforce in practice; therefore this is when your backup policy will save the day if data is destroyed as a result of an invasion.

USER INTERFACE

One of the major enhancements to Windows NT 4.0 was the adoption of the popular Window 95 GUI (Figure 8.7). Windows NT 4.0 was called the *Shell release* during beta testing because of the overlay of this Windows 95 interface. It is assumed that readers of this book understand how to use this interface and how to modify its look and feel. Unfortunately, not all users will have such knowledge. Therefore, to facilitate learning and reduce unnecessary user questions, system administrators might consider creating a default Windows NT scheme.

Future Windows NT interfaces will reflect the movement of related technologies such as a rumored move to a Web browser-like front end. Windows NT 5.0 may also have several faces depending on its application as a home, small business, or large commercial implementation.

Virtual DOS Machine

Another interface that will probably be employed by UNIX users for command line utilities is the VDM—the MD-DOS emulator bundled with Windows NT.

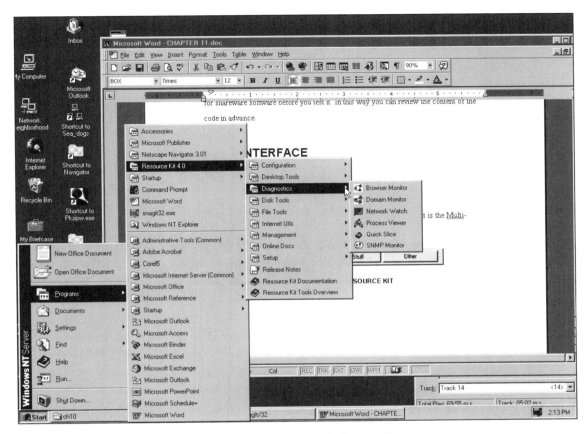

FIGURE 8.7.   Windows 95 User Interface Used in Windows NT

The first thing that UNIX users will notice is that the VDM permits the use of both DOS-like backslash and UNIX-style forward slash in defined paths. This is a nice little convenience for command line UNIX users. Many of the commands described in Appendix A are launched from the character-based VDM (Figure 8.8). In practical terms the VDM acts like a dumb terminal screen with regard to input and output. To access the VDM, select **Start ➞ Programs ➞ Command Prompt**.

Multi-Desktop for UNIX CDE Users

UNIX X-Windows users will feel comfortable with the transition to the Windows 95 interface. The point-and-click, drag, and drop functions are very similar if the user has worked with the Motif-based CDE. A nice utility is Multi-Desktop, which is shipped with the Windows NT Resource Kit (Figure 8.9). This utility

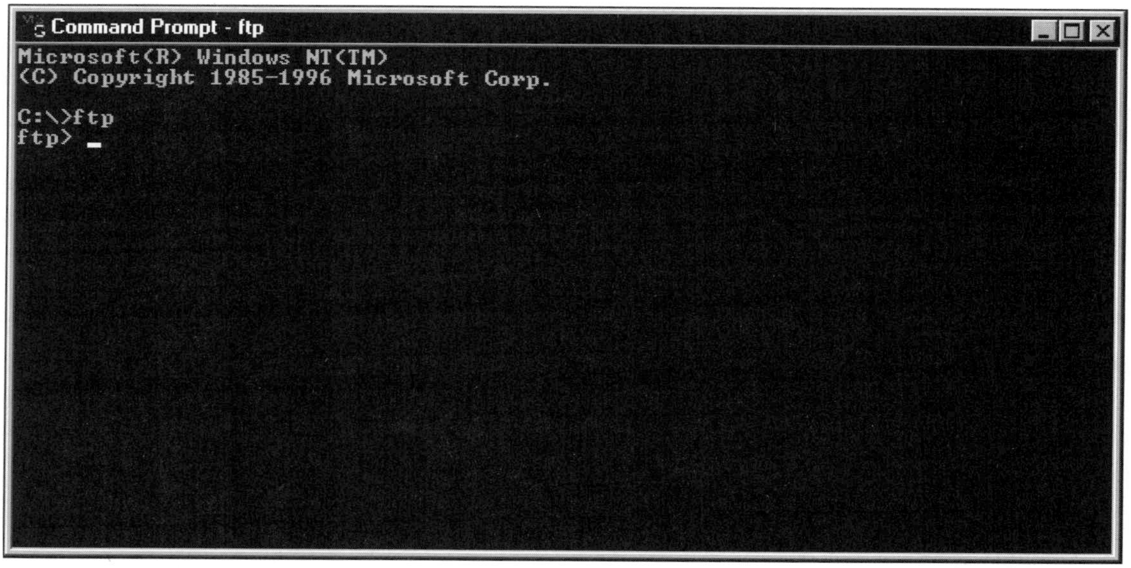
Command Prompt - ftp
Microsoft(R) Windows NT(TM)
(C) Copyright 1985-1996 Microsoft Corp.
C:\>ftp
ftp>

FIGURE 8.8. VDM Command Screen

permits the user to define multiple, concurrent desktops for different work activities and personal business.

REPLICATION SERVICE

Windows NT offers a facility known as Replication that permits the synchronization of directories, system files, databases, and other documents residing on one computer for duplication to other systems or the entire domain. This feature can be particularly helpful in a number of situations, including

- Shifting the processing load from a single computer to multiple systems
- Duplicating logon scripts that are not maintained by the PDC relationship or within the SAM database
- Archiving information across redundant systems

Replication involves duplication of selected information from a master source called the *export server* and download to one or more *import servers.*

ToolGroup
BobStuff
Other

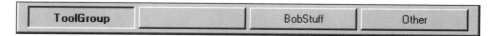

FIGURE 8.9. Microsoft Multi-Desktop from Resource Kit

The export server must be Windows NT Server 4.0, whereas the import servers can be Windows NT servers, workstations, or LAN Manager server boxes. The default export directory is defined as *\%systemroot%\System32\Repl\Export* and the default import directory is *\%systemroot%\System32\Repl\Import*. The export server can export only one directory tree for replication purposes. It is possible to lock subdirectories or individual files within the replication export directory tree so that they are not duplicated. The Replicator service checks the export server for changes at five-minute intervals, but if necessary you can change the interval parameter in the Registry to anything between one and sixty minutes.

There are three basic steps involved in creating a replication scenario:

1. Create a special user account in both the export and import servers.
2. Configure the export server with a defined export directory tree.
3. Configure the import servers with a defined import directory tree.

Creating the Replication User Account

A special user must be created to permit replication. The special replication user is not to be confused with the built-in Replicator group. There are a few rules that must be followed in creating this user. Invoke **User Manager for Domains** to create a new user as discussed earlier. The following specific items must be included in the definitions.

- Make the user part of the Domain Backup Operator, Domain Users, and Replicator groups.
- Set the password to the **never expires** setting.
- Make the account accessible 24 hours per day.
- Make sure that you use the same user name and password on both export and import servers. Remember that a user must be set up on the export server and all import servers.

Starting the Replication Services

After the special user account is established you need to next make sure that the Directory Replication service is running. To accomplish this task, select Start ➤ Settings ➤ Control Panel ➤ Services. In the Services window, select **Directory Replicator** from the Service list, then select **Start**.

While you still have the Services dialog box displayed (Figure 8.10), select the **Startup** button so that the Services dialog box for the Directory Replicator is displayed (Figure 8.11). Change the designation from **Manual** to **Automatic** so that the replication service is started the next time the system is booted.

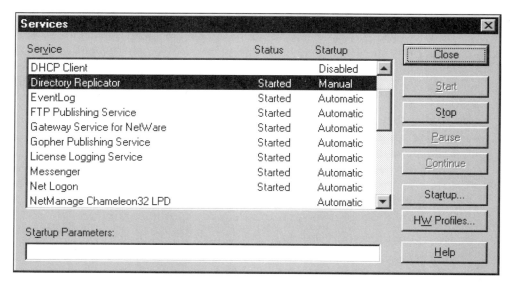

FIGURE 8.10.   Services Dialog Box

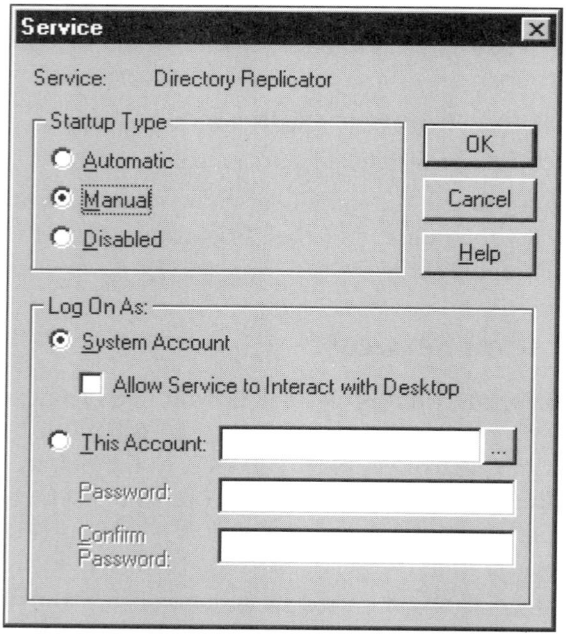

FIGURE 8.11.   Service Start-up Dialog Box

Preparing the Replication Export Server

The actual configuration of the Replication server involves two primary tasks: (1) defining the export directory tree with appropriate locks, as needed; and (2) identifying the import servers to receive the replicated data. To configure the export server, follow these steps:

1. Select **Start** ➤ **Settings** ➤ **Control Panel** ➤ **Server**.

2. In the Server window, select the **Replication** button. The Directory Replication dialog box should now be displayed (Figure 8.12).

3. Select the **Export Directories** radio button.

4. In the **From Path** field, enter the export directory if different from the default.

5. In the **To List** field, list all import servers and domains by selecting the **Add** button then choosing the servers or domains to add. By default, the **To List** field is left blank because it is assumed the replication is to take place within

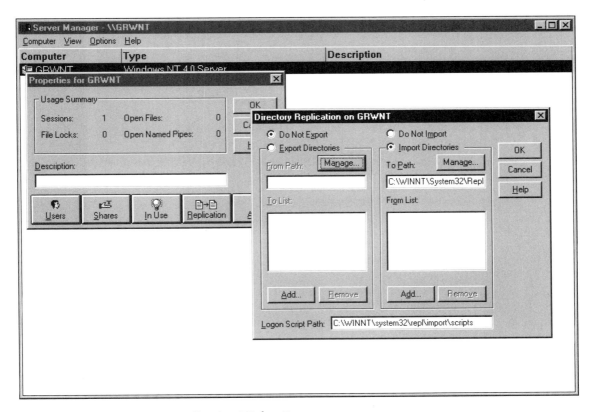

FIGURE 8.12.   Directory Replication Dialog Box

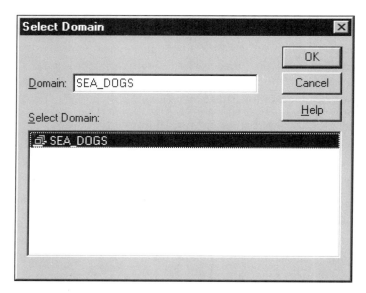

FIGURE 8.13.   Select Domain Dialog Box

the local domain. If you add other domains or systems, the local domain must also be listed to ensure its inclusion if desired. If you press the **Add** button, the Select Domain dialog box is displayed (Figure 8.13) so you may include domains and individual import systems.

If you want to control how specific subdirectories are handled, press the **Manage** button in the Directory Replication dialog box. The Manage Exported Directories window is now displayed (Figure 8.14). Select the **Add** or **Remove** button to manage specific subdirectories. From this window you may

- Select the button to lock a subdirectory from being exported
- Select the **Wait Until Stabilized** check box to instruct the export server to wait for two minutes before actually exporting the subdirectory
- Select the **Entire Subtree** check box if you want the entire subtree exported; otherwise only the first-level subdirectory is exported

All changes are retained when you select the **OK** button on the Directory Replication dialog box.

Preparing the Replication Import Server

The process of configuring the import server is very similar to the steps followed when creating the export server. You must establish an import directory

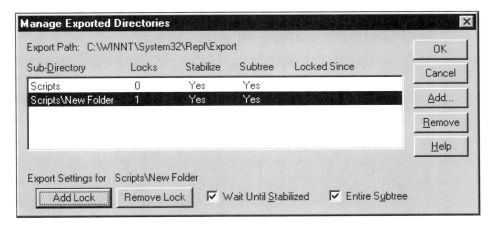

FIGURE 8.14.   Managed Exported Directories Dialog Box

point for replication and determine which export systems will be allowed to import the information. Use the following procedure.

1. Select **Start** ➤ **Settings** ➤ **Control Panel** ➤ **Server** ➤ **Replication**.

2. In the Directory Replication window, select the **Import Directories** radio button.

3. If the import directory is not the default *\%systemroot%\System32\Repl\ Import,* then change the path listed in the **To Path** field.

4. If you want to accept imports from other than the default local domain computer, select the **Add** button. The Select Domain dialog box now appears and you may add individual machines or other domains. Remember that the local domain must be added specifically if it is also to provide exports.

5. Finally, press the **Manage** button if you want to interact specifically with imported subdirectories, including adding locks to restrict the import.

CONFIGURING CLIENT COMPUTER SYSTEMS

Windows NT Server 4.0 supports an array of client machines, including old MS-DOS, Windows 3.1, and Macintosh computers. We center on the configuration of Windows 95, Windows NT Workstation, and UNIX clients. A brief description on the setup of the other systems is also provided. Connecting these machines via the TCP/IP network is the central focus because it is the common networking foundation between Microsoft operating systems and UNIX. Chapters 12 and 13 provide an in-depth review of the TCP/IP protocol. This section merely steps you through some of the related processes.

Windows 95, Windows NT Workstation, and UNIX-compatible Clients

The process of preparing Windows 95 and Windows NT Workstation client computers is very similar. By default they load the Windows Network and Windows NWlink networking stack. To connect a UNIX box, TCP/IP must be loaded explicitly. We center our discussion based on the assumption that eventual UNIX connectivity is required and a TCP/IP network is being used by default. The process involves three generic steps:

1. Configuring the network hardware
2. Configuring the selected network protocols
3. Connecting to the Windows NT 4.0 server

CONFIGURING THE NETWORK HARDWARE

The first task is to identify and load the drivers properly for the network cards installed on your client system. Compared with a similar task associated with the UNIX system, Microsoft has made the process relatively painless. To begin the process, select **Start** ➤ **Settings** ➤ **Control Panel** ➤ **Network** ➤ **Adapters** ➤ **Add**.

The Select Network Adapter dialog box (Figure 8.15) appears, from which you should select the type of network card adapter that is installed. In some cases, you need the original manufacturer's device driver set on diskette when prompted on screen.

You should follow the instructions in the subsequent set of dialog boxes to complete the adapter installation. We recommend that you refer to the manufacturer's manual for specific information relative to settings appropriate to your particular hardware.

CONFIGURING THE SELECTED NETWORK PROTOCOLS

The next step is to switch to the **Protocols** tab screen. (You can do this by selecting the Network icon from the Control Panel.) NetBEUI and NWlink protocols should already be visible (Figure 8.16). If you also plan to connect to a UNIX box, the future installation of TCP/IP is required. To include the TCP/IP stack, select **Add** and then select **TCP/IP Protocol** from the dialog box.

After the TCP/IP protocol is added, you need to configure the various elements. Chapters 12 and 13 detail the use and meaning of the IP address, DNS, WINS, Dynamic Host Configuration Protocl (DHCP), and routing (Figure 8.17).

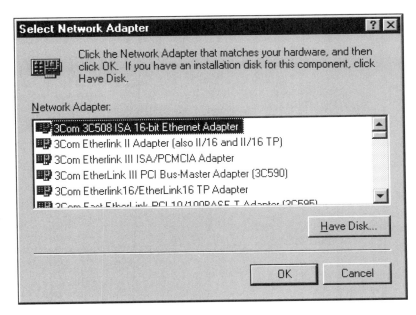

FIGURE 8.15.   Select Network Adapter Dialog Box

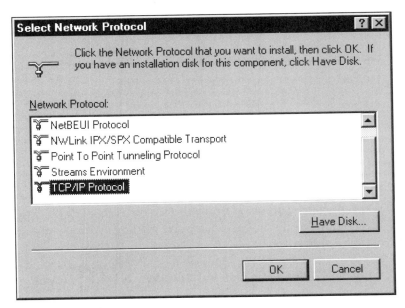

FIGURE 8.16.   Adding the TCP/IP Protocol

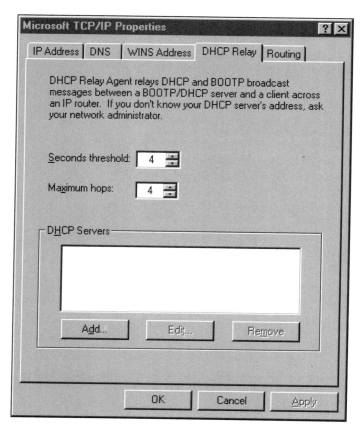

FIGURE 8.17.   TCP/IP Properties Dialog Box

Depending on your particular environment, each of these items must be completed correctly.

The next step is to bind the protocols to the network adapters. This is accomplished by moving to the **Bindings** tab from the Network window. Press the **Enable** button to bind all the network services (Figure 8.18). Alternately, you can enable and display only those protocols that you anticipate utilizing. It is recommended that you enable the binding sparingly to minimize computer resource utilization.

CONNECTING TO THE WINDOWS NT 4.0 SERVER

The final and perhaps most critical step is joining the workgroup or domain. This is done by selecting the **Identification** tab from the Network dialog box. You must enter the name of the local system and the name of the domain or

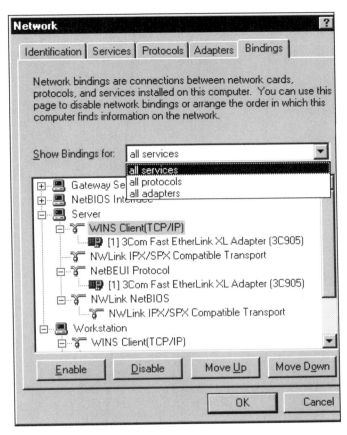

FIGURE 8.18.   Bindings Dialog Box

workgroup (Figure 8.19). Computer names must be unique for a given work-group or domain. When you press the **OK** button, this information is communicated to the network and you receive the appropriate acknowledgment from the workgroup or domain server.

NOTE   In a domain model, the system administrator must add the client/server to the list of hosts before connection can occur. This is done via the Server Manager on the domain server.

It is fairly straightforward to move a system from one workgroup or domain to another. From within the **Identification** tab, select **Change** and complete

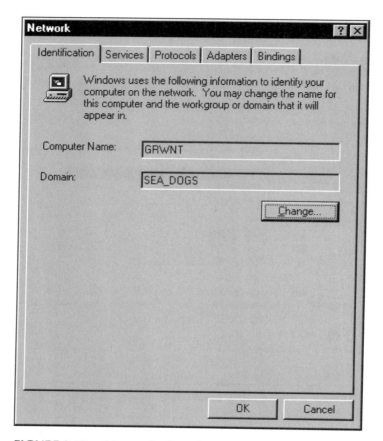

FIGURE 8.19.   Network Identification Tab

the information for the new workgroup or domain respectively (Figure 8.20). If you are logged on as the Administrator, then you can also create a user account on the domain from this dialog box by selecting the checkbox **Create a Computer Account in the Domain**.

NOTE   The look of some of the specific dialog boxes used in Windows 95 and Windows NT Workstation is different; however, the basic content required is generally the same. Refer to the on-line help provided with each dialog box for clarification. For additional information regarding the final step in connecting UNIX clients, see Chapters 12 and 13.

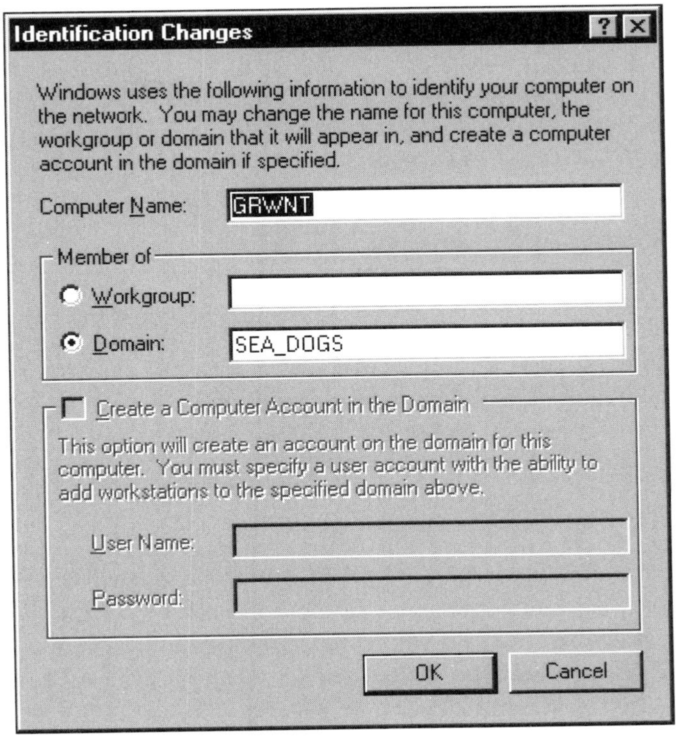

FIGURE 8.20.   Change in Network Identification

Installing Other Clients

An important feature of Windows NT Server 4.0 is the ability to support so many divergent network clients. For example, to install an MS-DOS client successfully, the creation of special network installation diskettes may be required. To create a network installation disk for a client computer you must have available the CD containing Windows NT Server 4.0 and the number of formatted 1.44-MB diskettes listed in Table 8.1.

Once equipped with these tools, continue as follows: **Start** → **Programs** → **Administrative Tools** → **Network Client Administrator**. The Network Client Administrator dialog box is now displayed (Figure 8.21). Select **Make Installation Disk Set**.

The next dialog box (Figure 8.22) asks for the path of the source media (in this case it is the path of your CD that contains Windows NT Server 4.0). After pressing **OK,** a dialog box appears that permits you to define the type of desired client software to be created.

TABLE 8.1.   Formatted Diskettes Required for Installation

Client product description	Number of diskettes
Network Client v3.0 for MS-DOS and Windows	2
Remote Access v1.1a for MS-DOS	1
TCP/IP 32 for Windows for Workgroups 3.11	1
LAN Manager	4
LAN Manager v2.2c for MS-DOS	4

After these diskettes are created, it is a generally a matter of rebooting from the target client system first and following the on-screen prompts to install and connect the computer to Windows NT Server 4.0.

BACKOFFICE SUITE

The Microsoft Windows NT BackOffice suite is an optional set of applications that greatly augments the scope of Windows NT Server 4.0. One of the components is the Exchange Server, which provides world-class e-mail services on groupware functions. We discuss the Exchange Server in Chapter 14 when we explore the interoperability of e-mail and communications involving UNIX and Windows NT. The other BackOffice packages also deserve a mention, although it is not in the scope of this book to provide a comprehensive review. An excellent resource on the topic was written by one of our contributors, Barrie Sosinsky, entitled *The BackOffice BIBLE* (published by IDG Books, 1997). Another source is Microsoft's Web page http://www.backoffice.microsoft.com. A summary of the BackOffice product suite follows.

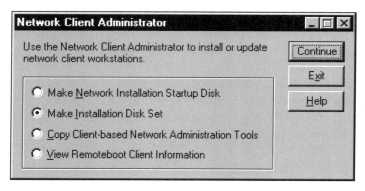

FIGURE 8.21.   Network Client Administrator Dialog Box

FIGURE 8.22.   Make Installation Disk Set Dialog Box

SQL Server 6.5

SQL Server has a long development legacy, beginning in 1988 under a joint development agreement between Sybase, Ashton-Tate, and Microsoft for OS/2. Soon after its acquisition by Borland International, Ashton-Tate severed the relationship. Microsoft then marketed the enhanced code for the Windows environment and Sybase introduced SQL Server for UNIX. In 1993, Sybase and Microsoft parted company, with each organization promoting their respective version. SQL Server embraces client/server relational database technology using structured query language (SQL) syntax. Due to the limitations of Intel-class processors, the Microsoft SQL Server has been relegated to departmental usage to date. This position is changing rapidly as a symmetrical processing architecture with faster chip performance makes enterprise-level database utilization possible with the Microsoft SQL Server.

Exchange Server 5.0

Exchange Server is an electronic mail system with built-in groupware. The most important additions to Exchange Server 5.0 in regard to the UNIX community is the bundling of the SMTP and the X.500 directory services. We examine the interoperability of the Exchange Server implementation with UNIX in Chapter 14. Figure 8.23 displays the Exchange Server client named Outlook.

System Management Server 1.2

The System Management Server (SMS) is an advanced suite of remote administration tools for the Windows NT configuration with specific attention to WAN and LAN functionality. SMS has an extensive troubleshooting capacity. It provides

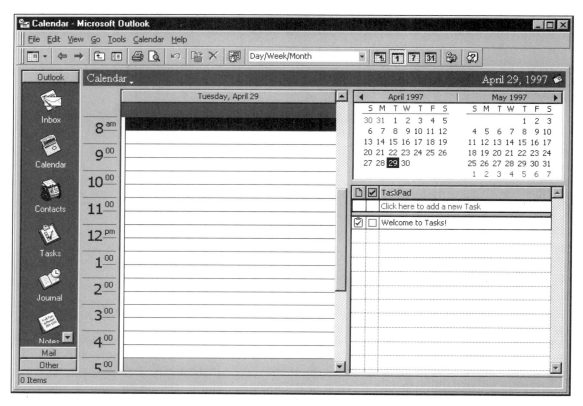

FIGURE 8.23.   Outlook Exchange Client Software

hardware and software inventory management and distribution functionality. Network protocol analysis is also included. SMS extends the already fine Windows NT performance-monitoring tool set. However, due to the complexity of this product, extensive planning of topology is recommended before implementation. Planning and deployment issues are discussed in Microsoft-published white papers that can be downloaded from `http://www.microsoft.com/SMSmgmt/`.

SNA Server 2.11

The SNA Server is Microsoft's accommodation to mainframe and AS/400 connectivity of the IBM System Network Architecture (SNA). SNA Server is first and foremost a gateway. Microsoft also provides an API to allow third-party software vendors the ability to write directly for the SNA marketplace.

Coexistence and Migration with UNIX and Windows NT

Operating system coexistence and integration is the primary focus of Part III, along with discussions of application porting issues. Part III begins with an examination in Chapter 9 of planning and deployment concepts. Chapter 10 centers on base-level technologies that facilitate operating system coexistence. The porting of UNIX applications to Windows NT is discussed in Chapter 11, with specific reference to application development tools.

- Chapter 9, Planning and Implementation Issues
- Chapter 10, UNIX and Windows NT Coexistence
- Chapter 11, Application Migration Issues

Chapter 9

Planning and Implementation Issues

In this chapter we examine the planning and implementation issues surrounding the introduction of Windows NT into a UNIX enterprise. We assume that the UNIX network is already in place and that the impacts to the enterprise involve Windows NT. As Windows NT enters the UNIX environment, a paradigm shift must occur. Three primary implementation alternative approaches generally surface either sequentially or concurrently:

1. **Coexistence**—How do you employ cooperative technologies?
2. **Integration**—What technologies facilitate interoperability?
3. **Migration**—Regarding legacy applications, how can you move from UNIX to Windows NT?

When faced with the task of coexisting, integrating, and migrating UNIX and Windows NT, a system administrator can easily become overwhelmed. Unfortunately, there is no clear blueprint for deploying and implementing a mixed or moving environment. Therefore, this chapter is not a definitive guide to coexistence, integration, or migration. Instead, its aim is to provide you with food for thought, information to help you develop a unique migration plan catered to your organization's needs and structure. The specific topics covered in this chapter include

- Conceptual views of where to begin
- Determining your organizational model
- Selecting a topological model
- Determining file system type
- Identifying server types

- Requirements for implementation
- Training
- Implementing the migration plan
- Postimplementation dilemmas

WHERE DO I START?

The entire issue of planning for a mixed operating system environment harkens the fabled question: Which came first, the chicken or the egg? Part of the reason that this type of planning seems so complex is that there is no clear top-down approach, such as executing one step at a time. In reality, you will probably be reviewing, defining, and executing several parts of the plan at the same time. Regardless, several issues must be resolved.

- What is the nature of your current UNIX enterprise?
- Does a single or multiple operating system environment make the best sense?
- Do you undertake the planning and deployment yourself or do you engage help?
- What organizational dynamics exist that will impact deployment?
- What network topological model should be employed?
- Where do you want the network to be in five years?

Understanding Your Current UNIX Environment

Reviewing your current configuration of hardware and software helps to determine issues that must be addressed as part of the migration. While reviewing your UNIX environment, you may want to determine answers to questions such as

- Do users access the UNIX system using dumb or character-based terminals, X-terminals, PCs running emulation software, or individual UNIX workstations?
- How are the users' terminals connected to the UNIX processor? Directly? Via a TCP/IP network, a modem, or other networking equipment?
- Develop a breakdown of the applications used on the system. Were they developed in-house or by a third party?
- How do you manage or migrate legacy software and hardware?
- How many physical locations are connected? Where are these locations? How many users are at each location?

- What other peripherals are connected (such as printers, fax machines, tape drives, modems)? Where are these peripherals physically located? How are they currently connected?

Single Versus Multiple Operating System Environments

After reviewing the current operating system environment, you need to determine how much of your enterprise you are going to migrate. Are you going to migrate the entire operation to one operating system or are you going to migrate only a portion so that you will be running multiple operating systems? A decision to migrate, coexist, or integrate presents both opportunities and costs. The ledger used to measure these benefits and risks is not just financial. A full scope of issues enters into the decision. Only in rare instances does an organization have sufficient resources to make an all-out move. Most organizations, however, do not have the luxury of abandoning existing equipment, software, and most importantly, people with older skills. Retrofitting and accommodating both equipment and people must enter into the scheme. Ultimately, technology is only as good as the people using the devices. Given the mix of available people skills, a long-term perspective on overall direction should be applied to formulate future buying decisions and training/support requirements.

ARGUMENTS FOR A SINGLE OPERATING SYSTEM ENVIRONMENT

The continued level of incompatibility of UNIX variants frustrates many technological officers. Despite much "lip service" given to the unification of UNIX by major vendors, the reality remains that the many flavors of UNIX create a mind-boggling nightmare for system administrators. For example, we could easily fill dozens of pages of text just detailing the differences between the latest versions of Hewlett-Packard HP-UX 10.x and IBM AIX 4.x. Is there any wonder that the prospect of a single-vendor world-class client/server operating system is so attractive? The ground swell for Windows NT has grown at least partially out of frustration with UNIX. Some information system managers have already jumped the UNIX ship and have implemented a policy of adopting a single-vendor operating system migration. When we speak of migration, the trend is unquestionably away from UNIX to Windows NT. (However, although it's rare, we have spoken to administrators who elected to deinstall Windows NT in favor of UNIX due to a belief that NT's functionality was oversold.) The following factors are among the reasons to opt for a single operating system environment.

- Both operating systems support Intel-class hardware and some RISC-based architectures
- The underlying TCP/IP network structure is practically identical
- Emulation programs exist on both UNIX and Windows NT to support the most popular applications originally designed for the other operating system
- Services such as electronic mail and remote printing can be configured to afford transparent interoperability
- User training on a single, familiar operating system is more cost-effective

ARGUMENTS AGAINST A SINGLE OPERATING SYSTEM ENVIRONMENT

As attractive as migrating appears on the surface, the costs in both human and computing resources cannot be understated. Further, there are types of enterprises where UNIX has the functional advantage. When considering the task of migrating solely to one operating system over the other, the following are a few of the reasons that seem to impinge negatively on such a decision:

- The two operating systems are not currently equal in terms of processing power or scalability
- Many mission-critical software applications do not run on both operating systems
- Disparity in the functionality and quality of user interfaces exists
- An enormous amount of initial user training is likely
- A high level of system administrative skill in both environments is required regardless of the operating system chosen
- The software development environments and APIs are radically different

SO WHAT SHOULD YOU DO?

There is no such thing as a one-size-fits-all operating system. Microsoft officials strongly urge a complete adoption of Windows NT, whereas most UNIX vendors are now supporting an integrated solution. Frankly, our biased recommendation for most enterprises is a mixed UNIX and Windows NT installation because of the unique functionality of the two operating systems. However, there are a few fundamental questions that need to be asked before making the decision, including

- What is motivating the change? Pressing business reasons or merely trend setting?

- What is the real cost of hardware and software, especially over a five-year period?
- What are the hidden costs, including the impact on people?
- Do the available technologies meet the mission-critical requirements of the organization?
- Can these changes be cost justified?

In-House Versus Third-Party Implementation

Another decision that must be made in the early stages is whether you should attempt to implement the migration plan using your own internal resources. Alternately, do you hire a third party, such as a solutions provider, to do it for you? Basically you need to decide whether the cost of the service provided by the third party is worth the benefit of using their labor and expertise to plan and execute your migration. Should you choose to utilize the services of a solutions provider, make sure that you select the company very carefully. While making the decision, the following are some suggestions to keep in mind.

- Planning and executing takes a significant amount of personnel resources beyond daily responsibilities. Can your organization manage to dedicate people to this task?
- Even if you choose to hire a solutions provider, you still have to provide personnel to work with the contractor. It is imperative that the solutions provider understand your business. In addition, it is critical for you to understand the environment the provider is implementing so that you can support it after the migration is complete.
- Will technical support be provided after the basic implementation and for how long? What is the cost of this support?

WHAT IS YOUR ORGANIZATIONAL MODEL?

It is easy to take the concept of planning for granted. Many technologists view the theory of planning as a fuzzy business school dark art. However, our system administrative associates believe that a comprehensive plan is worth its weight in dozens of haphazard and failed implementations. Yes, you could install Windows NT servers beside UNIX boxes and achieve instant connectivity with correct cabling and assigned IP addresses. In a very small environment, that may be all that is required. However, if any level of complexity exists within your enterprise, the solution will involve much more than coaxial cables and IP addresses.

This section discusses the importance of understanding the structure and processes of an organization and reviews the concepts of the workgroup and domain models. In addition, it makes suggestions regarding which model would be the best one to choose under certain circumstances.

If you thought it wasn't necessary to understand how a company or department is structured and how it operates, think again. Understanding the business processes, or at the very least understanding what questions to ask, is paramount in designing a computer network.

The Organizational Structure

How an organization is structured impacts the type of computing environment that should be put into place. If a company maintains a top-down management structure, then a traditional multiuser system could be an adequate computing solution. Central computer management generally reflects the system topology for a bottom-up organizational management style. For diverse concerns in which data is widely disseminated, a distributed computing environment is probably the best solution. When information is made widely available, a level of trust between employees is assumed. With computer systems, "trust" is established through permissions given to processes and file access. Therefore, the more closely overlapping the organization's management, the greater the requirement to establish "trusted" relationships between servers. In this latter case, understanding the basic manner in which UNIX and Windows NT differ in managing for both centralized and decentralized computing must then be considered.

When reviewing the organizational structure of your company, you may want to determine the answers to questions such as

- Is there a centralized management information system (MIS) or data processing department? Or does a data-processing function exist in each division?

- Does the organization have a single focus, such as with a law firm? Is the focus more diversified, such as with a manufacturing company?

- Do different departments have unique computing requirements? For example, a marketing department may require a graphical environment with the ability to create and display presentations such as slide shows. On the other hand an engineering department may need a more powerful processor to handle complex mathematical computations.

- How important is security to the structure of the organization? Does one department require a more secure environment than another?

- How critical is the flow of information between departments and divisions? Are they autonomous or is there intense interaction?

Organizational Processes and Dynamics

Every organization has its own dynamics. The computing requirements for a manufacturer are radically different from that of a finance house. The manner in which information is based can be very structured or completely ad hoc.

Process management breaks the functions, tasks, and responsibilities of a business into operations. By understanding how information flows through the organization, you are better able to identify the computing needs that different departments require for their processes. For example, the accounting, marketing, and manufacturing departments need access to customer information, but the human resources department does not. Human resources, in turn, has many processes that are confidential. This implementation should not be accessible by unauthorized employees. Understanding the business relationships between departments, and their processes, makes it easier to configure and implement the relative computer systems.

To design a network that meets the needs of its users and the business, you have to know and understand the answers to questions such as

- What are the critical business times? Daily, weekly, monthly, quarterly, or yearly? Or is a particular time of day more critical than others?

- Does the system need to be available twenty-four hours a day, seven days a week?

- What is the peak demand period and what does the system require to support this peak demand period?

- What information is considered confidential to a particular department or to the company as a whole?

- Are the users primarily located in a particular office or do they travel and thus require access from many locations?

- How many users are there?

- Do users need remote access? If so, how many?

- How many physical locations exist in the company? For example, are there multiple buildings in a single location or are there branch offices scattered nationally and/or internationally?

- What are the printing needs?

- What are the archival needs? How much data needs to be retained for future reference and for how long? How quickly will you be required to retrieve archived data?

- Do any processes require dedicated resources, such as a mission-critical and resource-demanding batch process?

- Which applications are used by a particular department or company? Are they written internally or purchased from a third party?
- Which applications/equipment must a department have without fail to conduct business?

SELECTING A TOPOLOGICAL MODEL

This section provides a review of the Windows NT workgroup model and the domain models that were originally discussed in Chapter 7. This analysis looks at the workgroup and domain models in the context of planning and implementation.

Workgroup Model

The workgroup model is simply a peer-to-peer relationship in which each host (computer) maintains its own copy of the SAM database. Users must be defined on all systems that they need to access. Consider using the workgroup model under the following conditions:

- When you need a low-cost alternative that utilizes older systems such as Windows for Workgroups, Windows 3.1, or Windows 95
- When management of the architecture is minimally centralized
- When your environment consists of ten or fewer computer systems
- When there is no need to establish global accounts
- When there is not a pressing need for a coordinated security policy
- When resources are not mission critical to daily business operations

Some examples of when a workgroup model might be appropriately installed within a larger organization include demo systems in sales and support departments, systems that are deployed for use at trade shows, systems installed for temporary functions, and systems that must be separated from the rest of the environment for security reasons.

Domain Models

In most cases you will need to select one or more domain models to implement in your organization. Remember that a Windows NT domain is a group of computer systems that consists of at least one Windows NT server. One of the servers, referred to as the PDC, contains the SAM database, which permits users to log on centrally to the domain.

SINGLE-DOMAIN MODEL

In this model the network consists of a single domain, so there is no need to establish trust relationships. A single domain contains both a PDC and one or more BDCs. Consider implementing this model when

- Yours is a small organization and there are less than twenty-six thousand users in the domain
- There is a need for both centralized account and resource management
- There is a centralized MIS department managing the network.

It is possible for an organization to have multiple, independent, single-domain models. In this instance there is no trust relationship between the domains, which creates a more secure and isolated environment. This type of model may also be used while phasing Windows NT into an organization, but be sure that there is an overall network migration plan first.

MASTER DOMAIN MODEL

The master domain model consists of a master domain containing the SAM database and one or more resource domains that trust the master domain. This model permits users to log on to the master domain and to access permitted resources in other domains. Select this model when your organization requires

- Less than forty thousand accounts in the domain. (Accounts consist of users, computer systems, and built-in and custom groups.)
- Centralized account management
- Decentralized resource management. (This model allows resources to be managed either by local administrators or by the system administrators.)
- Centralized MIS department
- The ability to manage security centrally

For example, if your organization consists of a main office with several branch offices, you may want to choose this model. The master domain would be located at the home office and the subdomains would be located in each of the branch offices. In this type of design, make sure that a BDC exists in each branch office to speed up the logon authorization process.

Another use of this model is in an organization with only one location. The master domain could be located in MIS; the subdomains could be located in each department, such as sales, marketing, and engineering.

MULTIPLE MASTER DOMAINS MODEL

The multiple master domains model is used primarily for large organizations that need several master domains to manage their user account database (SAM) effectively. In this model there is a bidirectional trust relationship established between each of the master domains. The subdomains (resource domains) trust each of the master domains with a one-way trust relationship. You may wish to select this model when your organization conforms to the following requirements:

- The organization needs to support more than forty thousand accounts (although it is possible to use this model with less users as well)
- The need for either centralized or decentralized account management. (All of the master domains can be administered from one location or from multiple locations.)
- The need for either centralized or decentralized resource management
- There is no centralized MIS department, such as when each division supports its own MIS activities

The multiple master domains model permits the organization to structure the network in the way that best fits its organizational structure. Perhaps the most common use of the multiple master domains model is in a large organization in which the number of users exceeds forty thousand. This model allows the organization to structure the network with room for expansion.

Another example of an organization in which the multiple master domain model may be appropriate is a company with a structure that is a combination of a functional and a divisional organization. In this type of organization each division manages its own sales, marketing, and data-processing functions, but relies on the company's corporatewide resources for human resources and accounting. Each division may have its own master domain, with another master domain defined for the corporatewide functions. Since there is a need to access other domains, there is a bidirectional trust relationship established between all of the master domains.

COMPLETE TRUST MODEL

The complete trust model creates a bidirectional trust relationship between all domains in the network. Rather than identify the situations when this model can be used, we choose to identify the reasons not to select this model.

- There is no central security control.
- Security and management of one domain is affected by how another domain is managed.

- The management of the trust relationships becomes unwieldy due to the large number of relationships that exist.

DETERMINING FILE SYSTEM TYPE

Another decision that must be made during the planning process is to determine which type of file system you will implement: FAT or NTFS. Reasons that you may choose to use the FAT file system include

- Compatibility with other operating systems such as DOS, Windows 3.1, Windows 95, Macintosh, NetWare, and OS/2
- The ability to boot Windows NT or DOS, Windows 3.1, Windows 95, or OS/2 from the same system (often referred to as the ability to *dual boot* operating systems)

Reasons that you may wish to select the NTFS file system include

- The ability to utilize the increased security available, including access controls and file permissions
- Faster processing
- Enhanced security
- The ability to use very large disks and very large files effectively
- The logging process, which facilitates system recovery

IDENTIFYING SERVER TYPES

In addition to identifying the domain model you are planning to use for your network, you also need to determine the types of servers that the domains will contain. Each domain must contain a PDC and at least one BDC. In most environments it is recommended that the PDC (running Windows NT Server) be dedicated to providing the directory services associated with the user account database (SAM). On the other hand, BDCs can provide other services, such as a print server, in addition to providing the backup services for SAM.

The SAM database is synchronized between the PDC and the BDC every five minutes. When the BDC is initially installed, the entire SAM database from the PDC must be copied to the BDC. We recommend that you install a BDC in the same location as the PDC so that the SAM is not copied over a slow remote connection.

Another consideration regarding the location of BDCs depends on the domain model chosen. In regard to the master domain model we discussed a scenario in which the PDC resided at the home office and there was a BDC located in each of the branch offices. By having a BDC located in each of the branch offices, the logon authentication process may occur faster, because the system does not have to deal with a network connection to the PDC. Remember that users are authenticated by the first available PDC or BDC.

If a server is not a PDC or a BDC, it is considered a member server. A member server can be any of the following types of servers:

- File server
- Print server
- Application server
- Communication server for e-mail, fax, and so on
- Database server, such as an SQL server
- Remote access server for modems
- Service servers, which include any other services provided for clients, such as DNS, DHCP, WINS, and so on

Depending on the memory, processing, and disk requirements of these services, it is possible for more than one service to exist on any one member server. However, there are some instances, such as with an SQL server, that the server should be dedicated to that one function.

REQUIREMENTS FOR IMPLEMENTATION

After you have chosen the domain model that best meets your organizational structure and dynamics, it is then time to evaluate what you already have in relation to what you need. This section provides a discussion on evaluating and determining hardware needs, concentrating on the computer systems to be used as servers. In addition, this section discusses software issues.

Hardware

When looking at hardware requirements for Windows NT servers, keep the following items in mind when evaluating current or new equipment.

- Is the system scalable? Is it flexible enough to be expanded to meet future needs?
- Are the components in the system on the Hardware Compatibility List provided by Microsoft? Choosing systems with components on this list may save you a lot of headaches in the long run.
- Choose a hardware vendor that has a good reputation and a solid warranty policy.

- What type of performance power do you need? Will an Intel-based machine be sufficient or does a RISC-based processor better suit your needs? Please note that if your applications are not available on a RISC platform, this is a moot point.

DETERMINING THE NUMBER OF DOMAINS

One of the determining factors in the evaluation of hardware is the size of the SAM database. A single domain can support a SAM that is 40 MB in size. Microsoft provides the following formula for calculating the estimated size of the SAM database in kilobytes:

$$(\text{no. of users} \times 1 \text{ KB}) + (\text{no. of computers} \times 0.5 \text{ KB}) +$$
$$(\text{no. of custom groups} \times 4 \text{ KB}) + (\text{no. of built-in groups} \times 4 \text{ KB})$$

where the number of computers refers to the number of computers running Windows NT Workstation or Windows NT Server that exist in the domain, the number of built-in groups is eleven, and the number of custom groups represents the groups that you define or plan to define for your system. To convert the size of the SAM database to megabytes, multiply the result of the formula by 0.001024.

To determine the minimum number of domains necessary to accommodate the size of your user base, divide the size of the SAM database in megabytes by forty and round up to the nearest whole number. For example:

No. of users = 50,000

No. of computers = 40,000

No. of custom groups = 200

No. of built-in groups = 11

The size of the SAM database = $(50,000 \times 1) + (40,000 \times 0.5) + (200 \times 4) + (11 \times 4)$, or 70,844 KB

The size of the SAM database in megabytes = $70,844 \times 0.001024$, or 72.5 MB

The minimum number of domains needed = 72.5/40, or two domains

HARDWARE REQUIREMENTS FOR WINDOWS NT SERVERS

Determining the amount of RAM required by a Windows NT server is critical to the planning process. Microsoft provides the following formula for calculating the approximate RAM size for a server:

16 MB + (no. of users × average no. of open files per user × average size of data files) + (average no. of applications run from the server × average size of data files)

TABLE 9.1.   Hardware Requirements for Domain Controllers

Users	SAM size (MB)	Minimum CPU	RAM (MB)
<3,000	5	486dx/33	16
7,500	10	486dx/33	32
10,000	15	Pentium or Alpha AXP	48
15,000	20	Pentium or Alpha AXP	64
20,000	30	Pentium or Alpha AXP	128
30,000	45	Pentium or Alpha AXP	166
40,000	60	SMP	197
50,000	75	SMP	256

To assist further in determining the hardware requirements for domain controllers, Microsoft publishes the guidelines listed in Table 9.1.

With regard to the PDC, it is our experience that although a Pentium system with 32 MB of RAM will perform the task sufficiently, 64 MB of RAM does a much better job. We believe that the real minimum should be a Pentium-class processor that clocks at 133 MHz, but 166 MHz or greater is preferred.

A BDC should be configured the same as a PDC. If the BDC is providing other services, you may want to reconsider the configuration. Table 9.2 gives some guidelines for determining RAM size for other types of Windows NT servers.

TABLE 9.2.   Determining RAM for Windows NT Servers

Service	Minimum RAM (MB)	Additional RAM	Comments
File servers	32	1 MB for each concurrent user	—
SQL Server	64	—	A Pentium-class 166 CPU is the minimum
Remote Access Server	32	2 MB for each concurrent user	—
TCP/IP services	—	4 MB for each service	—
Internet Server	32	—	64 MB works better
Exchange Server	32	—	I/O should be optimized

OTHER HARDWARE

The computers used as servers and workstations are just a portion of the hardware that must be considered as part of a migration plan. A number of other components that may exist in your current network must be reevaluated for inclusion in the new network. Some of these include

- Network components such as bandwidth, cabling, hubs, repeaters, routers, and switches
- Printers
- Modems
- Fax machines/boards
- Storage devices such as cartridge tapes or disks, optical disks, DAT tapes, digital linear tapes, hard disks

When evaluating these components for usability during and after the migration, you may want to consider the following items.

- Are the hardware components included on the Hardware Compatibility List provided by Microsoft? If not, contact the hardware vendor and obtain additional information.
- Are the current capacity levels of the hardware applicable to the new environment?
- Is the hardware still meeting the usage requirements or have the usage requirements changed?
- Will the equipment scale to meet projected needs?
- Will additional components be needed for the new configuration?

Software Concerns

When designing your network, software concerns can be just as critical as hardware concerns. For example, if you would like to use a RISC-based processor but a mission-critical application is not available on that platform, you obviously have to use an Intel processor for that particular application. The following is a list of questions to evaluate when addressing the software concerns of the network.

- How do legacy applications fit into the migration?
- Is in-house development work needed?
- Is development work required from third parties?
- How does existing user software fit? Does this software need to be upgraded as well?

- Are there any special resource needs for a particular application that must be included in the network plan?

Chapters 10 and 11 discuss the migration of application software in further detail.

TRAINING

If there ever was an example of which came first, the chicken or the egg, training is it. In an ideal world, the people planning for the introduction of Windows NT should be trained prior to developing the plan. It is important to understand both the old and new environments to develop a successful plan.

Users and administrators may be in for a culture shock as a result of the introduction of a new technology. While a number of the concepts are similar, Windows NT and UNIX are visually different. While application users may rejoice over the change to a more familiar interface, UNIX hacks may drag their feet. This section takes a look at the type of training that should ideally occur, then suggests different methods for conducting the training.

Types of Training

It seems like an impossible task to train an entire organization on a new computer system. The key is that different types of training occur at different times, and it is an ongoing process. The following identifies different types of training and when it should occur.

Administrator training – Ideally the individuals responsible for planning and execution should be trained before the plan is developed. The administrators, who have the most knowledge about the current environment, should understand the new environment as thoroughly as possible to develop a successful migration plan.

Developer training – The individuals responsible for converting applications to the new environment need to be trained early in the process. In fact, it is helpful to train them at the same time as the administrators, since their responsibilities will have an impact on the migration plan.

Help desk/technical support training – Oftentimes these individuals are the administrators' first line of defense. These are the people who are going to field the day-to-day questions from the users. Since they often have another perspective of the current system, they can often provide helpful insight into the development of a migration plan if trained early enough in the process. These individuals can also be enlisted to help train the user community. Therefore, their training should include not only an overview of the Windows NT operating system, but also how it will be implemented in the organization's environment.

User training – User training should occur before the user has to interact with the system, with a "refresher course" after the new system is in operation. Some basic topics that should be covered include logging on, file structure (where are my files?), printing files, application access, and how to get help.

Management training – Obviously management needs user training, but managers also need to understand the management aspect of the system changes. They are interested in the answers to questions such as: What is going to happen? When is it happening? How will it affect business? Who's responsible?

Training Methods

There are various training methods available. For the administrator, developer, and technical personnel, Microsoft offers a wide variety of courses including instructor-led courses, those offered at the Microsoft Online Institute, or self-paced courses. Descriptions of Microsoft training and certification programs can be found at Microsoft's Web site at www.microsoft.com.

Training for users and management can occur in classroom settings, departmental meetings, or on-line via e-mail. You need to determine what type of training works best for your user community. While some organizations prefer video training, others gain more from instructor-led training. The important task is to implement and execute a training plan that fits into the organization's budget. The better informed the users, the more successful the migration.

IMPLEMENTING THE MIGRATION PLAN

Now that you have evaluated your current environment, determined a new network topology, identified hardware and software concerns, and determined training needs, the next step is to figure out how to implement the migration. The following sections present ten tactical tips to help you implement the migration plan.

Tip 1: Publish the Plan, Including Policies and Procedures

Publishing a dynamic set of policies and procedures can help promote an early buy-in by both managers and end users. Feedback is very healthy during all phases of a migration or implementation program. The common belief that the information system manager or system administrator knows best is highly overrated. Contributions by user groups can often prove invaluable. It also prevents being blindsided by hidden agendas. It is easy for a system administrator to be too closely involved with the details of the implementation and to overlook some important issues. In addition, the system administrator may not completely understand how a particular person or department utilizes the computer system. The result of proceeding without having a plan corroborated is the possibility of implementing a system that does not meet users needs.

Tip 2: Leverage Current Investments

The conventional wisdom is to utilize current assets whenever possible. This is probably true when considering physical network connections and large hardware requirements. However, with the rapidly declining cost of workstation-class machines, it is often easier to buy new. There are times when it is possible to "recycle" the systems in one department to another department as needs change. The questions that need to be resolved are whether there is a cost benefit to a recycle plan or whether there are more resources (time, people) expended than the actual cost of purchasing new.

Tip 3: Determine Personnel Needs Early

In some locations, highly trained technical personnel are a rare commodity. Conduct a skill set survey. Managing a mixed- or single-operating system enterprise requires different skills. If you do not already have in place the mix of technical skills required to meet strategic objectives, it is never too early to begin the recruitment and/or training process. This is when professional temporary agencies come in handy. You may be forced to pay more per hour for these "leased workers," but you will not be burdened with long-term commitments when the rollout is completed.

Tip 4: Ensure Availability of Hardware, Software, and Funding

Securing the budget is one of the first major hurdles. Sometimes monies can be justified on the emotional basis that you simply need new equipment and software. More than likely, however, a plan to migrate or integrate operating systems must be cost justified. Can the organization perform its tasks with greater efficiency? Can the investment be justified in terms of productivity? Does it cost more to maintain the existing solutions? Are there any needed applications that the current system does not support?

Tip 5: Create a Test Environment

Wherever possible, test the migration in a lab environment prior to the actual implementation. The implementation will probably go much smoother if it is broken down into manageable sections and tested prior to the final implementation. After designing your network topology, you will be better able to determine how to phase in the migration while minimally disrupting day-to-day business. If possible, also include a pilot implementation for a portion of the installation that would allow actual users to test the implementation of the new environment. These pilot and test environments will also help with staging the implementation, which is discussed in the next tip.

Tip 6: Plan for Staging

When implementing a new program, retrofitting hardware and software becomes a daily task. The issue of staging arises. Do you unpack equipment at the user's workstation or preload and deliver? This may seem basic, but it has significant impact on the end user. If the first impression an end user gets is of technical people fumbling for any length of time, the recovery time for credibility is extended. We recommend using a staging area to preload whenever possible.

Tip 7: Get Others Involved in the Rollout

The actual rollout of systems should be well publicized and on a schedule that is not overly aggressive. Personnel assigned to interface with end users should be in the position to answer fundamental questions, and support must already be in place. You should count on problems. A rollout without a crisis is rare. That is why a reasonable schedule coupled with trained technical personnel are so essential in buffering against potential problems.

Tip 8: Plan Early for Operational Management

Once the initial rollout is in place, operational (or day-to-day) management complete with policies and procedures is required. The real job of the UNIX and Windows NT system administrator just begins here. It is critical that an aggressive and responsive approach be taken when those first problems occur. A quick and accurate response to the early problems helps to maintain and increase (hopefully) both user and management confidence and commitment.

Tip 9: Implement Training and Support Early

The requirement for training is directly related to the sophistication of your users and the complexity of the applications. Support follows the same principle. The variety of training and support mechanisms ranges from formal classroom experiences to on-line or videotape documentation. Take advantage of any training and support material offered by your vendors.

Begin training early. Support personnel should be trained prior to implementation, since they are your first line of defense with the user community. Having capable and specially trained individuals fielding questions provides the user with a higher comfort level that the new system can be incorporated into their daily business. Conducting internal information seminars for the user community before and/or shortly after rollout is also helpful. These information seminars can be conducted via printed material such as an "Implementation Update," via e-mail, or via short ten-minute presentations in department meetings. Keep this information exchange brief and practical, so that the chance of users retaining the information increases.

Tip 10: Use Audit and Performance-monitoring Tools

The final step in the planning process is to determine how system auditing and performance is to be conducted. Each version of UNIX supports a different tool set and monitoring methodology. Windows NT ships with tools that are consistent in look and feel. In subsequent chapters, we explore these tools. It is best to understand system auditing and performance-monitoring options early in your migration or integration process. Knowing what is available will allow you to instruct support personnel, users, and management on the information that can be gathered. Windows NT and some UNIX vendors support good tools for this purpose. Fortunately, third-party vendors are beginning to offer cross-platform monitoring and performance tools.

POSTIMPLEMENTATION DILEMMAS

Now that the planning and implementation is complete, the real fun begins. Expect the unexpected. Even a job well done will result in postimplementation dilemmas. Among those potential issues are the following:

- *Performance* – It is unfortunately all too common for system performance not to match the level advertised. This does not imply that vendors of hardware or software purposefully seek to misinform. Rather, the real-world impact of users and applications is difficult to project. Be prepared to make adjustments.

- *Users' behavior/resistance* – If you are a system administrator, then you understand the level of user unpredictability. (Keeping a drawer full of voodoo dolls representing some of your most troubled users is probably not a solution to this issue.) When making any change, expect some resistance. In some cases, resistance may be extreme. If problems arise, don't hesitate to seek management assistance. A well-placed word from a supervisor to a disgruntled employee on your behalf can work wonders.

- *Communication channels* – Keep managers and users informed of the plans and expected benefits. Establish your communication channels early and keep them open. Take extra care to inform the managers about understanding the needs and the benefits that are driving this migration. This understanding should lead to the managers' acceptance and enthusiasm, which will hopefully filter down to the other users. Understanding, acceptance, and knowledge *should* minimize complaints (at least we hope this happens).

- *Crisis management* – When migrating or integrating, only a rare installation transpires without an unexpected crisis. A good scout learns to be prepared. Good system administrators learn to pick themselves up when a crisis occurs and have plans to manage the unexpected.

- *Utopia not achieved* – Even when every item in the plan is implemented to perfection, there is no such thing as a computing utopia. Expectations of management and users are often higher than reality. When implementing, try not to raise false expectations. When the job is complete, don't be surprised when you hear a collective sense of disappointment. Unfortunately, sometimes the job of the system administrator is thankless.

Chapter

10

UNIX and Windows NT Coexistence

The issue of operating system coexistence is little different than integration. Coexistence implies managing two different environments that function in the same enterprise but may have little in common. Integration assumes interoperability. As preemptive network operating systems, Windows NT and UNIX fortunately share common ground for integration—primarily in mutually supported protocols and related services. Although we cannot help but mention some aspects of networking interoperability, this chapter focuses on technologies that facilitate coexistence. Specifically, we address the following technologies that aid coexistence:

- Accessing data across platforms
- User interface emulators, X11 servers, and the Intelligent Console Architecture (ICA) protocol
- Ported POSIX commands and utilities on Windows NT
- Database front ends to legacy software
- Remote system management tools
- Windows NT as a UNIX file server
- New clustering technologies

COOPERATIVE TECHNOLOGIES FOR SOFTWARE APPLICATION USE

The issue of sharing data and applications is central to UNIX and Windows NT coexistence. For example, there is no question that Windows-based products dominate the office automation (OA) market. Therefore, for users of UNIX systems, the availability of mainstream applications for office productivity solutions is limited. Even if UNIX users purchase a native OA solution from one of the handful of small UNIX software publishers, they will probably still need to access Windows applications sometimes. For example, if an Internet mail message contains an attached Microsoft Word document, reading the contents can be very daunting for UNIX users. If appropriate file filters are not available, the hapless UNIX user might "ftp" the file to another system and then gain access to that Windows-based computer. If the user has both a PC and an X-station available, the task is a bit less overwhelming. However, maintaining access to both systems is a very costly solution to what should be a straightforward activity. Fortunately, technology is rapidly emerging to facilitate the primary objectives of

- Gaining access to data across platforms
- Running Windows applications under UNIX
- Running UNIX applications under Windows NT
- Emulating environments to permit local access to applications designed for other operating systems

Accessing Data across Platforms

Users on UNIX and Windows NT systems can access flat file ASCII information using the common telnet facility. Assuming the user has an account on the foreign system, a telnet (network terminal) session can be established in a pure character-based mode. Files with appropriate read, write, or execute permissions can be viewed and otherwise manipulated without the need for additional software.

The telnet client function is available to the Windows NT user by typing `telnet` at **Command Prompt** (**Start** ➤ **Programs** ➤ **Command Prompt**). The telnet window is then displayed (Figure 10.1). The connection to the foreign system is accomplished by selecting **Connect** ➤ **Remote System** and completing the IP address or system name information as shown in Figure 10.1.

A UNIX telnet session to a Windows NT box is equally as easy. Remember, UNIX provides native client and server telnet components. The command line entry is simply

```
telnet {IP address of Windows NT | systemname of Windows NT system}
```

After the connection is made, the user can utilize a text editor like *vi* to open and manipulate data. Correct file permissions and ownership is obviously assumed. Using telnet between UNIX and Windows NT is essentially the same as a UNIX-to-UNIX telnet session.

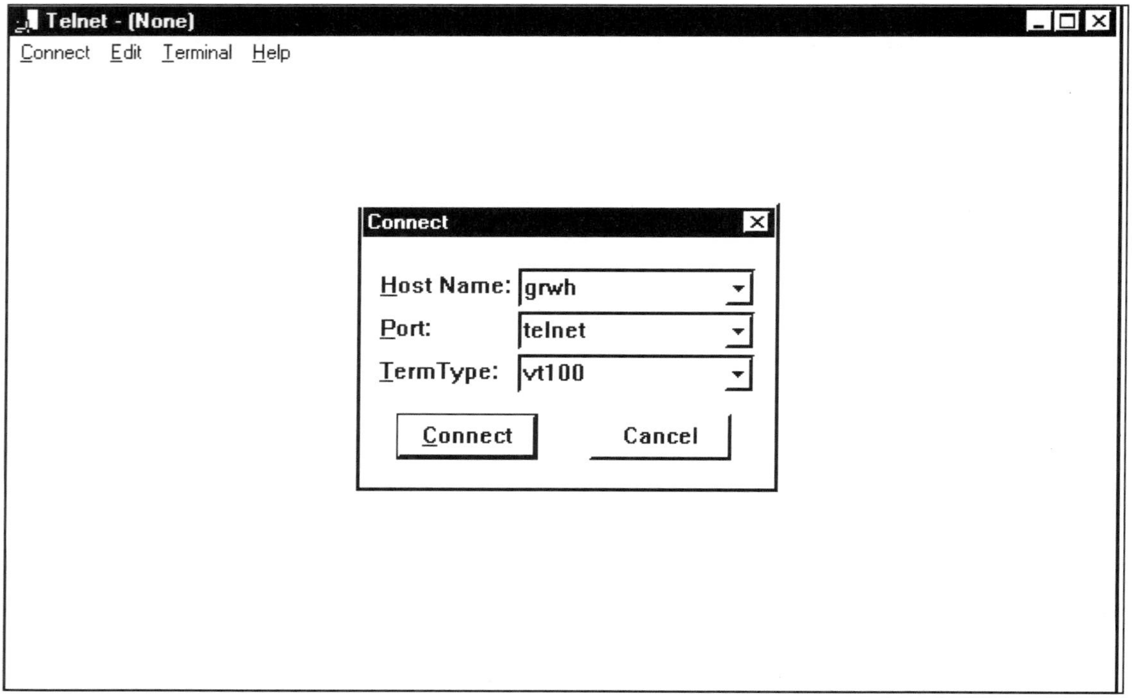

FIGURE 10.1.   Telnet Window

Moving Data across Platforms

Another base-level method of sharing data across UNIX and Windows NT is to use the *ftp* and *rcp* commands to copy data across platforms. Like the telnet client, FTP is shipped with the Windows NT Resource Kit and all variants of UNIX. The use of both *ftp* and *rcp* is covered in other sections of the book.

Running Applications from within Telnet

Character-based applications residing on either UNIX or Windows NT systems can generally be run under a standard telnet session. For example, we had no problem operating the character-based version of the Decathlon GOLDMEDAL office automation suite running on a Hewlett-Packard 9000 HP-UX system from a Windows NT telnet window. As far as the software was concerned, the Windows NT telnet session was no different than if a dumb terminal had been connected to the UNIX box. However, not all character-based applications will operate with equal ease. The key variable is the terminal emulation that the ap-

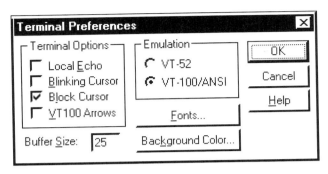

FIGURE 10.2.   Terminal Settings

plication expects to see. One of the traumas UNIX developers faced was designing applications that could handle the different settings of dozens of terminal types. The Windows NT telnet applet supports only two terminal definitions—the DEC VT52 and VT100. Fortunately, the definitions for the VT52 and VT100 are widely recognized by most UNIX applications. (However, these primitive emulations may not support features required by some applications, such as color and graphics.)

When using the telnet facility from Windows NT to UNIX box, it may be necessary to set the terminal configurations on both sides (Figure 10.2). We generally recommend the VT100 emulation for most application uses. To set the emulation from the Windows NT telnet applet, select **Terminal** ➤ **Preferences** ➤ **VT100/ANSI**.

After the terminal connection is established to the UNIX box, you may also need to set the terminal type before launching an application. Depending on the type of shell in which you find yourself, perform the following command line entry.

For ksh and sh environments, type

```
TERM=vt100; export TERM
```

For csh environments, type

```
set terminal vt100
```

Running Windows Applications under UNIX

UNIX users can employ two very different methods of running Windows applications from their native environments. The first involves emulators that simulate the MS-DOS and Windows environments natively on a UNIX system. The second method is through the use of the ICA network protocol to display an application running on the Windows NT server on a local UNIX terminal. The latter solution involves an additional layer of code on Windows NT Server 4.0 that transforms it into a true multiuser system.

Emulators

By definition, all emulation programs reside atop the native operating system, with a layer of code that simulates the I/O and other characteristics of another platform.

MS-DOS EMULATION

A number of DOS emulators were available with UNIX systems and were generally considered a requirement for Intel-class variants such as SCO and ESIX. These products worked reasonably well in supporting common DOS utilities largely due to limited memory management. Their ability to run DOS applications, however, was somewhat less satisfactory. These emulators are still handy for UNIX users needing to perform simple tasks such as formatting a DOS diskette and copying files to that media.

WINDOWS EMULATORS

Several products emerged in the early 1990s that resided on the X-Windows environment to provide support for a Microsoft Windows look and feel. The most successful of these products was developed by Sun Microsystems and is called *WABI*. It was made available on a wide variety of UNIX boxes. When WABI is invoked from within X-Windows, a Microsoft Windows environment window is displayed from which applications can be selected. The look and feel is very similar to the native Microsoft Windows 3.1 environment. With the use of WABI, Microsoft applications like Word and Excel can be run natively on a Sun box or an assortment of other UNIX X-Windows environments.

The WABI technology has two historic limitations. First, not all Windows applications will run successfully under WABI. While more recent versions of WABI have expanded the products supported, reports of difficulty still abound. Second, the performance of Windows applications running under WABI was much slower than what is experienced in native environments.

WISE EMULATION

A class of products based on the Microsoft-licensed Windows Interface Source Environment (WISE) supports the use of shrink-wrapped Windows applications on UNIX (Figure 10.3). Locus Computing Corporation's Merge utilizes WISE to support Windows applications on Intel-class UNIX systems. Insignia Solutions,

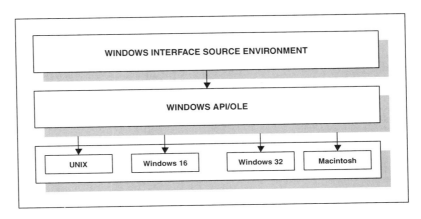

FIGURE 10.3.   WISE API Interface

Inc.'s Softwindows utilizes WISE for support on non-Intel-class UNIX environments. The WISE emulators actually utilize the Windows source code from Microsoft. The major advantage is that Microsoft OLE technology based on COM is supported. For example, when a UNIX user with an installed WISE emulator receives an Internet mail message with an attached Word document, it is possible to configure the system to load the *.doc* file and Word application seamlessly.

Running UNIX Applications under Windows NT

UNIX character-based applications can generally be displayed on a Windows NT system using a standard telnet session. However, X-Windows-based applications will require the X-Windows environment on Windows NT Server.

As we explained in Chapter 5, X-Windows uses a client/server model to separate the application logic from user input and displayed output. The X-Windows application is considered the client, whereas the server processes input and display output. This is an important concept because in order to display information on a Windows NT system, the X-Windows server components must be installed locally. This may be a little confusing from strictly a Windows NT vantage; after all, the objective is to use the Windows NT client to access a remote UNIX application. However, to display the application on the Windows NT console, the X-Windows server must be resident on the Windows NT client (Figure 10.4).

There are many commercial X11 servers available that permit the display of X-Windows applications within the Windows 95 GUI. For our money, we found several excellent X-Windows servers that deserve consideration. Hummingbird Communications has been in the X-Server market for many years and brings to

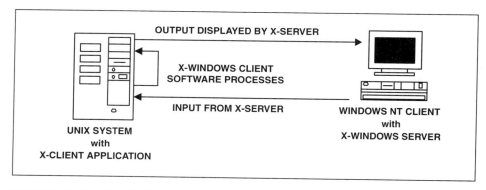

FIGURE 10.4.   X-Windows on Windows NT

the market a well-tested and solid offering. Relative newcomer Softway Systems offers a more economical and a little broader based X-Server (licensed from NetManage and also marketed as Chameleon) that supports Motif, OpenLook, VUE, and CDE. As to resource utilization, Softway's OpenNT X11 server gets the nod for lower memory and CPU usage in our tests. (Figure 10.5 shows several X-applications running under Windows NT using OpenNT.) Finally, DataFocus offers an excellent, although very expensive, X-Server with their NuTCRACKER development system (Table 10.1).

While discussing X-Windows, system administrators should also consider the use of CDE. As discussed earlier, CDE is a user interface that is now embraced by most UNIX vendors to provide a singular look and feel to UNIX application desktops. It is the UNIX answer to the Windows 95 interface. CDE is based on the Open Software Foundation's Motif widget set and Hewlett-Packard's VUE. TriTeal Corporation's (`www.triteal.com`) NTED is a good implementation of CDE for Windows NT systems. It resides on top of the WinFrame multiuser extension discussed next.

TABLE 10.1.   Selected List of X-Windows Servers for Windows NT

Product	Company	Web site
NuTCRACKER	Data Focus	`www.datafocus.com`
Exceed	Hummingbird Communications	`www.hummingbird.com`
Chameleon	NetManage	`www.netmanage.com`
PC-Xware	NCD	`www.ncd.com`
OpenNT X11 Server	Softway Systems	`www.softway.com`

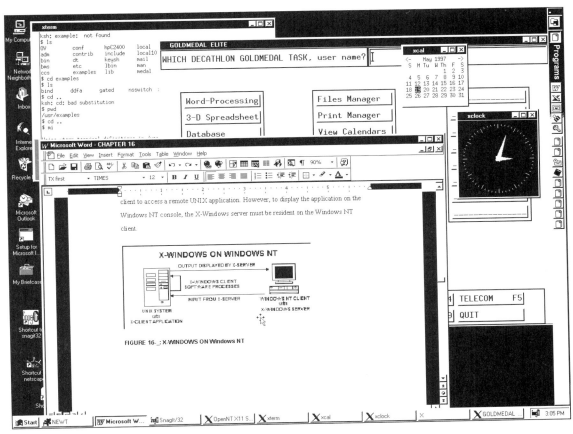

FIGURE 10.5.   Several X Applications Running under Windows NT

Multiuser Windows NT Emulation with ICA

Windows NT can be converted into a true multiuser system with the addition of a layer of code developed by Citrix Systems, Inc. Unfortunately, the current version only supports Windows NT 3.51 interface. Based on a source code license from Microsoft, Citrix's WinFrame technology permits remote access to 32-bit Windows applications akin to multiuser UNIX. Other products have been built on top of the WinFrame technology, including Insignia Solution's Ntrigue (www.insignia.com) and Tektronix's WinDD (www.tek.com).

The Tektronix WinDD transforms Windows applications into multiuser programs without the need for specific software emulation. According to Tektronix,

WinDD extends Windows NT into a server capable of supporting twenty-five to thirty concurrent users. UNIX workstations can function simultaneously as universal desktops because they are able to display both X-Windows- and Microsoft Windows-based applications. The WinDD approach has a number of strong advantages over emulation programs like WABI. First and foremost, application integrity is ensured because it runs in native environments. In addition, a single desktop can access distributed PC applications.

These products provide excellent Windows NT-to-UNIX application coexistence. UNIX users can log in to the "multiuser" version of Windows NT and display Windows applications locally. This technology achieves the same end results as utilizing X-Windows servers for Windows NT. The heart of the technology is ICA. Much like X-Windows separates the I/O functions from the logic of the application itself, ICA forces the application to run on the Windows NT server and to display on a UNIX client. In contrast to the X-Windows server handling input and display output, the ICA server provides the GUI instruction to the remote UNIX client.

In a white paper published by Tektronix, Inc., in 1996 entitled *Network Loading Characters of ICA-3 and X11,* it is reported that X11 sends three to ten times the number of bytes and six to ten times the number of Ethernet packets more than ICA. Compaq Computer Systems published similar findings in a report entitled *Configuring Compaq Servers in a Citrix WinFrame Environment* (Compaq Computer Systems, 1996). However, these findings are not without detractors. Vendors of X11 emulators make many claims that suggest that ICA does not offer appreciable advantages. In fact, some X11 vendors state that X-Windows emulators are more network efficient. We have operated both WinDD and X11 emulators on Windows NT boxes. Our experience suggests that X11 does seem to take greater network resources to perform similar tasks. This observation is based not on extensive benchmarking, but on more casual monitoring during power use. It is interesting to note that despite the apparent network traffic advantage to WinDD, most of our users still elect to use X11 emulators as the solution of choice. This is probably because most of us are old-time UNIX users and old habits die hard.

Because ICA does not require the bundling of packets of information for each input and output, it generally requires less network bandwidth than X-Windows. It should be recalled that the X-Windows protocol was designed for Ethernet networks with 10 Mb/s of wide bandwidth. This makes X relatively unacceptable in dial-up environments when serial constraints of 28.8-KB or 56.6-KB baud rates are common. Since ICA does not require the same bandwidth requirements, it may be a good choice for integrating environments when application accessibility to Windows NT applications is required.

UTILIZING PORTED POSIX APPLICATIONS AND UTILITIES

Another method of bringing UNIX and Windows NT into closer alignment is to have the operating systems provide similar or even identical utilities and functions. At this time, through third-party add-ons, Windows NT supports virtually any UNIX utility.

Standard POSIX Support from Microsoft

As shipped, the POSIX subsystem in Windows NT provides very little function. Microsoft states that POSIX applications have no direct access to any of the facilities and features of the Win32 subsystem, such as memory mapped files, networking, graphics, or dynamic data exchange. The extent of compliance is with the POSIX.1 C language API. To many critics of Microsoft, the only reason for the inclusion of the POSIX subsystem is to qualify for major US government contracts that require POSIX compliance. To that end, Windows NT meets exactly the POSIX compliance requirements and nothing more. However, the Windows NT Resource Kit does ship with source code and binary UNIX utilities including *ar, at, cat, chmod, chown, cp, grep, ld, ln, ls, mk, mkdir, mv, rm, sh, touch, wc, windiff,* and *vi.* Further and more importantly, the POSIX subsystem provides third parties a means of offering products that bridge the gap between Windows NT and UNIX.

Complete POSIX System with Third-Party Ports of POSIX

A number of quality third-party sources exist for POSIX utilities. Most common utilities are available as freeware or shareware from various Internet sites. Commercial packages like MKS Toolkit and Hamilton C Shell provide excellent System V4 and Berkeley version implementations respectively. Softway Systems's OpenNT, DataFocus's NuTCRACKER, and Consensys Computer's Portage also provide cross-platform development environments for migrating UNIX code to Windows NT. In Chapter 11 we discuss our experience with migrating applications using the OpenNT and DataFocus product suites. As to standard UNIX utilities, DataFocus simply bundles the MKS Toolkit. DataFocus's NuTCRACKER also resides on the Win32 subsystem and provides only the most widely used functions to support legacy UNIX software porting into a Win32 application. Softway's OpenNT replaces the Windows NT POSIX subsystem, and applications ported to it function under that subsystem and utilize only the Win32 console calls.

OPENNT: A COMPLETE POSIX SYSTEM

Softway's OpenNT is built in cooperation with Microsoft to provide a complete UNIX-like alternative to Windows NT. As previously stated, OpenNT replaces the POSIX subsystem and forms a cohesive environment for migrated UNIX applications. The OpenNT server meets native port specifications for POSIX.1 (operating system API interfaces), POSIX.2 (commands and utilities), and XPG4 (both API and commands/utilities). As to XPG4, OpenNT 2.1 expands functionality with the exception of internationalization primitives (which are expected by spring 1998). These specifications are often required in large federal government computer system procurements. Therefore, the ability to add compliant components easily to the otherwise limited Windows NT POSIX subsystem will gain much acceptance in many government, educational, and commercial installations.

When we installed the OpenNT server, we invoked the command prompt to test commonly used functions (Figure 10.6). After running through simple commands like *ls, cat, cd,* and *pwd,* we tried other commands that we initially did not expect to be supported, like *uname -a.* To our surprise, OpenNT handled our requests just like we would expect on a native UNIX system. The only distraction we noted was that the ksh prompt listed current drive and directory locally in a manner that was neither traditionally ksh- or MS-DOS-like.

```
OpenNT ksh                                                         _ □ ✕
$ ls
[              diff3       id           pathchk       tee
[              dirname     join         pax           test
awk            echo        kill         pg            touch
basename       ed          ksh          posixpath2nt  tr
bc             egrep       ksh.exe      pr            true
bp             elvis       ln           printf        tty
cat            env         locale       pwd           umask
cd             ex          localedef    read          uname
chgrp          expand      logger       rm            unexpand
chmod          expr        logname      rmdir         unifdef
chown          false       lp           sed           uniq
cksum          fgrep       ls           sh            uudecode
clear          file        mailx        sh.exe        uuencode
cmp            find        man          sleep         vi
comm           flip        mkdir        sort          virec
command        fold        mkfifo       split         wait
cp             gawk        more         ssimda        wc
ctags          getconf     mv           strerror      xargs
cut            getopts     nohup        strsignal
date           grep        ntpath2posix stty
dc             head        od           tail
dd             hexdump     paste        tar
diff
$
$ ▮
```

FIGURE 10.6.   Partial List of OpenNT Utilities and Commands

TABLE 10.2.   Selected List of Windows NT Freeware/Shareware for UNIX Integration

Product	Description
CRON	Equivalent to UNIX scheduling utility *cron*
Ntcrond	Enterprisewide scheduling *cron*-like program
WinPack32	Compression utility; includes *uuencode/uudecode*
WinSpace	Switch between multiple desktops
UNIX 95 Collect	Collection of UNIX utilities
Winsock RCP	Versions of *rcp*, *rsh*, and *rexec* utilities
Rshd	Remote shell daemon for Windows NT
Here	Web-based version of *finger* utilities
SendFile	32-bit console for sending ASCII text via SMTP
NetScan Tools	*nslookup*, *finger*, *ping*, *traceroute*, *whois*
Keep Connected	Autopings to keep connection alive
TJPing	*Ping*, *nslookup*, and *traceroute*
WinQVT/NeT	Includes *mail*, *telnet*, FTP, *rcp*, SMTP server
TFTP Client95	Trivial File Transfer Protocol (TFTP) client
VIM	Enhanced version of the *vi* editor

OTHER SOURCES OF UNIX COMMANDS FOR NT

In addition to commercially packaged suites, many individual utilities are available for download on the Internet. One of the best sources for Windows NT freeware downloads is Beverly Hills Software at www.bhs.com. Microsoft also provides an excellent list of free and commercial applications at www.microsoft.com/ntserver, as shown in Table 10.2. This table presents a selected list of Windows NT-supported products that a system administrator may find useful for UNIX integration or migration.

Windows NT Functions on UNIX

If transforming your Windows NT box into something that looks and operates like UNIX is not your cup of tea, then perhaps making your UNIX box a Windows NT clone might be attractive. Clearly, this proposition is not available to date. However, some movement in that direction is evident. For example, SCO has announced add-on products to their OpenServer line that emulate some Windows NT functions. The Common Internet File System extension permits Windows users to share files and printers using the core Windows NT networking protocol. On the other extreme, a freeware product that claims to emulate the NTFS file system layer for the LINUX operating system is posted on the Internet. This implementation can be downloaded from `www.informatik.hu-berlin.de/~loewis/ntfs/`.

DATABASE SOFTWARE INTEGRATION

The major vendors of database software have designed their current offerings to take advantage of client/server technology. The common use of SQL to manage data makes it easy for a Windows-based PC user to perform tasks on larger, UNIX-based database warehouse systems (Figure 10.7). There is no requirement for the local user to know anything about the operating system on which the database resides. When speaking of products from Oracle, Informix, and Sybase, the issues of integration across platforms is nearly mute. Fortunately, these vendors also have native client and server versions for both UNIX and

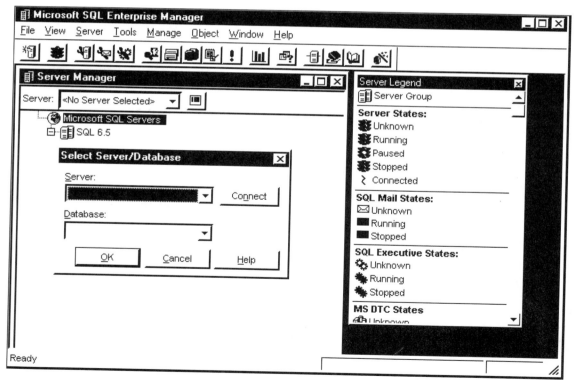

FIGURE 10.7.   Microsoft SQL Server Screen

Windows NT systems. In addition, the Windows NT BackOffice SQL Server provides a migration path from UNIX as system scalability improves. To complete this circle, UNIX client users can also access seamlessly Microsoft's SQL Server database on a Windows NT server. (It should be remembered that Microsoft's SQL Server and Sybase's SQL Server come from a common parentage and therefore have many common structures that facilitate UNIX and Windows NT interoperability.)

Windows NT includes open database connectivity (ODBC). This is an open interface that permits applications writers to implement vendor-neutral database clients. ODBC provides interfaces to more than fifty databases and is available through front-end development tools such as Visual Basic, Visual C++, Powersoft PowerBuilder, and Knowledgeware ObjectView. ODBC can be regarded as an event-driven buffer or gateway between client and server applications.

As of the writing of this book, UNIX clearly dominates the large-system database marketplace. Large data warehouses reside almost entirely in UNIX environments. However, this may change rapidly as Windows NT expands its scalability. By the time Windows NT Server 5.0 is released, the race for database dominance will be wide open.

It is outside the scope of this book to even begin to explore database theory or the use of SQL. However, the following is a list of activities that can be commonly undertaken within the context of database technology in both UNIX and Windows NT:

- Invoking SQL queries, calls, and transactions
- Formulating standard reports and retrieving data
- Viewing data and table flat file formats
- Limited tabling, indexing, and locking of data

REMOTE SYSTEM MANAGEMENT TOOLS

Another area of UNIX and Windows NT cooperative technologies is through the use of remote system management tools. The common thread for monitoring disparate systems is through the use of the Simple Network Management Protocol (SNMP)—a subset of TCP/IP.

Overview of SNMP

SNMP provides the ability to monitor any system utilizing TCP/IP. Therefore, as a means of integrating UNIX and Windows NT, the use of SNMP agent applications to monitor system activity is a natural extension. SNMP management software generally runs centrally to obtain client system data. The program essentially

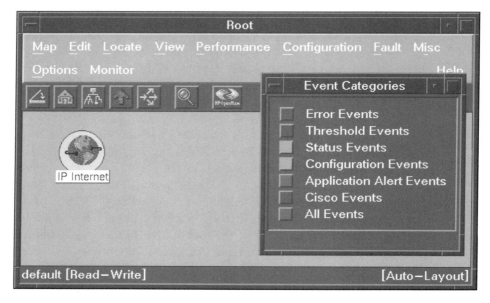

FIGURE 10.8. Hewlett-Packard OpenView Network Screen

collects information based on Management Information Base-II (MIB-II) data. For example, with the MIBs that are shipped with Windows NT, it is possible to obtain information about many of the items that are configured via the Control Panel.

Major UNIX vendors provide excellent add-on products to manage SNMP processes, including Hewlett-Packard's OpenView, IBM's NetView 6000, Sun's, SunNet, and Digital's PolyCenter NetView. These products monitor effectively network elements like bridges, routers, hubs, and switches. Hewlett-Packard's OpenView is available on both UNIX and Windows NT systems (Figure 10.8). This is an important development and represents another method for UNIX and Windows NT coexistence. Node monitoring of both operating systems can be viewed alternately by either environment through OpenView.

Systems Management Server

Microsoft's answer to SNMP monitoring is its BackOffice System Management Server (SMS). Like UNIX SNMP products, SMS does a good job of monitoring network elements like hubs and routers. The job of viewing signals from one PC to another based on console and agent MIB definitions is a singular component of SMS. One of the key tools is SMSTRACE, which examines where data packets have traveled (similar to the UNIX *traceroute* command).

In addition to SNMP network monitoring, the BackOffice SMS also provides quality system management support. One component is automated inventory and software inventory management across the Windows NT domain. Each system surveyed by the SMS database is assigned an SMS identification number (SMSID). This identification number and base-level inventory data are stored on the client system in the *sms.ini* file. SMS scans periodically for systems to determine what hardware and software has been added or deleted. If the system is unreachable, then this information is also reported to SMS, which maintains an inventory of hardware and software components for each machine.

Another valuable feature of SMS is its software distribution and installation services. Since commonly used applications can be automatically downloaded and installed on client machines, the time savings to system administrators can be enormous.

COMMON PERFORMANCE ISSUES

Products like the Microsoft Performance Monitor, Hewlett-Packard's *Glance-Plus,* Computer Associates' UniCenter, and IBM's Tivoli provide excellent snapshots of Windows NT and UNIX system activity respectively. The role of the system administrator is to optimize computer performance and to remove obstacles that otherwise inhibit proper activity. Whether we are discussing UNIX or Windows NT, there are four common areas in which system sluggishness generally occurs: memory, CPU, network, and disk I/O. When a system begins to respond sluggishly, it is easy to shoot from the hip and just begin upgrading hardware. While this may be the solution, in many cases this type of response is really like placing a Band-Aid on a disease. Therefore, a common-sense review of UNIX and Windows NT performance can prove helpful. We have elected to include a discussion on performance issues not because of any real or perceived interoperability, but because many performance issues are similar in UNIX and Windows NT.

UNIX and Windows NT Memory Performance

UNIX and Windows NT handle physical memory similarly. Problems surface when processes require more memory than what is physically available. When this occurs, the system begins paging or serving process requirements from disk. The simple fact is that disk access is significantly slower than RAM, and therefore when memory must be swapped to disk, the entire process becomes sluggish. Periodic monitoring of memory utilization is a task that every system administrator must undertake.

The Windows NT Performance Monitor measures memory in terms of pages per second (Figure 10.9). According to Microsoft, if the average is consistently greater than ten pages of data per second being written to disk, then a bottleneck probably exists. For Windows NT, it is important to monitor *memory availability* versus *committed* memory bytes. When committed bytes and the memory commit limit reach a maximum, then there is no more physical or swap room available. The system has now reached a critical state.

If you suspect that one process or application is hogging resources, both UNIX and Windows NT have tools that can help identify the problem area. The shareware UNIX program *top* (or *monitor* on IBM AIX) lists the greatest memory consumers in order (Figure 10.10). (In fact, finding memory hogs on UNIX systems is much harder than indicated. The best approach is to utilize UNIX accounting tools. However, a cheaper approach simply may be to add more memory.)

Windows NT also provides a command tool program called *pmon.exe* that shows process utilization. Once these processes are identified, then action can be taken, including killing the process in question. If the application or process is operationally critical, killing it is not an acceptable solution. In lieu of extreme measures, the system administrator can seek to schedule memory-intensive applications through *cron* or *at* during nonpeak hours. An effort can also be made to distribute these applications to other servers. If these solutions do not work, then adding memory is also advised, as is increasing swap or paging space.

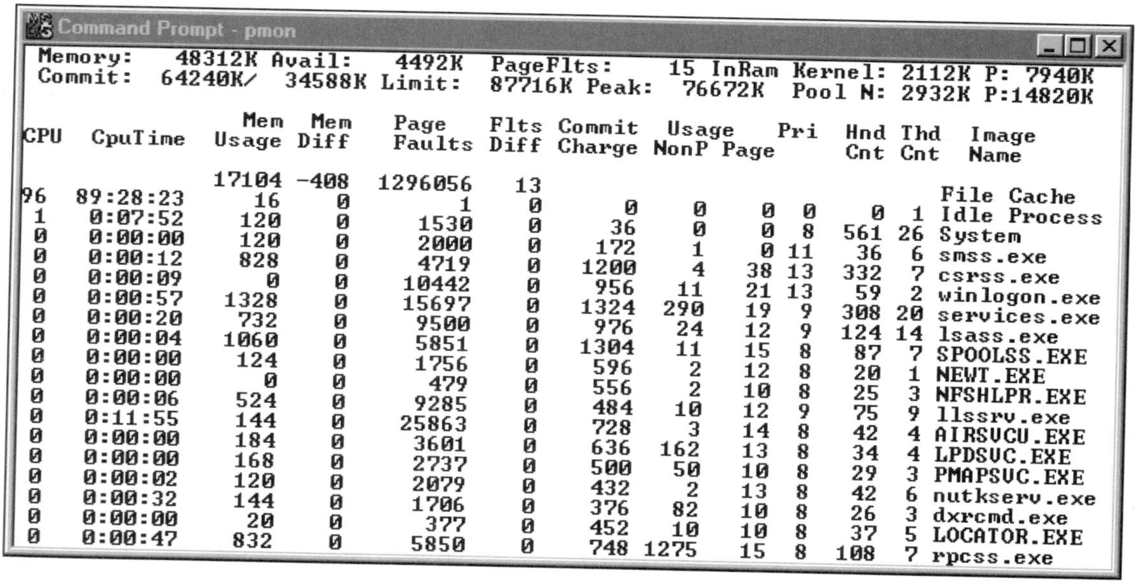

Command Prompt - pmon

Memory: 48312K Avail: 4492K PageFlts: 15 InRam Kernel: 2112K P: 7940K
Commit: 64240K/ 34588K Limit: 87716K Peak: 76672K Pool N: 2932K P:14820K

CPU	CpuTime	Mem Usage	Mem Diff	Page Faults	Flts Diff	Commit Charge	Usage NonP	Page	Pri	Hnd Cnt	Thd Cnt	Image Name
		17104	-408	1296056	13							File Cache
96	89:28:23	16	0	1	0	0	0	0	0	0	1	Idle Process
1	0:07:52	120	0	1530	0	36	0	0	8	561	26	System
0	0:00:00	120	0	2000	0	172	1	0	11	36	6	smss.exe
0	0:00:12	828	0	4719	0	1200	4	38	13	332	7	csrss.exe
0	0:00:09	0	0	10442	0	956	11	21	13	59	2	winlogon.exe
0	0:00:57	1328	0	15697	0	1324	290	19	9	308	20	services.exe
0	0:00:20	732	0	9500	0	976	24	12	9	124	14	lsass.exe
0	0:00:04	1060	0	5851	0	1304	11	15	8	87	7	SPOOLSS.EXE
0	0:00:00	124	0	1756	0	596	2	12	8	20	1	NEWT.EXE
0	0:00:00	0	0	479	0	556	2	10	8	25	3	NFSHLPR.EXE
0	0:00:06	524	0	9285	0	484	10	12	9	75	9	llssrv.exe
0	0:11:55	144	0	25863	0	728	3	14	8	42	4	AIRSVCU.EXE
0	0:00:00	184	0	3601	0	636	162	13	8	34	4	LPDSVC.EXE
0	0:00:00	168	0	2737	0	500	50	10	8	29	3	PMAPSVC.EXE
0	0:00:02	120	0	2079	0	432	2	13	8	42	6	nutkserv.exe
0	0:00:32	144	0	1706	0	376	82	10	8	26	3	dxrcmd.exe
0	0:00:00	20	0	377	0	452	10	10	8	37	5	LOCATOR.EXE
0	0:00:47	832	0	5850	0	748	1275	15	8	108	7	rpcss.exe

FIGURE 10.9. Windows NT PMON Performance Monitor

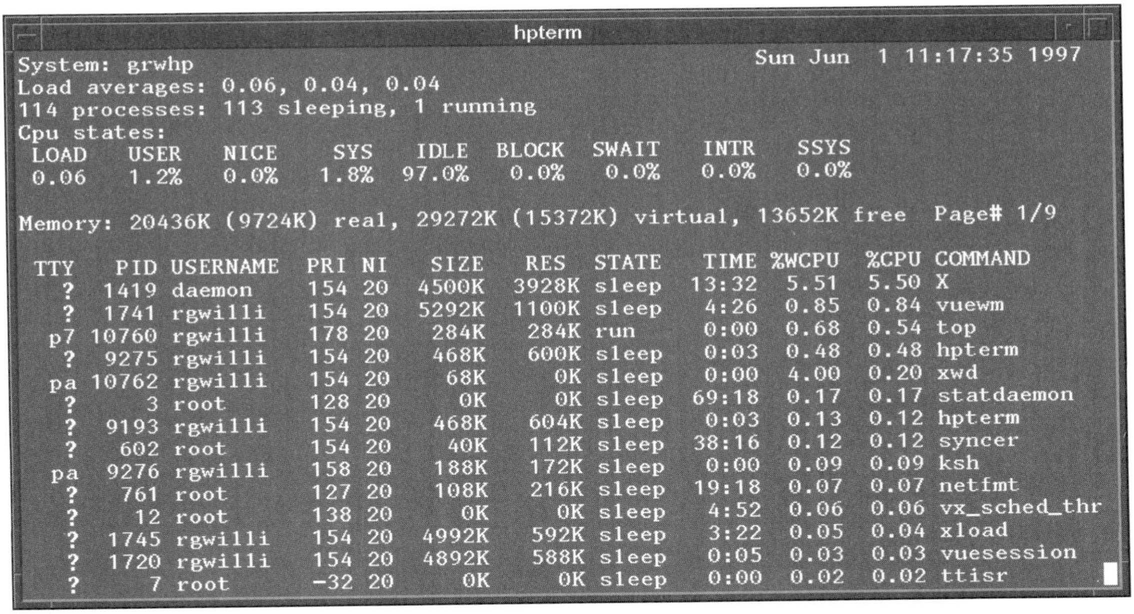

```
                                          hpterm
System: grwhp                                        Sun Jun  1 11:17:35 1997
Load averages: 0.06, 0.04, 0.04
114 processes: 113 sleeping, 1 running
Cpu states:
 LOAD    USER    NICE    SYS    IDLE   BLOCK   SWAIT   INTR    SSYS
 0.06    1.2%    0.0%    1.8%   97.0%   0.0%    0.0%   0.0%    0.0%

Memory: 20436K (9724K) real, 29272K (15372K) virtual, 13652K free  Page# 1/9

 TTY    PID USERNAME   PRI NI   SIZE    RES  STATE    TIME %WCPU  %CPU COMMAND
   ?   1419 daemon     154 20  4500K  3928K sleep   13:32  5.51  5.50 X
   ?   1741 rgwilli    154 20  5292K  1100K sleep    4:26  0.85  0.84 vuewm
  p7  10760 rgwilli    178 20   284K   284K run      0:00  0.68  0.54 top
   ?   9275 rgwilli    154 20   468K   600K sleep    0:03  0.48  0.48 hpterm
  pa  10762 rgwilli    154 20    68K     0K sleep    0:00  4.00  0.20 xwd
   ?      3 root       128 20     0K     0K sleep   69:18  0.17  0.17 statdaemon
   ?   9193 rgwilli    154 20   468K   604K sleep    0:03  0.13  0.12 hpterm
   ?    602 root       154 20    40K   112K sleep   38:16  0.12  0.12 syncer
  pa   9276 rgwilli    158 20   188K   172K sleep    0:00  0.09  0.09 ksh
   ?    761 root       127 20   108K   216K sleep   19:18  0.07  0.07 netfmt
   ?     12 root       138 20     0K     0K sleep    4:52  0.06  0.06 vx_sched_thr
   ?   1745 rgwilli    154 20  4992K   592K sleep    3:22  0.05  0.04 xload
   ?   1720 rgwilli    154 20  4892K   588K sleep    0:05  0.03  0.03 vuesession
   ?      7 root       -32 20     0K     0K sleep    0:00  0.02  0.02 ttisr
```

FIGURE 10.10.   UNIX-based *top* Performance Monitor

UNIX and Windows NT CPU Performance

Since both UNIX and Windows NT utilize the concept of processes and threads, the demand on the CPU can be both periodic and constant. When a process is waiting for input, no CPU time is being consumed. Certain applications such as word processors utilize intermittent CPU resources because they are directly dependent on user input. Databases that run background reports, on the other hand, may have a constant and overwhelming impact on the CPU.

As with memory, the system administrator is also charged with the responsibility of monitoring CPU performance. When CPU processes begin to spike, the system administrator can take several alternative actions. The simplest and least costly is to schedule high process-intensive applications to off-peak times. Whenever possible, distributing the processing load across several machines is also recommended. Upgrading processors to a higher clock speed or adding multiple processors should also be considered. It should be noted, however, that some poorly written applications still do not use multiple CPUs properly. Upgrading primary and secondary cache should also be considered. Particularly with database applications, make sure the software is optimized. Poorly designed SQL calls can use significant processing time.

UNIX and Windows NT Network Performance

While we discuss network optimizing in greater detail in Chapters 12 and 13, it is important to note that the network can also be an area of cyber congestion. Several items may generally account for such problems. Transport bandwidth is a very common problem source. If 56-KB connectivity is used where T1 transport rates are really required, then an obvious network slowdown will occur. By the same token, Ethernet cabling with its 10-MB limits might be logically replaced with FDDI or ATM in larger organizations. Another common problem relates to the physical network adapter. The use of an 8-bit network adapter in a 32-bit bus inhibits potential top performance. As with memory and CPU utilization, scheduling intensive network traffic to off-peak times can help. Further, if packet transmission is a major concern, the system administrator should examine the relative merits of protocol implementation and windows environments (such as X11 versus ICA).

UNIX and Windows NT Disk Performance

Disk performance boils down to one concept—the input and output of data. When dealing with disk performance you are generally talking about hardware configuration issues. Using mirrored or striped data sets permits the concurrent reading of data. An increase of physical RAM can also increase disk I/O through enhanced caching. On strictly the hardware side, the installation of faster disks and controllers together with proper bus architectures should be considered.

In Windows NT systems using FAT and some UNIX files systems, fragmentation can be a concern. Fragmentation involves the inability to find contiguous blocks of space for storage. As a result, the system is seeking pieces of information across the disk. The system administrator should utilize the defragmentation utilities available with Windows NT and UNIX. A general rule of thumb for all file systems is to allow 10% free space to avoid performance degradation.

NEW CLUSTERING TECHNOLOGIES

Clustering of servers is the latest technological battlefield that pitches UNIX and Windows NT against each other. While the concept of clustering has been widely used by companies like Digital (since the early 1980s on OpenVMS), it is becoming the focus for Microsoft to settle claims of scalability. Clustering technologies are rapidly emerging and appear to be moving in opposite directions. However, we believe in a short time that this will be another area of increasing importance for coexistence. The fact that billions of dollars are lost annually from computer downtime will force some level of convergence regarding inter-operable clustering technologies. Current movement within the UNIX commu-nity to standardize clustering APIs will predictably be addressed by Microsoft with its own set of APIs. Third parties will then step forward to form the neces-sary bridges. Look for this to happen in rapid succession.

A Brief Examination of Clustering

In general, a computer cluster is simply a group of otherwise independent sys-tems operating as a single, logical unit. Client systems function as if they were part of a single server. Clustering promises to reduce downtime and to expand system power. In some ways, clustering servers is equivalent to the function RAID sup-ports with disk drives. The utilization of clustering takes two basic forms:

1. *Scalability* – Clusters allow systems to share incremental additions of memory, CPUs, and storage devices. The sharing of resources permits the clus-ter to grow in relative power. Conceptually, when a cluster is overloaded, other servers can be added.

2. *Redundancy and accessibility* – The cluster also provides fail-over sup-port in the event of component failures (Figure 10.11). Should a processor fail,

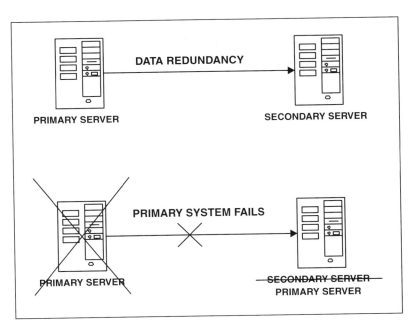

FIGURE 10.11.   Simple Cluster Fail-over

the mirrored system within the cluster provides storage access without loss or interruption. Since resources are shared, the availability of power to support applications is also enhanced.

The Future of Clustering

UNIX vendors have deployed successful clustering technology for some time. UNIX is particularly good in terms of its scalability functions. As to availability, UNIX systems also are ahead of Windows NT. However, to maintain this position major UNIX vendors are adding enhancements and calling for a unified clustering API. IBM is actively recruiting other UNIX vendors to license their Phoenix middleware. IBM's Phoenix API also supports a two-node cluster for the Windows NT environment. As of the writing of this book, vendors like Sun and SCO are actively talking to IBM about this clustering middleware and extending a broader API. In addition, these vendors have also announced enhanced clustering, like SunSoft's Full Moon suite, that will eventually offer Web-based extensions.

Microsoft is taking the criticism of its limited scalability to heart with a frontal attack on clustering by offering Wolfpack. Expected to be included in Windows NT 5.0, Wolfpack provides important although somewhat limited clustering functionality. The first release of Wolfpack is expected to be restricted to two-node fail-over support. Microsoft has a stated goal of sixteen-node scalability by mid 1998.

It is our belief that Microsoft will catch up rapidly with the clustering power already available within the UNIX community. We further believe that a convergence of APIs will permit greater interoperability between UNIX and Windows NT. How this eventually plays out is still a matter of debate and conjecture.

DISTRIBUTED FILE SYSTEM SERVER SUPPORT

In Part IV we detail the use of distributed file systems like NFS (Network File System) and SAMBA. In simple terms, these technologies permit remote access to partitions on a foreign system and appear to the user as if they are local. NFS, a Sun Microsystems-developed technology, has long been available for mounting file systems across UNIX boxes. Ports of this technology are widely and commercially available to permit UNIX files systems also to be mounted on Windows NT systems. SAMBA, a freeware product that may be downloaded at `http://lake.canberra.edu.au/pub/samba/samba.html`, permits the mounting of the Windows NT file system on UNIX boxes. Although we discuss these technologies later, it is appropriate here to suggest how distributed file systems can enhance interoperability as file servers. Using a Windows NT or

Addressing the Reality of Software Porting

The task of porting UNIX applications to Windows NT can vary radically in complexity. In some cases the scope might entail merely using a C compiler to achieve system compatibility. The other extreme case invokes a complete rewriting of code, saving only the base engineering specification. The thought of completely reengineering a complex UNIX application to run on Windows NT can be overwhelming and costly. Given the availability of excellent development tools, this approach is generally not necessary. However, if that is the only choice, then a general understanding of the scope of work is your first task. Regardless of the method to be used, porting an application involves resolving a number questions, including

- Must I maintain source code compatibility between the UNIX and Windows NT application versions?

- Will the new application be hosted on the POSIX or the Win32 subsystem?

- What elements of the code are expected to be incompatible with Windows NT?

- Is the user interface and application logic modular and generally separated or are they tightly intertwined?

- Are third-party libraries employed with the UNIX code and are these same libraries (or equivalents) available on Windows NT?

- How much time and resources are available?

- Is it practical to have a multiphased port that initially hosts the UNIX application on the Windows NT POSIX subsystem and is then eventually and fully ported to a full-blown Win32 application?

- Is a complete rewrite more practical than using layered, third-party development systems?

- Are there elements of the Microsoft Foundation Classes (MFC) functions (like printer, file, and help management) that can be used to replace certain UNIX application code elements?

- What tools are available for each phase of the development?

A discussion of porting should be a little more than theoretical. Therefore, in reviewing development tools for this book, we undertook the task of porting a large commercial C language-based application with various levels of complexity. We wanted to illustrate both the types of conditions you are likely to face plus provide a means of properly evaluating selected tools. The source code for the Decathlon GOLDMEDAL OA suite was utilized because the same code supports several dozen UNIX variants, and both character and X11/Motif user interfaces. We have direct experience porting this application suite and therefore can apply a baseline of understanding to what might be expected during the process. Due to the software's modular construction, it was possible to test both simple and heavily pointer-laden C language code. We believe that the 200,000+ lines of C source code mirror the range of complexity that will be faced in many application activities, including

- Simple C utilities with character-based output
- Code invoking fork() and exec() calls not supported by Windows NT
- Application logic that involves B-tree relational database structures, heavy network calls, and system I/O
- Code that invokes external scripts and common UNIX utilities
- User interface code that handles both character-based and Motif calls

The primary approaches we considered were to port the application to Softway Systems' OpenNT subsystem (recall that OpenNT replaces the standard Windows NT POSIX subsystem), port to the Win32 subsystem, and rewrite the application completely. The first two porting efforts were conducted with the help Softway Systems' OpenNT and DataFocus's NuTCRACKER development products respectively. It is important to note that both of these products require an additional C or C++ compiler. The third effort was attempted using the Microsoft Visual Studio 97 suite, which includes the Visual C++ product family. OpenNT also ships the gcc/gtt compiler with Version 2.1. (As to the latter effort, it was not possible to reengineer a large and complex program like GOLDMEDAL completely in a short period of time. Therefore, we only looked at a selected set of modules for our analysis.) As a final note, no attempt was made to examine device-specific code like modems or floppy drives. This would take some additional effort to map device types, and for the sake of this investigation we ignored these type of issues.

As a general statement, the porting effort involving simple character-based modules was successful with all three products. However, after more complex requirements were addressed, an added level of effort was required. This was particularly true on user interface issues. Therefore, before speaking directly about these porting tools, a brief discussion on the differences between X11 and Win32 is required.

A Brief Review of X11 and Win32

As stated before, simple character-based applications seem to port easily to Windows NT because the handling of screen output to terminals and to a DOS screen are comparatively similar. This is not true of the client/server nature of the X11 and console-based Win32 interface. The X11 server accepts requests from client applications using the standard API to invoke display actions (Figure 11.1). The communication between client and server is accomplished though the use of network sockets. The X11 client is the program that requests I/O support from the X11 server. Three levels of APIs exist to give the client software access to X11. The Xlib provides display primitives, the Xt toolkit provides greater display objects (called *widgets*) like menus, and Motif provides additional widget support and windows management. In most cases, the code that drives these API calls is separated from the logic of the program. For example, in a spreadsheet application, the mechanisms that calculate numbers are part of the program logic and remain in the back end. The display of the spreadsheet along with its fonts and graphics call the X11 API to permit I/O. X11 clients employ a continuous set of event loops that asks the X-Server for support. Once invoked, the application utilizes user interface callbacks. When a user selects a menu item, the X11 server accepts the input, passes it to an X11 client to invoke the specified application action, then passes the callback to the X11 server to display the result.

Although Win32 has many similarities to X software, the primary difference is that it does not observe the client/server display model. The Win32 API (Figure 11.2) provides the same basic functionality as Xlib, Xt tool kit, and Motif. Collectively, the application logic for Win32 applications is often separated and can be found in DLLs (Dynamic Linked Libraries). Because user interface and

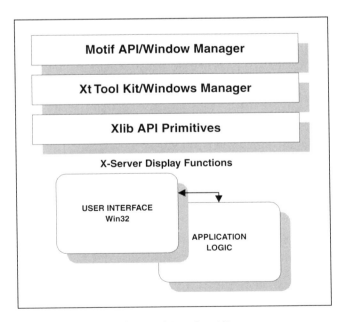

FIGURE 11.1.   Relationship of X Client
                          to Application Logic

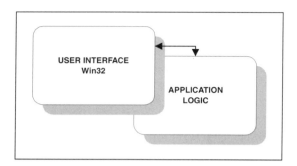

FIGURE 11.2.   Relationship of Win32
to Application Logic

application logic is often separated in both Win32 and X software, the task of mapping functions is possible.

MFCs provide a C++ framework to facilitate the separation of the user interfaces from the application logic. Events are processed as callback routines as in X11, but each component is treated as an object. MFC also incorporates common procedures like saving files, printing, and help functions. As a result, some of the application logic code inherent in many UNIX applications, such as online help, could be replaced in a Win32 port using MFC.

Windows NT utilizes the Graphical Device Interface (GDI) as a portion of the Win32 subsystem. The GDI is similar to Motif in that it provides windows management and widget object support. However, it is very different in structure from the UNIX Xlib, Xt tool kit, and Motif APIs. Fortunately, the GDI does include a "superset" of X-Windows features. It is beyond the scope of this book to specify these functions, but it is possible for the dedicated programmer to use these features in porting X applications to a native Windows NT environment.

The net impact of these differences is that moving an X11 application to Win32 involves matching display and other I/O calls. This is a daunting task to do without the use of porting tools. DataFocus's NuTCRACKER does a good job at this task. Alternately, you can elect to keep the application on the POSIX side and simply run the ported application on a Windows NT-based version of X11.

Porting to the POSIX Subsystem: A Look at the OpenNT Porting Solution

The OpenNT product family includes a comprehensive, low-cost software development kit (approximately $199 as of this writing). The OpenNT server also provides support for more than two hundred UNIX commands and utilities. This can be best described as a runtime variant of UNIX with a ksh and csh environment. In addition, an X11 server is available that supports CDE, Motif, and OpenLook window managers.

Softway Systems' OpenNT achieves its porting through the implementation of a full POSIX environment on Windows NT. Softway licensed the Windows NT source code to permit transparent subsystem support. The interaction with Win32 includes mandatory console calls, sockets, pipes, common file systems, and the ability to execute Win32 applications. You are utilizing a robust UNIX port that supports POSIX.1, POSIX.2, and XPG4. The latest versions of the product also include X11 libraries and Motif. Therefore, when porting native UNIX applications to Windows NT using OpenNT, you are basically moving a UNIX application to another UNIX environment—in this case, a subsystem of Windows NT. OpenNT achieves its porting and runtime environment through a complete implementation of a subsystem based on the POSIX standards and UNIX specifications. As a result, no Win32 API calls are required to port an application to Windows NT and a common source for Windows NT and UNIX is possible.

One of the most problematic issues in porting from UNIX to Windows NT is how to handle system calls that create parent/child relationships. The fork() and exec() calls are not supported by Windows NT. OpenNT nicely overcomes this issue by layering the POSIX structures that process parent/child calls.

The installation process for the OpenNT software development kit and related products is straightforward, using the standard Windows NT application installation **Control Panel** option or the **Run** facility. When configuring the software development kit, it is important that paths to include and library files are properly set in the Makefile created for the application port. Also, if you are installing the Command and Utility functions, make sure that you stop the Windows NT POSIX subsystem prior to copying the files. If you fail to stop the POSIX subsystem first, the installation will appear successful, but in fact will not be complete.

In attempting to port the GOLDMEDAL application suite using OpenNT, we were pleasantly surprised at the ease at which the character-based version moved across. With the exception of a half dozen minor code changes, the code compiled and linked to standard UNIX-like libraries effortlessly. The port appears stable. However, it is important to note that the application compiled strictly as a POSIX application. No effort to change support for things like local drives was considered. These types of changes must be coded by hand. The Motif version of the program required a little more effort (Figure 11.3). Some of the Xlib primitives needed to be redirected for the heavily graphical calls. The result was a stable application with the look and feel of Motif running with a Windows 95 graphic user environment. The port was really no more difficult than what we encountered when moving the code from HP-UX to an Intel-class SCO system. This is really not too surprising given the fact the OpenNT product keeps you in a POSIX environment.

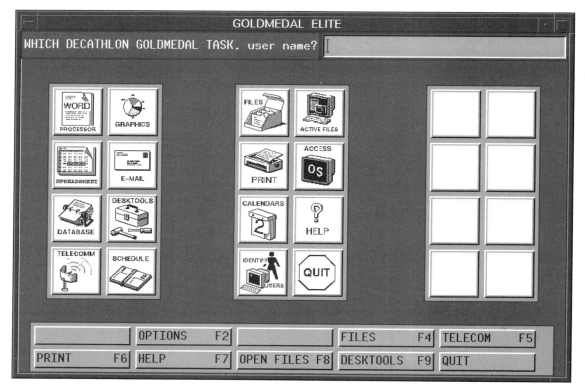

FIGURE 11.3.   Result of a UNIX-to-Motif Port Using OpenNT

If the application relies on third-party UNIX libraries or widget classes, then problems could arise with OpenNT. Most of these libraries are available on Windows NT, but only for the Win32 subsystem. The POSIX subsystem cannot invoke Win32 applications. Softway is encouraging third-party library vendors also to port to the POSIX subsystem. Since this task is relatively simple, you might see this current porting shortfall corrected over time.

If your goal is to migrate a POSIX application to Windows NT without the requirement for a Windows 95 look and feel, then the low-cost OpenNT solution is an excellent choice. It provides a robust porting environment that simply moves your current UNIX application to a UNIX-like subsystem. Applications ported using OpenNT are truly native Windows NT programs but they are not Win32 software. For most legacy applications, this is more than sufficient.

A final statement of caution is required before you decide to utilize the OpenNT solution set. All systems on which the ported applications are to run must also have OpenNT Lite installed as a minimum.

Porting to the Win32 Subsystem: A Look at the DataFocus NuTCRACKER Porting Solution

DataFocus Incorporated takes a considerably different approach to application porting. Unlike OpenNT, which provides a UNIX 95-compatible environment, NuTCRACKER simulates the most common UNIX calls and maps them directly to the Win32 subsystem. NuTCRACKER provides an API and not an emulation shell or subsystem replacement. This allows ported applications to have either a Motif/UNIX or Windows 95 look and feel. Further, because it resides within the Win32 subsystem, direct calls to other Win32 applications, tools, libraries, and objects can be made. The Microsoft Foundation Class (MFC) functions are directly addressable by NuTCRACKER; as a result, it is possible to abandon certain UNIX code in exchange for built-in facilities to generate menus, file I/O, print utilities, and on-line help.

NuTCRACKER is not a port of UNIX. For example, applications that require client/server calls will need to invoke a high-overhead vfork (for manual forking) or NutForkExec (for automatic forking and executing) procedure. The official position of DataFocus is that many specifications that are required for full POSIX and UNIX 95 compliance are not commonly utilized. As such, they have attempted to map the most common functions to Win32 and develop other calls independently. As a means of ensuring a wide range of support, DataFocus has elected to provide APIs for four variants of UNIX. When porting an application to Windows NT, it is advisable to set the appropriate cflags or #defines for the UNIX flavor that best matches your UNIX software (Table 11.1).

The NuTCRACKER approach is completed using its standard environment. As requirements evolve to make the application more Windows 95-like, then other native Windows NT development tools can be invoked. In fact, even in the initial port, Microsoft's Visual C++ environment can be utilized.

DataFocus utilizes several key third-party components to deliver its robust development system. NuTCRACKER utilizes SCO's Wintif technology to map X

TABLE 11.1.   NuTCRACKER UNIX Variant #define Macros

Variant	Macro	Description
POSIX.1	_POSIX_SOURCE	Compatibility with POSIX.1
POSIX.1/.2	_POSIX_C_SOURCE	Compatibility (partial) with POSIX.1 and POSIX.2
XPG4	_XOPEN_SOURCE	Compatibility with XPG4
Berkeley	_4.3_BSD	Compatibility with BSD
SVR4	_SVR4	Compatibility with UNIX System V, Release 4

primitives and Motif widgets to Win32. NuTCRACKER also provides more than 650 commands and utilities that they licensed from the MKS Toolkit. The company has done a fine job of integrating these components.

In our tests to port the GOLDMEDAL application suite, we found the migration of the character-based version to be a little more difficult than what was experienced with OpenNT (Figure 11.4). It should be pointed out that we exercised this tool a little harder than OpenNT in that we ran the compile four times, defining the code for System V.4, XPG4, POSIX.1, and BSD for each attempt. In each case we found that several of the calls that were normally found in two include header (*.h*) files required further definition. We also noticed a couple of missing library calls when we began the linking process. Again, we had to add the define information to the original source code. After these relatively minor changes in the code were made, all four ports were successful. The Motif version port was even easier. Since GOLDMEDAL only utilizes standard Xt tool kit and Motif 2.0 API calls, the mapping was straightforward. The resulting code appeared stable. However, the size of the NuTCRACKER-generated code was about 25% greater than that compiled with OpenNT. This

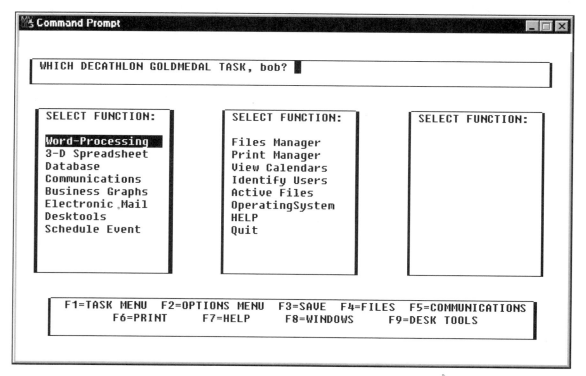

FIGURE 11.4.   Result of Character-based Port Using NuTCRACKER

fact is not too surprising in that the NuTCRACKER API transforms Motif calls to map to Win32.

It should be noted that applications ported to Windows NT using NuT-CRACKER require a runtime version of the DataFocus product on each work-station and server. This added cost should be factored into any decision to use this otherwise excellent tool set. (Ports to OpenNT also require a copy of the Lite version on target machines.)

Developers that plan to maintain both UNIX and Windows NT versions of the software should find the DataFocus solution a good, although a consider-ably more expensive, choice. However, the added ability to address the full Win32 subsystem is something that cannot be easily ignored. With this facility, developers may be constantly tempted to add Win32 enhancement to the code. When this occurs, the task of maintaining common UNIX and Windows NT source code obviously becomes more complex.

Other Potential Porting Alternatives

Other porting alternatives are available, depending on the type of application being ported and the desired results. These alternatives include using cross-platform development tools and rewriting the code using software such as Visual Studio 97.

CROSS-PLATFORM DEVELOPMENT TOOLS

Utilizing cross-platform C++ libraries is another approach that should be con-sidered. Essentially these products layer proprietary code over the native API to emulate a given environment. These types of products are best noted for their ability to provide a native look and feel to the same code running on different environments. Unfortunately, although these types of products permit easy prototyping and reasonably fast porting, they generally address only the lowest common denominators of functionality. In many cases such functions as DDE, OLE, and ActiveX are not supported. This approach can also add a considerable amount of overhead to an application. Since proprietary APIs are used, you are often locked into just those features that are supported by the libraries.

VISUAL STUDIO 97 FOR REWRITING

Another option is to rewrite the code. This may be your best choice if absolute adherence to the Win32 API is required as a long-term goal. Database applica-tions are another prime candidate for rewriting.

The Microsoft Visual Studio 97 suite is an excellent choice for two classes of migration. First, in situations when a completely native Windows NT environment is required, the Wizards can help automate the creation of a bug-free interface and application structure. The application logic can then be rewritten, or portions of the old code can simply be folded into the new structure. We took a small UNIX database application and used Visual Studio 97 to construct both a C++ and Visual Basic version of the application. We were able to take the simple sorting and data-storage logic of the UNIX application and integrate it easily into a new Windows application in a matter of an hour.

The second situation in which the Visual Studio 97 solution should be considered is with legacy database applications. The Enterprise version includes both Visual FoxBASE and the developer version of SQL Server. With these tools, it is possible to prototype most legacy databases required for use on Windows NT. Special consideration should be given to the use of Microsoft's VisualInter-Dev to develop Web-based interfaces to legacy applications.

USING OBJECTS

While porting is important, the use of the software components that communicate the data of the future is also a vital concern. The object is center stage in the war of technologies between Windows NT and UNIX. Windows NT defines itself as using objects as its base component. UNIX vendors are rapidly embracing the object paradigm. Not surprising, Microsoft and the UNIX community are promoting significantly different object architectures. Equally understandable, market forces are forcing these factions to work toward a common object solution set.

UNIX CORBA

CORBA is middleware that was developed by the Object Management Group (OMG). The OMG is a consortium of more than seven hundred companies, including IBM, Sun, Hewlett-Packard, Apple, Netscape, and Oracle. Microsoft is the notable exception. As a distributed object API, CORBA's design permits intelligent components to interact and discover other objects. CORBA defines an abstraction model that details logical components with their interfaces. This means that two CORBA-compliant objects can invoke each other's properties locally or on other machines. There are four primary elements to CORBA:

1. *Object Request Broker (ORB)* – This defines the object bus at the source code level (but not at the binary level).

2. *CORBA facilities* – This defines the application frameworks used by objects.

3. *CORBA services* – This defines the system-level object.

4. *Application objects* – These are objects and applications that are consumers of CORBA structures.

CORBA objects can be written in any language, providing that strict adherence to the specifications is maintained. Unfortunately, one of the current realities relating to CORBA technology is the extensions being added by companies like IBM that allow their objects to interoperate, but provide object communication to some other CORBA objects. CORBA is particularly valuable in the context of the Internet. It can help define how Web-based objects are loaded, manipulated, and modified. Netscape in particular is making CORBA a widely used client. It is bundling its version of the CORBA ORB as VisiBroker for Java ORB with every server. This automatically equates to more than twenty million CORBA-based installations. Other major vendors are equally as aggressive. JavaSoft is incorporating CORBA as the foundation for its Enterprise Java product. Oracle includes CORBA as part of its Network Computer Architecture. IBM, Hewlett-Packard, Digital, Novell, and many other vendors have announced CORBA-based products.

Microsoft COM and DCOM

The Component Object Model (COM) is Microsoft's base-level answer to CORBA. In mid 1996, the company introduced the distributed version—DCOM. COM defines how objects and their clients interact. These components can interact without an intermediary. In both Windows NT and UNIX, processes run separately from one another. If a client needs to communicate with other processes, then an IPC call must be made. COM intercepts the calls and transmits them to the other process. When these elements are resident on different computers, DCOM replaces the IPC with a network protocol (Figure 11.5). The primary enhancement is support for ActiveX components that can be embedded in Web pages. DCOM servers can run under both Windows NT and UNIX.

The theory behind the creation of object models is that they can be used repeatedly to communicate common functions. The battle between CORBA and COM hinges on the binary standards that define source code API parts. As an example of a COM object in action, consider using COM to embed a drawing into a word processor. The COM binary permits the drawing and word processor to communicate while maintaining their own process identities. The COM interface is comprised of six predefined primary components:

1. *COM clients* – As implied, COM clients make requests and services from COM objects.
2. *COM interfaces* – This functional prototype table describes the extent of functionality of the object.
3. *COM classes* – COM interfaces are implemented by COM code classes.
4. *IUnknown interface* – IUnknown supports the interface and object lifetime management.

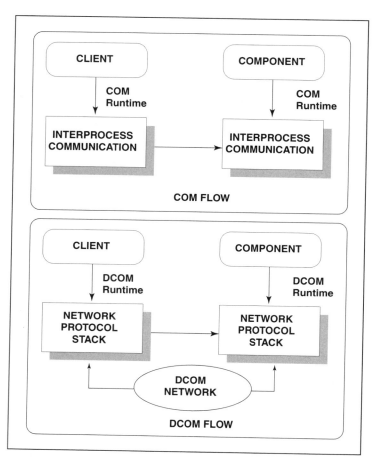

FIGURE 11.5.   COM and DCOM Relationship

5. *Class objects* – A meta class that maintains object inventory information and the raw data associated with the object.

6. *COM servers* – COM objects that operate within the sphere of the COM server, either as part of a DLL in-process event or external to the client process.

DCOM is little more than a network extension of COM. A very important concept is that the COM and DCOM objects separate the interface from the object logic. DCOM can employ multiple transport protocols including TCP/IP, IPX/SPX, NetBIOS, and the User Datagram Protocol (UDP). In addition, COM and DCOM objects can be written in any language, including C, C++, and Java. This means that DCOM objects, like CORBA, can also be platform neutral.

Examples of the Object Model

To understand the importance of having a commonly defined object model, simply consider how these objects will be used. If one of the considerations in moving code from UNIX to Windows NT is object maintenance, then the eventual confluence of CORBA and DCOM is vitally important. The following is a very small sample of how these models are being separately employed.

- Financial institutions are beginning to use CORBA objects to facilitate account management and bill payment.
- Web servers widely employ CORBA and DCOM (ActiveX) applets as embedded intelligent agents in home pages.
- Different application objects are embedded in a host application (like a word processor) and still retain separate process space and discrete operation.
- Database objects are shared to perform more rapid common transactions.

When the CORBA Bites COM

The original group that fostered CORBA is also in the forefront of bridging the gap with DCOM. The OMG has already announced a COM-to-CORBA link. In this case a COM component works as a proxy for a CORBA server and then transmits CORBA protocol messages. The OMG is now evaluating proposals for extending this link to DCOM. The real difference is that DCOM is a distributed technology and should be relatively easy to achieve. Even Microsoft is weighing in on the side of interoperability. During the March 1997 Object Work East conference, Microsoft executives agreed to the importance of a common DCOM and CORBA link. Microsoft supported the current proposal from Hewlett-Packard that takes network communication through DCOM protocols and uses the CORBA server to translate the data. The battlefield is somewhat mute in that COM and DCOM are not Microsoft-proprietary technologies at this time—the independent ActiveX Consortium controls them. Should these positive events continued to unfold, interoperability on the object front should be ensured.

HARDWARE MIGRATION

When we began writing this book we proposed including a section about migrating UNIX hardware elements to Windows NT. Unfortunately, after much analysis there is really not much to say except to suggest the following very commonsense notions.

- Most printers supported on UNIX can be utilized with Windows NT.
- Intel-class systems and Digital Alpha systems can be utilized with Windows NT (but not all CPUs).
- External devices such as modems, tape backup units, and CD-ROM can generally be salvaged and utilized with Windows NT (providing driver support exists).

Beyond these simple suggestions, the market for boat anchors that look like old computers is relatively narrow. Unfortunately, the loss of value on existing hardware with any migration effort is a harsh reality. The only positive aspect is that commodity-based PCs and devices are generally less expensive than traditional UNIX iron.

FINAL THOUGHTS

When considering any migration, the issue of software maintenance is a normal concern. A standard response is to maintain the legacy system until applications can be rewritten for the new platform. Obviously this may also be an alternative that must be applied in some UNIX-to-Windows NT migration efforts. Fortunately, there are also valid alternatives. Softway Systems offers a product line that permits the effortless porting of UNIX software to a greatly enhanced Windows NT POSIX subsystem. DataFocus, by contrast, provides a system call-mapping solution that permits the movement of UNIX source code to the Win32 subsystem. Finally, native Win32 development environments such as Microsoft's own Visual Studio 97 provide a framework for redeploying an entire application without having to rewrite the user interface and other components. As to hardware migration, the news is not quite as good. Although some devices can be put into place, the wholesale migration of hardware platforms is simply not a very viable alternative.

# Part V

Windows NT and UNIX Integration

As premier network operating systems, the cornerstone of UNIX and Windows NT integration rests on the common utilization of TCP/IP and related services. Chapters 12 and 13, respectively, provide an overview of network connectivity and how the TCP/IP suite can be used to assure greater interoperability. Chapter 14 examines the interrelationship of UNIX sendmail and internet mail with Microsoft's Exchange Server. Finally, Chapter 15 discusses the role Windows NT and UNIX play with the Internet and the specific management of Web servers.

- Chapter 12, UNIX and Windows NT Network Overview
- Chapter 13, UNIX and Windows NT Network Integration
- Chapter 14, Electronic Mail Integration
- Chapter 15, Windows NT and UNIX as Web Servers

Chapter
12
UNIX and Windows NT Network Overview

Contributed by Michael Borowski

The centerpiece of UNIX and Windows NT integration rests on the backbone of common networking functions. UNIX and Windows NT are both network operating systems with a wide range of supported protocols (Figure 12.1). These next two chapters center on the TCP/IP protocol suite. Specifically, Chapter 12 provides an analysis of the TCP/IP stack and how it is utilized by the respective operating systems, and Chapter 13 provides a hands-on review of the TCP/IP suite's setup and maintenance for both homogeneous and mixed UNIX/Windows NT enterprises.

System integration is best described as the ability to take multiple computing resources and utilize them together, thereby creating enhanced or entirely

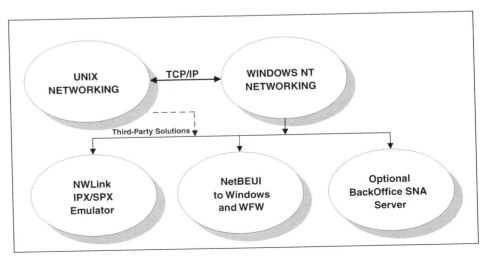

FIGURE 12.1.   Summary of Supported Network Protocols

new functionality. The network is the central component involved in providing interoperability to disparate operating systems. The ideal network technology provides robust support for all target platforms, rather than merely for propri- etary environments.

The TCP/IP protocol suite generally fits the definition of an idealized network technology. The Internet Protocol (IP) and the Transmission Control Protocol (TCP) have emerged as the common denominator for connecting otherwise dis- similar technologies. TCP/IP's early domination of the Internet, coupled with it becoming the de facto standard on which so many associated technologies are built, has resulted in its adoption by most vendors and platforms. The acceptance of this open standard by such a large community of developers and users has greatly stimulated the development of many useful computing applications uti- lized today. The primary emphasis of this chapter focuses on the nature of IP net- working as it is implemented in the Windows NT and UNIX environments. It is important to acknowledge that TCP/IP is operating system independent.

HISTORICAL BACKGROUND

In ancient computing history (circa 1968), the Department of Defense's Advanced Research Project Agency began the development of packet switching networks. These early networks primarily connected universities and defense agencies, and by the mid 1980s this *ARPAnet* evolved into an extended entity loosely referred to as the *Internet*. At that time, the National Science Foundation largely separated the Department of Defense's backbone (the MILnet) from a newly funded "Internet" infrastructure destined for commercial and civilian use. Today, this portion of the Internet is in part managed by a commercial entity—Advanced Network Services.

NOTE   Terminology Reference

Please note the following terms and contexts used in Chapters 12 and 13.

- The term *internet* refers to any instance of IP networking, isolated or otherwise.

- The term *Internet* (capitalized) refers to the more nebulous and global entity open to much of the world.

- The term *intranet* indicates an internet of known and finite proportions, such as one that spans a single organization and is usually accessible only to users within that boundary.

UNIX has largely been considered a network operating system (or NOS) since the very early 1980s when TCP/IP was first introduced into BSD variants.

The TCP/IP protocol suite and the UNIX operating system matured together, often hand in hand by the same developers. An elegant and seamless relationship emerged between the two, and today the protocol is as standard to UNIX as air-conditioning in Arizona. In fact, so intertwined is TCP/IP that configuring many of today's UNIX variants as *stand-alone* systems still requires the presence of certain basic networking services. TCP/IP is now included as a standard component in almost all UNIX derivatives.

On the other hand, early desktop operating systems, or more accurately those from Microsoft, initially embraced IP technology far less enthusiastically. DOS and early Windows-based systems tended to prefer more proprietary protocols. Early Windows network implementations were predominately Novell-based IPX/SPX or Microsoft-centric NetBEUI. The first real, reliable IP stacks came from third-party vendors such as Ftp Software, Inc. (`www.ftp.com`). Although Microsoft has made major strides in embracing TCP/IP, even Windows NT Server 4.0 falls short of implementing the entire TCP/IP suite.

In spite of the fact that IP networking seemed more of an afterthought to Windows 3.x, Microsoft owes much of its desktop dominance to the propagation of Windows as an IP client. Microsoft has come full circle. The company is now quite anxious to associate its name with the Internet in general and all the wonderful IP-based network applications that comprise it. Current Microsoft advertising promotes the Internet as if it were just one more application out of Redmond, and savvy marketing aside, some of the most useful TCP/IP applications now reside on Microsoft platforms.

PROTOCOL BASICS

Just as effective conversation between two individuals requires a mutual understanding of a single language, so too does any communication between computers. A protocol is a set of agreed-on rules and structures that control communication. The concept of a protocol is so rudimentary that we often do not appreciate its significance until it is missing. For instance, the use of punctuation in a paragraph is an example of a protocol in use. This section describes the fundamental elements of the IP and TCP.

Network Architecture

No self-respecting treatment of network architecture would be complete without the obligatory presentation of the Open Systems Interconnect (OSI) model. The OSI model attempts to outline each possible component involved with network communication in a sequential and hierarchical fashion (Figure 12.2). The OSI model is a *conceptual* model on which most network and protocol implementations do not precisely and strictly adhere. However, an understanding of

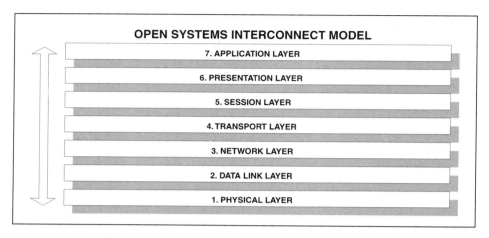

FIGURE 12.2.   The OSI Model

each part of the model helps us to grasp the roles of various networking components. As shown in Figure 12.2, the OSI model consists of seven layers.

PHYSICAL LAYER

The physical layer loosely refers to just about any characteristic of the hardware, such as signal voltages or cable and connector specifications. The sole objective of this layer is the transmission and reception of data in its raw and most simple form—bits or 1's and 0's. This is achievable on an amazing array of network mediums. Other, higher level layers are responsible for reassembling these bits into meaningful data. Standards such as Ethernet, RS232C, or X.25 dictate the requirements of this layer.

TCP/IP is a *hardware-independent* protocol suite and mostly indifferent to the physical layer. To help grasp the significance of this, think of language as a physically independent protocol. Human communication can be expressed by verbal speech, via hard-copy written text, or modulated into radio waves. It does not usually *require* particular characteristics inherent to any one of these substratas. Similarly, TCP/IP can also be expressed on a variety of physical media. This might include Ethernet hardware, infrared light, or serial and telephone lines. The attribute of hardware independence is extremely beneficial to a protocol frequently utilized to connect heterogeneous computing platforms, which tend to have highly varied hardware and physical connectivity issues. A tribute to IP networking is reflected by the number of physical layer media originally designed and intended for completely different protocols, but ending up predominately handling IP traffic instead. This in turn enables applications to interoperate with other systems and databases with little or no reengineering.

The physical layer does have a great impact on the *efficiency* of TCP/IP, as well as on the overall integrity of the network. The physical attributes of the hardware, media, and specifications at this level usually determine or limit the capacity and speed of the data transmitted.

DATA LINK LAYER

The data link layer changes the raw bit stream presented by the physical layer into data frames or blocks. This layer can also bring limited error control to the data stream. Just as in the physical layer, TCP/IP typically assumes the use of other standards to specify characteristics of the data link layer. Such independence allows TCP/IP to function on a network interface card using the IEEE 802 standard with almost identical functionality as it would on a parallel port with a custom driver.

NETWORK LAYER

The network layer presents the first active role for the IP. It is at this level that IP manages communication between the application layer and the lower physical or data link layers. The three primary roles of IP are as follows.

1. IP provides the Internet addressing scheme, or how network components may be identified.

2. IP defines a common structure or format for *datagrams*. A datagram is a packet of data as well as information describing that data (such as its destination, type, source, and size). Consequently, the IP also defines how the datagrams are interpreted.

3. IP also specifies how data is routed between Internet networks and addresses, especially on segmented or subdivided networks. This layer is used to connect multiple networks with different physical layers. For instance, a machine connected to both a token-ring and an Ethernet network can exchange IP traffic in a fashion completely transparent to the network applications.

TRANSPORT LAYER

The transport layer provides error detection and notifies the higher level application layer as appropriate. The transport layer may request the retransmission of bad or lost packets. This layer also works with the application layer in determining how to identify simultaneous traffic from multiple network applications. IP traffic between the two will typically use either the TCP or the User Datagram Protocol (UDP) and then associate each type of application with a specified port. All telnet traffic, for instance, traditionally resides on TCP port 23, whereas NFS traffic is typically defined on UDP port 2049.

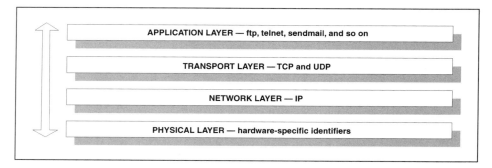

FIGURE 12.3.   Abbreviated Network Model Applicable to TCP/IP

SESSION LAYER

The session layer refers to the connectivity and management of network applications. This layer does not equate well to TCP/IP networks. With TCP/IP, the application and transport levels usually handle this functionality.

PRESENTATION LAYER

The presentation layer attempts to standardize the data format prior to passing it along to the network application's interface. Again, as in the session layer, TCP/IP networks tend to handle this role directly from within the application layer.

APPLICATION LAYER

The application layer can be thought of as any process or program that uses data received or sent through the network. It may have a user interface to allow control of the program or to act on its own. In a well-constructed network, this is the only layer apparent to users.

A MODIFIED NETWORK MODEL

There is little consensus on exactly how TCP/IP components map or equate to the OSI model. For Chapters 12 and 13 we perceive the network as comprised of just four layers, and we consider the physical and data link layers to be one layer (Figure 12.3).

The Transmission Control and Internet Protocols

The remainder of this section covers the configuration of the transport protocols (TCP and UDP) and the network protocol (IP) on both UNIX and Windows NT platforms. Later sections describe the attributes of various networking media and topology, and finally the applications that use these networks.

USER DATAGRAM PROTOCOL

Each layer of the network model adds a header of information to the data traversing the network. The network application sends a stream of data to the transport layer, which in turn appends to it a TCP or UDP header (Figure 12.4).

The UDP header contains only information pertaining to the source of the data and the data's destination. UDP receives no acknowledgment from the receiving end confirming that the data arrived correctly. Instead, UDP relies on the application or other network layers to guarantee reliable delivery, and retransmits the entire data packet when there is a failure. In some applications this is more efficient than establishing a verifiable transport-layer connection with the destination.

UDP does reside on defined ports, enabling the IP layer and the receiving end to determine which is the intended application for the data.

TRANSMISSION CONTROL PROTOCOL

Applications that require the transport layer guarantee and then verify that the data was received by the intended destination. Such applications must use TCP (Figure 12.5) rather than UDP. For this reason alone, TCP has become the preferred protocol.

TCP SEGMENT HEADER INFORMATION

TCP establishes a connection with the destination's transport layer and retransmits the entire data *segment* until an acknowledgment is received from the destination. The TCP header contains a checksum, which describes the data or number of bytes contained within the segment. The receiving end compares the checksum value against the amount of data actually received. Should the comparison show a mismatch, the segment is discarded and no acknowledgment is sent. The source retransmits any segments for which no acknowledgment is received.

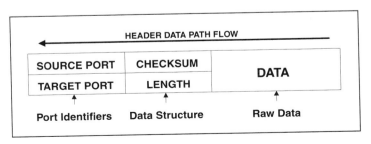

FIGURE 12.4.   UDP Header Information

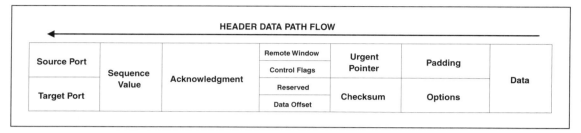

FIGURE 12.5.   TCP Header Information

The window portion of the header is sent from the receiving end and tells the transmitting side how much data it can accept. This window contains a zero if the receiver cannot handle any more data, and the sender then stops and waits for a larger value before continuing. The connection is closed when a segment is received with a special bit or control flag indicating there is no more data to be sent.

An additional function of the transport layer is determining the target application for the incoming data. On UNIX platforms, each network application (whether it is using UDP or TCP) has a corresponding port assignment defined within the */etc/services* file (Figure 12.6). This file may be edited from the normal conventions for various reasons, including security or the addition of new network applications.

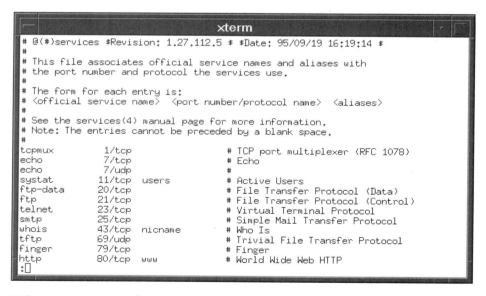

FIGURE 12.6.   Partial Listing of the UNIX */etc/services* File

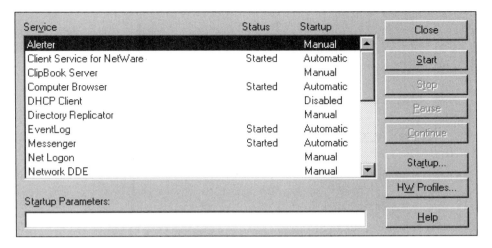

FIGURE 12.7.   Partial List of Windows NT Services (Port) Configuration

Windows NT also allows for control of TCP port services. A UNIX-like services file, similar to Figure 12.6, exists in the *%systemroot%\System32\Drivers\Etc* directory of the Windows NT operating system. However, it is far easier to use the Windows NT GUI interface provided within the **Services** selection (Figure 12.7) from the **Control Panel** (**Start** ➤ **Settings** ➤ **Control Panel** ➤ **Services**). The ability to determine the type of application for which the data is intended is extremely useful in creating firewalls and enforcing security.

IP Addressing

When data segments pass from the transport layer to the network layer, the IP appends its own header information and the new grouping becomes a datagram (Figure 12.8). The information contained in this header reflects the responsibility of the IP.

HEADER DATA PATH FLOW						
Version	Identification	Time to Live	Source Address	Destination Address	Padding	Data
Header Length	Flags	Protocol				
Service Type						
Datagram Length	Fragmentation	Checksum			Options	

FIGURE 12.8.   Internet Datagram

One of the foremost roles of the IP at the network layer is identifying or addressing a particular network and device. Sometimes referred to as a *node,* network devices include servers, desktop computers, network-interfaced printers, and even devices with the sole purpose of accommodating network traffic. The destination address describes where the information is to be sent and consists of a 32-bit value, separated into four octets.

NOTE   **A Word of Clarification**

There are two primary types of addresses that are discussed in this chapter. Do not confuse an IP address, the type discussed in this section and characterized by four numeric octets, with hardware- or medium access control (MAC)-level addresses used by the physical and data link layers.

- *19x.16x.1xx.1xx* – An IP address
- *08-00-09-93-2D-C8* – A MAC, hardware, or Ethernet link layer address

Part of an IP address defines the network and the other part defines the actual device. The portion of the 32-bit value allocated to each definition varies depending on the *class* of the address. Some classes allocate more bits for network definitions and fewer for nodes; others are capable of defining fewer networks but more individual nodes. The range of values available for either networks or nodes is referred to in this book as the *address space.* The class of an address is determined by the following three rules:

1. A class A address specifies a 0 as the first bit or a first byte less then 128. The first byte in a class A address defines the network, and the remaining bytes are available for assignment to individual nodes. The result is a mere 128 (0 to 127) potential class A networks, but an enormous number of hosts.

CLASS A ADDRESS

8-bit Network Address	24-bit Host Address
2x.	106.111.111

NOTE   There exists address space for 128 class A addresses (0 to 127), however it is important to note that the IP architecture reserves class A addresses 0 and 127 for special uses, resulting in 126 assigned class A networks.

2. Class B addresses contain a 1 and a 0 in the first two bits, or a value from 128 to 191 in the first byte. The 14 bits after the 1 and the 0 identify the individual networks, and the last 16 bits are available to specify node addresses. This equates to more potential network addresses than a class A address, but fewer addresses available for assignment to specific devices.

CLASS B ADDRESS

8-bit Network Address   24-bit Host Address

129.1xx.   111.111

3. Class C addresses begin with 1 1 0 in the first three bits, or a value of 192 to 223 in the first byte. The next 21 bits proceeding the 1 1 0 provide the range of network addresses, and the last 8 bits (the last byte in the address) are used to provide up to 254 hosts or node addresses.

CLASS C ADDRESS

8-bit Network Address   24-bit Host Address

192.1xx.111.   111

SUBNETTING

In some circumstances it can be useful to take a given address within a class and "move" or redefine the network and host portions. This creates additional *subnets* within an existing network space. Such implementations alter the available address space for networks and hosts. For instance, if your Internet service provider (ISP) assigned you a single class C address but you needed multiple IP networks, you might decide to break this single class C address into four subnets.

It is important to understand that the only hosts or device nodes capable of viewing and reaching these subnetted networks are either (1) those that have been explicitly told about *where* the subnet occurs (which portion of the address has been redefined as network bits, rather than host or device bits) or (2) those hosts with traffic that first travels through a device containing this information (such as a router).

Those devices that are to reside on a subnet must be configured with a *subnet mask*. A mask is a sort of blueprint used to define how the address space is divided between networks and hosts. This blueprint looks like a normal IP address, however the bits define the separation of the two address spaces (network and host), not an actual network or particular device. Subnet masks are usually simplified by being applied to entire bytes, rather than making the division at the bit level within a single octet. Let's look at the notation in Table 12.1 for default net masks without subnetting (the 255's denote network octets and the 0's denote host octets).

TABLE 12.1.   Submask Table

Class	Network mask
A	255.0.0.0
B	255.255.0.0
C	255.255.255.0

For example, a normal class B address with a default mask of 255.255.0.0 is broken down as

CLASS B ADDRESS

Network Address	Host Address
129.1xx.	13x.111

A *subnetted* class B address, however, with a mask of 255.255.255.0, would shift and be divided as

CLASS B ADDRESS

Class B Network Identifier	Network Address	Host Address
129.11x.	13x.	111

Using the subnet mask of 255.255.255.0 in conjunction with the class B address results in 254 different networks with a maximum of 254 devices on each, rather than a single network with potentially thousands of devices.

Similarly, to divide a single class C address into six separate networks, a subnet mask of 255.255.255.224 would result in the class C subnets shown in Table 12.2.

TABLE 12.2.   Class C Subnets

Subnet	Host address
19x.168.21.32	19x.168.21.33–62
19x.168.21.64	19x.168.21.65–94
19x.168.21.96	19x.168.21.97–126
19x.168.21.128	19x.168.21.129–158
19x.168.21.160	19x.168.21.161–190
19x.168.21.192	19x.168.21.193–222

REASON FOR SUBNETS

A host computer, router, or other piece of network hardware is frequently connected to multiple, physically different network media. In such a situation, each physical network may need to have its own unique network address. Subnetting allows this to happen without using an entire additional, conventional address. In addition to this and other physical layer concerns, dividing or partitioning a large address space into several smaller networks can make network management easier. In situations when nodes must communicate across subnets, different media, or with hosts assigned to different network addresses, the traffic must be *routed*.

Routing

Network communications between hosts residing on the same IP network and connected to the same physical segment can reach their intended destinations without routing. This is convenient on limited, isolated networks, such as those frequently found in a small organization. Any more complicated scenario frequently requires the network data to be "routed," or directed through a specific "gateway" to reach the appropriate destination. A route describes a destination through which different networks and hosts can be reached. A gateway resides on a UNIX or Windows NT server with multiple network interface cards (NICs), or a gateway might be a hardware device specifically intended for this function alone, such as a router. The rules describing how gateways and routers handle network communications are collectively referred to as *routing tables*.

NOTE   Routing of data is not necessarily limited to the network layer. Bridges and switches, for instance, can make routing decisions based on information at the data link layer.

USING NAMES

Identifying networks and devices with numeric addresses is fine for computers, although quite unwieldy for people. It would be quite unrealistic to expect users to remember the numeric addresses for all the systems that they utilize. Computer systems that utilize IP networking therefore allow the assignment of names to both host and network addresses. For instance, a computer with an IP address of 20x.20x.13x.8 might also be referred to as the node named *turbo*. This name refers to an actual computer on a specific network. When a user or application refers to turbo, the operating system uses a subsystem to identify which IP address is assigned to that computer or device. This process is called *name resolution*. The most basic form of name resolution on a UNIX system uses a file called */etc/hosts* (Figure 12.9).

Within a */etc/hosts* file, such as the one depicted in Figure 12.9, the lines beginning with a pound sign (#) are comments and are ignored by the system. We see that any network request for `localhost` or `loopback` will use the 127.0.0.1 network address. Any use of the name `turbo` or `turbo.petfinders.org` will use the address 207.203.138.8. Why are there two names for turbo? One is a system name and the other is a *fully qualified domain name*. There are many other ways of resolving names into network addresses. UNIX machines have fairly standardized processes for name resolution that apply to all network applications that run on them. Microsoft operating systems are capable of using many of the same subsystems. For now, know that in configuring and using a network, a name can be used to represent an IP address if it has already been added or set up for name resolution.

Many versions of UNIX extend the */etc/hosts* file with an */etc/networks* file that contains names that are resolved to the network portion of an IP address. Check the *man* pages or system documentation for details pertaining to the */etc/networks* file on a particular UNIX operating system.

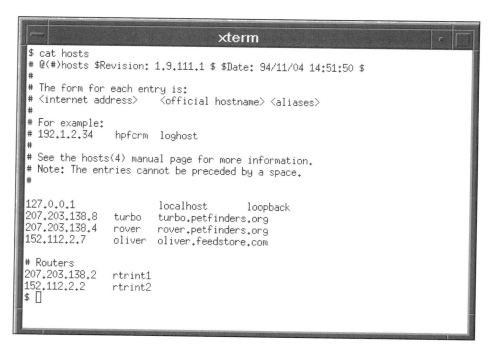

```
$ cat hosts
# @(#)hosts $Revision: 1.9.111.1 $ $Date: 94/11/04 14:51:50 $
#
# The form for each entry is:
# <internet address>    <official hostname> <aliases>
#
# For example:
# 192.1.2.34     hpfcrm   loghost
#
# See the hosts(4) manual page for more information.
# Note: The entries cannot be preceded by a space.
#

127.0.0.1               localhost       loopback
207.203.138.8   turbo   turbo.petfinders.org
207.203.138.4   rover   rover.petfinders.org
152.112.2.7     oliver  oliver.feedstore.com

# Routers
207.203.138.2   rtrint1
152.112.2.2     rtrint2
$ []
```

FIGURE 12.9.   Example of */etc/hosts* File

Just as Windows NT provides a UNIX-like services file, there also exists a hosts and networks file within the *%systemroot%\System32\Drivers\Etc* directory. Again however, there seems to be a tendency for some Windows network applications to ignore this system and attempt to build their own database of host names and addresses. The most common name resolution method of all is the DNS, and it is covered from various vantages in Chapters 13, 14 and 15.

AD HOC VERSUS REGISTERED DOMAIN NAMES AND ADDRESSES

When configuring an isolated network (one that is not connected to the Internet and uses a simple hosts file method for name resolution) there is no problem with using ad hoc host-naming schemes and IP addresses. Using host names such as *carol.accounting* or *server1* together with random IP addresses will work as long as the implementation adheres to the operational rules of the TCP/IP (subnets, masks, and so on). However, such methods are strongly discouraged under almost any circumstances, even if at present you cannot conceive of your network ever being connected to the Internet. By initially taking the time to obtain a proper domain name and network addresses, extraordinary conversion difficulties can be avoided down the road, and network growth can occur far less painfully. Having to revisit network configurations simply because an authorized domain name and network address was not initially obtained is a costly experience. If a network manager is bound and determined to use unsanctioned IP addresses and names, then the following guidelines are helpful:

- Use a protocol like BOOTP or DHCP to assign IP configurations dynamically for all equipment from a central source. This means that when there are changes to be made, they can be propagated through the network without having to visit each machine individually. These protocols and their particulars are discussed in Chapter 13.

- Some versions of UNIX have gateways that can be configured to "mask" local-side IP addresses so that all Internet-bound traffic appears to come from a single IP address. The gateway handles the translation.

- If none of the previous solutions is workable, then be certain to at least use one of the three IP address blocks that the InterNIC has specifically set aside or allocated for all private, non-Internet connected intranets:

  Class A – 10.0.0.0 to 10.255.255.255 (one network)

  Class B – 172.16.0.0 to 172.31.255.255 (sixteen different networks)

  Class C – 192.168.0.0 to 192.168.255.255 (256 different networks)

The processes of obtaining both a registered Internet domain name and an IP address into which the name resolves are two separate issues. The Internet Assigned Number Authority has contracted a commercial entity to handle address assignment in North America. Network Solutions, Inc. can be reached on the Internet at `http://rs.internic.net` or by phone at (703) 742-4777. Alternately, since class C addresses are becoming a rare commodity (remember IP version 4 has only a limited address space for each class), common practice is to obtain a block of addresses from your ISP. This is convenient at first; however switching ISPs at a later date may mean losing the originally assigned address space.

Having obtained a sanctioned IP address is only half the battle. A network needs a registered domain name. Unfortunately, an amazing number of names have already been taken. Again, one may start this process at the InterNIC or, more easily, have your ISP handle it. Should you opt for the latter, be certain the ISP registers your domain name with your corporation as the owner of the name, and not the ISP.

Physical Connectivity

The physical connectivity of multinetworked computer systems and devices is, for obvious reasons, a crucial aspect of integration. Remember that the TCP and IP are hardware independent, meaning they can be ported or made to run over almost any network. This is a major advantage because the UNIX and Windows NT operating systems frequently run on a wide variety of hardware and likewise use many different types of physical networks.

ETHERNET

The Ethernet is the most common type of LAN for TCP/IP. Two primary standards for Ethernet now exist: (1) Ethernet II jointly developed by Digital, Intel, and Xerox, and (2) IEEE standard 802.3. The difference between these two standards is largely inconsequential, as the two are almost completely compatible. The IEEE 802.3 Ethernet standard pertains to both the physical and the data link layers and describes the details of frame transmission and other interface particulars below the network layers containing the Transmission Control and Internet Protocols.

Ethernet interfaces (such as the card to which a network cable connects) are manufactured with a unique data link layer. These addresses are sometimes referred to as *Medium Access Control (MAC) addresses* and consist of a 48-bit, 6-octet, alphanumeric representation. Ethernet frames utilize these addresses to identify the source and destination interfaces. It is both interesting and useful to note that the first 23 bits of a MAC address identify the manufacturer of that interface. For instance, in the MAC address 08-00-09-93-2D-C8, the first three octets, 08-00-09, exist only on all Hewlett-Packard-manufactured interfaces (and thus usually identify a Hewlett-Packard computer or network device). A complete list of vendor assignments exists in IEEE RFC 1700.

ETHERNET MEDIA

Ethernet standards also identify the physical cable attributes and types fit for Ethernet traffic. The four most popular are

1. *10BASE2* – 10BASE2 is characterized by a thin coaxial cable with BNC-type connectors and attachments. One advantage of this older cable model is that systems can be easily "daisy chained" together, requiring fewer central hub ports, and in some cases fewer and shorter cable runs. Each coaxial interface has a T-shaped connector, and each of the two open ends requires either a cable segment to another interface or to a terminator plug. Each cable segment between interfaces can be as long as 185 to 200 m.

2. *10BASE-T* – 10BASE-T is the most commonly used cable specification today, and is characterized by unshielded twisted pair (UTP) wire. Each end of the cable normally has an RJ45-type connector that looks like the plug on a phone line, only larger. Normal designs require a dedicated cable running from a networked device's interface to a port on a hub. The 10BASE2 and 10BASE-T standards are rated for data speeds up to 10 Mb/s, although such throughput and speed are almost never actually achieved. Inexpensive transceivers or adapters can be used to connect most 10BASE-T interfaces to 10BASE-2 cables, and vice versa.

3. *10BASE-TX* – 10BASE-TX is one of several new standards, mostly utilizing various UTP cabling types, with data rates up to 100 Mb/s.

4. *Token-ring* – The token-ring cable standard actually comes from IBM rather than IEEE and runs over both an early version of heavily shielded "type 1" cable as well as UTP. Data rates exist for 4, 16, and 100 Mb/s.

OTHER NETWORK MEDIA

The Ethernet is far from being the only data link and physical layer medium on which TCP/IP can operate. There are many others types of substrate and cabling (such as phone lines or radio) that have various, different data link models to accommodate a particular medium's attributes.

Most networking implementations also adhere to some form of *topology* that impacts the overall cost, efficiency, reliability, and redundancy of the network. A *star topology,* in which all devices have their own dedicated run to a central hub, is perhaps the most popular. There are *ring* topologies, such as the one used by FDDI (100 Mb/s), and a point-to-point model that is frequently used to run TCP/IP over serial lines and modems (PPP; 2.8 Kb/s or more).

SPECIFIC, SUPPORTED TCP/IP SUITE COMPONENTS

The Internet Engineering Task Force (IETF) maintains the TCP/IP specifications of the InterNIC. In general, UNIX variants support the majority of the RFCs for the TCP/IP protocol suite. Windows NT Server supports the most commonly used elements. The following is a list of components common to both UNIX and Windows NT Server 4.0, many of which are defined in the appendices.

- *TCP/IP services and applications – ftp, echo, snmp, lpd,* and *chargen*
- *Utilities – ftp, lpr, finger, rexec, rsh, telnet,* and *tftp*
- *Basic protocols* – TCP, IP, ARP, UDP, ICMP, RAS, SLIP, and PPP
- *Interfaces* – Berkeley socket API (Winsocket) and RPC
- *Network tools – arp, ipconfig, lpq, netstat, ping, route, hostname,* and *traceroute*

FUTURE DEVELOPMENTS

TCP/IP is constantly evolving. The IETF of InterNIC is currently proposing additional changes. The current IP version 4 will be superseded by version 6. Anticipated changes include

- Shifting the support from 32-bit to 128-bit space for Internet addresses
- Improved organization of routing tables
- Automatic configuration of IP addresses
- Built-in user authentication and data encryption

FINAL THOUGHTS

It should be clear that TCP and IP are flexible network protocols with a longevity and usefulness that have revolutionized computing, with little changes to their core operation over many years—years that have seen other technologies come and go. The significance and value of TCP/IP as a tool for interoperation between Windows NT and UNIX is undisputed. As the industry acceptance of an open standard forges common networking, there are no inherent operating system dependencies embedded in the protocols. TCP/IP's vendor independence has provided all the attributes that make the technology so ideal for system integration. In this regard TCP/IP is a shining example of the benefits of open standards.

# Chapter 13

UNIX and Windows NT Network Integration

Contributed by Michael Borowski

This chapter covers the issues involved in integrating Windows NT and UNIX networks. Both the parameters and applications necessary for interoperability over a TCP/IP network are covered. Topics include

- IP network configuration
- Routing configuration
- Network applications configuration and use
- File and print sharing
- Network management
- Distributed computing
- Network security

CONFIGURING AN IP NETWORK

In the previous chapter the nature of an IP network was summarized. Those concepts apply to almost any computer or operating system using IP networking. We now turn our attention to the procedures for configuring connectivity with the Windows NT and UNIX operating systems in particular.

Fundamental IP Configuration Tasks

Each interface has a unique IP address and resides on an explicitly defined network that is described by its subnet mask. The following list outlines common information and network parameters that should be obtained prior to configuring either a Windows NT or UNIX operating system:

- The static IP address to be assigned to the interface (or dynamic host addresses; see the Dynamic IP Addressing with DHCP section)

- The net mask or subnet mask of the network to which the host is attached

- The computer's domain name and/or NetBIOS name specified during installation

- Any network adapter- and card-specific settings, such as IRQ, DMA, or I/O address

- The IP addresses for any default routers or gateways (only if on a routed network)

- The address of the Domain Name Service (DNS) server if name resolution is to be used

CONFIGURING WINDOWS NT TCP/IP INTERFACES

The first step in configuring Windows NT is to load the driver for the network adapter. (Note that when installing Windows NT, it is strongly recommended that the network adapter already be physically installed in the computer. This streamlines the network setup and forces a confirmation of the hardware during operating system installation.) Depending on the history and source of the computer system, this driver may or may not be installed already. If the car is already installed, then simply load the driver when prompted during the operating system installation. Otherwise, to begin the process, select **Start** ➤ **Settings** ➤ **Control Panel** ➤ **Network**.

If for some reason networking support has not been installed, a prompt is presented that gives the option of installing that portion of Windows NT. After support exists, the network window shown in Figure 13.1 appears and reflects the **Computer Name** and **Domain** that you designate.

First, select the **Adapters** tab in the Network window.

If a network adapter and driver are already present, as is the case in Figure 13.2, then you are ready to continue with configuring TCP/IP. If there is no adapter already installed, one can be added with the **Add** button. The administrator can either select from a list of presently available drivers or use a vendor-supplied driver with the **Have Disk** option (Figure 13.3). Some adapters can have their software program settings changed.

To finish installing the adapter, a system reboot may be required. Since the focus of this discussion is using TCP/IP to integrate a Windows NT machine with UNIX computers, return to the Network window by selecting **Start** ➤ **Settings** ➤ **Control Panel** ➤ **Network** and then select the **Protocols** tab (Figure 13.4). If you are prompted to restart the computer system, then follow that suggestion at that time.

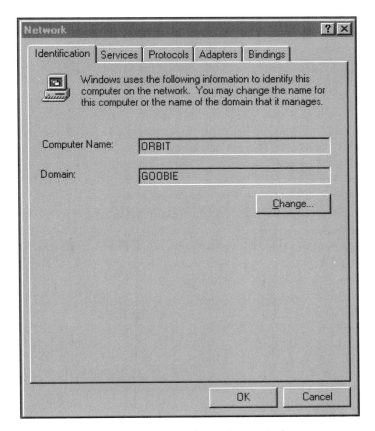

FIGURE 13.1.   Network Configuration Window

Select **TCP/IP Protocol** and then click on the **Properties** button (Figure 13.5). Should TCP/IP not already exist, the **Add** button provides the option of installing it. Removing unused protocols may conserve system resources.

Once the Microsoft TCP/IP Properties window is open, select the adapter card that is to be configured in the **Adapter** field, such as the [1] 3Com card in Figure 13.5. To configure static, permanent IP addresses, make certain that the **Specify an IP address** radio button is selected. The DHCP option is covered later. Now you can assign the IP addresses appropriate for this interface.

In the example in Figure 13.5, the first 3Com adapter on the Windows NT machine has been assigned an address of 129.106.138.144. Further, the interface exists with a subnet mask of 255.255.0.0. As discussed in Chapter 12, this subnet places the interface on a network using the first two octets (or first two groups of three numerics) as network identifiers and the last two octets as unique node or host addresses.

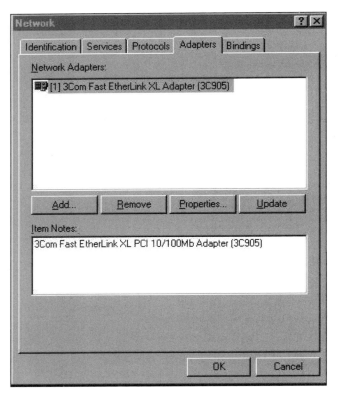

FIGURE 13.2.   Network Adapter Window

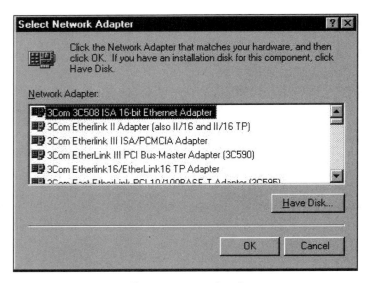

FIGURE 13.3.   Installing a Network Adapter

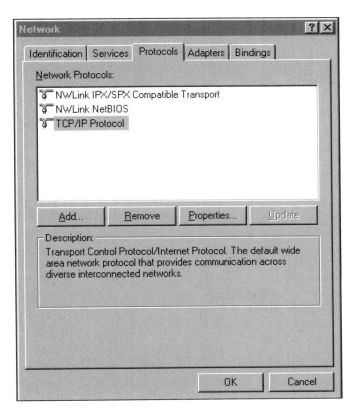

FIGURE 13.4.   The Microsoft Windows NT Network
                Protocols Window

Ideally there also should be some means for this machine to "talk" with
nodes and hosts on other networks. The **Default Gateway** field specifies that
all traffic *not* on the local network be sent and routed through the gateway
address—129.106.138.141. Obviously the gateway address must exist on the
same network and subnet as the local interface, and will usually be either a
hardware-only router or another Windows NT or UNIX system functioning as a
router with additional interfaces to other networks. (This type of a computer is
considered to be a *multihomed* computer.)

Additional Windows NT TCP/IP Interface Parameters

While at the Microsoft TCP/IP Properties window, let's consider optional IP configuration issues. The **Advanced** button within the **IP Address** tab provides
additional options (Figure 13.6).

From this window additional IP addresses and subnets can be added to a
single interface. This allows a single physical network connection to use and be
identified by multiple IP addresses that can operate on different logical net-

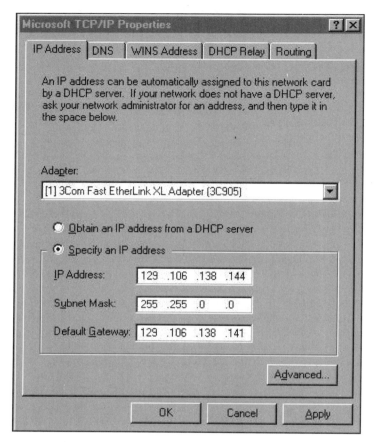

**FIGURE 13.5.   Windows NT TCP/IP Properties
Configuration Window**

works or subnets. It is usually advisable to use a separate physical interface for each IP address and network whenever possible, rather than bind multiple IP addresses and networks to a single interface, as has been done in the example in Figure 13.6. Using separate network cards reduces possible saturation or bottlenecking of a single, given network interface on heavily used systems, as well as simplifies routing and security concerns. However, the option to "bind" multiple IP addresses to a single interface card can be extremely useful in certain situations, such as when configuring host applications like Web servers to respond to multiple Universal Resource Locator (URL) or domain names.

Please note the selection box that allows for the configuration of additional gateways and routes to other networks and hosts. In Figure 13.6, a second, additional gateway of 129.106.138.140 has been configured to provide routing functions identical to the first default, 129.106.138.141. This tactic allows the 129.106.138.144 interface to communicate with other networks via a secondary

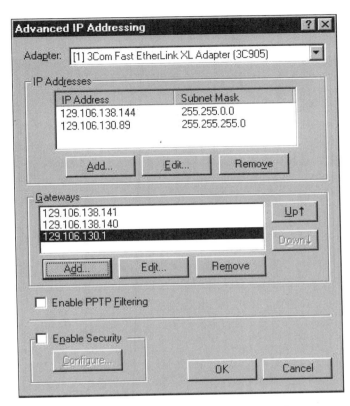

FIGURE 13.6.   Windows NT Advanced Interface Configuration Window

gateway if the first default gateway or router ever fails or experiences downtime. Also note that a third default gateway (129.106.130.1) has been added on the same subnet as the interface's second IP address (129.106.130.89) so that it too can transcend the local network.

Click on the **OK** button for this window and the previous one to configure and bind the specified settings to the interface. The interface is ready for use.

Displaying a Windows NT Interface Configuration
With Windows NT, the *ipconfig* command is used to display information pertaining to the configuration of an existing (installed) IP interface (Figure 13.7). The Windows NT command prompt syntax is

```
ipconfig [/? | /all | /release [adapter] | /renew [adapter]]
```

where /? displays the help message, /all displays complete or "full" configuration information, /release releases the IP address (DHCP) for the specified

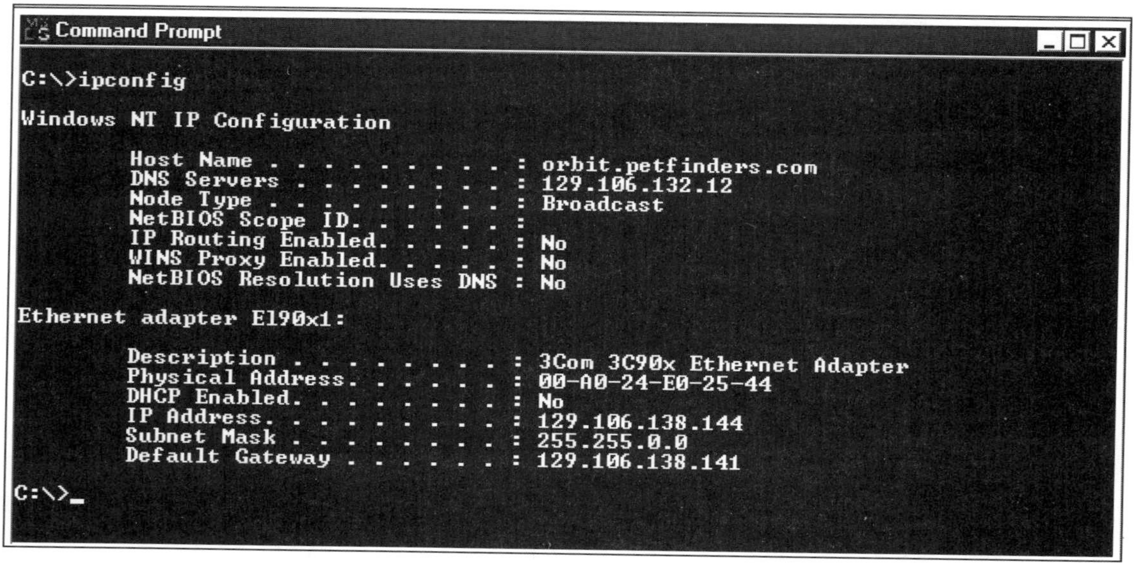

```
Command Prompt                                                    _ □ ✕

C:\>ipconfig

Windows NT IP Configuration

        Host Name . . . . . . . . . . : orbit.petfinders.com
        DNS Servers . . . . . . . . . : 129.106.132.12
        Node Type . . . . . . . . . . : Broadcast
        NetBIOS Scope ID. . . . . . . :
        IP Routing Enabled. . . . . . : No
        WINS Proxy Enabled. . . . . . : No
        NetBIOS Resolution Uses DNS : No

Ethernet adapter E190x1:

        Description . . . . . . . . . : 3Com 3C90x Ethernet Adapter
        Physical Address. . . . . . . : 00-A0-24-E0-25-44
        DHCP Enabled. . . . . . . . . : No
        IP Address. . . . . . . . . . : 129.106.138.144
        Subnet Mask . . . . . . . . . : 255.255.0.0
        Default Gateway . . . . . . . : 129.106.138.141

C:\>_
```

FIGURE 13.7. The Windows NT *ipconfig* Command

adapter, and /renew renews the IP address (DHCP) for the specified adapter. The default output contains information for *all* TCP/IP interfaces if none are defined explicitly as an argument to the command.

In Figure 13.7 *ipconfig* displays the IP host and domain name, a description of each adapter, the physical- or MAC-layer address discussed in the previous chapter, as well as the addresses for each interface, subnet mask, and default gateway. Additional useful information, such as where the host retrieves DNS and whether DHCP is enabled for a particular interface, is also displayed.

CONFIGURING UNIX TCP/IP INTERFACES

One of the more elegant aspects of UNIX is the treatment of most devices, including network interfaces, as zero-length special-character device files. On hardware manufactured with a specific UNIX operating system in mind, such as a Sun Sparc using Solaris or an RS/6000 using AIX, the network interface device files exist and are configured for the default hardware settings. Rarely do hardware settings need to be changed or new device files created in these circumstances. However, this is not often the case with UNIX derivatives on Intel platforms such as FreeBSD, SCO, or UNIX-like LINUX. These UNIX ports need to address and to support a wide variety of network interface cards (NICs) manufactured by many different vendors. In these instances the system administrator must sometimes change hardware settings, create new device files, and even update kernels.

NOTE   **A Few Words about Driver Support**

Manufacturers of NIC have a tendency to presume they will only be used on Microsoft Windows, Novell, or DOS platforms. Many cards come with drivers for these operating systems only and provide little or no support for UNIX.

Fortunately the developers of Intel-based UNIX operating systems have done an admirable job of developing their own support for an enormous range of third-party network cards. Before investing money in a NIC, check your operating system documentation or on-line help facilities (newsgroup or Web page) for recommendations on which cards provide the most seamless support.

Please note that some cards require IRQ, DMA, and address settings that are configurable only with vendor-supplied DOS software. These cards can usually be configured once from a DOS boot diskette or on a separate computer and only then used on a UNIX system. In some cases, this condition also exists with Windows NT.

After the UNIX kernel or operating system recognizes the existence of a network card, each interface will require its own unique identifier. Table 13.1 presents some examples. See your system documentation to determine, and create if necessary, the device identifiers for a specific network interface.

After the kernel and device support exist for a given network card, the *ifconfig* command is used to configure IP parameters and enable the network interface. With many UNIX operating systems there exist system administration utilities, or prompts during the operating system installation, that generate and configure the interface parameters. These utilities usually also add the local networking parameters to the *rc* or boot process so they will exist forevermore.

Knowing how to configure an interface from the command line serves most network administrators well. The common syntax for the UNIX *ifconfig* command is

```
ifconfig [device identifier] [IP address] netmask [Netmask]
```

TABLE 13.1.   Example of Interface Identifiers

UNIX variant	Interface
HP-UX	First interface card: lan0
FreeBSD	Intel EtherXpress interface: ix0
FreeBSD	First 3Com interface: ep0
FreeBSD	Second 3COM interface: ep1
LINUX	First interface card: eth0

The following are some usage examples, although the exact syntax and options may vary slightly between different UNIX operating systems. See your system documentation or *man* pages for further details.

```
# ifconfig ep0 207.203.138.8
```

configures the interface ep0 with the address 207.203.138.8; no netmask is used

```
# ifconfig ep0 207.203.138.8 netmask 255.255.255.192
```

same as the previous string except with a net mask of 255.255.255.192

```
# ifconfig lan0 207.203.138.8 down
```

disables the interface lan0

DISPLAYING A UNIX INTERFACE CONFIGURATION

The *ifconfig* command can also be used for checking the configuration of an existing network interface on most UNIX machines. Common syntax requires only the name of the interface as an argument, although some ports of UNIX will list information for all interfaces if none is explicitly defined as an argument. Entering

```
# ifconfig lan0 <enter>
```

under HP-UX, for instance, might provide the following information:

```
lan0: flags=863<UP,BROADCAST,NOTRAILERS,RUNNING>
inet 129.106.138.144 netmask ffff0000 broadcast
129.0.0.0
```

Such output tells the user that the lan0 interface is "UP and RUNNING" with an IP address of 129.106.138.144 and a net mask of ffff0000 (or 255.255.0.0).

TESTING THE INTERFACE

Both UNIX and the Microsoft NT operating systems can use *ping*—a program that necessitates a fundamentally sound network connection to verify further that the interface is available to application-layer programs. The *ping* program in its simplest form takes a destination as an argument, either an IP address or a resolvable host name, and sends a packet to that destination. *ping* then expects an "echo" or reply packet to be sent back. *ping* can be used from either the Windows NT command prompt, a third-party Windows NT GUI application, or from the UNIX command line (shown in Figure 13.8). The absolute path to the *ping* executable may vary from platform to platform.

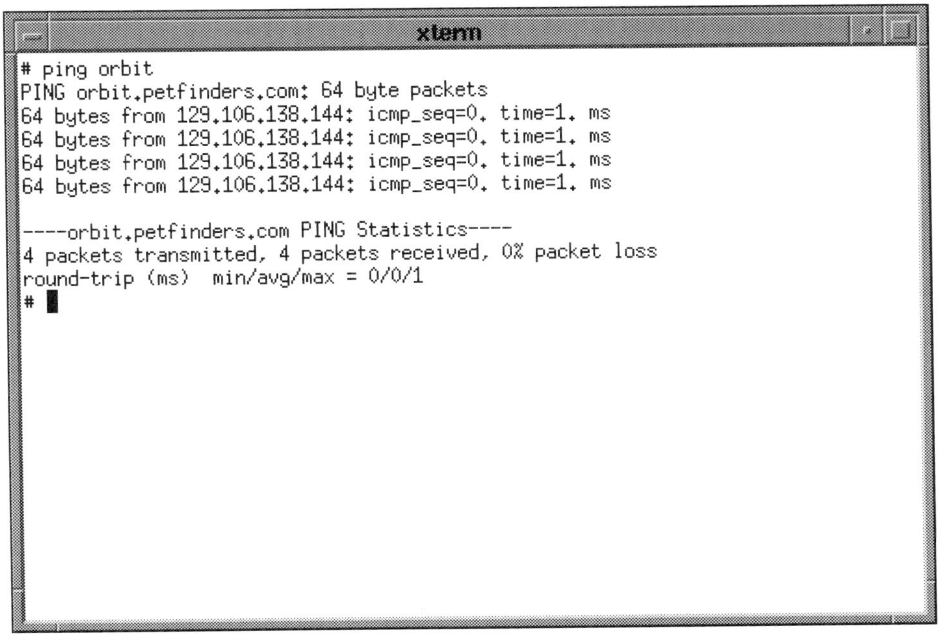

```
# ping orbit
PING orbit.petfinders.com: 64 byte packets
64 bytes from 129.106.138.144: icmp_seq=0. time=1. ms
64 bytes from 129.106.138.144: icmp_seq=0. time=1. ms
64 bytes from 129.106.138.144: icmp_seq=0. time=1. ms
64 bytes from 129.106.138.144: icmp_seq=0. time=1. ms

----orbit.petfinders.com PING Statistics----
4 packets transmitted, 4 packets received, 0% packet loss
round-trip (ms)  min/avg/max = 0/0/1
#
```

FIGURE 13.8.   The *ping* Network Application

Feedback from the command can also be useful in diagnosing connectivity problems. A *Network is unreachable* message may indicate that an interface or required route does not exist or is incorrectly configured on the local host. Packets sent but not "replying" sometimes indicate that even though the local host has a connection to the desired network, the remote target destination's interface is either down or does not have a working route back to the local interface.

Configuring Name Resolution

Thus far all configuration tasks have referenced IP addresses rather than host names. As mentioned in the previous chapter, *name resolution* is the process by which a computer takes a host name and matches it to an IP address that can be actually used on the network. If no explicit instructions pertaining to name resolution are given, then the local host file is used. Both Windows NT and UNIX servers can also be configured to provide name resolution via DNS.

This section does not cover how to configure an actual DNS server, but instead covers how to configure a Windows NT or UNIX system as a client, able to resolve host names by way of an external DNS server that is already configured. To continue, the IP address of at least a primary DNS server that is TCP/IP accessible must be obtained first.

WINDOWS NT DNS CLIENTS

To configure a Windows NT system to use DNS name resolution, select **Start ➤ Settings ➤ Control Panel ➤ Network** and the **Protocols** tab. Select the **TCP/IP Protocols** entry, click on **Properties**, then select the **DNS** tab (Figure 13.9).

The top two fields describe the local system's host and domain name. Simply click on the **Add** button to enter the IP address of a DNS server to be queried for name resolution. Multiple entries can be added, and by selecting an entry (highlighting it) each entry can be changed individually with the **Edit** button or removed from the list with the **Remove** button. The top entry is queried when name resolution is requested by an application. Should the first DNS server not be available, then each entry below it will be queried in descending order. The search order can be modified by selecting an entry and clicking the **Up** or **Down** buttons.

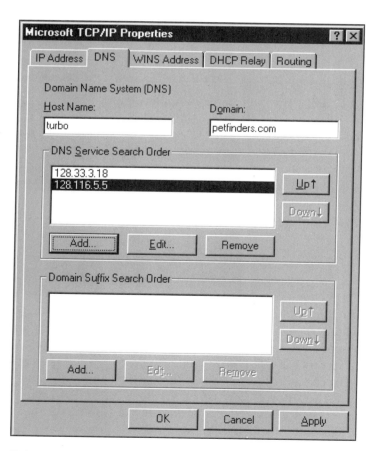

FIGURE 13.9.   Windows NT Network Properties
DNS Window

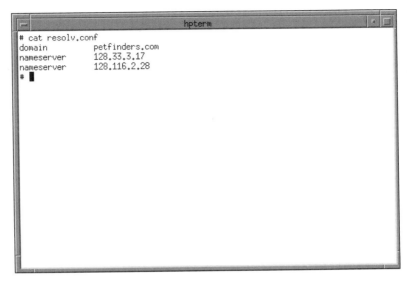

```
# cat resolv.conf
domain          petfinders.com
nameserver      128.33.3.17
nameserver      128.116.2.28
#
```

FIGURE 13.10.   A Sample */etc/resolv.conf* File

UNIX DNS CLIENTS

Most UNIX systems use a text file within the */etc* directory called *resolv.conf* to identify which DNS servers should be used for name resolution (Figure 13.10). Notice the absence of an "e" at the end of *resolv*. This anomaly will cause some confusion should */etc/resolve.conf* (with an "e") ever be edited mistakenly instead, so remember the correct filename.

As can be seen in the sample file in Figure 13.10, a *resolv.conf* file has a domain entry and list of DNS servers to be queried.

NOTE   Name Resolution

In addition to DNS, many UNIX systems can optionally utilize other subsystems for name resolution. Most prominent among these alternatives is *yellow pages* (also known as *NIS* and *NIS+*) or the conventional */etc/hosts* file. There is, however, no standard among various UNIX operating systems concerning which subsystem has priority. To clarify, some versions of UNIX can be configured to use one method of name resolution, such as */etc/hosts,* and then query a second or even third subsystem (perhaps DNS and then NIS) should the first fail to respond with the requested IP host name. Some versions of UNIX cannot utilize multiple methods concurrently, and among those that can there exists no standard way of defining the process or operation. For further details, see the variant-specific system documentation for your particular version of UNIX. Some third-party Windows NT TCP/IP suites also include NIS clients.

ROUTING CONFIGURATION

As noted in Chapter 12, the address space in any given class or subnet is limited. Whenever a network expands to the point where it must transcend multiple network addresses, then some form of routing must be implemented to forward packets between them. This is the case even when the networks share the same physical backbone. Other scenarios mandating IP routing exists when packets must traverse physical networks or data link layers (bridging). Providing security is another common use for routing and gateways. Firewalls in their most simple form are merely routers with more stringent rules regarding which packets are to be forwarded. Again it should be noted that most router-specific roles are implemented just as easily with either Windows NT or UNIX. Most routing protocols discussed later also operate on both operating systems. Fortunately the rules and methodologies for implementing a routed IP network are nearly the same regardless of the operating system or the hardware platform. Many configuration tasks and even some of the command syntax used to configure routing are nearly identical on both Windows NT and UNIX platforms.

Understanding a Routing Table

The previous sections described how to assign a default gateway under Windows NT. This allows the system to identify where to send any data with a destination that is not on the local network. The specified default gateway was required by Windows NT to create a default route. An examination of the routing table is now appropriate.

Both UNIX and Windows NT use the *netstat* command with almost identical syntax to display information regarding routes and TCP/IP connections. The command *netstat -rn* displays routing tables by IP address (Figure 13.11). The *-r* option tells the *netstat* command to display routes, the *-n* option tells *netstat* not to resolve IP addresses to host names. There are many other powerful options for *netstat* that display a wide array of additional useful information. Although the *-rn* argument appears almost universally, other options may differ from one flavor of UNIX to another. For this reason, see your system's *man* pages (UNIX), or type `netstat /h` (under Windows NT) for more information. At a minimum, *netstat -rn* on any platform should provide the following information:

- The network address for each communicated network or node to be communicated (or alternately a host address may also be used)
- The net mask for each network address
- The gateway address through which the network can be reached

- The IP address of the local interface that should be used to transmit packets to each network
- A metric or value describing the number of network "hops" required in the route. (Use a metric of 1 for a LAN or local address not needing a remote gateway, such as when both interfaces exist on the same IP network. This value increases for each router or gateway that must be crossed to reach a remote destination.)

NETWORK ROUTES

In Figure 13.11 we see that the 127.0.0.0 address is configured as a "loopback" interface for testing purposes of the IP subsystem. This system's IP interface has an address of 128.116.2.5 and a 255.255.0.0 net mask. It needs no router or remote gateway to reach other computers located on this same local network. This is reflected by the second routing table entry specifying that all traffic destined for 128.116.0.0 addresses use the system's own local interface as the "gateway."

If the computer's 128.116.2.5 interface tries to communicate with hosts on the 128.33 network, it must use a separate remote gateway. In Figure 13.11, any IP data destined for the 128.33 network is first sent to gateway 128.116.2.10, which then forwards the IP packets to the 128.33 network. This is called a *network route,* since it applies to any data intended for any host on the 128.33 network. A network

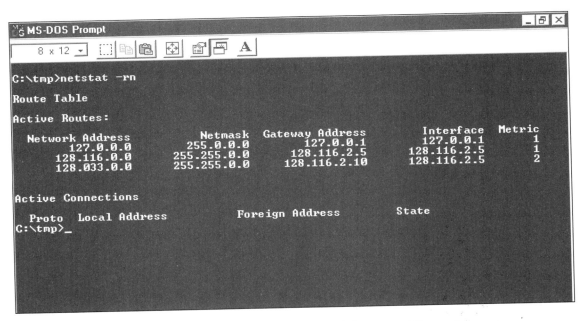

FIGURE 13.11. *netstat -rn* Output from a Windows NT Command Prompt

route makes routing decisions based only on the network portion of an IP address, providing a path to any host residing on that particular network.

HOST ROUTES

A host route exists as a path to an individual system and makes routing decisions based on an entire IP address. Notice the fourth entry in the routing table in Figure 13.12. Rather than displaying just the network, there is an entire IP address including the host portion (132.12) listed as a possible destination. This means that anytime IP data is sent to the host 129.106.132.12, the gateway 128.116.2.18 is used. This is different from the network route in the third entry, which uses the gateway 128.116.2.11 for any host residing on the entire 128.33 network.

Knowing that the system with this routing table has a local interface of 128.116.2.7, we can identify another host route. The second entry uses the loopback address as a gateway for internal IP communication sent to itself (128.116.2.7), rather than the actual interface. This may allow some local IP-dependent applications and subsystems to continue operating even in the event of a physical network or interface failure.

Observe that in the UNIX example in Figure 13.12 the *netstat -rn* output looks slightly different from previous examples. There is an entry displaying how many times each route is referenced (the Refs column) and how much IP traffic has traversed each route (the Use column). There is no net mask column displayed with the *-rn* arguments. In this particular version of UNIX a *-v* or verbose option must also be supplied to provide net mask information. Again, see your *man* pages for exact syntax on different platforms.

DEFAULT ROUTES

The default entry's gateway is used for all other destinations that reside on different networks and have no other specific routes defined. In Figure 13.12 the final entry lists `default` as a possible destination. With Windows NT and many varieties of UNIX, the host route has priority over a network route. The default route is used last, when and if there is no other match.

Windows NT uses 0.0.0.0 to indicate the default route rather than the actual word. Since just one default route is ever actually used, be certain to configure it only once.

Enabling IP Forwarding

For reasons of security, Windows NT and many UNIX operating systems are *not* enabled by default to forward IP packets or to act as a routers themselves. The default disabling of packet forwarding (regardless of rational routing tables

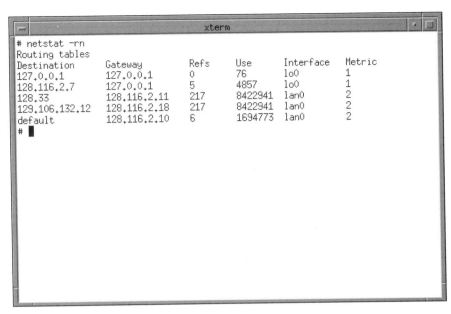

FIGURE 13.12.   A UNIX Routing Table Containing a Network, Host, and Default Route

established for that purpose) prevents inadvertent or overlooked gateways from popping up around the network each time a server is added. Having to enable systems explicitly for IP forwarding ensures that at least some sort of minimal acknowledgment is made prior to IP packets being allowed into an otherwise isolated network.

To illustrate enabling, let's examine Figure 13.13. The UNIX system and the Windows NT server can communicate with each other because the router acts

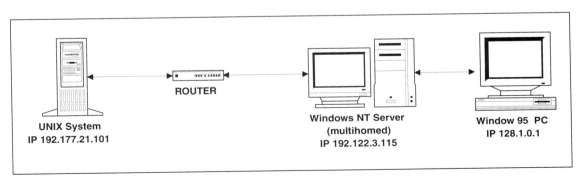

FIGURE 13.13.   Example of IP Forwarding

as a gateway, forwarding IP packets between the networks (192.177.21 and 192.122.3). The Windows NT server and the Windows 95 PC can also communicate directly with each other because they both have interfaces on the same network (128.1.0). With the UNIX system the following conditions are met.

- IP forwarding is *enabled* on the Windows NT server.
- The Windows NT server has appropriate host or network routes configured.
- The UNIX system and the Windows 95 PC also have appropriate default, host, or network routing tables.

Many UNIX servers must also have IP forwarding explicitly "turned on" prior to functioning as a gateway. Various mechanisms from file to kernel switches exist to control IP forwarding on UNIX platforms. Older versions of FreeBSD, for instance, required that the kernel be recompiled with a gateway option. Newer versions simply require a flag set in the *sysconfig* file at boot time. With most UNIX servers the system-specific documentation must be referred to since there is no standard convention for enabling UNIX to act as a gateway.

Enabling Windows NT IP Forwarding

On a Windows NT system, select **Start** ➤ **Settings** ➤ **Control Panel** ➤ **Network** and then select the **Protocols** tab. Select or highlight the **TCP/IP Protocol** option and click on **Properties**. From the Properties window, select the **Routing** tab (Figure 13.14).

Select the **Enable IP Forwarding** option and click the **OK** or **Apply** button. After the next reboot, the Windows NT system may forward IP packets and act as a router.

Modifying Static Routing Tables

Setting or determining routes explicitly for IP traffic to follow on a fixed and individual host or network basis is called *static routing*. This is in contrast to *dynamic routing*, when the process uses a special protocol or program to update and configure routes in an automated fashion. While dynamic routing is both necessary and invaluable in many environments, the ability to configure static routes manually is useful and should be understood prior to using a routing protocol. Like *netstat*, the command line syntax to add routes is also very similar on both Windows NT and most UNIX operating systems. Enough idiosyncrasies exist to justify using the *man* page for each particular UNIX operating system used. Syntax for making modifications to the Windows NT routing table is as follows:

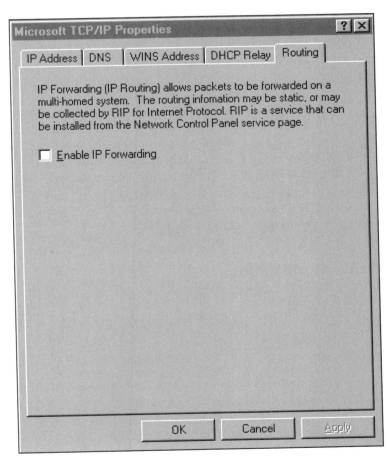

FIGURE 13.14.   The Routing Switch for Windows NT

```
route [-f] [-p] [command [destination] [MASK netmask]
[gateway] [METRIC metric]]
```

where –f indicates that all existing routes in the routing table should be cleared prior to building any additional routes, which may or may not be specified within the same command. Use –p if the route command is being used to build or add routes. The -p option indicates the route should become persistent and be recreated whenever the server or interface is restarted. When used in conjunction with the *print* command, all persistent routes are displayed.

The following four possible command options are specified to indicate the nature of the routing table modification.

- *print* – Prints the specified route as command output
- *add* – Adds the specified route
- *delete* – Deletes the specified route
- *change* – Modifies a specified route

The `destination` in the syntax indicates the target host, network, or default destination for which the route is to be used. If the `MASK` option is specified, then the specified `netmask` is applied to the route. `METRIC` is an optional key word that indicates the numeric routing metric or hops being supplied.

UNIX *route* command syntax is very similar but may vary slightly between variants. The *man* pages are the best source for any nuances. Common differences include UNIX systems requiring a "host" or "network" key word to indicate the type of route being created.

Route Table Modifications

Modifying a route table from the command line is fairly straightforward for both UNIX and Windows NT. For example, a route table for a UNIX system is modified as

```
route add host 128.1.0.5 128.0.0.1
```

In this example, a route to host 128.1.0.5 is created via the gateway interface at 128.0.0.1. Because no metric is specifically defined, a default metric of 1 is used.

Route modification for Windows NT is accomplished by invoking the command line and defining the route similar to

```
route -f -p add 128.3.0.0 mask 255.255.0.0 128.0.0.1 metric 2
```

In this example, the entire routing table is first flushed before a route to the 128.3 network is created via the 128.0.0.1 gateway. The –p option ensures that the route will always exist, even after a reboot. The metric of 2 indicates that IP traffic using this route will have to traverse a second router beyond the 128.0.0.1 interface.

```
route delete 128.1.0.5 128.0.0.1
```

In this example, the route to 128.1.0.5 using the 128.0.0.1 gateway is removed from the routing table. Most UNIX systems require both the destination and the gateway of the route to be removed be specified in the *delete* command, although some UNIX derivatives require only the destination as an argument.

Dynamic Routing Tables

As mentioned earlier, a routing protocol may be used to update routing tables dynamically. Windows NT version 3.51 and later support the static routes we have covered already. The use of the Multi-Protocol Router (MPR) for dynamic routing operations is also supported. MPR most commonly uses the extremely prevalent Routing Information Protocol (RIP) when dealing with IP traffic. In simple terms, RIP essentially broadcasts its routing tables at given intervals of time. Other routers using the protocol then use these broadcasts to update their own route information.

Most UNIX operating systems also provide mechanisms for dynamic routing, and UNIX in general has a long history of involvement with various methods and protocols. To date, chief among UNIX routing processes are the *gated* and the older *routed* daemons. Both daemons provide support for several routing protocols, including RIP. Since RIP is supported under both Windows NT (via MPR) and UNIX (*routed* or *gated*), it is a wise choice for a heterogeneous environment that includes both operating systems.

Using *traceroute* and *tracert*

It is sometimes useful in troubleshooting or design to trace the route or path that IP traffic takes to reach its destination. Using a tool such as *traceroute* (UNIX) or *tracert* (Windows NT) can show where a route or path breaks down and fails to reach its intended destination. The network utility *traceroute* now comes "standard" with most UNIX implementations. Windows NT comes bundled with *tracert,* although more feature-rich versions are available from third parties.

Typical command line syntax can include the executable and a destination for the route to be tested, although many additional options exist. These options can modify behavioral aspects, such as the maximal number of hops to traverse or the amount of time to wait for a route before timing out. Using these utilities with a direct connection to the Internet can be entertaining, as you may see traffic going to another state or country prior to reaching a destination just up the street.

Dedicated Hardware Versus Server Routing

In determining routing topology and implementation, a key decision is to resolve whether to utilize hardware or operating system-based software solutions. Hardware routers (such as those manufactured by CISCO or Bay Networks) and operating systems like UNIX or Windows NT with IP forwarding enabled are viable router solutions. Some networking purists, however, contend that this is not the case. They would argue that using a UNIX or Windows NT system to provide routing is an unworthy hack and that any professional or serious implementation requires equipment manufactured specifically for this purpose. The following are several advantages and disadvantages that should be considered when using servers to perform routing or to provide any other number of network services.

- *Cost* – Many organizations have old, unused 486 computer systems that need only have an additional interface card, possibly a memory upgrade, and a freely available UNIX operating system such as LINUX or FreeBSD installed to operate as a fully functional gateway or router. Even the cost of a new, custom-built server with preinstalled network software can be far less than many hardware-based routers. In addition to routing, several other network services such as DNS, mail, and even Web servers can also reside on similar configurations. Windows can also provide many of these services and may be easier for the novice to configure.

- *Performance* – When dedicated to providing a single network service such as routing, the Intel-based architecture scales fairly well. In even moderate-to-large enterprise environments a high-end Pentium processor possessing sufficient memory can frequently perform routing and other network tasks just as effectively as their RISC counterparts or most entry-level routers (such as those by CISCO). There is a breaking point where I/O constraints and the need for speed, switching capabilities, or other options exceed the capability of such systems and a specialty network device is required.

- *Turnkey Implementation* – One advantage of using a conventional router rather than a multihomed server is that a router typically can be dropped into a network with a minimum of fuss. Configuring a multihomed server with more than three network interfaces, on the other hand, may require somewhat more expertise. Many RISC platforms have a rather limited number of available card slots, and Intel servers tend to run out of available IRQs and DMA channels quickly.

CONFIGURING AND USING NETWORK APPLICATIONS

Configuring a working network with IP connectivity is done for the purpose of providing a framework on which useful applications can operate. Simply providing IP connectivity from both a UNIX and a Windows NT server to the same network goes a long way in terms of integrating the systems. This is an exigency and accolade owed at least in part to the early architects of TCP/IP. Connectivity and the use of common protocols is not enough, however. Interoperability really only becomes apparent when common applications are used.

In terms of IP networking, an application is any service above the presentation layer. Such a broad definition, however, can be misleading and obscures fundamental differences between network functions. It is for this reason that this section differentiates file/print servers from those servers providing multi-user, interactive, process-based applications. The former role, providing shared disk and printer resources, has been done fairly well by various network operating systems such as Novell for many years. UNIX's traditional advantage exists in its ability also to serve high-end user applications through such means as X11, or even character-based programs that may in part run on the server. In recent years Windows NT has evolved from having a predominantly file server role to one that can also serve interactive user applications. Much of Windows NT's success and potential comes from its growing ability to provide such expanded functional services.

Vendor-provided and Third-Party Application Suites

Significant differences between UNIX and Windows NT exist when considering

- Which network applications come with their respective operating system
- The robustness of these ports
- Which network applications need to be provided by third parties

Generally speaking, Windows NT's standard TCP/IP suite bundle is less robust than most UNIX variants. For example, Windows NT provides a telnet client but no server. Fortunately, excellent third-party versions are commercially available to fill this gap. In addition, some very fine shareware versions of many Windows network programs (especially the simpler ones such as telnet and ftp clients) are also readily available and cost little to nothing to obtain. The cost of using third-party applications depends on factors such as the reputation of the vendor, the quality and type of application, and the number of seats or network clients required.

While some commercial sources provide network applications on an individual basis, many others provide entire suites all bundled onto a single distribution. These suites may even include network applications traditionally only available on UNIX servers, such as *bootpd* or *nslookup*. The examples derived in this chapter were based on working with the excellent suite provided by Hummingbird Communications (www.hummingbird.com).

UNIX has a reputation for having a wide array of network applications already bundled into the operating system distribution. This potentially can save a great deal of money in some environments and minimizes the number of vendors, support relationships, and installation headaches. The occasional odd network application not included with a particular version of UNIX usually can be downloaded from an Internet site free of charge, and at most may simply require a recompile. This is the exception, however, and almost all programs reviewed here are standard with all UNIX varieties.

In stating that Windows NT has a less robust TCP/IP suite implementation, it is equally important to stress that the operating system bundles alternate network support for IPX/SPX, AppleTalk, and NetBEUI. To connect to these protocols, UNIX systems will also need to rely on third-party solutions. Therefore, it is improper to suggest that Windows NT Server is in any fashion anything but a world-class network operating system.

TCP/IP Interactive Remote Access Applications

Obtaining terminal access on a remote computer, as well as the ability to copy files interactively from one host to another, are among the most basic networking applications. An examination of some of these basic client programs is appropriate. In these scenarios the network "client" usually refers to the local program initiated to make a connection and is utilized by the user to communicate with the remote computer's server application.

TELNET

The telnet application is the most common program used to gain a command prompt, shell, or terminal access on a remote computer. Telnet clients come with almost every network operating system, including Windows NT, and can be used to access just about any UNIX server. While a user can "telnet" out of a Windows NT system, a third-party server must be installed or added to the Windows NT installation in order for it to host other system's telnet clients. Telnet clients tend to run equally well on either operating system and usually can be initiated from a command line.

In Figure 13.15, the local machine has used *telnet* to connect with the remote system *turbo*. Either an IP address or a valid host name can be passed as arguments to the *telnet* command. After a connection is established, a normal user account and password are utilized to gain access to the remote host.

A telnet connection to a UNIX host provides the opportunity to run almost any nongraphical application as though the user was logged onto the console itself. It can also be used to launch many other network applications.

In Figure 13.16, the Windows NT command prompt has been used to start a telnet session. Since no destination (IP address or host name) was passed as an argument, the telnet client window has come up without a connection. By using the **Connect** pull-down menu in the top left corner, a destination or remote host may be provided. Also shown are some of the terminal preferences that can be set optionally with this program. Third-party Windows telnet

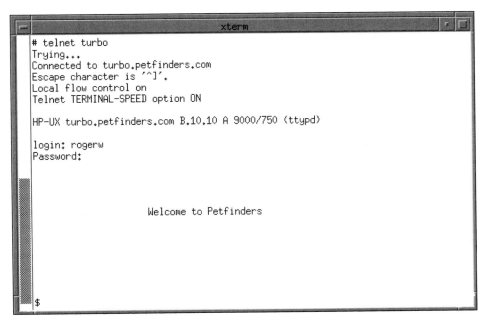

```
                                    xterm
# telnet turbo
Trying...
Connected to turbo.petfinders.com
Escape character is '^]'.
Local flow control on
Telnet TERMINAL-SPEED option ON

HP-UX turbo.petfinders.com B.10.10 A 9000/750 (ttypd)

login: rogerw
Password:



                         Welcome to Petfinders




$
```

FIGURE 13.15.   A UNIX telnet Session

clients typically have far more features and available terminal emulation types (Wyse, VT220, IBM 3151, and so on).

r PROGRAMS

The *r* programs refer to a number of mostly UNIX-centric network applications that perform many useful tasks and functions on remote hosts. The more robust third-party Windows NT networking suites also include some of the following *r clients*. Note that the following discussion of several various *r* programs relates to common usage, and that while the exact names and syntax vary between UNIX ports, they all tend to interoperate. Many of these utilities are covered in Appendix B. In addition, you can review the *man* pages for more a more detailed explanation of syntax on a particular platform.

rlogin

The *rlogin* command connects a local terminal to a virtual terminal on a remote system, providing remote access in much the same way as *telnet*. Execution syntax from the command line (UNIX) is simple:

```
rlogin remote-host [-l username]
```

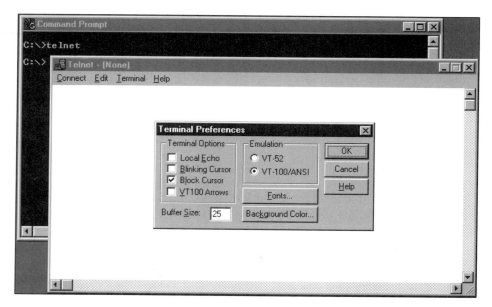

FIGURE 13.16.   The Windows NT telnet Client

where *remote-host* is the system name or IP address of the remote system with which to connect and [-1 *username*] specifies the login name the user utilizes on the remote system.

remsh, rsh, rexec

The *remsh* command, called *rsh* (BSD) or *rexec* on some UNIX ports, connects to a remote system and either executes a program or provides a shell prompt:

```
remsh remote-host [-l username] command
```

If no command to be executed on the remote shell is given, a shell prompt is provided and the program simply acts like *rlogin*.

rcp

The *rcp* command is used to copy files between a remote system and a local system. Note that the *ftp* program covered later is frequently a better choice for copying files over a network, although sometimes less flexible than *rcp* when integrating file-copy functionality into programs or shell scripts:

```
rcp [-p] source destination
```

where [-p] preserves the modification times and permissions on the copied file. The *source* and *destination* arguments take the form *remoteuser@-remotehost:filename*.

.rhosts and /etc/hosts.equiv

The UNIX *.rhosts* and */etc/hosts.equiv* files are security mechanisms of dubious integrity intended to provide remote access and authorization controls for many remote network client applications. The exact operation and reliability of these security systems vary by operating system. Essentially the files specify which remote systems and users are allowed to connect to the host with the equivalent "trust" of being local. For instance, if the host *turbo* has specified the root user on the remote server *orbit* as equivalent, then the root user on *orbit* can connect to *turbo* using a command like *rlogin* without having to supply a password. For all practical purposes the root user on *orbit* will have total root authority on both hosts. This can be dangerous because the security on a system employing equivalencies is only as good as the security on all the remote hosts it trusts. This problem can be compounded since each user may have a *.rhosts* file in their home directory, allowing remote equivalencies that are unknown to the system administrator or any of the other users. Entire hosts or only certain users on a given host can be trusted. The file format to specify trusted remote hosts and users can take the following form:

```
[hostname [username]] [#comment]
```

For example

```
grwhp       mborows      #Michael Borowski
grwhp       -bobw        #Robert Williams
```

Possible extensions include a plus sign, which matches all hosts or users, and a dash, which provides an exclusion match. In the previous example I have prevented Robert Williams from crashing my system by excluding him from access with a dash.

On most UNIX operating systems */etc/hosts.equiv* takes precedence over a user's *.rhosts* file. On some flavors of UNIX the absence of an */etc/hosts.equiv* file is a security breach in and of itself, so be certain to read the system documentation for particulars.

File Transfer Protocols

File transfer protocols, such as FTP, are used primarily to copy files between hosts. Decent security and authentication are provided *if the FTP server is properly configured.* A poorly configured FTP server is one of the most readily exploited security holes in many servers. Both FTP clients and servers are available with Windows NT and UNIX, although the server portion must be explicitly installed on Windows NT.

NOTE   To install FTP server on Microsoft Windows NT, launch the Network icon in the Control Panel and select the **Services** tab (Start ➤ Settings ➤ Control Panel ➤ Network ➤ Services), click **Add**, and then install the Microsoft Internet Information Server (IIS). During setup, be certain **FTP Service** is selected.

USING FTP CLIENTS

Like *telnet,* normal *ftp* program execution takes as a command line argument either the host name or the IP address of the remote server. Figure 13.17 shows a sample *ftp* session, and the syntax is nearly identical on both Windows NT and UNIX operating systems.

The line numbers on the left-hand side of the example in Figure 13.17 have been inserted only for the purpose of the following description and do not actually exist in an *ftp* session. In the first line, the user has executed the *ftp* program with instructions to connect with the host *turbo.petfinders.com*. After connecting, the user logs in with the same login name and password as used for

```
                                          xterm
  1  #ftp turbo.petfinders.com
  2  Connected to turbo.petfinders.com.
  3  220 turbo.petfinders.com FTP server (Version 1.7.112.3 Thu Oct 5 23:39:40 GMT 1995)ready.
  4  Name (orbit:root): rogerw
  5  331 Password required for rogerw.
  6  Password:
  7  230 User rogerw logged in.
  8  Remote system type is UNIX.
  9  Using binary mode to transfer files.
 10  ftp>pwd
 11  257 "/home/rogerw" is current directory.
 12  ftp>ls
 13  drwxr-xr-x  3 rogerw   users       1024 Sep 26  1996 utils
 14  drwxr-xr-x  5 rogerw   users       1024 Jan 17 15:19 webtools
 15  drwxr-xr-x  4 rogerw   users       1024 Apr 17 10:19 patches
 16  226 Transfer complete.
 17  ftp>cd patches
 18  250 CWD command successful.
 19  ftp> ls
 20  200 PORT command successful.
 21  150 Opening ASCII mode data connection for /usr/bin/ls.
 22  total 42
 23  drwxr-xr-x  2 rogerw   users       1024 Sep 26  1996 ospatch-2.5
 24  -rw-r--r--  1 rogerw   users      18293 Jan 17 15:19 ospatch-1.8
 25  226 Transfer complete.
 26  ftp>get ospatch-2.5
 27  200 PORT command successful.
 28  150 Opening BINARY mode data connection for jk (18293 bytes).
 29  226 Transfer complete.
 30  288293 bytes received in 0.00 seconds (4711.04 Kbytes/s)
 31  ftp>quit
 32  221 Goodbye.
 33  #█
```

FIGURE 13.17.   Example of an *ftp* Session

a normal terminal session and is presented with an ftp prompt. As seen in line 10, some shell-like syntax is even available. The *pwd* command tells the user that the working directory on the remote machine is the home directory for the user account being used. After doing a directory listing (line 12), the user changes to the *patches* directory (line 17) and retrieves a file called *ospatch-2.5* (the *get* command, line 26). The file is transferred to the local machine and into the same directory from which *ftp* was executed in line 1. The *put* command would have performed the reverse, transferring a local file into the working directory on the remote machine. Entering a question mark at the ftp prompt will also list all possible commands and operations.

GRAPHICAL FTP CLIENTS

One benefit of using a third-party FTP client, such as the ones provided by Hummingbird Communications, NetManage, Softway, DataFocus, Intergraph, and many other vendors, is that the FTP syntax is hidden by a user interface that allows the user to perform operations in a drag-and-drop file manager-like fashion (Figures 13.18 and 13.19).

THE TRIVIAL FILE TRANSFER PROTOCOL

The use of *tftp* is similar to *ftp,* however the trivial variety offers little in the way of security or user authentication. It is used predominantly to transfer configuration files directly between hardware components. For instance, many manufacturers of routers and networking hardware provide the option of upgrading the firmware, flash memory, or internal software via *tftp*. This allows the network administrator to retrieve updated software from a manufacturer's Web or FTP site and then "*tftp* it" down to the device. Firmware upgrades possible by this procedure are frequently needed to add new functionality and protocols, or to correct bugs that existed in the original hardware configuration software shipped with the equipment. All of this can be done from a single workstation, without having to visit each installation physically. Frequently a *tftp* program can also be used to *retrieve* a router or network device's user-defined configuration and save it as a backup file on another server. In the event the device somehow loses its configuration, the backup file can be simply downloaded back into the device rather than having to reconfigure the entire node (which could take far more time and effort). Another common use for *tftp* includes downloading configuration data to X-terminals and network printers.

tftp on Windows NT

The *tftp* program on Windows NT can be used to send a file to a remote destination or to retrieve files, but must be initiated on the Windows NT system:

```
tftp [-i] host [get | put] source [destination]
```

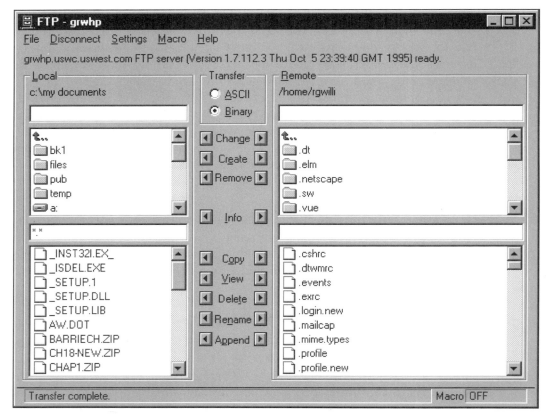

FIGURE 13.18.   Example of Windows NT-based FTP from NetManage

where -i indicates a binary file transfer (the default is ASCII), *host* specifies the local or remote system, [get | put] indicates file retrieval to the local system (*get*) or transferring a file to a remote system (*put*), *source* specifies the file to be transferred, and *destination* specifies where the file is to be transferred.

A TFTP server allowing remote devices to initiate and perform transfers to and from a Windows NT system can be acquired through third-party software.

tftp on a UNIX Operating System

Most UNIX systems offer a TFTP client functioning in a fashion similar to the Windows NT variety. They also provide a server process called *tftpd,* which allows remote systems to initiate transfers. Again, there is no user validation or authentication with *tftp*.

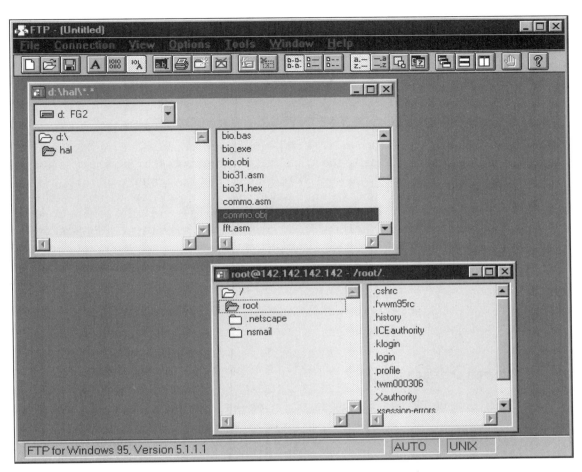

FIGURE 13.19.   Hummingbird Communications FTP Client for Windows

THE HYPERTEXT TRANSFER PROTOCOL AND WEB SERVICES

Chapter 15 details Internet- and Web-based services and products. However, in the context of the current discussion of file transfer, it is appropriate to summarize a few points. No technology has done more to promote use of the Internet and TCP/IP networks in general than the World Wide Web. It is therefore interesting to note that the Web's most basic and essential component, HTTP, is nothing more than a modified transfer protocol on some serious steroids, and a far more powerful interface.

Like the other network programs reviewed thus far, with HTTP there is a client portion that usually takes the form of a Web interface or browser such as Netscape Navigator and Microsoft's Internet Explorer. These clients are capable of processing HTTP, although fundamentally speaking the advent of the Web browser mostly just brought a useful interface to existing, long-established network programs and protocols like DNS, NTTP (news), SMTP, and FTP. More recently the Web has also prompted the development of entirely new protocols and network applications based on a common gateway interface (CGI) and Java.

WEB PROTOCOLS AS INTEGRATION TOOLS

Web protocols such as HTTP and Web-friendly languages such as Java also have the potential to make the single greatest contribution to the seamless integration of UNIX and Windows NT operating systems. Current trends in both application and operating system development are moving toward a browser-based model, just as software vendors are scrambling to create Web interfaces for existing applications. The simple act of creating a Web interface to an application also, in effect, seamlessly "ports" the program's user interface and client portion to any operating system with a standard Web browser. Coupled with the fact that the program languages performing most of today's server-side processing (such as Perl, TK, tcl) are increasingly available under both UNIX and Windows NT, Web and internet services become one of the most logical solutions to many integration issues.

FILE AND PRINT SHARING

Sharing file and print services may be the most fundamental role of network servers, and while it may be the operating system's ability to perform as an application server that determines its future, providing traditional file services is a substantial consideration. This section summarizes the two predominant technologies used for file sharing on a TCP/IP network with heterogeneous servers and workstations: NFS and SAMBA. Various methods of print sharing and using the network to provide remote backups are also addressed.

NFS

The Network File System (NFS) is a mature technology originally pioneered, in part, by Sun Microsystems. NFS functionality is included in most ports of UNIX and provides an inexpensive method for various UNIX servers to share file space transparently. In an NFS environment, a server *exports* a file system or portion of its local disk over the network to remote clients, which in turn *mount* the file system or drive space so that for all practical purposes it appears locally.

Since no NFS components are bundled with Windows NT platforms, reliance on third-party solutions is required. NFS client software allowing a Windows server or workstation to mount remote UNIX file space locally is widely available from many vendors at fairly reasonable prices. However, NFS server software for Windows platforms is not quite so prevalent and tends to be more expensive. Two excellent NFS products are Hummingbird's Maestro and Intergraph's AccessNFS.

SAMBA

SAMBA is a strong choice for Windows and UNIX (mixed) environments because it uses the same Server Message Block protocol as Microsoft and has been ported to almost every common flavor of UNIX. Using SAMBA on a UNIX system can also be a less expensive alternative to purchasing third-party NFS clients and servers for Windows workstations and Windows NT. Australian Andrew Tridgell originally developed SAMBA, and a distribution can be retrieved from either `ftp://samba.anu.edu.au/pub/samba/samba-latest.tar.gz` or `http://lake.canberra.edu.au/pub/samba/samba.html`.

Network Printing

There are many options and methods of performing network printing. Both UNIX and Windows NT support *lpd* (line printer daemon); therefore, a base level of printing interoperability exists. The Windows NT **Services** option available from the **Control Panel** supports the launching of *lpd*. The management of *lpd* on UNIX variants can vary significantly and requires reference to *man* pages. Most UNIX operating systems provide *lp* forward-style programs, whereby a print job can be sent to another remote UNIX server, that in turn places it into its local print queue. Many third-party vendors such as Qmaster and Network Instruments now provide programs that allow Windows NT servers to forward print jobs to the queues of remote UNIX servers. Both SAMBA and PCNFS provide remote print support over TCP/IP networks as well.

The Hewlett-Packard Jet-Direct products and technology also warrant mention here. With Jet-Direct a printer has either an internal interface card that plugs directly into the TCP/IP network, or the printer's parallel port can connect to a small, external network adapter. Both can be configured to use common network parameters such as IP addresses, net masks, and routes, so that any host or server on the network can reach it. Hewlett-Packard-provided software for both Windows NT and UNIX allows hosts and clients to send print jobs over the network directly to the printer itself, at network speeds, rather than forwarding the print jobs to another server's queue. The software also provides a great deal of additional value-added features, such as paper and toner status for some printer models. It should be further noted that Hewlett-Packard is not the only vendor to offer direct network print technologies. Many other vendors, such as Xyplex, offer comparable products.

NETWORK MANAGEMENT

There are many facilities aimed at managing the configuration, services, and resources in a networked environment. Some of these services have become mandatory for the operation of certain network clients, such as Web browsers that require DNS resolution. Other applications such as NIS are only valuable in certain environments with extreme characteristics. As a rule of thumb there is a very important question to be addressed prior to deciding on the implementation of a management service for assistance with a given task: Is the overhead of maintaining the management layer and associated applications greater than the effort required to handle the tasks manually by conventional means?

The answer is usually a factor of scale. In an environment with only a handful of servers and users for instance, with few day-to-day changes, implementing NIS to propagate user accounts and other services would not be worth the effort. However, if large growth is anticipated over time, then it might be far easier to implement the management service from the onset rather than retroactively integrating all the hosts at a later date.

DNS Servers

In the beginning of this chapter we described how to configure a UNIX or Windows NT system as a DNS client. Obtaining name resolution in this fashion rather than via a host file is rapidly becoming a necessary norm rather than a convenience. Both Windows NT and UNIX systems also make excellent DNS servers, without requiring extensive hardware resources. If providing DNS is the primary, dedicated function of a particular machine, then older hardware will usually suffice. A 486 with 32 MB of memory and an old ISA NIC can often be used with either operating system to make an adequate DNS server. Coupling such old hardware with a free UNIX operating system such as LINUX or FreeBSD provides an inexpensive solution that in many environments performs just as well as much more expensive hardware and software. The actual steps for configuring DNS software is beyond the scope of this text.

NIS and NIS+

Network Information Service (NIS), previously known as *yellow pages* or just *yp,* automates maintenance and preserves the consistency of common configuration files such as the *password, group, hosts,* and *services* files. For instance, in an environment with custom network applications being developed that operate on nonstandard TCP or UDP ports, ensuring that all machines are using the same */etc/services* file becomes critical. Historically the most predominant use of NIS was to centralize management of the */etc/hosts* and */etc/passwd* files on UNIX systems, instead of having to manage a separate copy of each file on every server. Use of NIS to propagate a single */etc/hosts* file for name resolution has declined in recent years as more intranets and local networks have adopted DNS services instead. With some amount of effort, the two can coexist. NIS is still a strong and popular solution for maintaining a single instance of almost any configuration file.

Dynamic IP Addressing with DHCP

The Dynamic Host Configuration Protocol (DHCP) has come into greater popularity in recent years for two primary reasons. As fewer network administrators are asked to manage greater numbers of nodes spread out over broader geographical areas, there is a need to simplify and centralize management tasks. Ideally this is done in such a way that configurations can be updated without having to visit each node physically or to assign network parameters explicitly on an individual basis. In addition to such convenience, it becomes apparent that greater flexibility in network configuration is being necessitated by new complications in Internet networking. Complications such as rapidly depleting address space, faster obsolescence of hardware, and transitory user requirements suggest that today's parameters across the enterprise will almost certainly need to be altered in the future. Further, traditional means of dealing with these issues results in extraordinarily expensive network management costs.

DHCP servers take logical network configurations and, on request, assign them to network clients on a single-session basis. For instance, instead of assigning each and every Microsoft Windows PC in a network a fixed and permanent IP address, you could instead configure the PCs at boot time to obtain an IP address from a predefined pool of address space on a DHCP server. In this way the administrator is saved the trouble of proactively propagating this parameter to each node or client. When the IP address is no longer in use, such as when the machine is turned off, moved, or discarded without the knowledge of the network administrator, the IP address is returned to the pool and made available again to other clients. In this way DHCP makes more efficient use of address space. When the foundation of the whole network changes and necessitates that an entirely new network space be used, then the network administrator need only modify the pool, or *scope,* on a single machine rather than alter manually every node across the enterprise. Be aware, however, that some nodes and systems such as routers, firewalls, proxies, and DNS servers usually need to retain a fixed IP address and are simply not candidates for DHCP. The majority of clients, however, can benefit from this technology.

Network Management Application Suites

The development and resale of enterprise-class network management suites and applications has become an enormous market. Many of these suites come shrink-wrapped and require heavy customization prior to being utilized in the target environment. It is also common to see large amounts of effort put into modifying an environment so it can accommodate the management application. A good shell or Perl programmer can often develop from scratch an optimized management program for a given task in less time than it takes to get a vendor-supplied product to work.

DISTRIBUTED COMPUTING

An understanding of how to maximize TCP/IP networks for resource sharing empowers both system administrators and developers alike. Inversely, misunderstanding network resource sharing presents the prospect of wasting a great deal of time and money relocating components or purchasing excessive hardware and application licenses. In many environments it simply does not make sense to purchase a DAT drive for every server when they can be shared across the network, or to purchase certain application licenses for each and every workstation when only a fraction of the users ever use the program concurrently. True distributed computing may save an organization a great deal of time and money, although dealing with all the factors involved can be both complicated and demanding.

Reasons for Distributed Computing

The functionality and advantages of sharing file systems between computer systems includes allowing one instance of data to be utilized by multiple users and programs, consuming less hardware resources, and in some situations even improving the overall performance of applications accessing that data. Such distributed data is different from distributed processing, during which the processor and memory usage for a given program or application occurs on multiple systems and may or may not operate against data on the local computer's hard drive. The following sections present alternatives in the way the network can be used to provide solutions to many common server resource issues.

DISTRIBUTED DATA

By using technologies such as NFS and SAMBA, discussed earlier, additional disk space can be easily added to a system over the network. There are two advantages—cost and availability. Many environments have servers scattered about the network with various and significant amounts of disk space that might otherwise go unused. Use of this space avoids having to purchase new drives and the accompanying scheduled downtime some platforms require for upgrades. Often a large amount of disk space is needed only temporarily and thus does not justify the expense of new, permanent drives. On some high-end enterprise systems using pseudoproprietary interfaces, supported disk drives are exceedingly more expensive than the more conventional drives that can be used on almost any Intel platform running Windows NT or a UNIX port. The less-expensive drives can be added to these systems and then made available to any server over the network. By making a single instance of the data available to multiple platforms, excessive redundancy of information as well as the accompanying file system maintenance and revision confusion may be avoided. Fewer peripheral devices such as tape drives may be needed, since existing resources can operate against other systems' local data.

There are two disadvantages to distributed data—speed and performance, and reliability.

- *Speed and performance* – Accessing data over a network usually introduces a latency that makes for slower access and throughput than would exist on a local drive and bus. The significance of this actuality varies based on a number of variables. In some rare situations, network-based file systems can actually provide *improved* performance.

- *Reliability* – A single network or server failure has a far greater potential to impact the availability of data resources to many more systems and users. Some applications and certain types of data are not supported or, in rare cases, cannot be used at all on a network file system.

INCREASED PROCESSING POTENTIAL

Distributed processing, including most client/server models, can be potentially much more complicated and difficult to implement than distributed data. The idea is to have multiple computers share the load of running programs under a single application rather than having the entire processing load reside on a single server. In some scenarios the programs running on a particular computer work with complete anonymity and without regard to the programs running on another system. Other applications require some sort of communication between the programs or processes running on each computer. One common example might include a program on a workstation handling all processing with regard to the user interface and program calculations, while a remote server processes the actual database queries.

Performance Issues in Distributed Computing

Processor, memory, and disk resources (both I/O and capacity) can all be distributed across TCP/IP networks; frequently this provides a method of relieving bottlenecks or resource shortages on any single given system. However, determining when or where an existing system has a bottleneck is far easier and much more apparent than determining whether distributing the resources over multiple, networked servers will actually alleviate rather than exacerbate the problem. The right decision is never as apparent as it seems. Each solution introduces different dependencies, and oftentimes one performance problem is simply exchanged for another.

A BRIEF WORD ABOUT NETWORK SECURITY

Network security in a mixed Windows NT and UNIX environment opens up numerous complexities beyond what exists in a homogenous environment. The reason for this is not because existing security mechanisms for the respective operating systems no longer apply, but rather because at times they must be loosened to interoperate. It is commonly accepted that less stringent and more flexible operating environments are also by nature less secure. Each additional networking service and connection presents another potential security hole. Keep in mind too that with third-party network servers a certain amount of faith is placed in the developers and vendors of the product.

Most vendors of UNIX operating systems support forums and Web or FTP sites that include various patches and fixes to prevent promiscuous interface behavior, corruptible sendmail features, and countless other potential security breaches. Windows NT is a more shrink-wrapped operating system, but it is still just as vulnerable. Contrary to a great deal of marketing propaganda, Windows NT is not inherently more secure than its UNIX counterparts. Furthermore, the default security parameters of an operating system should never be assumed to be correct.

Chapter 14
Electronic Mail Integration

Contributed by Mark E. Walla

Electronic mail has long been the cornerstone of organizational communication, especially within the UNIX community. E-mail is based on a simple concept of data flowing from sender to recipient. Through adherence to basic rules such as address conventions, mail can be passed from one computer through a maze of networks to a remote recipient anywhere in the world. Until very recently, the existence of different protocols and conventions employed by a variety of proprietary e-mail systems hampered seamless communication. Then came the overwhelming popularity of the Internet and its de facto e-mail backbone—the Simple Mail Transfer Protocol (SMTP) and UNIX sendmail. Despite the presence of many competing technologies such as X.400, UNIX-based SMTP has emerged as the clear international standard on the Internet and elsewhere. Microsoft recognized this trend with the release of the Windows NT BackOffice Exchange Server 5.0 groupware suite. In addition to maintaining other protocols, Exchange Server also includes native SMTP support.

The focus of this chapter is the integration between UNIX sendmail and Windows NT BackOffice Exchange 5.0 e-mail services, even though there are many other commercial applications that support SMTP. As a member of the BackOffice product family, Exchange Server 5.0 should be considered an optional extension to Windows NT. Despite the concentration on Exchange Server, it is our belief that this discussion will provide the basis for mail connectivity involving other Windows NT-based products and UNIX systems.

The audience for this chapter is system administrators who need a base-level understanding of SMTP structures and methods for properly configuring UNIX sendmail and Windows NT BackOffice Exchange Server. This chapter is not intended as an end user how-to guidebook. Therefore, we ignore discussions on available clients, such as elm or Outlook, and their respective utilization.

Before venturing into discussions about UNIX and Windows NT integration based on SMTP, it is appropriate to acknowledge that neither UNIX nor Windows NT is confined to this protocol. Windows NT BackOffice Exchange Server 5.0 also maintains native interfaces to other protocols such as cc:Mail and MS-Mail. UNIX systems can communicate with other applications such as UUCP and a variety of vendor-specific proprietary systems.

Windows NT BackOffice Exchange Server 5.0 can interface directly to UNIX sendmail via the Internet Mail Service SMTP connector, allowing clean and relatively simple integration between the two products. This chapter is divided into three primary sections, each consisting of the following specific topics:

1. Understanding basic mail concepts
   - Concepts of the mail transfer agent (MTA) and mailer user agent (MUA)
   - Understanding the SMTP model
   - Internet mail address conventions
   - Site and return address
   - Incoming and outgoing mail routing
   - Error handling with the Postmaster
2. Integrating UNIX and Windows NT Exchange Server
   - Case study scenarios
   - Specific configuration requirements for sendmail and Exchange
3. Advanced Topics
   - Understanding the DNS
   - Post Office Protocol, version 3 (POP3) mail retrieval and alternative mail site designs

UNDERSTANDING BASIC E-MAIL CONCEPTS

Consider Figure 14.1 as a means of visualizing the flow of e-mail between two mail server applications. SMTP is the transmission backbone between the UNIX sendmail and Windows NT Exchange mail servers and/or the interface to the Internet. Mail client software fulfills the dual purpose of providing the user with the ability to compose messages as well as to send and retrieve messages through their respective servers. As discussed in greater detail later, this transfer can occur through propriety protocols or through defined interfaces like the POP3 client/server protocol.

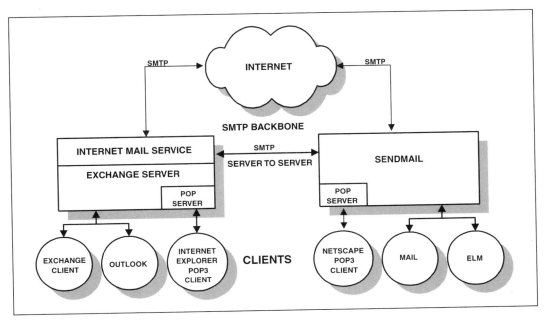

FIGURE 14.1.   Example of Basic E-mail Structure

Understanding the Concept of Mail Agents

E-mail services including SMTP utilize two generic types of mail "agents." The first type is a user-based client commonly known as the *mail user agent*. The MUA primarily provides the user with an editor to compose and read e-mail. This client-side agent creates local repositories on the host to store received mail and archive all sent mail until deleted. Examples of MUA applications are UNIX's *mailx* and Microsoft's *Outlook*. The second mail agent is a server application that is responsible for transmitting data, commonly known as the *mail transfer agent*. The MTA is responsible for delivering and receiving. Examples of MTAs are Microsoft's *Exchange Server* and UNIX's *sendmail*. The MUA contacts the MTA to transport a message to its destination when the composition is finished (Figure 14.2).

An MTA performs the SMTP send and receive functions. After the MTA receives a transmission from the MUA, the MTA resolves the mail message's destination IP address and establishes a transfer session with the designation MTA. The two MTAs must be able to understand each other. Both sendmail and Exchange Server are MTAs that implement a delivering and receiving agent for SMTP over TCP/IP (Figure 14.3). They both follow the SMTP model to ensure message delivery and integrity.

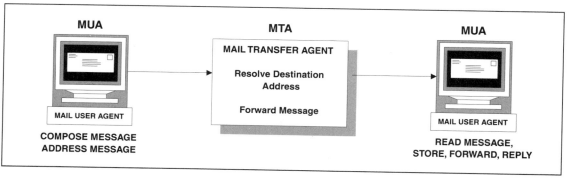

FIGURE 14.2.   Simplified View of Mail Agents

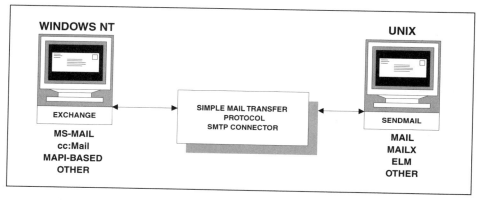

FIGURE 14.3.   View of Exchange-to-sendmail Mail Flow

Understanding the SMTP Model

The SMTP model is the basis for integrating UNIX and Windows NT mail systems. SMTP has undergone a number of evolutions. The specification is established by the Internet Engineering Task Force (IETF) of the Network Information Center. The complete specification for SMTP is defined in IETF RFC 821, available at www.freesoft.org/CIE/index.html. SMTP establishes two-way communication between hosts through a defined set of commands (Figure 14.4). These commands force mail agents both to receive and to acknowledge a mail message to ensure reliable mail delivery. We discuss the model from a high level, but the complete explanation of these commands and specification is derived from RFC 821.

When the MUA initiates the action to transmit an e-mail message, SMTP begins a series of communications. Figure 14.4 illustrates some of the basic commands sent between an SMTP sender and receiver, while Figure 14.5 provides a

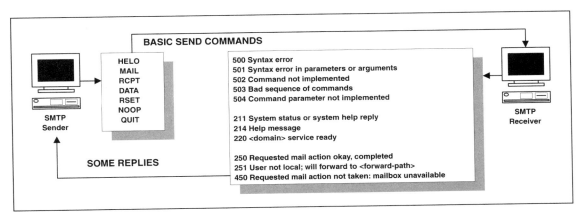

FIGURE 14.4.   Flow of Commands in SMTP

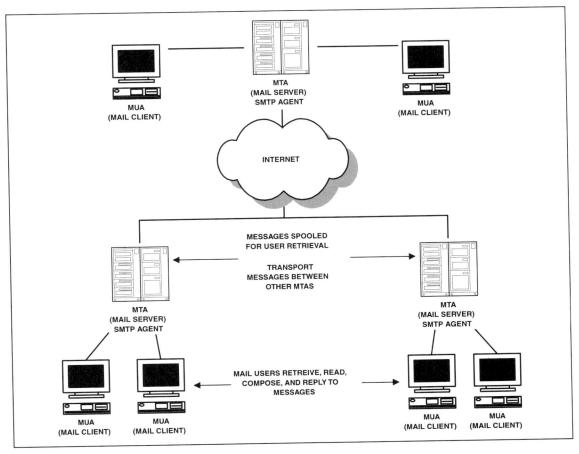

FIGURE 14.5.   View of SMTP Agents in an Internet Enterprise

more global view. The SMTP sender transmits a send command, such as HELO, to the SMTP receiver through the transport connection. The SMTP receiver should then reply with one of the predefined replies, such as the 250 okay reply, to acknowledge the sender's command. There are several defined "procedures" for the SMTP mail model, but we shall only cover a basic mail transaction that involves opening a connection, sending a mail message, and closing the connection. The following code contains an example mail transaction using the verbose option for the UNIX-based sendmail application. In our discussion involving UNIX and Windows NT we assume this activity occurs over TCP. However, it should be noted that an SMTP session could be handled over several transport protocols, including TCP, NCP, NITS, and X.25. The following examples take place over the TCP transport service using port 25, as specified in RFC 821.

Let's first dissect the SMTP process with the sample message shown here. The numbers in the parentheses to the right match the explanation that follows.

```
# /usr/lib/sendmail -v mwalla@unint.com
This a test message
.
mwalla@nthost.unint.com... Connecting to nthost.unint.com. (ether)...
220 nthost.unint.com Microsoft Exchange Internet Mail Service
5.0.1457.7 ready
>>> HELO unixhost.unint                                          (1)
250 OK                                                           (2)
>>> MAIL From:root@unixhost                                      (3)
250 OK - mail from <root@unixhost>
>>> RCPT To:mwalla@nthost.unint.com                              (4)
250 OK - Recipient mwalla@nthost.unint.com
>>> DATA                                                         (5)
354 Send data. End with CRLF.CRLF
>>> .
250 OK
>>> QUIT                                                         (6)
221 closing connection
mwalla@nthost.unint.com... Sent (OK)
```

As shown here, SMTP consists of three primary components (connect, transmit, and close), and each component involves six actions. The connection sequence is shown in the first two statements.

(1) The transmission channel is opened with the HELO <SP> <domain> <CRLF> from the sending SMTP host.

(2) The receiving SMTP host then acknowledges this command and ensures that the host name matches its own name and verifies that a connection is now open.

The next three steps involve the actual transmission transaction.

(3) The sending SMTP host first sends the *MAIL* command with the sender's mailbox address and entire return path (in case the message has been relayed through more than one host). This allows the receiving host to notify the sender if problems occur with message delivery.

(4) The second mail transaction is the RCPT <SP> TO:<forward-path> <CRLF>, which identifies one recipient for the mail message. The receiving host must verify that the recipient exists and has a mailbox on the system. If this is true, a 250 OK reply is sent to the sending SMTP host.

(5) When all commands receive valid responses, the sending SMTP host sends the third command—DATA <CRLF>. If this command receives the 354 reply, then the entire mail message text is sent, followed by a line with a single period, <CRLF>. <CRLF>.

Finally, the session is closed.

(6) After the message data is received, a 250 OK reply is sent by the receiving SMTP host. The transmission channel is closed when the sending SMTP host sends the *QUIT* command and the session termination is acknowledged.

Internet Mail Addressing

A mail address is specified by a rigid format in which the message is routed to a *userid* (or login name) on a host called *hostname*. There are the two major parts of the Internet mail address. On the left side of @ is the user ID, which uniquely identifies a user at a site. To the right of @ is a host name, which identifies the host that receives the mail message (Figure 14.6). This receiving MTA must be able to communicate with the sending MTA. The host name must also be fully qualified and mapped to a valid IP address when the SMTP sender attempts to map this name to an IP address. The most prevalent method for resolving an Internet address—DNS—deserves consideration. DNS is discussed in greater detail in the Advanced Topics section in this chapter.

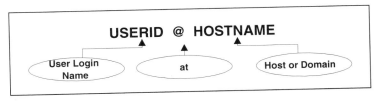

FIGURE 14.6.   Dissection of a Simple Mail Address

Understanding the Site Address

Most organizations prefer a uniform address for everyone at a site or an enterprise. Ideally, all e-mail addresses should be in the form

```
USERID @ COMPANY.COM
```

This means your site address, *company.com,* needs to resolve to the IP address of a mail server at your site. A detailed discussion of mail exchanger (MX) records in the Advanced Topics section in this chapter demonstrates how backup mail servers can handle the mail connection when the primary one does not respond. So if MX records are used, *company.com* resolves to a backup mail server if the primary mail server is down.

NOTE   **How to Get a Registered Domain Name**

Each country maintains its registration of domain names. The first step in selecting a domain name is to determine if it is available. An excellent search tool for this purpose is located at `http://http.demon.net/external/ntools.html`. There are a variety of searches that can be conducted for free. Once you have determined that a name is still available, it must then be registered. This can also be done over the Internet. In the United States, domain name registration is managed by InterNIC and involves a $100 fee. The InterNIC Registration Tool is available at `http://rs.internic.net/cgi-bin/itts`.

Return Addresses

Mail messages are composed of a body and a header. The header is appended to a mail message to provide the message's return address, sending address, date and time, and the complete mail route. This header information is tacked on by the MTA. You use the MTA to configure the return address. The return address usually includes the sender's user ID, @, and the sending MTA's fully qualified host name in the following format:

```
SENDERUSERID @ SENDINGHOSTNAME
```

In this case the SENDINGHOSTNAME should be *company.com,* without a specific host name appended to it. In this way replies to the e-mail messages will find their way back to the mail server.

Figure 14.7 demonstrates how a site address can be used to maintain a consistent reply address for all users, and to maintain specific host anonymity. Each mail server, mailserver1 through mailserver3, is configured to send the same

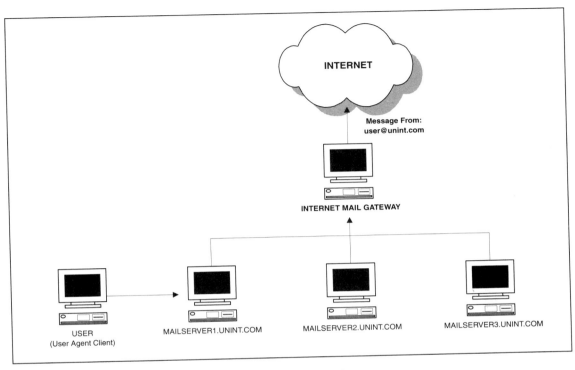

FIGURE 14.7.   Example of Uniform Site and Return Addresses

reply host name, *@unint.com*. This means that the user sending a message to a friend on the Internet via the MTA on mailserver1 has a reply address of *user@unint.com*. All messages from the *unint* site have the same reply address. Specific mail server names are hidden from external mail recipients, and the right side of @ remains consistent for all mail addresses. The specific steps for identifying a single-reply address are discussed later in the chapter.

Incoming Mail Routing

Now that all mail messages have a consistent return address, you must be able to route these incoming mail messages to the appropriate user. The MTA sending a message to your site over the Internet must be able to match the site address to an IP address. This IP address should correspond to an interface on your site's Internet mail gateway. The details of this name-to-IP address mapping are covered in the Advanced Topics section in this chapter. After the foreign MTA delivers the mail message to your Internet mail gateway, some internal mail routing needs to be handled. The incoming mail message has a destination host name, *@company.com,* that is the same for every user at the site. How do you know to which mail server to forward the message? We cannot figure this out with only the destination host name. The destination user ID must be mapped to the mail server, where the user maintains a mailbox. The Internet mail gateway MTA is responsible for mapping user IDs to the mail server. The sendmail application can accomplish this with the *aliases* configuration file. Scenario 5 in the sample scenario section that follows presents a sample *aliases* file and describes how it is used to find the destination mail server.

Outgoing Mail Routing—The Mail Relay

Now that we have discussed some addressing issues and incoming mail routing techniques it might prove helpful to talk about outgoing mail. When sending mail messages to the Internet, external host names must be resolved by accessing name servers on the Internet. For security and convenience it is a good idea to centralize this name resolution process to one host connected to the Internet. You can remove the name resolution burden from internal mail servers by forwarding all outbound e-mail to this one central mail server. This host, referred to as the *mail relay,* would then be handling all outgoing mail messages, regardless of their destination, and would be responsible for resolving e-mail addresses. This funneling of all outgoing traffic through one host puts the burden of resolving external names in one place and simplifies the site's structure.

Postmaster Error Handling

A configuration parameter required by RFC 822 for mail systems is that a postmaster be specified. The primary purpose of the postmaster is to resolve errors and in many cases return improperly addressed or otherwise undeliverable messages. The postmaster stamps the header of an undeliverable message, which is returned to the sender.

REVIEWING SENDMAIL AND EXCHANGE
THROUGH SAMPLE SCENARIOS

With a basic understanding of how SMTP works, the next step is to understand the components necessary to implement your mail strategy. In this discussion we take a generic look at how mail flows internally and externally. Armed with these examples, we then explore the specific configuration items that must be addressed in both UNIX sendmail and Windows NT Exchange Server 5.0 to ensure connectivity. For advanced individual configuration needs you will need, consult other resources, such as *Sendmail* by Bryan Costales and Eric Allman (O'Reilly & Associates, Inc., 1994) and *Using Microsoft Exchange Server* by Sal Collora (editor), Kent Joshi, Mark Kapczynski, and Ruben Perez (Que Corporation, 1996).

The preceding section summarizes the theory of transport agents, user agents, Internet mail addressing conventions, and how the destination address is determined from the mail address. The discussion now shifts to bringing these basic concepts into focus for the purpose of implementation. A great way to identify overlapping configuration issues needed for integration is to walk through several mail flow scenarios. The reason for providing these examples is simply to place into a real-world context the system configuration discussions that follow.

Figures 14.8 and 14.9 illustrate a simplified flow of e-mail within and external to UNI/NT Technologies, a company using the *unint.com* domain name. Figure 14.8 demonstrates several messaging scenarios involving sendmail and

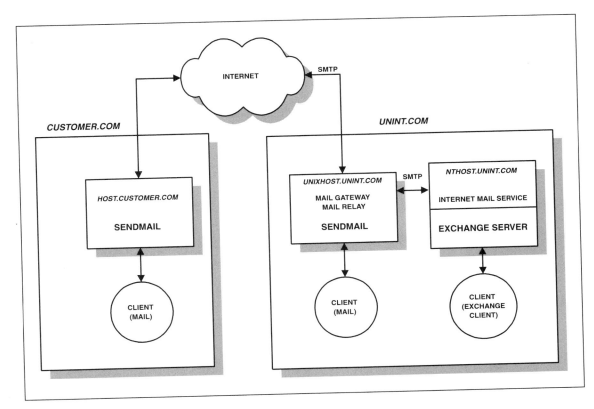

FIGURE 14.8.   The Unint Site

Exchange integration. For the sake of simplicity, the site is shown in a minimal configuration with one UNIX mail server, positioned as the mail gateway to the Internet, and one Windows NT Exchange mail server. *Unixhost* is configured as the mail gateway and all messages entering the *unint.com* site flow through this mail server. This server distributes each incoming mail message to the appropriate mailbox. *Unixhost* is also designated as the mail relay for all mail servers at the site and performs Internet name resolution for outgoing mail.

Scenario 1: Exchange Client E-mails Local sendmail Client

An Exchange client sends a message to someone in another department who uses a sendmail client, such as mailx or elm (Figure 14.9). The destination e-mail address *unixuser@unint.com* needs to be routed to the user's mailbox based on the user ID *unixuser*. When the Exchange server receives the message from the Exchange client, the destination user ID is not known as a local user. The Exchange server forwards the message to its designated mail relay *unixhost* via an SMTP session with its Internet mail service. *Unixhost* compares the user ID with local users and delivers the message locally to *unixuser*'s mailbox.

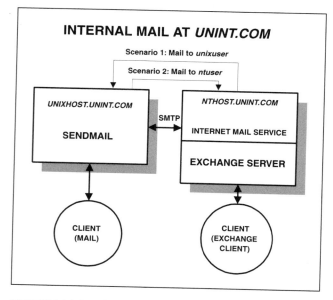

FIGURE 14.9.   Scenarios 1 and 2

Scenario 2: sendmail Client E-mails Local Exchange Client

A sendmail client sends a message to someone using an Exchange client, such as Outlook (see Figure 14.9). The message is destined for *ntuser@unint.com*. The sendmail application recognizes this as a local address and consults the *aliases* configuration file to identify *ntuser* with its fully qualified host name, *nthost.unint.com*. Sendmail then forwards the message to *nthost.unint.com* via an SMTP session with the Internet Mail Service on the Windows NT host. The Exchange server recognizes the local user name and sends it to *ntuser*'s mailbox for client retrieval.

Scenario 3: Exchange Client E-mails Off-site Customer on the Internet

An Exchange client mailing a message to another site on the Internet sends its message to the Exchange server with the destination address *offsite_user@customer.com*. The Exchange server sends the nonlocal address to its mail relay *unixhost. Unixhost* attempts to resolve the host name *customer.com* using DNS. The local name server cannot resolve the name and must access a root name server on the Internet, at *unint.com*'s ISP. Eventually an IP address is found for the destination host name *customer.com*. A detailed explanation of this name resolution is covered in the Advanced Topics section in this chapter. An SMTP session is opened with the mail server for *customer.com* and the message is sent to the *offsite_user*'s mailbox based on the customer's mail site configuration.

Scenario 4: sendmail Client E-mails Off-site Customer on the Internet

This scenario is the same as scenario 3, without involving the Exchange server. Sendmail receives the message from its client, resolves the host name using an Internet name server, and sends the message to *customer.com*. The user ID is resolved at the foreign site.

Scenario 5: Off-site Customer E-mails Local sendmail Client or Exchange Client

The off-site customer replies to a message from *ntuser@unint.com*. Their call to DNS eventually references MX records for *unint.com*. The highest priority MX record references the *unixhost*'s IP address. (MX records are discussed in greater detail in a later section.) The mail server at *customer.com* opens an

SMTP mail session with *unixhost* and sends the message. *Unixhost* references its *aliases* configuration file, as shown here, and forwards the message to *nthost.unint.com*. If the message had been destined for *unixuser@unint.com*, *unixhost* would have delivered the message locally or found an entry in the *aliases* file and forwarded it to the appropriate sendmail server. The Outlook client in Figure 14.10 displays the header for the message coming from *off-site_user*. The header is handy for retracing each link of an e-mail message's journey. The following explanation expands the *offsite_user* message header.

```
##
#  Sendmail Aliases File
##

# RFC 822 requires that every host have a mail address "postmaster"
postmaster   : root

# System Administration aliases
operator     : root
uucp         : root
daemon       : root
```

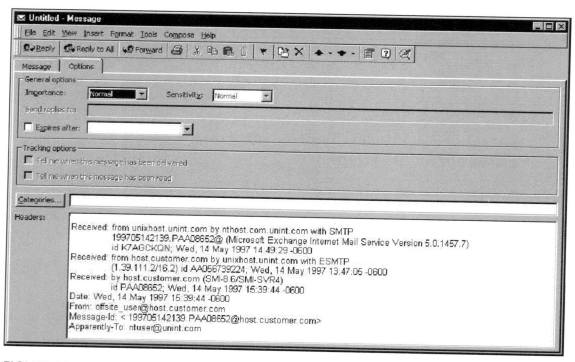

FIGURE 14.10.   Exchange Mail Verbose Output

```
# Site aliases
ntuser      : ntuser@nthost.unint.com
ntuser2     : ntuser2@nthost.unint.com
```

- *Line 1* – Received: from *unixhost.unint.com* by *nthost.unint.com* with SMTP 199705142139.PAA08652@ (Microsoft Exchange Internet Mail Service version 5.0.1457.7)
- *Line 2* – id K7AGCKQN; Wed, 14 May 1997 14:49:29 -0600
- *Line 3* – Received: from *host.customer.com* by *unixhost.unint.com* with ESMTP
- *Line 4* – (1.39.111.2/16.2) id AA056739224; Wed, 14 May 1997 13:47:05 -0600
- *Line 5* – Received: by *host.customer.com* (SMI-8.6/SMI-SVR4)
- *Line 6* – id PAA08652; Wed, 14 May 1997 15:39:44 -0600
- *Line 7* – Date: Wed, 14 May 1997 15:39:44 -0600
- *Line 8* – From: *offsite_user@host.customer.com*
- *Line 9* – Message-Id: < 199705142139.PAA08652@*host.customer.com*>
- *Line 10* – Apparently-To: *ntuser@unint.com*

The message route from *offsite_user* to *ntuser* is followed by reading the header information in Figure 14.10 from the bottom up. The message originates from a remote client and is received by the remote host, as seen in line 5. This remote host appears to be running sendmail version 8.6 for a System V, release 4 UNIX platform, evident from line 5. Line 3 indicates the message is then sent to *unixhost* using extended SMTP (ESMTP). *Unixhost* then maps the user *ntuser* to the Exchange server (*nthost*) from the *aliases* file and sends the message to the *nthost* as shown by line 1. It should be noted how tight control over local message routing is maintained in one central location, the *aliases* file.

SENDMAIL AND EXCHANGE CONFIGURATION DETAILS

The configuration details that follow are pertinent to integrating Exchange and sendmail. The actions required are relatively simple. To facilitate an understanding of the process, we have broken the tasks out separately and pinpointed the actions that must be taken with both UNIX sendmail and Windows NT Exchange Server sequentially. The following configuration issues are addressed:

- Base-level configuration for sendmail and Exchange
- Mail relay configuration
- Site address configuration
- Postmaster configuration

Base-level Configuration

This section discusses the basic configuration necessary for implementing both UNIX sendmail and Windows NT Exchange Server. We also discuss briefly the *nslookup* command as a tool for testing host name lookups and identifying MX records.

SENDMAIL BASE-LEVEL CONFIGURATION

Sendmail requires mainly two configuration files: *aliases* and *sendmail.cf*. These files, as well as the sendmail program itself, are located in different directories depending on the UNIX variant in use. Some common locations are */usr/ucb, /etc/mail,* and */usr/lib.* Check the system documentation or utilize the UNIX *find* command to locate these files. When the *aliases* file is changed, sendmail must be sent the *-bi* option to reread the aliases file:

```
#/usr/lib/sendmail -bi
```

The sendmail process must be stopped and restarted to reread the *sendmail.cf* file. This file is read only once during the life of the process. You must first kill the existing daemon by identifying its process number and then issuing the *kill* instruction:

```
#ps -ef | grep sendmail
```

This returns a line similar to the following:

```
root     196    1 0  May 20 ?    0:04 /usr/lib/sendmail -bd -q1h
```

Then issue the *kill* command and restart the process just as it was running before being killed. In this case sendmail was running in the daemon mode (*-bd*) with queuing every hour (*-q1h*):

```
#kill 196
#/usr/lib/sendmail -bd -q1h
```

Running the *sendmail* command with the recipient and text message at the command line is a great way to send mail messages without utilizing a user agent. The text message must be terminated with a period in the first column followed by a <CRLF> to send the message and end standard input (more specifically <CRLF>.<CRLF>):

```
#/usr/lib/sendmail user@hostname
This is a test message
.
```

Sending a mail message using the sendmail verbose option displays all SMTP communication that occurs between the sendmail application and the destination SMTP host:

```
# /usr/lib/sendmail -v mwalla@unint.com
This a test message
.
mwalla@nthost.unint.com... Connecting to nthost.unint.com (ether)...
220 nthost.unint.com Microsoft Exchange Internet Mail Service
5.0.1457.7 ready
>>> HELO unixhost.unint
250 OK
.
.
```

The lines beginning with >>> are SMTP-defined commands sent from the sendmail application to the Windows NT Exchange Server. The line with 250 is a response from the Exchange Server.

EXCHANGE BASE-LEVEL CONFIGURATION

Start the Microsoft Exchange Administrator by selecting **Start ➤ Programs ➤ Microsoft Exchange ➤ Microsoft Exchange Administrator**.

From the left pane of the Microsoft Exchange Administrator window, select **Configuration ➤ Connections**. The available Exchange connections are displayed in the right pane of the Microsoft Exchange Administrator window (Figure 14.11). The Internet Mail Service is the SMTP connector of interest. Double-click this selection to display its configuration (Figure 14.12).

The Internet Mail Service Properties window displays configuration parameters relevant to the SMTP connector. The **Routing** tab displays the destination address formats that are accepted when rerouting is activated. This rerouting is necessary when using POP3 Exchange Server support. Only destination e-mail addresses with the host name portion matching these formats are accepted at this server site. All others are forwarded to the mail relay or alternately to a DNS server to resolve the host name, and are then forwarded accordingly. Destination address formatting is also managed at the individual mailbox level and should not be confused with the "site-level" configuration.

To ensure that the Internet Mail Service for Microsoft Exchange is running correctly, use telnet to connect to port 25 on the Windows NT mail server. The following code verifies that the SMTP agent is running on the host.

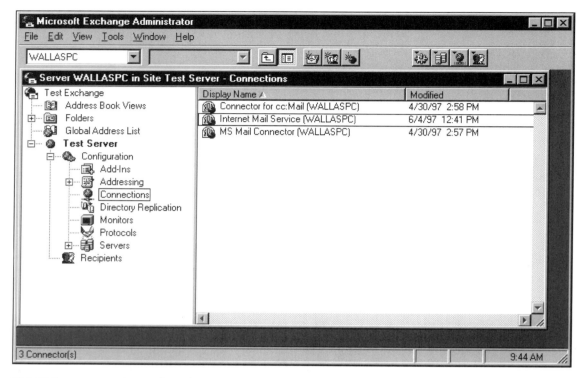

FIGURE 14.11.   Microsoft Exchange Administrative Tool

```
# telnet nthost 25
Trying 151.116.25.155...
Connected to nthost.unint.com.
Escape character is '^]'.
220 nthost.unint.com Microsoft Exchange Internet Mail Service
5.0.1457.7 ready
QUIT
221 closing connection
Connection closed by foreign host.
#
```

Notice that the initial response to the telnet connection indicates Microsoft Exchange. Make sure that this is the SMTP application that you want running on this mail server.

Also, be sure that only one SMTP server is running on the Windows NT server by checking the started processes from the Control Panel Services window (**Start** ➤ **Settings** ➤ **Control Panel** ➤ **Services**; Figure 14.13).

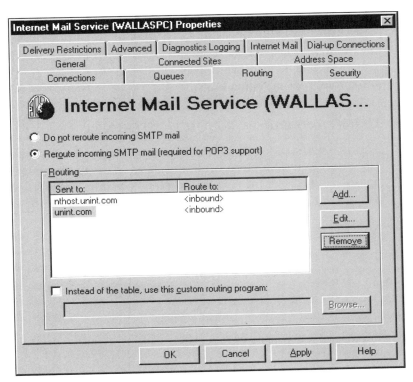

FIGURE 14.12.   Exchange Mail Service Properties

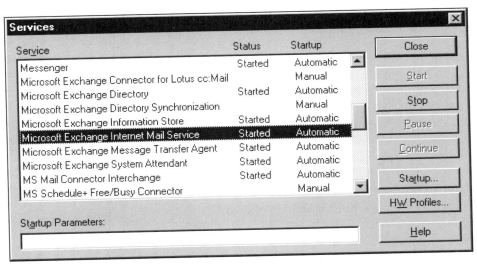

FIGURE 14.13.   Windows NT Services Dialog Box

The Microsoft Exchange Internet Mail Service must be started. No other SMTP-type mail server products should be running. Whenever changes are made to the Internet Mail Service configuration, the process must be stopped and restarted. The Services window is where you should stop and start the service, using the **Stop** and **Start** buttons.

USING *nslookup* FOR QUICK REFERENCE

The *nslookup* command is useful for testing host name lookups and identifying MX records. It is important to verify the existence or nonexistence of these records and ensure mail is being routed correctly. To test for MX records type the following:

```
#nslookup
Default Server: domainnameserver.unint.com
Address: 184.112.3.52

>nthost
Server: domainnameserver.unint.com
Address: 184.112.3.52

Server: nthost.unint.com
Address: 184.112.3.48

>set type=mx
>nthost.unint.com

Server: domainnameserver.unint.com
Address: 184.112.3.52

*** No mail exchanger (MX) records available for nthost.unint.com
>
```

This verifies that there are no MX records for our Windows NT server. Any mail message destined for this host will not be rerouted using DNS.

Mail Relay Configuration

Depending on the UNIX variant you are using, different changes must be made to the sendmail configuration to specify a mail relay. This section gives guidelines for changing the *sendmail.cf* file for two different UNIX variants. In addition, this section describes specifying a mail relay for the Windows NT Exchange Server.

SENDMAIL MAIL RELAY CONFIGURATION

To specify a mail relay for the sendmail application, modify the *sendmail.cf* file. For HP-UX 10.10/ HP sendmail (1.39.111.2/16.2), the DS macro should be set to your relay host name. The portion of S0 should be uncommented so that all outgoing messages include the mail relay in the destination route:

```
# SMTP relay for unresolved @ addresses
DSrelayhost.domain.com

S0:
.
.

# Users must choose at most one of the following lines to pass
#   unresolved SMTP addresses to the SMTP relay or UUCP relay
#R$+<@$+>        $#tcp$@$S$:$1<@$2>      user@domain to SMTP relay
```

The SunOS 5.5 version of sendmail (SMI-8.6) involves setting the DR macro and ensuring the following line is uncommented from rule S0:

```
# major relay host
DRmailhost

S0:
.
.

R$*<@$+>$*       $#$M $@$R $:$1<@$2>$3      user@some.where
```

To change the file accurately, review the *sendmail.cf* file for your version of sendmail and follow the instructions outlined by the comments contained in the *sendmail.cf* file. Refer to the *man* pages for setup specifics on other UNIX variants.

EXCHANGE MAIL RELAY CONFIGURATION

To specify a mail relay for the Exchange Server, launch the Internet Mail Service window and select the **Connections** tab (Start ➤ **Programs** ➤ **Microsoft Exchange** ➤ **Microsoft Exchange Administrator** ➤ Connections ➤ **Internet Mail Service** ➤ **Connections**; Figure 14.4).

Select the **Forward all messages to host** radio button in the Message Delivery box and enter the fully qualified name of the relay host. The option to use DNS is also readily available from this window as long as it has been configured on the current Exchange host system.

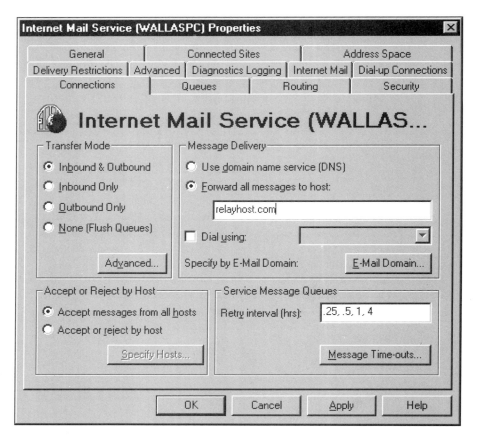

FIGURE 14.14.   Connections Tab of the Internet Mail Service Properties
Dialog Box

Site Address Configuration

A site address should be configured in order to establish both a consistent
sender's address for outgoing messages and a reply address. This section discusses the steps necessary to accomplish this configuration for both UNIX
sendmail and Microsoft Exchange Server.

SENDMAIL SITE ADDRESS CONFIGURATION

Configure the site address hiding in the *sendmail.cf* file. The intention here is
to is to maintain a consistent sender's address for all outgoing messages. For
the HP-UX 10.10/ HP sendmail (1.39.111.2/16.2) version, uncomment the DY

macro and append your domain name as we have done with the *unint.com* domain in the code that follows. (For other UNIX variants, consult the *man* pages prior to configurating the *sendmail.cf* file.):

```
# site hiding: local sender identified as user@my_site
instead of user@my_host
DYunint.com

S11

..
R$+                     $:$1<@$?Y$Y$|$w$.>      add local domain
```

For the SunOS 5.5 version of sendmail (SMI-8.6), you have to add the DY macro and modify rule 11 to something similar to the following:

```
# add new macro, all sender's addresses will now end
with only our domain.
DYunint.com

S11:

..
R$+             $@$Y                    user@yourdomain
```

Now the sender's address or reply address will be *sender@yourdomain* without the inclusion of the sender's specific host name.

EXCHANGE SITE ADDRESS CONFIGURATION

The ability to modify the site address for Exchange can be accessed using two different methods from within the Microsoft Exchange Administrator. The first method, in the Site Addressing Properties window, can be accessed by selecting **Configuration** ➤ **Site Administration** ➤ **Site Addressing** (Figure 14.15). This brings up the e-mail addresses for the site. Here you may change default mail addresses for newly created accounts. You must also decide whether or not this new e-mail address will be assigned to all current e-mail accounts. SMTP e-mail recipient addresses can be resolved for each user from this spot. The new e-mail address would also become every user's reply address.

Select the SMTP site address from the **E-mail addresses** field and press the **Edit** button. You may now change your site address for all users on this server or just affect newly created e-mail accounts. If you apply the address to all users, the new address will be set as the return address for all e-mail accounts on this server.

When editing the SMTP site address, the SMTP Properties window is displayed (Figure 14.16). At this point, enter the site host name portion of the e-mail address.

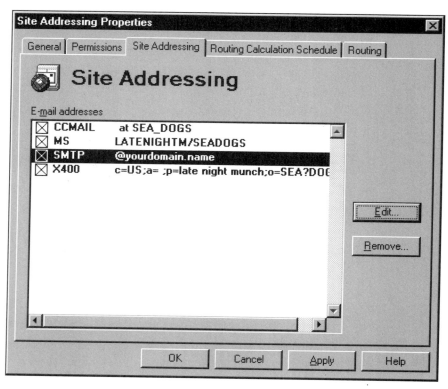

FIGURE 14.15.   Exchange Site Addressing Properties Dialog Box

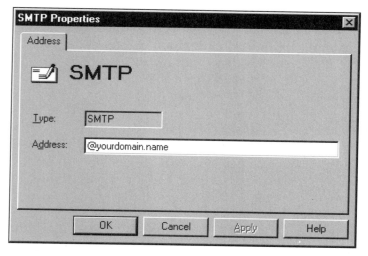

FIGURE 14.16.   SMTP Properties Dialog Box

This brings us to the second method for modifying a site's address—the individual recipient's Properties window. Access this window from within the Microsoft Exchange Administrator by selecting **Recipients** and then double-clicking on the desired user. When the user's Properties window appears, select the **E-mail Addresses** tab (Figure 14.17).

In Figure 14.17 the SMTP address *mwalla@unint.com* is set as the reply address. To change this, select an address that is not bold and press the **Set as Reply Address** button. The other SMTP addresses are very important for determining which destination address formats will be accepted by this mailbox. An incoming e-mail message must have a destination address matching one of the formats in this recipient's Properties window if it is to be delivered to this mailbox.

To add a new SMTP incoming message format, select the **New** button and choose **Internet Address**. Enter the new address format in the Internet Address Properties window (Figure 14.18).

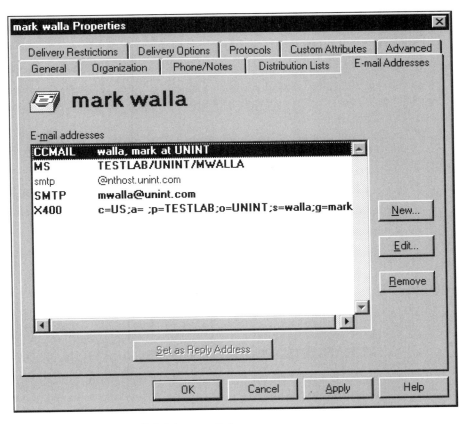

FIGURE 14.17.   E-mail Addresses Tab

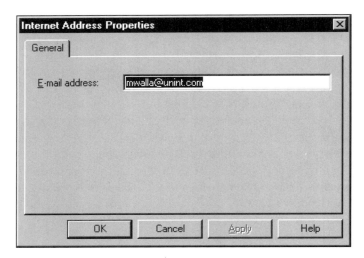

FIGURE 14.18.   Internet Address Properties Dialog Box

Postmaster Configuration

There are times that any mail system has undeliverable mail. The warnings that result should be delivered to a single recipient, called a postmaster. This section discusses configuring a postmaster for both UNIX sendmail and Microsoft Exchange Server.

SENDMAIL POSTMASTER CONFIGURATION

To specify the user ID that will receive undeliverable headers on both the HP-UX and SunOS sendmail systems, use the *sendmail.cf* configuration file. Simply specify the user with the following macro:

```
OPuser_name
```

Another common option is to leave this option as the default: OPPostmaster. In the *aliases* file assign the Postmaster to the user you desire to receive Postmaster complaints, such as:

```
Postmaster : root
```

EXCHANGE POSTMASTER CONFIGURATION

The Exchange server also has a configurable postmaster that receives undeliverable message warnings. Access it by selecting **Microsoft Exchange Administrator** ➤ **Connections** ➤ **Internet Mail Service** ➤ **Internet Mail** (Figure 14.19).

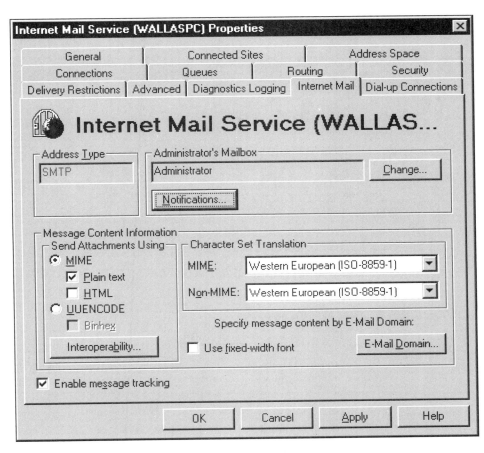

FIGURE 14.19.   Internet Mail Tab

The **Administrator's Mailbox** field can be changed to any user, but is set to the Administrator's account as default. The **Notifications** button presents some interesting options (Figure 14.20).

Most of the options available in the Notifications dialog box should be selected during the testing phase of your site to ensure messaging problems are sent to the postmaster. As the system administrator you need to know where failures occur, especially during the early days of deployment. As the installation matures you may elect to reduce the amount of problem notification. However, if you do elect to deactivate these options it is recommended that you reinstate them periodically on a regular basis to ensure system health.

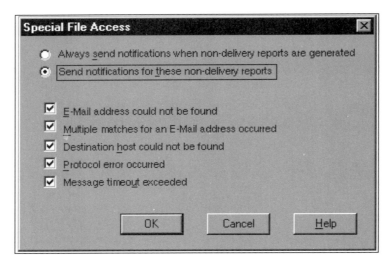

FIGURE 14.20. Notifications Dialog Box

ADVANCED TOPICS

In addition to understanding how to connect UNIX sendmail systems with Windows NT Exchange servers, several other related concepts should be mentioned. The resolution of names and IP addresses within an enterprise and across the Internet can be handled by a variety of directory services. In this chapter we confine our review to the DNS. Another topic that deserves attention is the POP. Clients can use POP to retrieve messages from mail servers that support this standardized protocol.

DNS and How It Relates to Mail Systems

This section discusses how names are resolved for transmission of mail across a network. Any computer or device connected to a network running IP has an assigned IP address. Data can be sent to another host by simply forwarding the information to a router on the Internet. This router then forwards the packet to other routers, based on its routing tables. Eventually this packet enters the host interface that answers to your destination IP address. When using TCP on top of the IP network layer, a connection can be made between the destination host and the sending host. This means an IP destination address can translate to a mail communication session between two hosts.

The role of the DNS is to match a host name with the defined IP address. This "name" must be a fully qualified host name or a domain name that resolves to a particular IP address. Domain names are organized in a top-down fashion, from general to specific (Figure 14.21).

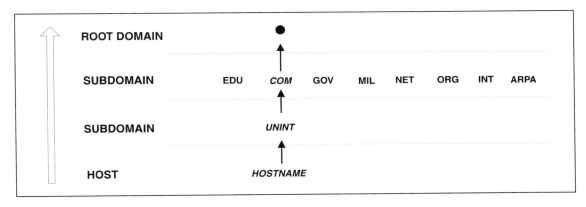

FIGURE 14.21.   Hierarchy of Domain Name Construction

Figure 14.21 depicts this hierarchy, reading from bottom to top. The fully qualified host name for *host* in the *unint* subdomain would be *host.unint.com*. The root domain is indicated by the period on the far right of the qualified name. This is usually omitted from e-mail addresses and host names, but is necessary in DNS configuration files. The *com* portion is, in this example, the highest subdomain under the root domain, indicating a commercially assigned domain name. In our example we have used a real company name and registered domain name—*unint*. *Unint* is a private corporation that requested allocation of this subdomain name from the Network Information Center. The *host* portion of the name is a host within the *unint* subdomain that is assigned an IP address for one of its network interfaces. This fully-qualified host name can be used to reference this IP address by accessing a domain name server with a configuration file similar to the following:

```
; specify the name server (NS) for the unint.com domain
unint.com.                              IN      NS      domainnameserver.unint.com.

; map host names to IP addresses (A)
unixhost.unint.com.                     IN      A       18x.11x.2xx.x46
nthost.unint.com.                       IN      A       18x.11x.2xx.x48
hostname.unint.com.                     IN      A       18x.11x.2xx.x50
domainnameserver.uninit.com.            IN      A       18x.11x.2xx.x52

; host name aliases (CNAME)
unixhost.unint.com.                     IN      CNAME   mailgateway.unint.com.
nthost.unint.com.                       IN      CNAME   mailgatewaybak.unint.com.

; map hosts to a mail exchanger (MX)
unint.com.          IN      MX      0       mailgateway.unint.com.
unint.com.          IN      MX      10      mailgatewaybak.unint.com.
```

This is not a complete configuration file for a DNS server, but it gives you a basic understanding of name resolution and mail exchange routing. The first set of parameters designates the host *domainnameserver.unint.com* as the name server for the *unint.com* domain. The second set of parameters map fully qualified host names to IP addresses. When a host asks its DNS server for an IP address, the search begins. When a name server cannot resolve a host address, it asks other servers recursively. For a more detailed description of name resolution please refer to other resources, such as *DNS and BIND* by Paul Albitz and Cricket Liu (O'Reilly & Associates, 1994).

The host name alias section provides alternate names for hosts. A host with an alias can be referenced with either its own name, assigned with the A record, or with an alias name, created with a CNAME record. Both names will reference the same IP address. This is useful when "aliasing" a host name to a service that it performs. The *unixhost* performs the preferred mail exchange function for *hostname*. You could rename the mail exchange by simply modifying one CNAME record for *mailgateway* and change it from *unixhost* to another host name. All hosts referencing *mailgateway* as the preferred mail exchange now point to the newly assigned alias for *mailgateway*.

NOTE   In the following discussion we use the term *mail exchange* or the abbreviation *MX*. This term is used specifically in terms of the DNS process. It should not be confused with the product name of Microsoft Exchange.

MX records are essential for rerouting e-mail to the appropriate mail servers. A request to resolve a host name returns the address of another host if an MX record exists for the host. In Figure 14.22, seven primary steps take place.

1. The sending host contacts its local domain name server and attempts to resolve the destination host name *unint.com*.

2. The local domain server queries the root domain server on the Internet. The root name server returns the *.com* name server address.

3. The local domain server then queries the *.com* name server on the Internet. The *.com* name server returns the address of the *.com.unint* name server.

4. The local name server then queries the *.com.unint* name server on the Internet. The MX records for the receiving site reside there. The previously mentioned sample configuration file also resides on this name server. This would probably be at the receiving site's ISP. The *.com.unint* name server observes from its configuration files that *unint.com* has two MX

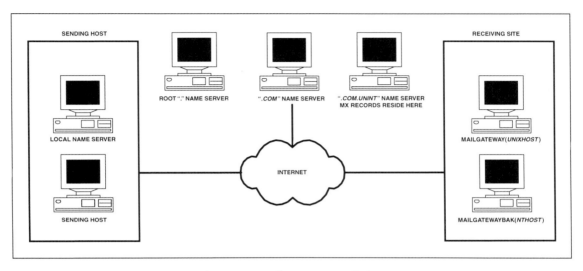

FIGURE 14.22.   How MX Records Route Mail to Your Mail Gateways

records for this host. The lower the MX record number, the higher the priority.

5. The preferred mail exchange *mailgateway.unint.com,* otherwise known as *unixhost.unint.com,* and the second choice mail exchange *nthost.unint.com* are returned to the sending host.

6. The sending host then tries to open an SMTP mail session with *unixhost*.

7. If this fails, it tries *nthost*.

This example should give you some insight into DNS, the most prevalent Internet name resolution method. Mail destined for a host may be rerouted to another. In this way mail responsibilities can be off-loaded to a few designated mail servers or mail exchanges.

POP3 Mail Retrieval

The previous mail designs involve MUAs that are specifically oriented toward their respective MTAs. These mail clients must speak the proprietary language of their server application. This can lead to operating system dependencies, implying that a UNIX mail server requires a UNIX mail client and a Windows NT mail server requires a Windows NT client. Some mail servers also require delivery to the user's client mailbox within a specified period of time. If your client system is portable and often not connected to your network, this would be a problem.

Enter POP3 (defined in RFC 1725) as a possible solution to these problems. The origin of POP stems from the UNIX environment where it used to be required to maintain an MTA and MUA on the same platform. POP allowed the "thin" client to shed this requirement and only support a POP client. This protocol sends a series of commands and responses to TCP port 110 and establishes a POP3 session. Once the user ID and password have been validated, the POP3 session enters a *transaction state*. The client can now issue several commands relating to mail retrieval. These commands enable the client to list, retrieve, and delete messages from the POP mail server. However, these commands are only oriented toward retrieving mail messages. The POP client must send messages using the SMTP model (Figure 14.23). It is interesting to note that the SMTP session only requires a valid user ID and no password. So if you know someone else's user ID and server, you can send mail through their server. POP3 does have password verification, securing message retrieval.

Using a POP client frees the user to choose a mail server, independent of the mail application server software (Figure 14.24). A POP client can have an account on the Exchange or sendmail mail servers, since they both support POP3. If you wished to stick with the mixed MTA environment (Exchange and sendmail), your site design will probably not change much. However, POP clients on Netscape and Internet Explorer browsers free the user from the mail server application/client requirements. You could then choose either Exchange or sendmail and have all users access this one server (or servers) running the same MTAs.

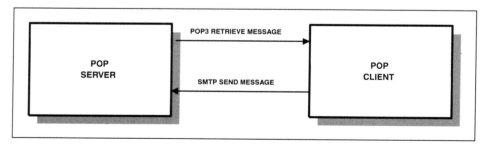

FIGURE 14.23.   POP Receives Messages with POP3 and Transmits with SMTP

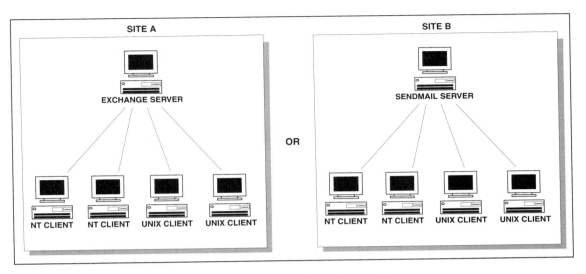

FIGURE 14.24.   POP Permits Mail Movement without Integration

FINAL THOUGHTS

E-mail is an essential part of personal and commercial life. Fortunately, transparently moving messages between UNIX and Windows NT can be achieved easily using the SMTP backbone between sendmail and Exchange Server. The level of effort required configuring UNIX sendmail and Windows NT BackOffice Exchange Server 5.0 is minimal and straightforward. Other shareware and commercial e-mail products can also be used to achieve the same end.

15
Windows NT and UNIX as Web Servers

Contributed by Barrie Sosinsky

With the unprecedented growth of the Internet, system administrators of UNIX and Windows NT enterprises often find themselves also in the role of Web master. Fortunately, the functions performed by Web servers are fundamentally the same on both UNIX and Windows NT. This chapter provides information necessary for getting started with the selection, installation, configuration, and maintenance of both Windows NT and UNIX Web servers. Specifically we examine the following major topics:

- Background on Web server technology
- Windows NT as a Web server platform
- UNIX as a Web server platform
- Basic issues of Web server security

BACKGROUND ON WEB SERVER TECHNOLOGY

The first HTTP service that signaled the beginning of the World Wide Web ran on a matte black NeXT machine at the CERN high-energy physics laboratory in Geneva, Switzerland in 1990. This accomplishment was one of several firsts made possible by Steve Jobs's company's seeding of academic institutions with their workstation. NeXT runs a variant of Mach 5 UNIX, based on the system developed at Carnegie Mellon University.

UNIX has been the operating system of choice for the large majority of Web servers worldwide. As previously stated, among the many UNIX vendors supplying hardware are Sun Microsystems, Digital, Silicon Graphics, and Hewlett-Packard. The leading software packages for UNIX Web servers are CERN's originally distributed W3C software, Apache, and the National Center for Supercomputing Applications (NCSA) server, the latter of which was developed at the University of Illinois's Supercomputing Center. All three of these programs are freeware, and together they account for roughly 63% of the Web server market as of June 1996. Other popular UNIX software packages are Netscape's Communications Server, GNN Server, and the Spry Web server, all of which with the exception of GNN Server are commercial products.

UNIX Web servers continue to offer performance advantages, and they are especially suitable for large Web sites. However, UNIX Web servers are often difficult to manage and maintain. For administrators with UNIX backgrounds, these UNIX Web servers continue to make good sense. As Web technology has grown more popular, Web server software that runs on other operating systems such as Windows and Macintosh have become increasingly more popular. They require much less specialized knowledge to set up and maintain and are generally cheaper to implement.

The dramatic improvement in Windows NT system software, and its emergence as an enterprise-strength network operating system coupled with the relatively low cost of Windows NT Server hardware, have made this platform an increasingly popular alternative to UNIX solutions. Windows NT offers many of the multitasking network capabilities, and some of the security and maintenance options found on the graphical versions of UNIX. Web server software and services are tightly integrated into Windows NT and run as threads in a multi-threaded architecture, as does this software on UNIX. Windows NT provides a set of tools for managing and executing threads on a server.

For most people Windows NT Server is easier to learn than UNIX. So today, while Windows NT Web servers are still a minority component of the Web server hardware/software market, Windows NT Web solutions are the fastest growing segment in the Web server marketplace.

With approximately 100 million Windows 3.x and Windows 95 systems in use today many network administrators already have a long experience maintaining and managing those machines. Much of that knowledge translates into common knowledge of Windows NT Server, and is a strong argument for the adoption of Windows NT Server as an enterprise solution.

This chapter describes the features and options available in setting up and running a Windows NT Web server, and highlights some of the differences you'll find when compared with their UNIX counterparts. Among the Web server topics covered are

- Software selection
- Performance
- Configuration
- Security

WINDOWS NT OPERATING SYSTEM FEATURES

The Windows NT operating system was designed to be both modular and extensible. Figure 15.1 shows the Microsoft BackOffice family of products and how they relate to the Windows architecture. Both current and future Microsoft products are shown in this overview.

Web services run as threads in Windows NT's multitasking environment. You have control over prioritization and execution of these threads, and can start and stop services using the Services Control Panel. Windows NT supports a multiprocessing hardware platform, and any Windows NT Web server can make use of the additional horsepower that this enables. Four processor systems are common, and the operating system will support up to thirty-two concurrent processors in operation. Specific system software and drivers need to be installed to make anything greater than four processors operate correctly.

Web servers specifically designed as Windows NT services have a performance edge over applications that run on Windows NT without consideration of the services management feature. You'll find that software like the Microsoft Internet Information Server and Netscape FastTrack and Enterprise Server are

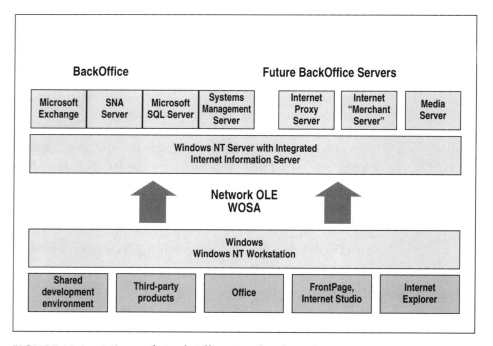

FIGURE 15.1.   Microsoft BackOffice Family of Products

fast for this reason. Other packages that are slower aren't as well integrated into Windows NT's core architecture.

Web servers also run applications, both small and large. Some of these applications enable search engines or database connectivity. There are three common ways in which Web servers deliver up dynamic data to client browsers: Server-Side Includes (SSI), Common Gateway Interface (CGI) scripts, and APIs. CGI is commanded by scripting languages and full programming languages. Web server software can be programmed for additional capabilities. Perl and JavaScript are examples of scripting languages in use. Java, Visual Basic, and even C are used as compiled programming languages. SSI doesn't include a full programming capability and is thus limited in its utility. For more powerful control of Web server software, Windows CGI or Win CGI is used on Windows NT and Windows 95 to allow rapid application development tools like Visual Basic and Delphi to exchange spooled data between the server and the CGI program. CGI is supported by virtually every Web server on Windows, but is notorious for slow performance. Normally the number of CGI applications in use at any Web site is highly limited.

To improve Web server performance, Web server vendors are releasing their own proprietary APIs in native code. Microsoft offers the Internet Server API (ISAPI) as part of Windows NT. There are several other companies that have released APIs, including Netscape's NSAPI and O'Reilly's WSAPI. Both the Internet Information Server (IIS) and Process Software's Purveyor software use ISAPI. Netscape's NSAPI is published and available to other vendors. Using NSAPI vendors can add the basic functions found in Netscape's family of Web servers to their products. O'Reilly's WSAPI provides tools for developing dynamic Web pages, as well as access to some ISAPI modules.

An API can perform the functions of any CGI script, as well as allow for additional functionality to be programmed in later, and offers greatly improved performance. In comparisons done on identical programs using CGI and ISAPI, the API-programmed functions ran five times faster and with fewer system resources consumed. You get this performance boost because ISAPI applications are composed of DLLs that load into the same memory space as the Web server and thus reside locally so no I/O is required.

The downside to using an API is that it is more difficult to program than CGI, especially if the function isn't contained in the API and must be coded by hand. You must also learn to work with process synchronization, multithreading, direct protocol programming, and error handling—areas that are not normally addressed in CGI.

To make their APIs easier to program, both Microsoft and Netscape server products come with scripting built into them. LiveWire comes with both the Netscape Enterprise Server and the Netscape FastTrack Server. Microsoft IIS comes with the Internet Database Connector, which is an application that runs using ISAPI. There are also many third-party tools available for scripting Netscape's and Microsoft's APIs.

Java is another programming facility used for providing database connectivity and other application processes. Unlike CGI, SSI, and the proprietary APIs just discussed, Java runs in a way that is most often independent of server software. When a Java applet is called from an <APPLET_> tag in an HTML page, the applet is downloaded from its stored location and executed locally on the client. Most major browsers, such as Navigator 3 and Microsoft Internet Explorer 3 (and later), are Java enabled. There are some instances, such as Netscape's server software and later versions of Microsoft IIS, however, where the software includes a built-in Java interpreter. This allows Netscape's server software to run Java applets on the server side, which can be a performance boost. Java applets can connect to database servers by accessing database APIs that some vendors have released. A common standard in use is the Java Database Connectivity API layer, which is the functional equivalent of the Microsoft Open Database Connectivity (ODBC) standard.

Configuring TCP/IP for Windows NT Web Servers

Windows NT may be used in both heterogeneous and homogeneous networks. Among the many network protocols, Windows NT supports native NetBEUI, TCP/IP, NetWare IPX, and even the AppleTalk protocol without requiring special configuration. You can be running one or all of these protocols in a network stack and thus support diverse clients. Since UNIX, DOS, and Macintosh clients support TCP/IP, when Windows NT Server is running as a Web server it can provide support for each of them. TCP/IP was designed to be a central service in Windows NT, and as things appear to be developing, TCP/IP seems to be *the* central protocol in the Windows NT network protocol stack.

Additionally, in a heterogeneous network environment a Windows NT Web server can provide Web services for NetWare clients in a NetWare network or for clients in a LAN Manager network. For Internet/intranet clients, Windows NT Server not only runs TCP/IP, but also manages several services that provide for dynamic addressing of clients from a pool of available addresses. These services, described in the next few sections, make Windows NT Server attractive as a Web server.

Web-related Naming and Addressing Services

To review, Windows NT uses a system of domains to partition an enterprise into logical units. A domain can be administered locally or through a master domain involved in a trust relationship, if a master domain is set up. Each domain contains a number of groups, both local and global, some of which may be defined and some of which are built into the system. User accounts are created and added to appropriate groups to limit access. Additionally, each machine in an enterprise is assigned a name and internally assigned a unique security ID. A security database (SAM) on a domain's Primary Domain Controller stores all of this information. Any Backup Domain Controller contains a replicated copy of the SAM. The SAM maintains what is called an Access Control List or ACL.

TCP/IP specifies a set of internetworking protocols that convert data transmission into addressed packets. TCP/IP relies on the routing of packets to specific servers based on a unique 32-bit IP address. Part of an address identifies a host in an Internet session, which is the server side of a client/server architecture. The host then routes packets to the computer with the specific address that is requested. To set up a Windows NT Web server you must assign a unique TCP/IP address to the server. You must also assign unique numbers to each of the clients on the network. These are networking issues, but if you are setting up a Web server for an intranet you may be tasked with configuring this system yourself.

As previously discussed, there are three different classes of Internet host addresses:

- *Class A* – This class can assign up to 16,777,214 host IDs. Large companies or networks take class A Internet network addresses. There are very few class A networks available.
- *Class B* – This class allows 16,382 network IDs on the Internet, which can have 65,534 host IDs assigned to each.
- *Class C* – This network class offers 2,097,150 network IDs with 254 attached host IDs. Most organizations take a class C scheme assignment.

Each Web server is assigned a unique IP address by the ISP from its pool of addresses. For sites large enough to have direct access to the Internet, an address is assigned by InterNIC directly. For an enterprise a pool of addresses is assigned composed of a set of consecutive numbers. Each node must be unique while active in a session. Since TCP/IP addressing is a networking issue, and doesn't represent the direct focus of this chapter, refer to Chapters 12 and 13 for a full explanation of these principles.

In some cases there are enough assignable addresses so that a server and client may have their addresses hard-wired in the Network Control Panel. More often than not, the number of IP addresses assigned are not sufficient to provide for permanent assignment to a computer, but must be rotated among the clients on a network as they request an Internet connection from a Windows NT Web server.

Windows NT Server provides for several services that allow an administrator to assign TCP/IP addresses to their network clients from an available pool and, once assigned, to provide for name resolution or mapping of a TCP/IP address to a domain name.

The Dynamic Host Configuration Protocol (DHCP) is a method used on Windows NT for assigning IP addresses and other operating parameters from an assigned pool of addresses called its *scope*. When DHCP running on Windows NT Server as a network service gets a request for a TCP/IP address from a new and unassigned client, it provides an available address with a lease. That machine uses the address for the duration of the lease. For small networks, leases may be many weeks or months. Medium-size networks with adequate nodes typically assign leases of two to eight weeks. For large networks with a short supply of TCP/IP addresses, DHCP leases can be in the range of several hours down to a session time. You can determine the range of addresses in use on a DHCP server by entering the *ipconfig /all* command in the Run dialog box.

In an intranet environment, you can assign any valid TCP/IP addresses you choose. Of course, if you then set up an Internet access for network nodes you will have to rework your addressing scheme. In an intranet, DHCP is of less value. Even though Microsoft has advertised DHCP as a service with low administrative overhead, small network managers may find DHCP, which is installed via the Network Control Panel, to be somewhat daunting and may prefer to manage their Windows NT server and nodes manually.

Name Resolution: DNS and WINS

Windows NT Server uses two different methods to perform name resolution between TCP/IP addresses and domain names: Domain Name Service (DNS) and the Windows Internet Naming Service (WINS). Both of these systems operate as tightly integrated services on a Windows NT server.

WINS, which is installed through the Network Control Panel, uses a central directory service to match computer names to their assigned IP address. WINS solves the problem of using NETBIOS names for TCP/IP addresses. When a WINS client boots, it announces its presence to the WINS server and provides the primary and secondary WINS server addresses. When you run DHCP as well as WINS, you can let DHCP provide the addresses for primary and secondary servers automatically. Typically all computers are registered with WINS servers, as this provides routable access to machines in an enterprise. The WINS server directory is replicated to its other replication partners.

The DNS translates domain and host names on a Windows NT Server network to IP addresses, and vice versa. It is DNS that can translate an IP address into *www.microsoft.com* without the user knowing the exact IP address when requested by the resolver, which is part of the TCP/IP stack. DNS is only required to resolve addresses on your network site. It is the host's responsibility to resolve address requests on a remote site.

DNS uses a hierarchical distributed database, and multiple DNS servers may be run in an enterprise and the database replicated. The DNS server address is either configured by an administrator or assigned by your ISP. DNS information is stored on the domain name server. DNS is enabled by specifying the DNS options in a configuration dialog box during TCP/IP installation.

Many small networks do not require DNS, as their DNS services are maintained at the ISP. For small networks that require a naming service, an older system using a *hosts* file (such as the */etc/hosts* file of UNIX) can be used to list IP addresses and their hosts on each line of a text file. The TCP/IP resolver will then read the *hosts* file line by line, with each line interpreted as a record to find the appropriate assignment or name. *Hosts* files are really only useful for small networks, as changes in network configuration and assignments rapidly make its maintenance a nightmare. Therefore, even Windows NT enterprises that aren't connected to the Internet will run DNS.

Both DNS and WINS take a friendly computer name and return the appropriate IP address for that name. The difference between the two is that a computer's NETBIOS name is resolved by DNS, whereas an administrator enters the host name into the WINS directory. Since Windows domains and the Internet naming convention use different syntax and conventions, two different resolving services are required. All of these naming and addressing services may or may not be run on the same Windows NT server that runs your Web, FTP, Gopher, or e-mail service. For a more technical presentation of naming and addressing issues, refer to *Building NT Sites with Windows NT* by Jim Buyens (Addison-Wesley Developers Press, 1996).

Windows NT Network Security and Web Servers

All of the Web software in popular use on Windows NT Server today make full use of the GUI. Since the Windows NT operating system allows for security and access control to be set through users and groups at the operating system level, this task is already built into Windows NT. What most Windows NT Web servers add to this security scheme is the second layer of permissions that enables a group (permissions are set for groups and not specific users per se) to access specific files and folders. IIS, Commerce Builder Pro, and the Purveyor Encrypt Web Server offer to build on Windows NT's Control Panel to provide user and group security. NetWare Web Server is integrated into the Novell Directory Services.

To provide file and directory permissions in Web server software that inherit the Windows NT security scheme, such as the IIS, you need to install

Windows NT over an NTFS file system instead of the older MS-DOS standard FAT file system.

When installing a Windows NT Web server like Microsoft IIS, the following steps are helpful in securing your server.

- Review the rights of the user accounts, and membership and privileges of the Administrator group.
- Use the NTFS file system and set appropriate folder and file access privileges.
- Make passwords difficult to sniff, and modify them often.
- Set directory and file access in the Windows NT Explorer. Set user accounts and group privileges in **User Manager for Domains**, in the **Administrative Tools** program, as shown in Figure 15.2.
- Enable auditing and maintain strict account policies.

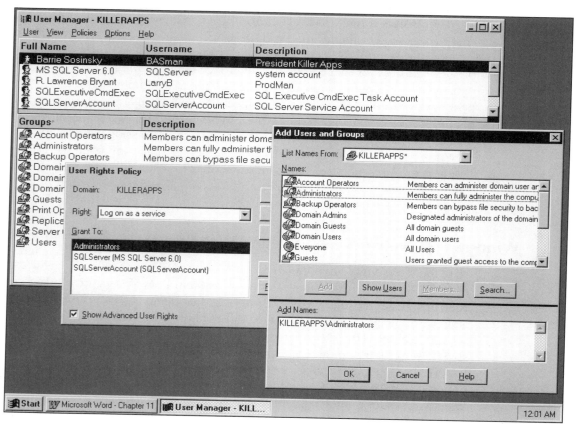

FIGURE 15.2.   Windows NT's User and Group Accounts Set in the User Manager Application

- Limit the services running on any Windows NT server running Web server software.
- Check the permissions to network shares carefully.

Some Web server software offers you an additional layer of user accounts and groups. In those instances you have the opportunity of separating access and privileges of Web users from domain accounts. This can be very valuable for the Administrator group of a Web server, because it allows that group to manage the Web server very securely without interference from domain administrators. The reverse is also true. Web site administrators will not have access to full privileges to alter domain accounts.

Secure Web services is one area of great activity at the moment, as a number of companies are introducing secure Web server systems aimed at Internet commerce. In addition to authentication through password and user name access (a challenge/response system), systems use Secure Sockets Layer (SSL), which encrypts passwords and data. SSL is slow. Access can also be given based on a TCP/IP address. SSL includes the use of certificates to authenticate Web communication. A certificate authority like Verisign authorizes these certificates.

The two common secure protocols in use on the Internet are the Secure Hypertext Transfer Protocol and Netscape's Secure Sockets Layer (SSL). SSL is becoming the standard and has been licensed by Microsoft. The Microsoft Commerce Server, a more robust version of IIS, also includes the Microsoft's Private Communications Technology as the authentication technology.

When an SSL client sends information to a server, the two essentially "handshake" the data to decide the greatest security level that both support and then authenticate services for one another. SSL encrypts and decrypts the data in a format specified by the protocol. Information requested and then returned over the Internet is fully encrypted.

Microsoft is developing secure electronic transactions using a technology they call *Secured Transaction Technology*. There is a system of digital signatures and verification in which both the server and the client can identify themselves. On-line credit card transactions are actually safer using this technology than they would be at a store, because a clerk at the store never sees the credit card number. Instead it is passed directly to the bank issuing the credit approval. Another protocol in development, the *Secure Payment Protocol,* will allow secure payment with bank cards over the Internet. These combined protocols are now part of a single standard referred to as *Secure Electronic Transactions*.

IIS comes with a Key Manager utility to create a digital key in the SSL security scheme. In a two-step process you first generate a key pair and then use the SSL certificate assigned to your server or client. The Key Manager creates two files: a key file with the key pair and the certificate request file. No one can break your signature because both parts are secure and only you hold both parts. Your generated key is created and held by you. The certificate given to you by the certification authority is unique and registered. Only when all of these pieces are combined is the encrypted key enabled.

To complete the process you use the Key Manager to enter all of the information. Then a digital signature is created and assigned. A server's digital signature can be assigned to a single IP address or to any and all of the virtual servers you have running on your network. Also, once you enable the digital signature, all of your Web services in IIS are signed as part of the SSL feature.

WINDOWS NT HARDWARE OPTIONS

In theory, any computer that can run Windows NT Server can serve as a Web server. Windows NT Server supports the following processor types: Intel 486/33 MHz or higher, Pentium or Pentium Pro, as well as RISC-based systems such as the Digital Alpha AXP.

Windows NT Web servers benefit from a fully configured server with an adequate memory footprint. The requirement for almost all Web server software is simply that Windows NT run on the computer you wish to designate as a Web server. However, there are definitely different configurations required for a low-, medium-, or high-traffic Windows NT Web server. When comparing these different performance requirements for the Intel family of microprocessors, the following configuration represents an average requirement for Windows NT Server 4.x.

- *Low traffic* – Use a 486DX2 66-MHz processor with 24 MB of RAM. A system of this type might allow for up to ten to twelve concurrent users.

- *Medium traffic* – Use a Pentium with a 90-MHz processor with 32 MB of RAM. A configuration of this nature when connected with a fractional T1 line and appropriate dial-in hardware support can support about fifty concurrent Internet sessions, along with the number of dial-up users that the system allows.

- *High traffic* – Use a Pentium with a 160-MHz processor with 64 MHz of RAM or more, as a minimum.

For very high-traffic sites running Windows NT 4.x as their operating system, consider using a Pentium Pro 200-MHz computer, a multiprocessor computer, or a fast RISC chip such as a Digital Alpha machine.

As a general rule of thumb, Windows NT Server 4.0 requires a bare-bones minimum of 16 MB to run, with 24 MB recommended. An additional 8 MB of

RAM is required for full TCP/IP operation and for the FTP server software. A Web server typically requires an additional 6 MB of RAM to operate. If a medium-traffic Web server has fifty running sessions, those sessions use about 12 MB to manage. Add 4 MB for Web server utilities that monitor activity and for e-mail software. Taken as a whole, you can see that for any production Web server you really require about 54 MB if you run all of the services described in this chapter. If you add a database to the mix for Web/database connectivity and management, such as Microsoft SQL Server 6.5, then you should consider using a Pentium with 96 MB of RAM for a production Web site.

Windows NT Server version 3.x, and notably 3.5.x, has lower memory requirements. The requirements for low-, medium-, and high-traffic installations on this older version of the operating system are 16, 24, and 32 (and greater) MB of RAM. Installing more RAM and letting Windows NT Server manage it is often a relatively easy way to improve Web server performance.

One aspect of Web performance that typically gets overlooked in specifying a Web server is a speedy hard drive. Windows NT is very tolerant of hard disk types and bus configurations and will operate with most industry-standard equipment. However, the speed of disk access and the type of bus will be the next most significant factor in performance beyond processor type and installed RAM. Windows NT's current disk configuration of choice is SCSI-2. Other fast disks using a bus-mastering technology, such as EISA, are also good choices.

WINDOWS NT WEB SERVER SOFTWARE

Web server software running on a server takes requests from Web browsers using Hypertext Transfer Protocol (HTTP) transmitted by TCP/IP packets and returns information to that client browser. The request represents a single transaction in a client/server architecture, so that when the Web server software retrieves the file and transmits the data, the connection is broken. All information, whether it be associated graphics, sound, video, or binary files, is processed in this same manner.

Regardless of your evaluation of the relative merits of the UNIX and Windows NT operating systems or the hardware on which each runs, there is no doubt that there is considerably more and better Web software being released for the Windows NT environment than for UNIX. In the sections that follow you will find an explanation of some of the features of the more popular Web server software and listings of prices and manufacturers. This area is very changeable, so you may want to contact some of the vendors listed to obtain their most recent product information.

There is a trend in the Windows NT Web server software area to merge Web software with the operating system and other common server functionality.

You see this in the bundling of the Microsoft IIS with Windows NT Server packages. Also, you should anticipate new Web server software with additional capabilities included beyond simple HTTP. Expect to see database connectivity tools and programming languages built directly into Web server software. About half of the Web server packages available today come with facilities for authoring HTML content contained therein. For example, Netscape Gold has a simple authoring package included, and IIS has an editor for existing content. Some packages include some site management facilities for locating content files, and for checking and validating hypertext links, although that is less common. As an example, Netscape's LiveWire, which is part of the Enterprise Server and an option in FastTrack, has a site management capability, as does O'Reilly's Web-View. Typically, packages that don't come with authoring and site management features include a companion product like HotDog, or in the case of IIS, Front-Page, that provides this functionality.

Common Features

The Web server software typically manages the information it is tasked with processing, such as HTML pages, graphics, word processor documents, and the like. There are facilities for specifying content directories, default documents, and other information in most Web server software. With the exception of user-submitted forms, most information flows from the Web server to the client browser.

For most Windows NT Web server software packages, the following features are typically found and are of value.

- *Services* – Many Web server software packages support HTTP (the native protocol of the Web), as well as FTP for file transfer, Gopher, e-mail software, and so forth.

- *Remote administration* – This feature lets you control and administer Web services from a remote server or workstation in a domain.

- *Scripting tools* – Although CGI is an industry standard and all Web server software supports these executable files written in Perl, DOS batch files, or compiled C programs, CGI is slow to process. Some vendors' software supports proprietary APIs that preprocess HTML requests before submitting them to the Web server and postprocess data that depends on session information.

- *Database connectivity* – Microsoft supports the ODBC standard. This standard installs what amounts to a data "device driver" that translates a request for data typically in the form of an SQL query into a format that a particular database can understand. ODBC drivers exist for Microsoft Access, Visual

FoxPro, and SQL Server, dBASE IV, Oracle, and even spreadsheets like Excel. With ODBC installed, a user can open a browser, compose a query in an HTML form, and then have that query submitted and translated to the database. ODBC also allows for the data to be returned in a format that can provide for dynamic Web page creation, which allows for a customized response to that query.

- *Server-Side Includes* – SSI is a command embedded in HTML comment strings that can add dynamic elements such as the time or date, or a fixed SQL database query. SSI is typically executed slowly.

- *Text indexing and search engines* – Some Web server software provides for indexing and a private search function. Your site is indexed, and a search page is included in your site. Microsoft provides these functions in its Index Server software, but many other Web server products have these functions built into the Web server package. You may wish to experiment with the Microsoft Index Server, which was code-named *Tripoli* in its development stage. This software can index a Web site in minutes and make it fully searchable. To download a copy of the Index Server, go to `http://www.microsoft.com/ntserver`. Tripoli uses ISAPI and in-stalls the scripts necessary to operate, along with sample Web pages. After installation you may create a search index against which queries may be placed.

- *Virtual servers* – This feature lets multiple IP addresses and domain names be routed to the same host computer. Using the virtual server function a Windows NT Web server appears to the outside world as if it were two or more separate Web servers. When you enable this feature on Windows NT, the TCP/IP stack handles requests for all of these virtual servers without the necessity of installing multiple network cards each with their own IP address. The feature is called *multihoming,* and each virtual server can have its own domain name in a DNS service. Nearly all Web server software comes with this capability.

- *Logging and performance monitoring* – Windows NT has a rich event model that supports event logging to Windows NT Server in several transaction logs. Often these log files can be analyzed to see who has accessed your ser-ver, for how long, what's been accessed, and so forth. The information can be exported to common data formats for more sophisticated analysis to a database or spreadsheet. When properly used, transaction logs can help a Web administrator manage a Web site for better performance.

As an example of the kind of logging that you can do with Microsoft IIS, you can configure each of its three services (Web, FTP, and Gopher) to enter an event into a tracking log. Among the data that can be tracked are the client's IP addresses, the service requested, and the resource required. The log is maintained as a standard Windows NT Event Log, or as a SQL Server database file, with conversion of the first to the second for further analysis. This allows for report generation, performance monitoring, configuration, optimization, capacity planning, content assessment, as well as security auditing. If you do extensive logging you will notice a performance lag, as there is considerable activity writing the data to disk.

As an example of a log entry, considering the following record:

```
155.53.94.24, -, 12/10/96, 18:23:59, W3SVC, INETSRV12,
159.53.82.2, 220, 250, 1492, 200, 0, GET,
/Guido/home/index.htm, -,
```

The parameters tracked here are the following: client IP address, client user name, date, time, service, computer name, IP address of server, processing time (milliseconds), bytes received, bytes sent, service status code, Windows NT status code, name of operation, and target of operation. Therefore, you can read this example as: an anonymous client at 155.53.94.24 gave a *get* command for *index.htm* at 6:23 P.M. on December 10, 1996, from the virtual server at 159.53.82.2.

Microsoft IIS ships with a log conversion utility that converts a log from the default format into the NCSA Common Log File or EMWAC format. The utility also provides DNS replacement of IP addresses with domain names.

Windows NT Server has several utilities for monitoring performance. The system relies on *event counters*, a system by which different events are recorded to the log. Administrators can define different counters to aid them in evaluating server and network performance. Windows NT maintains three different event logs, and the analysis of event logs can allow an administrator to fine-tune Windows NT Web server performance. Several third-party packages build on this system of events, counters, and log analysis.

One utility that comes with Windows NT Server, the Performance Monitor, can be used to do real-time analysis of these events. Windows NT also has strong third-party support for utilities that manage and tune Windows NT Server in its many different roles, of which providing Web services is just one.

Microsoft IIS

Microsoft IIS ships free with every copy of Windows NT Server. You can't beat the price. It is also available for free as a download from the Microsoft Web site at http://www.microsoft.com/ie/. A version of IIS is also available for Windows NT Workstation that provides for full functionality, but by license limits the number of simultaneous connections. A stripped-down version of IIS is contained as part of Microsoft FrontPage, a Web page creation and site management package, and is installable on Windows 95. Microsoft also sells a version of IIS called the Merchant server, which provides for secure commercial transactions, as well as a proxy server. IIS, Merchant server, and the proxy server are all marketed as part of the Microsoft BackOffice suite of products.

IIS runs as a service on Windows NT Server. Setting up IIS is a relatively simple operation, making it easy to install the three important services it provides:

1. Web services
2. FTP services
3. Gopher services

IIS can work with ODBC drivers to communicate between IIS and data sources like SQL Server.

IIS provides you with services useful in setting up a Web site to manage multiple domains and multiple clients. A virtual server capability lets a single IIS Web server host multiple sites securely. Each domain on the Web looks as if it is an individual server. This feature makes IIS on Windows NT Server a favored solution of many ISPs.

Virtual servers are also used to service different divisions in an organization. For example you could assign department addresses so that *sales.mycompany* *.com* and *finance.mycompany.com* are mapped to different virtual servers. Each domain gets its own IP address pool and is registered in the DNS. To set up a virtual server, open the **Directories** tab of the Properties window for that IIS server in the Microsoft Internet Service Manager and specify which IP address applies to each directory you add. Figure 15.3 shows you the Internet Service Manager (**Start** ➤ **Programs** ➤ **Microsoft Internet Server** ➤ **Internet Service Manager** ➤ **select the desired computer** ➤ **Properties** ➤ **Service Properties** ➤ **Directories** ➤ **Add**).

The World Wide Web, FTP, and Gopher services in IIS can all make two or more directories available to clients based on their ability to access that directory as set by their user account. Virtual directories can include two or more directories in different physical locations, but require that each directory be in the same domain as the IIS server. Each service (World Wide Web, FTP, or Gopher) must have a home directory with a default document, but any of the publishing directories can be a virtual directory.

Using virtual directories in IIS, an administrator can distribute files across the volumes of a server, or other servers on a network. The connected user sees a virtual directory in which a tree or hierarchical display is built from aliases, and it appears in the appropriate local or network directories. Any request for service (a file or Web page) is routed by the virtual file system and is sent to the

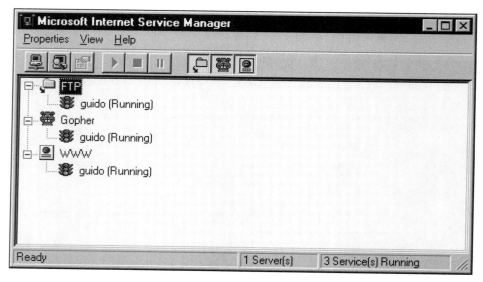

FIGURE 15.3.   IIS and the Internet Service Manager

physical location on the virtual tree. Therefore, administrators can manage a distributed Web site from more than one location and have at their disposal all of the network resources for their Web site activities.

Virtual directories are configured in the Microsoft Internet Service Manager, a utility that comes with IIS. The **Directories** tab of the Properties window is where you specify virtual directories, their physical location, and their current status. You can also set up a service called *multihoming,* in which each virtual directory is mapped to a separate IP address and domain name.

One nice feature of IIS is bandwidth throttling. This feature lets you control the activity of your IIS server by setting the number of channels or connections that may be active. If you are approaching the connection limit, additional requests are refused until the activity decreases below the threshold you set. One setting lets you delay requests when IIS is close to the threshold. Then some requests are delayed so that the usage of the site is maximized. Bandwidth throttling is turned on in the **Advanced Properties** tab of the IIS server in the Internet Service Manager.

IIS has a feature called *directory browsing* that lists files and directories as a set of hypertext links that can be activated in a Web browser. What you see looks similar to what you see in an FTP service. Directory browsing is useful for folders with many documents, especially when documents are in a format other than HTML. Files can be downloaded without being viewed. As with FTP services, you need to designate a default document or directory when you enable directory browsing.

Unlike other vendors that have incorporated page design and site management tools into their Web server software, Microsoft has made a conscious choice to separate these functions. Microsoft FrontPage fills in these missing features for many users. In fact, Microsoft bundled FrontPage into beta versions of Windows NT 4.0, along with the copy of IIS that they include standard in all Windows NT Server packages.

Netscape Commercial Servers

Netscape offers several different versions of their Web server software. The two most widely distributed are Netscape FastTrack Server and Netscape Enterprise Server. They replaced the best-selling Communications Server and the Commerce Server. FastTrack is meant to provide a quick installation and be suitable for the larger majority of Web server sites. While not reputed to be as easy to install as IIS, O'Reilly WebSite Professional, and Process Software's Purveyor Encrypt WebServer, FastTrack is noted for its strong performance, low price, and for its access to advanced features like SSL 3.0. Only IIS offers performance as fast as FastTrack.

The Netscape Enterprise Server adds additional features that might be of interest to large sites. There are tools for content creation and site management included, and some of these features are groupware enabled. Among the many features in the product are system-monitoring utilities, client-side authentication, a search engine from Verity, and support of SNMP. As noted previously, the Enterprise Server ships with LiveWire, which allows for strong support of content management. There is also a document check-in and check-out feature, as well as document version control. Netscape Web servers and browsers are both Java enabled, and support both Java and JavaScript.

Netscape's Web server software is the most widely available software on the market today. There are versions running not only on Windows NT, but also on several variations of UNIX, including HP-UX, IBM's AIX, SGI's Irix, and Sun's Solaris. All of these versions come with the Netscape Server Manager (NSM), which is configured inside a copy of the company's browser, Netscape Navigator.

When tested against each other several months back on Windows NT 3.51 and Sun Solaris, Enterprise Server ran substantially faster for small client loads of up to twenty clients. As the number of clients increase, the differences in performance between the two platforms diminish dramatically. These tests were done on single-processor systems and might vary in multiprocessor systems.

Configuration of Enterprise Server is a point-and-click affair, although reviewers found the interface awkward to use. For example, although it is easy to create users and groups, there is slow access to directories. Another issue is that the defined users and groups are separate from the Windows NT network operating system users and groups. This makes it necessary to define and to manage separate user account lists and associated passwords. Administration of this additional layer is an extra chore, although there can be extra benefits to the added security it provides. You can also filter requests to your server based on IP addresses, a host computer's name, or the rights you assign to user accounts for specific directories. FastTrack and Enterprise Server support server-side certificates, with the latter product also supporting client-side certificates.

Netscape Service Manager (NSM) provides you with the capability of setting up virtual servers. It also allows you to tune the performance of their Web servers by controlling the number of processes that run and the number of threads that are executing on your server. FastTrack provides access logs and error logs, but it does not let you log events such as CGI execution, network I/O, or HTTP header fields—features available with IIS. The Enterprise Server does allow for CGI event logging and a programming feature that lets an administrator log nearly any kind of transaction.

Netscape's Web server software is noted for the programming capabilities that come with it. This software is a strong candidate for any Web site to which custom applications are being delivered. In addition to allowing CGI scripting and access to WinCGI, you can also use C to access and manipulate NSAPI. The incorporation of a Java interpreter in both the Netscape browser and server is also a valuable feature. LiveWire also lets you create compiled applications in JavaScript.

The Enterprise Server can be purchased as part of a $3,995 package called *Netscape SuiteSpot*. This package comes with Netscape Mail, News, Proxy, and Catalog servers. Included with SuiteSpot is also LiveWire Pro, a development version of LiveWire that is bundled with the Informix Online Workgroup Server. Netscape has SuiteSpot positioned as a complete intranet solution. Netscape purchased Collabra and intends to add Collabra Share to SuiteSpot to provide support for the Lightweight Directory Access Protocol (LDAP), which is a directory services standard that is being widely adopted in the industry. When this integration is complete, SuiteSpot will be better positioned to compete with Microsoft Exchange and Lotus Notes in the groupware category.

Popular Windows NT Web Server Packages

Having reviewed the two top market leaders for Web server software on Windows NT, this section surveys briefly the other packages that are available. Among the many Web server packages available on the market today, the following sections represent those that have a measurable market share. Some of these products run on both Windows NT and UNIX, and when that is the case it is noted. Otherwise, this section is Windows NT specific.

COMMERCE BUILDER PRO

This package offers virtual servers, a macro language, chat room, and a proxy server. It can run on either Windows 95 or Windows NT. A subsequent product, Merchant Builder, was slated to replace Commerce Builder Pro. Commerce Builder Pro allows you to create user and group accounts, as well as perform IP address filtering on client requests. Commerce Builder Pro supports SSL for client/server authentication and encryption. This product also supports virtual servers. It comes with a proprietary macro language to connect to an ODBC data source. Commerce Server Pro costs $995 and comes from The Internet Factory, Pleasanton, CA; tel. (800) 229-6020; `www.mortimer.com/ifact`.

EMWAC SERVER

This freeware software is available for both Windows NT and UNIX. EMWAC has been developed further into Purveyor Encrypt WebServer, which is described next. There are several features common to most Web servers that are missing in EMWAC, such as virtual servers, access control, SSL, and proxy server support. However, for someone wanting easy installation and setup, along with free software, EMWAC might be a reasonable first place to start. EMWAC offers WAIS searches, forms support, CGI scripting, and image maps. You can obtain the latest version of EMWACS from the European Microsoft Windows NT Academic Centre at `emwac.ed.ac.uk/html/internet_toolchest/https/contents.htm`. If you wish to enable WAIS searches in this product, you should get the WAIS Toolkit from `ftp://emwac.ed.ac.uk/pub/waistool`.

ENCRYPT WEBSERVER

Purveyor Encrypt WebServer is a fully developed version of the EMWAC Web server, with nearly all of the missing features of the latter product added to it. Included in the product are site and content management tools, ISAPI support, and local and remote server management tools. WebServer is easy to install, and has been well reviewed. It taps into the Windows NT security scheme, and uses Windows NT's user and group accounts for server access. A version of WebServer called Purveyor IntraServer ($1,395) comes bundled with InfoAccess's fine content conversion tool (HTML Transit), as well as a database connectivity tool (WebDBC) from Nomad Development. You can obtain information on Purveyor Encrypt WebServer from Process Software Corporation, Framingham, MA; tel. (800) 722-7770; `www.process.com`.

NETWARE WEB SERVER

Novell's NetWare Web Server is marketed for Novell NetWare networks and is positioned primarily as an intranet server. On Windows NT, NetWare Server was among the fastest products tested; certainly competitive with both Netscape and Microsoft Web server products. The current product does not have full access control support and does not support virtual servers, virtual paths, and SSL. There are also no site management tools that come with this package. Novell is planning to add these features into future versions of the product.

The NetWare Web server is an NLM and it runs on top of a NetWare 4.x server. When purchased, the NetWare Web server includes a runtime version of NetWare 4.1. Installation and setup are reputed to be easy, and the server taps into NetWare Directory Servers to provide security based on user and group access to directories. The product supports CGI and Perl scripting, has a Basic interpreter, supports Java applets and JavaScript and the Novell Local Common Gateway Interface, but has no database connectivity. NetWare Web Server costs $995, and information can be obtained from Novell, Orem, UT; tel. (800) 638-9273; www.novell.com.

WEBSITE PROFESSIONAL

O'Reilly and Associates' WebSite Professional is a product in the top tier of Web servers. It has many impressive features, a strong programming and development environment, and the best management interface on the market. You'll find that not only SSI, CGI, but WSAPI (which is compatible with ISAPI) is supported. The Cold Fusion Standard for ODBC is also supported in the product.

WebSite comes with content and site management tools, a text-indexing tool, and an outstanding document set. It would be a good choice for a small Web site, but its poor performance probably precludes use as an industrial-strength product in larger Web sites. WebSite runs on Windows NT Server, Windows NT Workstation, or Windows 95. Unlike Microsoft IIS, which has a concurrent user restriction on Windows NT Workstation, WebSite has no such restriction.

WebSite is relatively easy to manage locally, but somewhat difficult to manage remotely. The product is particularly strong in setting up virtual servers and in mapping URL paths to physical directories. You can set access control to specific URL paths, and create user and group accounts. WebSite Professional does not use the Windows NT security system's account database. Security features also include SSL and the Certificate Manager for server-side certificates.

LOTUS DOMINO

Relatively new to the Web server market is Lotus Domino. For anyone using Lotus Notes as groupware, Lotus Domino offers connectivity to the many features included in Notes, like database and document management.

UNIX-BASED WEB SERVERS

UNIX is where the Web phenomenon started. It is therefore not surprising that so many excellent Web servers are available for UNIX variants. Two of the earliest and still most accessible Web servers are the Apache Group's HTTPd and the NCSA's HTTPd (Table 15.1). Although the first to be developed, the NCSA HTTPd currently employs parts of the Apache code. Both of these Web servers can be downloaded in both binary and source code format. Due the nature of variations between UNIX releases, it is suggested that you download the source code and compile it on your native machine. Numerous other commercial Web servers for UNIX are available from companies like Netscape.

Brief Considerations in Installing the UNIX Web Server

The scope of this book does not permit a comprehensive review of all the issues involved in installing and configuring a UNIX-based Web server. However, we hope this section provides a framework for base-level Web installation.

Most UNIX systems assume that the Web server is located in the *usr/local/ etc/httpd* directory. Move the downloaded source from NCSA or Apache to */usr/local/etc* and uncompress and untar the distribution. The *httpd* subdirectory should be automatically created. If the location of the NCSA Web server is to be different from the default, you will need to change the #define for HTTPD_ROOT to the new location in the *config.h* file. You will also need to run the *uname −a* command to identify the UNIX platform. Once this is accomplished, execute the *make* command to compile the code. For the Apache Web

TABLE 15.1.   Sample List of Freeware UNIX Web Servers

Web server	Download URL	Licensing
Apache HTTPd	/Web/httpd/Unix/apache_httpd	Free for any use
NCSA HTTPd	ftp://ftp.ncsa.uiuc.educ	Free for internal and educational use

server you must also edit the configuration file and specify the type of UNIX. This is done by uncommenting (removing the pound sign) before all references to your variant of UNIX. Once this is accomplished, run *./Configure* followed by the *make* command.

There are many other configuration issues that must be considered. The documentation that is provided with the Web servers and located on the home pages for Apache and NCSA are good sources of these issues. Cornelius Cook's excellent article, entitled "Configuring a Minimal Web Server," in the August 1996 issue of *Sys Admin* magazine (*Sys Admin* CD-ROM 1992–1996, © 1997) is recommended reading. Items to consider include

- Reflecting changes in the server location in all related configuration files and identifying directories like *htdocs*
- Changing the port number in *httpd.conf* to above 1024 if you are not root; 8000 is a good option
- Ensuring that the timeout value is adequate. (When transferring large files, the length of the timeout must be sufficient to accommodate slower modem transfers.)
- Considering security issues by removing the ExecCGI and FollowSymLinks from options and by turning off the CGI alias facility in *cgi-bin*
- Making directories accessible externally by creating aliases in the *srm.conf* file

One of the final considerations when configuring a UNIX Web server is to determine if the daemon should be launched manually or at system start-up. To start the Web server automatically at boot time, the initialization scripts for the system must be modified. As we describe in earlier chapters, the *rc.d* scripts vary between UNIX variants. Therefore, modify the initialization scripts in accordance with the instructions provided in the system *man* pages.

Securing the UNIX Web Server

One of the most critical issues for any system administrator turned Web master is securing the system. Providers of Web servers have dedicated, extensive resources to help the process of securing the site. Despite these efforts, horror stories abound regarding unwanted intrusions. The Web server and the client browser establish a virtual TCP connection. The browser requests data that is then provided by the server. The browser in turn displays the interpreted information. At any point in this process security can be violated by sophisticated devices like network sniffers and through simple holes left by sloppy permission settings.

The major push in securing the TCP transmission of Web-based data is focused on the socket layer. The evolving SSL standard discussed earlier in the context of the Windows NT IIS is equally applicable to UNIX systems. Residing on top of the Berkley sockets, SSL verifies bilaterally the identity of the client browser and server and encrypts the resulting transferred data. SSL was designed by Netscape and is widely licensed by many organizations, including Microsoft. The full specifications for SSL are available on the Netscape home page (`www.netscape.com`). In brief, the relationship between the SSL client and server verifies certain attributes including the protocol level, an identification for the session, the compression methodology, and the cipher suite used. This is done when the ClientHello and ServerHello messages are successfully exchanged. At this stage, a security certificate is sent for the duration of the session. If the server requests a certificate, the client must either respond with a corresponding certificate or a no-certificate alert (nonsecure client site).

The other portion of the SSL technology is the use of encryption and the exchange of public cryptographic keys. SSL employs the U.S.-patented RSA algorithm. Again, a discussion of cryptography is outside the scope of this book. However, the Netscape home page's description of SSL is a good starting resource. In addition, the RSA reference documentation can be obtained from the Internet at `www.rsa.com`.

If you plan to utilize the Apache Web server discussed earlier, then the installation of the SSL patch is appropriate. It is recommended that you compile the regular Apache server first before installing the SSL patch. This ensures that a stable, unrestricted Web server can function on your UNIX or Windows NT box. The SSL patches can be applied once the Apache daemon is running. The patch is available from `www.apache.org`.

FINAL THOUGHTS

UNIX and Windows NT system administrators may rapidly find themselves also wearing the hat of Web master. Clearly most Web servers are currently hosted on UNIX systems. While many in the UNIX community point to the availability of faster systems as a reason for UNIX dominance, this is more an accident of history than clearly technological reasons. In recent months Windows NT has made a dramatic surge in the Web server marketplace for two reasons: (1) Microsoft bundles the Internet server with Windows NT Server 4.0, and (2) the majority of graphical development tools are being released for the Windows environment. In many organizations of the near future, Web server hosting could well be found in mixed UNIX and Windows NT enterprises. Fortunately, the technology base for supporting Windows NT and UNIX Web servers and related security issues are very similar, which means coexistence issues are greatly reduced.

Part V

Epilogue and Quick Reference Guides

Part V begins with a look at the future of Windows NT and UNIX in Chapter 16. The appendices comprise the remainder of the part. Appendix A details common Windows NT commands and utilities. Appendix B examines UNIX commands and utilities. When similar commands and utilities are available on the other operating system, cross-reference comments are provided.

- Chapter 16, A Look at the Future
- Appendix A, Windows NT Commands and Utilities
- Appendix B, UNIX Commands and Utilities

Chapter 16

A Look at the Future

The crystal ball of old is probably as good a tool as any in projecting the future of network operating systems. In the process of writing this book we constantly found that technological innovations were moving so rapidly that the present and future began to blur. By the time the ink dries on this page, many of the items we have discussed will be outdated by operating system patches and replacements. Therefore, the best we can hope to achieve is to provide a preview of things we believe will develop over the coming months and next several years. In this chapter we briefly examine the following:

- Anticipated developments within the UNIX community
- A preview of Windows NT 5.0

ANTICIPATED UNIX DEVELOPMENTS

For the first time in its history of innovation, the UNIX community finds itself in the position of playing defensively against a formidable opponent. In some key technological areas, UNIX is beginning to lag behind Windows NT. As a result, a number of UNIX vendors and the industry standards organization—the Open Group—have announced aggressive initiatives. We briefly explore some of these initiatives here. However, there are two basic conclusions that can be generalized from current activities:

1. Efforts to create a unified operating system environment under the Single UNIX Specification, version 2 (UNIX 98) will gain strength.
2. The UNIX community will ultimately remain divided because of the independent extensions continuing to be developed by major vendors.

447

Open Group's Unification Initiative

The Open Group is a combined organization comprised of the older X/Open, Ltd., and the Open Software Foundation. It is this organization that has the mantle of branding operating system variants with the UNIX name. Only those operating systems that conform to the Single UNIX Specification can be branded as UNIX 95 (also known as Spec 1170) compliant. The Open Group has published the Single UNIX Specification, version 2 API for future branding of UNIX 98, beginning sometime in 1998. The technical specifications are available on the Open Group's Web site (`www.opengroup.org`). The new specification is part of ISO/IEC 9945-1:1996(POSIX) and embraces the "classic dot one" IEEE standard POSIX.1-1990 with numerous others extensions including IEEE standard POSIX.1b-1993 (Realtime) and IEEE Standard POSIX.1c-1995 (Pthreads). ISO/IEC 9899: 1990/Amendment 1:1995, and FIPS 151-2 are also incorporated. We could obviously fill dozens of pages listing the associated specifications. For those with a real interest, use the Web site as your reference point. The following represents a brief list of the more important aspects of the new API and associated announcements:

- *Advanced UNIX real-time features* – This includes specifications on synch and asynch I/O, shared memory, signals, priority schedulers, memory locking, message queues, file synch, mapped files, and memory protection.

- *Real-time threads features* – This includes specifications for priority execution, inheritance and protection, process sharing, thread functions, and stack size and attributes. The plan also calls the incorporation of the Aspen Threads extensions.

- *64-bit initiative* – The programming API for 64-bit application development includes C data types, conformance of integers to 32-bit length, removal of other 32-bit dependencies, longs and pointer use 64-bit length, and data size neutrality.

- *ISO C language alignments* – Enhancements to the ISO C Amendment 1: 1005 (Multibyte Support) are included for international application support.

- *Dynamic linking* – Based on the SVR4 DLL functions, addition functions are provided in the API to support DLLs.

- *Support for large files* – This will replace more than twenty file-handling commands to permit files of a size larger than 2 GB.

- *Other initiatives* – The Open Group is sponsoring a host of other initiatives independent of UNIX 98 but connected directly to the promotion of open systems, including enhanced specifications for XPG4, Year 2000 alignments, expanded CDE functionality, and broadened security.

Other UNIX Initiatives

The list of initiatives announced by UNIX operating system vendors are too numerous to cover fully. The following is a sampling of some of the activity within the UNIX community:

- *Hewlett-Packard/SCO* – These two companies are working to produce a layer of code that will permit binary compatibility for UNIX applications.

- *IBM/Hewlett-Packard/SCO Internet initiatives* – Among the many activities centering on Internet tool integration are SCO embedding Netscape, IBM embracing the Lotus Domino toolkit, and Hewlett-Packard supporting the Just-In-Time Compiler for Java.

- *Sun's modular operating system* – Solaris 2.6 will be the last numbered release of this UNIX variant from Sun Microsystems. Future versions will focus on what is called the power server, intranet server, and connection server.

SNEAK PREVIEW OF WINDOWS NT 5.0

The preliminary specifications are emerging from Microsoft for Windows NT Server 5.0. If Microsoft can achieve its stated goals, then the UNIX community may have additional reasons for concern. When reviewing the scheduled enhancements, it is obvious that many of the new functions are aimed squarely at UNIX strengths. Many of the current advantages of UNIX will simply evaporate. While there is no guarantee that all of these features will actually see the light of day, the following are among the most likely functional improvements in Windows NT Server 5.0 and the Window NT product family:

- *Improved multiuser capabilities* – With the current nickname *hydra,* the mythical multiheaded beast of ancient lore is transformed into a multiuser environment. Microsoft will provide capacity for all Windows clients while Citrix will provide client software for UNIX, MACOS, and other environments. Hydra's commercial name is Terminal Server, and it is an add-on to Windows NT 4.0.

- *Support for network computers* – As a direct assault on the network computer threat, Windows NT 5.0 will support remote booting and multiuser access to network PCs.

- *Zero-administration initiative* – Hoping to lower the cost of operating system management, Microsoft plans to include a number of automated administrative functions. Zero Administration Windows provides automatic system updates, application installation, "roaming user" management, central lockdowns, and other snap-in tools.

- *64-bit architecture* – Applications will have increased virtual memory address space from the current 4-GB limit to 32 GB. This is limited to the Digital Alpha version and Enterprise versions supporting the forthcoming HP/Intel MERCED chip set.

- *Active and distributed directory services* – Active directory support is promised for standards like LDAP, DNS, and HTTP. A partial implementation of X.500 is also foreseen. This model will be both distributed and hierarchical. It will also support programming APIs such as Java, Visual Basic, and C/C++.

- *Distributed security* – Public key security support is targeted for inclusion. Using the X.509 standard, this will enhance the ability to conduct commerce on a vastly improved, secure network.

- *Command line scripting* – Old UNIX professionals will love this feature. Direct command line access to management functions is targeted at existing UNIX system administrators.

- *Disk volume control* – Scaling disk storage and dynamically shifting volumes has long been a hallmark of UNIX. Windows NT 5.0 takes scalable storage device management to yet another step.

- *Distributed file system* – The Distributed File System is Microsoft's answer to NFS. With this technology, logical directories can be mounted within a hierarchical view across the network.

- *Server-based plug-and-play* – This permits dynamic reconfiguration of devices and drivers across the network.

- *Web-based user interface* – A more Web browser-style user interface will also be included. This will ensure compatibility with the ever-increasing popularity of the Internet. Internet Explorer 4.0 is represented as this new interface.

- *Enhanced clustering technology* – Seeking to ensure greater system availability and fault tolerance, Windows NT 5.0 will expand its system clustering functionality to greater system support.

FINAL THOUGHTS

The UNIX community continues to make innovative technical strides. The operating system should maintain a bright future. However, the continuing lack of consolidation will only hurt the operating system in long the run.

Microsoft's Windows NT 5.0 is a major advancement that will greatly enhance its appeal to traditional UNIX users. If supported hardware platforms can keep the same pace, we could envision that Windows NT will seriously erode the traditional UNIX marketplace.

The major challenge to both UNIX and Windows NT is Sun Microsystems' JAVA operating system. The network computer paradigm has appeal on many fronts. Both Microsoft and the UNIX community recognize this fact and are rapidly including elements of network computer technology into their platforms.

Ultimately, the future will be determined by how you vote with your dollars. We only hope that this book has provided some basis for making a decision that best meets your future computing needs.

Appendix A

Windows NT Commands and Utilities

Appendix A is a reference tool for users and system administrators. It defines and discusses a number of procedures as well as commands with options that are used in the day-to-day operation of a Windows NT system. When appropriate we have cross-referenced alternative UNIX-based commands.

Since one of the objectives of this appendix is to give UNIX professionals a quick reference point for operating within Windows NT, both command line and graphical versions are referenced. The commands and utilities have been broken down into the following categories:

- Backup commands
- Comparison commands
- Compression commands
- Display commands
- File management commands
- File manipulation commands
- Miscellaneous commands
- Networking commands
- Ownership commands
- Print commands
- Search commands
- System management commands

Within each category, various commands and procedures are discussed. We distinguish between procedures and commands as follows:

- Procedures are methods for accomplishing a task using the Windows NT graphical interface.

- Commands are executed within the Virtual DOS Machine (VDM) at the command prompt.

- In some categories we provide both methods to give the system administrator a broader view of the capabilities of Windows NT.

Within Windows NT two methods are available to review the file hierarchy: one using the My Computer icon and its accompanying windows and the other using Windows NT Explorer. We have chosen to focus primarily on Windows NT Explorer, which is accessed by selecting **Start → Programs → Windows NT Explorer**. Procedures that can be completed using the My Computer windows will be referenced as appropriate. The VDM or command prompt is accessed by selecting **Start → Programs → Command Prompt**. In this mode, Windows NT is not case sensitive, so commands and their parameters and options may be entered in either lower- or uppercase. We have chosen to use lowercase for these types of commands as a matter of style. In addition, Windows NT has a series of commands referred to as *net commands*. These commands are available to assist the system administrator in maintaining the network that is an inherent part of Windows NT. These commands are distributed among the other sections when appropriate. Within the networking section we define each of the *net* commands and also provide a cross-reference to where a complete description of each command is located in this appendix.

The following syntax conventions are used here.

- Command names are shown in lowercase letters. This convention is used primarily to give consistency for command names between this appendix and other chapters.

- *Lowercase italic* letters are used to represent the variables that must be replaced in the command, such as *filename,* which must be replaced with the actual file name on which the command will operate.

- [Brackets] surround those parameters or options that are optional.

- {Braces} surround a list of items, options, or parameters from which you must choose one.

- The pipe symbol (|) separates options from which you must choose one. In this case the pipe works like an OR—one or the other.

Regarding the UNIX alternatives that are provided, remember that Windows NT employs a POSIX-compatible subsystem and does provide some common UNIX utilities. The Resource Kit provides some "POSIX clones," which are commands that perform the same functions as their UNIX counterparts but they do not utilize the POSIX subsystem. These cloned commands are *cat, cp, ls, mv, touch, wc,* and *vi.* A more detailed discussion on POSIX can be found in Chapter 10.

This appendix is a reference tool that classifies some of the daily tasks that system administrators must accomplish. For more detail on a particular command or procedure, please refer to Windows NT Help, which can be accessed from the **Start** menu or from the window within which you are working.

BACKUP COMMANDS

A user can back up data to several different types of media: tape, floppy, and hard disk. This section describes both the VDM command options as well as the graphical procedures for backing up data on a Windows NT system. This section also discusses methods of restoring data from a backup.

Backing Up Data to Floppy or Hard Disk

To back up files to a DOS-formatted floppy, you can use either the My Computer windows or Windows NT Explorer. First select the files by clicking on them. (Remember, to select multiple files hold down <Ctrl> as you click the left mouse button). After all the files are selected, utilize the mouse to drag the files to the appropriate drive designation, such as A:. Basically you are "copying" files to a floppy. This same procedure is followed when backing up files to a hard disk.

Another alternative for backing up files to floppy disk is to use the VDM command *backup.* The *backup* command backs up files from one disk to another, and the disk can be either a hard disk or a floppy disk. The syntax of this command is

```
backup source-file destination-drive: [options]
```

The `source-file` parameter can consist of the letter of the drive and a colon (e.g., C:), the directory name, the name of a file, or any combination of the three. The `destination-drive` parameter is the letter of the drive that will contain the backed up files, such as A:.

Files are backed up to files named: *BACKUP.nnn* and *CONTROL.nnn,* where *nnn* is the sequential number of the disks used during the backup. For example, if the backup takes two disks, the files on the first disk would be named *BACKUP.001* and *CONTROL.001,* and the files on the second disk would be named *BACKUP.002* and *CONTROL.002.*

The options for the *backup* command are listed in Table A.1.

TABLE A.1.   *backup* Options

Option	Qualifier	Description
/s		Includes the contents of all subdirectories in the backup
/m		Backs up only those files that have changed since the last backup. This is determined by the archive attribute that is contained in every file. Also, after the file is backed up, the archive attribute is turned off in the source (or original) files.
/a		Appends backup files to an existing backup. This option is valid only if the original backup was created using a version of the *backup* command from MS-DOS version 3.3 or later. If this option is not used, old files on the backup disk are deleted before the backup begins.
/f	:*size*	Formats the backup disk to the default drive size or the *size* specified. This option is only valid when the *format* command is in the current path. If the /f option is not specified, the *backup* command formats disks to the size of the default of the drive. The *size* qualifier is in kilobytes and can be one of the following: 160, 180, 320, 760, 1200, 1440, or 2880.
/d:*date*		Changes backup files on or after *date,* where *date* is in the default format for your system as defined by the *country* command
/t:*time*		Changes backup files on or after *time,* where *time* is in the default format for your system as defined by the *country* command
/l	:*drive:path\logfile*	Creates a log file to record the date, time, and files of the backup operation. If *drive, path,* or *logfile* are not named, a log file named *BACKUP.LOG* is created in the root directory of the source file drive. The *drive* specified should not be a removable drive. If the file *BACKUP.LOG* already exists, the log information is appended to the existing file.

EXAMPLE OF THE *backup* COMMAND

To back up the directory *emily\school\homework* to an unformatted 720-KB floppy that is in the A: drive and to record the backup log in the default file, enter the following command:

```
backup C:\emily\school\homework A: /f:720 /l
```

NOTE   Other Alternatives

Windows NT Resource Kit 4.0 provides some alternatives for backing up to hard disk. The *scopy* command enables the user to copy the files and directories of an NTFS file system to another disk location while keeping the security on those files. Another command is *robocopy,* which the Resource Kit describes as an "enhanced network file-copying utility." This command enables the user to make a copy of a directory and all of its contents either on the same system or on another system on the network. Please refer to Windows NT Resource Kit 4.0 documentation for more information regarding these commands.

Backing Up Data to Tape

There are two methods of executing the Windows NT backup for tape backups. One is accomplished using the graphical interface and the other by using the *ntbackup* command at the command prompt. Both methods are discussed here.

Both of these backup methods allow the user to back up volumes, directories, and files from either NTFS or FAT file systems. Options are available to select the type of backup (copy, daily, differential, incremental, normal), verify the data backed up, append to existing backups, back up data to multiple tapes if necessary, and to create a backup log. Restore options are also available and are discussed in this section in Restoring Files from Tape.

A user must be a member of the Administrators group or the Backup Operators group to create a backup tape.

USING THE GRAPHICAL METHOD FOR TAPE BACKUPS

The graphical backup procedure is accessed by selecting **Start** ➤ **Programs** ➤ **Administrative Tools** ➤ **Backup**. To run the backup there are several tasks that must be completed: selecting and preparing the tape, selecting the files to be backed up, and defining the backup options.

Windows NT

Selecting and Preparing the Tape

It is necessary to select a tape drive only if there is more than one connected to the system.

1. From the Backup window, select **Operations ➤ Hardware Setup**.
2. Within the Hardware Setup dialog box, select the desired tape drive.
3. Click the **OK** button.

In some cases you must ready the tape for use by erasing or retensioning it. To erase a tape, follow the steps outlined here.

1. From the Backup window, select **Operations ➤ Erase Tape**.
2. Select **Quick Erase** to erase only the tape label. This method leaves previous data on the tape and is less secure because that data can be accessed.
3. Select **Secure Erase** to erase all data on the tape.

Some tapes should be retensioned prior to using them the first time or after they have been used a specified number of times. Please refer to the manufacturer's information for the tapes and tape drives to determine if you must complete this step. To retension a tape, select **Operations ➤ Retension Tape** from the Backup window.

Selecting the Files to Back Up

To back up all files on one or more volumes (or drives), click in the check box in front of the drives you desire in the Drives window, which is part of the Backup window. To select individual files, execute the following.

1. Within the Drives window, double-click on a drive to view the files on that drive. A separate window for that drive will display, looking very similar to the Windows NT Explorer window.
2. To view files in a particular directory, double-click the directory.
3. To select a directory to back up, click the check box for that directory. By selecting a directory, all files and subdirectories in that directory are automatically selected.
4. To remove a file from the selection, click the check box to remove the "x." If any files or subdirectories within a directory are not marked for backup, the check box for the directory is shaded gray.

After you have selected the files to be included in the backup, either click the **Backup** button or select **Operations ➤ Backup** from the menu bar.

Defining the Backup Options

By selecting the **Backup** button, the Backup Information window displays. The following describes the fields available for user input.

1. The system determines if the tape in the drive contains data or if it is blank. If it is blank, the **Replace** operation button is selected. If the tape contains data, the user must choose **Append** or **Replace**. Append adds the backup to a tape without destroying previous backups on the tape. Replace overwrites existing data on the tape.

2. Enter the name of the tape in the **Tape Name** field when replacing data on the tape. The default tape name is "Tape created on *date*," where *date* is the current date. This field is not available for the **Append** option.

3. Select **Verify After Backup** to execute the verify function after the backup is complete. The verify function compares the files on the backup with the original files to ensure that no errors occurred during the backup process.

4. Select **Backup Local Registry** to back up the critical Windows NT Registry. This can only be selected if the local drive is marked for backup. We recommend that you always select this option when backing up the local system.

5. Select the **Restrict Access to Owner or Administrator** check box to ensure that only the owner of the tape or a member of the Administrators or Backup Operators group can restore data from this tape. This option increases the security of the data and is only available when **Replace** is selected.

6. Select the **Hardware Compression** check box to compress the data as it is backed up. This option is only available if the tape drive supports hardware compression.

The next section of the Backup Information window contains information pertinent to each backup set. A backup set contains the files that have been selected from a single drive or volume. If files in more than one drive are selected, there will be more than one backup set identified—one for each drive. The following steps must be completed for each backup set.

1. Select the **Drive** to define the information for each backup set. If only one drive was selected for backup, no selection is necessary here.

2. Enter the **Description** for this backup.

3. Choose the **Backup Type**: Normal, Copy, Differential, Incremental, or Daily.

Windows NT

The last section of the Backup Information window pertains to the backup log.

1. Enter the name of the **Log File** you wish to use for this backup or choose one from the available list.

2. Select **Full Detail** to log all information, including the start and stop of the backup operation, errors, and the names of the files and directories that are backed up.

3. Select **Summary Only** to log only summary information about the backup. This option does not include the file and directory names.

4. Select **Don't Log** if you do not wish to create a log file.

After all the options have been selected, click the **OK** button to execute the backup and display the Backup Status window.

Monitoring the Backup Status

The Backup Status window displays the status of the backup, which includes the name and number of the files and directories being backed up. It also displays the number of corrupt files encountered and the number of files skipped in the backup. The backup log provides more detailed information regarding these types of errors. The **Summary** section shows when the backup was started and if it was completed successfully.

From this window a user can stop the backup prematurely by selecting the **Abort** button. The system asks the user if it should complete the backup for the current file before aborting. If not, the file is designated as corrupted on the backup.

When more than one tape is necessary to complete the backup, an Insert New Tape dialog box displays.

USING *ntbackup* ON THE COMMAND LINE

The *ntbackup* command can be used within the VDM as a command at the prompt or within a batch file to achieve the same results as the graphical backup. There are several different formats of this command, but the primary syntax is

```
ntbackup backup path [options]
```

The *backup* parameter must be included except for the other variations of the syntax as shown later. The *path* parameter should contain the path or paths of the directories to be copied to the backup tape. Table A.2 identifies options available for the command. These options can be entered in any sequence.

To erase a tape, enter the following command:

```
ntbackup /nopoll
```

TABLE A.2. *ntbackup* Options

Option	Qualifier	Description
/a		Appends the data to the end of an existing backup tape. The default option is to "replace" the data on the tape with the new backup.
/b		Backs up the Registry from the local system
/d	*"text"*	Enters the description for the backup set between the quotes in place of the variable *text*
/e		Includes exceptions only in the backup log. The default is to create a fully detailed backup log.
/hc:on		Turns on hardware compression; not valid if the /a option is used
/hc:off		Turns off hardware compression; not valid if the /a option is used
/l	*"filename"*	Creates a log file as *filename*. The path can be included as part of *filename*.
/r		Restricts access to the data on the backup tape to members of the Administrators group and the Backup Operators group; must not be used with the /a option
/t	*type*	Specifies the backup *type*, where *type* can be one of the following values: copy, daily, differential, incremental, or normal
/tape:*n*		Identifies the number of the tape drive to use, where *n* can be a value from 0 through 9. This option is necessary only if there is more than one tape drive on the system.
/v		Verifies the data after it has been backed up

No other options are available with the /*nopoll* switch. This format of the command requires user input and cannot be used in a batch file.

To eject a tape, the following syntax may be used:

```
ntbackup eject /tape:n
```

The /*tape:n* option is only necessary if there is more than one tape drive installed on the system. The variable *n* can be a value from 0 through 9, designating which tape drive should eject the tape.

Windows NT

Example of the ntbackup Command

To back up and verify the C: drive, including the local Registry and restricting access to the Administrators and Backup Operators groups with a fully detailed log of the backup in the file *C:\winnt\backup.log,* enter the following command:

```
ntbackup backup c: /b/r/l "c:\winnt\backup.log"
```

Restoring Data from a Floppy Disk

If you created your floppy backup using Windows NT Explorer, restore files by selecting them, then dragging them to the restore location. If the floppy backup was created using the *backup* command on the command line, invoke the VDM and utilize the *restore* command. The syntax for the *restore* command is

```
restore source-drive: dest-drive:[path/[filename]] [options]
```

The `source-drive:` is the drive where the backup is located. The `dest-drive:` is the drive where the files will be restored. The `path` is the directory where the files will be restored. This path must be the same as the directory from which the files were backed up. The `filename` is the name of the file or files to be restored. To name multiple files, use wildcard characters as part of the `filename` parameter. Table A.3 lists the *restore* command options.

TABLE A.3.   *restore* Options

Option	Description
/s	Restores all subdirectories and their files
/p	Prompts the user restoring the file for confirmation if the file being restored is read-only or if the file has changed since the last backup
/b:*date*	Restores files that have been modified on or before *date*
/a:*date*	Restores files that have been modified on or after *date*
/e:*time*	Restores files that have been modified at or before *time*
/l:*time*	Restores files that have been modified at or after *time*
/m	Restores files modified since the last backup
/n	Restores files that do not exist on the destination
/d	Produces a list of the files that will be restored without actually restoring them

EXAMPLE OF THE *restore* COMMAND

To restore any files that were accidentally deleted from the *c:\emily\school\homework* directory using the backup that was created in the previous backup example, enter the following:

```
restore a: c:\emily\school\homework\*.* /n
```

Restoring Files from Tape

To restore files from tape the user must first select the files to restore, then identify any of the restore options and then the restoration will take place. Restoration actually takes place from the Backup window accessed by selecting **Start → Programs → Administrative Tools → Backup**.

SELECTING THE FILES TO BE RESTORED

To select the files to be restored, execute the following:

1. After inserting the tape, double-click the Tapes icon. This will open the Tapes window.
2. To load the tape catalog, select **Operations → Catalog**.
3. To display the contents of the catalog, select the icon representing the tape you wish to restore.
4. Click the check box for all items to be restored. Clicking a directory will automatically select all files and subdirectories within it.
5. After all the files have been selected, click the **Restore** button.

SELECTING RESTORE OPTIONS

After clicking the **Restore** button, the Restore Information dialog box displays. This window displays the name of the tape and backup set as well as the creation date and the owner who created the backup. Complete the following appropriate information.

1. Enter **Restore to Drive**, which is the drive to which the data should be restored.
2. Enter an **Alternate Path**, if the files are to be restored to a directory different from the one from which they were backed up.
3. Check **Restore Local Registry** if you wish to restore the Registry file. This option is only available if the Registry was backed up.
4. Check **Restore File Permissions** if you wish to retain the original file and directory permissions. This option is only available for NTFS file systems.

Windows NT

5. Check the **Verify After Restore** option to compare the restored files against the files on tape to ensure that the restore procedure was error free.

6. Enter or select the **Log File** that will contain messages. If you do not want a log, select **Don't Log**. Select **Full Detail** to record the names of all the files and directories restored, or select **Summary Only** to record summary information only.

After completing the restore information, select the **OK** button to begin the restore process. If the backup contains multiple tapes, the restore procedure will request that a particular volume be mounted to read the tape catalog. This catalog is usually stored on the last tape.

The command *ntbackup /missingtape* entered at the command line will rebuild the catalog of a tape. This is usually necessary when there is a missing tape in a multiple-tape backup.

UNIX Alternatives

The UNIX commands that are available to back up and restore data are

- *cpio* – Backs up or restores data using tape, diskette, or disk
- *dd* – Backs up or restores data using tape, diskette, or disk. This command allows the user to identify block sizes of both input and output devices.
- *tar* – Backs up or restores data to tape, floppy disk, or disk

COMPARISON COMMANDS

Within a windowing environment a user can compare files visually by displaying two files in separate windows and comparing them by sight. The only utilities available within the base Windows NT system are executed from the command line. Two commands that compare files are the *fc* and the *comp* commands. In addition, the Windows NT Resource Kit provides a graphical equivalent to the UNIX *diff* command called WinDiff (**Start ➤ Programs ➤ Resource Kit 4.0 ➤ File Tools ➤ File and Directory Comparison**).

fc Command

The *fc* command enables a user to compare two files when both files are in either an ASCII or a binary format. The differences between the files are displayed. The syntax of the command is

```
fc [options] file1 file2
```

The files, *file1* and *file2,* can be just a filename; a path with a filename; or a drive, path, and filename in the format *drive:path\filename*. In addition, file1 and file2 can contain the wildcard characters * and ?. When using a wildcard character in file1, the *fc* command compares each file found with file2. In other words, it compares many files with one file. When using a wildcard character in file2, the command compares file1 with a file with a corresponding name in file2's location.

Table A.4 lists the *fc* command options.

TABLE A.4.   *fc* Options

Option	Description
/a	Used only for ASCII comparisons and provides the output display in abbreviated form. Only the first and last lines of each set of differences are displayed.
/b	Compares binary files. This option is automatically the default for files with *.EXE, .COM, .SYS, .OBJ, .LIB,* and *.BIN* extensions. The files are compared by byte and differences are output in the format *xxxxxxxx: yy zz,* where *xxxxxxxx* is the address of the bytes being compared in hexadecimal, *yy* is the contents of the byte from file1, and *zz* is the contents of the byte from file2.
/c	Ignores the distinctions between upper- and lowercase
/l	Compares ASCII files. This is considered the default for all files except those mentioned in the */b* option. The comparison is executed line by line and the differences are output in the following format: the name of file1, then the lines of file1 that differ from file2, then the first line that matches between the two files, the name of file2, the lines of file2 that differ from file1, then the first line that matches between the two files. After a difference is found, the command tries to resynchronize the two files.
/lb*n*	Sets the size of the internal line buffer to *n*. The default size is 100 lines. If the number of consecutive differences is greater than *n*, the command terminates.
/n	Displays the line numbers; used only for ASCII files
/t	Does not treat tabs as spaces. The default is to treat tabs as spaces.
/w	Treats consecutive tabs and spaces as one space. Does not compare tabs and spaces at the beginning and end of a line.
/*nnnn*	The file is considered to be resynchronized when *nnnn* number of consecutive lines match. Otherwise, matching lines are displayed as differences. The default value for *nnnn* is 2.

EXAMPLES OF THE *fc* COMMAND

To compare two binary files with the names *test.exe* and *test1.exe,* the command can be entered two different ways:

```
fc /b test.exe test1.exe
```

or

```
fc test.exe test1.exe
```

In this example both formats are acceptable, because a file with a *.exe* extension is assumed to be binary by default.

To compare the files *autoexec.bat, autoold.bat,* and *autoex3.bat* to the file *newauto.bat,* enter the following:

```
fc auto*.bat newauto.bat
```

Suppose that as a system administrator you needed to compare some test result files with a *.tst* extension in the *C:/test* directory with files of the same name in Bob's test directory on the D: drive. You could enter

```
fc c:/test/*.tst d:/bob/test/*.tst
```

comp Command

Another comparison command available through the VDM command line is the *comp* command. This command compares the content of the files by byte. Output consists of error messages of the format

```
Compare error at OFFSET xxxxxxxx = yy = zz
```

where *xxxxxxxx* is the memory address of the differing bytes, *yy* is the contents of the bytes in file1, and *zz* is the contents of the bytes in file2. The addresses and contents are in hexadecimal format unless an option (Table A.5) is specified to display them in decimal or character format.

TABLE A.5.   *comp* Options

Option	Description
/a	Displays the differences between the files in character format
/d	Displays the differences between the files in decimal format instead of hexadecimal
/l	Displays the line number of the differences instead of the number of the byte offset
/n=*num*	Compares the first *num* lines of both files. This is used particularly when two files are different sizes
/c	Ignores upper- and lowercase distinctions

The syntax of the *comp* command is

```
comp [file1] [file2] [options]
```

The files file1 and file2 can be the names of two files, including as necessary the drive designation as well as the directory path. The wildcard characters of * and ? can be used to compare multiple files.

EXAMPLE OF THE *comp* COMMAND

To compare the first fifteen (15) lines of the files *newtest.log* and *oldtest.log,* displaying the line numbers of where the differences occur, enter the following:

```
comp newtest.log oldtest.log /n=15 /l
```

WinDiff

The Windows NT Resource Kit provides a graphical tool that compares two files, as shown in Figure A.1.

UNIX Alternatives

UNIX enables users to compare files using a number of different commands.

- *cmp* – Compares binary files
- *comm* – Compares sorted files to determine the lines that are common
- *diff* – Compares two files for differences
- *diff3* – Compares three (3) files for differences
- *sdiff* – Compares two files for differences and provides side-by-side output display
- *dircmp* – Compares two directories for similarities and differences
- *uniq* – Searches file for unique and duplicate lines

Windows NT

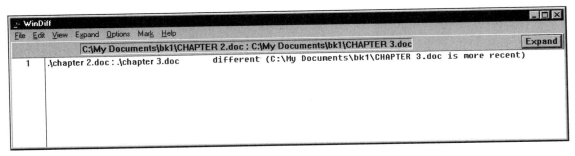

FIGURE A.1.   Windows NT Resource Kit WinDiff

COMPRESSION COMMANDS

Each file within the Windows NT NTFS file system contains a compression attribute. This attribute identifies (1) that a file should be stored as compressed or (2) that it is already compressed. It is recommended that this attribute be selected for large files that are not used frequently. When this attribute is selected, files are automatically compressed when they are saved, and decompressed when accessed for use. (Remember that this compression technology is not available with the FAT file system.)

This compression attribute can be set from within the My Computer windows or through Windows NT Explorer. From Windows NT Explorer, select the file for which you wish to view or set the compression attribute. Next, from the menu bar select **File ➤ Properties**. Within the Properties window for the file select the **General** tab if it isn't already displayed. Within the **General** tab, there is a **Compressed** check box in the **Attributes** section. To compress or decompress a file, click in this check box.

As an alternative to using the **File** menu bar item, you may select the file and click the right mouse button. From the menu that displays, select **Properties**.

compact Command

The *compact* command allows the user to set or display the compression attribute on NTFS files from the VDM command line. The syntax of the command is

```
compact [options] [filename]
```

The `filename` parameter can actually be the name of a file or a directory. In a directory, the compression attribute indicates that any new files added to the directory will automatically have their compression attributes set, thereby compressing the new files. This does not, however, change the compression attribute for files that already exist in the directory. Wildcard characters can be used as part of the `file` parameter.

If no options are used or no filenames are entered, the compression attribute for the current directory is displayed. Table A.6 describes the available options.

EXAMPLES OF THE *compact* COMMAND

To set the compression attribute on the directory *\ellen\oldfiles* as well as any of its subdirectories, enter the following:

```
compact /c /s c:\ellen\oldfiles
```

TABLE A.6.   *compact* **Options**

Option	Qualifier	Description
/c		Compresses the named files
/u		Uncompresses the named files.
/s	*:directory*	Compresses or uncompresses all subdirectories for *directory*. The *:directory* qualifier is optional. The default is the current directory.
/i		Ignores any errors that occur
/f		Forces *filename* to be compressed or uncompressed. The main use for this option occurs when a file is only partially compressed or uncompressed and the system administrator needs to complete the task.

To remove the compression attribute from the directory *d:\bob\contracts,* enter

```
compact /u d:\bob\contracts
```

Remember that this command only removes the attribute from the directory and does not affect any of the files and subdirectories currently in the directory *\bob\contracts*.

UNIX Alternatives:

The standard UNIX commands for compressing and uncompressing files are

- *compress* – Compresses files using adaptive Lempel-Ziv coding
- *pack* – Compresses files using Huffman coding
- *pcat* – Displays files compressed using the *pack* command
- *uncompress* – Expands files created using the *compress* command
- *unpack* – Expands files compressed using the *pack* command
- *uudecode* – Expands files created using the *uuencode* command
- *uuencode* – Converts binary files for mail transmission
- *zcat* – Displays files compressed using the *compress* command

Other commands also exist, most notably *gzip,* which is a freeware program available from the GNU Project at `www.gnu.ai.mit.edu`.

Windows NT

DISPLAY COMMANDS

The display commands cover a variety of functions. Examples include displaying the contents of files, the properties of files, lists of files, help files, and organizing displays into a sequence the user desires. This section describes the procedures and commands available to accomplish these tasks.

Displaying the Contents of Files

Windows NT primarily uses installed applications to enable a user to look at the contents of a file. The Windows NT Registry maintains a list of installed applications and attempts to match file extensions to appropriate software so that the file can be viewed in native format. When you double click on a file within the Windows NT Explorer, the file opens within the application. If the file type is unknown, the Open With window is displayed, which allows the user to select the application that should be used to open the file.

The Notepad and WordPad applications that are part of the base Windows NT system allow the user to display and create text or ASCII files. These applications are accessed by selecting **Start** ➤ **Programs** ➤ **Accessories** ➤ **Notepad** or **WordPad**.

From the VDM command line, two commands are available for displaying files: *more* and *type*. The *more* command displays long files one screen at a time, while the *type* command just displays the entire contents of a file and is usually used only for short files.

more COMMAND

The *more* command is used to display long text files from within the command prompt window. The file displays one screen at a time. The basic syntax of the command is

```
more [options] [file(s)]
```

The `file(s)` parameter is not necessary when data is passed to the *more* command from another command using the pipe symbol (|). When the `file(s)` parameter is used, it can be in the format of one or more filenames, including the drive designation and path if they are necessary. Table A.7 presents the *more* command options.

If the /e switch is used, then the commands listed in Table A.8 may be used whenever the —More— prompt displays.

TABLE A.7. *more* Options

Option	Description
/e	Enables the "extended" features, which allow the user to control how the file is displayed by entering commands whenever the —More—prompt displays. These commands are identified in Table A.8.
/p	Expands any form-feed characters
/s	Consolidates multiple blank lines into one blank line
/t*n*	Substitutes *n* spaces for each tab
+*n*	Starts displaying the first file in the *file(s)* list at line *n*

TABLE A.8. *more* Commands

Command	Description
Space bar	Displays the next page of text
<ENTER>	Displays the next line of text
f	Displays the next file in the *file(s)* list
p*n*	Displays the next *n* lines
s*n*	Skips *n* lines
?	Displays the commands that are acceptable at the—More—prompt. In other words, this is the help function.
=	Displays the line number
q	Quits

type COMMAND

The *type* command simply displays the contents of one or more files similar to the UNIX *cat* command. The syntax of the command is

```
type file(s)
```

The `file(s)` parameter can consist of just the filenames entered with the drive designation and path name if they are necessary. Multiple files in the `file(s)` list are separated by spaces. Remember to enclose the filename in quotes when entering filenames that contain spaces as a part of the name.

Windows NT

UNIX Alternatives

Commands in UNIX that enable a user to display the contents of a file are

- *cat* – Displays or creates a file
- *head* – Displays the beginning of the file
- *more* – Displays the file one screen at a time
- *pg* – Displays the file one screen at a time
- *tail* – Displays the end of a file

Displaying Attributes and Properties of Files and Folders

Windows NT provides graphical and character VDM-based methods of displaying the file and directory hierarchy of a system and its network. The graphical methods available are through the My Computer windows, Windows NT Explorer, and the Network Neighborhood. The Network Neighborhood allows the user to display the files and directories available on the network. It is accessible either from its desktop icon or through Explorer. This section describes the file and folder views available through Windows NT Explorer as well as the *dir* command that is available at the command prompt.

When displaying the file hierarchy using Windows NT Explorer, the left pane shows the top level of the hierarchy for the desktop. Directories have file folder icons and are referred to as *folders*. To view the subdirectories, use the left mouse button to click on a box containing a plus (+) sign. When the subdirectories are displayed, this box will contain a minus (–) sign. To display both the files and the subdirectories of a particular folder, select the folder by clicking it with the mouse. The contents of the folder will display in the right pane of the window (Figure A.2).

To view detailed information about each file in the **Contents of** pane, select **View ➤ Details** from the menu bar. This detailed information includes the name of the file, the size in bytes, the file type, the date it was last modified and the attributes associated with it. The attributes can be Archive (A), Read-only (R), Hidden (H), System (S), or Compressed (C). The Compressed attribute only displays on NTFS file systems.

It is important to note that by default certain file types are omitted (or hidden) from the Explorer hierarchical display, such as system (.*SYS*) and application extension (.*DLL*) files. To show all files automatically or to view a list of the

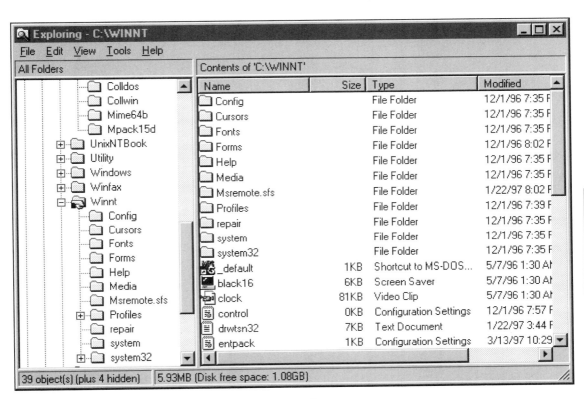

FIGURE A.2. Windows NT Explorer Primary Window

file types that are hidden, select **View → Options → View** tab. Select the **Show all files** option to display all files.

There are four ways to sort the files in the **Contents of** pane for viewing: by name, type, size, or date. To change this display sequence, from the menu bar select **View → Arrange Icons**, then select the desired sort order.

There are two different ways to view the properties and attributes of a particular folder. After selecting a file or folder in the **Contents of** pane, do the following.

1. Click the right mouse button or select **File** from the menu bar.

2. Select **Properties**.

3. Within the Properties window, select the **General** tab.

Figure A.3 displays the **General** tab for a file in a Windows NT system using the FAT file system. If the NTFS file system were used, there would also be a Compressed attribute.

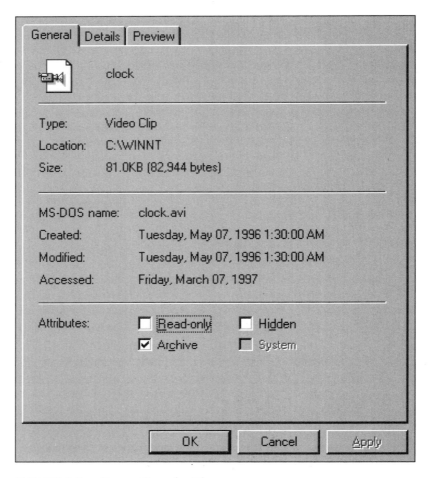

FIGURE A.3.   Properties of a File

dir COMMAND

The *dir* command is available from the command prompt, and it gives the user the ability to display file and directory properties and attributes via the command line. The default output display of the *dir* command includes the volume label and serial number of the disk, a listing of the current or selected directory, the total number of files listed, the total size of the files listed, and the amount of space remaining on the disk. The listing for each file or directory includes the size of the file in bytes as well as the date and time that the file was last modified. In addition, if the file has an extension it is displayed following the filename. An example of a portion of the *dir* command output is presented in Figure A.4.

```
⌐ Command Prompt                                                    _□×
C:\Program Files\Accessories>dir
 Volume in drive C is AUNKF08ABA
 Volume Serial Number is 581A-340D

 Directory of C:\Program Files\Accessories

10/29/96   02:40p        <DIR>          .
10/29/96   02:40p        <DIR>          ..
07/11/95   09:50a               311,808 MSPAINT.EXE
07/11/95   09:50a               183,296 WORDPAD.EXE
07/11/95   09:50a               820,224 BACKUP.EXE
07/12/96   03:35p        <DIR>          HyperTerminal
11/13/96   10:26a        <DIR>          ImageVue
               7 File(s)       1,315,328 bytes
                            36,077,568 bytes free
```

FIGURE A.4.   VDM Directory Listing

The syntax of the *dir* command is

```
dir [file(s)] [options]
```

Neither the `file(s)` nor the `options` parameters are required. Without these parameters the *dir* command just displays the default information for the current directory. The `file(s)` parameter can be one or more filenames or directories. The format for this parameter can be just the file or directory name or it can include the drive designation as well as the path using the standard syntax of `drive:path\filename`. Separate multiple filenames with spaces, commas, or semicolons. In addition, the wildcard characters * and ? may be used as part of the `file(s)` parameter. (Note that with wildcards, unlike the early versions of DOS that require *.*, in Windows NT a single * is used like UNIX.)

The *dir* options are listed in Table A.9.

TABLE A.9.   *dir* Options

Option	Qualifier	Description
/a	:*attributes*	Displays only those files that match *attributes*. The default (which is without the /a switch) displays all files except those with the hidden or system attribute set. The *attributes* qualifier is optional. When not used, the *dir* /a command displays all files, even hidden and system files. The colon is optional as well. Multiple attributes may be entered in any order as long as there are no spaces between them, but only files that match all of the attributes are displayed. The following is a list of acceptable values for the *attributes* qualifier. A minus sign in front of the attribute displays all files that do not match that attribute. Acceptable values are *a* (files that have the archive or backup attribute set), *-a* (files that do not have the archive attribute set), *d* (directories only), *-d* (files only, no directories), *h* (hidden files), *-h* (files that are not hidden), *r* (read-only files), *-r* (files that are not read-only), *s* (system files), and *-s* (nonsystem files).

continued

Windows NT

TABLE A.9.   *dir* Options *(Continued)*

Option	Qualifier	Description
/b		Does not display any heading or summary information. Do not use in conjunction with the /*w* option.
/d		Displays the files and directories in columns, sorting by column
/l		Displays any unsorted files and directories in lowercase letters
/n		Displays the following information for each file and directory: date and time last modified, whether the file is a directory or not, the size of the file, and the name of the file or directory. This is the default format for the *dir* command. Should the user wish the filenames to display on the left, enter this option as /-*n*.
/o	:*order*	Displays the files sorted based on the order given. The default (without the /*o* switch) is to display the files and directories in the order they are stored. Using the /*o* switch without any order specified displays the directories sorted alphabetically, then the files sorted alphabetically. The colon is optional. The following is a list of the acceptable values for *order*. These values may be entered in any order and combination as long as there are no spaces between them. The sort order is defined by the order of the values, such that the first-order value will be the primary sort key, the next one is the secondary sort key, and so on. Acceptable values are *d* (sort in ascending order by date and time, oldest first), -*d* (sort in descending order by date and time, newest first), *e* (sort alphabetically by file extension), -*e* (sort in reverse alphabetical order by file extension), *g* (display with directories grouped before the files), -*g* (display with directories grouped after the files), *n* (sort alphabetically by filename or directory name), -*n* (sort in reverse alphabetical order by name), *s* (sort in ascending order by size, smallest first), and -*s* (sort in descending order by size, largest first).
/p		Displays only one screen at a time. Any key can be pressed to display the next screen.
/s		Displays all occurrences of the filename given in the directory specified, as well as its subdirectories. Obviously this option requires the use of the `file(s)` parameter.
/t	:*time*	Displays the selected *time* for each file, where *time* can be *c* for the creation time, *a* for the time the file was last accessed, or *w* for the time that the file was last written. When used in conjunction with the /*od* or /*o-d* option, it identifies the time field that is used for sorting.
/w		Displays the directory contents in wide format, which contains up to five columns of file and directory names.
/x		Displays the MS-DOS names for the files before the NT names. Remember that NT allows longer file names than the MS-DOS 8.3-character limit. The format of the display is similar to that of the /*n* option.

Windows NT allows a user to create his own default results for the *dir* command through use of the *dircmd* environment variable. To set the default switches that would be executed automatically whenever *dir* is entered at the command line, enter the following:

```
set dircmd=options
```

where `options` is any of the switches identified in Table A.9. These switches are considered the default until they are reset or Windows NT is restarted. To override the default for a single command, just enter a minus sign (–) before the switch. For example, if the command *set dircmd=/n* was entered and the user wanted to see the shorter, wide listing for a directory that contains a large number of files, type `dir /-n/w`. Please refer to the *set* command for more information regarding setting, overriding, and clearing environment variables.

Examples of the dir Command

Suppose as a system administrator you are familiar with the recursive capabilities of UNIX and wish to enter a command in Windows NT that is similar to the UNIX *ls -lR | more* command. You could enter the following while residing in the root directory:

```
dir /s/n/o/p
```

This command would produce a long alphabetical listing of all files, directories, and subdirectories, and would pause at the end of each screen of information. The directories would display first, then the files.

To display files in the current directory that have the attributes of both hidden and system, enter the following:

```
dir /ahs
```

or

```
dir /a:hs
```

To display all files with a *.doc* extension in the current directory and its subdirectories, enter the following:

```
dir *.doc /s
```

UNIX Alternative

The UNIX *ls* command displays information about files and directories on the system, including file and directory names, permissions, size, ownership, and date the file was last modified.

Windows NT

echo COMMAND

The *echo* command is used primarily in batch files either to enable or disable the command echoing feature, or to display a message to the screen. The syntax of the command is

```
echo [options]
```

Using *echo* without any `options` displays whether the *echo* feature is either turned on or off. The *echo* options are listed in Table A.10.

UNIX Alternative

The *echo* command in UNIX outputs a string or message to standard output or the terminal screen.

Displaying Help

Windows NT provides both graphical and command line methods of displaying help documentation to the user. The graphical version of help is accessed from the **Start** menu by choosing **Start ➤ Help** (Figure A.5).

The Help Topics: Windows NT Help window displays, containing three tabs.

1. **Contents** – This tab displays a table of contents of help categories available. Double-click on the book icon for a particular entry to display subtopics.

2. **Index** – This tab provides an alphabetical index of help topics. The user can select a topic from the list or enter a portion of the topic to locate it more quickly.

3. **Find** – This tab enables the user to search the on-line documentation for any references to the words or phrase entered.

help COMMAND

Through the command line the *help* command can be used to display help information about Windows NT commands. This form of help does not include information on the NT *net* commands. The syntax of the command is

```
help [command]
```

The `command` parameter is the name of the command for which you wish information. Omitting the `command` parameter creates a display of each command available, along with a brief description.

TABLE A.10. *echo* Options

Option	Description
on	Turns the echo feature on. In other words, displays (or echoes) each command as it is executed.
off	Turns the echo feature off. Typing *echo off* on the command line removes the prompt from screen.
message	Displays *message* on the screen. This command is usually used in batch files following an *echo off* command.
.	A period displays a blank line. The syntax for this option is *echo.* with no spaces between the word echo and the period.

Windows NT

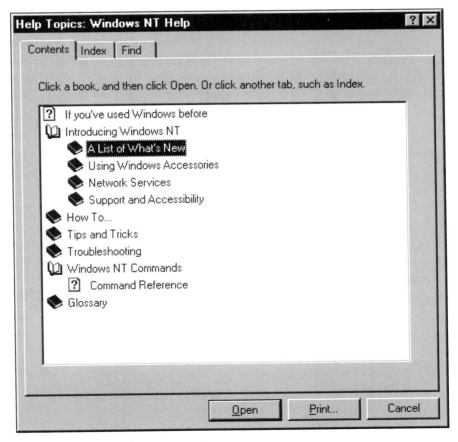

FIGURE A.5.   Windows NT Help

As an alternative to typing *help* then the command name, the user can use the */?* switch after the command. For example, *dir /?* and *help dir* both give help information for the *dir* command.

net help COMMAND

The *net help* command provides help information for the Windows NT *net* commands. There are two acceptable formats for this command:

```
net help [command]
net command {/help | /?}
```

The *command* parameter can contain one of three values:

1. A *net* command, such as *net account, net start, net user,* and so forth
2. The word *services,* which would provide a list of network services that the user executing the command can start
3. The word *syntax,* which provides information on interpreting the syntax used in the *net help* documentation

net helpmsg COMMAND

The *net helpmsg* command provides the user with more information regarding a net error message. The syntax of the command is

```
net helpmsg number
```

The *number* parameter is the number of the net error message. The net error messages are displayed in the following way:

```
NET ####: Message
```

where #### is the number that you would include in the *net helpmsg* command.

UNIX Alternatives

There are three methods of displaying help information within UNIX.

1. The *man* command displays on-line documentation.
2. The *?* or *help* options are available as parameters for some commands.
3. By entering a command with the incorrect syntax, the correct syntax is often displayed as part of the error message.

FILE MANAGEMENT COMMANDS

The file management commands and procedures are those that allow a user to create, remove, copy, move, and rename files and directories. These tasks may be completed using graphical methods via Windows NT Explorer or the My Computer windows. The Network Neighborhood windows permit some of these actions to occur for resources shared across the network, provided that the user has the permission to execute the requested task. Windows NT Explorer is the application we use for most explanations.

Displaying Path Names

While in Windows NT Explorer, users can view the full path name of their current location within Explorer by selecting **View** from the menu bar, then selecting **Options** ➤ **View**. Within the **View** tab, select the **Display the full path in the title bar** option. This, by the way, is the default setting.

If you wish to determine the current directory while at the command prompt, type *cd* then press <Enter>. This command displays the current directory.

UNIX Alternative

To display the current path in a UNIX system, type *pwd* at the prompt.

Creating and Removing Folders

Windows NT provides VDM commands as well as graphical procedures for creating and removing directories or folders. This section discusses both types of procedures.

CREATING FOLDERS

New folders can be created through the Windows NT Explorer as well as through the My Computer windows using the same procedure. To create a folder (or directory) from Windows NT Explorer, execute the following.

1. Select the folder that will contain the new directory.

2. Select **File** from the menu bar.

3. Select **New**.

Windows NT

4. Select **Folder**.

5. Within the **Contents of** pane of the Explorer screen, a new folder icon displays at the bottom of the file list with the name New Folder. Enter the name of the new folder.

mkdir Command

The *mkdir* command enables the user to create a directory from the command line. Another name for this command is *md*. The syntax is

```
mkdir directory-name
```

or

```
md directory-name
```

The `directory-name` parameter is the name of the folder (or directory) you wish to create. The drive designation may be included as part of `directory-name` as well as the path, should you wish to create a subdirectory. For example, suppose the current directory is the root directory on the C: drive and you wish to create the folder *budget* in the *year97* directory on the D: drive. To create this directory without moving from the current location, enter

```
mkdir d:\year97\budget
```

UNIX Alternative

The command to create directories in UNIX goes by the same name—*mkdir*.

REMOVING FOLDERS

Windows NT provides several ways to remove folders through either Windows NT Explorer or the My Computer windows. Removing a folder places it in the Recycle Bin, where it can be accessed until the Recycle Bin is cleared. In other words, folders are not permanently removed from the system until the file is removed from the Recycle Bin.

The simplest way to remove a folder is to select the folder then press `<Delete>`. A confirmation message similar to the following displays: "Are you sure you want to remove the folder and move all its contents to the Recycle Bin?" The user must respond by selecting either **Yes** or **No**.

Another way to remove a folder using Windows NT Explorer is to execute the following steps.

1. Select the folder.
2. Select **File** from the menu bar.
3. Select **Delete**.

Step 2 is not necessary if you select the folder by using the right mouse button. Clicking the right mouse button displays a menu that also contains the **Delete** option.

As an alternative, the user can select the folder, then while holding down the left mouse button can drag the folder to the Recycle Bin icon and release the mouse button. This moves the folder to the Recycle Bin. If you want the folder to be removed permanently from the system, hold <Shift> down while dragging the folder to the Recycle Bin.

rmdir Command

The *rmdir* command deletes the given directory. Another name for this command is *rd*. The syntax of both commands is

```
rmdir directory-name [/s]
```

or

```
rd directory-name [/s]
```

The `directory-name` parameter is the name of the directory or folder you wish to delete. It can contain both the drive designation as well as the path name if they are necessary.

The */s* switch is optional and enables any files and subdirectories contained within the folder to be deleted as well. If the */s* switch is not used, the directory must be empty of any files before it can be removed.

UNIX Alternatives

There are two commands that can remove directories in UNIX:

- *rmdir* – Removes an empty directory
- *rm* – Removes directories and files

Moving between Folders

Moving between folders within Windows NT is as simple as selecting a different folder with the mouse. Within Windows NT Explorer you may select the folder either in the **All Folders** pane or in the **Contents of** pane. Within the My Computer windows, just click on the icon representing the folder or the folder name.

chdir COMMAND

The *chdir* command enables the user to display the name of the current directory as well as to change to a different directory. Another name for this command is *cd*. The syntax of both commands is

```
chdir [/d] [[drive:]directory-name]
```

or

```
cd [/d] [[drive:]directory-name]
```

The parameters */d* and *drive:directory-name* are optional. If neither are entered, the *chdir* command displays the name of the current directory, including the drive designation.

The */d* switch changes the current drive designation. The *drive: directory-name* parameter identifies the new drive and directory. The drive designation is only entered when necessary. Using a double period (..) in place of the directory name changes the directory from the current one to its parent.

UNIX Alternatives

The following are some related commands in UNIX:

- *cd* – Changes to a new directory
- *pwd* – Displays the current directory

Creating and Removing Files

This section provides procedures and commands for creating and removing files within Windows NT.

CREATING FILES

Files are usually created within Windows NT via an application, such as Notepad, WordPad, or any other installed application. From within Windows NT Explorer and the My Computer windows, selecting **File** ➜ **New** provides a list of the types of files that you can create based on the applications installed on your system. In addition, the MS-DOS editor, *edlin,* is available from the command prompt. The *vi* editor is also shipped with Windows NT. For details on the use of *vi,* see Chapter 5.

UNIX Alternatives

UNIX provides several commands for creating files:

- *cat* – Creates new files as well as displays existing files
- *ed* – One of the editors available on UNIX systems
- *vi* – The most used editor on UNIX systems

REMOVING FILES

The procedure for removing files is the same as that for removing folders. The simplest way to remove a file is to select it then press <Delete>. To remove a file using Windows NT Explorer, execute the following steps.

1. Select the file.
2. Select **File** from the menu bar.
3. Select **Delete**.

Step 2 is not necessary if you select the file by using the right mouse button. Clicking the right mouse button displays a menu that also contains the **Delete** option.

As an alternative the user can select the file then drag it to the Recycle Bin icon. This moves the file to the Recycle Bin. If you want the file to be removed permanently from the system, hold <Shift> down while dragging the file to the Recycle Bin or simply press <Shift> and <Delete> simultaneously.

To select multiple files for deletion, hold down <Ctrl> while selecting the files with the mouse, then drag the files to the Recycle Bin.

del and erase Commands

The *del* command deletes or erases files from the system. Another name for this command is *erase*. The syntax is

```
del file(s) [options]
```

or

```
erase file(s) [options]
```

TABLE A.11. *del* Options

Option	Qualifier	Description
/a	*:attributes*	Deletes those files that match the attributes *r* for Read-only, *h* for Hidden, *s* for System, and *a* for Archive. A minus (–) sign may be used in front of any of these options to identify those files that do not match the given attribute.
/f		Forces read-only files to be deleted
/p		Requires the user to confirm whether a file should be deleted or not by displaying the following prompt: *file*, Delete (Y/N)? Answering **Y** will delete the file; **N** will not. (To abort the *del* command altogether, press <Ctrl-C>.)
/q		Does not prompt for confirmation. This is the default option.
/s		Deletes the files listed from not only the current directory, but also from the subdirectories

The `file(s)` parameter identifies the names of the files to be removed from the system. The parameter can contain the drive designation and the directory path in the format *drive:path\file*. More than one file can be deleted using the same *del* command by separating multiple filenames with spaces, commas, or semicolons. The *del* options are presented in Table A.11.

The wildcard characters * and ? can be used when specifying files to delete. It is important that these are used with care to reduce the risk of deleting critical files.

UNIX Alternative

The UNIX command *rm* removes files and directories from the UNIX system.

Copying and Moving Files

There is a difference between copying and moving a file. The copy procedure creates a duplicate of the original file in another location so that more than one copy of the file exists, while the move procedure places the original file in another location without making a duplicate of it.

Windows NT provides both graphical and command line methods for copying and moving files. The graphical method using the Windows NT Explorer application provides the user multiple ways of copying and moving files, such as using the menus or using the drag and drop method. In addition, this application enables a user to copy/move files within the same disk, between disks, or across the network. The following sections discuss both the graphical and command line procedures for these tasks.

COPYING FILES

To copy a file using the drag-and-drop method within Windows NT Explorer, execute the following steps.

1. Display the file in the **Contents of** pane.
2. Make sure that the destination directory is visible in the **All Folders** pane (or start another copy of Explorer and display the destination directory in the **Contents of** pane).
3. Select the file you wish to copy.
4. Hold down `<Ctrl>` and drag the file to its destination.

Remember, to select multiple files, hold down `<Ctrl>` while selecting the files.

To use the menu bar in Windows NT Explorer to copy files, execute the following steps.

1. Select the files.
2. Select **Edit** ➤ **Copy** or press `<Ctrl-C>`.
3. Select the destination directory.
4. Select **Edit** ➤ **Paste** or press `<Ctrl-V>`.

Selecting the files with the right mouse button displays a menu that contains the **Copy** menu choice as well.

Copying an executable file (one that has a *.exe* or *.com* extension) may create a shortcut. A shortcut is a link to the executable that gives the user an alternative way of executing the program. Shortcuts are often dragged and dropped to the main screen so that the user can bypass the menus.

copy Command

The *copy* command copies the source file or files to the destination defined. In addition, the *copy* command can be used to combine the contents of files. The syntax for this command is

```
copy [/a|/b] source-file [/a|/b] dest-file [/a|/b] [options]
```

Windows NT

where *source-file* is the name of the file to be copied. It can take the form of simply the filename or can be extended to include the drive designation and the directory path as necessary. In addition, *source-file* can actually be a device.

The parameter *dest-file* is the name of the destination file, which takes the form of the filename, is extended to include the drive designation and the directory path, or is a device name such as COM1 or LPT1. If *dest-file* is omitted, a file with the same name, creation date, and time as *source-file* is created in the current directory and on the current drive. If a file with that name already exists, an error is displayed.

The parameter [/a|/b] indicates whether the file is ASCII (*/a* switch) or binary (*/b* switch).The default value is binary when copying files and is ASCII when combining files. When the [/a|/b] switch is entered before *source-file*, all items that follow use that flag until a different [/a|/b] switch is entered. The new [/a|/b] switch applies to the *source-file* that immediately precedes it as well as any *source-files* that follow it. Placement of the */a* or */b* option after *source-file* or *dest-file* results in different copy procedures. Table A.12 explains the differences that result according to the placement of these switches on the command line.

When *dest-file* is a device, it is recommended that the */b* switch be used so that special control characters are copied to the device as data. If the */a* switch is used in this instance, the ASCII copy might cause those control characters to be interpreted, thus providing unpredictable results.

Two additional options are available, as indicated in the syntax line as *options,* as defined in Table A.13.

TABLE A.12.   *copy* Options /a and /b

Option	Used after *source-file*	Used after *dest-file*
/a	Copies all data in the file up to the first end-of-file character. The end-of-file character is not copied. The data is considered to be in ASCII format.	Adds an end-of-file character to the end of *dest-file* as the last character.
/b	Copies all data in the file, including the end-of-file character. The data is considered to be in binary format.	Does not add an end-of-file character to the end of *dest-file*.

TABLE A.13. *copy* Options

Option	Description
/n	Uses the MS-DOS filename format of *filename.ext* when copying files with longer names
/v	Performs verification of each file copied. If an error occurs, a message is displayed. This switch causes the *copy* command to execute more slowly.

EXAMPLES OF THE *copy* COMMAND

To copy the file *budget.xls* from the C: drive to the directory *d:\financial\year97*, enter the following:

```
copy budget.xls d:\financial\year97
```

Suppose that you wish to copy an ASCII file up to the first end-of-file character and output it to a file with the end-of-file character added. The command would be

```
copy demo.txt /a newdemo.txt /a
```

Combining Files with the copy Command

A user can combine files using the *copy* command. To instruct the *copy* command to combine files, multiple source files are entered separated by a plus (+) sign. Remember that the default file type is considered to be ASCII when combining files. Should you need to combine binary files, the */b* switch would need to be entered. An example of the syntax for combining files is

```
copy [/a|/b] source-file1 [+ source-file2 [/a|/b]
[+ source-file...]] dest-file [/a|/b] options
```

Instead of entering multiple source file names, wildcard characters can also be used to designate multiple files to be combined.

A special use of the plus (+) sign parameter allows the user to update the date and time of the file to the current date and time without changing the contents of the file. The syntax to accomplish this task is

```
copy [/a|/b] source-file+ ,,
```

EXAMPLES OF THE *copy* COMMAND USING THE COMBINING OPTION

Suppose that a department manager wants to combine all of his employees' monthly status reports for April into one file. She could enter

```
copy grwapr.rpt + ebgapr.rpt + eegapr.rpt April.rpt
```

If all of these files were in the same directory, another variation of this command could be entered:

```
copy *apr.rpt April.rpt
```

xcopy Command

The *xcopy* command is more comprehensive than the *copy* command. *xcopy* allows the user to copy not only files and directories, but also the subdirectories. The syntax of the command is

```
xcopy source-file [dest-file] [options]
```

where *source-file* is the names of the files to be copied as well as their locations. This parameter must include either a drive designation or a directory path. The *dest-file* parameter is the destination of the files you want copied. It may include the name of the file as well as the drive designation and the directory path as necessary. The *dest-file* parameter is optional. If it is not included, the source files are copied to the current drive and directory. The destination files automatically have the archive attribute set.

The *xcopy* command options are presented in Table A.14.

EXAMPLE OF THE *xcopy* COMMAND

To copy the directory *budget* and all of its files and subdirectories to the *year97* directory, creating a directory named *budget* at the same time, enter

```
xcopy \budget \year97 /i/s/e
```

where the */i* switch creates a directory named *budget* under the *year97* directory, the */s* switch copies both files and subdirectories, and the */e* switch ensures that empty subdirectories get copied as well.

TABLE A.14.   *xcopy* Options

Option	Qualifier	Description
/a		Copies only those source files with the archive attribute set. Using this switch does not cause the archive attribute to change.
/c		Ignores any errors as they occur
/d	:*date*	Copies only those files with a modification date the same as or after the :*date* qualifier. The :*date* qualifier is in the format of MM-DD-YY. The :*date* qualifier is optional. If it is not used, this option copies only those files that are more recent than any existing destination files.
/e		This option must be used with the */s* and */t* options and allows empty subdirectories to be copied as well as those containing files.

TABLE A.14.   *(Continued)*

Option	Qualifier	Description
/exclude	:*filename*	Does not copy the files contained in *filename. filename* is a file that can contain one pattern per line without the use of wildcard characters. A file is not copied when any portion of `source-file` matches a line in *filename*.
/f		Displays both the source filename and the destination filename during the copy
/h		Includes files that have the hidden and system attributes set. The default is to not copy these file types.
/i		Creates a directory called *dest-file* if the `source-file` contains wildcards or if the `source-file` is a directory and if `dest-file` does not exist. All `source-files` are then copied to the `dest-file` directory. When this option is not set, the *xcopy* command prompts the user to identify the `dest-file` as a file (F) or a directory (D).
/k		Copies the `source-files` without changing the read-only file attribute. The command automatically removes the read-only attribute whenever this option is *not* used.
/m		Similar to the */a* option; copies files with the archive attribute set, but the difference lies in the fact that the */m* option turns off the archive attribute on the `source-files` after the copy
/n		Copies files using the short filename format of *filename.ext*. This is required when copying files to a system that can only handle the shorter filenames.
/p		Displays a confirmation prompt prior to creating the destination file
/q		Does not display messages
/r		Enables the command to copy over read-only files
/s		Copies both directories and subdirectories. Empty directories and subdirectories are not copied. When this option is omitted, subdirectories are not copied.
/t		Does not copy files under subdirectories. Only copies the subdirectories themselves. Must use with the */e* switch to copy empty subdirectories.
/u		This is the update option. When used, this option only copies those files that already exist at the destination, thereby updating them.
/w		Displays a message that requires the user to press any key to start the copy process.
/z		Copies files over the network in restartable mode.

Windows NT Resource Kit Alternatives

There are two other copy utilities that are part of Resource Kit 4.0:

- *robocopy* – A program that copies entire directory trees either within the same system or across the network

- *scopy* – A program that copies files and directories within NTFS file systems while keeping the security settings

UNIX Alternatives

The following are some UNIX alternatives to the Windows NT *copy* command:

- *cp* – Copies files to new destinations
- *cat* – When used in conjunction with the > > (append) symbol, creates files

MOVING FILES

To move a file using the drag-and-drop method within Windows NT Explorer, execute the following steps:

1. Display the file in the **Contents of** pane.
2. Make sure that the destination directory is visible in the **All Folders** pane (or start another copy of Explorer and display the destination directory in the **Contents of** pane).
3. Select the file you wish to move.
4. Drag the file to its new destination, if it is on the same disk as its current location. Otherwise, hold down <Shift> while dragging the file to force the move. If <Shift> is not held down, a copy will occur instead of a move.

Remember, to select multiple files, hold down <Ctrl> while selecting the files.

To use the menu bar in Windows NT Explorer to move files, execute these steps:

1. Select the files.
2. Select **Edit** ➤ **Cut** or press <Ctrl-X>.
3. Select the destination directory.
4. Select **Edit** ➤ **Paste** or press <Ctrl-V>.

move *Command*

The *move* command actually moves files from one directory to another. The files will no longer exist in their original location. The syntax for this command is

```
move source-file(s) dest-file
```

The *source-file(s)* parameter represents the files that you wish to move. It can be just the filename or it can include the drive designation and directory as necessary. Wildcard characters can be used to move multiple files.

The *dest-file* parameter represents the new location of the files. It can be a new filename or it can include a new drive designation or new directory path as necessary. Wildcard characters can be used here as well, such as in a situation when you need to change the extension of a number of files to a new extension.

UNIX Alternative

The comparative UNIX command for the WINDOWS NT *move* command is *mv*.

RENAMING FILES OR FOLDERS

To rename the file using Windows NT Explorer, execute the following steps:

1. Select the file or folder.
2. From the menu bar, select **File ➤ Rename**.
3. Enter the new name for the file or folder.

or

1. Select the file or folder by using the right mouse button to display a menu.
2. Select **Rename**.
3. Enter the new name for the file or folder.

rename *Command*

The *rename* command permits the user to change the name of a file or directory without changing its location. In other words, filenames cannot be changed across drives or directories with this command. If the location needs to change as well as the name, either the *copy* or *move* command must be executed. The syntax for both formats of this command are

```
rename oldfile newfile
```

or

```
ren oldfile newfile
```

Windows NT

The *oldfile* parameter is the name of the file that you wish to change. It may include the drive designation and directory path to identify its location if necessary. The *newfile* parameter is the new name for the file. This parameter may not include a drive or path. If a file already exists with the *newfile* name, an error will be displayed. Wildcard characters (* and ?) can be used in either the *oldfile* or *newfile* parameter.

UNIX Alternative

The UNIX *mv* command is used to rename files.

Determining File Type

Windows NT Explorer automatically attempts to identify a file type. The file type is displayed in the Type column of the **Contents of** pane as long as a detailed view is selected (**View** ➤ **Details**). Another method of displaying the file type is to look at the properties of the file by selecting **File** ➤ **Properties** ➤ **General**. You may also select the file with the right mouse button, then select **Properties** ➤ **General**.

UNIX Alternative

The UNIX *file* command identifies the file type.

FILE MANIPULATION COMMANDS

While UNIX allows the user to modify the contents of a file from the command line using utilities like *cat, vi,* and *paste,* Windows NT turns that type of file manipulation over to individual applications. For instance, text file data can be manipulated within the Notepad and WordPad applications by using **Edit** from the menu bar and selecting **Cut** to delete text, **Copy** to copy text, and **Paste** to insert the text that is residing in the buffer as a result of cut or copy.

There are several commands that may be entered at the command prompt that allow the manipulation of files, such as *attrib, copy,* and *sort. Attrib* permits the user to change file attributes. The *copy* command permits the user to combine files. The *sort* command sorts data. The *attrib* and *sort* commands are discussed here. The *copy* command was discussed in the previous section.

attrib Command

The *attrib* command allows the user either to display or change a file's attributes. A file may have the following attributes: archive, compressed, hidden, read-only, and system. The compressed attribute is only available on NTFS file systems and cannot be altered using this command. The syntax of the *attrib* command is

```
attrib [attributes] filename [/s]
```

To display the attributes associated with a particular file, neither the `attributes` parameter nor the /s switch would be entered. In other words, the syntax would be `attrib filename`. The `filename` parameter is the name of the file, with the drive designation and path included when necessary. The /s switch is used when setting or changing attributes and it instructs the command to change not only the files in the current directory but also the files in the subdirectories. As with most commands, the wildcard characters * and ? may be used to designate multiple files to affect.

Table A.15 identifies the acceptable values for the `attributes` parameter. More than one attribute can be set within a single command. Also, if a file has the system or the hidden attribute currently set, the system and hidden attributes must be removed before any other attribute to that file can be modified.

EXAMPLE OF THE *attrib* COMMAND

To add the archive attribute to all the files in the current directory, enter

```
attrib +a *.*
```

TABLE A.15.   Attribute Values

Attribute	Description
+a	Adds the archive attribute
-a	Removes the archive attribute
+h	Adds the hidden attribute
-h	Removes the hidden attribute
+r	Adds the read-only attribute
-r	Removes the read-only attribute
+s	Adds the system attribute
-s	Removes the system attribute

Windows NT

sort Command

The *sort* command arranges the data that is input into the command then outputs the result to either the screen, a file, or a device. The *sort* command accepts input from another command, from a file, or from data entered onto the terminal screen. The syntax of the command can be one of the following:

```
sort options < infilename > outfilename
command | sort options > outfilename
```

The `infilename` parameter is the name of the file containing the data to be sorted. The drive designation and directory path may be entered as necessary. The `outfilename` parameter is the name of the file containing the sorted data. Once again, the drive designation and the directory path may be entered as necessary. The `command` parameter is a command with output that is sorted using the *sort* command. Two options are available, as shown in Table A.16.

If the `command` or `infilename` parameters are omitted, then the *sort* command takes input as it is entered on the screen by the user until a `<Ctrl-Z> <Enter>` sequence is encountered. If the `outfilename` parameter is omitted, then the sorted data displays on the screen.

UNIX Alternatives

UNIX utilizes the following commands to manipulate the data in a file:

- *cut* – Extracts one or more columns of data from a file
- *join* – Combines the contents of two files based on a common field
- *paste* – Pastes corresponding lines from files into columnar format
- *sort* – Sorts data according to the options given
- *split* – Splits a file into multiple files

TABLE A.16. *sort* Options

Option	Description
/+n	Sorts the data based on the character in column n. The default sort is based on the character in column 1.
/r	Executes a reverse sort, either in reverse alphabetical order or in reverse numerical order

MISCELLANEOUS COMMANDS

This section discusses commands and procedures that enable users to set the date and time, log in as another user, enter a chat mode, and send messages.

Setting and Displaying Date and Time

On a standard Windows NT desktop the current time displays in the bottom right corner of the task bar. To display the current date, move the cursor until it points at the time display. The current date displays. To modify this date, double-click on the time and the Date/Time Properties window displays (Figure A.6). Within the **Date & Time** tab, the user can modify the current date as well as view a calendar for the month and year selected. In addition, the user can modify the time from this window. An alternate way of displaying the Date/Time Properties window is by selecting **Start ➤ Settings ➤ Control Panel ➤ Date/Time**.

To change the format of how a date or the time is displayed, select **Start ➤ Settings ➤ Control Panel ➤ Regional Settings**. In the Regional Settings

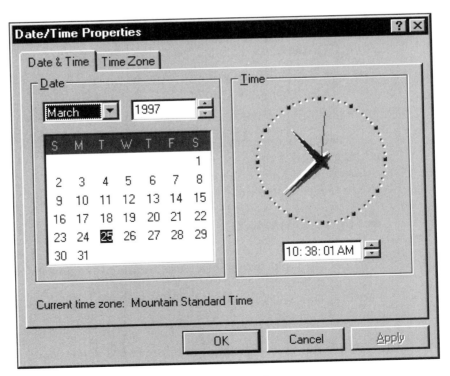

FIGURE A.6.   Date/Time Properties Window

Properties window, select either the **Date** or **Time** tab as appropriate. Within these tabs, you can, for example, change the time format to a twenty-four-hour clock or change the date to the format yy/mm/dd.

One other method of displaying the date and time is accessed by selecting **Start ➤ Programs ➤ Accessories ➤ Clock**. The VDM command line also offers options to assist in displaying and changing the date and time. These are discussed next.

date COMMAND

The *date* command allows the user either to display or to change the date. The syntax of this command is

```
date [mm-dd-yy]
```

If the *mm-dd-yy* parameter is omitted, the current system date is displayed. Entering *mm-dd-yy* sets the date to the value you enter. Acceptable values for the month or *mm* parameter are 1 through 12; for the day or *dd* parameter, 1 through 31. The year or *yy* parameter can be 80 through 99 or 1980 through 2099. If you prefer, the dashes (-) separating the month, day, and year can be replaced with either a period (.) or a slash (/).

time COMMAND

The *time* command allows the user either to display or to change the system time. The syntax for this command is

```
time [hrs:[min[:sec[.hun]]]][AP]
```

When no parameters are entered, the current system time is displayed. In addition, it gives the user an opportunity to change the time if necessary. If users do not wish to enter a new time, they just press <Enter>. If it is necessary to change the time, the syntax identified in Table A.17 is used.

net time COMMAND

The *net time* command allows the user to synchronize the time across the network between the current system and another domain (or computer). In addition, this command allows the user to display the time for any system on the network. The syntax for this command is

```
net time [\\computername | /domain[:domainname]] [/set]
```

When no parameters are given, the *net time* command displays the time from the system that is considered to be the time server. The */set* parameter

TABLE A.17.   *time* Options

Option	Description
hrs	Enter the hour in either regular or twenty-four-hour format. Acceptable values are 0 through 23.
min	Enter the minutes, ranging from 0 through 59
sec	Enter the seconds, ranging from 0 through 59
hun	Enter the hundredths of a second, ranging from 0 through 99
AP	Enter A for A.M. or P for P.M. This field is not necessary if the twenty-four-hour format is used.

is optional and is required only when you want to change the time. When /set is omitted, the time on the system named is displayed. When used, /set synchronizes the time on the current system with the time on the system named.

The *computername* or the /domain:*domainname* identifies the system for which to display the time or the system from which the current system's time is synchronized. The *domainname* portion of the /domain:*domainname* parameter is optional.

Windows NT Resource Kit Additional Programs

The Windows NT Resource Kit has several additional programs to help with managing the time on a Windows NT system.

- *timeserv* – This program is only available in the Windows NT Server Resource Kit and it enables the administrator to identify a primary and secondary time source, and then have all workstations and servers in the network synchronize their time with the main time source. This program is also accessed by selecting **Start ➤ Programs ➤ Resource Kit 4.0 ➤ Configuration ➤ Time Service for NT**.

- *timezone* – This program enables the administrator to update the daylight savings time information for a particular time zone in the Registry.

- *tzedit* – This is a program that can be used to create or edit time zone entries in the Date/Time Properties window. This program is also accessed by selecting **Start ➤ Programs ➤ Resource Kit 4.0 ➤ Configuration ➤ Time Zone Editor**.

Windows NT

UNIX Alternatives

UNIX utilizes the following commands to set and display date and time:

- *date* – Displays and sets the date and/or time for the current system
- *cal* – Displays a monthly or yearly calendar

Logging In as Another User

To log in as another user you must first access the Windows NT Security window by pressing `<Ctrl-Alt-Del>`. This window displays who you are currently logged in as, the name of the current domain, and the date and time you logged into the system. Select the **Logoff** button to log off as this user.

UNIX Alternatives

UNIX utilizes the following commands to log in as another user:

- *login* – Permits a user to log in as another user, provided that the user knows the other user's password
- *logname* – Displays the current login name based on the contents of the LOGNAME environment variable

Chat Mode

Windows NT provides the Chat application to allow users to conduct conversations with each other. A user accesses the Chat Application by selecting **Start** ➤ **Programs** ➤ **Accessories** ➤ **Chat**. To initiate a conversation, select **Conversation** ➤ **Dial** from the menu bar and the Select Computer window displays. Either enter the name of the computer of the person with whom you wish to chat or select one from the list.

When someone has sent you a chat message, the **Chat** button displays on the task bar. To respond to the message, click the **Chat** button, then select **Conversation** ➤ **Answer**.

While researching some problems that we were having with this utility, we were introduced to Microsoft's NetMeeting software, which enables you to communicate with people over the Internet or over an intranet. The version of the software that supports Windows NT has the Internet phone feature along with multiuser data conferencing. The multiuser data conferencing feature allows for the sharing of applications, an electronic whiteboard, a text-based chat facility, and binary file transfer. For more information on this software, access www.microsoft.com/netmeeting.

UNIX Alternatives

- *talk* – Allows users to chat with each other within a local system or across a network

- *write* – Allows users to communicate interactively

Sending Messages

It is important for a system administrator to be able to communicate electronically with the users of the system. While an e-mail system allows this, there are times that the message must be displayed immediately to the users, such as in the case of emergency system shutdowns. There are several ways within Windows NT to accomplish this.

To send a message to all users connected to any machine in a domain, select **Start** → **Programs** → **Administrative Tools** → **Server Manager**. The Server Manager window displays. First select the domain or domains to receive the message. From the menu bar select **Computer** → **Send Message**. Enter the message in the Send Message window and select **OK**. The Messenger Service (which is a default service) must be running in order to send messages.

net name COMMAND

The *net name* command adds, deletes, or displays names that are authorized to receive messages. These names are used only for messaging and must be unique from any other name existing throughout the network. Windows NT acknowledges three types of names: computer names, user names, and messaging names that are set up by the *net name* command. To execute the *net name* command, the Messenger Service must be running. The syntax of this command is

```
net name [name [/action]]
```

Executing the *net name* command without any parameters displays a list of all names that can accept messages on this computer. The *name* parameter is the unique name that is authorized to receive messages and can be fifteen (15)

characters in length. Acceptable values for the /action parameter are /*add* or /*delete,* which instructs the command to add or to delete the messaging name entered. The /action parameter is optional, with /*add* being the default.

Example of the net name Command

To add the messaging name *techsupport* to the computer, you can enter one of the following commands:

```
net name techsupport /add
```

or

```
net name techsupport
```

net send COMMAND

The *net send* command works in conjunction with the Messenger service and enables you to send messages on the network to users, computers, and messaging names. Only those users connected to the network and running the Messenger service will receive the message. The syntax of the command is

```
net send destination message
```

The message parameter contains the message that will be delivered. The message should be contained in quotes if it contains special characters, such as a slash. In addition, there can be up to 128 characters in the message.

The values for the destination parameter are described in Table A.18. The destination parameter is required and must contain one of the values listed.

TABLE A.18.   *net send* Options for the **destination** Parameter

Option	Qualifier	Description
*		Sends the message to all names in the user's group
/domain	:*domainname*	Sends the message to all names in either the current domain or in the domain or workgroup given by the :domainname parameter
name		Enter the user name, the computer name, or the messaging name of the recipient of the message for the variable *name*. Names that include spaces should be enclosed in quotes.
/users		Sends the message to all users connected to the server.

UNIX Alternative

The *wall* command allows the system administrator to broadcast a message to all users connected to the system.

NETWORKING COMMANDS

In this section we review some of the networking commands and procedures that are available on Windows NT. Since one of the keys to the coexistence of UNIX and Windows NT is TCP/IP, we have concentrated on those commands that are related to the TCP/IP networking services. In fact, to access many of these commands the TCP/IP service must be installed on the Windows NT system.

This section also discusses how to connect to a system via modem and how to determine and set the host name for the system. In addition we identify the Windows NT *net* commands. Each command is identified in this section, although the detailed description of the command may appear in another section of this appendix. When this is the case we reference the section that contains the detailed description of the *net* command.

Although many of the TCP/IP commands for Windows NT have the same name as the UNIX commands, please check the on-line help documentation for the respective system, since the options available for the commands may be slightly different based on the capabilities of each operating system.

For more information on networking, please refer to Chapters 12 and 13 as well as to Windows NT Help.

HyperTerminal

The HyperTerminal application is bundled with Windows NT and enables a user to dial out to another computer via a modem. It is accessed by selecting **Start → Programs → Accessories → HyperTerminal**. The following steps identify how to set up and connect to a remote location.

1. When accessing the HyperTerminal application, the Connect Description window displays to allow the user to define the connection.
2. Within the Connect Description window, enter the name of the connection you wish to make, such as Microsoft BBS, then select the **OK** button.
3. After **OK** is selected, the Connect To window displays. This window contains the fields **Country Code, Area Code, Phone #,** and **Connect Using**. These fields identify the number you wish to call using the modem installed on the system.

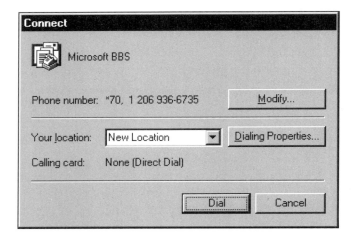

FIGURE A.7.   The Connect Window

4. After entering the phone number as well as modifying any other field, the Connect window displays (Figure A.7).

5. The Connect window allows the user to modify the phone number as well as change the configuration of the local modem, including the baud rate, data bits, and parity. These settings are accessed by selecting the **Modify** button.

6. By selecting the **Dialing Properties** button, users can define the properties about the location from which they are dialing, including whether there are any dialing prefixes to access an outside line or to turn off call waiting (Figure A.8).

7. By selecting the **Dial** button, the status of the modem displays (Figure A.9), such as Disconnected.

8. Selecting **Dial Now** initiates the connection process.

To transfer files between the systems, select **Transfer** from the menu bar then select **Send File** to send a file or **Receive File** to receive one. Within each of these options, the transfer protocol can be selected. To terminate a session, select the disconnect icon from the tool bar or select **Call ➤ Disconnect** from the menu bar.

UNIX Alternative

The *cu* command allows the user to connect to and communicate with a remote system. In addition, it permits the user to transmit and receive data.

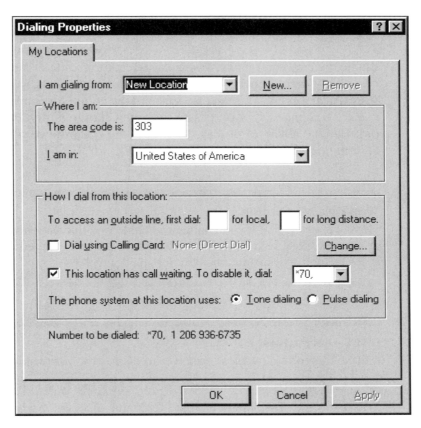

FIGURE A.8.   Dialing Properties Window

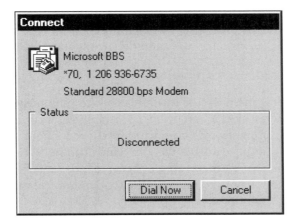

FIGURE A.9.   Displaying the Modem Status

Windows NT

Determining and Setting the Host Name

The host name is defined as the name of a device that is on the network. This can be the computer name. To display the computer name, select **Start ➤ Settings ➤ Control Panel ➤ Network**. Within the Network window, select the **Identification** tab. This tab displays both the computer name and the domain name. To change either of these, select the **Change** button. Windows NT also provides the ability to display the host name from the command prompt by entering *hostname*.

Windows NT Caution

Please be aware that if you change the name of a domain controller, you need to reinstall software on all other servers in the domain. We recommend that you avoid changing domain names on domain controllers.

UNIX Alternatives

UNIX offers the following alternatives to display the host name:

• *hostid* – Displays the ID number of the host machine in hexadecimal
• *hostname* – Displays or changes the name of a host machine

ftp Command

Using the *ftp* command enables a user to transfer files between systems. Both systems must have ftp installed and running. The syntax for this command is

```
ftp [options] [hostname]
```

where *hostname* is the name or IP address of the remote system with which you wish to communicate. When given, *ftp* establishes a connection with that system. Otherwise, *ftp* goes into command mode waiting for the user to enter a command. A list of the available *ftp* commands can be retrieved by entering *help* at this point. Due to the number of commands available, we do not discuss them in this book but recommend that you either use the help feature or refer to Windows NT Help.

Table A.19 lists the *ftp* options.

TABLE A.19.   *ftp* Options

Option	Qualifier	Description
-d		Turns on the debugging option, which displays all *ftp* commands that are passed between the systems
-g		Turns off filename "globbing," which means that wildcard characters are not expanded
-i		Turns off interactive prompting, which means that *ftp* automatically executes a given command for all filenames entered
-n		Does not allow automatic login when the initial connection is made. Instead, it requires the user to log on to the remote system.
-s	:*filename*	Enters as the *filename* qualifier the name of a file that contains *ftp* commands that are executed immediately on connection. Do not include any spaces in this parameter.
-v		Does not display responses from the remote system
-w	:*size*	Changes the size of the transfer buffer to *size*. The default is 4,096.

UNIX Alternative

UNIX also supports the *ftp* command to allow users to transfer files. Check your UNIX documentation for the parameters and settings necessary to run *ftp* on UNIX systems.

netstat Command

The *netstat* command displays protocol statistics and current TCP/IP connection information. The syntax for this command is

```
netstat [options]
```

Used without any options, the output includes the following:

- *Proto* – Displays the protocol used by the connection, such as TCP/IP
- *Local address* – Displays either the IP address or host name of the local system as well as the number of the port used by the connection. This is displayed in the format *name:port*. An asterisk displays in the **Port** field if the port hasn't been established yet.

- *Foreign address* – Displays either the IP address or the host name of the remote system as well as the port number. The display is in the format name:port.
- *State* – Displays the state of the TCP/IP connection. Examples of the contents of the **State** field are **CLOSED, ESTABLISHED,** and **LAST_ACK**.

The *netstat* options are listed in Table A.20.

U

UNIX Alternative

The UNIX *netstat* command displays configuration and status information about the network.

TABLE A.20. *netstat* Options

Option	Qualifier	Description
-a		Displays the status of all connections and listening ports
-e		Displays Ethernet statistics
interval		Displays statistics after each *interval,* where *interval* is the number of seconds between capturing statistics. To terminate the display, enter <Ctrl-C>. This option should be the last one on the command line.
-n		Displays addresses numerically. For example, displays the IP address instead of the host name.
-p	*protocol*	Displays the connections for the protocol given. Acceptable values for protocol are *tcp* and *udp*. If the *-s* option is also used, *icmp* or *ip* are also acceptable values.
-r		Displays the network routing tables
-s		Displays protocol statistics for *tcp, ucp, icmp,* and *ip*. To reduce the number of protocols displayed, use this option in conjunction with the *-p* option

ping Command

The *ping* command is used to test and verify network connections. It sends Internet Control Message Protocol (ICMP) packets of data to a remote computer and waits for a reply. By default, four of these packets are transmitted and validated when received. The syntax of this command is

```
ping [options] hostname(s)
```

where *hostname(s)* is the remote computers for which you wish to test the network connections. The *hostname* parameter may contain either the host name itself or the IP address.

The *ping* options are presented in Table A.21.

TABLE A.21. *ping* Options

Option	Qualifier	Description
-a		Converts numerical addresses to their corresponding host names
-f		Includes a flag in the data packet that instructs the gateways not to fragment the data
-i	*time*	Sets the **Time-to-live** field in the echo request packet to *time,* where *time* can be a value from 0 to 255
-j	*list*	Routes the data packets through up to nine host names contained in *list*. This option allows loose source routing, which means that intermediate gateways may separate consecutive hosts. This option cannot be used in conjunction with the *-k* option.
-k	*list*	Routes the data packets through up to nine host names contained in *list*. This option allows strict source routing, which means that intermediate gateways may not separate consecutive hosts. This option cannot be used in conjunction with the *-j* option.
-l	*length*	Sends a data stream containing the number of bytes specified by *length* to each host. The default value is 64 and the maximum value is 8,192.
-n	*count*	Sends *count* number of data packets. The default value is 4.
-r	*count*	Records the route of the outgoing and returning data packets for the number of hosts specified by *count*. The variable *count* can be a value from 1 to 9.
-t		Keeps sending data packets to the host names specified until the command is terminated by \<Ctrl-C\>
-v	*type*	Sets the **Type of Service** field to *type*
-w	*time*	Sets the timeout interval to *time* milliseconds

UNIX Alternative

The UNIX version of the *ping* command allows the user to test the performance of the network, especially when there are suspected problems.

rcp Command

The *rcp* command copies files between networked machines, including UNIX systems. Windows NT must be the system that initiates the command. Other systems must be running *rshd,* which is the remote shell daemon, as well as have the *rcp* utility installed. The syntax for this command is

```
rcp [options] host.user:srcfile(s) host.user:dest-file
```

where `host.user:srcfile(s)` is the name of the file to be copied to another system. This parameter breaks down as follows:

- `host` – This is the name of the source computer system. The host name is only required if the source system is different than the system from which the command is executed. It is also required in the event that a specific user name must be entered. The host can be either the host name or the IP address.
- `user` – This is the login name of the user whose files are being copied. The user name is required when the host is entered as an IP address. It must also be used to copy files that belong to another user.
- `srcfile` – This is the name of the file being copied. The `srcfile` parameter may contain the entire path if necessary to identify where the file is located, if it isn't in the current directory or in the user's login directory when `host.user` is used.

The parameter `host.user:dest-file` is the name of the destination file or directory to which the file is copied. If more that one `srcfile` is listed, `dest-file` must be a directory. The `host.user` portion identifies the remote system as well as the login name of the destination system. If the `host.user:dest-file` parameter is omitted, the local system is considered the default. Table A.22 presents the *rcp* options.

In order for the *rcp* command to be successful with UNIX, the *.rhosts* file must exist in the user's home directory on the remote computer. This file contains the host name of the local system as well as the user's name. It is also recommended that the host name of the local system be included in the remote system's */etc/hosts* or */etc/hosts.equiv* file.

TABLE A.22.   *rcp* Options

Option	Description
-a	Copies the files in ASCII mode. This is the default mode.
-b	Copies the files in binary mode
-h	Copies files that have the hidden attribute set. By default, files with the hidden attribute are not copied even if they are specifically requested.
-r	Copies the contents of a directory and its subdirectories. This is considered a recursive copy. Both the `srcfile` and the `dest-file` should be directories.

UNIX Alternative

UNIX has both the *rcp* command as well as the *rshd* daemon. This combination allows UNIX not only to initiate the *rcp* command, but also to be a remote system. Remember that Windows NT can only be the system that initiates the *rcp* command unless the Windows NT Server Resource Kit's Remote Shell service (*rshsvc.exe*) is installed. Also, the command syntax is different for *rcp* on UNIX and Windows NT systems.

rsh Command

When the rsh service is running, the *rsh* command permits a user to execute commands on a remote system. The syntax of the command is

```
rsh hostname [options] command
```

where `hostname` parameter is the name of the system on which you wish to run a command and `command` contains the command to be run on the remote system. The *rsh* options are listed in Table A.23.

When running the *rsh* command from a Windows NT Server, the primary domain controller (PDC) must be available to validate the name of the user currently logged in. Also, to access remote UNIX systems, a *.rhosts* file should exist in the user's home directory on the remote system. The *.rhosts* file contains both the host names and the login names of those computers and users who have access to this remote system.

TABLE A.23.   *rsh* Options

Option	Qualifier	Description
-l	*user*	Logs on to the remote computer using the name represented by *user*. When this option is not used, logs on as the user executing the *rsh* command.
-n		Redirects the input to NULL

UNIX Alternative

The UNIX *rsh* command performs the same functions, but the command has a slightly different syntax.

telnet

Using telnet enables a user to connect to and communicate with another system using its own protocol. To access telnet within Windows NT, select **Start** ➤ **Programs** ➤ **Accessories** ➤ **Telnet**. To connect to a remote system, execute the following steps:

1. From the menu bar, select **Connect**.
2. Select **Remote System**.
3. Within the Connect window, select or enter **Host Name, Port,** and **TermType** (terminal emulation type).
4. Select **Connect**.

From the **Terminal** menu, select **Preferences** to define default preferences such as cursor type, terminal emulation, and fonts.

With the VDM, you simply type `telnet` to launch the Telnet window. It is important to understand that this is a telnet client only. To accept telnet sessions from other systems, the Telnet Server must be installed, which is included with Windows NT Resource Kit 4.0.

UNIX Alternative

UNIX provides a *telnet* command that enables a user to connect to and communicate with a remote system.

Displaying Users Connected to a System

To display users connected to the current server, execute the following steps:

1. Select **Start** ➤ **Settings** ➤ **Control Panel** ➤ **Server**.
2. Select the **Users** button to display the User Sessions window.
3. The top half of the User Sessions window displays the users connected to the current server.
4. Select a particular user and the system displays the shared resources to which the user is connected in the bottom half of the window.

To access the User Sessions window for a particular server, execute the following.

1. Select **Start** ➤ **Programs** ➤ **Administrative Tools** ➤ **Server Manager**.
2. From the Server Manager window, select the desired computer.
3. From the menu bar, select **Computer** ➤ **Properties**.
4. At the bottom of the Properties window, select **Users**.

Disconnecting Users

To disconnect a particular user from a server, do the following.

1. Select **Start** ➤ **Programs** ➤ **Administrative Tools** ➤ **Server Manager**.
2. Select the desired computer.
3. From the menu bar, select **Computer** ➤ **Properties**.
4. At the bottom of the Properties window, select **Users**.
5. Select the user you wish to disconnect from the User Sessions window.
6. Select the **Disconnect** button.

To disconnect all users from the server, select the **Disconnect All** button.

Using the *net session* command provides these functions from the command prompt. This command is described in the following section, *net* Commands.

net Commands

Windows NT provides a series of commands that may be executed from the prompt or within batch files. These commands are referred to as *net* commands. While many of these procedures may be performed through the graphical interface, sometimes users prefer to use the command line interface instead.

All of the *net* commands are identified here with at least a brief description. When necessary, we reference the section of this appendix where a more detailed definition of the command is found.

Windows NT

TABLE A.24. Common *net* Command Options

Option	Description
/no	Automatically responds to any prompt that the *net* command issues with a no. An alternative format for this option is /*n*.
/yes	Automatically responds to any prompt that the *net* command issues with a yes. An alternative format for this option is /*y*.

There are some common options that are available for all *net* commands. These are described in Table A.24.

net accounts COMMAND

The *net accounts* command allows authorized users to update the user accounts database. In addition, this command facilitates modifications to the password and logon requirements for all users. For this command to execute properly, the Net Logon service must be running on the system containing the accounts you wish to change. For detailed information about this command, please refer to the System Management Commands section of this appendix.

net computer COMMAND

The *net computer* command enables the user to add or delete computers from the domain database. It can only be executed from an NT server. These modifications to the database are automatically forwarded to the primary domain controller. The syntax for this command is

```
net computer \\computername option
```

where *computername* is the name of the computer to add to or delete from the domain database. The *option* parameter can contain one of two options (Table A.25).

These functions can also be accomplished through the Server Manager window: **Start ➤ Programs ➤ Administrative Tools ➤ Server Manager**. Another alternative for accessing the Server Manager window is to select **Start ➤ Run** and enter *srvmgr \\hostname*, where the *hostname* parameter is optional.

TABLE A.25. *netcomputer* Options

Option	Description
/add	Add the computer name to the domain
/del	Deletes the computer name from the domain

Windows NT

Example of the net computer Command

To delete the computer *incy* from the domain, enter the following:

```
net computer \\incy /del
```

net config COMMAND

Executing the *net config* command without any parameters displays the services that are both configurable and running. With the appropriate parameters and options, this command enables a system administrator to change the settings permanently for the service while it is running.

Two variations of the *net config* command are *net config server* and *net config workstation*. Both of these commands are discussed here.

net config server Command

The *net config server* command either displays or modifies the settings of the Server service. Changes are made while the service is running and are permanent. The syntax of this command is

```
net config server [options]
```

Executing the *net config server* command without any options displays the current settings for the Server service. The *net config server* options are presented in Table A.26. An example of the output display is shown on the next page.

TABLE A.26.   *net config server* Options

Option	Qualifier	Description
/autodisconnect	:*time*	Sets the maximum amount of *time* that a user's login session can be idle before it is automatically disconnected. Acceptable values for *time* are -1 to 65535 minutes. The default is fifteen minutes. Setting *time* to -1 instructs the service to never disconnect an idle user.
/hidden	:{yes | no}	Determines whether the computer name of the server will display on the lists of servers or not depending on whether yes or no is entered as the qualifier. The default is no.
/srvcomment	:"*text*"	Defines a message that can be displayed in many Windows NT windows as well as with the *net view* command. The qualifier *text* can be forty-eight (48) characters long. Please note that the quotation marks are required.

```
Server Name                     \\INCY
Server Comment
Software version                Windows NT 4.0
Server is active on             NetBT_NDISLoop1  (204c4f4f5020)
NetBT_NDISLoop1 (204c4f4f5020)
Server hidden                   No
Maximum Logged On Users         Unlimited
Maximum open files
  per session                   2048
Idle session time (min)         15
The command completed successfully.
```

EXAMPLE OF THE *net config server* COMMAND

To disconnect users after 30 minutes of idle time, enter the following command:

```
net config server /autodisconnect:30
```

net config workstation Command

The *net config workstation* command either displays or modifies the settings of the Workstation service. Changes are made while the service is running and are permanent. The syntax of this command is

```
net config workstation [options]
```

Executing the *net config workstation* command without any options displays the current settings for the Workstation service on the local computer. Table A.27 presents the *net config workstation* options. An example of the output display appears on the next page.

TABLE A.27.   *net config workstation* Options

Option	Qualifier	Description
/charcount	*:bytes*	Sets the number of *bytes* of data to be collected prior to sending them to a communication device. Acceptable values for *bytes* are 0 to 65535. The default is 16 bytes.
/chartime	*:msec*	Sets the number of milliseconds (*msec*) for collecting data prior to sending it to a communications device. Acceptable values for *msec* are 0 to 65535000. The default is 250 msec.
/charwait	*:sec*	Specifies the number of seconds (*sec*) to wait for a communication device to become available. Acceptable values for *sec* are 0 to 65535. The default is 3600 sec.

```
Computer name                \\INCY
User name                    Administrator
Workstation active on        NetBT_NDISLoop1 (204C4F4F5020)
Software version             Windows NT 4.0
Workstation domain           BOOK
Logon domain                 BOOK
COM Open Timeout (sec)       3600
COM Send Count (byte)        16
COM Send Timeout (msec)      250
The command completed successfully.
```

If both the /charcount:bytes and /chartime:msec options are used, Windows NT sends data to a communication device based on whichever parameter is fulfilled first.

net continue COMMAND

The *net continue* command reactivates a service that has been suspended by the *net pause* command. Services are restarted without canceling a user's connection. For more detailed information regarding this command, please see the System Management Commands section of this appendix.

net file COMMAND

The ability to share files between computer systems and users is at the heart of a networked system. These shared files can be periodically left open and locked (prohibiting access). The *net file* command enables the user to display both the names of any open shared file and the number of locks on that file. In addition, this command can both close shared files and remove file locks. The syntax for the *net file* command is

```
net file [options]
```

When used without any options, the *net file* command displays a listing of all shared open files on the server as well as the number of locks of file. There are two possible options available, and they are presented in Table A.28.

TABLE A.28.   *net file* Options

Option	Description
id	Enter the ID number of the file, which is found in the first column of the net file listing that displays all open files
/close	Closes the file represented by *id;* must be used in conjunction with the *id* option

Windows NT

net group COMMAND

The *net group* command permits the addition, display, or modification of global groups on Windows NT Server domains. In addition, this command can only be run from systems that are Windows NT Server domains. Users who work together or who have the same requirements for system use are usually classified as members of the same group.

It is important to remember that the *net group* command deals with *global* groups. In essence, this means that the group can only contain users from the domain in which it was created, but this group can be assigned privileges from anywhere in the network as long as there is a trust relationship between the other domains. For more detailed information regarding this command, please refer to the System Management Commands section.

net help COMMAND

The *net help* command provides help for the Windows NT *net* commands. It displays a listing of all of the commands or detailed information on a requested command. This command is discussed in more detail in the previous Display Commands section.

net helpmsg COMMAND

The *net helpmsg* command displays an explanation for the requested Windows NT error message. This command is discussed in more detail in the previous Display Commands section.

net localgroup COMMAND

The *net localgroup* command enables the addition, deletion, or modification of local groups. It is important to remember that a local group can contain users from the domain in which the local group was created, as well as global users and global groups from other domains that have a trust relationship with the local group's domain. A difference between a local group and a global group is that a local group can only be assigned privileges in its own domain whereas a global group can be assigned privileges in trusted domains. For more detailed information regarding this command, please refer to the System Management Commands section.

net name COMMAND

The *net name* command adds, deletes, or displays names that are authorized to receive messages. These names are used only for messaging and must be unique from any other name existing throughout the network. Windows NT acknowledges three types of names: computer names, user names, and messaging names that are set up by the *net name* command. To execute the *net name* command, the Messenger service must be running. For more information regarding this command, please refer to the previous Miscellaneous Commands section.

net pause COMMAND

The *net pause* command is used to suspend a Windows NT service or resource. Pausing a service instead of stopping it enables current users to continue working while prohibiting new users from gaining access. System administrators sometimes pause a service prior to stopping it to warn users and give them an opportunity to finish what they are doing. To reactivate a service that has been paused, use the *net continue* command. For more detailed information regarding this command, please refer to the System Management Commands section.

net print COMMAND

The *net print* command displays information about both printer queues and printer jobs. In addition, print jobs can be deleted, put on hold, or reactivated. This command is described in more detail in the Print Commands section.

net send COMMAND

The *net send* command uses the Messenger service to send messages to users, computers, and messaging names set up on the network. This command is described in more detail in the previous Miscellaneous Commands section.

net session COMMAND

The *net session* command provides a listing of the current connections between the local computer and its clients. It also enables an administrator to disconnect sessions. When a user contacts a server from a client computer and logs on successfully, a session between the client and the server is established.

The syntax for this command is

```
net session [\\computername] [/delete]
```

The *net session* command can only be executed from a server. When running this command without any parameters, the display contains the following information regarding each session on the local computer: computer name, user name, client type, number of open files, and the idle time.

The \\computername parameter is the name of the computer for which you wish to list sessions. When running the *net session* command specifying

computername, the following information is displayed: user name, computer name, guest logon, client type, session time, idle time, and a listing of all the shared resources connected to the user. This listing includes the share name, the type of resource, and the number of open files.

Use the */delete* parameter to disconnect a session with *computername*. If the *computername* parameter is not used, the /delete parameter disconnects all sessions associated with the server.

net share COMMAND

The *net share* command displays, creates, or deletes shared resources. After a shared resource is created, it is available immediately as a shared resource and it remains shared until it is deleted. There are several syntax formats for this command:

```
net share sharename [options]
net share sharename=drive:path [options]
net share {sharename | drive:path } /delete
```

When the *net share* command is executed without any options or parameters, it displays the following information for all shared resources on the local system: the share name for the resource, the device name or path of the resource, and a comment field.

The *sharename* parameter contains the name that the network uses to refer to the shared resource. The command *net share sharename* displays the following information about the share: share name, path, remark, maximum number of users, and the users connected to the share.

When you need to establish a directory share, use the parameter *sharename=drive:path,* where *sharename* is the network name for the directory and *drive:path* is the absolute path of the directory being shared. Remember to enclose *drive:path* in quotes if there is a space in the directory name.

Table A.29 lists the *net share* options.

Examples of the net share Command

Enter the following to share the directory *c:\customers* with the name *contacts,* to limit the access to a maximum of fifteen users, and to include a comment:

```
net share contacts=c:\customers /user:15 /remark:
"Contact Information"
```

A task force has concluded its work so the resource that was shared is no longer needed. To remove the share for the task force, enter

```
net share taskforce /delete
```

TABLE A.29.   *net share* Options

Option	Description
/delete	Stops sharing the resource identified by either *sharename* or *drive:path*
/users:*number*	Sets the maximum number of users that can access a shared resource at the same time to *number*. This option cannot be used in conjunction with the */unlimited* option.
/unlimited	Allows an unlimited number of users to access a shared resource simultaneously. This option cannot be used in conjunction with the */users:number* option.
/remark:*"text"*	Defines a comment, *text,* to be associated with the shared resource. Be sure to surround the text of the comment with quotes.

net start COMMAND

The *net start* command either displays services that are currently running or starts a new service. For more detailed information about this command, please see the System Management Commands section.

net statistics COMMAND

The *net statistics* command displays network statistics information for either the Workstation service or the Server service. The syntax of the command is

```
net statistics [service]
```

Running the *net statistics* command without specifying a service displays a list of those services that are running and for which there are statistics. Acceptable values for the `service` parameter are the words *Workstation* and *Server* (not the actual name of the server or workstation). An alternative format for this command is `net stats service`.

Running `net statistics server` displays the following statistics for the local server:

- The number of sessions that were started, timed out, or terminated due to an error
- The number of kilobytes sent and received
- The average response time of the server
- The number of system errors, and permission and password violations
- The number of files and communication devices accessed

- The number of print jobs spooled
- The number of times that the memory buffer was exceeded

Executing *net statistics workstation* displays the following statistics for the local workstation:

- The number of bytes and server message blocks received and transmitted
- The number of read and write operations
- The number of read and write operations that failed
- The number of network errors
- The number of connections to shared resources that were successful and the number that failed
- The number of reconnections to shared resources
- The number of sessions started, failed, and disconnected
- The number of failed operations
- The total use count and the total failed use count

net stop COMMAND

The *net stop* command stops the Windows NT service named. This command is described in more detail in the System Management Commands section.

net time COMMAND

The *net time* command allows the user to synchronize the time across the network between the current system and another domain (or computer). In addition, this command allows the user to display the time for any system on the network. This command is described in more detail in the previous Miscellaneous Commands section.

net use COMMAND

The *net use* command either connects a computer to a shared resource or disconnects a computer from a shared resource. In addition, this command can be used to display all the shared resources currently connected to a computer. There are several syntax formats for this command:

```
net use [devicename] [\\computername\sharename[\volume]]
[password] [/user:[domainname\]username] [[/delete] |
[persistent:{yes | no}]]
net use devicename [/home[password]] [/delete:{yes | no}]
net use [persistent:{yes | no}]
```

Executing the *net use* command without any options displays all of the shared resources that are currently connected to the computer (Figure A.10).

Table A.30 defines the options that are valid for use in all syntax formats of the command.

The third syntax format of the *net use* command is *net use persistent:* {*yes* | *no*}. When *yes* is used, all connections that currently exist are reestablished at subsequent logins. When *no* is entered, any subsequent connections are not saved and therefore are not reestablished at subsequent logins.

Examples of the net use Command

To disconnect from the printer designated by LPT2:, enter

```
net use lpt2: /delete
```

To connect to the shared resource *g:\Sales\Contacts* as the user *bosco,* enter

```
net use g:\Sales\Contacts * /user:bosco
```

The asterisk (*) forces a password to be entered at a prompt before allowing the connection to occur.

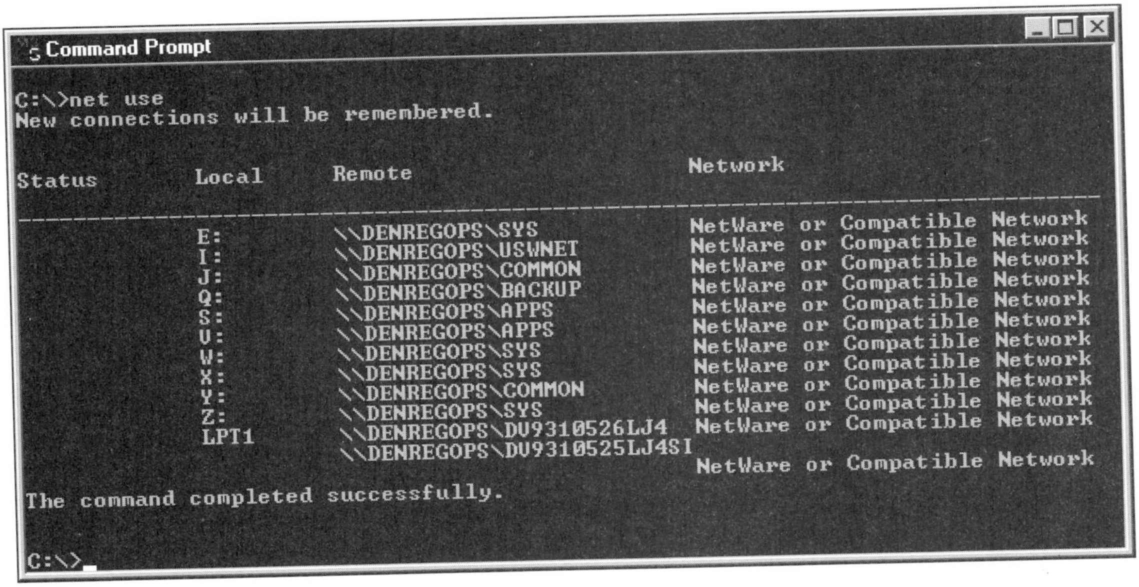

```
Command Prompt                                                    _ □ ×

C:\>net use
New connections will be remembered.


Status       Local      Remote                    Network
─────────────────────────────────────────────────────────────────────────
             E:         \\DENREGOPS\SYS            NetWare or Compatible Network
             I:         \\DENREGOPS\USWNET         NetWare or Compatible Network
             J:         \\DENREGOPS\COMMON         NetWare or Compatible Network
             Q:         \\DENREGOPS\BACKUP         NetWare or Compatible Network
             S:         \\DENREGOPS\APPS           NetWare or Compatible Network
             U:         \\DENREGOPS\APPS           NetWare or Compatible Network
             W:         \\DENREGOPS\SYS            NetWare or Compatible Network
             X:         \\DENREGOPS\SYS            NetWare or Compatible Network
             Y:         \\DENREGOPS\COMMON         NetWare or Compatible Network
             Z:         \\DENREGOPS\SYS            NetWare or Compatible Network
             LPT1       \\DENREGOPS\DU9310526LJ4   NetWare or Compatible Network
                        \\DENREGOPS\DU9310525LJ4SI
                                                   NetWare or Compatible Network
The command completed successfully.


C:\>
```

FIGURE A.10.   *net use* Information Window

Windows NT

TABLE A.30. *net use* Options

Option	Qualifier	Description
devicename		Enter the name of the device that will be connected or disconnected. Acceptable values for *devicename* are D: through Z: for disk drives, LPT1: through LPT3: for printers, or an asterisk (*), which is utilized to assign the next-available device designation. Executing the command *net use devicename* displays information about the connection made to the shared resource *devicename*.
computername *sharename*	*volume*	Enter the name of the computer that controls the shared resource for *computername*, which can be no longer than fifteen characters. Enter the network name for the shared resource for *sharename*. The *volume* qualifier contains the name of a volume on a NetWare server and can only be used if either the Client Services for NetWare or the Gateway Services for NetWare is installed.
password		Enter the password necessary to access the shared resource. Utilizing an asterisk (*) in place of the password forces a prompt for the password. Utilizing an asterisk is often preferred, since the password is not visible on the screen when it is entered in response to the prompt. This option can only be used after the *computername\sharename* option.
/user:*name*		Make the connection using the user, *name,* instead of the currently logged on user. A domain different than the current one can be specified as part of *name* (/user:*domainname\name*).
/delete		Disconnects the connection to the shared resource. It also removes it from the list of persistent connections. This option cannot be used in conjunction with the */persistent* option.
/persistent {yes | no}		Identifies whether a connection is persistent or not. Entering *yes* saves each connection made as a persistent connection so that the connections are reestablished at each login. Entering *no* stops saving the current connection and all future connections; only existing connections are reestablished at the next login. The current persistent setting remains the default until it is changed. Once a connection is considered persistent, it can only be removed from the recurring list by using the */delete* option.
/home		Connects users to their home directory

net user COMMAND

The *net user* command adds, modifies, and deletes user accounts. It also displays information about a specific user account or lists all user accounts on the system. Executing this command at a Windows NT server updates the user accounts (SAM) database on the PDC. That data is then replicated to the BDCs. For more detailed information regarding this command, please refer to the System Management Commands section.

net view COMMAND

The *net view* command displays the resources being shared on the computer. Depending on the parameters selected, a listing of computers in the current domain or a listing of all domains in the network displays. The syntax of this command can be one of the following:

```
net view \\computername
net view /domain:domainname
```

Entering the *net view* command without parameters produces a list of all computers in the network. Specifying a computer name for the *computer-name* parameter produces a listing of all resources shared with that computer. Using the /domain:*domainname* parameter and specifying a particular *domainname* produces a listing of all resources shared with the computer in the named domain. Omitting *domainname* produces a listing of all domains in the network.

A special format of this command displays all the servers available on a NetWare network. The syntax is

```
net view /network:nw
```

OWNERSHIP COMMANDS

The concepts of file ownership and file permissions are drastically different between Windows NT and UNIX. Chapters 6 through 8 discuss sharing resources, assigning user rights, assigning share permissions, and assigning file and directory permissions. This section highlights the steps necessary to access these types of functions.

Assigning User Rights

Rights define the tasks that users can perform. Default rights are assigned based on the groups to which a user belongs. Rarely is it necessary to change these default rights. The list on the next page defines how to display and change these rights.

1. Select **Start** → **Programs** → **Administrative Tools** → **User Manager for Domains**. Or select **Start** → **Run**, then enter *usrmgr* in the **Open** box.

2. From the User Manager window, select **Policies** → **User Rights**.

3. Selecting a right from the Rights dialog box displays the groups and users that have been granted those rights in the **Grant To** box.

4. To add a group or user to the **Grant To** list for a specific right, select the **Add** button.

5. The Add Users and Groups window displays. Specify here the users or groups you wish to add.

6. To remove a group or user from a particular right, select the group or user from the **Grant To** list, then select the **Remove** button.

Sharing a Directory

To create a directory share, you must be a member of the Administrators group or the Server Operators group. The following steps are based on using Windows NT Explorer, but the My Computer windows could be used as well.

1. From Windows NT Explorer, utilize the right mouse button to select the directory you wish to share.

2. Select **Sharing** from the menu that displays.

3. Within the **Sharing** tab of the Properties window, select **Shared As**.

4. Enter the **Share Name**, which can be a maximum of twelve characters.

5. Enter a **Comment** if desired.

6. Select a **User Limit** of either **Maximum Allowed** or a specified number of users.

7. If this particular directory is already shared and you wish to create an additional share, select the **New Share** button to enter the new share information.

Sharing Permissions

The next step in creating a directory share is to set the share permissions if desired. Share permissions are primarily used in FAT file systems since they are the main security vehicle available. While you can set share permissions for an NTFS file system, the file and directory permissions are much more inclusive.

The Access Through Share Permissions window is displayed by selecting the **Permissions** button from the **Sharing** tab of the directory's Properties window.

Execute the following to add permissions to a share.

1. Select the **Add** button to display the Add Users and Groups window.
2. Select the desired domain from the list in the **List Name From** box.
3. Select the **Show Users** button to display the accounts in the domain.
4. Select from the **Names** list the name for which permissions are to be added.
5. Select **Add** to add the name to the **Add Names** list.
6. From the **Type of Access** list, select the desired permission.
7. Select **OK**.

To modify share permissions, do the following.

1. From the Access Through Share Permissions window, select from the **Name** list the name with the permissions you wish to change.
2. From the **Type of Access** list, select the new permissions.
3. Select **OK**.

To remove permissions from a share, do the following.

1. From the Access Through Share Permissions window, select from the **Name** list the name of the user or group whose permissions you wish to remove.
2. Select **Remove**.
3. Select **OK**.

Directory and File Permissions

Directory and file permissions may only be set on NTFS file systems. Users can grant permissions for files and directories that they own. Administrators can manage file and directory permissions as well, although it may be necessary for them to "take ownership" of the file or directory in order to do so.

The procedures for assigning permissions to directories and files are the same with one exception. You can set/change the permissions for multiple files at one time, but you can assign permissions on only one directory at a time. Remember, to select multiple files from the Explorer window, hold down <Ctrl> and select the files with the left mouse button.

To access the Permissions window for either files or directories, execute the following.

Windows NT

1. From Windows NT Explorer, select the file or directory with the right mouse button.

2. Select **Properties** from the displayed menu.

3. Select the **Security** tab from the Properties window.

4. Select the **Permissions** button.

If you selected multiple files, you can access the Permissions window by selecting **File ➤ Properties ➤ Security ➤ Permissions**.

The Permissions window displays the names of the users and groups that have permission to access the file or directory as well as the type of access granted. Windows NT provides the following predefined standard permissions for directories: No Access, List, Read, Add, Add & Read, Change, and Full Control. The standard permissions for files are No Access, Read, Change, and Full Control. It is also possible to assign special permissions to both directories and files.

ADDING PERMISSIONS

Do the following to enable additional users and groups to gain access to a particular file or directory.

1. From the Permissions window, select the **Add** button.

2. From the Add Users and Groups window, select from the **List Names From** list the domain that contains the users or groups you wish add.

3. Select the **Show Users** button to display a list of the users and groups in the selected domain.

4. Double-click on the group or user you wish to add.

5. From the **Type of Access** list, select one of the standard permissions or **Special Directory Access** or **Special File Access**.

6. If you select either **Special Directory Access** or **Special File Access**, another window displays that allows you to create your own file access parameters based on the permissions selected.

7. Select **OK** to add the users and groups to the **Name** list.

8. For directories, you can select whether or not you want the permissions defined to replace those on all subdirectories and any existing files. If no explicit action is taken, the permissions on existing subdirectories and files will retain their original values. Any newly created directories inherit the permissions of their parent directory.

9. Select **OK**.

CHANGING PERMISSIONS

To change permissions, do the following.

1. From the Permissions window, select from the **Name** list the group or user whose permissions you wish to change.
2. From the **Type of Access** list, select the new permissions.
3. Select **OK**.

Taking Ownership of a File or Directory

When the Take Ownership permission is enabled, as in the case of a user or group that has the Full Control standard permission invoked, an administrator or authorized user can take ownership of a file or directory. To take ownership, execute the following.

1. From Windows NT Explorer, select the file or directory with the right mouse button.
2. Select **Properties** ➔ **Security** ➔ **Ownership**.
3. A dialog box displays appropriate to your permissions.
4. Select the **Take Ownership** button if displayed.

UNIX Alternatives

As stated earlier, the concept of UNIX file ownership and permissions is different than Windows NT. The following are the UNIX commands that relate to file ownership and permissions:

- *chgrp* – Changes the name of the group associated with a file or a directory
- *chmod* – Changes the permissions of a file or a directory
- *chown* – Changes the owner of a file or a directory

PRINT COMMANDS

Within Windows NT a printer can be set up as a local printer that is attached to the local system or set up as a network printer. This section provides an overview of the steps used to create a printer, send files to print, determine the status of a print job, manage printer operations, and define the properties of a printer.

Creating a Printer

In this section we define creating a printer as installing a printer so that it is accessible to both users and applications. Windows NT simplifies this process with the Add Printer Wizard. There are three ways of accessing this wizard.

1. From the My Computer icon, double-click the Printers folder.
2. Select **Start** ➤ **Settings** ➤ **Control Panel** then double-click the Printers folder.
3. Select **Start** ➤ **Settings** ➤ **Printers**.

Printers can be created in different ways: as a local printer and as a remote printer. To create a local printer, from the Add Printer Wizard do the following.

1. Select the **My Computer** button, then click **Next**.
2. Choose the port to which the printer is connected from the **Available Ports** list, then click **Next**.
3. Choose the manufacturer and printer from the lists provided, then click **Next**.
4. Before selecting **Next** in the previous step you may select the **Have Disk** button to install the printer driver at this point. If a printer driver is necessary, you have the opportunity to install it later as well.
5. Enter a name for the printer that your users will understand and recognize. In this window you may also designate whether this printer will be the default printer for the system. Select **Next**.
6. If the printer is to be shared over the network, select **Shared** and either accept the shared printer name displayed or enter one that you prefer. Remember, if this printer is to be available to MS-DOS and Windows 3.x users, be sure the name is consistent with their file-naming restrictions of eight characters before the period and three characters after the period (*filename.ext*).
7. If sharing the printer over the network, select the operating systems that will access the printer, then select **Next**.
8. Choose whether you wish to print a test page or not. Select **Yes** to print the test page; select **No** to bypass it.
9. Select **Finish** to complete the installation.
10. At this point, the Wizard may request that you insert the media that contains the print drivers for the operating systems that you selected. Just follow the instructions on the screen.

Creating a remote printer is often referred to as connecting to a network printer. This printer can either be new or already be installed elsewhere on the network. To accomplish this, access the Add Printer Wizard then follow these steps.

1. Select **Network Printer Server**, then select **Next**.
2. The Connect to Printer windows displays. Choose from the **Shared Printers** list the network printer to which you wish to connect, then select **OK**.
3. Select **Finish** to complete the installation.

UNIX Alternatives

To add printers to a UNIX system we recommend that you utilize the system administration utilities available on your UNIX variant (such as SMIT for AIX systems). Utilizing these utilities is the best way to configure any special enhancements that the manufacturer included.

As an alternative, *lpadmin* can be executed from the command line to define printers and devices.

Sending Files to Print

To ensure that a file is printed correctly, we recommended that you use the print facility provided by the application that created the file. From within a Windows-based application, select the Printer icon to send a file to the default printer. To select a specific printer, select **File ➤ Print** from the menu bar.

For file types that are recognized by Windows NT, a file can be dragged and dropped onto the icon for the desired printer. To accomplish this, select **Start ➤ Settings ➤ Printers** to display the icons for all available printers. Then, using either Windows NT Explorer or the My Computer windows, select a file, drag it to the appropriate printer icon in the Printers window, and release the mouse button (drop it).

lpr COMMAND

The *lpr* command enables a user to print to a computer that is running the LPD server. This command enables a user on a Windows NT system to print to a printer installed on a UNIX system. The syntax of this command is

```
lpr –Sserver –Pprinter [options] filename
```

where *filename* is the name of the file to be printed. All other parameters and options are described in Table A.31.

Windows NT

TABLE A.31.   *lpr* Options

Option	Qualifier	Description
-S	*server*	Enter the name of the computer where the printer is attached for the variable *server*. This is a required parameter.
-P	*printer*	Enter the name of the printer in place of the variable *printer*. This is a required parameter.
-C	*class*	Enter the *class* of the print jobs to list the contents of the banner page. This is an optional parameter.
-J	*jobname*	Enter the name of the print job in place of the variable *jobname*.
-O	*option*	The variable *option* describes the type of file to be printed. The default is a text file. An l (lowercase L) is entered to signify a binary file, such as a PostScript file. In this case the option would be *-Ol*.

print COMMAND

The *print* command enables the user to print a text file. Printing occurs in the background. The syntax for this command is

```
print [/d:device] filename(s)
```

Executing the *print* command without any options or parameters displays a list of the files currently in the print queue.

The first parameter, /d:*device*, is optional and designates the name of the print device. Acceptable values for *device* are LPT1, LPT2, and LPT3 for parallel ports; COM1, COM2, COM3, and COM4 for serial ports; and *servername\sharename* for a network printer where *servername* is the name of the server and *sharename* is the name of the shared printer resource. The default value for /d:*device* is PRN, which is the same as LPT1, the first parallel port.

The *filename(s)* parameter is optional and should include the name of the file or files to be printed. Multiple filenames are entered separated by a space. The *filename* parameter may include, if necessary, a drive designation and path name in the format of *drive:path\filename*.

As a note of interest, PostScript files are printed using the *copy* command not the *print* command. For example, *copy file.ps lpt1:* prints a PostScript file on lpt1.

UNIX Alternatives

The primary command that is used to send files to the printer is the *lp* command. Some variants of UNIX have their own print commands, such as *enq* in the AIX system. Some versions of UNIX (especially BSD variants) utilize the *lpr* command.

Determining Printer Status

To determine the status of files in the print queue, select **Start → Settings → Printers**, then double-click on the printer for which you want status information. A status window for that printer displays containing the following information for each print job currently printing or waiting to print:

- **Document name** – At a minimum, the name of the file being printed. It may also contain the name of the application that created the file.
- **Status** – If nothing displays in this field, the file is waiting to print. Otherwise, some status messages that may display include printing, spooling, paused, and deleting.
- **Owner** – The logon name of the owner of the document
- **Pages** – The number of pages in the document
- **Size** – The size of the document in bytes
- **Submitted** – The date and time that the print request was submitted
- **Port** – The port where the printer is connected

lpq COMMAND

The *lpq* command displays status information for a print queue on a host computer that is running the LPD server. The syntax of this command is

```
lpq -Sserver -Pprinter [-l]
```

The *lpq* options are presented in Table A.32.

net print COMMAND

The *net print* command displays information about both printer queues and printer jobs. In addition, print jobs can be deleted, put on hold, or reactivated. There are two formats for this command. The syntax of the first format is

```
net print \\computername\sharename
```

Windows NT

TABLE A.32.   *lpq* Options

Option	Qualifier	Description
-S	*server*	Enter the name of the computer with the printer attached for the qualifier *server*. This is a required parameter.
-P	*printer*	Enter the name of the *printer* to identify the queue for which you wish to display status information. This parameter is also required.
-l		Prepares a detailed status report

TABLE A.33.   *net print* Parameters

Parameter	Description
\\computername	Enter the name of the computer sharing the print queue
\sharename	Enter the name of the specific print queue. This parameter is optional. When it is not entered, the *net print \\computername* command displays all print queues on this computer.

This format of the command displays the following information for each print queue: the name of the print queue, the number of jobs in the queue, and the status of the queue. For each job in the queue, this command displays the user name, the job number, the size of the job, and the job status. Table A.33 defines the parameters.

The syntax for the second format of the *net print* command is

```
net print [\\computername] job# [options]
```

This format of the command displays information about a specific job number or enables you to control it. The \\computername parameter is optional and if used should contain the name of the computer sharing the printer queue. The job# parameter is required and should contain the number of the print job in question. This number is part of the print queue listing that can be displayed using the *net print \\computername* command. Table A.34 describes the options.

Examples of the net print Command

To display all print jobs in the marketing print queue on the computer *incy,* enter

```
net print \\incy\marketing
```

TABLE A.34.   *net print* Options

Option	Description
/delete	Deletes a print job (*job#*) from the printer queue
/hold	Puts a hold on a print job (*job#*) that is waiting in the print queue. This job does not print, but stays in the print queue until it is released or deleted.
/release	Releases the print job (*job#*) that has been put on hold

To delete print job no. 12 from the computer *incy,* enter

```
net print \\incy 12 /delete
```

UNIX Alternatives

Utilize the system administration utilities available on your UNIX variant to display the status of print jobs and print queues or use the *lpstat* command.

Managing Printer Operations

Once a document is in the print queue, several operations can be executed to control the printing of the document. These operations include pausing and resuming the printing of a printer or a document, restarting documents from the beginning, and canceling documents.

PAUSING AND RESUMING A PRINTER

Pausing a printer stops the printer from printing files, but the printer continues to accept files into the print queue. To pause a printer, do the following.

1. Select **Start** ➤ **Settings** ➤ **Printers**.
2. Double-click the icon for the desired printer.
3. From the selected printer's window, select **Printer** ➤ **Pause Printing**.
4. The title bar of the window will display Paused.

To resume printing, select **Printer** ➤ **Pause Printing** from the Printer window.

PAUSING AND RESUMING THE PRINTING OF A DOCUMENT

To put the printing of a particular document on hold, execute the following.

1. Select the desired document from the Printer window.
2. From the menu bar, select **Document ➤ Pause**.
3. The status column for the document displays Paused.

Do the following to resume printing of the document.

1. Select the paused document from the Printer window.
2. From the menu bar, select **Document ➤ Resume**.

RESTARTING AND CANCELING A DOCUMENT

To restart the printing of a document from the beginning, do the following.

1. Select the document to be restarted from the Printer window.
2. From the menu bar, select **Document ➤ Restart**.

Do the following to remove a document from the print queue (i.e., cancel it).

1. Select the document to be canceled from the Printer window.
2. From the menu bar, select **Document ➤ Cancel**.

UNIX Alternatives

The cleanest way to control spooled print jobs is through the use of the system administrative tool available with your UNIX variant. Alternately, utilize these command line utilities:

- *accept* – Accepts print requests into the spooler
- *cancel* – Cancels or removes a file from the print queue
- *disable* – Disables the identified printer. Files can still go into the spooler.
- *enable* – Enables the specified printer to begin printing files
- *reject* – Does not accept print requests for the specified spooler

Defining Printer Properties

To define or modify the default behavior of a printer, the printer properties must be modified. There are two ways to access the printer properties. First, select **Start** ➤ **Settings** ➤ **Printers**. Then using the right mouse button, select the desired printer icon. From the menu that displays, select **Properties**. The second method is to double click on the desired printer icon to display the Printer window, then select **Printer** ➤ **Properties** from the menu bar.

The Properties window displays with six tabs. A brief description of each tab and its contents follows.

- **General** – Contains comment and printer location information. Also enables you to configure a separator page, configure a print processor, or print a test page.
- **Ports** – Enables the addition, deletion, and configuration of ports. This tab can be used to create a printer pool that consists of more than one printer device of the same type connected to the same print server.
- **Scheduling** – Defines the times that the printer is available for printing. This tab also has options to configure the spooler operation, such as whether to start the printing of the document before it is completely spooled.
- **Sharing** – Defines whether a printer is shared over the network
- **Security** – Defines or displays parameters for the following three security areas: permissions, auditing, and ownership
- **Device settings** – Displays a hierarchical list of the printer's hardware features and allows changes to the settings of these features based on the content of the printer driver

LPD Service

The LPD Service (lpdsvc), referenced as the TCP/IP Print Service within Windows NT, enables Windows NT to receive print jobs from remote clients such as UNIX systems. This service is a part of the Windows NT Server Resource Kit and is installed by selecting **Start** ➤ **Settings** ➤ **Control Panel** ➤ **Network** ➤ **Services**. Within the Services window, select **Add**. From the **Network Service** list, select **Microsoft TCP/IP Printing**, then select **OK**. At this point follow the instructions on the screen, which include inserting the Windows NT Server Resource Kit CD-ROM so that additional files may be installed. Once the files have been installed, you must restart the computer to utilize the newly installed files and programs.

To start the LPD Service, select **Start** ➤ **Settings** ➤ **Control Panel** ➤ **Services**. From the list, select **TCP/IP Print Server**, then click **Start**. Once this service is available, the administrator can create a TCP/IP printer on this Windows NT Server that can accept print jobs from UNIX systems.

Windows NT

SEARCH COMMANDS

Windows NT provides the ability to search for files and folders as well as to search files for a specific string of text. This search facility can be accessed in three ways:

1. By selecting **Start** ➤ **Find** ➤ **File or Folders**

2. From within Windows NT Explorer by selecting **Tools** ➤ **Find** ➤ **Files or Folders**

3. From within the My Computer window, by first selecting a folder, then selecting **File** ➤ **Find**

Accessing the Find utility by any of these methods displays the Find: All Files window. This window consists of three tabs: **Name & Location**, **Date Modified**, and **Advanced**.

Name & Location Tab

The **Name & Location** tab of the Find: All Files window (Figure A.11) enables a user to specify the name of a file to locate in the **Named** box. The filename can contain the wildcard characters * and ?. In the **Look in:** box, the user can identify the directory in which to begin the search. The **Browse** button provides a directory tree to assist the user in selecting the folder for the starting point of the search.

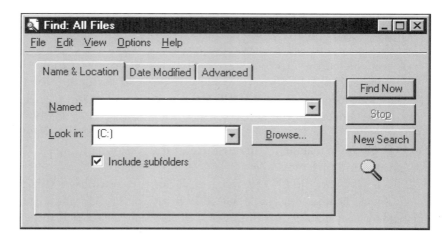

FIGURE A.11.   Finding Files—Name & Location Tab

By default, the *findstr* command displays the lines of the files that match the specified string. This display may vary based on the options selected. A list of the options is described in Table A.37.

EXAMPLES OF THE *findstr* COMMAND

Assume that a user was looking for a particular e-mail message that had a subject of "Mary's Retirement Party." To search all of the saved e-mail messages, even those in subdirectories, and display the filename that contains the message, enter

```
findstr /s /i /m /c:"Mary's Retirement Party" *.*
```

To display the line numbers of the lines that contain the acronym GOSIP in the *govt.txt* file, enter

```
findstr /n GOSIP govt.txt
```

UNIX Alternatives

UNIX provides the following search commands:

- *find* – Locates files and directories with specified search criteria
- *grep, egrep,* and *fgrep* – Three command variations that search the contents of text files
- *strings* – Searches binary and object files for a specified pattern.

SYSTEM MANAGEMENT COMMANDS

System management commands are those commands that assist the system administrator while keeping the system running smoothly on a day-to-day basis. This section includes such topics as disk management; process management; password, user, and group management; and service management.

Disk Management

System administrators must keep track of how disks are being utilized and how they are performing so that they can make informed decisions regarding the maintenance of current disks as well as the need for additional disks. Windows NT provides both graphical and command line functions that assist in these tasks.

DISK ADMINISTRATOR

Windows NT provides the graphical utility Disk Administrator to assist in the management of the various disks installed on the system. Some of the tasks performed by the Disk Administrator include creating and deleting partitions and volume sets, formatting and labeling volumes, providing status information, and making and changing drive letter designations. This section discusses only the status information that is available.

To access the Disk Administrator, select **Start** ➤ **Programs** ➤ **Administrative Tools** ➤ **Disk Administrator**. The Disk Administrator window displays, showing disk configuration information for each disk currently installed on the system. This configuration information is displayed graphically and includes the size, file system type, and drive letter designation for each partition. CD-ROM drives are also displayed.

By selecting **View** ➤ **Volumes** from the menu bar, more information is provided. The volumes display is in columnar format and contains the following information:

- Drive letter with an icon depicting a hard disk or a CD-ROM
- Name of the volume
- Total capacity of the volume
- Amount of free space available
- Percentage of free space available
- File system type such as FAT or NTFS
- Fault tolerance of the volume
- Volume type
- Fault tolerance overhead
- Status

While in either the volumes view or the disk configuration view, select a particular volume, then select **Tools** ➤ **Properties** from the menu bar to provide additional information as well as some tools. Select the **Tools** tab to access the Error-checking, Backup, and Defragmentation tools.

chkdsk COMMAND

The *chkdsk* command can be used by members of the Administrators group and provides the user with a status of the disk as well as a list of errors. Errors are corrected by invoking the options selected by the user. In order for the errors to be displayed and corrected accurately, the drive being checked should be locked. This means that no files are open and in use. If the drive is not locked, the *chkdsk* command offers the user the option of automatically exe-

TABLE A.38.   *chkdsk* Options

Option	Description
/f	Fixes the errors found on the disk. The disk must be locked for files to be fixed; otherwise, the disk is checked at the next reboot.
/v	Displays the name of each file as it is checked
/r	Identifies any bad sectors, then tries to recover any information that is readable

cuting the command at the next reboot. In this instance, errors are automatically corrected.

The syntax for this command is

```
chkdsk [drive:][[path\]filename] [options]
```

Running *chkdsk* without any parameters or options displays a status report for the current disk drive. The `drive:` parameter is the letter designation of the drive you want checked. As an alternative on volumes that are formatted with the FAT file system, the `path\filename` parameter can be entered to designate one or more files that need to be checked for fragmentation. Wildcard characters can be utilized to specify multiple files.

The *chkdsk* options are presented in Table A.38.

diskperf COMMAND

The *diskperf* command starts and stops the system disk performance counters. It works in conjunction with the Performance Monitor (**Start ➤ Programs ➤ Administrative Tools ➤ Performance Monitor**). The syntax for this command is

```
diskperf [-y[e] | -n] [\\computername]
```

When the *diskperf* command is executed without any parameters, it displays whether the disk performance counters have been activated. The other options are described in Table A.39.

UNIX Alternatives

The following UNIX commands concern disk management:

- *df* – Displays the amount of free disk space
- *du* – Displays disk utilization information
- */etc/fsck* – Provides a file system check and repair on all or selected file systems

TABLE A.39.   *diskperf* Options

Option	Qualifier	Description
-y	e	Flags the disk performance counters to start the next time the system is rebooted. These counters continue to collect data until they are turned off using the *-n* option. Use the *e* qualifier only to measure the performance of the drives in a striped disk set. To revert to the standard performance measurements, re-execute the command with just the *-y* option.
-n		Stops gathering the disk performance information after the next reboot
computername		Enter the name of the computer on which to start or stop the disk performance counters. When the *-y* or *-n* options are omitted, this option displays whether the performance counters have been activated for the specified computer.

Process Management

This section describes tasks related to the running of processes and applications on the local system. Included in this discussion are tasks such as scheduling programs to run at specified times, terminating applications and processes, displaying active applications and processes, and monitoring the performance of processes and the local system.

at COMMAND

The *at* command works in conjunction with the Schedule service and enables commands and programs to be executed in the background at a predefined date and time. (The Schedule service is started by selecting **Start** ➤ **Settings** ➤ **Control Panel** ➤ **Services**. In the Services window, scroll down the list of services until **Schedule** displays, select it then select the **Start** button.) In addition, the user executing the *at* command should be a member of the Administrators group on the local system. The two syntax formats for the *at* command are

```
at [\\computername] [[id] [/delete [/yes]]]
at [\\computername] time [/interactive] [/every:date |
/next:date] "command"
```

When the *at* command is executed without any options, it performs two functions. First it displays a list of the scheduled commands, consisting of the status of the command, the identification number, the day it is scheduled to run, the time that it is scheduled to run, and the actual command. Second, running the *at* command without any options synchronizes the scheduler with the system clock. This is advantageous to ensure that the commands are executed at the proper time, especially after the system clock has been adjusted. Both required and optional options are described in Table A.40.

Since the *at* command runs in the background, it is a good idea to redirect the results of the command to a file using the redirection symbol (>).

Examples of the at Command

To display the network statistics for the server every Monday, Wednesday, and Friday at 10:00 A.M., enter the following:

```
at 10:00 /every:M,W,F "net statistics server > srvrstat"
```

The *srvrstat* file will be placed in the system's root directory.

To delete a scheduled job, first determine the ID number by running the *at* command without any options. If the ID number is 3, enter the following command:

```
at 3 /delete
```

COMMAND SCHEDULER

The Command Scheduler is an application that is part of the Windows NT Resource Kit 4.0. It provides the user a graphically based method of scheduling commands or programs to be run at a designated date and time. To access the Command Scheduler, select **Start → Programs → Resource Kit 4.0 → Configuration → Command Scheduler**. Another alternative is to run *winat* at the command line or command prompt. Both the Schedule and Workstation services must be running to access this application.

The WinAt window displays for the local system and lists all commands that are scheduled to be run. To view the programs scheduled to run on a remote computer, select **File → New** from the menu bar, then enter the name of the remote computer.

To add a program to the schedule, select **Edit → Add** from the menu bar. The Add Command window displays, giving the user the opportunity to enter not only the command but specifics as to when the command should run. The information captured is similar to the parameters for the *at* command discussed earlier.

TABLE A.40.   *at* Options

Option	Description
computername	Enter the name of the remote system on which to schedule the command. The default (without the parameter) is to schedule the command on the local system.
id	Enter the ID number of the scheduled command. The ID number is displayed when the *at* command is run without any parameters. To display information specific to this particular job number, enter the *at id* command.
/delete	Deletes the scheduled command represented by *id* or deletes all scheduled commands on the computer. Use the */yes* option in conjunction with the */delete* option to respond *yes* automatically to any prompts that the */delete* option provides.
time	Enter the time when the command is to run using the format of hours:minutes where acceptable values are 00:00 through 23:59. The hours must be in twenty-four-hour format.
/interactive	Permits the scheduled command to interact with a logged on user's desktop while the command is running. Be sure to use this option only when you are sure that a user will be logged on. It is not a good idea to use this option when scheduling off-hour backups.
/every:*date*	Executes the scheduled command on every specified day of the week (M, T, W, Th, F, S, Su) or specified days of the month (1 through 31). Make sure that you separate multiple date entries with commas. The default is the current date.
/next:*date*	Executes the scheduled command on the next-specified day of the week (M, T, W, Th, F, S, Su) or next-specified days of the month (1 through 31). Make sure that you separate multiple date entries with commas. The default is the current date.
"*command*"	Enter the command to be run at the scheduled day and time, where *command* is a Windows NT command, a program (files with extensions *.exe* or *.com*), or a batch program (files with extensions *.bat* or *.cmd*). For all types of commands except those with a *.exe* extension, enter *cmd /c* in front of the command. Use only absolute path names when path names are required. When specifying remote computers, use the *computername\sharename* designation rather than the assigned remote drive letter. It is strongly recommended that you enclose the command in quotes.

UNIX Alternatives

UNIX can schedule commands and programs to be run at predetermined times by using either the *at* command or the *crontab* command.

TASK MANAGER

The Task Manager enables a user to display and control the processes and applications running on the local system. In addition, it provides the user a way to monitor the performance of the system.

To access the Task Manager, use the right mouse button to click the task bar. The task bar displays at the bottom of the screen by default and displays the **Start** button as well as a list of the open windows on the desktop.

There are three tabs within the Task Manager: **Applications**, **Processes**, and **Performance**. Each of these are discussed briefly here.

Applications Tab

The **Applications** tab displays the name and status of those applications that are currently running on the local computer. Three functions are available within this tab: ending a task, switching to a task, and starting a new task.

Ending a task is the same as terminating an application. To end a task, do the following.

1. Select the application you wish to terminate.
2. Click on the **End Task** button.

An alternative to selecting a task from the task bar is to utilize the Task Manager to switch to another task. Do the following to switch to another task.

1. Select the application to which you wish to switch.
2. Click on the **Switch To** button.

An alternative to starting a task from the desktop or from the **Start** menu is to utilize the Task Manager to start a new program. To start a new task, execute the following:

1. Select the **New Task** button.
2. Enter the name of the new task or select **Browse** and browse through the available programs, then select one.

Windows NT

Processes Tab

The **Processes** tab displays information about the processes currently running on the local system. The default information that displays for each process includes the name of the program, the process ID number, the CPU and CPU time, and the memory usage. To display additional or different information, select **View ➤ Select Columns** from the menu bar.

To end or kill a process, first select the process, then click the **End Process** button at the bottom of the window. As an alternative, select the process using the right mouse button, then select **End Process** from the menu that displays.

To change the priority for a process, select the process using the right mouse button. From the menu that displays, select **Set Priority**, then choose one of the following priorities: Realtime, High, Normal, or Low.

UNIX Alternatives

UNIX commands related to process management include

- *kill* – Terminates a process
- *nice* – Changes the priority of a command
- *ps* – Displays a list of all active processes

Performance Tab

The **Performance** tab allows the user to monitor the performance of the local computer. Information, displayed numerically or graphically, includes CPU usage and history; memory usage and history; the total number of threads, handles and processes; and physical and kernel memory information.

Windows NT also provides a configurable performance monitor that can be accessed by selecting **Start ➤ Programs ➤ Administrative Tools ➤ Performance Monitor**.

UNIX Alternative

Depending on the UNIX variant, several system performance utilities are available, including *sar* and *top*.

Password and User Management

User and password management on any system entails many facets. Windows NT is no exception. Perhaps because it is a networking system, user management becomes even more involved. This section highlights just some aspects of user management such as setting and changing passwords and adding, changing, displaying, and deleting users.

If you are a member of either the Administrators, the Domain Admins, or the Account Operators group, functions for user account management can be accessed by selecting **Start** ➤ **Programs** ➤ **Administrative Tools** ➤ **User Manager for Domains**. As an alternative, you can select **Start** ➤ **Run**, then enter

```
usrmgr [\\computername | domainname]
```

where *\\computername* is the name of a specific remote computer and *domainname* is the name of a specific domain where the user either is or will be located. Running the *usrmgr* command without any parameters displays a list of the users in the same domain as the user that is executing the command. This is the same default as accessing **User Manager for Domains** from the **Administrative Tools** menu.

To display users in another domain, select **User** ➤ **Select Domain** from the User Manager window and enter either the name of the desired domain or the name of the desired computer.

ADDING USER ACCOUNTS

Selecting **User Manager for Domains** from the **Administrative Tools** menu displays the User Manager window. The user's domain is displayed in the title bar of the window. To add a new user account, do the following.

1. From the menu bar, select **User** ➤ **New User**.

2. The New User window displays. In this window enter the logon name for the user, which can be a maximum of twenty characters, including both upper- and lowercase letters, numbers, and punctuation. Invalid characters are = + [ ] / \ < > ; : ' " * ?. If you are operating in an integrated environment you may wish to establish a logon name that is acceptable to all systems on the network. For example, UNIX, DOS, and Windows 3.1 systems restrict the length of the login name to eight characters; therefore, in a mixed environment you may want to keep all logins to eight characters.

3. Enter a full name for the user as well as a description. The **Description** field is optional.

4. Set up an initial password for the user if desired.

5. Select the appropriate password criteria: user must change the password at next logon (default), user cannot change the password, or password never expires.

6. Select the **Account Disabled** box to disable the account. You may want to select this on initial setup if you are creating an account to be used as a template account to set up other users or if you are setting up the account a period of time before the user actually needs it.

At the bottom of the screen there are six icon boxes that further define the properties associated with this user account. A brief description of each of these selections follows.

- **Groups** – Assigns the groups to which the user belongs
- **Profile** – Assigns user profile information such as the path of the user's profile, the name of the logon script if used, and the paths for the local and network home directories
- **Hours** – Defines the days and times that the user can access the network
- **Logon To** – Defines the computers that the user can utilize to log on to the network
- **Account** – Defines when the account expires (if ever) and whether the account is local or global
- **Dialin** – Defines whether the user has permission to connect to the network via dial-in

After you have completed all of the desired user configuration information, select the **Add** button in the New User window to add the user to the user account database. Another way to add user accounts is to use the Administrative Wizard: **Start ➤ Programs ➤ Administrative Tools ➤ Administrative Wizards ➤ Add User Accounts**.

MODIFYING USER ACCOUNTS

You may access any of the user account information in two ways. From the User Manager window, double-click on the user you wish to modify. As an alternative, select the user, then select **User ➤ Properties** from the menu bar.

You may make the same changes to multiple users in the following way. From the User Manager window, hold down `<Ctrl>` and select all of the users you wish to modify, then select **User ➤ Properties** from the menu bar.

DELETING USER ACCOUNTS

There are three alternatives for disabling access to a particular user account: locking it out, disabling it, and deleting it.

1. Account lockout occurs after a specified number of bad logon attempts. Lockout parameters are set for a particular user by selecting **Policies** → **Account** from the User Manager window. An administrator can unlock an account from the User Properties window, which is accessed by double-clicking on the user from the User Manager window.

2. To disable an account, double-click on the user in the User Manager window. Select the **Account disabled** button in the User Properties window.

3. To delete an account permanently, select the user in the User Manager window. From the menu bar, select **User** → **Delete**.

net user COMMAND

The *net user* command allows an administrator to perform many of the previously discussed user management tasks from the command line or command prompt. This command adds, modifies, and deletes user accounts. It also displays information about a specific user account or lists all user accounts on the system. Executing this command at a Windows NT server updates the user accounts database on the PDC. That data is then replicated to the BDCs.

There are three syntax formats for this command:

```
net user [username [password]] [options] [/domain]
net user username password /add [options] [/domain]
net user username [/delete] [/domain]
```

Using the *net user* command without any parameters or options displays a listing of the user accounts set up for the current system. Using the *net user* command with only the `username` parameter displays information specific to that user account. The display contains information such as the expiration date of the account, password-related information like expiration dates, the name of the user's logon script and profile, the user's home directory, the date of the last login, and the name of the user's local and global groups. Tables A.41 and A.42 define both the parameters and the options available for these commands.

Examples of the net user Command

The syntax

```
net user emilyg * /add /times:M-F,08:00-18:00
/workstations:incy,sales,techsupp,mktg
```

sets up a user named *emilyg* prompting for a password. This user is permitted to log in Monday through Friday from 8:00 A.M. until 6:00 P.M. from the workstations named *incy, sales, techsupp,* and *mktg.*

TABLE A.41. *net user* **Parameters**

Option	Description
username	Enter the name of the user account to be added, changed, deleted, or displayed. A *username* can contain a maximum of twenty characters.
password	Enter the password for the user account. This parameter is used either to set up a password for a new account or to change the password for an existing account. The password can consist of a maximum of fourteen characters and must conform to the password specifications defined by the *net accounts* command. Entering an asterisk instead of the actual password forces a prompt for the password. In this instance, the password is not displayed on the screen while it is entered.
/domain	Specifies that the command be executed on the PDC of the current system's domain. This parameter should be used only from Windows NT workstations that are members of a Windows NT server domain.
/add	Adds the *username* to the user account database. The *password* parameter is required with this function.
/delete	Deletes the *username* from the user account database.

To delete the user *bosco* from the system, enter

```
net user bosco /delete
```

If you would like to deactivate *bosco* instead of deleting him altogether, enter

```
net user bosco /active:no
```

UNIX Alternatives

UNIX does provide some command line commands such as *adduser, usermod,* and *userdel* that enable an administrator to add, change, and delete users, but these tend to differ between UNIX variants. A system administrator's best bet is to utilize the system administrative menus and tools provided with your specific UNIX variant, such as SMIT in AIX and SAM in HP-UX.

TABLE A.42.   *net user* Options

Option	Description
/active:{yes | no}	Entering *yes* activates the user account. Entering *no* disables the user account, prohibiting the user from accessing the server. The default is *yes*.
/comment:"*text*"	Enter a comment up to a maximum of forty-eight characters for *text*.
/countrycode:*nnn*	Enter the numeric value for the operating system country code for *nnn* to display the user's help and error messages in a different language. Using 0 signifies the default country code.
/expires:*date*	Enter the date that the account will expire. Acceptable values for *date* are *never*, which specifies that the account will never expire, or a date in the default format defined by the country code. Examples of date formats are mm/dd/yy, dd,mm,yyyy, mmm,dd,yy. The month can be either numeric or alphabetic. The year can be two or four digits. Either slashes or commas can be used to separate the components of the date.
/fullname:"*name*"	Enter the user's full name for the variable *name*.
/homedir:*path*	Enter the path for the user's home directory for the variable *path*. The path specified must already exist.
/homedirreq:{yes | no}	Enter *yes* to specify that a home directory is required. Enter *no* if it is not.
/passwordchg:{yes | no}	Enter *yes* to identify whether a user can change his password. Enter *no* if a user cannot. The default is *yes*.
/passwordreq:{yes | no}	Enter *yes* to require a password for a user. Enter *no* if a password is not required. The default is *yes*.
/profilepath:*path*	Enter for *path* the path name for the user's logon profile.
/scriptpath:*path*	Enter for *path* the path name of the user's logon script.
/times:*time*	Enter the time of day that a user can log on to the system. Acceptable values for *time* include *all* (a user can always log on), a space or blank (a user can never log on), and days and times in the format *day,hour*. Days are the days of the week either spelled out or abbreviated as M, T, W, Th, F, Sa, and Su. Hours can be either in twelve-hour or twenty-four-hour format. When the twelve-hour format is used, use one of the following to designate A.M. or P.M.: am, pm, a.m., p.m. Days and times are separated with commas. If multiple days and times are listed, separate them with semicolons. There should be no spaces. An example of the different formats is */times:M,8am-5pm ,12pm-8pm;W,13:00-17:00*.
/usercomment:"*text*"	Enter a comment for the variable *text*.
/workstations:*name(s)*	Substitutes for *name* a list of the workstations from which a user can access the network. A maximum of eight workstations can be listed separated by commas. Using an asterisk or not providing a list identifies that the user can log on to the network from any computer.

Windows NT

PASSWORD MANAGEMENT AND ACCOUNT POLICIES

To increase security, Windows NT provides the ability to set password restrictions. These restrictions are considered part of the account policy. To define these restrictions by user or group of users, execute the following.

1. Select a user or group of users from the User Manager window.
2. From the menu bar, select **Policies ➤ Account**.
3. Within the Account Policy window, set the restrictions as desired. These include minimum and maximum password age, minimum password length, and password uniqueness.
4. Select whether or not the user must log on to change the password.

The Account Policy window also allows the administrator to set the account lockout parameters for the user. The administrator can set the number of invalid logon attempts that may occur before the account is locked out. The account remains locked until either the administrator unlocks it or a specified amount of time passes. The account is unlocked through the User Properties window. The Account Policy window also permits the ability to determine whether or not remote users should be forcibly disconnected from the server when their logon hours have expired.

CHANGING A PASSWORD

To change your own password while you are logged on to the system, press <Ctrl-Alt-Del> keys simultaneously. The Windows NT Security window displays. Select the **Change Password** button to change your password for any of the domains to which you have access. You are only permitted to change your password when the restrictions defined in the Account Policy window are met.

net accounts COMMAND

As an alternative to the Account Policy window, the *net accounts* command allows authorized users to update the user accounts database. In addition, this command facilitates modifications to the password and logon requirements for all users. For this command to execute properly, the Net Logon service must be running on the system containing the accounts you wish to change. The syntax for this command is

```
net accounts [options]
```

When *net accounts* is run without any options, the current settings for password, logon limitations, and domain information are displayed. Table A.43 presents the *net accounts* options. Executing *net accounts* with no options displays results as shown in Figure A.14.

TABLE A.43. *net accounts* Options

Option	Qualifier	Description
/forcelogoff	:*minutes*	Defines the number of *minutes* that a user has before the system automatically logs him off after the expiration of either the account or login time. The variable *minutes* can be numeric or the value *no*. The value *no* is the default and it does not allow a forced logoff. When a numeric value is entered for *minutes,* a warning is sent to the user.
/minpwlen	:*length*	Defines the minimum password *length* for a user account password. Acceptable values for *length* are 0 to 14, with 6 being the default.
/maxpwage	:*days*	Defines the maximum *days* that a password is valid. Acceptable values for *days* are 1 to 49, 710, and *unlimited*. The value of *unlimited* means that the password does not expire. In addition, the value used here must be greater than the value defined for the /minpwage option.
/minpwage	:*days*	Defines the minimum number of *days* that must pass before a user can change his password. Acceptable values for *days* are 0 to 49 and 710, with the default being 0. A value of 0 means that no limitations are set.
/uniquepw	:*number*	Defines the *number* of password changes that must occur before a password can be reused. Acceptable values for *number* are 0 to 8, with 5 being the default.
/domain		Updates the user accounts database based on the parameters given for the PDC of the current domain. Omitting this parameter updates the database on the current system.
/sync		Synchronizes the user account database in the following manner. When executed from the PDC, all BDCs are synchronized. When executed from a BDC, the backup is synchronized with the primary. This option can only be used with the /domain option.

Windows NT

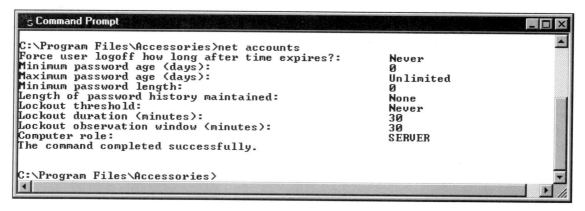

FIGURE A.14.   *net account* Screen

Examples of the net accounts Command

Consider the following examples. To synchronize the user account databases on all member servers, enter

```
net accounts /sync
```

Suppose that you are currently using a Windows NT workstation and wish to set the minimum password length to ten characters for the domain to which the workstation is connected. You would enter

```
net accounts /minpwlen:10 /domain
```

UNIX Alternative

The UNIX *passwd* command enables the administrator to set or change the login password. Depending on the UNIX variant that is used, password restrictions may be set using the system administrative tools available for that system.

Group Management

The User Manager window is also employed to add, display, modify, or change both global and local groups. The groups that are automatically displayed in the bottom half of the User Manager window are those groups that are defined for the current domain.

To add a global group, select **User ➤ New Global Group**. Enter the name and description of the group, then select the users that will be part of the group.

To add a local group, select **User ➤ New Local Group**. Enter the name and description of the group, then select **Add** to choose the names of the users and groups that will be a part of this local group.

To modify the properties of either a local or a global group, double-click the desired group or select the group then **User ➤ Properties** from the menu bar.

To create a new group with the same members as another group, select the model group from the User Manager window, then select **User ➤ Copy** from the menu bar. You are prompted to enter the new group name and description. The **Members** box contains the same list of users and groups as the model group.

To delete a group, select the group then select **User ➤ Delete** from the menu bar. Only groups that have been created by the domain administrator can be deleted. Built-in groups (those created by the installation of Windows NT) cannot be deleted.

An alternative way to add and modify groups is to access the Administrative Wizard that performs those functions. Select **Start ➤ Programs ➤ Administrative Tools ➤ Administrative Wizard ➤ Group Management**.

net group COMMAND

The *net group* command permits the addition, display, or modification of global groups on Windows NT Server domains. In addition, this command can only be run from systems that are Windows NT Server domains. Users who work together or who have the same requirements for system use are usually classified as members of the same group.

It is important to remember that the *net group* command deals with *global* groups. In essence, this means that the group can only contain users from the domain in which it was created, but this group can be assigned privileges from anywhere in the network as long as there is a trust relationship between the other domains.

There are three syntax formats for this command:

```
net group [options]
net group groupname [options]
net group groupname user(s) [options]
```

When the *net group* command is executed without any options, the display includes the name of the server as well as the name of each group on the server. When the group name is displayed it is preceded by an asterisk. The asterisk in front of the group name assists the user in differentiating group names from user names when both are displayed. Table A.44 presents the *net group* options.

TABLE A.44.   *net group* Options

Option	Qualifier	Description
groupname	/comment:"*text*" or /*action*	Enter the name of the group (*groupname*) you wish to add, modify, or delete. When used without any qualifiers (*net group groupname*), the users within that group are displayed. When used with just the qualifier /comment:"*text*", the comment *text* is added to the existing *groupname* entered, where *text* can be forty-eight characters long and must be enclosed in quotes. The /*action* qualifier either adds the *groupname* as new or deletes it. Acceptable values for /*action* are /*add* or /*delete*. When using the /*add* qualifier, the /comment:"*text*" option can be used, as well as in the format *net group groupname* /*add* /comment:"*text.*"
user(s)	/*action*	List the *user(s)* that are to be added to or deleted from *groupname* based on *action*. Acceptable values for /*action* are /*add* or /*delete*. If more than one user is entered, separate them with a space.
/domain		Causes the *net group* command to execute on the PDC of the current domain. The default (without this option) is to execute the command for the local computer. This option can be used with any of the syntax formats and is necessary only when executing the command from a workstation that is a member of a Windows NT server domain.

Examples of the net group Command

To display all the users in the group *sales1,* enter

```
net group sales1
```

To add a comment to the record for the group *sales1,* enter

```
net group sales1 /comment:"Direct Sales Personnel"
```

To add a group called *sales2* and include a comment, enter

```
net group sales2 /add /comment:"Indirect Sales Personnel"
```

To delete the user *gregh* from the group *sales1* and add him to the group *sales2,* enter

```
net group sales1 gregh /delete
net group sales2 gregh /add
```

net localgroup COMMAND

The *net localgroup* command enables the addition, deletion, or modification of local groups. It is important to remember that a local group can contain users from the domain in which the local group was created, as well as global users and global groups from other domains that have a trust relationship with the local group's domain. A difference between a local group and a global group is that a local group can only be assigned privileges in its own domain whereas a global group can be assigned privileges in trusted domains.

There are three syntax formats for the *net localgroup* command:

```
net localgroup [options]
net localgroup groupname [options]
net localgroup groupname name(s) [options]
```

When the *net localgroup* command is executed without any options, the display includes the name of the server as well as the name of each local group on the server. Table A.45 lists the *net localgroup* options.

TABLE A.45.   *net localgroup* Options

Option	Qualifier	Description
groupname	/comment:*"text"* or */action*	Enter the name of the local group (*groupname*) that you wish to add, modify, or delete. When used without any qualifiers (*net localgroup groupname*), the users and global groups within the local group *groupname* are displayed. When used with just the qualifier /comment:*"text"*, the comment *text* is added to the existing *groupname* entered, where *text* can be forty-eight characters long and must be enclosed in quotes. The */action* qualifier either adds the *groupname* as new or deletes it. Acceptable values for */action* are /add or /delete. When using the /add qualifier, the /comment:*"text"* option can be used, as well as in the format *net localgroup groupname /add /comment:"text."*
name(s)	/action	List the *name(s)* that are to be added to or deleted from *groupname* based on *action*. Acceptable values for *name* include either local users, or users on trusted domains or in global groups. If more than one name is entered, separate them with a space. Acceptable values for */action* are /add or /delete.
/domain		Causes the *net localgroup* command to execute on the PDC of the current domain. The default (without this option) is to execute the command for the local computer. This option can be used with any of the syntax formats and is necessary only when executing the command from a workstation that is a member of a Windows NT server domain.

EXAMPLES OF THE *net localgroup* COMMAND

To display all the users in the group *tech1,* enter

```
net localgroup tech1
```

To add a comment to the record for the group *tech1,* enter

```
net localgroup tech1 /comment:"Primary Tech Support Team"
```

To add a group *tech2* and include a comment, enter

```
net localgroup tech2 /add /comment:"Secondary Tech Support Team"
```

To add the names *nancyd, phill* from the helpdesk domain, and global group *sales2* to the local group *tech2,* enter

```
net localgroup tech2 nancyd helpdesk\phill sales2 /add
```

UNIX Alternatives

The concept of groups is more advanced in Windows NT than in UNIX. To add or change a user's group membership, the administrator must alter the */etc/groups* file manually or utilize the system administrative menus available on the particular UNIX system. The *groups* command displays the groups to which users belong. The *chgrp* command changes the group that owns a specified file.

Displaying Users on the System

Accessing **Start ➤ Programs ➤ Administrative Tools ➤ User Manager for Domains** displays a list of the users defined for the current or selected domain. To display the users that are currently connected to the system, you are actually displaying session connection information. To display this information, select **Start ➤ Settings ➤ Control Panel ➤ Server**. At the bottom of the Server window are five buttons. Selecting the **Users** button displays the User Sessions window. The top half of this window displays the users connected to the current server. For each user that is connected, the following information displays:

- **Computer** – The name of the computer from which the user connected
- **Opens** – The number of open files belonging to the user
- **Time** – The amount of time the user has been connected
- **Idle** – The amount of time elapsed since the user accessed the connection
- **Guest** – Whether or not the user is logged on as Guest

When you select a particular user, the bottom half of the screen displays the shared resources to which the user is connected. To access this screen for a particular server, select **Start** ➤ **Programs** ➤ **Administrative Tools** ➤ **Server Manager**. The Server Manager window for the local domain displays. To display the user sessions for a particular system, do the following.

1. Select the desired computer.
2. Select **Computer** ➤ **Properties** from the menu bar.
3. Select **Users** at the bottom of the Properties window.

DISCONNECTING USERS

To disconnect a particular user from a server, execute the following steps.

1. Select **Start** ➤ **Programs** ➤ **Administrative Tools** ➤ **Server Manager**.
2. Select the desired computer.
3. Select **Computer** ➤ **Properties** from the menu bar.
4. Select **Users** at the bottom of the Properties window.
5. Select the user you wish to disconnect from the User Sessions window.
6. Select the **Disconnect** button.

To disconnect all users from the server, select the **Disconnect All** button.

net session COMMAND

As an alternative to the User Sessions window, executing the *net session* command from the command line provides a listing of the current sessions between the local computer and its clients. It also enables an administrator to disconnect sessions. When a user contacts a server from a client computer and successfully logs on, a session between the client and the server is established. For more detailed information regarding this command, please refer to the previous *net* Commands section.

U

UNIX Alternatives

The following commands enable a UNIX administrator to display users connected to the system as well as to disconnect them:

- *who* – Displays the users logged on to the system
- *ps* – Displays all the processes associated with a user
- *kill* – Kills all process IDs associated with the user. Killing just the login process terminates a user's connection but may leave some extraneous orphan processes.

Windows NT

Service Management

Windows NT provides a number of processes, called *services,* that perform specific functions. To access a list of the services installed on the system, select **Start** ➤ **Settings** ➤ **Control Panel** ➤ **Services**. The Services window displays. From this window an authorized user can start, stop, pause, continue, and display the status of the various services. There are also *net* commands that perform the same functions. The related *net* commands are described here.

net continue COMMAND

The *net continue* command reactivates a service that has been suspended by the *net pause* command. Services are restarted without canceling a user's connection. The syntax of this command is

```
net continue service
```

Acceptable values for the `service` parameter for standard NT services follow. Other services may be acceptable depending on what is installed on the system:

- file server for macintosh (at the Windows NT Server level only)
- ftp publishing service
- lpdsvc
- net logon
- network dde
- network dde dsdm
- nt lm security support provider
- remoteboot (at the Windows NT Server level only)
- remote access server
- schedule
- server
- simple tcp/ip services
- workstation

net pause COMMAND

The *net pause* command is used to suspend a Windows NT service or resource. Pausing a service instead of stopping it enables current users to continue working while prohibiting new users from gaining access. System administrators sometimes pause a service prior to stopping it to warn users and give them an opportunity to finish what they are doing. To reactivate a service that has been paused, use the *net continue* command.

The syntax for this command is

```
net pause service
```

The *service* parameter is required and can be one of the following standard services. Other services may also be available depending on the configuration of your system:

- file server for macintosh (at the Windows NT Server level only)
- ftp publishing service
- lpdsvc
- net logon
- network dde
- network dde dsdm
- nt lm security support provider
- remoteboot (at the Windows NT Server level only)
- remote access server
- schedule
- server
- simple tcp/ip services
- workstation

net start COMMAND

The *net start* command either displays services that are currently running or starts a new service. The syntax for this command is

```
net start service
```

Executing the *net start* command without the *service* parameter provides a list of the services that are currently running. The *service* parameter is the name of the service you wish to start. If the name of the service contains more than one word, be sure to enclose the service name in quotes. Table A.46 identifies the Windows NT services that may be started with this command, along with a brief description.

net stop COMMAND

The *net stop* command stops the Windows NT service named. The syntax of this command is

```
net stop service
```

TABLE A.46.   Windows NT Services

Service	Description
Alerter	Enables alert messages to be sent to specific users and users connected to the server. Must be used in conjunction with the Messenger service.
Client Service for NetWare	Available only on a Windows NT workstation when Client Service for NetWare has been installed. Starts the Client Service for NetWare.
ClipBook Server	Enables cutting and pasting over the network
Computer Browser	Enables browsing computers over the network. Also enables the computer starting the service to be browsed by other computers on the network. Alternative command: *net start browser*.
DHCP Client	Allows IP addresses to be retrieved from a DHCP (Dynamic Host Configuration Protocol) server
Directory Replicator	Ensures that designated files are the same on all requested servers. These files and servers must be set up prior to starting this service. Alternative command: *net start replicator*.
Eventlog	Logs any type of system, security, or application event that requires a notification sent to users. This service cannot be stopped or paused and must be running to use the Event Viewer.
File Server for Macintosh	Allows file sharing with Macintosh computers; only available on Windows NT servers
FTP Publishing Service	Available only if the Internet Information Server is installed
Gateway Service for NetWare	Available only if the Gateway Service for NetWare is installed
Lpdsvc	Enables UNIX clients to print via a printer connected to a Windows NT computer; available only if TCP/IP has been installed
Messenger	Enables a computer to receive messages
Microsoft DHCP Server	Provides network clients with IP addresses. Available only on Windows NT servers and if both TCP/IP and the DHCP server have been installed. Alternative command: *net start dhcpserver*.
Net Logon	Verifies requests to log on and controls copies of the user accounts database in the domain. Service is started on all servers in a domain that uses a copy of the domain's user accounts database. Alternative command: *net start netlogon*.
Network DDE	Starts the Network Dynamic Data Exchange service

TABLE A.46. *(Continued)*

Service	Description
Network DDE DSDM	Starts the Network Dynamic Data Exchange Share Database Manager service
Network Monitor Agent	Enables remote monitoring of a client machine's network communication
NT LM Security Support Provider	Available only if the NT LM Security Support Provider is installed
Print Server for Macintosh	Enables printing from Macintosh computers; available only on Windows NT servers
Remoteboot	Permits networked computers to load the operating system from the server; available only on Windows NT servers
Remote Access Connection Manager	Allows remote access to the network through a dial-up connection; available only if the Remote Access Service is installed
Remote Access ISNSAP service	Available only if the Remote Access Service is installed
Remote Access Server	Available only if the Remote Access Service is installed
Remote Procedure Call Locator	Allows applications to use the Microsoft RPC name service; also manages the RPC name service database
Remote Procedure Call Service	Allows applications to use dynamic end points; also manages the endpoint map database
Schedule	Enables use of the *at* command to start programs at a specified time
Server	Enables a computer to share resources on the network, such as files and printers. In addition, it provides RPC support.
Simple TCP/IP services	Activates the TCP/IP services of Character Generator, Daytime, Discard, Echo, and Quote of the Day; available only if TCP/IP and the simple TCP/IP service are installed
SNMP	Enables a server to report its status to the SNMP management system; available only if both TCP/IP and SNMP are installed
Spooler	Starts the Spooler service
TCP/IP NetBIOS Helper	Enables NetBIOS over the TCP/IP service; available only if TCP/IP is installed
UPS	Manages the uninterruptible power supply (UPS) that is connected to the computer
Windows Internet Name Service	Enables the mapping of computer names to TCP/IP addresses for networked client systems; available only on Windows NT servers
Workstation	Enables a computer to connect to and communicate with network resources

Windows NT

Executing the *net stop* command without the `service` parameter displays a list of the valid services. The `service` parameter can be any of the standard services listed here, as well as any services that were installed on your system:

- Alerter
- Client Service for NetWare
- ClipBook Server
- Computer Browser
- Directory Replicator
- File Server for Macintosh (only on Windows NT Server)
- FTP Publishing Service
- Gateway Service for NetWare (only on Windows NT Server)
- Lpdsvc
- Messenger
- Microsoft DHCP Server (only on Windows NT Server)
- Net Logon
- Network DDE
- Network DDE DSDM
- Network Monitor Agent
- NT LM Security Support Provider
- OLE
- Print Server for Macintosh (only on Windows NT Server)
- Remote Access Connection Manager
- Remote Access ISNSAP Service
- Remote Access Server
- Remote Procedure Call Locator
- Remote Procedure Call Service
- Schedule
- Server
- Simple TCP/IP services
- SNMP
- Spooler
- TCP/IP NetBIOS Helper
- UPS
- Windows Internet Name Service (only on Windows NT Server)
- Workstation

Other System Management Tools

This section discusses other system management tools that are of interest to administrators and users.

LOGGING OFF A SYSTEM

To log off of a system, press `<Ctrl-Alt-Del>` simultaneously. This displays the Windows NT Security window. To log off, select the **Logoff** button. After logging off, you can log in again as the same user or as a different user.

UNIX Alternatives

Press `<Ctrl-D>` to log off of a UNIX system.

The *su* command permits you to log in as another user while remaining connected to the system with your current login.

The *login* command also allows a user to log in to the system. This command prompts for a password if one is set up for the user.

SHUTTING DOWN THE SYSTEM

There are two ways to shut down the system: select **Start** ➤ **Shutdown** or select **Shutdown** from the Windows NT Security window, which is accessed by pressing `<Ctrl-Alt-Del>`.

UNIX Alternatives

Commands that can be used to shutdown a UNIX system are

- *shutdown* – Shuts down the system after broadcasting a message to users that the system will be shut down.
- *init 0* – Shuts down the system without warning
- *init 6* – Shutsdown and restarts the system

DEFINING ENVIRONMENT VARIABLES

There are times when a user or an administrator must define or change environment variables for the system, such as setting default paths and defining temporary directories. To set or change the environment variables, select **Start** ➤ **Settings** ➤ **Control Panel** ➤ **System**. Within the System Properties window, select the **Environment** tab. Only administrators may change **System Variables**. Users or administrators may change the **User Variables**.

To change a variable, select it and it displays in the **Variable** and **Value** fields at the bottom of the screen. Make whatever changes are necessary, then select **Set**.

To add a variable, just enter the variable and its value in the appropriate fields, then select **Set**.

To delete an environment variable, select it, then select **Delete**. In all cases, select **OK** to exit the window. Changes made to the system variables are effective the next time the computer is restarted. Changes made to the user variables are effective the next time the user logs on to the computer.

UNIX Alternative

The *env* command displays the user's current environment. To set an environment variable on systems using the Korn or Bourne shell, use the format `variable=value; export variable`. For example, `TERM=vt100; export TERM`. Systems using the C shell utilize the *set* command to set environment variables.

UNIX Commands and Utilities

This appendix is designed as a reference tool for users and system administrators. It defines and discusses a number of commands and their options that are used in the day-to-day operation of a UNIX system. Even though UNIX systems do have graphical interfaces available to accomplish many tasks, we concentrate on the more universal procedures associated with executing commands from the command line. When appropriate we cross-reference Windows NT alternative commands.

We break down the commands into the following categories:

- Backup commands
- Comparison commands
- Compression commands
- Display commands
- File Management commands
- File Manipulation commands
- Miscellaneous commands
- Networking commands
- Ownership commands
- Print commands
- Search commands
- System management commands

Within each category we discuss the individual commands and their options. We also give examples of many of the commands. When appropriate we give the Windows NT alternative for the command. This alternative takes the form of a graphical method of executing the command, the command line method, or both. The Windows NT command line procedures are executed from the Virtual DOS Machine (VDM), and the command line is accessed within Windows NT by selecting **Start** ➤ **Programs** ➤ **Command Prompt**. This cross-reference will help system administrators who are working with both environments.

One of the frequent complaints about UNIX concerns its cryptic command names. In this appendix we include a more descriptive name for the UNIX command in parentheses when appropriate. This should assist you in becoming more familiar with the UNIX command names.

The following syntax conventions are used in this appendix.

- In the tables detailing various command options, we use *italic* typeface to represent variables that must be replaced in the command structure. For example, *filename* represents a parameter variable that must be replaced with an actual file name.
- In the text the command name itself is in *italic* typeface so it can be recognized easily.
- In the text command parameters are printed in `monospace` type in order to distinguish the references to the parameters from the explanation in the text.

NOTE   **A Word on UNIX Variants**

Not all commands and options are the same with different UNIX variants. We have elected to use UNIX System V.4 as our baseline in writing this chapter. We do recommend that you check the documentation available for your UNIX operating system, including the *man* pages, to confirm the options that are available for each command on your particular variant of UNIX. When possible, we tried to denote the differences between variants.

BACKUP COMMANDS

An important duty that usually falls to the system administrator is backing up critical files in preparation for system failure or just plain human error. UNIX offers a variety of commands that perform the backup function. In addition, several of the UNIX variants have created their own backup utilities that expand the options available. We recommend that you check out what is available within the system administrative tools supplied by your variant.

We have included in this section commands that are suitable for archiving as well as for backup making. The commands *tar* and *cpio* are actually considered archival commands because they fill holes in sparse files with null bytes. Therefore, when these files are restored, they may require more disk space than when they were originally backed up. Although the *dd* command can be considered a backup command, it retains information about the physical layout of the file system being backed up. This may create a problem if you attempt to restore the data to a device with different characteristics. We have chosen to list these commands here because they are available on all UNIX variants. As stated earlier, many UNIX variants contain their own backup and restore utilities, such as *backup* and *restore, dump* and *restore,* and *ufsdump* and *ufsrestore.* We recommend that you check your system documentation to determine the backup and restore commands that best suit your needs.

cpio (copy in/out) Command

The *cpio* command copies files on to or off of tape, disk, or diskette. In addition, this command can be used to move files around on a local system. There are actually three different formats of the command: *cpio -i,* which copies files "into" the system from a tape or disk; *cpio -o,* which copies files "off of" the system onto a tape or a disk; and *cpio -p,* which copies files within the local system, "passing" them from one directory to another. The syntax of each of these formats is given here along with a brief explanation of what the command does. Table B.1 describes all of the options available and designates for which formats the options are valid.

cpio -i COMMAND

The syntax of the *cpio -i* command is

```
cpio -i options pattern
```

The *cpio -i* command copies files "into" the system off of a tape or disk. If a `pattern` is given, any filenames that match `pattern` are copied. Otherwise, the entire contents of the media are restored to the system. It is recommended that the pattern be contained in quotes to ensure a proper match. In addition, metacharacters (e.g., *, ?, !, []) can be used as part of the pattern. While restoring files, if the file on the system is newer than the one being restored, then the file is bypassed and not restored.

cpio -o COMMAND

The syntax for this format of the *cpio* command is

```
cpio -o options
```

TABLE B.1.   cpio Options

Option	Qualifier	Description	-i	-o	-p
-a		Resets the access times of the input files after they have been copied		x	x
-B		Uses 5,120 bytes per record as the block size for either input or output. The default is 512 bytes. Data must be input to or output from a character special device.	x	x	
-c		Inputs or outputs the header information in ASCII format	x	x	
-d		Creates directories if they do not exist	x		x
-E	*list*	Restores any files listed in the file *list* from the backup	x		
-f		Restores those files that do *not* match the pattern	x		
-H	*format*	Either inputs or outputs the header information based on *format*. Choices available for the qualifier *format* include *crc* (ASCII header with expanded device numbers), *odc* (ASCII header with small device numbers), *ustar* (IEEE/P1003 Data Interchange Standard), or *tar* (*tar* command format).	x	x	
-I	*list*	Restores the files from the file *list*	x		
-k		Bypasses any I/O errors of corrupted headers	x		
-l		Does not copy the files to the new directory but links them instead			x
-L		Follows symbolic links when backing up or copying files		x	x
-m		Does not change the file modification time	x		x
-M	*message*	Displays *message* when switching media when the end of media is reached. The variable *%d* used in *message* displays as the numeric identification of the media. This must be used with either the -*I* or -*O* options.	x	x	
-O	*file*	Outputs the backed up files to *file*		x	
-r		Renames files interactively.	x		
-s		Swaps bytes within each half word	x		
-S		Swaps half words within each word	x		
-t		Displays the contents of the backup	x		
-u		Restores or copies files regardless if the destination contains a newer file or not (in other words, copies unconditionally)	x		x
-v		Displays a list of the files being copied, restored, or backed up (verbose option)	x	x	x
-V		Another version of the verbose option, but instead of a list of files, outputs to the screen a period for each file input or output. This lets the user know that the command is working.	x	x	x
-6		Restores a UNIX 6th Edition format file, which is an old format	x		

This *cpio* command outputs a list of files to tape or disk. The list of files can come from standard input or can be piped from another command such as *find*. The output of this command must be redirected to the device, such as a tape or a diskette. For example, a system administrator performs a backup of users' files on a monthly basis in which she backs up files that have been changed within the last thirty days. To execute this type of backup using *cpio*, she would enter

```
find /usr -ctime -30 -print | cpio -ov > /dev/rmt/0m
```

cpio -p COMMAND

The syntax for this format of the *cpio* command is

```
cpio -p options directory-name
```

This *cpio* command actually copies within a system to another directory. In other words, this version of the command works similar to the *cp* command. The files are copied to *directory-name*. Therefore, any source directories become subdirectories in *directory-name*.

Examples of the cpio Command

In the *cpio -o* section, we gave an example of how to back up users' files. Suppose that the user *bosco* somehow deleted all of the files in his financial directory, then started adding some new files to the directory. To restore his files, ignoring any files currently in the directory, the system administrator would enter

```
cpio -iduv "bosco/financial" < /dev/rmt/0m
```

The *d* option is used to create directories if necessary. The *u* option is used to restore files unconditionally even if they already exist in the destination directory.

For an example of the *cpio -p* command, suppose a user named *sarah* has left the company and the system administrator needs to transfer her customer files to the user *emily*. To accomplish this the system administrator would change to the */usr/sarah* directory and then enter the following:

```
find customer -print | cpio -padm /usr/emily/client2
```

This command resets the access times of Sarah's files to their original access times, creates directories if necessary, and maintains the modification times of Sarah's files.

Windows NT Alternative

To back up files to tape, select **Start** ➤ **Programs** ➤ **Administrative Tools** ➤ **Backup**. After a tape is inserted, it displays in the Backup window. From this window, select the **Window** command menu to choose the drives and the volumes to be backed up. Select drives, files, and folders by clicking on the check box. Select the **Backup** button. In the Backup Information window, enter the tape name and conditions of the backup.

To restore files from tape, select **Start** ➤ **Programs** ➤ **Administrative Tools** ➤ **Backup**. Within the Backup window, select the files to restore, then select the **Restore** button.

To back up files to a floppy, use the My Computer icon or Windows NT Explorer to select the files then drag them to the appropriate drive designation, like A:. This works just like copying files.

Another alternative for backing files up to floppy disk is to use the VDM command line *backup* command.

dd Command

The *dd* command is often the preferred method of backup because it can handle variable block sizes. This may become necessary when moving data from one type of raw device to another. It is also useful in transferring data either to or from non-UNIX systems.

The syntax of this command is

```
dd option=value option=value ...
```

The *dd* command allows any number of *option=value* parameters. Options are available to identify input files and output files, as well as many others (Table B.2). If the output file is omitted, the input files are copied to standard output.

With the options in Table B.2, the value n can be increased using the following conventions.

- To increase n by 1,024, follow n with the letter k.
- To increase n by 512, follow n with the letter b.
- To increase n by 2, follow n with the letter w.

TABLE B.2.   *dd* Options

Option	Value	Description
bs	*n*	Sets both the input and output block sizes to *n*. If the input and output block sizes differ, use the *ibs* and *obs* options instead.
cbs	*n*	Defines *n* as the logical record length in bytes for conversion purposes. Must be used in conjunction with *conv types ascii, ebcdic, ibm, block,* or *unblock*.
conv	*types*	Converts input based on *types*. One or more types can be listed and separated by commas. The types are *ascii* (convert ebcdic to ascii), *ebcdic* (convert ascii to ebcdic), *ibm* (convert ascii to ebcdic using IBM proprieties), *block* (convert variable-length records to fixed-length records), *unblock* (convert fixed-length records to variable-length records), *lcase* (convert uppercase to lowercase), *ucase* (convert lowercase to uppercase), *noerror* (ignore up to five errors in a row), *swab* (swap every pair of bytes), and *sync* (pad input blocks until they reach the value of *ibs*).
count	*n*	Copies *n* input blocks
files	*n*	Copies *n* input files
ibs	*n*	Defines the input block size as *n* bytes. The default is 512 bytes.
if	*file*	Takes the input from *file*. If omitted, standard input is assumed.
obs	*n*	Defines the output block size as *n* bytes. The default is 512 bytes.
of	*file*	Outputs files to *file*. If omitted, standard output is assumed.
iseek	*n*	Skips to the *n*th block from the beginning of the input file. The input file should be a disk file.
oseek	*n*	Skips to the *n*th block from the beginning of the output file.
skip	*n*	Skips to the *n*th block from the beginning of the input file. Works best with magnetic tape input files.

UNIX

EXAMPLES OF THE *dd* COMMAND

To convert all uppercase letters to lowercase, the following command could be entered:

```
dd if=/usr/bosco/letter of=/usr/bosco/newletter conv=lcase
```

To copy the first ten files off of a backup tape to the existing directory */home/data,* enter

```
dd if=/dev/rmt0 of=/home/data files=10
```

tar (tape archive) Command

The *tar* command is often referred to as a tape archive command. Do not let the name limit your use of the command. It can be used to back up and restore files to tape, floppy diskette, or even another directory on the current system.

The syntax of this command is

```
tar function options filelist
```

A *function* parameter must be specified first (Table B.3) with the options (Table B.4) following. A unique formatting convention is used with the *tar* options. All of the options are grouped together with the qualifiers following in their respective order. When entering the command on the command line, no space is entered between the desired *function* and its *options*.

TABLE B.3. *tar* Functions

Function	Description
c	Creates a new backup
r	Adds *filelist* to an already existing backup
t	Displays the table of contents of the backup. If *filelist* is omitted, displays all files; otherwise, only displays *filelist* if it exists on the backup.
u	Adds to (or updates) the backup if *filelist* is not already on the backup or if *filelist* has a more recent modification time
x	Restores (or extracts) files from the backup. If there is no *filelist,* restores all files.

TABLE B.4. *tar* Options

Option	Qualifier	Description
A		Changes absolute filenames to relative filenames. This option is not available on all UNIX variants.
b	*n*	Sets the blocking factor to *n*, where *n* can be from 1 to 20. The default is 1.
f	*file*	Copies `filelist` to or restores it from *file*. This file can be an actual file or a device name. If the value of *file* is a minus sign, this option uses standard input or standard output depending on the function chosen.
k		Enter the size in kilobytes of the device. Use this option to have *tar* identify when the device is filled and to prompt for the next floppy or tape. This option is not available on all UNIX variants.
l		Displays error messages when links cannot be followed
L		Follows symbolic links
m		Does not change the modification times on restoration. The modification time is the time the file was extracted.
n		Tells *tar* that the device is not a tape drive. This option is not available on all UNIX variants.
o		Modifies the owner and group of the file on restoration to those of the user executing the command
v		Verbose option. Displays files as they are backed up or restored. An *x* is displayed as they are restored (extracted). An *a* is displayed as they are backed up.
w		Forces the user to confirm whether the file should be backed up or restored. Enter *y* to confirm the file or any other letter to deny it.

EXAMPLES OF THE *tar* COMMAND

To back up *bosco*'s financial directory to floppy disk, enter

```
tar cvf /dev/rfd0 /usr/bosco/financial
```

To view the contents of a tape to determine if it is the appropriate one, enter

```
tar tvf /dev/rmt/0m | more
```

Windows NT Alternative

To back up files to tape, select **Start** ➤ **Programs** ➤ **Administrative Tools** ➤ **Backup**. After a tape is inserted it displays in the Backup window. From this window, select the **Window** command menu to choose the drives then select the volumes to be backed up. Select drives, files, and folders by clicking on their check box. Select the **Backup** button. In the Backup Information window, enter the tape name and conditions of the backup.

To restore files from tape, select **Start** ➤ **Programs** ➤ **Administrative Tools** ➤ **Backup**. Within the Backup window, select the files to restore, then select the **Restore** button.

To back up files to a floppy, use the My Computer icon or Windows NT Explorer to select the files then drag them to the appropriate drive designation, like A:. This works just like copying files.

Another alternative for backing up files to floppy disk is to use the VDM command line *backup* command.

COMPARISON COMMANDS

There are times when it is necessary to compare files to determine their similarities and their differences. UNIX offers a number of commands that assist in the comparison process.

cmp (compare) Command

The *cmp* command compares two files and displays the byte and line number where the difference occurred. This comparison command works best with binary files.

The syntax of the command is

```
cmp options file1 file2
```

Table B.5 presents the *cmp* command options.

The message "EOF on *filename*" displays when one file is shorter than the other. The *filename* will be the name of the shorter file. If there are no difference between the files, no output will display. By default, only the first byte of the difference is displayed. To show more information, utilize one of the options discussed in Table B.5.

TABLE B.5.   *cmp* Options

Option	Description
-l	For each difference found in the file, displays a long listing containing the decimal byte number of the location where the difference is found and displays, in octal, the contents of the differing bytes
-s	Does not create any display; in other words, executes the command silently. Instead, outputs only one of the following exit codes: 0, if the files are the same; 1, if the files are different; or 2, if they are inaccessible.

EXAMPLES OF THE *cmp* COMMAND

To compare two compiled program files to determine if they are the same, enter

```
cmp /home/oldfiles/program1 /home/newfiles/program1
```

An example of the output of the *cmp* command is

```
/home/oldfiles/program1 /home/newfiles/program1 differ: char 5, line 1
```

Windows NT Alternative
Using the VDM command line, enter the *fc /b* command to compare binary files.

comm (common) Command

The *comm* command compares two sorted files to determine which lines are common between them. The standard output of this command consists of three columns: unique lines in the first file, unique lines in the second file, and lines common to both files.

The syntax of this command is

```
comm options file1 file2
```

Table B-6 lists the *comm* command options.

Using a hyphen (-) in place of either *file1* or *file2* replaces that file with data taken from standard input.

TABLE B.6.   *comm* Options

Option	Description
-1	Does not display column 1 (the lines unique to *file1*)
-2	Does not display column 2 (the lines unique to *file2*)
-3	Does not display column 3 (the lines common to both *file1* and *file2*)
-12	Displays only column 3 (the lines common to both files)
-13	Displays only column 2 (the lines unique to *file2*)
-23	Displays only column 1 (the lines unique to *file1*)

EXAMPLE OF THE *comm* COMMAND

Suppose that there is a new version of an application to install, and as a system administrator you wish to determine which filenames are different between the current version and the new update. After creating files that contain a sorted list of the files for both versions, you enter the following command:

```
comm -3 update current
```

The output of this command displays files that are unique to the application *update* in column one and files that are unique to the *current* application in column two.

diff, diff3, and *sdiff* Commands

UNIX offers three different comparison commands that output the differences between files. The *diff* command compares two files for differences. The *diff3* command compares three files for differences. Finally, the *sdiff* command allows a side-by-side comparison of two files.

diff COMMAND

The *diff* command displays the lines that differ between *file1* and *file2*. The lines for *file1* begin with a < (less than) sign. The lines for *file2* begin with a > (greater than) sign. An easy way to remember which output line is associated with which file is to associate *file1* with a smaller number, thus it is tagged by the less than (<) symbol.

The syntax of the command is

```
diff options directory-options file1 file2
```

The parameters *file1* and *file2* can be either two files, a file and a directory, or two directories. If they are files, the *diff* command compares the files line by line. To compare a file against standard input, replace one of the filenames with a – (minus sign). If one of the filenames is a directory, the *diff* command compares the file to the file with the same name in the directory. In other words, it compares *file1* to *directory/file1*. If both filenames are directories, it compares each file that has the same name in both directories. The directory compare identifies files that are unique to one directory, and sub-directories that exist in both directories.

The *diff* command options are listed in Table B.7. As discussed, *file1* and *file2* can be directories. If this is the case, the options listed in Table B.8 are available.

TABLE B.7.   *diff* Options

Option	Qualifier	Description
-b		Ignores multiple blank characters or blanks that appear at the end of a line. Combines multiple blanks into one blank.
-c		Displays the differences with three lines of output. Cannot be combined with the following options: -C, -e, -f, -h, and -n.
-C	*x*	Similar to the -c option except displays *x* lines of output. Cannot be combined with the following options: -c, -e, -f, -h, and -n.
-e		Generates a script that can be input into the *ed* editor to recreate *file2* from *file1* with the use of the editor's *a, c,* and *d* commands. Cannot be combined with the following options: -c, -C, -f, -h, and -n.
-f		Generates a script in reverse order, which recreates *file1* from *file2*. This script cannot be input into the *ed* editor. Cannot be combined with the following options: -c, -C, -e, -h, and -n.

continued

TABLE B.7.   *diff* Options *(Continued)*

Option	Qualifier	Description
-h		Executes a minimal comparison. This is not a complete comparison. The *-e* and *-f* options are not available with this option. Even though files of any length can be used as input, this command works best for files with small numbers of differences. Cannot be combined with the following options: -c, -C, -e, -f, and -n.
-i		Does not differentiate between upper- and lowercase.
-n		Counts the number of changed lines. This is similar to the *-f* option. Cannot be combined with the following options: -c, -C, -e, -f, and -h.
-t		Expands tabs for output. This helps to preserve command line indentation.
-w		Ignores *all* spaces and tabs. More comprehensive than the *-b* option.

TABLE B.8.   *diff* Directory Options

Option	Qualifier	Description
-l		Provides a long format with comparative displays for each file beginning at the top of the page (or screen)
-r		Compares common files in subdirectories; in other words, executes a recursive compare
-s		Displays a listing of files that are identical
-S	*filename*	Compares files alphabetically beginning with *filename*

Examples of the diff Command

To determine which files are identical between the *financial* and *budget* directories, enter the following:

```
diff -s financial budget
```

For the remainder of the *diff* examples assume the contents of `file1` and `file2` are as described in Table B.9.

TABLE B.9.   Example Files

file1	file2
apple	apple
banana	blueberry
cucumber	Kiwi

The output of the command *diff file1 file2* is

```
2,3c2,3
< banana
< cucumber
--
> blueberry
> Kiwi
```

Notice the first line of the output is similar to the *ed* command to modify the file. To create an actual *ed* script to recreate `file2` from `file1`, the command is

```
diff -e file1 file2
```

This command outputs the following:

```
2,3c
blueberry
Kiwi
```

Windows NT Alternatives

Using the VDM command line, enter the *fc* command with the appropriate options to compare the contents of two files. A graphical comparison program, WinDiff, is available through the Windows NT Resource Kit 4.0 (**Start ➤ Programs ➤ Resource Kit 4.0 ➤ File Tools ➤ File and Directory Comparison**).

diff3 COMMAND

The *diff3* command includes the ability to add a third file to the comparison. The designators used to distinguish between each file in the output are listed on page 586.

TABLE B.10.   *diff3* Options

Option	Description
-e	Creates an *ed* script to merge the differences between `file2` and `file3` into `file1`
-E	Same as *-e,* except the lines different between all three files are marked with < >
-x	Creates an *ed* script to merge into `file1` any differences between all three files
-X	Performs the same function as the *-x* option except lines different between all three files are marked with < >
-3	Creates an *ed* script to merge into `file1` any difference between `file1` and `file3`.

- = = = = if all three files are different
- = = = =1 if *file1* is different
- = = = =2 if *file2* is different
- = = = =3 if *file3* is different

The syntax of this command is

```
diff3 options file1 file2 file3
```

The *diff3* command options are listed in Table B.10.

Example of the diff3 Command

For the purpose of the *diff3* examples, the contents of the test files are as displayed in Table B.11.

The output of the command *diff3 file1 file2 file3* is

```
====
1:2,4c
  banana
  cucumber

2:2,4c
  blueberry
  Kiwi

3:2,3c
  Kiwi
  watermelon
```

TABLE B.11.   Example Files

file1	file2	file3
apple	apple	apple
banana	blueberry	Kiwi
cucumber	Kiwi	watermelon

sdiff COMMAND

The *sdiff* command compares only two files for similarities and differences, but displays the output in columnar format (side by side). Table B.12 describes the format of the output that is produced. The syntax of the *sdiff* command is

```
sdiff options file1 file2
```

The *sdiff* command options are listed on Table B.13.

TABLE B.12.   *sdiff* Command Output

Column 1	Column 2	Explanation
Line of file1	Line of file2	These lines are identical.
Line of file1	<	The line only exists in file1.
>	line of file2	The line only exists in file2.
line of file1 |	line of file2	A vertical bar displays between the two lines to signify that the lines are different.

TABLE B.13.   *sdiff* Options

Option	Qualifiers	Description
-l		Displays the lines of *file1* that are identical. There is no need to display the same line in *file2*.
-o	*filename*	Outputs lines that are identical between *file1* and *file2* to *filename*. Sends to standard output (the screen usually) only the lines that are different. The user can edit *filename* by using the commands listed in Table B.14.
-s		Omits identical lines
-w	*x*	Changes the length of a line from the default of 130 to the value of *x*

UNIX

To edit the *filename* created with the *-o* option, the edit commands in Table B.14 may be used. A % prompt displays, denoting when the commands can be entered.

Example of the sdiff Command

The example uses the files listed in Table B.15.

The command *sdiff file1 file2* gives the following result:

```
apple                apple
banana     |         blueberry
cucumber   |         Kiwi
date                 <
eggplant             <
```

TABLE B.14.   *sdiff* Edit Command Options

Option	Description
e	Modifies an empty file
e b	Edits both columns
e l	Edits the left column
e r	Edits the right column
l	Adds the left column to the end of *filename*
q	Quits editing
r	Adds the right column to the end of *filename*
s	Omits printing identical lines
v	Prints identical lines. This option is used to turn off the *s* option.

TABLE B.15.   Example Files

file1	file2
apple	apple
banana	blueberry
cucumber	Kiwi
date	
eggplant	

dircmp (directory compare) **Command**

The *dircmp* command compares two directories and reports their similarities and differences. The syntax of the command is

```
dircmp options directory1 directory2
```

The *dircmp* command options are presented in Table B.16.

TABLE B.16.   *dircmp* Options

Option	Description
-d	Automatically executes the *diff* command on files that differ between the two directories
-s	Omits the display of identical files
-wx	Changes the width of the display line from 72 to the value of x.

When no options are chosen, the output contains a listing of the files that exist only in `directory1` and only those in `directory2`. The output display then identifies the files that are named the same, whether their contents are the same or different. Subdirectories of the same name are just noted as directories. The output displays page headings that describe the contents of the page.

EXAMPLE OF THE *dircmp* COMMAND

The following command will output only the files that are different between the two directories and will execute the *diff* command on files of the same name with contents that differ.

```
dircmp -ds newdir olddir > cmpout
```

uniq (unique) **Command**

Although the *uniq* command does not compare files, it does compare lines within a file. The *uniq* command searches for unique lines as well as duplicate lines. Duplicate lines that are adjacent in `file1` are removed from the file and one of each of the duplicate lines is displayed on standard output. If a `file2` is named, these lines are output to `file2`. The input file (`file1`) must be sorted.

The syntax of this command is

```
uniq option file1 file2
```

The option field may only contain a single option, not a combination of several options (Table B.17).

UNIX

TABLE B.17.   *uniq* Options

Option	Description
-c	Displays the number of occurrences of a line and then the line itself
-d	Displays only the lines that are repeated more than once. Unique lines (ones that occur only once) are not displayed.
-u	Displays/outputs only unique lines (those that occur only once)
-x	Omits the first x fields in a line during a comparison, where fields are space or tab delimited
+x	Omits the first x characters of a field

EXAMPLE OF THE *uniq* COMMAND

To determine how many times each user is logged in, enter

```
who | cut -d" " -f1 | sort | uniq -c
```

COMPRESSION COMMANDS

The compression commands permit users to reduce the size of files. These commands can be beneficial for archiving data because a compressed file requires less storage space. Also a compressed file takes less time to transmit electronically. The commands necessary to compress a file and to expand a compressed file are reviewed.

We limited ourselves to the commands that are standard on most UNIX variants. However, there are a few excellent freeware tools available. The most common are *zip* and *gzip* from the GNU Project at *www.gnu.ai.mit.edu*.

Whereas UNIX provides a number of compression utilities, Windows NT relies primarily on third-party applications such as *pkzip* to handle file compression, especially when it is configured with a FAT file system. In this section we refer to a couple of compression utilities embedded in Windows NT, but these are usable only with the NTFS file system.

compress Command

The *compress* command compresses files using a methodology called *adaptive Lempel-Ziv coding*. This method reduces the size of the file somewhat. The compressed file retains the same filename but has a .Z added as an extension. In other words, the original file is replaced with the file with the .Z extension. For example, after the file *total* is compressed, a file named *total.Z* exists

TABLE B.18. *compress* Options

Option	Qualifier	Description
-b	*n*	Reduces the number of bits used in the compression coding process. Acceptable values for *n* are 9 through 16, with 16 being the default. In essence this option causes a less compressed file (i.e., it will be larger than without this option) that enables a user to uncompress a file in a limited address space.
-c		Outputs the compressed file to standard output rather than renaming it with a *.Z* extension
-f		"Forces" the output of the *filename.Z* file, overwriting it if it already exists
-v		Outputs the percentage that *filenames* were reduced

instead of the original *total* file. Compressed files are expanded using the *uncompress* command.

The syntax of the command is

```
compress options filename(s)
```

Table B.18 lists the *compress* command options.

Windows NT Alternative

When Windows NT is configured with NTFS, access My Computer or Windows NT Explorer. From within either of these windows, select the file or folder, then select **File → Properties**. In the Properties window, click on **Compressed** in the **Attributes** section.

Using the VDM command line, the *compact* command compresses a directory or a file as well as displays the compression state of a file or directory. This command only works for files stored in an NTFS file system.

uncompress Command

This command expands files created by the *compress* command back to their original size. The command assumes the *.Z* extension so it can be omitted. The syntax of the command is

```
uncompress -c filename(s)
```

The *-c* option is not required and actually just outputs the expanded file to standard output, which is what the *zcat* command does.

Windows NT Alternative

Using the VDM command line, the *compact* command decompresses files when they reside in an NTFS file system.

pack Command

The *pack* command compresses files using a minimum redundancy methodology referred to as *Huffman coding*. The output replaces the original file with the packed file, distinguishing it by a *.z* extension. It is recommended that the total number of blocks be greater than three blocks to gain any benefit in packing the file.

The syntax of the command is

```
pack options filename(s)
```

The options for the *pack* command are presented in Table B.19.

TABLE B.19.   *pack* Options

Option	Description
-	Displays statistical information such as the number of times each byte is used, the relative frequency of use, and the byte code
-f	Forces the compression of the file even if the compression doesn't actually reduce the file size by much

Packed files can be viewed using the *pcat* command and expanded using the *unpack* command. Some conditions under which a file cannot be packed follow. These conditions are output in the form of error codes/messages.

- *filename* is already packed.
- *filename* is too long so that the *.z* extension cannot be added (keep *filename* to twelve characters).
- *filename* has links.
- *filename* is actually a directory.

- *filename* cannot be opened.
- No disk storage space is saved by the packing of *filename*.
- *filename.z* already exists.
- The *.z* file cannot be created.

unpack Command

The *unpack* command expands files that were compressed using the *pack* command. The syntax of the command is

```
unpack filename(s)
```

The *unpack* command assumes the *.z* extension on *filenames*. The newly expanded file replaces the *.z* file in the directory.

pcat Command

The *pcat* command displays files compressed with the *pack* command. The syntax of the command is

```
pcat filename(s)
```

The *filename* can be the name of the file with or without the *.z* extension. If a user redirects the output of the *pcat* command to another file, the user is actually creating an unpacked version of the file.

For example, if a user wants to unpack the file *budget.z,* one command that accomplishes this is

```
pcat budget.z > budget95
```

uuencode Command

The *uuencode* command is used to convert binary files into a format that allows them to be transmitted via e-mail. The encoded file contains only the printable ASCII characters as well as the permissions and name of the file. This command can take input from standard input.

The syntax of the command is

```
uuencode infilename outfilename
```

The `infilename` parameter is the actual file being converted. This field is not entered if *uuencode* is accepting input from standard input. The `outfilename` parameter is the filename that is stored in the encoded file as well as the name of the file after it is decoded.

UNIX

The *uuencode* command and its counterpart, *uudecode,* are often used in commercial mail packages to encapsulate binary attachments to mail messages for transmission to its destination.

uudecode Command

The *uudecode* command extracts files that have been converted using *uuencode*. The output filename and permissions are obtained from within the encoded file. The syntax of the command is

```
uudecode filename
```

The *filename* parameter is the name of the encoded file.

zcat Command

The *zcat* command displays files compressed with the *compress* command. The syntax of the command is

```
zcat filename(s)
```

The *filename* can be the name of the file with or without the .Z extension. If a user redirects the output of the *zcat* command to another file, the user is actually creating an uncompressed version of the file.

For example, if a user wants to decompress the file *financial.Z,* one command that accomplishes this is

```
zcat financial.Z > finances
```

DISPLAY COMMANDS

Within UNIX there are a number of ways to display information on the screen depending on the user's requirements. A user can display the beginning of a file, the end of a file, a page of a file, and the entire file. In addition, a user can list files in a variety of different sequences. This section examines the display commands.

cat Command

The *cat* command actually does more than just display files. It can also be used to create files or combine them. Files are created from scratch by entering information on standard input, which is usually the terminal screen. Input is terminated by entering <Ctrl-D>. To combine files, the > or >> operators can be

TABLE B.20.   *cat* Options

Option	Description
-e	This option must be used in conjunction with the *-v* option to display $ at the end of each line.
-s	Does not display an error message when a file cannot be found. In BSD UNIX variants, this option ignores blank lines.
-t	This option must be used in conjunction with the *-v* option to display tab characters such as ^I (`<Ctrl-I>`) and form-feed characters as ^L (`<Ctrl-L>`).
-u	Displays the output of a file as unbuffered
-v	Displays any nonprintable characters, including control characters, that are in the file. This excludes tabs and form feeds unless the *-t* option is also used. The formats for nonprintable characters are control characters = ^x, a DEL (delete) character = ^?, and non-ASCII characters = M-x, where x is the character represented by the seven low-order bits.

used. The > operator can combine several files into a new file, whereas the >> operator causes one file to be appended to another.

The syntax of the *cat* command is

```
cat options file(s)
```

The *cat* command options are listed in Table B.20.

EXAMPLES OF THE *cat* COMMAND

To display a file, enter

```
cat file1
```

To create a new file on the terminal screen, enter

```
cat > newfile
```

Then enter the contents of the file. When finished, enter `<Ctrl-D>` to end the file and stop running the *cat* command.

To combine two files into a single new file, enter

```
cat file1 file2 > newfile2
```

To add a third file to the already created *newfile2,* enter

```
cat file3 >> newfile2
```

Windows NT Alternative

Files can be viewed within Windows NT by using the Notepad or WordPad programs. Access these using the following menu selections: **Start → Programs → Accessories → Notepad** or **WordPad**.

Files can also be viewed using the VDM *type* command line option.

echo Command

The *echo* command writes a string to standard output (usually the terminal). The output of an *echo* command can be piped to another command or redirected to a file. The full path name of the command is */bin/echo*.

The syntax of the command is

```
echo -n string
```

If both *-n* and `string` are omitted, *echo* just returns a new line. The *-n* option suppresses the new line after the `string` is output to standard output (usually the terminal screen.) For the *-n* option to work properly, the user's PATH must list */usr/ucb* before */usr/bin*.

Within the Bourne and C shells there is another *echo* command that is a built-in shell. The */bin/echo* command and the *echo* built-in shell command in the Bourne shell support escape characters as part of the string. When using these escape characters, be sure to enclose them in quotes so that they are interpreted properly by the *echo* command. Table B.21 presents these escape characters.

The C shell version of the *echo* command does not support escape characters. To ensure that you are not executing the C shell built-in *echo* command, enter `/bin/echo` instead of just `echo`.

EXAMPLES OF THE *echo* COMMAND

To display a message to standard output (your own terminal screen), enter

```
echo "This is my message."
```

To send a two-line message to another terminal, enter

```
echo "Hello, user! \n Please log off! " > /dev/tty00
```

To display the value of the environment variable TERM, enter

```
echo $TERM
```

TABLE B.21.   Escape Characters Used by the *echo* Command

Escape Character	Description
\0*nnn*	*nnn* is the octal number for an ASCII character, which can be from one to three digits long
\b	Backspace character
\c	Same as the *-n* option; omits the new line at end of the string
\f	Form feed
\n	New line
\r	Carriage return
\t	Tab character
\v	Vertical tab
\\	Backslash

Windows NT Alternative

Utilize the *echo* command available through the VDM command line. This command can be utilized in a batch file or directly on the command line.

head Command

The *head* command displays the first ten lines of the requested files by default. This command is useful for taking a cursory look at the contents of a file.

The format of the command is

```
head -n file(s)
```

where *−n* is the number of lines to be displayed. The *−n* option is optional and is necessary only if the number of lines to be displayed is different than ten.

ls (list) Command

The best way to list the contents of a directory is with the *ls* command. A user can list the contents of an entire directory or information about selected files. This command is powerful because users can decide which list format best suits their current needs. In addition, metacharacters can be used as part of the command.

UNIX

The syntax of this command is

```
ls options filename(s)
```

Using the *ls* command without any `options` (Table B.22) or `filenames` lists alphabetically the names of the files and subdirectories in the current directory.

EXAMPLES OF THE *ls* COMMAND

A user is having trouble remembering the filename for the last file he created today. To help him determine the filename, enter

```
ls -lt | more
```

Since a long listing of a directory has the potential of taking more than one screen to display, the example is piped to the *more* command so that only a page (or screen) of the listing displays at a time.

A user is having difficulty removing a file and the system administrator suspects that there is a nonprintable character in the filename. To confirm this, she enters

```
ls -lq
```

Windows NT Alternative

A listing of directories and files can be displayed by clicking on the My Computer icon. An alternative to this method is the Windows NT Explorer program, found by selecting **Start ➤ Programs ➤ Windows NT Explorer**.

Within VDM, the *dir* command is available via the command line.

man (manual) Command

The *man* command is used to display the on-line documentation for UNIX commands as well as system codes, system calls, file formats, and device and driver information.

The syntax of this command is

```
man options section topic
```

A `topic` must be entered unless you are using the *-k* and *-t* options described in Table B.23. When no `section` is given with `topic`, the first occurrence of `topic` is displayed. (In some variants of UNIX all occurrences of

TABLE B.22. *ls* Options

Option	Description
-a	Lists all files, even hidden ones that are identified by a period preceding the filename
-A	Same as the -a option, but does not display the "." (current directory) and ".." (parent directory) entries
-b	Displays any nonprintable characters in octal format (\xxx)
-c	Lists files in ascending sequence by modification time (the last time the file or inode was modified). This must be used in conjunction with the *-t* option.
-C	Lists files in columnar format, where the files are sorted alphabetically down the columns. This is the default format in SV4, but it is not the default in older UNIX variants.
-d	Does not list the content of a directory, only its name
-F	Appends an identifier to specific file types: / to directories, * to executable files, and @ to symbolic links
-f	Evaluates each *filename* as a directory, which means that the directory name slot of the inode is read. The files are output in the order they appear in the directory. This option works like *-a*, and options *l*, *r*, *s*, and *t* are ignored.
-g	Does not display the owner name. Similar in format to the *-l* option.
-i	Displays the inode number for each file in the first column.
-l	Displays a long, detailed alphabetical list containing the following information: mode, links, owner, group, size in bytes (or major, minor numbers for special files), modification time, filename, and symbolic link path name. In addition, the total number of blocks in the directory is displayed at the top of the list.
-L	Lists the name of the file or directory referenced by a symbolic link
-m	Lists the files across the page separated by commas
-n	Similar to *-l*, except displays the Group ID (GID) and User ID (UID) numbers instead of the group and owner names
-o	Similar to *-l* except the group name is not displayed
-p	Attaches a forward slash (/) after directory names so that they are recognized more easily
-q	Substitutes nonprintable characters with a question mark
-r	Lists files in reverse order. Used by itself, this option lists files in reverse alphabetical order, but used in conjunction with the -t option, it lists by oldest modification date first.
-R	Lists all directories and subdirectories. This is called a *recursive listing*. This could be a multiple screen display, so be sure to pipe it to the *more* or *pg* command.
-s	Displays the size of the files in 512-byte blocks instead of bytes
-t	Lists files in the order of modification times with the newest file first
-u	Sequences files by the access time, newest first. Must be used in conjunction with the *-t* option.
-x	Displays files in rows
-1	Displays one item for each line (Note this option is the number one not the letter l.)

UNIX

TABLE B.23.   *man* Options

Option	Qualifier	Description
-		Utilizes the *cat* command to display the documentation to the screen. If this option is not used, *more -s* is the default screen display utility utilized.
-a		Displays all pages in the documentation that match the `topic` entered. This option is not available in all UNIX variants.
-f	*filename(s)*	Accesses the on-line manual and outputs a summary for all *filename(s)*. The only option that can be used in conjunction with this one is -M.
-k	*keyword(s)*	For each *keyword* found, outputs to standard output the header line as it appears in the documentation file. The only option that can be used in conjunction with this one is -M.
-M	*pathname*	Searches the manual stored in *pathname* instead of the default directory set by MANPATH, which is usually */usr/share/man*.
-s	*section*	Required with the Solaris 2.x UNIX variant if entering a *section* number from 1 to 8.
-t		Utilizes *troff* to format the *man* page display
-T	*macro*	Utilizes *macro* to output the *man* pages. The default that *man* utilizes is *tmac.an*

`topic` are displayed.) To access other sections, a `section` number from 1 to 8 should be entered.

In order for the *-k* option to work on some UNIX variants, the command *catman -w* must be run first to create the index file */usr/share/man/whatis*. Our recommendation is to try to execute the *man -k keyword* command first. If no results are returned, check the *man* pages of your system for *catman*. Some UNIX variants use the program */usr/lib/makewhatis* instead of *catman*.

EXAMPLES OF THE *man* COMMAND

To display all commands related to mounting a file system, enter

```
man -k mount
```

To create a text file of the command *ps* that can be input to an editor on either DOS or UNIX, enter

```
man - ps | col -b > outfile
```

The *col –b* command is necessary to strip out the backspaces that would display as ^H in the outfile, making it difficult to read.

Windows NT Alternative

The Help function provides on-line documentation regarding commands and procedures to Windows NT users. Access **Help** from the **Start** menu. The **Find** tab within Help is useful for locating commands or topics.

more or *page* **Command**

The *more* command enables the user to display large files one screen at a time. To move to the next screen of information, the user presses the spacebar. Another name for this command is *page*. The *terminfo* file is used to determine the terminal characteristics for formatting data on the screen.

The format of the command is

```
more options filename(s)
```

or

```
page options filename(s)
```

The *more* or *page* command options are listed in Table B.24. While within the *more* command, there are a number of commands that can be used to move around in the file. There is no need to press <Enter> after these commands because they are interpreted immediately. In addition they do not echo back to the screen. Only / and ! display. These internal commands are outlined in Table B.25.

Windows NT Alternative

Within VDM use the *more* command. It operates very similarly to the UNIX version. If the Notepad or WordPad editors are used to display a file, this type of a *more* command may not be necessary.

UNIX

TABLE B.24.   *more* or *page* **Options**

Option	Description
-c	Clears each window before displaying the next page. The default is to scroll the next page on the screen. The -c option is viewed as being the fastest.
-d	At the end of each screen, displays: Press space to continue, 'q' to quit. This message may differ between UNIX variants. The default prompt is usually "More."
-f	Counts lines logically rather than by screen. In other words, counts a long line that wraps to several lines on the screen as one line. This command is used primarily when the input to *more* is coming from *nroff*.
-l	Ignores form-feed characters (^L). The default is to pause at each form feed like the *more* command pauses at the end of a screen.
-n	Changes the size of the window. In other words, changes the number of lines that display per screen. The default display size for a 24-line terminal is 22 lines.
-r	Displays control characters in the file using the format ^c (caret character). For example, displays ^M for carriage returns. Please note that for SCO systems, ^M is the only control character that -r displays. The rest are displayed using the -v option. This option does not exist on some UNIX variants.
-s	Omits the display of multiple blank lines; instead, only displays one blank line for many
-u	Does not display/interpret backspace (^H) or underline characters. This option should be used when the display terminal does not interpret underline characters properly.
-v	Displays control characters and unprintable ASCII characters in the file using the format ^c (caret character). This is similar to the -r option.
-w	Does not exit until the user presses a key
-num	Makes the size of the window *num* lines.
+line	Starts displaying the file at *line* number.
+/pattern	Searches for *pattern*, then begins the display two lines before the first occurrence.

TABLE B.25. *more (page)* **Internal Command Options**

Option	Description
spacebar	Displays the next screen of text
\<Enter\>	Displays the next line
h or ?	Displays help
x	Displays *x* more lines
d or \<Ctrl-d\>	Displays down eleven lines. If a number *x* is entered prior to *d,* displays down *x* number of lines. For example, 10d displays down 10 lines.
*x*z	Changes the window size to *x* lines
*x*s	Skips down *x* lines
*x*f	Skips down *x* screens
b or \<Ctrl-b\>	Goes back to the previous screen
=	Displays the current line number
v	Starts *vi* at the current line
*x*pattern/	Finds the *x*th occurrence of *pattern,* then begins the display two lines before it. The default value of *x* is 1 (one).
*x*n	Finds the *x*th occurrence of the last pattern used. If *x* is omitted, finds the next occurrence of the last search pattern entered.
'	Starts searching where the last search ended. If no search has been conducted, goes back to the beginning of the file.
x:n	Goes to the next file if *x* is omitted or is set to 1. Otherwise, goes to the *x*th next file listed in the command line.
x:p	Goes to the previous file if *x* is omitted or set to 1. Otherwise, goes to the *x*th previous file listed in the command line.
:f	Displays the current filename and line number
.	Repeats the previous command
!*shell*	Starts the shell command named *shell*. If % is utilized, the current filename replaces % in *shell*. If ! is utilized, the previous shell replaces !.
/*pattern*	Searches for *pattern*
q or Q	Quits

UNIX

pg **Command**

The *pg* command is similar to the *more* and *page* commands. There are a few differences in the *pg* options versus the *more* options. The primary difference is the ability to move forward and backward within the file, reviewing information that has already been displayed. Another difference is that when formatting data for the screen, the *pg* command uses the *termcap* file for terminal definitions. (The */etc/termcap* file is often used for terminal definitions on BSD-based systems such as SunOS.) Whether the *more* command or the *pg* command is better to use is a matter of personal preference.

The syntax of the command is

```
pg options filename(s)
```

Table B.26 presents the options for the *pg* command. While within the *pg* command, there are a number of internal command options that can be used to move around in the file, as listed in Table B.27.

TABLE B.26.   *pg* Options

Option	Qualifier	Description
-c		Clears each window before displaying the next page. The default method is to scroll to the next page. The -c option is viewed as being faster than not using this option. If the terminal definition does not support "clear screen," the screen will scroll regardless if this option is entered.
-e		Displays the next file automatically after the end of the first one is reached. The default is to pause between files.
-f		Does not break up long lines. The default is to wrap lines that are longer than the screen width. The default can create a problem if special characters, such as control characters, are split.
-n		Considered a "quick key" option, this option allows the user to press just the command letter and not <Enter> while viewing the file. There are times that <Enter> is required regardless if this option is specified.
-p	*string*	Changes the prompt between pages of a file to *string*. Utilize *%d* to display the page number. The default prompt is a colon.
-s		Displays messages and prompts in reverse video (also referred to as *standout mode*)
-num		Makes the size of the window *num* lines. The default is usually 23 lines for a 24-line screen.
+line		Starts displaying the file at *line* number
+/pattern		Searches for *pattern,* then begins displaying at the line of the first occurrence

TABLE B.27.   *pg* Internal Command Options

Option	Description
<Enter>	Displays the next line
h	Displays help
+x or -x	+x, Displays forward x pages; -x, displays backward x pages
+xl or -xl	+xl, Scrolls forward x number of lines; -xl, scrolls backward x number of lines
l	Begins display at line number l
+d or -d	+d, Scrolls forward half of a screen; -d, scrolls backward half of a screen. <Ctrl-d> can be used instead of d.
.	Redisplays the current page/screen. Another option is to use <Ctrl-L>.
$	Displays the last screen of the file
x/*pattern*/	Searches for the xth occurrence of *pattern*. The search begins after the current page and continues to the end of the file. <Enter> must be pressed even if the -n option is requested. The first match displays at the top of the screen. Follow the search pattern with an m to leave the displayed match at the middle of the screen. Or follow the search pattern with a b to display the match at the bottom of the screen. A t after the pattern returns the displayed match to the top of the screen.
x^*pattern*^ or x?*pattern*	Searches for the xth occurrence of *pattern*. The search goes backward and begins before the current page, and continues to the beginning of the file. <Enter> must be pressed even if the -n option is requested. The first match displays at the top of the screen. Follow the search pattern with an m to leave the displayed match at the middle of the screen or follow the search pattern with a b to display the match at the bottom of the screen. A t after the pattern returns the displayed match to the top of the screen.
xn	Goes to the xth next file listed in the command line; ignored if there is only one file listed
xp	Goes to the xth previous file in the command line
xw	Changes the display to have a screen size of x lines
s*filename*	Saves displayed data as *filename*
!*command*	Passes *command* to the shell. <Enter> must be pressed after *command* even if the -n option is requested.
Ctrl-\	Stops displaying data and displays the prompt. A <BREAK> key works the same way.
q or Q	Quits

UNIX

printf Command

The *printf* command enables a user to print a string of information based on a defined format. This command is often used in shell scripts to print messages to the user or to explain error messages further.

The syntax of this command is

```
printf format string
```

The *string* variable is optional. Often another command pipes data to the *printf* command for printing on standard output.

The *format* variable can be text, escape sequences, or a combination of predefined arguments. These arguments can take the format of

```
%(flag)(x.y)conv-char
```

Let's break down this syntax. The percent sign is required and signifies that an argument follows. The *flag* parameter is optional. When it is used, it can have three different formats as described in Table B.28.

The next argument is *x.y*, where *x* represents the field width and *y* represents the precision for numeric values or the maximal field width. This argument is optional and explained more fully in Table B.29.

The last argument is required and is *conv-char* or *conversion character*. The conversion character defines the type of output and its format. Table B.29 discusses each available conversion character.

EXAMPLES OF THE *printf* COMMAND

A simple example of the *printf* command is as follows:

```
printf ("\n\n*** DDS Meeting Scheduler ***\n")
```

This command will print two empty lines, the text *** DDS Meeting Scheduler ***", then another empty line.

TABLE B.28.   *printf* flag Options

Option	Description
–	Prints the data left justified
+	Identifies a signed result, either a + for positive or a – for negative
#	Requests an alternate format (see Table B.29)
%	Outputs a percent sign

EXAMPLES OF THE *cp* COMMAND

To make a backup copy of the *budget* file while preserving its permissions and modification times for future reference, type

```
cp -p budget budget.sav
```

To make a complete backup of some application software before installing some new software, type

```
cp -r /usr/medal /usr/backup
```

To copy several files to the user *bosco*'s financial directory and prompt before overwriting, type

```
cp -i forecast budget /usr/bosco/financial
```

Within X-Windows-based window managers like CDE, a file can be copied by selecting the file with the mouse in the directory window, dragging the file to its destination, and releasing the mouse. This method works whether a file or a directory is selected.

Windows NT Alternative

To copy a file, which means that the original file still exists, select a file while within either the My Computer window or Windows NT Explorer. Once selected, continue to hold down the left mouse button and drag the file to its new destination while simultaneously holding down <Ctrl>. If the user drags the file without holding <Ctrl>, the file is moved to its new destination (unless that destination is on another disk). Multiple files can be selected for copying by holding down <Ctrl> while selecting the source files with the mouse.

From within the My Computer or Windows NT Explorer window a user can also utilize the **Edit** menu to copy the file. Select the file, select **Edit** from the menu bar, then select **Copy**. At the destination, the user would once again select **Edit**, then **Paste**.

Using the VDM command line, the *copy* or *xcopy* command could be executed.

dirname (directory name) Command

The *dirname* command outputs to standard output the path name of the file entered, excluding the information after the last slash (/). The syntax of this command is

```
dirname pathname
```

For example, if the following was entered on the command line

```
dirname /usr/bosco/financial
```

the result */usr/bosco* would be returned to the screen.

This command is most often used in shell scripts in conjunction with shell variables.

file Command

The *file* command outputs the file type of the files listed. The file type is determined by testing the data in the file. This test usually includes a check against the file types in the magic file, which is */etc/magic* unless otherwise designated. Some of the file types that can be found include text (or ASCII) file, directory, symbolic link, data, empty, and c program. The syntax of this command is

```
file options filename(s)
```

The *file* command options are presented in Table B.32.

TABLE B.32.   *file* Options

Option	Qualifier	Description
-c		Checks the format of the magic file. No output regarding file types is displayed.
-f	*name*	Executes the *file* command for all files listed in the file *name*
-h		Ignores symbolic links. This option is the default on some UNIX variants.
-L		Follows symbolic links
-m	*name*	Uses *name* as the magic file

EXAMPLES OF THE *file* COMMAND

To list the files in the */tmp* directory that are empty, enter

```
file /tmp/* | grep empty
```

Using the magic file */etc/magic2*, determine the type of the files in */usr/bosco/list*:

```
file -f/usr/bosco/list -m/etc/magic2
```

Windows NT Alternative

Windows NT identifies the file type for the user automatically. If Windows NT cannot determine the file type, it asks the user to identify it.

ln (link) Command

One concern of every system administrator at one time or another is the amount of disk space available on the system. Another concern is customizing applications for each user. UNIX provides a way to alleviate these concerns somewhat. Suppose there is an office application to which all users have access and it is executed by typing `medal` at the prompt. One type-A personality would prefer to type just `m` to execute the application rather than type the longer `medal`. The *ln* command allows the system administrator to give the user what he wants while minimally affecting disk space usage.

Another use of *ln* is to hide the real location of files, directories, or applications. The symbolic link is employed to access applications or files that appear to the user as local, but they are actually located elsewhere, such as in another file system. The system administrator can move or switch the location of a file or application easily as required.

The *ln* command creates a reference to the file with another name. It does not create another copy of the file; it just creates a separate directory entry. In this type of link, often referred to as a *hard link,* the files share the same inode and the same blocks on disk. A hard link cannot occur over disk partitions (file systems). For a link to occur over disk partitions (file systems), a symbolic link must be executed. A symbolic link is a file that contains a pointer to the path name of the original file.

The syntax of the *ln* command is

```
ln options source-file(s) destination-file
```

The `destination-file` parameter can be a directory. If it is a directory, then a link named `source-file` is created in the directory.

Table B.33 lists the *ln* command options.

EXAMPLES OF THE *ln* COMMAND

To keep the type-A personality happy in the scenario described above, type

```
ln /bin/medal /bin/m
```

Now all users can benefit from the shortened command.

TABLE B.33.   *ln* Options

Option	Description
-f	If the `destination-file` already exists, overwrites it with the link (i.e., forces the link)
-n	If the `destination-file` already exists, does not create the link
-s	Creates a link across file systems. This is referred to as a *symbolic link*. When there is a symbolic link, the link reference is displayed when using the *ls -l* command. Please note that this option often does not exist in older versions of UNIX.

To create a symbolic link of the files *March* and *April* to the *Year96* directory in the file system */home,* type

```
ln -s March April /home/Year96
```

mkdir (make directory) Command

The *mkdir* command permits the user to create a directory anywhere that the user has write permission. The syntax of the command is

```
mkdir options directory-name(s)
```

Table B.34 presents the *mkdir* command options.

TABLE B.34.   *mkdir* Options

Option	Qualifiers	Description
-m	*permissions*	Defines *permissions* for the `directory-names` being created. The *permissions* are in the octal format, like 644.
-p		Creates all of the `directory-names` listed, even the parent directory if it doesn't exist already

EXAMPLES OF THE *mkdir* COMMAND

To create two directories named *Mutt* and *Jeff* with permissions of -rw-r--r--, enter

```
mkdir -m 644 Mutt Jeff
```

To create the directory *customer* with a subdirectory of *letters,* enter

```
mkdir -p customer/letters
```

Windows NT Alternative

Within Windows NT, directories can be created using the Windows NT Explorer application or the My Computer window by selecting **File** ➤ **New** ➤ **Folder** from the menu bar.

mount and *umount* Commands

These commands are found in the */etc* or */sbin* directory and enables devices (usually removable ones such as floppies and CD-ROMs) to be accessible to users by "mounting" the file system to a directory. A user with root or superuser permission, such as the system administrator, should be the only person who can execute these commands.

mount COMMAND

This *mount* command permits access to a removable file system by "mounting" it to a directory. For example, to access files on a CD-ROM, the CD-ROM must be mounted as a file system first.

The syntax of the command is

```
/etc/mount options device-name directory
```

The */etc/mount* command options are listed in Table B.35.

TABLE B.35.   *mount* Options

Option	Qualifier	Description
-F	*fstype*	Identifies the type of file system, *fstype,* that is to be mounted if it differs from the system's root file system. Some common file system types are AFS (Acer Fast File), DOS, EAFS (extended Acer Fast File), HS (High Sierra CD ROM), and XENIX.
-r		Mounts the file system as read only
-v		Instructs the command to be verbose. In other words, while the command is executing, comments and status information are displayed on standard output (normally the terminal screen).

UNIX

The *mount* command can be executed without any options (i.e., */etc/ mount*). When this is done, the command returns what is currently mounted on the system in the following format:

```
Directory on Device Permission on Day Date Time Year
```

The following is an example of how root is mounted on one of our test systems:

```
/ on /dev/root read/write on Mon Dec 10 8:34:56 1996
```

The directory to which a device is mounted should already exist and contain no files. If the directory does contain files, they are not accessible while the device is mounted. Although there are times that a system administrator may need to mount devices manually, we strongly recommend the use of the system administrative tools available on the system, such as SMIT or SAM. These tools ensure that access to removable devices is successful.

Examples of the mount Command

To mount a CD-ROM as read only, enter

```
/etc/mount -r /dev/cd0 /cdrom
```

To display what is currently mounted on the system, enter

```
/etc/mount
```

umount COMMAND

This command removes access to the removable file system. The */etc/umount* command should be executed before the physical device is removed or changed. In other words, to access a different CD-ROM, the first one must be unmounted, then physically removed, then the new CD-ROM must be mounted. If the device or file system is in use when the system administrator tries to unmount it, the system will return a message similar to *mount device is busy*.

The syntax of the command is

```
/etc/umount device
```

Example of the umount Command

To unmount the CD-ROM used in the */etc/mount* example, enter

```
/etc/umount /dev/cd0
```

Windows NT Alternative

In most cases devices are available when a user needs them, but occasionally a user may need to start or stop a device. To accomplish this, select **Start** ➤ **Settings** ➤ **Control Panel** ➤ **Devices**.

mv (move) Command

The *mv* command performs two functions. First, it changes the name of a file by renaming it. Second, it moves files or directories from one place to another. It is important to understand the difference between the *mv* and *cp* commands. With the *cp* command, the source file is duplicated in the destination file (i.e., the source file still exists). With the *mv* command, the source file becomes the destination file (i.e., the source file no longer exists as the source file).

The syntax of the *mv* command is

```
mv options source-file(s) destination-file
```

Table B.36 presents the *mv* command options. If the destination file already exists, the *mv* command overwrites it unless one of the options listed in Table B.36 is used. Both the `source-file` and the `destination-file` can be directories.

TABLE B.36.   *mv* Options

Option	Description
–	Used when either the `source-` or the `destination-file` begins with a minus sign
-f	Some files have permission settings that restrict access by certain users. This "force" option forces the move to the `destination-file` regardless of the permissions and does not display any prompts.
-i	Requests the user to respond to a prompt with *y* before overwriting a `destination-file` that already exists

EXAMPLES OF THE *mv* COMMAND

To rename the file *budget* to *budget96,* type

```
mv budget budget96
```

UNIX

To rename the directory *data* to *results,* type

```
mv data results
```

To move the files *January* and *February* from the *results* directory to bosco's *financial* directory, type the following after changing to the *results* directory:

```
mv January February /usr/bosco/financial
```

Windows NT Alternative

To move a file (which means that the original file no longer exists in the source location), the user can select a file while within either the My Computer window or Windows NT Explorer. Once selected, continue to hold down the left mouse button and drag the file to its new destination, as long as the new destination is on the current disk. To force a move rather than a copy to occur, the user must hold down <Shift> while dragging the files.

Using the VDM command line, the *move* command can be executed.

pwd (present working directory) Command

The *pwd* command is very useful to users and system administrators alike. Quite simply, it displays the complete path name of the user's current working directory. The format of the command is

```
pwd
```

Windows NT Alternative

To ensure that the full path name of a file is displayed while in Windows NT Explorer or My Computer, select **View** ➤ **Options** ➤ **View**. From the **View** tab, make sure the option for displaying the full path name is checked.

rm (remove) Command

The *rm* command provides the ability to remove files from the system. A user can only remove files from directories for which he has write permission. A remove is permanent. A user cannot access a file once it has been removed.

The format of the command is

```
rm options file(s)
```

The *rm* command options are listed in Table B.37.

TABLE B.37.   *rm* Options

Option	Description
-f	Does not prompt for confirmation when removing write-protected files
-i	For each file to be removed, prompts for confirmation. A *y* response removes the file, while an *n* response does not.
-r	In this case, the file listed is a directory. This option removes the directory and all of its files and subdirectories (remove recursively). Use this command carefully. It is easy to remove critical files accidentally with this command. We recommend never using wildcard characters (especially *) in conjunction with this option.
—	Use this option when the `file` begins with a minus sign.

Windows NT Alternative

Windows NT provides several methods for deleting files: dragging the file to the Recycle Bin, highlighting the file and pressing <Delete>, and highlighting the file and then selecting **File ➤ Delete** from the menu bar. In all cases the file is moved to the Recycle Bin, where it remains until the Recycle Bin is emptied.

If the user does not wish the file to be saved temporarily in the Recycle Bin, hold down <Shift> while dragging the file to the Recycle Bin.

rmdir (remove directory) Command

The *rmdir* command provides a more cautious way of removing directories from the system. This command only deletes directories that are empty.

The format of this command is

```
rmdir options directory-name(s)
```

The *rmdir* command options are listed in Table B.38.

TABLE B.38. *rmdir* Options

Option	Description
-p	Removes the *directory-name(s)* listed, but also removes the parent directory if it becomes empty as well
-s	Used in conjunction with the *-p* option. Does not display any error messages that are a result of the *-p* option.

Windows NT Alternative

Windows NT deletes directories just as it deletes files, by moving them to the Recycle Bin, where they remain until the Recycle Bin is cleared.

wc (word count) Command

The *wc* command counts characters, words, or lines in a file or files. A common manner of using this command is to use standard input in place of the file.

The syntax of the command is

```
wc options filename(s)
```

Table B.39 lists the *wc* command options.

TABLE B.39. *wc* Options

Option	Description
-c	Counts the number of characters
-l	Counts the number of lines
-w	Counts the number of words

EXAMPLES OF THE *wc* COMMAND

To determine the total number of files and directories in a directory, enter

```
ls | wc -w
```

Please note how the *filename* parameter is omitted from this example. This is because the *wc* command is taking its input from the piped (|) output of the *ls* command.

To determine the number of lines in a program, enter

```
wc -l program.c
```

FILE MANIPULATION

UNIX offers the ability to manipulate the contents of files in a variety of ways. A user can extract specific information from one file and add it to another. In addition, a user can sort files, check the spelling of files, and split a file into multiple files. Once the following commands are learned, a user can manipulate data to create the desired results.

Because of the graphical user interface within Windows NT, many of the commands discussed in this section do not have comparable commands within Windows NT directly. However, most of these commands can be executed within the Notepad or WordPad editors. These editors allow a user to manipulate data/text using options such as **Cut** and **Paste** from the **Edit** menu.

cut Command

The *cut* command allows the user to extract specific fields or columns of data from one or more files. The user can identify the field delimiter for which to search to determine the beginning and end of a field. If a *filename* is omitted from the command, perform the *cut* command on standard input.

The syntax of this command is

```
cut options filename(s)
```

Table B.40 presents the options for the *cut* command. It is important to understand that either the *-c* or the *-f* option is required when using the *cut* command.

EXAMPLE OF THE *cut* COMMAND

The system administrator would like to create a reference file that contains each user's login, user ID, group ID, and comment field. To do this, enter the following command:

```
cut -d: f1,3,4,5 /etc/passwd > userinfo
```

The file *userinfo* will contain output in the following format:

```
login:UID:GID:comments
```

TABLE B.40.   *cut* Options

Option	Qualifier	Description
-c	*columns*	Extracts the *columns* specified. The *columns* qualifier is an integer. Multiple columns are separated by commas, and a range of columns is separated by a hyphen.
-d	*c*	Identifies the delimiter character *c* for which to search to mark the beginning and end of each field. The default delimiter is the tab character. Be sure to surround the delimiter character with quotes, especially if it is a special character. This option must be used with the *-f* option.
-f	*fields*	Extracts the *fields* specified. The *fields* qualifier is an integer. Multiple *fields* are separated by commas, and a range of fields is separated by a hyphen.
-s		Ignores lines in the file that have no delimiters. This option must be used with the *-f* option.

join Command

The *join* command "joins" the contents of two files based on a matched common field. The two files must be sorted. When a common field is contained in a line in each file, those two lines are combined into a single line following the common field. The output of the *join* command goes to standard output or can be redirected to a file.

The syntax of the *join* command is

```
join options file1 file2
```

Table B.41 lists the *join* command options.

EXAMPLE OF THE *join* COMMAND

Now the system administrator would like to add the group name to the *userinfo* file created in the *cut* example presented earlier. To add the group name, enter the following:

```
join -t: -j1 3 -j2 3 -o 1.1 1.2 1.4 1.3 2.1 userinfo /etc/group > userinfo2
```

This command joins the two files on the group ID field (field 3 in both *userinfo* and */etc/group*). The output is in the following format:

```
login:UID:comment:GID:Group Name
```

TABLE B.41. *join* Options

Option	Qualifiers	Description
-a	*n*	List the lines in file *n* that don't contain a match on the common field. The qualifier *n* can be a 1 for `file1` or a 2 for `file2`. If *n* is omitted, this option displays the lines in both files that don't contain a match on the common field.
-e	*string*	Includes *string* in the output in place of an empty output field
-j	*n x*	On matched lines, outputs fields from file *n* beginning with field *x*. The qualifier *n* can be a 1 for `file1` or a 2 for `file2`. If *n* is omitted, outputs fields from both files beginning with the field *x*. Fields are numbered starting with one.
-o	*n.x n.x n.x*	Creates the output line using file *n* and field *x*. Include as many of the *n.x* combinations as necessary to create the appropriate output. Be sure to include the field number for the common field if it is to be displayed in the output.
-t	*d*	Uses *d* as the field delimiter for both the input and output files

UNIX

paste Command

The *paste* command adds corresponding lines from files into a column-formatted output file. The input can be one or more files whereas the output is a single file. The columns in the output file are separated by a tab unless specified otherwise with the options (Table B.42).

The syntax of this command is

```
paste options file(s)
```

EXAMPLE OF THE *paste* COMMAND

To output the contents of a file into four columns, a user could enter the following command:

```
paste -s -d"\t\t\t\n" file1
```

The *-s* option pastes each pair of sequential lines together, while the *-d* option formats the output using the tab (\t) as a column separator.

TABLE B.42.   *paste* Options

Option	Qualifier	Description
-		Uses standard input for this input file
-d	'*d*'	Uses '*d*' to separate the columns. The following escape sequences can be used as well as any other character: \n for newline, \t for tab, \ for backslash, and \0 for a null character. The qualifier '*d*' can be used more than once in a command line to identify different separators for each column. The default separator is a tab.
-s		Combines each pair of sequential lines into one line. This option is for use within a single file.

sort Command

The *sort* command sorts the lines of the named files into the order identified by the *options* (Table B.43). The default sort order is alphabetical. The syntax of this command is

```
sort options file(s)
```

EXAMPLE OF THE *sort* COMMAND

To sort the *userinfo2* file created in the *join* example given earlier by the user ID number, enter the following:

```
sort -t: +1n -2 userinfo2
```

The *-t* option gives the field separator as a colon (:) and the *+1n* instructs the command to sort in numeric sequence beginning with field 1 and ending at the beginning of field 2 (*-2* option). Remember to count the fields beginning with zero!

Windows NT Alternative

Utilizing the VDM command line, execute the *sort* command.

TABLE B.43. *sort* Options

Option	Qualifier	Description
-b		Does not include spaces and tabs at the beginning of a line in the sort; ignores them
-c		Checks the *files* to determine if they are already sorted. If so, this option terminates the command without creating output files.
-d		Does not include punctuation in the sort (e.g., the way a dictionary is sorted)
-f		Ignores upper- and lowercase distinctions for the sort
-i		Does not include nonprintable characters in the sort. Nonprintable characters are those that have an ASCII value from 040 to 176.
-m		Merges the *files* when more than one file is listed. This option assumes that the files are already sorted.
-M		Interprets the first three characters as a month designation (i.e., sorts by month)
-n		Sorts in numerical order
-o	*filename*	Stores sorted output in *filename*. The default is standard output.
-r		Sorts in reverse order depending on the sort option chosen
-t	*d*	Separates fields in the output with the delimiter *d*. The default delimiter is tab.
-u		Outputs duplicate lines in the input file once
-y	*memory*	Defines the amount of memory (in kilobytes) allocated to the *sort* command. If no memory is specified, this option automatically allocates the maximum.
-z	*size*	Defines the maximum number of bytes than can be included in one line (i.e., defines the length of the longest line)
+x.y		Skips to the *x*th field to begin sorting at character *y* and sorts to the end of the line unless the option -*x.y* is present. If *y* is omitted, this option sorts on the first character of field *x* only. Starts counting fields in a line with the number zero. In other words, the first field is field zero, the second field is field one, etc. This option must be used in conjunction with one of the following options: *b, d, f, i, n,* or *r*.
-x.y		Ends the sort at field *x*, character *y*. If this option is not entered, the end of the line is considered the end of the *sort* key.

UNIX

spell Command

The *spell* command is a spellchecker that is available on UNIX systems. The system dictionary is stored in */usr/lib/spell*. The syntax of this command is

```
spell options file(s)
```

The options for the *spell* command are presented in Table B.44.

TABLE B.44.   *spell* Options

Option	Description
-b	Checks also for the British spelling of words
-l	The *spell* command by default follows the paths of all included files, namely the *troff* macros of *.so* and *.nx*, unless they begin with the path */usr/lib*. This option does not ignore the */usr/lib*-included files.
-v	Includes all words in a dictionary list, even those included in the definitions of the dictionary entries
+*custom*	Enter for *custom* the name of a custom dictionary that contains sorted words used to expand the system dictionary. This command checks words against the system dictionary as well as the *custom* list. The format of this file should include only one word per line.

EXAMPLE OF THE *spell* COMMAND

Suppose that you created a technical document that contained a number of acronyms. To spell check the document against the system dictionary as well as your own acronym dictionary, enter the following command:

```
spell +/usr/bosco/Acronyms techdoc
```

split and *csplit* Commands

The *split* and *csplit* commands split the contents of an input file into one or more output files depending on the options used. These commands are useful for breaking large files into more manageable components.

split COMMAND

The *split* command splits an input file based on a specified number of lines. The input file is not altered in anyway. The split file is output into the necessary number of output files with the default names of *xaa, xab, xac,* etc. If an output name is given on the command line, the output name is appended with *aa, ab, ac,* etc., to accommodate multiple output files.

The syntax of the command is

```
split -n infilename outfilename
```

The *-n* option represents the number of lines that each `outfilename` should contain. If this option is omitted, the system assumes that `infilename` should be broken into 1000 line segments.

If the input is coming from standard input, use a minus sign as `infilename`.

Example of the split Command

To split a large program file called *biggie* into manageable sections of 100 lines per file, enter the following command:

```
split -100 biggie biggie
```

This will name the output files: *biggieaa, biggieab, biggieac,* etc., until the end of the file is reached.

csplit COMMAND

The *csplit* command differs from the *split* command in that it separates `infilename` into different *outfilenames* based on the parameters given. These parameters could be a count of lines (similar to split) or a match on a particular pattern. The *csplit* command provides a little more flexibility to the user.

The syntax of this command is

```
csplit options infilename parameters
```

A maximum of one hundred *outfilenames* can be created and are named *xx00* through *xx99* unless the *-f* option (Table B.45) is selected. The parameters are listed in Table B.46.

Example of the csplit Command

To split the *techdoc* file into separate chapter files, the *csplit* command can be used to match on the word Chapter. Each Chapter has about a hundred lines. The command to split this file is

```
csplit -fChapter techdoc /Chapter/+100
```

TABLE B.45.   *csplit* Options

Option	Qualifier	Description
-f	*outfilename*	Creates the output files with the names *outfilename00* through *outfilename99*
-k		Keeps all *outfilenames* created even if an error occurs during processing. If this option is not specified, all *outfilenames* are deleted from the system when the command terminates with an error.
-s		Suppresses all character counts. By default the *csplit* command prints the number of characters for each *outfilename* created.

TABLE B.46.   *csplit* Parameters

Parameter	Description
/pattern/+x	Matches *pattern* then outputs lines from the *pattern* line to the *x*th line. If *x* is omitted, this parameter outputs lines beginning with the current line and going up to the line containing *pattern*. The current line then becomes the line containing *pattern*.
/pattern/-x	Matches *pattern* then outputs lines beginning with the *x*th line above the *pattern* up to the line containing the *pattern*. If *x* is omitted, this parameter outputs lines beginning with the current line and going up to the line containing the pattern.
%pattern%	Matches *pattern* only and doesn't output extra lines
lines	Creates *outfilename* containing the current line up to the line number *lines*. The current line then becomes the line represented by the parameter *lines*.
{x}	Performs the parameters *x* times. This parameter can follow any of the other parameters. A new file is created when the pattern is matched or the number of lines is reached.

tr Command

The *tr* command can substitute one string for another or delete characters in a file. The command takes input from standard input and creates output in standard output. The syntax of the command is

```
tr options string1 string2
```

Table B.47 lists the *tr* command options.

TABLE B.47.   *tr* Options

Options	Description
-c	Changes the characters in *string1* to their ASCII counterparts (001 to 377)
-d	Deletes characters found in *string1* from the input
-s	Reduces repeated characters in *string2* to one character for output

The data, *string1,* are the characters that are matched and must be translated, whereas *string2* represents the result of that translation.

To represent a range of ASCII characters, utilize the format *[c1-cn],* where *c1* represents the first character and *cn* represents the last character.

To represent repeated characters use the format *[c*n],* where *c* is the character and *n* is the number of repetitions of it. If *n* is zero or omitted, the command assumes a large number of the characters represented by *c*. Using *n* as zero is useful for padding *string2*. It is important to remember that *string2* must be the same length as *string1.*

A \ (backslash) followed by one to three digits represents an octal value of a character.

EXAMPLES OF THE *tr* COMMAND

To substitute uppercase letters for lowercase letters in a file, enter the following:

```
tr "[a-z]" "[A-Z]" < file1 > newfile1
```

To remove all carriage return characters from a file, enter the following:

```
tr -d "\015" < oldfile >newfile2
```

MISCELLANEOUS COMMANDS

The commands in this section are some that are useful but did not fit easily into any of the other categories.

cal (calendar) Command

The *cal* command permits a user to output a monthly or a yearly calendar to standard output. The syntax of this command is

```
cal month year
```

Both the *month* and *year* parameters are optional. If they are not entered, *cal* displays the calendar for the current month based on the system date. If the *year* parameter is entered, *cal* displays a twelve-month calendar for the *year* entered beginning in January. If both the *month* and the *year* are entered, a calendar for that *month* and *year* is displayed. Acceptable values for *month* are 1 through 12 and for *year* are 1 through 9999 (so the year 2000 and beyond will not be a problem.)

Windows NT Alternative

To display the calendar for the current month, select **Start** ➤ **Settings** ➤ **Control Panel** ➤ **Date/Time**.

date Command

The *date* command has two different formats that perform two separate functions. One format of the *date* command allows the user to output the date in a format that she specifies. The second format allows a superuser to set the date and time for the system.

SETTING THE DATE

Executing the *date* command without any options (Table B.48) simply displays the date to the user. The syntax of the date command that sets the system date is

```
date options string
```

TABLE B.48.   *date* Options for Setting the Date

Option	Qualifier	Description
-a	*s.f*	Adjusts the system clock in small increments until it is *s* seconds away from the current time. The *f* qualifier defines the small increments as a fraction of a second. To slow down the clock, place a minus sign in front of the *s.f* qualifier.
-u		Sets the time using Greenwich Mean Time

The `string` parameter actually can contain three separate numeric fields: day, time, and year. These fields can be used only in the following combinations: time; day and time; and day, time, and year. The formats for these fields are described in Table B.49.

TABLE B.49. *date* Fields

Field	Description
day	The *day* field consists of a two-digit month and a two-digit year formatted as *mmdd*. The default is the current day and month.
time	The *time* field consists of a two-digit hour and a two-digit minute formatted as *HHMM*. The hour field is in the twenty-four-hour format (e.g., 1:00 P.M. is entered as 13).
year	The *year* field can be either a four-digit field for the full year or a two-digit field for the last two digits of a year. (It looks like this portion of UNIX systems can handle the year 2000 and beyond). The default is the current year.

Examples of Setting the Date

To change the time on the system to 3:30 P.M., enter

```
date 1530
```

To change the day to February 14 and the time to 9:00 A.M., enter

```
date 02140900
```

To change the day to February 2, the time to 12:00 noon, and the year to 2000, enter

```
date 020212002000
```

Windows NT Alternative

Select **Start** ➤ **Settings** ➤ **Control Panel** ➤ **Date/Time**. Within the Date/Time Properties window change the date and time as desired, then select the **Apply** button.

To set the date and time via the VDM command line, use the *date* and *time* commands with the appropriate parameters.

DISPLAYING THE DATE

The *date* command that displays the date has the following syntax:

```
date -u +format
```

The *-u* option is not required, but when entered it displays the time using Greenwich Mean Time. The `format` parameter can contain text strings (we recommend that you surround these with quotes) and any of the variables described in Table B.50.

Examples of Displaying the Date

To display "Today is Valentine's Day, February 14th," enter

```
date +"Today is Valentine's Day, "%B %e"th"
```

To display the current time using the twelve-hour format with afternoon designated as p.m. and including the time zone, enter

```
date +"%r %Z"
```

This command displays the time in the following format:

```
03:30:45 p.m. MST
```

Windows NT Alternative

To change the display format of the time, select **Start** ➤ **Settings** ➤ **Control Panel** ➤ **Regional Settings** ➤ **Time**.

To display the time from the VDM command line, enter the command *time* with no parameters.

To display the time on the desktop in Greenwich Mean Time, select **Start** ➤ **Programs** ➤ **Accessories** ➤ **Clock**. Within the Clock window, access **Settings** from the menu bar.

To change the display format of the date, select **Start** ➤ **Settings** ➤ **Control Panel** ➤ **Regional Settings** ➤ **Date**.

To display the date from the VDM command line, enter the command *date* with no parameters.

login Command

The *login* command allows a user to sign on to a system. In most cases a user is prompted for a password after entering her login name. The system admin-

TABLE B.50.   *date* Format Variables

Variable	Description
%a	Displays the abbreviated weekday name
%A	Displays the full weekday name
%b	Displays the abbreviated month name
%B	Displays the full month name
%c	Displays a country-specific date and time format. The default format is displayed as Sun Jan 12 12:30:00 MST 1997.
%d	Displays the day of the month using a zero before single digits, like 01
%D	Displays the date in the format mm/dd/yy
%e	Displays the day of the month with a space before single-digit days
%h	Displays the abbreviated month name
%H	Displays the hour in twenty-four-hour format using numbers from 00 to 23
%I	Displays the hour in twelve-hour format using numbers from 01 to 12
%j	Displays the Julian date using numbers from 001 to 366
%m	Displays the month of the year using numbers from 01 to 12
%M	Displays the minutes using numbers from 00 to 59
%n	Inserts a new line into the output display
%p	Displays morning and afternoon times as a.m. or p.m. The default is A.M. or P.M.
%r	Displays the time in the following format: HH:MM:SS a.m., where HH is in the twelve-hour format
%R	Displays the time in the HH:MM format, where HH is in the twenty-four-hour format
%S	Displays the seconds using numbers from 00 to 61, where 61 allows leap seconds
%t	Inserts a tab into the output display
%T	Displays the time in the following format: HH:MM:SS, where HH is in the twenty-four-hour format
%U	Displays the number of the week in the year using the numbers 00 to 53, where the week begins on Sunday
%w	Displays the day of the week using the numbers 0 through 6, with Sunday being 0 and Saturday being 6
%W	Displays the number of the week in the year using the numbers 00 to 53, where the week begins on Monday
%x	Displays the date in country-specific format
%X	Displays the time in country-specific format
%y	Displays the last two digits of the year using numbers from 00 to 99
%Y	Displays the year as four digits
%Z	Displays the time zone (e.g., MST)

UNIX

TABLE B.51.   *login* Options

Option	Qualifier	Description
user		Signs on using the login name *user*
-d	*tty*	Identifies the path name of the login port *tty*

istrator creates the login name for each user. This login name is stored in the *etc/passwd* file. The syntax of the command is

```
login options env-var=value
```

Table B.51 lists the *login* command options.

The parameter `env-var=value` allows the user to set an environment variable to a specific value at login time. More than one of these parameters can be entered. The PATH and SHELL variables cannot be set at this time.

EXAMPLE OF THE *login* COMMAND

To log in to a system as *bosco* and set the TERM environment variable to vt100, enter the following:

```
login bosco TERM=vt100
```

Windows NT Alternative

Access the Windows NT Security window by pressing `<Ctrl-Alt-Del>` simultaneously. Then select the **Logoff** button to log in as another user.

logname Command

The *logname* command displays the current login name by accessing the LOGNAME environment variable, which is set at time of login. The syntax is simply *logname*.

Windows NT Alternative

Access the Windows NT Security window by pressing `<Ctrl-Alt-Del>` simultaneously. The **Logon Information** is displayed, including the current **DOMAIN/username**.

mail Command

The *mail* command allows users to read and send mail from the command line without the use of a fancy interface. After entering the *mail* command and pressing <Enter>, the user can enter a question mark to display a summary of the commands available within *mail*.

READING MAIL

The syntax of the command to read mail is

```
mail options
```

Table B.52 lists the *mail* read options.

TABLE B.52.   *mail* Read Options

Option	Qualifier	Description
-e		Determines if there is mail without displaying it. If there is mail, an exit status of 0 is returned. If there isn't any mail, the exit status is 1.
-f	*mailbox*	Reads mail from *mailbox* instead of the user's default mailbox
-F	*user(s)*	Forwards all mail to the *user(s)* listed.
-h		Displays a list of messages instead of just the latest message
-p		Displays all messages without pausing in between messages
-P		Includes all header lines when displaying messages
-q		Quits the mail command when an interrupt signal is received
-r		Displays messages in reverse order, oldest to newest

SENDING MAIL

The syntax for sending mail is

```
mail options user(s)
```

The *user(s)* parameter is the login name of the users you wish to receive the mail message. Table B.53 lists the *mail* send options.

TABLE B.53.   *mail* Send Options

Option	Qualifier	Description
-m	*string*	Inserts "Message-Type: *string*" line at the beginning of the mail message text. The *string* qualifier can be text that defines the message type.
-t		Inserts a "To:" line in the heading of the message to display the recipients of the mail message
-w		Does not wait for the remote transfer program to complete before sending mail to remote users

Windows NT Alternative

The Microsoft Exchange application provides mail services to users of Windows NT. To access, select the **Inbox** icon.

mesg Command

The *mesg* command enables you to determine whether or not to allow other users to send messages to your terminal. The syntax of this command is

```
mesg options
```

Executing this command without options (Table B.54) displays whether or not your terminal is accepting messages. The default state of each terminal is to accept messages. A user with root permission (a superuser) can send a message to any user regardless of how the user has the terminal set.

TABLE B.54.   *mesg* Options

Option	Description
n	Prohibits users from sending messages to your terminal
y	Enables users to send messages to your terminal

talk Command

The *talk* command is UNIX's version of the discussion (or chat) rooms that are available through the on-line providers such as America Online, CompuServe, Prodigy, and Microsoft Network. This command divides your screen into two windows, allowing you to type your messages in the top window while the recipient's response displays in the bottom window. The syntax of this command is

```
talk user@hostname port
```

The only required parameter is *user,* which is the login name of the user with whom you wish to communicate on the local system. If the user with whom you wish to communicate is on a remote system, you would enter *user@hostname,* where *hostname* is the name of the remote system.

Use the *port* parameter to identify the specific port (tty line) that the *user* is currently employing. This parameter is helpful if the user is logged on more than once. (Of course that rarely happens—Ha!)

To redraw the screen, press <Ctrl-L>. To exit the discussion, press <Ctrl-D>.

Windows NT Alternative

To have a conversation with a user on another machine, select **Start** ➤ **Programs** ➤ **Accessories** ➤ **Chat**.

wall Command

The *wall* command allows a user to send a message to all users. It is used particularly by the superuser to notify users of an imminent system shutdown.

The syntax of the command is simply *wall.* After entering the command and pressing <Enter>, the user can type in the message to be broadcast. To terminate and send the message, the user must press <Ctrl-D>, which designates the end of the file.

write Command

The *write* command is yet another command that allows a user to communicate interactively with another user. The syntax of the command is

```
write user port
```

The *user* parameter is the login name of the user with whom you wish to communicate. The *port* parameter is optional and identifies the tty line (port) that the *user* is employing. This parameter is useful when a person is logged in more than once.

After entering the *write* command and pressing <Enter>, any text that is entered up until the end of the file (EOF) is sent to the *user*. The EOF character is <Ctrl-D>, which instructs the command to end and send the message. In order for the receiving user to respond, he must initiate his own *write* command.

NETWORKING COMMANDS

The networking commands discussed encompass a wide variety of activities. They assist the user in contacting other systems (both UNIX and non-UNIX), transferring files, and managing networks. This is an ever-expanding area of UNIX as networking and communications become more critical to daily business. Be sure to check the *man* pages and system administrative documentation to determine other commands and command options available to your variant of UNIX.

cu (call UNIX) Command

The *cu* command enables the user to call up a system via a telephone line with a modem or a direct connection. The system can be remote or local, UNIX or non-UNIX. Besides allowing the user to connect to other systems, this command also allows the user to interact with the system, including transferring files.

The syntax of the command is

```
cu options dest
```

The following sections discuss the *cu* command in three parts: connect, transmit and receive. First, the command must connect to the system. Once connected, the command permits the user to transmit and receive data.

CONNECTING WITH THE *cu* COMMAND

The first parameter that needs to be completed is *dest,* the value for the destination of the connection (Table B.55). The *dest* parameter is optional based on other *options* requested.

The options available for the *cu* command are listed in Table B.56.

TABLE B.55. *cu* dest **Values**

Value	Description
sysname	Enters the *uucp* system name (*sysname*) for the connection. The *uuname* command provides a list of the valid *uucp* system names. The *cu* command accesses the connection information from the */usr/lib/uucp/Systems* file. This destination should not be used with the *-l* or *-s* options described in Table B.56.
telno	Enter the telephone number to dial.

TABLE B.56. *cu* **Options**

Option	Qualifier	Description
-b	*n*	Set the bits to *n*, which can be a value of 7 or 8.
-c	*name*	Connects to the system *name*. This name must be part of the *uucp Devices* file.
-d		Displays/outputs diagnostics
-e		Sends data to the remote system with even parity
-h		Uses local echo to communicate with other systems that expect terminals to be set to half-duplex mode
-l	*line*	Uses the device, *line*, to connect and communicate with the other system. Do not use this option with a *sysname* destination.
-n		Prompts the user to enter the telephone number
-o		Sends data to the remote system with odd parity
-s	*n*	Sets the speed of transmission (the baud rate) to *n* (e.g., 2400, 9600, 14400). The default is *Any*.
-t		Dials an ASCII terminal with parameters that are set to auto answer

TRANSMITTING WITH THE *cu* COMMAND

The transmit process begins after a connection is made. While in the transmit process, the *cu* command reads data from standard input and transmits it to the connected system. An exception to this process is the command structure that is available within the *cu* command. Commands begin with a tilde (~) and are described in Table B.57.

UNIX

TABLE B.57.   *cu* Transmit Commands

Command	Parameter	Description
~.		Ends the conversation
~!		Escapes to an interactive shell on the local system
~!*cmd*		Runs the *cmd* command on the local system using *sh -c*
~$*cmd*		Runs the *cmd* command on the local system but sends its output to the remote system
~%cd		Changes directories on the local system
~%take	*infile outfile*	Copies *infile* from the remote system to *outfile* on the local system. The *outfile* parameter is optional. If it is not entered, *infile* is the name of the new file on the local system.
~%put	*infile outfile*	Copies *infile* from the local system to *outfile* on the remote system. The *outfile* parameter is optional. If it is not entered, *infile* is the name of the new file on the remote system.
~~*line*		Sends ~*line* to a remote system. This command allows a user to transmit a command to a second remote system that was connected to the first remote system via *cu*.
~%b		Sends a BREAK signal to the remote system
~%d		Toggles the debug mode on or off
~t		Displays the termio values for the local system
~l		Displays the termio values for the communication line
~%ifc		Toggles the control protocols DC3/DC1 and XON/XOFF on or off. Another command that accomplishes this is ~*%nostop*.
~%ofc		Toggles the output flow control on or off

RECEIVING WITH THE *cu* COMMAND

The *cu* receive process reads the data from the remote system and outputs it to standard output. Remember that data preceded by a tilde (~) are treated as commands.

Examples of the cu Command

Suppose you need to dial out on a 14,400-baud modem to the telephone number 555-3232, but you need to dial 9 to access an outside line. The command would be

```
cu -s14400 9=5553232
```

To connect to a system named *bashful* that is set up within *uucp,* enter the following:

```
cu bashful
```

To connect to a system using a direct connection line, the following can be entered:

```
cu -s9600 -l/dev/ttya
```

Windows NT Alternative

The HyperTerminal application within Windows NT permits dial-up access via a modem to another computer. Select **Start ➤ Programs ➤ Accessories ➤ HyperTerminal**. Within HyperTerminal, select **File ➤ Properties**. The telephone number is entered under the **Connect To** tab. Select the **Configure** button to set the baud rate, parity, and stop bits.

ftp (file transport program) **Command**

The *ftp* command enables a user to transfer files to and from a remote system using the File Transfer Protocol. This protocol supports ASCII and binary file transfers, with ASCII being the default type between dissimilar systems. However, if *ftp* determines that the systems are similar, the binary file transfer protocol becomes the default. A more detailed discussion of *ftp* in the context of TCP/IP is provided in Chapters 12 and 13. The syntax of this command is

```
ftp options hostname
```

The `hostname` parameter is the name of the remote system with which you wish to communicate. When given, *ftp* establishes a connection with that system. If the *hostname* is not entered, *ftp* goes into command mode and waits for the user to enter a command. A list of the available *ftp* commands can be retrieved by entering *help* at this point. Due to the number of commands available, we do not discuss them in this book but recommend that you either use this help feature or refer to the *man* pages for *ftp*. The *ftp* command options are listed in Table B.58.

TABLE B.58.   *ftp* Options

Option	Description
-d	Turns on the debug option
-g	Turns off filename "globbing," which means that metacharacters in file and directory names are not expanded
-i	Turns off interactive prompting, which means that *ftp* automatically executes a given command for all filenames entered
-n	Does not allow automatic login when the initial connection is made. Instead, requires the user to log on to the remote system.
-v	Displays all messages from the remote system.

Windows NT Alternative

From the VDM command line, use the *ftp* command. This version of the command behaves similarly to the UNIX version.

hostid Command

The *hostid* command displays the ID number of the host machine in hexadecimal. The command is found in the */usr/ucb* directory and its syntax is simply *hostid*.

hostname Command

The *hostname* command displays the name of the host machine. The syntax of the command is

```
hostname newname
```

Only a superuser can enter the *newname* parameter, which changes the name of the host machine to *newname*.

Windows NT Alternative

Select **Start** ➤ **Settings** ➤ **Control Panel** ➤ **Network**. Within the Network window, select the **Identification** tab. The **Computer Name** field displays the host name. To modify the host name, select the **Change** button.

Using the VDM command line, the *hostname* command will display the name given to the current computer.

netstat (network status) Command

The *netstat* command displays configuration and status information about the network. Several different outputs occur depending on the options chosen (Table B.59). The syntax of the command is

```
netstat options parameters
```

Table B.60 lists some parameters that can be used in conjunction with the options.

If no options are selected, a status report of active sockets is displayed. The socket display (created with the *-a, -A,* or *-n* options) contains local and remote addresses, the size of the send and receive queues in bytes, the protocol used, and the status of this protocol.

The interface display is created using the following options: *-g, -i, -I,* and *-n*. This display contains the packet statistics regarding the number of transfers, errors, and collisions, along with the interface network address and the maximal transmission unit. When the *interval* parameter is entered, the display contains not only a summary of all interfaces since the last system boot but also a cumulative total for each *interval*.

The routing table display can contain the following depending on the options selected: the available routes with their status, the route's destination network, the netmask, and the gateway to be used.

Windows NT Alternative

From the VDM command line, enter the *netstat* command. This version of the *netstat* command is similar to the UNIX version.

UNIX

TABLE B.59. *netstat* Options

Option	Qualifier	Description
-a		Displays the status of all sockets. Do not use with the following options: -g, -i, -I, interval, -m, -M, -p, -r, and -s.
-A		Includes the protocol control block address in the output display. This display includes only active sockets when no other options are selected. Do not use with the following options: -g, -i, -I, interval, -m, -M, -p, -r, and -s.
-f	*addr*	Displays statistics for *addr,* which can have a value of *inet* or *unix* (address families, AF_INET or AF_UNIX). This option can be used in conjunction with the following options: -a, -A, and -s.
-g		Displays multicast information for network interfaces. Only the AF_INET address family is valid. Do not use with the following options: -m, -M, and -p. Can be used with the *-i* option.
-i		Displays the status of network interfaces. Do not use with the following options: -m, -M, and -p. Can be used with the *-g* option.
-I	*interface*	Displays information concerning *interface*. This option can be used with the following options: -g, -i, and -n.
-m		Displays the statistics captured by the network memory management programs. Do not use this option with any others.
-M		Displays the multicast routing tables. To display the multicast routing statistics, combine this option with the *-s* option. Do not use the -M option with -m or -p.
-n		Displays the network address numerically instead of symbolically. This display includes only active sockets when no other options are given. This option can be used with these other options: -a, -A, -i, -r, and -v.
-p	*protocol*	Displays the statistics for *protocol,* where *protocol* can be one of the following values: *arp, icmp, igmp, ip, probe, tcp,* or *upd.* Do not use with the -m option.
-r		Displays the network routing tables. When used in conjunction with the *-v* option, the network masks are displayed. When used with the *-s* option, the routing statistics are displayed. Do not use this with the following options: -g, -i, -I, interval, -m, -M, and -p.
-s		Displays the statistics for all protocols. Do not use this with the following options: -g, -i, -I, interval, -m, and -p.
-v		Displays the network masks in the route entries. This option can only be used in conjunction with the *-r* option.

TABLE B.60. *netstat* **Parameters**

Parameter	Description
interval	Accumulates and displays interface statistics for the given time *interval* of seconds. The *interval* parameter can be used in conjunction with the -g, -i, -I, and -n options.
kernel	Displays statistics for *kernel*. The default value is the default kernel on the system, such as *vmunix, unix,* etc.
mem	Displays the statistics using *mem*. The default value of *mem* is */dev/kmem*.

ping Command

The *ping* command is a tool that allows the system administrator to test the performance of the network when there are suspected problems. This command sends an echo request packet containing 64 bytes to the requested host once every second. When the *ping* command successfully communicates with the requested system, acknowledgment information is displayed to standard output. No output is displayed when there is no response from the receiving system. This is generally the first command to be used to determine if a network node or element is accessible. It is much like checking the power cord on a piece of hardware. When the *ping* command terminates, summary information is displayed.

The syntax of this command is

```
ping options host packet-size
```

The *host* parameter is required and can be either the host name or the system's Internet address. The *host* parameter can also be a broadcast address, in which case all systems that receive the broadcast should respond to the echo packet

The *packet-size* parameter is optional and is used only when it is necessary to modify the default size of 64 bytes. The acceptable values are from 8 to 4095 bytes; but if the value is less than 16 bytes, timing information is not displayed.

The *ping* command options are listed in Table B.61.

Windows NT Alternative

From the VDM command line, enter the *ping* command. This version of the *ping* command behaves similarly to the UNIX version.

TABLE B.61.   *ping* Options

Option	Qualifier	Description
-i	*addr*	This option is used when the host is a multicast address. If entered, the echo request is sent from the address *addr*. If this option is not entered, the echo request is sent from the default address defined in the route configuration.
-n	*count*	Defines the number of packets (*count*) transmitted before terminating the *ping* command. Zero is the default, where *ping* keeps running until receiving an interrupt signal. This option should follow the `host` and `packet-size` parameters.
-o		Includes the IP record route option in the outgoing packets so that the output display contains a summary of the routes taken. This option is valid only for those hosts that utilize the IP record route option.
-p		This option must be used in conjunction with the *-v* option and a large packet size. It displays the new path maximum transmission unit whenever the message "Datagram Too Big" is received.
-r		Sends the echo request directly to `host` bypassing routing tables
-t	*ttl*	Use this option only for multicast addresses. Sets the time-to-live field in the echo request packet (datagram) to *ttl,* where *ttl* is a value from 0 to 255. The time-to-live field defines the maximum number of systems through which the packet can be sent. For example, a *ttl* of 0 limits the datagram to the local system. A *ttl* of 1 (which is the default) limits the transmission to systems that are directly connected to the default interface address (or the address specified by the *-i* option).
-v		Displays other packets received in addition to the echo request packets

rcp (remote copy) Command

The *rcp* command copies files between networked machines. The format of the command is

```
rcp options host:pathname/srcfile username@host:pathname/destfile
```

The `host:pathname/srcfile` parameter identifies the file (or files) that are to be copied to another system. The *host* variable is optional but useful in helping the user keep the systems straight in her mind. The *pathname* variable is only necessary if the `srcfile(s)` is in a directory other than the current one.

The `username@host:pathname/destfile` parameter identifies the user, machine, path, and filename where the source file is to be copied. The *username* variable is only necessary if the user's login name on the destination machine differs from the source machine. The `host` parameter is required because it identifies the host name of the destination system. If the `username@host` variable is omitted, the destination is the local machine. The `pathname` variable is required only if you want the source file copied to a directory other than your home directory. If the `destfile` variable is omitted, the destination file will have the same name as the `srcfile`. The *rcp* command options are listed in Table B.62.

To use the *rcp* command between systems, the user's home directory of the remote system should contain a *.rhosts* file listing the host name of the local system. An alternative is to include the host name of the local system in the remote system's */etc/hosts.equiv* file.

TABLE B.62.   *rcp* Options

Option	Description
-p	Keeps the modification times, access time, and permissions of the `destfile` the same as those for the `srcfile(s)`.
-r	Does a recursive copy. In other words, if both the `srcfile` and `destfile` are directories, this option copies files and subdirectories as well.

EXAMPLES OF THE *rcp* COMMAND

To make a copy of your *budget* directory in your home directory on the system *bashful,* enter the following:

```
rcp -r budget bashful:
```

UNIX

Suppose that your login name on *bashful* was *bosco2* instead of *bosco*. In addition, you wanted the budget directory to be placed in the directory *year96* without changing the modification times. This command would be

```
rcp -pr budget bosco2@bashful:/usr/bosco2/year96
```

Windows NT Alternative

From the VDM command line, the *rcp* command can be executed. This command is similar to the UNIX version. The remote system that is communicating with the Windows NT system must contain a *.rhosts* file in the user's home directory that lists the Windows NT system. If the remote system is a UNIX system, the UNIX system must have the *rshd* daemon running as well as have its own copy of the *rcp* command. The Windows NT system must be the one that initiates the *rcp* command.

Using the graphical side of Windows NT, select a host system from the Network Neighborhood icon, then drag and drop the files into the appropriate place within the My Computer window.

rlogin (remote login) Command

The *rlogin* command allows a user to log in to a remote system from his login session on the local system. The syntax of this command is

```
rlogin options hostname
```

The `hostname` parameter is the name of the remote machine. If a user does not want to enter a password at login on the remote machine, the `hostname` must be included in the *.rhosts* file located in the user's home directory or in the */etc/hosts.equiv* file, both on the remote machine

The options for the *rlogin* command are listed in Table B.63.

Windows NT Alternative

To log in remotely to another computer on the network, access the Network Neighborhood icon, then double-click on the remote computer you wish to access.

TABLE B.63. *rlogin* Options

Option	Qualifier	Description
-8		Sends 8-bit data to the system instead of 7-bit data
-e	*c*	Defines the escape character as *c*. The default escape character is the tilde (~). Using this escape character will disconnect the user from the remote system. As a rule of thumb, users should log out properly rather than using the escape character.
-l	*user*	Use this option only if the login (*user*) name on the remote system is different than the login name on the local system.

rsh (remote shell) Command

The *rsh* command connects to a remote system and either executes a specified command or prompts the user for a remote login. This command is found in the */usr/ucb* directory. The syntax of this command is

```
rsh options hostname cmd
```

The `hostname` parameter is the name of the remote system and is a required parameter. The `cmd` parameter is a command that the user wants to execute on the remote machine. If metacharacters are used, be sure to enclose them in quotes. The `cmd` parameter is optional. If it is not used, the remote system prompts for a remote login.

The *rsh* command options are listed in Table B.64.

TABLE B.64. *rsh* Options

Option	Qualifier	Description
-l	*user*	Connects to the remote system using the login name *user*
-n		Redirects input to */dev/null*.

UNIX

Windows NT Alternative

The *rsh* command can also be entered on the VDM command line. It is similar in function to the UNIX *rsh* command. To run commands via *rsh*, the remote computer must have the *rsh* service running, such as *rshd* on UNIX systems.

ruptime (remote uptime) Command

The *ruptime* command displays the status of machines in a local area network. The syntax of the command is

```
ruptime options
```

Table B.65 lists the *ruptime* options.

In order for the *ruptime* command to run properly, the *rwhod* daemon must be active. This daemon results in traffic on the network every several minutes and can take up progressively more bandwidth as the number of hosts increases, thereby making it cost prohibitive as the network grows.

TABLE B.65. *ruptime* Options

Option	Description
-a	Displays all users, even those that have been idle more than 1 hour
-l	Displays status sorted by load average
-r	Sorts in reverse order depending on the sort option chosen
-t	Sorts the status by uptime
-u	Sorts the status by the number of users

rwho (remote who) Command

The *rwho* command is similar to *who* except that it displays the users logged in for all systems in the local area network. The syntax of this command is

```
rwho -a
```

The *-a* option lists all users even if they have been idle for more than 1 hour. The default (without the *-a* option) displays users who have been active within the last hour.

In order for the *rwho* command to run properly, the *rwhod* daemon must be active. This daemon results in traffic on the network every few minutes and can take up progressively more bandwidth as the number of hosts increases, thereby making it cost prohibitive as the network grows.

telnet Command

The *telnet* command allows a user to connect to another system and to communicate using its own protocol. The syntax of the command is

```
telnet options hostname port
```

Both the *hostname* and *port* parameters are optional. When entered, *telnet* connects to the *hostname* through the *port* identified. The *hostname* can either be entered as the name of the remote system or as that system's Internet address. Once connected, the user enters telnet input mode, which allows him to interact with the remote system beginning with logging in, if the system requires such a step. If desired, the user can enter *telnet* command mode by entering the *telnet* escape character of ^ [(the <ESC> key).

If the *hostname* and *port* parameters are not entered, then *telnet* executes in the command mode. This mode is identified by the prompt *telnet>*. In this mode, a user can supply the name of a host to which to connect by using the *open* command. A number of other commands are available and can be obtained by entering a question mark at the *telnet>* prompt. Due to the number of commands available, we do not discuss them in this book but recommend that you either use this help feature or refer to the *man* pages for *telnet*.

The *telnet* command options are listed in Table B.66.

TABLE B.66.   *telnet* Options

Option	Qualifier	Description
-8		Transfers data at 8 bits from the local tty
-e	*c*	Changes the escape character for *telnet* command mode to *c*. The default value is ^ [(the <ESC> key).
-l		Forces the user to enter a login name and password on the remote system

Windows NT Alternative

The *telnet* command can be executed from the VDM command line. This version of *telnet* behaves similarly to the UNIX version.

uucp (UNIX to UNIX copy) Command

The *uucp* command does exactly what its expanded name implies—copies files between UNIX systems. This copy can be on a local system or between the local system and a remote system. Although the concept behind the command is simple, *uucp* actually has a number of options (Table B.67), files, and related commands that enable some complex tasks to occur. With the appropriate files configured, the *uucp* command connects to the remote system via dial-up or direct connection as well as transfers the files.

TABLE B.67.   *uucp* Options

Option	Qualifier	Description
-c		This is the default option that instructs the command not to copy the *srcfile* to the /usr/spool (or /var/spool) directory prior to transferring the file to the destination system.
-C		Copies files to the /usr/spool (or /var/spool) directory prior to transferring them. This options then allows a user to access the original file for such tasks as modification or decompression while waiting for the file to be transferred.
-d		Creates directories that do not exist at the destination. This is the default.
-f		Does not create directories that do not exist
-g	*x*	Sets the priority for the transfer to *x*, where *x* can be a letter or a number, with *a* and *1* being the highest priorities
-j		Displays the *uucp* job number
-m		Sends mail to the user that executed the command to notify her that the transfer is complete
-n	*name*	Sends mail to the user, *name*, when the transfer is complete. This user can be on the remote system.
-r		Places this *uucp* job in the queue but does not begin the transfer
-s	*statfile*	Outputs the status of the transfer to the file *statfile*. This option overrides the -*m* (mail) option.
-x	*n*	Turns on the debug level to *n*, where *n* is a value from 0 to 9, with 9 producing the most debugging output

We define just a few of the options available here. With increased use of the Internet and FTP's *put* and *get* commands, use of *uucp* has become virtually obsolete. When it is used, its management is complex and entails a number of other commands and files. For more complete information on *uucp,* we refer to the *man* pages or one of the books on *uucp,* such as *Using and Managing UUCP* by Grace Todino (O'Reilly and Associates, 1987) or *Managing UUCP and Usenet* by Tim O'Reilly and Grace Todino (O'Reilly and Associates, 1992).

The syntax of the *uucp* command is

```
uucp options srcsys!srcfile destsys!destfile
```

The only required parameters are the actual file names. The `srcsys` (source system) and the `destsys` (destination system) can be either a local system or a remote one. When transferring a file, *uucp* transfers the execute permissions of the `srcfile` and gives the destination file read-write permission for all (owner, group, and others).

uuname Command

The *uuname* command is a *uucp*-related command that displays the names of systems defined within *uucp*. The syntax of the command is

```
uuname options
```

The *uuname* options are listed in Table B.68.

TABLE B.68.   *uuname* Options

Option	Description
-c	Displays the system names that are known to the *cu* command. These are probably the same as those known by *uucp*. A difference would only occur if there are two *Systems* files defined—one for *cu* and one for *uucp*.
-l	Displays the node name for the local system

OWNERSHIP COMMANDS

The ownership commands provide ways for a user or system administrator to change the following characteristics of a file: the owner, the group, and the permission modes. In addition there are commands in this category that allow the user to display the groups to which the user belongs as well as a listing of user and group ID numbers. Finally, there is a command that allows a user to set the default permission mode for new files.

When reviewing the Windows NT alternatives in this section, keep in mind that file ownership and file permissions differ in concept from that of UNIX. For additional information on Windows NT file ownership and permissions, review Chapters 6 and 7.

chgrp (change group) Command

The *chgrp* command changes the group ownership on files that the user owns. Naturally a superuser can change the group ownership on any file. The syntax of the command is

```
chgrp options newgrp filename(s)
```

The *newgrp* parameter is either the group ID number or group name as identified in the */etc/group* file. Two options can be used when required (Table B.69).

TABLE B.69.   *chgrp* Options

Option	Description
-h	Includes symbolic links when changing the group. The default is to change groups only on those files referenced by a symbolic link.
-R	Sets *newgrp* for all files and subdirectories in a directory; in other words, sets *newgrp* recursively

Windows NT Alternative

To modify share permissions, access either the My Computer window or Windows NT Explorer. Select the file/folder to modify. Click the right mouse button, then select **Sharing** from the menu. Select the **Permissions** button. At this point a group can be added and the **Type of Access** can be changed.

chmod (change mode) Command

The *chmod* command changes the permission modes for files and directories. Only the owner of the file or a superuser can change its permissions. The syntax of this command is

```
chmod option mode filename(s)
```

There is only one *option* for this command and it is the recursive option *-R*. The *-R* option sets recursively the mode for all files, subdirectories, and their files in the directory entered on the command line.

There are basically two ways to set the mode parameter: using a symbolic permission designation or using an octal reference. The symbolic permission designation combines character codes that identify which mode to change, how to change it, and to what to change it. The format for this type of mode is *who how what*. Tables B.70 through B.72 give the acceptable values for these variables.

TABLE B.70.   *who* **Values for** *chmod* **Mode Variable**

Value	Description
u	Changes the modes for the user
g	Changes the modes for the group
o	Changes the modes for others
a	Changes the modes for all (user, group, and other). The who value can be omitted. If it is, all is the default.

TABLE B.71.   *how* **Values for** *chmod* **Mode Variable**

Value	Description
+	Adds the permission to the ones that already exist for *filename*
-	Removes the permission from the ones that already exist for *filename*
=	Changes the permissions for *filename* to the value given

TABLE B.72.   *what* **Values for** *chmod* **Mode Variable**

Value	Description
r	Sets the permission to read
w	Sets the permission to write
x	Sets the permission to execute
s	Sets the user or group ID
t	Sets the sticky bit
u	Sets the permissions to the user's current permissions
g	Sets the permissions to the group's current permissions
o	Sets the permissions to the other's current permissions
L	Sets mandatory locking

UNIX

A three-digit octal number can be entered as the mode to set the permissions for filenames. This octal number can be calculated from the following values: 4 for read, 2 for write, and 1 for execute. Table B.73 gives a complete breakdown of various octal mode values.

There is an optional octal digit that can precede the permission mode. This digit has the following values: 4 to set the user ID at execution time, 2 to set the group ID at execution time or to set mandatory locking and 1 to set the sticky bit.

EXAMPLES OF THE *chmod* COMMAND

To change the permissions of the file budget to read-write for any user, enter the following using the symbolic method:

```
chmod a=rw budget
```

or

```
chmod =rw budget
```

To change the permissions using the octal mode, enter the following:

```
chmod 666 budget
```

To add execute permission to the group permissions for the application program *sales,* enter the following:

```
chmod g+x sales
```

Assuming that the permissions on the sales file were originally read-write-execute for the user, read for the group, and read for others, to add execute permissions for the group as in the previous symbolic example you would enter the following:

```
chmod 754 sales
```

TABLE B.73.   Octal Permission Values

Permission Level	Permissions	Octal Setting
None	---	0
Execute only	--x	1
Write only	-w-	2
Write and execute	-wx	3
Read only	r--	4
Read and execute	r-x	5
Read and write	rw-	6
Read, write, and execute	rwx	7

To set the group ID at execution time in this example, enter the following:

```
chmod 2754 sales
```

Windows NT Alternative

Keep in mind that the concept of file permissions is different between Windows NT and UNIX. The following highlights several methods for changing share permissions.

To modify share permissions, use either the My Computer icon or Windows NT Explorer. After selecting the file or folder, select **File ➤ Properties ➤ Sharing ➤ Permissions**.

To modify share permissions using the administrative wizards, select **Start ➤ Programs ➤ Administrative Tools ➤ Administrative Wizards ➤ Managing File and Folder Access**. At this point, choose either **On my computer** or **On another computer**, then click on the **Next** button. Select the specific file or folder then change the permissions.

Additional permissions can be set for NTFS file systems. These permissions rest on top of the share permissions. From Windows NT Explorer, select the file. Click the right mouse button. Select **Properties ➤ Security Tab ➤ Permissions**.

chown (change owner) Command

The *chown* command allows the user to change the owner of files that he owns. Naturally a superuser can change the owner on any file. The syntax of the command is

```
chown options newowner filename(s)
```

The *newowner* parameter is either the user ID number or the login name as identified in the */etc/passwd* file. There are two options that can be used when required (Table B.74).

TABLE B.74.   *chown* Options

Option	Description
-h	Includes symbolic links when changing the owner. The default is to change owners only on those files referenced by a symbolic link.
-R	Sets *newowner* for all files and subdirectories in a directory. In other words, sets *newowner* recursively.

UNIX

groups Command

The *groups* command displays the groups to which the executing user belongs. Optionally this command displays the groups to which the requested user belongs. The syntax of the *groups* command is

```
groups username
```

The *username* parameter is an optional parameter.

id Command

The *id* command displays your login name, user ID number, group name, and group ID number. The syntax of the command is

```
id -a
```

The *-a* option is not required, but when used it displays all groups.

Windows NT Alternative

Access the Windows NT Security window by pressing `<Ctrl-Alt-Del>` simultaneously. When the **Logon Information** window displays, the **DOMAIN/ username** also displays.

umask Command

The *umask* command can be used to set the default permissions for all newly created files. Additional information on *umask* is covered in Chapter 3. This command is often part of a user's *.login* or *.profile* file, so that *umask* is set at login time. The syntax of the command is

```
umask mask
```

The *mask* parameter is optional. When it is omitted, the *umask* command displays the current default permission modes for newly created files.

The *mask* parameter, when entered, is a three-digit octal code. The possible values of the *mask* parameter are listed in Table B.75.

EXAMPLE OF THE *umask* COMMAND

To set your default file permissions so that you have read-write-execute permissions, your group has read-only permissions, and others have no permissions, enter the following:

```
umask 037
```

TABLE B.75.   Summary of *umask* Settings

Permission Level	Permissions	Octal Setting
None	---	7
Execute only	--x	6
Write only	-w-	5
Write and execute	-wx	4
Read only	r--	3
Read and execute	r-x	2
Read and write	rw-	1
Read, write, and execute	rwx	0

PRINT COMMANDS

Printing commands are critical to any system. Any user or system administrator needs to know how to create a paper copy of a file. This section discusses those commands necessary to print files and to manage the printers and printing processes. The commands described here are considered to be the standard UNIX V.4 print commands. Some older versions of the commands include *lpr* (to print files), *lprm* (to remove files), and *lpq* (to display the print status). These commands still exist in some UNIX variants. In addition, some UNIX variants have added their own print commands, such as *enq* on AIX systems. Check your *man* pages to determine which commands are valid for your system.

cancel Command

The *cancel* command allows print jobs to be canceled (removed) from the print queue. Requests can be canceled using the print ID number, the printer name, or by the login name of the user who executed the print request.

The syntax of the command is

```
cancel options printer
```

When entering *printer,* the print job that is currently printing on that *printer* is canceled. Table B.76 presents the *cancel* command options.

EXAMPLE OF THE *cancel* COMMAND

To cancel the print job number 231 owned by *bosco* and printing on the *ink-jet* printer, enter the following:

```
cancel 231 ink-jet -u bosco
```

TABLE B.76.   *cancel* Options

Option	Qualifier	Description
id		Enter the *id* of the print job to be canceled. The identification number of the print job can be found using the *lpstat* command.
-u	*name*	Cancels the print request that is currently printing for the user *name*.

Windows NT Alternative

To display the print queue, select **Start** ➤ **Settings** ➤ **Printers**. At this point double click on the desired printer. From the print queue, select the print job to cancel, then select **Document** ➤ **Cancel**.

lp (line printer) Command

The *lp* command allows a user to send files to the defined printers. Files can be named on the command line or come from standard input. Each print request (i.e., each file to be printed) is given an identification number that can be used by other commands to manage the printing process.

The syntax of this command is

```
lp options filename(s)
```

A minus sign can be used as one of the *filenames* to signify that one of the print requests comes from standard input. Table B.77 lists the *lp* command options.

EXAMPLE OF THE *lp* COMMAND

To omit printing the banner when sending a financial report to the printer, *ink-jet,* enter the following command:

```
lp -d ink-jet -o nobanner financial
```

TABLE B.77.   *lp* Options

Option	Qualifier	Description
-c		Outputs (or copies) `filenames` to the print queue. The default option is to link files. Linking means that changes made to the file between the time the file is sent to the printer and the time that it is printed are reflected in the hard-copy output. In the case of the -c option, these changes would not be output; the file is printed as it was when it was sent to the printer.
-d	*prtr*	Outputs filenames to the printer named *prtr*
-f	*form*	Prints *filename* using *form* defined with the command *lpforms*; *form* is usually a preprinted form
-H	*action*	Prints *filename* following the special instructions denoted by *action*. There are three possible values for *action: hold, resume,* and *immediate.*
-i	*ID*	Changes the print options for the print *ID*s listed. The new options follow the *-i* option.
-m		Sends a mail message to the user when *filename* has completed printing
-n	*copies*	Identifies the number of *copies* to print
-o	*option(s)*	Turns on *option(s)* for a specific printer. These *options* can vary between different printers and versions of UNIX. Multiple *options* can be listed but each one must be preceded by -o. Some common options are: *nobanner* (don't print banner page), *nofilebreak* (no form feed between files), *cpi=c* (print *c* characters per inch), *lpi=l* (print *l* lines per inch), *length=n* (define page length as *n* lines or *n*i inches), and *width=n* (define page width as *n*i inches or *n* characters).
-P	*pages*	Prints *pages* listed
-q	*priority*	Assigns *priority* number (from 0 to 39) to the print request, with 0 being the highest priority
-s		Does not output messages to standard output, such as the printer ID number for the request
-S	*char-set*	Uses the character set, *char-set,* during the printing of this request
-t	*title*	Outputs *title* on the banner page
-w		Displays a message on the user's terminal when the request has been printed

UNIX

Windows NT Alternative

One method of printing a file is dragging its icon to the printer icon. To access the printer icon, select **Start** ➤ **Settings** ➤ **Printers**.

Otherwise, select the Print icon or **File** ➤ **Print** from within the application that created the file.

lpstat (line printer status) Command

The *lpstat* command shows the status of the files waiting to be printed (files in the spooler or print queue). The syntax of the command is

```
lpstat options
```

If no *options* are listed (Table B.78), the status of all print requests sent by the current user is displayed.

Windows NT Alternative

To display the available printers, select **Start** ➤ **Settings** ➤ **Printers**. Double-click on a printer to display information about the printer and its queue. Using the options available in this window, the printer status is displayed as well as the ability to change the priority of a print job.

lptest Command

The *lptest* command, which is found in the */usr/ucb* directory, outputs all printable ASCII characters to standard output. It is used to test terminals as well as printers. The syntax of the command is

```
lptest width lines
```

The *width* parameter is the width of a line, with the default being 79 characters. The *lines* parameter is the number of lines printed during the test, with the default being 200 lines.

TABLE B.78. *lpstat* Options

Option	Qualifier	Description
-a	*printers*	Displays the acceptance status of the *printers* listed (i.e., whether the printer is accepting print jobs or not). Multiple *printers* can be separated by commas or separated by spaces if enclosed in double quotes.
-c	*classes*	Displays information about the printer *classes* listed. Multiple *classes* can be separated by commas or separated by spaces if enclosed in double quotes.
-d		Displays the name of the default printer
-D		Displays the printer description. Must be used with the *-p* option.
-f	*forms*	Confirms that the *forms* listed are defined in the system. Multiple *forms* can be separated by commas or separated by spaces if enclosed in double quotes. A *-l* option used after the *-f* option displays information about the *forms* that are available.
-o	*list*	Displays the status of the print jobs in *list*. The *list* can include printer names, class names, or printer IDs. Using the *-l* option after this option provides a more detailed listing.
-p	*printers*	Displays the status of *printers,* where *printers* is a list of printer names. Multiple *printers* can be separated by commas or separated by spaces if enclosed in double quotes.
-r		Displays whether the print scheduler is active or not
-R		Displays where a print job falls in the queue
-s		Displays a print status summary, including default printer, printer names, device names, and whether the print scheduler is active
-S	*sets*	Confirms that the character *sets* listed are valid
-t		Displays all (total) status information
-u	*users*	Displays a status of all print requests for the *users* listed. Multiple *users* can be separated by commas.
-v	*printers*	Lists the device names of the printers listed. Multiple *printers* can be separated by commas or separated by spaces if enclosed in double quotes.

UNIX

SEARCH COMMANDS

UNIX provides a collection of powerful search commands that permit both the location of files and identification of data within files. Used in combination with other UNIX commands, these search programs support file and process manipulation. By contrast, Windows NT supports a set graphical search functions; however, they cannot be combined easily with other programs to invoke more complex results. The following search commands are examined:

- *find* – Locates files and directories with specified search criteria
- *grep, egrep,* and *fgrep* – Three related commands that examine the contents of flat files
- *strings* – Searches binary and object files for a specified pattern

UNIX also supports other programs that are designed to carry forth search and pattern identification such as *awk* and *sed* (streaming editor), which are discussed briefly in Chapter 5.

find Command

Almost everyone has experienced the problem of losing track of a file on a computer system. The UNIX *find* command enables a user or system administrator to locate that file using a number of conditions or options. One of those options is to specify where to limit the search. A user can either search the entire system or start with a specific directory. In other words, the *find* command performs its searches based on the UNIX system directory structure.

One word of warning though: the *-print* option must be used (with the exception of HP-UX) if the user wants the results displayed on the screen. If -*print* is not used and the output is not redirected to a file or piped into another command, the results of the search are lost.

The *find* command uses the following syntax:

```
find searchpath(s) option(s) with qualifiers
```

Using special operators, the scope of the *find* command expands. The special operators include !, which finds everything *except* what is requested in the options (remember if using the C shell to use \!), and parentheses can group options together (remember to use the backslash '\(and \)').

The *find* command options are listed in Table B.79.

TABLE B.79.   *find* Options

Option	Qualifier	Description
-atime	*n* or *+n* or *-n*	Finds all files, beginning with the search path, that were accessed exactly *n* days ago. Uses *+n* for files accessed more than *n* days ago or *-n* for less than *n* days ago. It is important to note that using the *find* command with the -atime option changes the access time on all files accessed.
-ctime	*n* or *+n* or *-n*	Finds all files, beginning with the search path, that were changed exactly *n* days ago. Uses *+n* for files changed more that *n* days ago or *-n* for files changed less than *n* days ago. "Changed" refers to any change made to the file including the contents, permissions, ownerships, and links.
-depth		Skips the directories and evaluates the files first, then goes back and evaluates the directories
-exec	*command* {} \;	For each file found that matches the criteria in the *find* command, executes the *command*. The {} \; must be included after the command to ensure the command executes on found files.
-follow		Outputs the directories found while following symbolic links
-fstype	*name*	Finds the files that are on the file system *name*
-group	*name* or *n*	Finds all files that match the group name *name,* or finds all files that match the group ID number *n*
-inum	*n*	Finds the files that match the inode number *n*
-links	*n*	Finds the files that have *n* number of links
-local		Restricts the search to the local system
-mount		Restricts the search to those files on the same file system as the search path
-mtime	*n* or *+n* or *-n*	Finds all files beginning with the search path that were modified exactly *n* days ago. Uses *+n* for files modified more that *n* days ago or *-n* for files modified less than *n* days ago. "Modified" refers to the content of the file.
-name	*pattern*	Finds all files with the name that match *pattern*. Metacharacters can be used, but then enclose the entire *pattern* in single quotes.
-newer	*filename*	Similar to the *-mtime -n* option, except that this option finds all files that have been modified more recently than *filename*
-nogroup		Finds all files that are owned by a group that is not listed in the */etc/group* file
-nouser		Finds all files that are owned by a user that is not listed in the */etc/passwd* file

continued

UNIX

TABLE B.79.   *find* **Options** *(Continued)*

Option	Qualifier	Description
-o		Works as an OR option when combined with two other options
-ok	*command* {} \;	Similar to the *-exec* option, except that the user has control over whether the command is executed or not. To execute the command a *y* for yes must be entered at the prompt.
-path	*file*	Allows the user to specify the path of the directory to be surveyed. Works the same as *-name*.
-perm	*nnn*	Finds all files with permissions that match *nnn,* the octal representation of the permission. For example, 777 matches -rwxrwxrwx. A minus sign before *nnn* acts as a wildcard. For example, -070 matches -***rwx***, where * can be any permission.
-print		Outputs all matches to standard output, which is usually the terminal screen. If this option is not used and the output is not redirected, the results of the *find* command are not readily visible.
-prune		Prunes the directory tree; in other words, it instructs the *find* command to discontinue searching lower in the directory tree. This option is usually used in conjunction with the *-o* option.
-size	*n* or *c*	Finds files with a size that is *n* blocks in length. If the *c* qualifier is used, it finds files with a size that is *c* characters in length.
-type	*t*	Finds files with a file type of *t*, which can be one of the following values: *b* (block special file), *c* (character special file, like devices), *d* (directory), *p* (named pipe or fifo), *l* (symbolic link), or *f* (regular file).
-user	*name* or *ID*	Finds files that belong to the user *name* or *ID*

EXAMPLES OF THE *find* COMMAND

To locate all of the files named *budget* on the system, type

```
find / -name budget -print
```

If you wish to limit this search to the */usr* directory, then type

```
find /usr -name budget -print
```

To find the *budget* file owned by the user *bosco,* enter

```
find /usr -name budget -user bosco -print
```

To output *bosco*'s *budget* file to the printer, type

```
find /usr/ -name budget -user bosco -exec lp {} \;
```

A system administrator suspects that two different users have the same user ID number of 200. To locate them in the */etc/passwd* file, type the following:

```
egrep 200 /etc/passwd
```

TABLE B.81.   *egrep* **Options**

Option	Qualifier	Description
-b		Includes the block number where the pattern is found
-c		Provides counted statistics as to the number of times the pattern is found
-e	*pattern*	This option is useful if the search *pattern* begins with a minus sign.
-f	*filename*	Searches for the patterns that are identified within *filename*
-h		Outputs only the matched lines and ignores the filename (opposite of *-l*)
-i		Ignores case sensitivity (upper-/lowercase letters) in the search
-l		Lists only the names of the files (not lines) where the pattern is found
-n		Outputs both the line and the line number. This option is ignored if used in conjunction with -c, -b, -l, or -q.
-q		A quiet mode that exits the command with a 0 status when it detects a match; all other output is suppressed.
-s		If damaged or unreadable files are found, suppresses the output of error messages
-v		Prints those lines that do not have the pattern present
-x		Extracts matches only when the entire line is the same as the search item

UNIX

fgrep (fast global regular expression printer) COMMAND

The *fgrep* command provides the ability to search files for a pattern that contains a string of text. It is faster than either *egrep* or *grep* because it only allows text strings and does not include metacharacters. The syntax of the command is

```
fgrep option(s) desired_pattern file(s)
```

The *fgrep* options are listed in Table B.82.

TABLE B.82.   *fgrep* Options

Option	Qualifier	Description
-b		Includes the block number where the pattern is found
-c		Provides counted statistics as to the number of times the pattern is found
-e	*pattern*	Use this option when the search *pattern* begins with a minus sign.
-f	*filename*	Searches for the pattern that is identified in *filename*
-h		Outputs only the matched lines and ignores the filename (opposite of -*l*)
-i		Ignores case sensitivity (upper-/lowercase letters) in the search
-l		Lists only the names of the files (not lines) where the pattern is found
-n		Outputs both the line and the line number. This option is ignored if used in conjunction with -c, -b, -l, or -q.
-q		This is a quiet mode that exits the command with a 0 status when it detects a match. All other output is suppressed.
-s		If damaged or unreadable files are found, suppresses the output of error messages
-v		Prints those lines that do not have the pattern present
-x		Extracts matches only when the entire line is the same as the search item

Examples of the fgrep Command

To find all occurrences of the word UNIX in `file1` regardless of case, enter

```
fgrep -i UNIX file1
```

A user has created a long document that contains a number of acronyms. This user has created a file named *Acronym* and wants to use this file to search his document for all of the acronyms and display the line numbers as well. To do this using *fgrep,* type the following:

```
fgrep -nf Acronym document
```

strings Command

The *strings* command is useful as a search command because it provides the ability to search object or binary files. This command, developed by the University of California at Berkeley, displays lines with four or more ASCII (printable) characters followed by a new line or a null character. It is useful in identifing the contents of an unknown object file. Note that the *strings* command only searches the initialized data section of files unless specified otherwise.

The syntax of the *strings* command is

```
strings options file(s)
```

The *strings* command options are listed in Table B.83.

TABLE B.83.   *strings* Options

Option	Qualifier	Description
-a		Searches the entire file. Does not limit the search to initialized data.
-o		Before each line, display the offset number
-n	*number*	Changes the search to display lines with *number* of printable characters. The format of this option can also be -*number*.

UNIX

Examples of the strings Command

To determine the content of a binary file, type the following:

```
strings file1
```

To restrict your search of the file to display lines with eight printable characters, type the following:

```
strings -8 file1
```

Windows NT Alternative

When a user double-clicks on a file within the Windows NT Explorer application, Explorer attempts to identify each file automatically for the user. Selecting different file types executes different applications, perhaps giving the user a peek at the contents of an unknown file.

SYSTEM MANAGEMENT COMMANDS

A system administrator is often the chief, cook, and bottle washer of the computer systems for which she is responsible. Any assistance that the operating system can give her with managing the day-to-day operations as well as coping with special circumstances is greatly appreciated. We classified a group of commands as System Management Commands because these are the commands that assist the system administrator in making the system operate more smoothly.

at Command

The *at* command enables a command or series of commands to be executed at a specified time. The commands may be entered from standard input, may be input from a file, or may be piped from another command. There are two syntax formats for the *at* command:

```
at option-set1 time
```

or

```
at option-set2 jobid
```

When you want to accept commands from standard input to run at a specified time, enter the following at the command prompt:

```
at command with appropriate options
commands that you wish to execute
EOF character, such as a ^d (<Ctrl>d)
```

A message in the following format is sent to standard error:

```
job jobid.queue at time
```

where `jobid.queue` is the number of the job and the queue in which it is located and `time` is the date and time that the job will execute. On some UNIX variants this message will be mailed to the user that executed the *at* command. The *at* options for set 1 are presented in Table B.84 and `time` values are listed in Table B.85.

The second format of the *at* command (`at option-set2 jobid`) enables you either to list jobs in the queue or remove them. The `jobid` parameter contains the job ID number of the job in question. The *at* options for set 2 are listed in Table B.86.

It is important to note that users can only use *at* if their login name is in the */usr/lib/cron/at.allow* file. If the login name is in */usr/lib/cron/at.deny,* then the

TABLE B.84. *at* Options, Set 1

Option	Qualifier	Description
-f	*filename*	Executes the commands listed in *filename*
-m		Sends a mail message to the user who executed the *at* command to notify when the job has been completed

TABLE B.85. Values for the *time* Parameter

Parameter	Description
time	This is a required parameter that identifies the time that you want the job to execute. The *time* parameter can be in the following formats: *h, hh, hhmm,* or *hh:mm,* where *h* and *hh* represent hours and *mm* represents minutes. A twenty-four-hour clock is assumed unless the time is followed by the qualifiers *am* or *pm*. In place of an actual time, one of the following key words may be used: *midnight, noon,* or *now*.
date	This parameter is optional and can consist of either the day of the week or a specific date. Enter the name of the day of the week in its entirety or as the standard three-character abbreviation, such as Monday or Mon. The format for the date is *month day, year*, where *month* is either spelled out or abbreviated (January or Jan), the *day* is a number, and the *year* is optional. As an alternative, one of two key words can be used in place of the date: *today* or *tomorrow*.
increment	This parameter permits you to specify a time or date relative to the current one. The format is *+num keyword*, where *keyword* can be either *minute, hour, day, week, month,* or *year* and *num* is the amount of time relative to the current time. For example, entering *now +30 minute* would execute the job thirty minutes from now. The keyword *next* can be used to indicate an increment of +1. For example *next day* would be the same as using the designation tomorrow.

UNIX

user is denied access to *at*. If neither the *at.allow* or *at.deny* files exist, then only root has access to *at*. If there is no *at.allow* file and there is an *at.deny* file but it is empty, then everyone has access to *at*. Please note that the location of

TABLE B.86.   *at* Options, Set 2

Option	Description
-l	Lists all pending jobs with their job ID number. Entering the *jobid* number lists the information specific to that particular job.
-r	Must be used in conjunction with the *jobid* parameter, removes the job specified from the queue

these files may vary depending on the UNIX variant used. Some suggested locations are */usr/lib/cron, /var/spool/cron,* and */var/adm/cron.*

We also recommend that you check the *at* command *man* pages on your particular variant of UNIX to determine if all of the options listed here are available or if there are any additional options.

EXAMPLES OF THE at COMMAND

To execute the shell script *audit* at 6:00 P.M. tomorrow, enter one of the following formats:

```
at -f audit 6:00pm tomorrow
cat audit | at 1800 next day
```

To schedule a backup for Friday at noon from the command prompt, enter

```
at noon Friday
find /usr/sarah/customer -print | cpio -padm /usr/emily/client2
<Ctrl>d
```

Please note that this backup is actually copying files from one directory to another.

batch Command

The *batch* command differs from the *at* command in that it schedules the commands entered from standard input to be run immediately or as soon as the system load permits. The format of the command as entered from standard input is

```
batch
commands to be run
EOF entered via a <Ctrl-d> or its equivalent
```

crontab Command

The *crontab* command is actually a method of managing the *cronfile*, which is a chronological table that identifies when programs are to be run automatically. The *cronfile* in conjunction with the *cron* program enables programs to be run on a scheduled basis such as every Friday at 3:00 A.M. The *crontab* command enables a user to activate a particular *cronfile* or to change the contents of a *cronfile*. A *cronfile* can exist for each user as well as for the system.

There are two formats for this command. The first one is

```
crontab filename
```

This format activates the cronfile *filename*, so that the system begins tracking and automatically starts programs based on the contents of *filename*. If *filename* is omitted, *crontab* activates the login user's cronfile.

The second format is

```
crontab options username
```

This format of the command allows for the creation, modification, listing, and removal of a user's *cronfile*. The `username` parameter is optional and necessary only if a user is modifying another user's *cronfile*. This can only occur if the permissions are set appropriately.

It is important to note that users can only use *crontab* if their login name is in the */usr/lib/cron/cron.allow* file. If the login name is in */usr/lib/cron/cron.deny*, then the user is denied access to *crontab*. If neither the *cron.allow* or *cron.deny* files exist, then only root has access to *crontab*. If there is no *cron.allow* file and there is a *cron.deny* file but it is empty, then everyone has access to *crontab*. Please note that the location of these files may vary depending on the UNIX variant used. Some suggested locations are */usr/lib/cron, /var/spool/cron, /etc/cron.d,* and */var/adm/cron*.

The *crontab* command options are listed in Table B.87.

TABLE B.87.   *crontab* Options

Option	Description
-e	Creates or modifies the user's cronfile
-l	Lists the contents of the user's cronfile
-r	Removes the user's cronfile

UNIX

TABLE B.88.   *cronfile* Field Description

Field	Description
M	Minutes; enter the minutes of the hour that the command line is to execute. Acceptable values are 0 to 59.
H	Hours; enter the hours that the command line is to execute. Acceptable values are 0 to 23.
D	Day of the month; enter the days of the month that the command line is to execute. Acceptable values are 1 to 31.
M	Month; enter the months that the command line is to execute. Acceptable values are 1 to 12.
W	Days of the week; enter the days of the week that the command line is to execute. Acceptable values are 0 to 6, with 0 being Sunday;1, Monday; etc.
command line	Enter the command line for the program or shell that is to execute.

A cronfile consists of list of single-line commands that automatically execute at a specific time, which is included as part of each command line. The format of a line in a cronfile is as follows:

```
M H D M W command line
```

Table B.88 describes each field of this cronfile format.

Each of the time fields can contain a single number, multiple numbers, a range, or an asterisk. Multiple numbers are separated by commas. A range is indicated by a dash between the beginning number of the range and the ending number. An asterisk is used to represent any value. There must be a value in each of the fields.

It is recommended that the log file for *cron* be cleared out periodically. A suggested method of accomplishing this follows. Be sure to confirm where *cron/log* resides on your system.

```
tail /var/cron/log >> /var/cron/cron.log.save
cat /dev/null > /var/cron/log
```

EXAMPLES OF *cronfile* ENTRIES

Suppose the system administrator has both the Decathlon Data Systems' GOLDMEDAL Elite and GOLDMEDAL WorkGroup programs installed on the system. Both applications have a *RECYCLE* directory for each user that needs to be emptied on a periodic basis. Since most users have access to the WorkGroup program for electronic mail, their *RECYCLE* directories need to be cleared once a week, whereas the *RECYCLE* file for Elite users need only be cleared twice a month. The *cronfile* could contain the following two entries:

```
15 3 * * 6 /usr/wgroup/cleanup
30 3 1,15 * * /usr/medal/cleanup
```

In the first line, the program */usr/wgroup/cleanup* will run every Saturday at 3:15 in the morning. In the second example, the program */usr/medal/cleanup* will run the first and fifteenth days of the month at 3:30 in the morning.

EXAMPLES OF THE *crontab* COMMAND

Suppose a system administrator would like to make some changes to the system or root *cronfile,* but she wants to make sure that she does not corrupt the active *cronfile* in the process. The system administrator could enter the following command:

```
crontab -l > /tmp/root
```

This command outputs a copy of the root *cronfile* to the file */tmp/root*. The system administrator can edit */tmp/root* without affecting the permanent file. When she is satisfied with the changes, she can execute the following command to activate the new root *cronfile*:

```
crontab /tmp/root
```

Windows NT Alternative

The *at* service performs a function similar to UNIX's *cron*. To activate it, select **Start** ➤ **Settings** ➤ **Control Panel** ➤ **Services**. To enter options into the *at* service, utilize the VDM command line and the *at* command.

The Windows NT Resource Kit contains a graphical application that permits you to schedule jobs. To access, select **Start** ➤ **Programs** ➤ **Resource Kit 4.0** ➤ **Configuration** ➤ **Command Scheduler**.

df (disk free) Command

The *df* command displays the amount of free disk space available in the named file system or directory. The available disk space is displayed in blocks and inodes. This command is named *bdf* on systems with the HP-UX variant of UNIX.

The syntax of the command is

```
df options directoryname
```

TABLE B.89. *df* Options

Option	Description
-b	Displays only the number of kilobytes that are free (available)
-e	Displays only the number of inodes that are available. This is the same as the number of files that are free.
-g	Displays the file system block size, fragment size, total blocks, and free blocks
-k	Displays the disk allocation in kilobytes
-l	Displays information for local file systems only
-n	Displays the name of all file systems when used without any other options
-t	Displays the total amount of space allocated to *directoryname,* as well as the amount of free space
-V	Echos the command but does not execute it

The `directoryname` parameter can be the actual name of a directory, the directory name of a file system, the device name of a disk, and even the directory name of a resource that is not local, but is accessible by NFS or RFS. If no options or directory names are given, the *df* command displays the amount of disk space free on each file system.

The options for the *df* command are listed in Table B.89.

EXAMPLES OF THE *df* COMMAND

The following is the output from a *df* command without any options:

```
/         (/dev/root    ):      24396 blocks    33116 i-nodes
/u        (/dev/u       ):      60934 blocks    24608 i-nodes
/home     (/dev/home    ):     780150 blocks    63850 i-nodes
```

For each file system defined in */etc/mnttab* the *df* command displays the total number of available (or free) blocks and inodes.

Entering the command *df -t* will result in the following output for each mounted file system:

```
/         (/dev/root      ):      24396 blocks    33116 i-nodes
                      total:     358738 blocks    44848 i-nodes
/u        (/dev/u         ):      60934 blocks    24608 i-nodes
                      total:     235520 blocks    29440 i-nodes
/home     (/dev/home      ):     780148 blocks    63849 i-nodes
                      total:     827818 blocks    65488 i-nodes
```

This command displays the available (or free) blocks and inodes (or files) as well as the total number of blocks and inodes (the total number used plus the total number free).

Windows NT Alternative

To display both the total capacity as well as the total free space on a disk, select **Start** ➤ **Programs** ➤ **Administrative Tools** ➤ **Disk Administrator**. Within **Disk Administrator**, select **View** ➤ **Volumes**.

For another alternative, select the My Computer icon, then select **View** ➤ **Details**. Once the disk is highlighted, the status bar shows total free space as well as total capacity for the disk.

du (disk usage) Command

The *du* command displays the number of blocks used by directory. A block is considered to be 512 bytes. If no *directoryname* is given, usage is displayed for the current directory only.

The syntax of the command is

```
du options directoryname(s)
```

Table B.90 lists the options for the *du* command.

TABLE B.90.   *du* Options

Option	Description
-a	Displays disk usage for each file in the directory, including subdirectories
-f	Displays only the disk usage for the files in the current file system
-r	If the command is unable to access a particular file or directory (probably due to the permissions), displays the message "cannot open" by the file
-s	Displays only the total number of blocks used for each directory
-u	Ignores files with more than one link

UNIX

EXAMPLES OF THE *du* COMMAND

The following is the output from the command *du -a /usr/bob*. Remember, the -*a* option includes subdirectories in the display. The first column displays the number of blocks for the file or directory listed in the second column.

```
2   /usr/bob/.profile
0   /usr/bob/.lastlogin
2   /usr/bob/.odtpref/ScoSession/dynamic
12  /usr/bob/.odtpref/ScoSession/xrdb.stop
16  /usr/bob/.odtpref/ScoSession
18  /usr/bob/.odtpref
32  /usr/bob/trash/.xdtdirinfo
34  /usr/bob/trash
4   /usr/bob/Initial.dt
2   /usr/bob/XDesktop3
62  /usr/bob
```

The following is the output from the command *du /usr/bob*. Notice how only the sizes of directories are given.

```
16  /usr/bob/.odtpref/ScoSession
18  /usr/bob/.odtpref
34  /usr/bob/trash
62  /usr/bob
```

Windows NT Alternative

To determine the amount of disk space used by a file or a directory, select the My Computer icon. From the **View** menu, select **Details**. After selecting a drive volume, such as **C:**, the bottom status bar displays the total number of bytes used for the particular directory level selected.

To determine the size of a particular directory (folder), select the directory (folder), then select **File → Properties**. The Properties window displays the total disk space used for the folder, plus eleven of its subdirectories. Individual file sizes can be displayed in the same manner.

If you prefer, the Windows NT Explorer application can be used instead of the My Computer selection.

Using the VDM command line, change to the directory in question and use the *dir /s* command.

env (environment) Command

The *env* command displays the current values of the environment variables defined for the current login session. Environment variables define the defaults and parameters for a particular session.

The syntax of the command is

```
env option variable=value command
```

When *env* is executed without any parameters, the values of all environment variables are displayed. This command may also be used to set values for new or existing environment variables. The new environment is displayed as the change is made. If the `command` parameter is entered, the `command` is executed under the current environment, including any changes made as part of the *env* command line.

There is only one option available with the *env* command. It is the – option, which instructs the system to ignore the current environment completely.

EXAMPLES OF THE *env* COMMAND

The following is the sample output from an *env* command without any parameters. This form of the command just displays the current environment.

```
COLUMNS=80
DISPLAY=scosysv:0.0
HOME=/
LINES=25
LOGNAME=root
MAILER=scomail
PATH=/bin:/etc:/usr/bin:/tcb/bin:/usr/dbin:/usr/ldbin:/
usr/bin/X11
SHELL=/bin/sh
TERM=ansi
TZ=PST8PDT
USER=root
```

To change the value of the environment variable TERM only during the execution of the program */usr/medal/medal,* enter the following:

```
env TERM=vt100 /usr/medal/medal
```

Windows NT Alternative
Select **Start** ➤ **Settings** ➤ **Control Panel** ➤ **System** ➤ **Environment** to view and set environment variables with Windows NT.

finger Command

The *finger* command displays information about users listed. This includes any of the information contained in the *.plan* and *.project* files found in the user's *HOME* directory.

The syntax of the command is

```
finger option(s) username(s)
```

Table B.91 lists the *finger* command options.

TABLE B.91. *finger* Options

Option	Description
-b	Does not include the home directory and shell for *username(s)* in the display
-f	Omits the headings from the display. Used in conjunction with the *-s* option.
-h	Does not include the *.project* file in the display
-i	Displays the idle format, which displays the amount of idle time for each active terminal
-l	Displays the long format. This is the default option when a `user name` is entered. It includes the home directory, the login shell, the *.plan* and *.project* files, along with all of the information displayed by the *-s* option.
-m	Matches on `username(s)` exactly. Does not include the ability to match on first or last names.
-p	Does not include the *.plan* file in the display
-q	Quick format; displays only the login, the tty, and when the last login occurred
-s	This short format displays the following information in columns: login, full name, tty, idle time, when the last login occurred, the office location, and phone number. The full name, office location, and phone number come from the comment field for the user in the */etc/passwd* file.
-w	Does not display the user's full name. Must be used in conjunction with the *-s* option.

If the `username` is not entered, the *finger* command is executed on the current login. When the *-m* option is omitted, the `usernames` can be either the login name or the first or last name of the user. If the first or last name is used, the *finger* command displays information about all users that match one of those components.

EXAMPLES OF THE *finger* COMMAND

The following is the output for the command *finger ellen*. Notice that two listings are given since the name *ellen* occurs twice in the */etc/passwd* file in the comment field (displayed here as In real life).

```
Login name: ellen      In real life: Ellen Beck Gardner
Directory: /usr/ellen Shell: /bin/sh
Last login Wed Apr 24, 1996
No Plan.

Login name: ebg        In real life: Ellen Beck Gardner
Directory: /usr/ebg   Shell: /bin/sh
Last login Wed Apr 24, 1996
No Plan.
```

The following is the output for the *finger -i* command, which displays the idle time for each terminal currently logged in:

```
Login     TTY      When               Idle
root      *tty02   Thu Dec 19 10:13   270 days
root      ttyp0    Thu Dec 19 10:13   238 days
root      ttyp1    Thu Dec 19 10:13
root      ttyp3    Thu Dec 19 10:22   1 hour 23 minutes
```

The following is the output for the *finger -s* command. The Office column contains no information because the comment field in the */etc/passwd* file contains no office information. Also, root is displayed here several times because this is a system running X-Windows.

```
Login     Name       TTY    Idle   When         Office
root      Superuser  *02    270d   Thu 10:13
root      Superuser  p0     238d   Thu 10:13
root      Superuser  p1            Thu 10:13
root      Superuser  p3     1:23   Thu 10:22
```

Windows NT Alternative
To display the amount of idle time for each user, select **Start** ➤ **Settings** ➤ **Control Panel** ➤ **Server** ➤ **Users**.

fsck (file system check) Command

The *fsck* command provides a way of auditing the file system for errors or inconsistencies. It ensures that the data in the superblock and in the inodes are in sync with the actual directory structures. In addition, the *fsck* command can resolve some of the problems that are found. Most UNIX variants run *fsck* automatically at boot time or during a reboot after an abnormal system termination, so only in rare circumstances should a system administrator have to run this command manually.

The *fsck* command identifies file system problems such as

* Blocks identified as being free (not in use) when they actually are in use
* Blocks identified as being in use when they are actually free
* A block of data assigned to multiple files
* Differences between the inode size and the actual number of data blocks for a file
* Discrepancies between the number of inodes and the actual number of entries in a directory
* Inodes that contain data but are not associated with any directory. These are considered to be "lost" files.

When discrepancies are found in the file system, the *fsck* command identifies them and attempts to correct the problems based on the response from the system administrator. The syntax for this command is:

```
fsck options filesystem
```

The *fsck* command is normally found in the */etc* directory, but it may reside in another location such as in */usr/sbin* depending on the UNIX variant in operation. The `filesystem` parameter contains the name of the special file for the file system. The *fsck* command is commonly run without the `filesystem` parameter, so that all file systems that are listed in the file system table (e.g., */etc/fstab* or */etc/checklist*) are checked. It is important to note that all file systems except for root must be unmounted to run the *fsck* command. To perform a file system check on the root file system, the system administrator should take the system to the single-user run level.

The options available for the *fsck* command vary depending on the UNIX variant that you are running. Table B.92 identifies some of the more common options, but we recommend that you check the *fsck man* pages for your system before running this command manually.

TABLE B.92.   *fsck* Options

Option	Qualifier	Description
-F	*type*	Identifies the file system type that you are checking, such as UFS. If this option is not entered, the information is retrieved from the file system table, such as */etc/fstab*.
-n		Lists all of the problems found but does not correct them. In other words, answers no to all prompts.
-p		This option is one of the most frequently used. It automatically corrects problems that do not affect a file's contents.
-y		Responds yes to all prompts, resulting in all problems being corrected automatically. Although this option sounds like the best bet, it should be used with caution. You may not be pleased with the corrections that are made automatically.

Windows NT Alternative

Windows NT provides tools to check the performance and reliability of various disks installed on the system by selecting **Start ➤ Programs ➤ Administrative Tools ➤ Disk Administrator**.

In addition, the *chkdsk* utility can be executed from the command line to check each disk for errors and correct them optionally.

init (initialize) Command

The *init* command starts (or spawns) processes. It does not spawn just any process, only those identified in the */etc/inittab* file. The best way to understand the functions of the *init* command is to understand what happens when a UNIX system is started (or booted).

During the boot process, the *init* command is executed. This command uses data in */etc/inittab* to determine what processes need to be started. One of those processes is defined by the *initdefault* line in */etc/inittab*. This process identifies the default run level for the system. Table B.93 identifies all possible run levels in the system.

TABLE B.93.   Run Levels

Run Level	Description
0	Shutdowns the system to prepare for power off
1	This is similar to single-user mode (level s or S) in that only the system administrator can access the system via the system console. All file systems are mounted and accessible.
2	This is multiuser mode. All users can log in and all file systems are mounted. There is no networking available.
3	This is a multiuser mode that allows remote file sharing. Remote file systems are mounted and accessible in this state. This is the state that is used when NFS and RFS are invoked. Networking is enabled in this run level.
4	This mode is available as a special run level that is defined by a user or by user applications.
5	This run level is referred to as the *firmware mode* and is used primarily for hardware and firmware updates.
6	This level performs a system shutdown and automatically reboots the system to the *initdefault* run level
s or S	This is similar to run level 1, the single-user mode. When a system goes to this run level from run level 2 or 3, all file systems remain mounted. This level is commonly referred to as *maintenance mode* and permits the installation of software without allowing users to log in.
q or Q	Reads */etc/inittab* and spawns any newly added processes
a, b, c	Doesn't change the current run level but executes the identified line (a, b, or, c) in the */etc/inittab* file

If the *initdefault* line is omitted from the */etc/inittab* file, the system requests the entry of a run level.

The syntax of this command is

```
init level
```

where `level` is one of the run levels identified in Table B.93.

The processes that are spawned by *init* have a parent process ID number of 1. The only time that */etc/inittab* is reexamined to determine if other processes need to be spawned is when one of the processes it spawned terminates, when a power failure signal is received, when a run level change is requested, or when the *init q* or *init Q* command is executed.

This command differs from the *shutdown* command in that it does not give users any warning when the run level is about to change. To change the run level gracefully, we recommend using the *shutdown* command.

The *telinit* command can be linked to the *init* command in some UNIX variants.

kill Command

The *kill* command is a quick way of terminating one or more active processes. To kill a process you must have superuser privileges or own the process. The *kill* command resides both in the */bin* directory and as part of the Bourne, Korn, and C shells. The only difference between the two commands is the ability to terminate processes by process group IDs rather than by process IDs. Chapter 3 extends the discussion of kill, including information about runaway processes, zombies, and restarting system processes.

The syntax of the command is

```
kill option(s) IDnumber
```

Table B.94 lists the *kill* command options. The `IDnumber` parameter usually contains the process ID number.

TABLE B.94.   *kill* Options

Option	Description
-l	When only this option is used, displays a list of the *kill* signal numbers and symbolic signal names
-signalnumber	Sends *signalnumber* to the PID listed to terminate the process. Which signal should be used depends on the process being killed and the desired results. A *kill -9* terminates the process completely. A list of the signal numbers is found in Table B.95. The signal name can also be used.

Windows NT Alternative

To access Windows NT Security, press `<Ctrl-Alt-Del>` simultaneously. From the Windows NT Security window, select **Task Manager**. Choose the **Applications** tab to select an application to terminate or choose the **Processes** tab to select a process to terminate.

UNIX

TABLE B.95.   Signal Commands

Signal Number	Signal Name	Signal Description
1	SIGHUP	Hang-up signal
2	SIGINT	Interrupt signal
3	SIGQUIT	Quit signal
4	SIGILL	Illegal instruction signal
5	SIGTRAP	Trace trap signal
6	SIGIOT	IOT instruction signal
7	SIGEMT	EMT instruction signal
8	SIGFPE	Floating point exception signal
9	SIGKILL	Absolute kill
10	SIGBUS	Bus error
11	SIGSEGV	Segmentation violation
12	SIGSYS	Bad argument to a system call
13	SIGPIPE	Write to pipe, but no output to read it
14	SIGALRM	Alarm clock signal
15	SIGTERM	Software termination (this is the default)
16	SIGUSR1	User-defined signal 1
17	SIGUSR2	User-defined signal 2
18	SIGCLD	Child process died
19	SIGPWR	Restart after power failure

Note that these signals may change depending on the UNIX variant in use.

nice Command

The *nice* command allows the system administrator either to raise or lower the priority of a command and its parameters when it is executed.

The format of the command is

```
nice -n command with parameters
```

The *-n* option allows the user to set a niceness level from 1 to 19. If the *-n* option is omitted, a niceness level of 10 is assumed. The higher the value of *n*, the lower the priority. If the user is a superuser, he can increase the priority by entering a negative niceness number. The niceness level only remains in effect for the command entered.

EXAMPLE OF THE *nice* COMMAND

A system administrator wants to increase the priority of a print job by three levels. The following command needs to be entered:

```
nice -n3 "lp budget"
```

nohup (no hangup) Command

The *nohup* command allows a command to continue executing even if a user logs out. In other words, the *nohup* command ignores the HUP (hang-up) signal. The syntax of the command is

```
nohup command with parameters &
```

The ampersand (&) requests that the command be run in the background so that the user is returned to the prompt while the command continues to execute. If a user uses the C shell, the *nohup* command is not necessary because *nohup* is built into the shell. The Bourne shell allows the output to be redirected. If output redirection is not specified, the default is *nohup.out*. In other words, instead of error messages going to standard out, they are redirected to *nohup.out*.

EXAMPLE OF THE *nohup* COMMAND

Suppose that the system administrator must dial in to some remote locations to support them. In one case a critical month-end maintenance program called *cleanup* did not run properly and must be restarted. Since this program takes more than an hour to process, the system administrator does not wish to remain logged in to the remote site for that long. Therefore, he enters the following command to activate the program before logging out:

```
nohup cleanup &
```

passwd (password) Command

The *passwd* command allows a user to set her own login password. If used by a superuser, it allows the superuser to change any user's password. The use of password aging and related security issues are covered in the UNIX primer chapters, Chapters 3, 4, and 5.

The syntax of the command is

```
passwd options loginname
```

The *passwd* command options are listed in Table B.96.

UNIX

TABLE B.96.   *passwd* Options

Option	Description
-a	Displays information about the password for all users. Must be used in conjunction with the *-s* option. The `loginname` parameter should be omitted. This parameter is available to superusers only.
-d	Deletes the password for `loginname`. The user is no longer required to enter a password at login time. Only superusers can use this parameter.
-f	Forces the password to expire for `loginname`. The user will be required to set up a new password at the next login.
-l	Locks the password for `loginname`. Users will not be allowed access until the lock is removed.
-n	Sets the number of days that must pass before `loginname` can change his password again.
-s	Displays the following password information: 1. login name; 2. NP for no password, PS for password, LK for locked; 3. the date the password was last changed; 4. the number of days that can transpire before `loginname` can change the password again; 5. the number of days before password expiration; 6. the number of days before the password expires that the system should warn `loginname` that the password is about to expire.
-w	Sets the number of days before password expiration that the system should warn `loginname` that the password is about to expire
-x	Sets the number of days for password expiration. A value of -1 disables password aging. A value of 0 forces password expiration.

EXAMPLES OF THE *passwd* COMMAND

A user suspects that someone has been using his login. The user can change his password by entering `passwd` at the prompt. If the system does not allow the user to change the password, the system administrator can force the password to expire for the user *bosco* by entering

```
passwd -f bosco
```

The next time the user *bosco* tries to log in, the system will require that he change his password.

The only reason that the system would refuse to change a password for a user is if the parameter that sets the number of days between password changes has not yet been reached. To confirm this value, the system administrator could enter

```
passwd -s bosco
```

Field number 4 contains the number of days allowed between password changes. In the following example of the *passwd -s* output, twenty days must pass before *bosco* can change his password:

```
bosco    PS    12/31/96    20    42
```

Windows NT Alternative

Access the Windows NT Security window by pressing *<Ctrl-Alt-Del>*. Once the Security window displays, select the **Change Password** button.

An administrator can change any user's password by selecting **Start ➤ Programs ➤ Administrative Tools ➤ User Manager for Domains**. Double-clicking on the desired user displays the User Properties window, which permits modification of the password and days-to-expiration information.

Using the VDM command line, the *net user* command enables authorized users to add or change a password whereas the *net accounts* command allows the administrator to define or change password restrictions.

ps (process status) Command

The *ps* command provides a status on all active processes. A variety of information is available depending on the options selected.

The syntax of the command is

```
ps options
```

If no *options* are requested (Table B.97), the *ps* command displays the following fields for the current terminal (the terminal that executed the *ps* command): process ID number, terminal ID, cumulative execution time, and command name.

When using the options *g, p, s, t,* and *u,* either separate the items in the list with commas or enclose them all in double quotes.

EXAMPLES OF THE *ps* COMMAND

To find all of the users running the executable GoldMedal, enter the following:

```
ps -ef|grep GoldMedal
```

TABLE B.97.   *ps* Options

Option	Qualifier	Description
-a		Lists all processes not associated with a terminal and those that are not group leaders
-d		Displays all processes except process group leaders
-e		Displays *all* processes
-f		Displays a complete listing of information about each process. This listing includes User ID, Process ID, Parent Process ID, CPU utilization, start time, tty, elapsed time, and command executed.
-g	*list*	Displays process information for group leader ID numbers contained in *list*. Group leaders are processes for which the PID is the same as the process group ID number, as in the case of a login shell.
-j		Displays the process group ID and session ID
-l		Displays a long listing
-p	*ID(s)*	Displays process information only for process *IDs* listed
-s	*session(s)*	Displays process information only for *session* IDs identified
-t	*terminal(s)*	Displays process information only for *terminal(s)* listed
-u	*name(s)*	Displays process information only for user *name(s)* listed

To display all of the processes that the user *bosco* has running, enter the following:

```
ps -fubosco
```

Windows NT Alternative

Access the Windows NT Security screen by pressing <Ctrl-Alt-Del> simultaneously. Select the **Task Manager** button. To view applications that are running, select **Applications**. To view the processes that are running, select **Processes**.

shutdown Command

The *shutdown* command is found in the */usr/sbin* directory and allows an authorized user to change the run level of the system or prepare the system for power-off. The shutdown routine terminates currently running processes before changing the run level.

The syntax of the command is

```
shutdown options
```

Table B.98 lists the *shutdown* command options.

TABLE B.98.   *shutdown* **Options**

Option	Description
-gx	Before beginning the shutdown routine, gives users a grace period of x seconds to allow them to finish logging out. If this option is not used, the default grace period is sixty seconds.
-ir	Sends the desired run level r to the *init* command. If this option is omitted, the system goes into single-user mode (s). Other values for r are 0 to shutdown the system for power-off, 1 to bring the system to single-user mode with all file systems mounted, 5 to halt the system and go into firmware mode, and 6 to halt the system then automatically reboot.
-y	Does not send the message: Are you sure you wish to shutdown the system?

The *shutdown* command automatically notifies the users that the system will be shutdown in *g* seconds (the amount of the grace period, usually sixty seconds). After the grace period, another message is sent notifying users that the system is being shutdown now. The system actually waits another *g* seconds before finally beginning the shutdown process.

Windows NT Alternative

Select Start ➤ Shutdown. Select **Shut down the computer**.

UNIX

size Command

The *size* command displays the size of an object file in bytes by section. The sections include *.text, .data, .bss,* and *.comment.* The syntax of the command is

```
size option objectfile(s)
```

Table B.99 lists the *size* command options.

TABLE B.99.   *size* Options

Option	Description
-f	Outputs the size, name, and total size for each section
-F	Outputs size, permission settings, and total size for sections that are loadable
-n	Outputs sizes for sections that cannot be allocated or loaded
-o	Displays output in octal instead of decimal
-V	Displays the version number of the size command
-x	Displays output in hexadecimal instead of decimal

If *objectfile* is not actually an object file, the following message will display:

```
size:    filename    bad magic
```

EXAMPLES OF THE *size* COMMAND

To determine the "size" of the executable GoldMedal, enter the following:

```
size -f GoldMedal
```

The output from the command is

```
829876(.text) + 106608(.data) + 67472(.bss) +
55776(.comment) = 1059732
```

sleep Command

The *sleep* command is one that is often used in shell scripts. It instructs the system to wait the prescribed number of seconds before continuing and executing the next command.

The syntax of the command is

```
sleep seconds
```

EXAMPLE OF THE *sleep* COMMAND

Suppose you were monitoring the process table to troubleshoot a problem with a particular user's processes. To do this you could enter the following shell script at the command line:

```
while true
do
        ps -fubosco
        sleep 5
done
```

This script would keep displaying the process status for the user *bosco* every five seconds.

stty Command

The *stty* command defines the terminal options for the current device. The format of the command is

```
stty option(s) mode(s)
```

If the command is executed without any `options` (Table B.100) or `modes` listed, it displays the settings for the current terminal.

The `mode(s)` parameter allows the user to set values for various terminal characteristics. The modes can be broken down into categories such as control modes, input modes, output modes, local modes, control assignments, combination modes, hardware flow control modes, and window size. Utilize the *man* pages on your system to learn the various mode parameters that are available for your UNIX variant.

A common use of the *stty* command is to define the erase character as a destructive backspace. For example, suppose that when a user presses the backspace key on a terminal a ^H displays instead of deleting the previous character as expected. To correct this situation, enter the command *stty erase ^H* to set the erase character to ^H, which is the control sequence that a backspace normally transmits.

TABLE B.100. *stty* Options

Option	Description
-a	Displays all option settings
-g	Displays the current settings

su Command

When performing the duties of a system administrator, there are times you must login as a specific user to research a problem. The *su* command provides an alternative to logging out of one login and logging in again under a different user.

The syntax of the command is

```
su option loginname shell-options
```

The simplest way to run the command is to run it without any *options* or *loginnames*. This logs you in as a superuser, a user with the same permissions and privileges as a root login. If a *loginname* is specified, you have the same permissions and privileges as the user you specified. Be careful, though, since the operating environment (*env*) is the same as the original login name. If you want the environment to change as well, be sure to use the – (minus sign) option. This option actually changes the environment to the user's environment by executing his login shells.

The *shell-options* parameter allows the user to pass different arguments to the shell or to name the shell to be used. If no shell is named on the command line or in the user's */etc/passwd* entry, the default shell */bin/sh* is used. For example if the user is running the *sh* shell, *-r shell-option* will run the restricted shell; *-c shell-option* allows a particular command to be run.

Each use of the *su* command is logged into the file */usr/adm/sulog*.

EXAMPLE OF THE *su* COMMAND

Suppose that a system administrator would like to run the program */usr/medal/medal* as if the user *bosco* was running it. To do this without actually logging in as *bosco,* enter the following:

```
su - bosco -c "/usr/medal/medal"
```

tee Command

The *tee* command is used as part of a piped command line and allows a user to continue sending the output of the originating command to standard output while also capturing the data in one or more files. The syntax for this command is

```
tee options filenames
```

The *tee* command options are listed in Table B.101.

TABLE B.101.   *tee* Options

Option	Description
-a	Appends the standard output from the originating command to *filenames*
-i	Ignores interrupts

EXAMPLES OF THE tee COMMAND

Suppose you want to create a file of all the processes the user *bosco* had running at a particular time but you also want to see those same processes displayed on your screen. Using the *tee* command you could enter

```
ps -fubosco | tee boscopro
```

If later in the day you wanted to check *bosco*'s processes again and append them to the same file you would enter

```
ps -fubosco | tee -a boscopro
```

uname Command

The *uname* command displays the name of the local UNIX system. With the options detailed in Table B.102, this command can also display the hardware name, the processor type, the node name, and the operating system release and version.

The syntax of this command is

```
uname options
```

TABLE B.102.   *uname* Options

Option	Description
-a	Displays information included in all of the options
-m	Displays the hardware name
-n	Displays the node name
-p	Displays the processor type
-r	Displays the release number of the operating system
-s	Displays the system name. This is the default option.
-v	Displays the version of the operating system

UNIX

The *uname –a* option is particularly useful when you have multiple telnet sessions open. It is very easy to forget which remote system is associated with which telnet window. There is simply nothing worse than performing a task on the wrong remote host. By invoking the *uname –a* command, the identification of the remote host is displayed.

Windows NT Alternative

To display the name of the local system, select **Start** ➤ **Settings** ➤ **Control Panel** ➤ **Network**. Within the Network window, select the **Identification** tab. The **Computer Name** is the name of the local system.

Also, using the VDM command line, enter the *hostname* command to derive the same results.

who Command

The *who* command is used to determine the login status of the system. Common questions that can be answered with the use of this command are the following: Who is logged in? Are any users logged in but inactive? Who is currently logged in on a particular terminal? When was the last time the system was rebooted?

The syntax of the command is

```
who option(s) filename
```

Table B.103 lists the options for the *who* command. When the *who* command is executed without any options or files, it displays only the fields of login name, terminal, and time. The optional `filename` is a file that can provide additional information about logins. The default for the optional file is */var/adm/utmp* or */etc/utmp*. A common selection for filename is */etc/utmp,* which contains information about all logins since the file was created.

EXAMPLES OF THE *who* COMMAND

To determine when the system was last booted, enter

```
who -b
```

The output will be similar to the following:

```
. system boot Dec 19 12:17
```

Appendix B   UNIX Commands and Utilities   701

TABLE B.103.   *who* Options

Option	Description
-a	Displays the output of all options
-b	Displays when the system was last rebooted
-d	Displays information about processes that have been terminated
-H	Includes headings in the display output
-l	Lists all inactive terminals
-n*x*	Uses this option in conjunction with the *-q* option to display *x* number of users per line
-p	Displays any processes that are currently active and that have been spawned previously by *init*
-q	Displays only the names of the users logged in
-r	Displays the current run level
-s	Displays not only who is logged in but the time and line fields as well
-t	Displays when the system clock was last changed using the date command
-T	Displays whether you can write to a terminal or not. Displays a plus sign for a terminal to which you can write, a minus sign for those that cannot, and a question mark for those undetermined.
-u	Displays terminal usage time. A period means that the terminal has had activity within the last minute. The term *old* means that the terminal has had no activity for more than twenty-four hours, therefore it is safe to assume that it is idle. The time value displayed in this field is the amount of time the terminal has been idle (seen no activity).
am i	Displays the name of user executing the command. This may be different than the login name depending on whether the *su* command was used.

To display who is currently logged into the system and to include titles in the output, enter

```
who -H
```

The output will be similar to the following:

```
NAME      LINE  TIME
root      tty02 Jan 05 12:25
root      ttyp0 Jan 05 12:26
root      ttyp1 Jan 05 12:26
```

UNIX

To determine the current run level, enter

```
who -rH
```

The sample output is

```
NAME    LINE            TIME            IDLE   PID   COMMENTS
 .      run-level 2     Dec 19 12:17    2      0     S
```

To display terminal usage, enter

```
who -uH
```

An example of the output is

```
NAME    LINE            TIME            IDLE   PID   COMMENTS
root    tty02           Jan 05 12:25    0:50   512
root    ttyp0           Jan 05 12:26    old    586
root    ttyp1           Jan 05 12:26    .      629
```

Windows NT Alternative

To view a list of active users, select **Start** ➤ **Programs** ➤ **Administrative Tools** ➤ **Server Manager**. Within the Server Manager window, select the computer for which you want to display a list of all active users. Then, from the menu bar, select **Computer** ➤ **Properties** ➤ **Users**.

Using the VDM command line, enter the *net sessions* command to list the sessions between a local computer and the clients connected to it.

Index